PEOPLE OF THE COVENANT

PEOPLE OF THE COVENANT

An Introduction to the Hebrew Bible

FOURTH EDITION

HENRY JACKSON FLANDERS, JR.
Baylor University

ROBERT WILSON CRAPPS
Furman University

DAVID ANTHONY SMITH
Furman University

New York   Oxford
OXFORD UNIVERSITY PRESS
1996

Oxford University Press

Oxford   New York
Athens   Auckland   Bangkok
Calcutta   Cape Town   Dar es Salaam   Delhi
Florence   Hong Kong   Istanbul   Karachi
Kuala Lumpur   Madras   Madrid   Melbourne
Mexico City   Nairobi   Paris   Singapore
Taipei   Tokyo   Toronto

and associated companies in
Berlin   Ibadan

Published by Oxford University Press, Inc.
198 Madison Avenue, New York, New York 10016

Oxford is a registered trademark of Oxford University Press, Inc.

Library of Congress Cataloging-in-Publication Data

Flanders, Henry Jackson.
People of the covenant : an introduction to the Old Testament /
Henry Jackson Flanders, Jr., Robert Wilson Crapps, David Anthony
Smith.—4th ed.
p.   cm.
Includes bibliographical references and indexes.
ISBN 0-19-509370-4 (alk. paper)
1. Bible.   O.T.--History of Biblical events.   I. Crapps, Robert
W., 1925–   .   II. Smith, David Anthony, 1928–   .   III. Title.
BS1197.F47   1995
221.9'5—dc20   95-16121

1 3 5 7 9 8 6 4 2
Printed in the United States of America
on acid-free paper

Preface

Few fields of professional study have received more scholarly attention in recent years than the Hebrew Bible, commonly known to Christians as the Old Testament. The fourth edition of *People of the Covenant* intends to take account of these new studies, updating earlier editions to give the serious but beginning student a reliable introduction. The authors, themselves persons of religious faith and ordained clergy in a major Protestant denomination, assume that the Hebrew Bible refracts the religious pilgrimage of a particular people within a specific historical framework. We further assume that their struggles with basic human issues typify the concerns of those in other times and places who wrestle with the same fundamental questions of human existence.

As in earlier editions, this one uses the historical thread to weave together materials that do not always fit neatly into a historical framework. After an initial presentation on the nature of biblical literature, the book of Genesis is treated as a theological prelude to Israel's story. Subsequent chapters are organized around epochs in Hebrew life. But this is not a technical history of Israel. For us, as for Israel, history is the vehicle for developing self-consciousness in relation to God. Hence the reader will find an emphasis on the meaning that a people gave to persons and events in its attempt to manage life's struggles. What were the human issues at stake in Israel's memory and preservation of its history, and how did the nation understand God to be related to these problems? How did ancient circumstances and thought influence its perception and interpretation of those issues? How do literary forms and structures found in the Hebrew Bible lay bare these struggles? Are Israel's resolutions appropriate or helpful to contemporary persons or groups who face identical or similar questions? Answers to these questions demand the gathering of data from whatever sources are available: historical, archeological, literary, sociological, and anthropological studies, data that elaborate the ancient world and Israel's place in it, literary analysis of individual books of the Hebrew Bible and the larger canon, and reflective judgment on theological ideas that permeate the literature. And, further, careful students, whatever their theological perspective, must be critically aware of the myriad psychosocial factors brought to the interpretive situations.

The authors assume, then, that the Hebrew Bible is unique religious literature in the sense that it comes out of the religious pilgrimage of an ancient people who struggled with complex human issues in relation to its God. We further assume that light shed on these materials from whatever source will enhance their meaning for the contemporary student who vests them with religious authority. Both the Jewish and Christian communities have accorded these materials such status, and consequently the Hebrew Bible has profoundly influenced Western life and culture. The drama of the Hebrew Bible has been acted out in a specific historical context, but it has also continued to be reenacted as persons have attempted to face life's cold realities.

The approach to Israel's story taken in *People of the Covenant*, the selection and omission of materials, and interpretive conclusions are distinctly the responsibility of the authors, but we obviously are indebted to many. To our teachers remote and recent, to colleagues, especially to Professor Jeffrey Rogers of the Furman religion faculty, who have most often been gentle but candid in their suggestions, to Furman administrators who have encouraged and supported the project, to the library staff of Furman University, and to our students who have also been our teachers, we express our gratitude.

No textbook on the Hebrew scriptures ought to replace the reading of the primary materials—the biblical documents themselves. We have, therefore, provided biblical references to encourage reading the Hebrew Bible alongside the textbook.

The readers of the earlier editions will easily recognize major updating of interpretation, additions, clarification, and alterations in this edition. Further, the bibliography has been thoroughly updated and rearranged to make it more useful. References in the general bibliography have been organized by subject and type and cross-referenced with bibliographies at the end of each chapter, themselves considerably expanded. The author index will assist the reader in finding complete bibliographical references. Inserts within chapters will assist the student to reflect on relationships and to clarify relevance to contemporary life. Maps, charts, illustrations, chronololgy charts, and glossary have been expanded and an author index added.

The authors subscribe to nonsexist language and have sought to use such language throughout. The serious student needs to recognize the dominance of a patriarchal orientation in the Hebrew Bible and avoid either sacralizing the ancient Hebrew cultural emphasis or transfering it into the contemporary scene. We have attempted to take seriously the development of a feminine hermeneutic in biblical studies and incorporate that perspective in understanding the Hebrew Bible.

The scripture quotations contained herein are from the New Revised Standard Version Bible, copyright © 1989 by the Division of Christian Education of the National Council of Churches of Christ in the U.S.A. Used by permission. All rights reserved.

Illustrations credited to *Illustrator* Photo are copyrighted by the Sunday School Board of the Southern Baptist Convention. All rights reserved. Used by permission.

Waco, Texas	H. J. F., JR.
Greenville, South Carolina	R. W. C.
January 1996	D. A. S.

Contents

PEOPLE OF THE COVENANT

1

Structure and Interpretation
of the Hebrew Bible

People of the Covenant is a study of a collection of ancient Hebrew religious literature that is sacred to Judaism and Christianity and to some extent to Islam. The works in this collection form the Hebrew Bible and part of the Christian Bible. To Jews this collection is known by several names, the earliest of which was *ha Sefarim* (the books). Early Greek-speaking Jews translated this Hebrew name as *ta biblia*, hence "the Bible." In the Middle Ages the designations *Miqra* (Reading) and *Sifre ha Qodesh* (the Holy Books) were frequently used. The most common Jewish name for their scriptures is *Tanak*, a word formed from the initial letters of the three sections of the Hebrew scriptures as divided by Jews—*Torah* (Law), *Nevi'im* (Prophets), *Kethu'bim* (Writings).

Christians know these works as the Old Testament (Old Covenant), a name that distinguishes them from the distinctively Christian works that form the second division of the Christian scriptures, the New Testament (New Covenant). These titles denote historical sequence, not superiority of one over the other. For Judaism and Protestant Christianity, the contents of *Tanak* and Old Testament are the same, although they are numbered and arranged differently. The differences are merely formal and easily explained. Judaism counts as one book some works that Christianity divides into two or more books. The difference in arrangement is accounted for by the early church's use of Greek translations of the Hebrew scriptures that followed a different order from the Hebrew originals. One of the results, for example, was that books from the *Kethu'bim* were interspersed with the prophetic collection in the Christian Old Testament.

There is a more significant difference between the Protestant Old Testament and that of the Roman Catholic Church. The Catholic Old Testament includes additional works, Jewish writings of importance in late Hebrew biblical history (c. 200–100 B.C.E.) that did not become part of the Jewish scriptures. These writings were used by early Christians and the Catholic Church subsequently

3

included them in its scriptural collections. Catholics call these works deuterocanonical—that is, their sacred character was not universally recognized from
the beginning. In Catholic Bibles the deuterocanonical books are interspersed
with the other canonical books, although many English editions of the Hebrew
Bible present them as a separate collection.

Thus, although there are variations in Jewish, Catholic, and Protestant collections of the Hebrew Bible, basically the materials form a common body.

THE STORY OF ISRAEL IN THE HEBREW BIBLE

The Hebrew scriptures are diverse and complex throughout, but the literature
has in common an orientation toward history and a deep religious faith. Its
primary concern is to interpret the workings of God within the events of Israel's
history. Through its pages run the scientific, theological, and psychological
ideas of the day, but their elaboration is not its focus of attention. The Hebrew
Bible centers on the action of God in the affairs of human beings as they react
to deity and seek to interpret the meaning of divine action for life and faith.
Even though it deals with the affairs of Israel in history, it is a history book
only in the sense that history is the context in which the acts of God are described.

The Israelite Understanding of History

In the Hebrew Bible, history is the arena of God's activity. God is understood
to be actively involved in the life of the Israelites and that involvement is the
focus of their sacred writings. The various writers of the Hebrew Bible observed
events as persons of faith; they wrote as persons of faith. For them the essence
of history was the revelation of God, and consequently their understanding of
history was colored by their understanding of God. Israel's sacred literature is
first and foremost a presentation of the acts of God in its history. From this
starting point, the Hebrew scriptures report Israel's response to its various
experiences of God.

Thus, in the Hebrew Bible history and faith are inextricably combined. On
one hand, belief in God's continual action in the things that happened to the
nation shaped Israel's self-consciousness. Remembered events in Israel's history molded the theological thought of the people—its understanding of itself
in relationship to its God. On the other hand, the mind of Israel, with its
orientation toward God, caused the memory of that history to be viewed in a
particular way. Israel's religious mind was ever active in selecting, arranging,
interpreting, and revitalizing historical memories until they finally took the
form in which we now have them. Thus, both event and religious interpretation
of event were incorporated in the telling of Hebrew history.

This theological orientation means that the final written record is the product of theological selection and interpretation. History so written sometimes makes factual summary difficult, if not impossible. Such history at times obscures distinctions between historical data and later meanings attached to those data, but these distinctions are not always necessary for the understanding of religious truth contained in the writing.

The Crucial Moment

This merging of history and faith is typified in the way that two prominent events are treated. These events are the exodus from Egypt and the establishment of covenant with God at Sinai. Together they form the crucial moment in Israelite history. Deliverance from Egypt is the mighty act by which God emphatically demonstrates special concern for Israel. All that preceded this moment is interpreted in its light, and it gives meaning to everything that follows. Covenant making at Sinai was the divine revelation of God's requirements and Israel's acceptance of them. Both Israel's conception of God and its awareness of its own destiny can be traced to that time when God delivered it from bondage in Egypt and made it God's own people by entering into covenant with it at Sinai. Thus, knowledge of God comes neither through reasoned argument nor observing natural order, but through remembering God's deeds in history, especially in the crucial moment.

Survey of the History of Israel

From the perspective of God's mighty act in delivering slaves from Egyptian bondage and establishing a distinctive relationship with them, Israel tells its story. The story is set in the context of ancient Near Eastern history and provides the narrative framework of the Hebrew scriptures. The narrative begins with traditions about the movement of patriarchal and matriarchal ancestors out of Mesopotamia into Canaan (an ancient name for western Palestine, especially the area west of the Jordan River valley). The central figures are Abraham and Sarah, Isaac and Rebecca, Jacob and Rachel and Leah, and Joseph. In Canaan Israel's ancestors lived as seminomads in the central hill country and in the desert wilderness to the south of Jerusalem. During a time of drought and famine, they moved into Egypt where adequate food was available. Settling there, they were at first accepted by the Egyptians but eventually were enslaved and made to do hard labor for the Egyptian government. Under the leadership of Moses these Israelites, as they called themselves, escaped Egypt to return to Canaan. They spent about a generation wandering in the desert wilderness. Most important among the events of this period was the religious experience they had at Sinai, the holy mountain of God. There they became the people of Yahweh, the name by which God was intimately known by the Israelites.

Joshua then succeeded Moses as leader of the Israelites and led them into

Canaan. There, joined by some kindred tribes that had not gone into Egypt, the Israelites began to make the land their own. As they were establishing themselves in Canaan, Joshua loosely organized the Israelites into a religious confederacy of twelve tribes, each of which had considerable political and economic independence. The unifying factor was their faith in the same God—Yahweh. This religio-political organization served Israel well for more than two centuries while they were securing their hold on Canaan. Then increasing pressure from enemies made necessary a more efficient and centralized political organization.

A monarchy was eventually established with Saul as king. Under his successor, David, Israel became a very strong nation. The unified nation, however, was short-lived. It began to decline during the reign of Solomon, David's son and successor, and at Solomon's death split into two kingdoms, Israel in the north and Judah in the south. These kingdoms, weakened by the division, were increasingly threatened by the great empires of the ancient Near East. Judah and Israel were small nations in the midst of great powers. Their destinies were largely determined by the international affairs of Egypt, Syria, Assyria, Babylon, Persia, and Greece. After two centuries, the northern kingdom was overrun by Assyria and many of its inhabitants were scattered across the East. Soon thereafter the southern kingdom became a vassal of Assyria and remained so until the Assyrian empire fell before the rising power of Babylon. Then Babylon became the oppressor of Judah and soon Nebuchadnezzar, king of Babylon, destroyed Jerusalem, the capital of Judah, and carried the leaders and many of the Judeans to Babylon as captives. However, Babylon then lost her world supremacy to the Persian empire under whose benevolent rule the exiles of Judah were allowed to return home, to rebuild Jerusalem, and to restructure their way of life. When Greece replaced Persia as the dominant power of the East, the restructured nation continued as a modest nation, even enjoying a period of relative independence, before falling under Roman control.

This brief summary of Israel's story may be sketched as follows:

A. Patriarchal period, c. 2000–1700 (Genesis 12–50)[1]
B. Period of national formation, c. 1700–1000 (Exodus, Numbers, Joshua, Judges)
   1. Sojourn in Egypt, c. 1700–1300
   2. Exodus from Egypt, c. 1300
   3. Sinai Covenant, c. 1280
   4. Conquest of Canaan, c. 1250–1200
   5. Tribal Confederacy, c. 1200–1020

---

[1]The dates listed here are worked out by correlations between biblical and ancient Near Eastern archeological and inscriptional materials. The earlier dates are approximate. From c. 1000 B.C.E. on, they are more precise.

C. Monarchy, 1020–587 (Samuel, Kings, Chronicles)
   1. United monarchy, 1020–922
   2. Divided monarchy, 922–587
      a. Israel, 922–722
      b. Judah, 922–587
D. Exile in Babylon, 597–538.
E. Restoration and reconstruction, 538–63 (Ezra, Nehemiah)
   1. Under the Persians, 538–332
   2. Under the Greeks, 332–167
   3. Independence, 167–63
   4. Under the Romans, from 63

Narrative Traditions of Israel's History

This story of Israel is preserved in the Hebrew Bible in the books indicated in the parentheses above. However, behind these biblical books are some great narrative traditions—theological interpretations of Israel's "historical" experience. These narratives focus on Israel's experiences with God. Each narrative is a collection and careful blending of many different traditions with the intention of showing how the past has meaning for the present. In Israel these narratives were preserved and recited because each contributed to the broad picture of God's work in Hebrew history and together made up the entire story. The tellers and organizers of the materials were not necessarily participants in the described events. They were "theologians" who looked back at the past with interpretive eyes. They were addressing their interpretation of God's work in Hebrew history toward answering the religiously important questions, Who are we? and What are we to do? They did so with specific reference to God's divine presence in their experiences. Although the primary purpose of the narratives is not historical, they do provide an overview of the history of ancient Israel and describe the context in which other material in the Hebrew Bible developed. These narratives are preserved in six major collections:

1. *Narratives of creation and fall (Genesis 1–11).* These narratives provide a theological background or preface for understanding the rest of the Hebrew story. They include stories about the creation of the world and about the sinful condition of humankind. These profound statements about the beginnings of humankind and the beginning of sinfulness present the fundamental human predicament addressed by God's work through Israel's history.

2. *Patriarchal and matriarchal narratives (Genesis 12–50).* Stories about Abraham and Sarah, Isaac and Rebecca, Jacob and Rachel and Leah, and Joseph relate the migrations of these founding ancestors in Mesopotamia, Haran, Canaan, and Egypt to set the scene for the exodus event. Their focus is theological. The patriarchs are representative figures typifying all that Israel should be. Their stories introduce covenant and salvation themes. Through patriarchs,

as through Israel, God begins a work that will redeem Israel and subsequently bless all humanity. The presence in the narratives of the antiheroes, Lot and his wife, Esau, Laban and his sons, and Joseph's brothers who sold him into slavery, emphasizes that neither covenant nor salvation are achieved without struggle.

3. *Narratives of the exodus, the giving of the Law of Sinai, and the wilderness wanderings (Exodus and Numbers).* Here the two key events, the exodus from Egypt and the establishment of a covenant with God at Sinai, bring God's purposes into full view and define how Israel should respond. Deliverance from Egypt is described as the mighty act of God demonstrating God's concern for the oppressed people of Israel. The Sinai covenant represents Israel's understanding of its own identity as a people set apart and how it should respond to what God had done. The stories in Numbers describe wilderness wanderings of the Israelites and show that from the beginning the "people of the covenant" responded to God in faith mixed with doubt and self-will. Nonetheless God is faithful even when the covenant community is unfaithful.

4. *The story of Israel in Canaan (Joshua, Judges, Samuel, Kings).* A long and carefully edited collection of traditions tells about Israel's settlement in Canaan (Joshua) and about its national life, first as a religious confederacy (Judges and Samuel), then as a united monarchy (1 and 2 Samuel, 1 Kings), and finally as a divided monarchy (1 and 2 Kings). This long narrative comes from the time of the Babylonian exile and interprets Israel's life in Canaan as a series of increasing failures to be the faithful people of God. Exile in Babylon, therefore, is God's judgment on a sinful people. The point of view taken in the narrative is essentially that of the book of Deuteronomy, which promises blessings to the obedient and punishment to the disobedient. For this reason this "history" of Israel is often called the deuteronomic history.

5. *Narratives about the worship of God in Jerusalem (1 and 2 Chronicles).* These narratives are based on those in Samuel and Kings and emphasize Israel's worship of God in Jerusalem. They focus on Jerusalem as the sacred center of Israel's life and the significance of ritual to a community understood essentially as a theocracy, a nation over which God rules. Emphasis is placed on the institutions and rites of the ritual life of Israel and on those who made significant contributions to it. Both are considered essential to the stability and continuity of culture. Without them there can only be chaos.

6. *Narratives of restoration (Ezra and Nehemiah).* The narratives in Ezra and Nehemiah are closely related to the books of Chronicles, carrying the story into the period during and after the return from exile in Babylon. Their concern is with the rebuilding of Jerusalem and the temple there and with the restoration and purification of Jewish ritual essential to the real restoration of Israel.

Together, these six narratives tell and retell the story of Israel from patriarchal beginnings through restoration of Jewish life in Palestine after the Babylonian exile. Several collections of laws are interspersed in these narrative traditions: (1) the Decalogue (Exodus 20:1–17 and Deuteronomy 5:6–21); (2) the Covenant Code, a collection of civil and religious laws (Exodus 20:22–23:33); (3) the Ritual Decalogue (Exodus 34:10–26); (4) legislation concerning priests and worship (Exodus 25–31, Leviticus 1–27, Numbers 1–10, 28–31, and 33–36); (5) the Deuteronomic Code (Deuteronomy 12–27).

These codes include laws of all kinds, but all are understood as divine laws. They have been given by God as divine guidance about the way Israel should live in relation to God (ritual laws) and in relation to fellow humans (social laws).

Other Hebrew Scripture Materials

The "history" narratives together with the interspersed law codes compose about half of the Hebrew Bible. The remainder includes a wide variety of materials, all of which took shape in and had religious importance for the Israelite community of faith whose life is chronicled in the narrative traditions.

Prophetic Materials (Collections of Prophetic Teachings and Sermons). These make up a large portion of the Hebrew Bible. These materials are found in books bearing the names of Israel's great prophets: Isaiah, Jeremiah, Ezekiel, and the Book of the Twelve (Hosea, Joel, Amos, Obadiah, Jonah, Micah, Nahum, Habakkuk, Zephaniah, Haggai, Zechariah, Malachi). The prophets intended to hold Israel responsible for the quality of its life as a covenant people, and therefore their writings contain pronouncements of judgment and promises of hope. These pronouncements are usually made in a powerfully persuasive form of poetry commending faithfulness, demanding justice, and advocating love.

Worship Materials (Psalms and Lamentations). The Psalms are a grand collection of Israel's prayers and praises expressing worshipful trust in God. They are a treasury of Israelite piety. Their setting is the Jerusalem temple both before and after the Babylonian exile. The psalms reflect the many moods of Israel's faith: joy, thanksgiving, praise, hope, despair, dismay. Lamentations is a collection of liturgical poems used at an annual solemn commemoration of Jerusalem's fall to the Babylonians. In prophetic tones these laments express the community's grief over the fall of the city, the destruction of the temple, and the exile of many into captivity.

Wisdom Materials (Proverbs, Job, and Ecclesiastes). In these books sages speak about life's guidance and meaning. Proverbs states principles by which religious persons should live. It aims for harmony of life in a harmonious universe. Careful observance of its maxims was thought to guarantee the well-being of individuals and of society at large. In contrast, Job and Ecclesiastes raise serious questions about the meaning of life. In the tragic later years of Israel's history these books challenge traditional understandings. Job is a poetic dialogue about the meaning of divine presence. Do persons gain anything from being obedient to God? Easy answers are rejected in the face of the hard realities of life. With similar questioning the sage of Ecclesiastes chases after meaning without satisfaction.

Didactic Narratives (Ruth, Jonah, Daniel and Esther).   These are stories told to instruct or explain. Ruth and Jonah challenge the Jews of the postexilic period to rise above exclusive provincialism and to accept their non-Jewish neighbors. Daniel and Esther are stories about faithfulness in the face of persecution and hardship.

Song of Songs.   This collection of poetry belongs to a category by itself. It celebrates the beauties, intimacies, and joys of human love.

All these materials—historical narrative or wisdom writings, prophetic proclamation or poetic song, prayer or lament—represent the rich diversity of the Hebrew scriptures and all weave together majestically Israel's memory of her past and her faith conviction that God has been at work in that past.

ORIGIN AND DEVELOPMENT OF HEBREW BIBLICAL LITERATURE

The writing of a work in the Hebrew Bible differs considerably from the production of a modern book. A modern book results from a rather direct and intentional plan. Consider, for example, this textbook. There are three authors. Each first wrote a specific section. Then each read and edited the sections written by his two colleagues. Then the original writer edited his own materials in light of his colleagues' suggestions. Finally the completed text was edited by the publisher, proofs were printed and checked, and the book was finally printed, bound, and published. Inasmuch as this is the fourth edition, the procedure has been followed four times by the same three authors and in a relatively short period of time.

In contrast, note the way the Hebrew Bible came into being. First, the Hebrew scriptures are obviously not a single book, but a collection of materials of many kinds. Second, these materials were over a thousand years in the making, many of them originating and being passed on in oral forms. Third, the authors and editors were numerous and many are unknown. They did not have the modern pride and possessiveness of authorship. All of this is true not only of the Hebrew Bible as a whole but of most of the books within it. Much of the narrative materials went through long stages of oral tradition, being transmitted from generation to generation with a great degree of respect, reverence, and accuracy. Only gradually were they gathered into larger collections.

In this way ancient traditions were preserved, passed on, and collected in the period before Israel became literary-minded. "As we read the literature of the Old Testament, therefore, we do well to remind ourselves constantly that its stories were made to be told, its psalms to be sung, its oracles to be spoken with authority, its laws to be the memoranda of authorities in a court of appeals."[2]

The "historical" narratives originally focused on individual persons of faith (in Genesis: the patriarchs and matriarchs; in Exodus: Moses, Aaron, Miriam, and Jethro; in Samuel and Kings: Samuel, Saul, David, and Solomon). Stories of these individuals were combined into an epiclike story of Israel. God plays a prominent role in the narratives because Israel believed God was guiding both the individuals and the nation not as a distant, but as an immanent presence. The stories were early treasured as religious possessions of tribal and local communities. Subsequently the materials could be incorporated into the great narrative traditions of Israel to demonstrate God's working in Israel's history. By this slow process of narrative development, Israel was expressing its religious faith; the literature was thus sacred literature. Guided by this benchmark, superficial items were eliminated; the important was emphasized; the precise word was selected. By the time of the Israelite monarchy, when literary activity began to flourish in Israel, there was already in existence a great reservoir of material, both oral and written, from which writers could draw.

The process of selecting, remembering, organizing, expanding, and editing was typical not only of Israel's historical materials, but also of all of the materials that became part of the Hebrew scriptures. Collections of laws, songs, prophetic utterances, and wisdom materials were made by individuals or groups particularly interested in each of these types of literature. The legal minds in Israel expanded the basic codes of law into the extensive legal corpus now found in the Hebrew Bible. Around a basic code of law (that of Moses), judges, scribes, and legal-minded priests gathered an ever-increasing amount of legal material. They sought to keep the law code up-to-date and adapted it to meet changing historical, social, and economic circumstances. Ancient and modern laws often stood side by side in the same code. Because Moses was looked upon as the "great lawgiver" and laws enacted by Moses lay at the root of the developed code of Israel, the entire legal corpus came to be called Mosaic law. Just as all United States law can be called constitutional because it is in the spirit of the Constitution (although some of it obviously arose long after the Constitution was written), so all of Israel's law, both early and late, could be called Mosaic because it was written in the spirit and tradition of Moses.

In a similar way the temple prophets and singers grouped the psalms for use

---

[2]Nielsen, *Tradition*, p. 19. Persons in the Near East have retained exceptional skill in memory and recitation; some Arabs can repeat the entire Qur'ān from memory, even though they can neither read nor write.

in the worship life of Israel. In these collections they intended to supply what was necessary for every form of worship. The psalms are the hymns and prayers of Israel's worship in the Jerusalem temple both before and after the Babylonian exile. The Psalter, therefore, like the law code, contains materials from almost every period of Israel's history and presents a cross section of its religious life.

Likewise the book of Proverbs represents reflections on the religious and moral life made by numerous sages over a quite long period. Wisemen grouped wisdom sayings current in Israel and then expanded these collections by including material from the wisdom literature of other peoples of the ancient world. Wisdom literature flourished in Egypt and Mesopotamia as well as in Israel, and the Hebrew Bible recognizes the international flavor of wisdom. Included in the book of Proverbs are collections attributed to Agur and Lemuel, both of whom were Arabs; and certain sections of the book reflect the Egyptian wisdom book of Amenemope,[3] as well as the wisdom sayings in the Mesopotamian story of Ahikar.[4]

A similar developmental process is true of Israel's prophetic books. Seldom, if ever, were these works the product of a single author intentionally composing a book. Prophets were more speakers than writers, and few were concerned to give their message written form. Their sermons were reported by followers and later developed into books, often including historical and biographical data about the prophets. The book of Isaiah, for example, contains prophetic oracles (short sermons) from an eighth-century Jerusalem prophet and also oracles from his disciple-successors working in the sixth and fifth centuries during and after the Babylonian exile. The book of Jeremiah reflects different stages of Jeremiah's own editing, the contributions of his scribe and friend Baruch, and the editorial work of other prophetic hands.

These examples indicate that the composition of the Hebrew Bible was an extremely complicated process to which many Jewish thinkers contributed. The following sketch may help to put the development of Israel's literature in the framework of Hebrew history:

1. Patriarchal period, 2000–1700. No literary activity can be traced to this period. Oral, tribal, ancestral traditions were shaped and circulated.
2. Period of national formation, 1700–1000. Continuation of the oral tradition and, late in the period, the beginning of literary collection: Song of Deborah (Judges 5); Song of Miriam (Exodus 15:21); liturgical confession (Deuteronomy 26:5–10); and early legal and cultic traditions (Exodus 20:1–17).
3. United monarchy, c. 1020–922. Collection of tribal traditions, later expanded and edited into great epic traditions of the history of all Israel; expansion of legal and cultic traditions. Toward the end of this period the first epic of Israel's beginnings

---

[3]A collection of proverbs and precepts dating from the tenth to the sixth centuries B.C.E. See Pritchard, *Texts*, pp. 421ff.

[4]A collection of Aramaic proverbs from the end of the Assyrian Empire.

(the Yahwistic tradition) was edited in Judah; traditions from David's reign, particularly the court history in 2 Samuel 9–20 and 1 Kings 1–2; beginning of wisdom literature; continuing expansion of legal and cultic traditions.

4. Divided monarchy: Israel and Judah coexisting, 922–722. Second epic of Israel's beginning (the Elohistic tradition); earliest prophetic narratives (Elijah and Elisha materials); early historical materials from Israel and Judah; continued development of legal and cultic material.

5. Divided monarchy: Judah alone, 722–587. Collection of prophetic oracles of Amos, Hosea, Micah, Isaiah, Jeremiah (not all these books, but major portions thereof; each book contains some later additions, some contain considerable later additions); earliest form of Deuteronomy and the deuteronomic history of Israel in the land (Joshua–2 Kings); continued growth of legal and cultic materials.

6. Exile, 597–538. Ezekiel, Deutero-Isaiah (chaps. 40–66); priestly tradition of Israel's origins; collection of Psalms, elaboration of wisdom materials; Lamentations.

7. Postexile, 538–63. Late prophetic writings; apocalyptic literature in Daniel; Ruth and Esther; Job and Ecclesiastes; Chronicler's history work.

Thus the literature of Israel took shape as persons of faith brought together materials of enduring religious value. As the collections were being made, the believing community was gradually moving to the acceptance of this literature as the authoritative "word of God."

In two or three sentences, write your belief concerning the inspiration of the Bible. What implications does this discussion about the development of the Hebrew scriptures have for your understanding of inspiration?

CANON AND CANONS

As one or another of these collections came to be important to the worship life of a segment of the people of Israel, it would be looked upon as religiously authoritative and binding. In it the people recognized the authentic voice of authority speaking to them. In other words, it was regarded as scripture. The technical term used to describe collections so regarded is "canon," and the process by which collections come to be looked upon as authoritative is called "canonization." The word "canon" is a transliteration of a Greek word traced to an old Babylonian word meaning "reed." The reed was one of the earliest measuring devices, and thus the word "canon" came to designate a "measuring rod" and, finally, "that which regulates, rules, or serves as a norm or pattern for other things." In this sense it was applied to the Hebrew Bible. Materials were looked upon as authoritative, as scriptural, when they met a certain standard—that is, when they proved themselves in one way or another to be the authentic voice of religious authority speaking to human beings.

The canonization of the Hebrew scriptures was a long and somewhat complicated process. It had its beginnings when various groups of the Israelite people preserved stories, laws, prophetic oracles, songs, proverbs, and so forth, in which the community clearly recognized the voice of God. In other words, the very process of selectivity and preservation had canonical overtones.

There were probably many reasons behind the preference for some works over others. Unfortunately we do not fully know what they were. Time seems to have been an essential factor in turning treasured religious writings into canonical authorities. Few books were canonized until long after they had been written. Religious usage seems to have been another primary criterion. The books included were those that had found their place in the worship life of the people and those that provided divine guidance for individual and corporate life. The majority of Hebrew scripture was probably accepted through common consent long before it was formally canonized. Canonization was more a process of popular acceptance than of official action.[5] "No party, denomination, or hierarchy in Jerusalem or elsewhere would have the power to foist off on the people a literature which held little meaning or value for them."[6] Popular acceptance must have been a powerful influence leading to official acceptance.

Canonization of Torah (Law).   Eventually collections of the Hebrew scriptures did come. We may describe the process in terms of the major divisions of the Hebrew Bible. The earliest collection to achieve canonical status was Torah (Law). When a priest Ezra led a revival of Hebrew faith in the early part of the fifth century, he used a collection of Law to appeal to the populace for faithfulness. Evidently both Ezra and the people accepted this law, probably Torah, as religiously binding.

Further, the Samaritans, a mixed race of Jews and Assyrians, accepted only Torah as their scripture. These folk were detested by Jews and there was a distinctive breach between the two communities by the end of the fifth century. It seems logical to conclude that Torah had achieved canonical status before such a division occurred. These data suggest that Torah was considered canonical by about 400 B.C.E.

Canonization of Nevi'im (Prophets).   A collection of prophetic writings seems to have become canonical about two centuries later than Law, about 200 B.C.E. Of course, prophetic sayings and sermons were taken seriously by the prophets' followers from the outset. These disciples of men like Isaiah, Jeremiah, Amos, and Hosea firmly believed that the prophets were speaking for God, even when their messages spoke of approaching disaster as God's judgment on the nation. The early followers collected and preserved the words

---

[5]Josephus, an early Jewish historian, uses the term "popularity" in reference to sacred books in *Against Apion*, I, 28–46.

[6]Sanders, *Canon*, p. 33.

of their hero, but when history demonstrated the truth of their message of judgment, prophetic works took on authority in the wider community.

The first clear evidence of the existence of a defined prophetic collection comes from the second century B.C.E. The Wisdom of Jesus ben Sirach alludes to the books of Joshua, Judges, Samuel, Kings, Isaiah, Jeremiah, Ezekiel, and the Twelve Prophets. Presumably ben Sirach knew a collection of the prophets. When a grandson of ben Sirach translated his grandfather's work from Hebrew into Greek in 132 B.C.E., he added a prologue in which he spoke of "the law, and the prophets and others that have followed in their steps," and "the law itself, the prophecies, and the rest of the books." These expressions indicate both that the prophetic collection had already achieved a status similar to that of Torah and that the third section of the canon was beginning to take shape.

Canonization of Kethu'bim (Writings). The third section of the Hebrew canon seems not to have been accepted widely until the end of the first century C.E. The ben Sirach reference suggests some movement in that direction and NewTestament references confirm a growing authority for the Writings. Luke 24:44 speaks of "the law of Moses, and the prophets, and the psalms," and in Matthew 23:35 "from the blood of innocent Abel to the blood of Zechariah" means the whole range of Hebrew scripture. The New Testament references date from the last quarter of the first century C.E. At about the same time the Jewish historian Josephus refers to five books of the law, thirteen books of the prophets, and four books containing hymns to God and precepts for the conduct of human life. These references imply collections already well established. The third section of the Hebrew canon seems to have been widely accepted by the end of the first century C.E.

Jamnia (c. 90 C.E.)

Many have attributed a final and formal shaping of the Hebrew canon to decisions reached in discussions c. 90 C.E. among rabbis at Jamnia or Jabneh, a Jewish center of learning on the Palestinian coast. Jamnia had replaced Jerusalem as a focal point of Jewish leadership after Jerusalem was destroyed by the Romans in 70 C.E. We only know, however, that rabbis there discussed whether or not certain books should be "reserved" (i.e., restricted from public reading). They apparently were discussing an already widely accepted collection of Torah, Nevi'im, and Kethu'bim and made no official rulings. The sense of canonical authority actually came in the freedom of the Jewish community as a whole, rather than being imposed on that community by some hierarchy of religious leaders.[7]

---

[7]On the whole question of what happened at Jamnia/Jabneh, see Jack P. Lewis, "What Do We Mean by Jabneh?" in Leiman, *Canon.*

The Alexandria Collection and the Apocrypha

While the Palestinian Jews were completing their canon of scripture, a similar phenomenon was occurring at Alexandria in Egypt. The Jews there shared Greek culture and hence translated the Hebrew scriptures into Greek. For these Alexandrian Jews, Torah seems to have been the only portion given absolute authority. However, they included in their sacred writings collections of Nevi'im and Kethu'bim along with certain other works not accepted by the Palestinian Jews. No single manuscript of these collections has survived. This makes it difficult to determine their extent, particularly because they seem to have varied from community to community. Certain works not in the Hebrew collection were taken over by the early Christian church from these Greek collections (many were used by New Testament writers) and passed from Greek into the Latin Bible.

When Jerome translated the Bible into Latin in 382 C.E., he included the extra works but with some reservations. He himself used the term "Apocrypha" ("hidden things") for those books that were not part of the Hebrew scriptures. He felt they could be read for edification but should not be used for confirming the authority of church dogmas. In spite of this distinction, however, Jerome included the extra works in his translation because of the church's use of them. Jerome's translation was called the Vulgate and became the official Bible of the Roman Catholic Church. During the Protestant Reformation of the sixteenth century C.E., the reformers accepted only those books included in the Palestinean canon. In his translation of the Hebrew Bible into German, Luther included the additional books but placed them together at the end of the Hebrew Bible under the title "Apocrypha." At the Council of Trent (1546 C.E.) the Catholic Church reaffirmed the canonical authority of the Vulgate translation. The additional books were included in some Protestant collections as late as the King James Version in 1611 C.E.

Roman Catholic scholars refer to these additional books as "deuterocanonical" without implying that they are less important or authoritative. Generally Protestants assign Apocryphal books inferior status, often ignoring them. Nonetheless, these are important for understanding the historical, literary, and theological development of Jewish thought between 200 B.C.E. and 100 C.E., a period for which any light is welcome.

Figure 1.1. The books of the Apocrypha.

I Maccabees	Baruch, including Letter of Jeremiah
II Maccabees	Susanna
I Esdras	Bel and the Dragon
II Esdras	Song of the Three Holy Children
Wisdom of Jesus ben Sirach or Ecclesiasticus	The Rest of Esther
Judith	Prayer of Manasses
Tobit	Book of Wisdom or Wisdom of Solomon

The Pseudepigrapha

The term "Pseudepigrapha" applies to certain Jewish writings of the period from 200 B.C.E. to 200 C.E. found in neither the Hebrew Bible nor the Apocrypha. For a time these writings were popular in certain branches of the early Christian church. There is no established collection of the Pseudepigrapha, and modern editors of these ancient works make various arrangements of the materials. Among the more noted pseudepigraphical writings are Enoch, Psalms of Solomon, Testament of the Twelve Patriarchs, and Assumption of Moses. Like books of the Apocrypha, those of the Pseudepigrapha are of primary value for a period for which data are scarce and additional information welcome.

We can see then that the development of an "official" canon was more the development of several canons, as reflected in Figure 1.2. Further, an official canon does not always coincide with a personal canon—those books that persons of faith choose as particularly appropriate for their own inspiration and guidance. Also Hebrew literature included religious materials that did not make it into any canon. Numerous books now lost are quoted or otherwise embodied in the canonical books.[8] This literature was valued for a while and some of it enjoyed religious status, but for reasons unknown to us was not cherished enough to be incorporated into an authorized collection.

TEXTS AND VERSIONS OF THE HEBREW BIBLE

As soon as Judaism accepted the Hebrew scriptures as canonical, every effort was made to preserve them as accurately as possible. For the many centuries before the invention of the moveable-type printing press in 1456 C.E., copies of the Hebrew scriptures were made by hand. This difficult and tedious work was assigned to dedicated scribes who made every effort to do their work as accurately as possible.

The Hebrew Text

The language in which most of the Hebrew Bible was originally written is Hebrew. For a small part of it, Aramaic was used. The Aramaic sections are Genesis 31:47; Jeremiah 10:11; Ezra 4:8–6:18; 7:12–26; and Daniel 2:4–7:28. Like most other Semitic languages, Hebrew and Aramaic are written from right to left. All twenty-two letters of their alphabet were consonants and the early manuscripts of the Hebrew scriptures were written without vowels.

---

[8]For example, the Book of Jasher (Joshua 10:13; 2 Samuel 1:18), the Book of the Wars of Yahweh (Numbers 31:14), the Book of the Acts of Solomon (1 Kings 11:41), Chronicles of the Kings of Judah (1 Kings 14:29), Chronicles of the Kings of Israel (1 Kings 14:19), and others.

TANAK

Torah

1. Bereshith (Genesis)
2. Shemoth (Exodus)
3. Wayiqra (Leviticus)
4. Bemidbar (Numbers)
5. Debarim (Deuteronomy)

Nevi'im (Former)

6. Joshua
7. Shofetim (Judges)
8. Samuel
9. Melakim (Kings)
10. Isaiah
11. Jeremiah
12. Ezekiel
13. TereAsar (The Twelve)
    Hosea
    Joel
    Amos
    Obadiah
    Jonah
    Micah
    Nahum
    Habakkuk
    Zephaniah
    Haggai
    Zechariah
    Malachi

Kethu'bim

14. Tehillim (Psalms)
15. Job
16. Mishle (Proverbs)
17. Ruth
18. Shir Hashirim (Song of Songs)
19. Qoheleth (Ecclesiastes)
20. Ekah (Lamentations)
21. Esther
22. Daniel
23. Ezra–Nehemiah
24. Dibre Hayamim (Chronicles)

ROMAN CATHOLIC AND ORTHODOX

Pentateuch

1. Genesis
2. Exodus
3. Leviticus
4. Numbers
5. Deuteronomy

History

6. Joshua
7. Judges
8. Ruth
9–10. I and II Samuel
11–12. I and II Kings
13–14. I and II Chronicles
15–16. Ezra and Nehemiah
17. Tobit*
18. Judith*
19. Esther, including The Rest of Esther

Poetry and Wisdom

20. Job
21. Psalms
22. Proverbs
23. Ecclesiastes
24. Song of Solomon
25. Wisdom of Solomon*
26. Ecclesiasticus (Wisdom of ben Sirach)*

Prophets

27. Isaiah
28. Jeremiah
29. Lamentations
30. Baruch, including The Letter of Jeremiah**
31. Ezekiel
32. Daniel, including The Rest of Daniel*; Susanna*, Song of the Three Holy Children*, Bel and the Dragon*
33. Hosea
34. Joel
35. Amos
36. Obadiah
37. Jonah
38. Micah
39. Nahum
40. Habakkuk
41. Zephaniah
42. Haggai
43. Zechariah
44. Malachi
45. I Maccabees*
46. II Maccabees**

*Apocryphal in Protestant canon
**Roman Catholic only

PROTESTANT

Pentateuch

1. Genesis
2. Exodus
3. Leviticus
4. Numbers
5. Deuteronomy

History

6. Joshua
7. Judges
8. Ruth
9–10. I and II Samuel
11–12. I and II Kings
13–14. I and II Chronicles
15–16. Ezra and Nehemiah
17. Esther

Poetry and Wisdom

18. Job
19. Psalms
20. Proverbs
21. Ecclesiastes
22. Song of Solomon

Prophets

23. Isaiah
24. Jeremiah
25. Lamentations
26. Ezekiel
27. Daniel
28. Hosea
29. Joel
30. Amos
31. Obadiah
32. Jonah
33. Micah
34. Nahum
35. Habakkuk
36. Zephaniah
37. Haggai
38. Zechariah
39. Malachi

Figure 1.2. Jewish and Christian canons of the Hebrew Bible.

The manuscripts were originally written on scrolls made of leather or papyrus, a kind of "paper" made from the stem of a fibrous Egyptian plant. Not until the third and fourth centuries C.E. did the "book with pages" or codex form appear. With its ease of reference and capacity for enlargement through the addition of pages, the codex soon replaced the awkward scroll, but for official worship Jewish communities continued to use manuscripts in scroll form. Manuscripts, both in scroll and codex form, were manually reproduced by one of two methods. Either a scribe copied by sight a manuscript he had before him or a single scribe would read a manuscript to a number of scribes who recorded what they heard. The latter method produced more copies in a shorter time, but the former was usually more accurate. Both methods were subject to errors; scribes could get tired with the tedious work, lines or words could be misread, or read words could be misunderstood. In spite of the intense dedication of the scribes to their work, errors would creep into the text.

Realizing that mistakes did occur, Jewish scribes devised elaborate schemes to safeguard the text. As a rule, new manuscripts were corrected against the original from which they had been copied. In addition, an extensive system of checks and counterchecks was established to determine the accuracy of every new manuscript. The importance of the materials and the great concern for accuracy in preserving a consonantal text gave considerable status to the dedicated scribe.

The Jewish scholars who copied and safeguarded the manuscripts were called Sopherim ("men of the book") and Masoretes ("men of the Masora"). The Sopherim had their beginning sometime in the fourth century B.C.E. and continued their work until the early Christian era. They copied manuscripts, marked doubtful passages, added marginal notes giving alternate readings that they thought were more correct than those in the body of the text, and divided the manuscripts into sentences and sections for liturgical usage. The Masoretes continued and elaborated this project. They collected and catalogued errors found in the text, noted every unique form, and counted the letters of the individual books. All this information they gathered and placed in the margins of manuscripts, thus surrounding the text with a protective hedge, which they called the *Masora,* thus their name Masoretes, "men of the Masora."

In addition the Masoretes in the seventh to ninth centuries C.E. added vowels and accents to the texts. This was perhaps their greatest contribution, because thereby they preserved the full grammatical structure of the Hebrew language. By the seventh century C.E. Hebrew had become a book language. Because the written language used only consonants, the full structure of the language was in danger of being forgotten. The Masoretes, who knew the sound and structure of the language from memory, devised a system of vowels to be inserted in the existing consonantal texts above, below, or in the middle of the consonantal characters.

The work of the Sopherim and Masoretes gradually produced a somewhat

Figure 1.3. Portion of a tenth-century C.E. Hebrew manuscript opened to Leviticus 5:18–6:5. Notations around the columns are the Masora. Vowel points and accents appear within the text. (Courtesy of the British Library, MS. OR 4445)

standardized text looked upon as authoritative. Because the books were sacred, it was important to have a trustworthy text. During the tenth century C.E., two main families of Masoretes flourished in Palestine, that of ben Asher and that of ben Naphtali. The texts produced by these two families were quite similar, although they differed in certain details. For a time the two texts were rivals, but in the twelfth century C.E. the text of ben Asher was accepted as standard. The consonantal form of this text was written by a certain ben Buja and later was given vowels by ben Asher in 1008 C.E. It is the oldest extant manuscript of the entire Hebrew Bible and is the basis for modern editions of the Hebrew text.

Copyists faithfully destroyed old, worn-out manuscripts from which they had made new copies (they were too sacred to leave lying around), and so it was by accident that any ancient copies were preserved. Until recent years the onlyHebrew manuscripts predating 1008 C.E. were a tiny first-century C.E. fragment containing a few verses from Exodus 20 and Deuteronomy 5 and 6, a codex of the Prophets written in 895 C.E., a codex of Torah dated 820–850 C.E., a collection of sixth-century C.E. miscellany from a synagogue storeroom in Cairo, and two unresearched collections in Russia.

Since 1947, however, a large number of manuscripts have been discovered in a series of caves near Qumran on the western plateau above the Dead Sea. The materials were hidden there toward the end of the first century C.E. by a Jewish community threatened by the Romans. They hoped to be able to reclaim them when the threat was past. However, their hope was unfulfilled and the manuscripts remained hidden until they were accidentally discovered centuries later. The discovery brought to light a wealth of Hebrew manuscripts. Among the newfound scrolls, all of which date from the first or second century B.C.E., are portions (often only scraps) from every book of the Hebrew Bible except Esther. Relatively complete scrolls of Isaiah, Leviticus, and Psalms have been found, along with sizable portions of a number of other books. These Dead Sea Scrolls represent one of the most significant finds ever made for the textual study of the Hebrew scriptures.

Ancient Versions

The preservation of the Hebrew biblical materials entails not only the story of its copying, but also its translation into numerous languages. Various communities of Jews and Christians were unaccustomed to using Hebrew and hence the materials were translated into other languages to meet their needs. Some of the more important of these translations are the Greek, Aramaic, Syriac, and Latin.

Greek. Translations into Greek were the earliest and most significant translations. They are commonly known as the Septuagint, or LXX. The ancient and legendary Letter of Aristeas claimed that the Septuagint was an official project of the Greek government of Egypt around 200 B.C.E. According to this letter, seventy-two learned Jews, brought from Palestine to Alexandria and isolated on an island in the harbor, completed their task in seventy-two days. They were supposed to have worked in pairs and to have finished thirty-six copies of the Hebrew Bible at the very same time and without variation in the Greek. This would have been quite an accomplishment. The story, of course, is pure fantasy. Actually, the Septuagint was produced to meet the needs of the Jewish population in Egypt whose language was no longer Hebrew but Greek. There is no single Septuagint, but a collection of translations, whose translators varied greatly in practice and ability, knowledge of Hebrew, and style.[9] The work of translation took place over a long period of time. Torah was translated around 250 B.C.E., but the translation of the remaining books was not completed until the first century C.E. The Septuagint included more books than were in the Palestinian canon, a collection commonly known as Apocrypha.

The Bible of the early Christians was these Greek translations and most Hebrew scripture quotations found in the New Testament came from them. The Septuagint influenced both the Latin versions and modern English trans-

[9]See Wurthwein, *Text,* pp. 36–37.

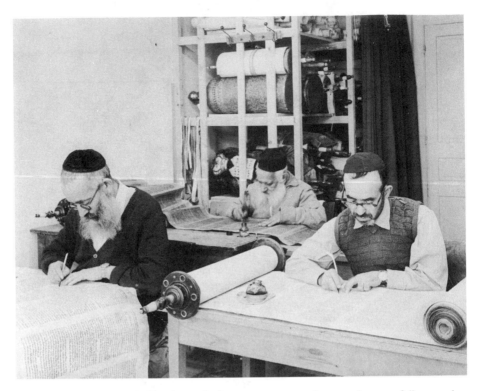

Figure 1.4. Modern scholars, in much the same way as ancient copyists, carefully reproduce biblical manuscripts. (Courtesy of Israel Office of Information)

lations. The names of many of the books in the Hebrew Bible came from the Septuagint, as for example, Genesis, Exodus, Deuteronomy. Other Greek versions are also known, but they are not as important.

Aramaic.   Hebrew ceased to be spoken by the Jews in the postexilic period; Aramaic became the common language. Hebrew scriptures continued to be read in the synagogues, but the reading was accompanied by an oral Aramaic paraphrase so the people could understand. Gradually these paraphrases were standardized. They were called "targums" and were more free explanations of the Hebrew text than literal translations. Early in the Christian era these were put into writing. The most important of the targums are the Targum of Onkelos (the Torah) and the Targum of Jonathan (the Prophets).

Syriac.   When Christianity spread into the interior of Syria in the late first or early second century C.E., the Hebrew Bible was translated into Syriac. This version probably was carried by the first Christian missionaries to India and China.

Latin.   Two Latin translations are significant. Around the end of the second century C.E. a series of Latin translations of various Hebrew biblical books began to circulate in the Latin-speaking churches of northern Africa. These early translations are generally called the Old Latin version. Their roughness and disunity made them unsatisfactory, and in 382 C.E. Pope Damasus commissioned Jerome to produce an official revision. His translation, called the Vulgate, was based on the Hebrew, the Old Latin, and the Septuagint. It met with considerable opposition when it appeared, but by the seventh century it had become *the* Bible of the Roman Catholic Church. The Vulgate used the Septuagint, and so it included the Hebrew Apocrypha.

English Versions

Wyclif.   The translation of the Bible into English became important during and after the Protestant Reformation with its emphasis on the availability of religion to common folk. The first complete translation into English was made by followers of John Wyclif, "the father of English prose, the morning star of the Reformation, the flower of Oxford scholarship," who demanded that the Bible be made available to Englishmen in their mother tongue. This translation was completed around 1382 C.E. and was based on the Vulgate.

Tyndale and Others.   The first English translation based on the original languages was produced around 1525 C.E. by William Tyndale. The first printed edition of the Bible in English, the Coverdale Version, appeared in 1535. These were followed by the Great Bible (1539), the Geneva Bible (1560), and the Bishops' Bible (1568). Catholic scholars in the French cities of Douai and Rheims produced a translation from the Vulgate into English (1610), commonly called the Douai Version.

The King James.   In 1611 a group of translators commissioned by King James I of England completed a work of seven years and gave the English-speaking world the Bible described on its title page: "The Holy Bible: Containing the Old Testament and the New: Newly translated out of the Original tongues: and with the former translations diligently compared and revised by his Majestie's special Commandment."

Immediately it replaced the Bishops' Bible in official use and, after fifty years or so, it replaced the Geneva Bible in popular use. For three and a half centuries the King James Version (KJV) has remained an "accepted Bible" of English-speaking Protestantism. Its staying popularity with many persons has produced sacred associations with its superb literary style.

Other English Translations.   The discovery after 1611 of a great number of ancient biblical manuscripts made desirable further translations utilizing these materials. The first of these were the English Revised Version of 1885 and the American Revised Version of 1901. These translations, while not measuring up to the superlative literary character of the King James, are more accurate. Other steps in translation were taken with the publication of the widely accepted Revised Standard Version (RSV, 1954), the Roman Catholic Jerusalem Bible (JB, 1966), the New English Bible (NEB, 1970), the New International Version (NIV, 1978), and the New Revised Standard Version (NRSV, 1989). The translation process will likely continue as language changes and as new data emerge from study of available manuscripts. In the ongoing process the traditions of ancient Israel are continually being made alive in the contemporary community of faith.

METHODS USED IN THE INTERPRETATION OF THE HEBREW BIBLE

Biblical scholarship has developed some methods of study that help the interpreter to understand the meaning of a text. Some of the Hebrew scriptures' stories, many of its psalms and proverbs, and some of its prophetic sayings are rather easy to understand. Other sections are much more difficult. They all come from a context and represent a worldview in many ways different from our own. Any scriptural text is better understood if one knows something about the context out of which it came, how it was shaped, the kind of literature it is, the literary style and devices its author used, and how it was used by those who preserved it. Scholarly research that provides some of this information greatly enriches our understanding and appreciation of the Hebrew Bible.

The methods of study used in Hebrew biblical research are called *criticisms*, in the sense of "careful analyses." In this sense "criticism" has no negative connotation. The scriptural texts are assumed to be important religious documents, which become more valuable as they are carefully analyzed and studied. The various methods used in scholarly analysis may be grouped under two headings: (1) textual criticism and (2) interpretative criticism. Textual criticism is concerned only with the wording of the text. Inasmuch as the original manuscripts are not available, how may we with reasonable certainty reconstruct the exact wording of the text? The form of the text, not its interpretation, is the focus of textual criticism. Interpretative criticism is concerned with various methods that help the interpreter understand the meaning and relevance of a text.

Textual Criticism

Basic to all further study of the Hebrew Bible is an analysis of the accuracy of its text. This analysis is necessary because even the best manuscripts of the Hebrew scriptures contain scribal errors. The diligent work of the Sopherim and the Masoretes tried to eliminate copyist mistakes, but they still occurred.

There are a number of variant readings for almost every Hebrew scripture passage. If one had a dozen ancient manuscripts of a passage, their comparison with each other would reveal numerous differences in spelling or wording. Some differences would be minor and others would be significant for the meaning of the passage. A reader using one of the recent translations of the Hebrew scriptures, such as the NIV or NRSV, will notice numerous footnotes about textual matters. An interesting example is found in the NIV note on Exodus 1:5. This translated verse reads: "The descendants of Jacob numbered seventy in all; Joseph was already in Egypt." The footnote that refers to the word "seventy" points out that this is the number that occurs in the Masoretic text, but that the Dead Sea Scrolls and the Septuagint have instead "seventy-five." The note also mentions the reference to this verse in Acts 7:14 where the number is also "seventy-five." Apparently the Acts reference was taken from the Septuagint.

Textual differences like these were largely the inevitable consequence of the manual reproduction of the biblical manuscripts. Even in printed texts, where control is strict, mechanical errors occur. They were much more common in handwritten copies. Occasionally there are differences that represent intentional changes made by a scribe or an editor to preserve an intended meaning.

Scribal mistakes are usually divided into three categories: errors of the eye, errors of the ear, and inclusions into the text of marginal notes. *Errors of the eye* occurred when manuscripts were being copied by sight and a scribe misread the text or failed to follow his place accurately. Thus he might advertently change a letter (a number of Hebrew letters look alike); or repeat a letter, word, or phrase; or omit a letter, word, or phrase. In Leviticus 20:10 the phrase "if a man commits adultery with the wife of" occurs twice in Masoretic text and the repetition is probably a scribal mistake. Compare the translations of this verse in the KJV, the NRSV, and the NIV:

> KJV: And the man that committeth adultery with *another* man's wife, *even he* that committeth adultery with his neighbour's wife, the adulterer and the adulteress shall surely be put to death.
>
> NRSV: If a man commits adultery with the wife of his neighbor, both the adulterer and the adulteress shall be put to death.
>
> NIV: If a man commits adultery with another man's wife—with the wife of his neighbor–both the adulterer and the adulteress must be put to death.

The words in italics in the KJV were added by the translators to smooth out awkwardness occasioned by repetition of the phrase "commits adultery with."

In 1 Samuel 14:41 the Septuagint has an entire line not found in the Masoretic text. Compare the KJV and the NIV, which are based on the Hebrew text, with the NRSV, which adds the additional line from the Septuagint:

> KJV: Therefore Saul said unto the Lord God of Israel, Give a perfect *lot*. And Saul and Jonathan were taken: but the people escaped. [The word "lot" was supplied by the translators on the basis of the context.]

NIV: Then Saul prayed to the Lord, the God of Israel, "Give me the right answer." And Jonathan and Saul were taken by lot, and the men were cleared.

NRSV: Then Saul said, "O LORD God of Israel, why have you not answered your servant today? If this guilt is in me or in my son Jonathan, O LORD God of Israel, give Urim; but if this guilt is in your people Israel, give Thummim." And Jonathan and Saul were indicated by the lot, but the people were cleared.

Errors of the ear occurred when manuscripts were being reproduced by dictation, an economical but less accurate method of copying. In these cases the scribes in dictating or in hearing dictation did not clearly distinguish between letters and words that sound alike. A good illustration of this kind of mistake is the well-known verse from Psalm 100: "It is he that hath made us and not we ourselves" (KJV). The word here translated "not" is the Hebrew word *lo'*. Another Hebrew word, *lo* (to him), would have almost the same sound and makes better sense in the verse: "It is he who made us and we are his" (NRSV).

Marginal notations were sometimes shifted from the margin into the text by a scribe who mistakenly thought that thereby he was correcting an error made by a previous copyist. Believing that his predecessor had corrected an inadvertent omission by placing the omitted section in the margin, the second scribe would move it back into the text.

A clear example of this is found in Genesis 10:13–14 in a list of descendants of a certain *Egypt:* "Egypt became the father of Ludim, Anamim,Lehabim, Naphtuhim, Pathrusim, Casluhim (whence came the Philistines), and Caphtorim" (author's translation). In a list of seven names, there is comment on only one. The comment was probably in the margin of a manuscript being used by a copyist who put the elaborating comment into the text—but after the wrong word. The Philistines did not come from Casluhim, but from Caphtorim.[10] The NRSV moves the comment to its proper place.

Copy one page of this text and then check carefully for errors you might have made.

The book of Jeremiah illustrates a textual problem of a different kind. The length and order of the Septuagint text differs considerably from the Masoretic text. This is not a matter of scribal mistakes, but of a different editorial tradition. Resolution of this difference goes beyond the textual question and raises a question about canonicity. Which version of Jeremiah should be part of the canon of scripture? Both Judaism and Christianity have usually given preference to the Masoretic version. To say the least, such a problem suggests that the textual and canonical shape of scripture is a complicated matter and demands the best discipline of textual scholarship.[11]

---

[10]See Amos 9:7.

[11]The issue of the longer and shorter endings of Mark and the place in the Gospel of John of the story about the woman taken in adultery, John 7:53–8:11, raise similar questions.

Because textual mistakes did frequently occur in the tedious process of preserving the manuscripts, modern scholarship has been concerned to recover the best possible form of the text of the Hebrew scriptures. A careful method of textual analysis has been developed: *textual criticism*. Its methodology is essentially the systematic comparison of all available ancient manuscript traditions both in Hebrew and in translations. The Masoretic text is the standard. Other Hebrew manuscripts are classified into "families" according to their text forms or patterns. Where textual differences occur, the various "families" of the Hebrew text and the various translated versions are studied together, for the purpose of determining both how the differences came about and which of the possible wordings represents the best text.

One of the most exciting archeological finds of all times was the discovery of the Dead Sea Scrolls, in large part because they provide an early form of the text of the Hebrew scriptures. These scrolls predate all other manuscripts of the Hebrew scriptures by many centuries. With their help scholars have solved some textual problems; others have been raised. In both respects the Dead Sea Scrolls have stimulated textual studies. The new manuscript finds have contributed to an increasing knowledge of the form of Hebrew biblical texts. The tasks of textual criticism, however, are unfinished; unresolved textual problems remain. Modern scholarship, however, has been amazingly successful in recovering a reliable text of the Hebrew Bible and contemporary translations profit from their work.[12]

Interpretative Criticism

Textual criticism provides a reliable text; interpretative criticism builds on that foundation. Interpretation aims to recover the historical context and literary character of any passage under consideration. The Hebrew Bible grew out of the rich life of the Israelite community of faith; an imaginative understanding of its materials begins with a sense of what the Hebrew scriptures meant in the lives of those persons who created, shaped, and preserved them. Reconstruction of the ancient environment may help make ancient religious literature come alive as expressions of real life and hence make the materials relevant to modern readers. The biblical interpreter may be compared to a good historical novelist who imaginatively creates a believable context for a story, one into which readers can enter and understand. So the biblical interpreter aims to place narratives, hymns, prophetic and wisdom sayings, law codes, and so forth, in the setting from which they come. Important questions of who, what, where, when, why, and how are asked to help us see how influential the community's situation was on the shaping of the sacred texts and how vital the

---

[12]Many modern translations contain footnotes that give the uninitiated reader a key to both where problems lie and how the translator has resolved them.

sacred texts were in the life of the community. These interpretive methodologies may be divided into two interdependent categories: (1) those types of
criticism that reconstruct the "place in life" (*Sitz imLeben*) of a text and
(2) those that define its literary character and meaning.

Reconstructions of the Place in Life.   Several types of interpretive analysis
attempt to understand biblical texts in terms of their role in the life of ancient
Israel. Four methods concern us here: historical criticism, source criticism,
form criticism, and sociological/anthropological criticism.

HISTORICAL CRITICISM. Historical criticism assumes that every scriptural
writing has a history of its own, originating in and developing in certain historical circumstances. Historical criticism tries to recover this history by answering questions about authorship, audience addressed, circumstances that
occasioned the writing, and the unity of books or other units of material in the
Hebrew scriptures. A good example of historical criticism is offered by the
book of Isaiah. When analyzed by this methodology, it appears to fall into three
major sections, each coming from a different time in Israel's history. The first
part of the book in the main contains oracles, or short sermons, from Isaiah,
a prophet who lived in Jerusalem in the eighth century B.C.E. He warned Judah
of judgment in the midst of an imminent crisis brought on by the westward
advance of Assyrian conquests. The audience: the proud, selfish leaders of a
nation that has forgotten social and religious obligations to God and neighbor.
The contents of these chapters themselves clearly tie many of Isaiah's words
to particular events during this threatening time. Beginning with chapter 40,
however, both the setting and the mood of the prophetic preaching change and
the style of the oracles is quite different. The enemy is no longer Assyria but
Babylon and punishment is no longer a threat but a judgment already in process and about to end. The prophetic word has now become a promise of return
from exile and restoration. The third section of the book, beginning with chapter 56, presupposes that exiles have returned from Babylonian captivity and
are restoring normal life in and around Jerusalem.

Historical criticism suggests that these materials in the book of Isaiah come
from a number of prophetic spokesmen whose work spanned several centuries.
Those who worked after the eighth century adapted the theological insights of
Isaiah of Jerusalem and applied them to their own audiences. In this way the
prophetic word was kept alive and vital for changed times and circumstances.
When the collection of prophetic literature was gathered and edited, these
materials were related to each other as belonging to the same important prophetic school of thought.

SOURCE CRITICISM. This methodology tries to get behind a work as it now
stands to the sources out of which it is composed. A source critic identifies
strata within a work by characteristics of style, vocabulary, emphases, and so
forth. Once identified, the critic then asks about each source questions like

those asked by historical criticism. In effect, source criticism is a subdiscipline of historical criticism. The identification of four major strata of sources in the Torah (Genesis–Deuteronomy) is one of the outstanding achievements of this method.

The basic collection of laws and stories with which the Hebrew scriptures begin is a multilayered interpretation of Israel's early history and of its sense of responsibility to God and neighbor. In Torah we have not just one point of view from one fixed point in time, but several tellings of the patriarchal and matriarchal and Mosaic stories. Each of these stresses the importance of the ancestral experience of God for its own time and community.

This kind of analysis approaches scripture as dynamic literature that must be relevant to every generation in turn. The Hebrew Bible grew and changed through time with a vitality that confronted the people of each new era with the will of God.

FORM CRITICISM. This approach first sets the bounds of a text that can stand with clear meaning apart from its context. Then it is concerned with (1) the literary form of a text as it now stands, (2) the probable earlier oral form behind the text, (3) the life setting in which such a text was appropriate, and (4) the pattern shared with similar texts in the Hebrew Bible and elsewhere in the ancient world. For example, certain forms of speech are connected with and appropriate for courts of law. In many ancient Israelite towns, court was held in the open public square near the city gate (Amos 5:10; Ruth 4:1). Court procedure and language would have been familiar to most residents. Therefore, when a prophet used language of the courts, hearers easily understood the seriousness of the accusation being brought against them. Form criticism has helped us identify certain prophetic oracles as "prophetic law suits" and to hear them with something of the immediacy of judgment felt by their ancient hearers.

A clear illustration appears in Micah 6:1–8. First, the prophet as prosecutor asks Israel, the accused, to present its case before witnesses:

> Hear what Yahweh says:
> Rise, plead your case before the mountains,
>   and let the hills hear your voice.
> Hear, you mountains, the controversy of Yahweh,
>   and you enduring foundations of the earth;
> for Yahweh has a controversy with his people,
>   and he will contend with Israel.

Next God testifies:

> O my people, what have I done to you?
>   In what have I wearied you? Answer me!
> For I brought you up from the land of Egypt,
>   and redeemed you from the house of slavery; . . . .

> O my people, remember now what
> > Balak king of Moab devised,
> > what Balaam the son of Beor answered him,
> and what happened from Shittim to Gilgal,
> > that you may know the saving acts of Yahweh.

The people present a defense:

> With what shall I come before Yahweh,
> > and bow myself before God on high?
> Shall I come before him with burnt offerings,
> > with calves a year old?
> Will Yahweh be pleased with thousands of rams,
> > with ten thousands of rivers of oil?
> Shall I give my first-born for my transgression,
> > the fruit of my body for the sin of my soul?

This defense is then refused by the prophet prosecutor:

> He has told you, O mortal, what is good;
> > and what does Yahweh require of you
> but to do justice, and to love kindness,
> > and to walk humbly with your God?

Did the prophets actually deliver these oracles in the court setting of the city gate? One can imagine that they did. Even if they did not, the judicial character of these oracles is unmistakable. The use of court language by the prophets in condemning injustice must have been both a stern reminder of Israel's responsibility to a system of justice believed to have been revealed by God and a strong condemnation of abuses of that system.

Form criticism also enables us to distinguish different types of psalms and to assign them to appropriate occasions in the worship life of Israel. Psalm 24, for example, is a hymn used in a liturgical procession entering the Jerusalem temple:

> The earth is Yahweh's and all that is in it,
> > the world, and those who live in it;
> for he has founded it on the seas,
> > and established it on the rivers.

> Who shall ascend the hill of Yahweh?
> > And who shall stand in his holy place?
> Those who have clean hands and pure hearts,
> > who do not lift up their souls to what is false,
> > and do not swear deceitfully.
> They will receive blessing from Yahweh,
> > and vindication from the God of their salvation.
> Such is the company of those who seek him,
> > who seek the face of the God of Jacob.

> Lift up your heads, O gates!
> > and be lifted up, O ancient doors!
> > that the King of glory may come in.

Who is the King of glory?
>   Yahweh, strong and mighty,
>   Yahweh, mighty in battle.
Lift up your heads, O gates!
>   and be lifted up, O ancient doors!
>   that the King of glory may come in.
Who is this King of glory?
>   Yahweh of hosts,
>   he is the King of glory!

Priests carrying the Ark, God's portable throne, approach the temple into which they are welcomed with shouts of God's glory. A hymn like this belonged to joyful ritual celebration of God's kingship.

In contrast, Psalm 60 comes from a solemn time of national crisis:

O God, you have rejected us, broken our defenses;
>   you have been angry; now restore us!
You have caused the land to quake;
>   you have torn it open;
>   repair the cracks in it, for it is tottering.
You have made your people suffer hard things;
>   you have given us wine to drink that made us reel.

You have set up a banner for those who fear you,
>   to rally to it out of bowshot.
Give victory with your right hand, and answer us,
>   so that those whom you love may be rescued.

God has promised in his santuary;
>   "With exultation I will divide up Shechem,
>   and portion out the Vale of Succoth.
Gilead is mine, and Manasseh is mine;
>   Ephraim is my helmet;
>   Judah is my scepter.
Moab is my washbasin;
>   on Edom I hurl my shoe;
>   over Philistia I shout in triumph."
Who will bring me to the fortified city?
>   Who will lead me to Edom?
Have you not rejected us, O God?
>   You do not go out, O God, with our armies.
O grant us help against the foe,
>   for human help is worthless.
With God we shall do valiantly;
>   it is he who will tread down our foes.

In somber mood this lament cries out for God's deliverance from national enemies.

Form criticism has also enriched our understanding of the art of biblical narratives. Israel's way of speaking about God was to tell stories about God's

deeds. These narratives are of many different kinds, so the better we understand their style and structure, the better we will be able to know their significance in the religious life of Israel and their meaning for us as part of scripture.
This approach to narratives often reveals the process by which Hebrew biblical
traditions were gathered and shaped. It points out smaller units embedded in
a longer narrative and emphasizes their importance for understanding the
larger narrative. For example, Deuteronomy 26:5–9 is a short confession of
faith recited with the offering of the firstfruits of harvest:

> A wandering Aramean was my ancestor; he went down into Egypt and lived there
> as an alien, few in number, and there he became a great nation, mighty and
> populous. When the Egyptians treated us harshly and afflicted us, by imposing
> hard labor on us, we cried to Yahweh, the God of our ancestors; Yahweh heard
> our voice and saw our affliction, our toil, and our oppression. Yahweh brought
> us out of Egypt with a mighty hand and an outstretched arm, with a terrifying
> display of power, and with signs and wonders; and he brought us into this land,
> a land flowing with milk and honey.

A similar confession is found in Deuteronomy 6:20–24:

> When your children ask you in time to come, "What is the meaning of the decrees
> and the statutes and the ordinances that Yahweh our God has commanded you?"
> then you shall say to your children, "We were Pharaoh's slaves in Egypt, but
> Yahweh brought us out of Egypt with a mighty hand. Yahweh displayed before
> our eyes great and awesome signs and wonders against Egypt, against Pharaoh
> and all his household. He brought us out from there in order to bring us in, to
> give us the land that he promised on oath to our ancestors. Then Yahweh com-
> manded us to observe all these statutes, to fear Yahweh our God, for our lasting
> good, so as to keep us alive, as is now the case . . . ."

The form critics who first emphasized the importance of these credos/creedal
statements believed them to be the bases around which larger narratives were
formed.[13] Recently, however, it has been suggested that these credos and others like them are summaries in easily remembered form of the massive narratives of Torah. The credo in effect condenses the various stories about Israel's
ancestors, the exodus from Egypt, the giving of the law at Sinai, and the settlement in Canaan.[14] Torah took shape in the worship life of the community.
In either case the confession of God's significant deeds in its history was at the
heart of Hebrew worship.

SOCIOLOGICAL/ANTHROPOLOGICAL CRITICISM. This is yet another method
for placing texts from the Hebrew Bible in their context. It approaches the
texts from the perspective of the social sciences. As our knowledge of the world
and culture of the ancient Near East has increased, biblical scholarship has
begun seriously to point to the important roles that culture plays in shaping
life and literature. The significance and consequences of social change is a good
example. What happens to Israel's institutions when the people move from a

---

[13]See von Rad, "The Form-critical Problem of the Hexateuch," in *Problem*.
[14]See Douglas A. Knight, "The Pentateuch," in Knight and Tucker, *Bible*, pp. 263–67.

nomadic to an agricultural to a mercantile society? Or, what changes are necessary when Israel's homeland is destroyed and they are carried into exile in a foreign land? Such changes affected all aspects of Israel's life: the relationship between classes, the nature of political and religious leadership, the location and nature of Israel's worship, the structure and application of law codes, and the way they selected, preserved, and interpreted religious texts. Other examples are the conditions of the middle and lower-class people, changes in the economy, the infiltration of foreign elements into Israelite culture, and so forth. Considering factors like these and using data from the biblical materials and utilizing the vast amount of socioeconomic information being provided by the so-called "New Archeology" (see the discussion in Chap. 2), sociological interpreters have made significant contributions to our understanding of early Israelite life, the "conquest" of Canaan,[15] the institutions of the monarchy, and the nature of prophecy.

Other scholars influenced by anthropological studies of primitive or traditional peoples are beginning to make exciting suggestions about Israel's life and culture. They subject the life and thought and religion of the biblical Israelites to the same scrutiny with which field anthropologists study primitive or traditional communities in Africa, Asia, the Americas, and the Pacific islands. Then, comparing the cultures at points where there are similarities, they use the anthropological data to interpret the biblical data. This method of "comparative inquiry" points out that "humans in different times and places struggle with similar sorts of issues, such as the meaning of existence, human sexuality, the difference between genders, the question of what happens at death, and so forth.[16] Therefore, even though different peoples have different histories and contexts, their cultures inevitably have features in common.

Comparative inquiry has already helped us better to understand biblical ideas about impurity and circumcision; and clean and unclean persons, foods, and practices;[17] and the importance of sacred space and time. The method further promises to help us understand (1) the importance of proverbs as a method of educating youths about adult responsibilities—that is, proverbs as a means of social control; (2) the nature, context, and ceremony of ritual healing; and (3) the roles of prophets and priests in matters like these. It may provide us additional data about the significant roles of women in patriarchal societies.

Methodologies To Define the Literary Character and Meaning. The methodologies discussed so far have been "excavative"—that is, they are concerned with the background, form and structure, and development of texts. All these enhance our understanding of the history that lies behind the texts in the

[15]See Gottwald, *The Tribes of Yahweh: A Sociology of the Religion of Liberated Israel, 1250–1050 B.C.E.* (Orbis, 1979).

[16]Eilberg-Schwartz, *The Savage in Judaism*, p. 101.

[17]See Mary Douglas, *Purity and Danger*, (Routledge & Kegan Paul, 1966), chap. 3.

Hebrew Bible. Other critical methodologies deal with the texts as they were finally shaped.

REDACTION CRITICISM. Redaction criticism or editorial criticism is concerned with the way the writers of the materials, as we now have them, selected, combined, and arranged already existing materials to express special concerns and emphases. Every combination of traditions has a literary life and purpose of its own, shaped by the theological interests of the redactor or editor. Redactors are interpreters of the materials out of which they structure a text. Thus, new meaning is given to a variety of materials of differing points of view.

A good example is the way in which the deuteronomic narrator used his source materials in producing 1 and 2 Kings. The narrator cites his own sources for the reigns of Israelite and Judean kings—"the book of the acts of Solomon" (1 Kings 11:41), "the Book of the Chronicles of the Kings of Israel" (1 Kings 14:19), and "the Book of the Chronicles of the Kings of Judah" (1 Kings 14:29). He combined these materials with stories about prophetic figures who often stand against the royal policies of the kings. In so doing, he shaped a new work that makes particular theological evaluations about Israel's life in the land of Canaan. Rather than merely chronicling the reigns of the kings, the redactor interprets them in light of a certain understanding of God's commitment to and claims on the people of Israel as a people of the covenant. The narrator in Chronicles uses many of the same materials as the deuteronomic narrator, including the deuteronomic materials in Samuel and Kings, to make a different interpretation and application. Redaction criticism analyzes the way the redactors as creative theologians used the sources they were editing to suit their individual purposes. Redaction criticism also demonstrates that already in the early stages of development of the materials in the Hebrew scriptures there were important attempts to interpret and apply significant religious texts in changing historical contexts.

LITERARY CRITICISM. This approach to biblical texts studies them in the perspective of their literary type or genre. The literary critic may be interested in the date, authorship, historical or nonhistorical character, or setting or context of the materials, but these matters are decidedly secondary in this methodology. The primary concern is the type of literature that is being studied and reflection on the way the genre influences interpretation. The basic literary genres are, of course, poetry and prose although a sharp line cannot be drawn between the two everywhere in the Hebrew Bible. Each category has many variations or subtypes, and selected examples will illustrate their character, content, and style. A simple systematic classification of poetry and prose types gives some feeling for the richness of Israelite literature.[18]

---

[18]This procedure is followed in the form-critical sections of the introductions of Eissfeldt, Weiser, and with modifications Sellin-Fohrer. Koch (*Growth*, pp. 25–26) points out some of the disadvantages of this kind of classification. These disadvantages, however, are not significant for an introductory study of the Hebrew Bible.

1. *Poetry.* In Israel poetry as a literary type is probably older than prose. It was characteristic of early peoples who ascribed special power and effectiveness to fixed formulas with rhythmic wording and sound. Poetry in Israel often retains the power of an utterance objectively directed to change a situation. For example, the formula of priestly benediction in Numbers 6:24–26 undoubtedly intended to create the ends about which it speaks:

> Yahweh bless you and keep you:
> Yahweh make his face to shine upon
> you, and be gracious to you:
> Yahweh lift up his countenance upon
> you, and give you peace.

The same intention is present in the commissioning of a prophet in Jeremiah 1:9–10:

> Now I have put my words in your mouth,
> See, today I appoint you over nations and
> over kingdoms,
> to pluck up and to pull down,
> to destroy and to overthrow,
> to build and to plant.

Most Hebrew poetry has advanced beyond this practical purpose of affecting a certain life situation, but it has its roots in that sort of dynamic attempt to deal with reality.

Out of these roots Israel developed an extensive poetic literature in which certain characteristics are distinguishable. It is clear that rhythmic arrangement was typical. Hebrew songs were sung to the accompaniment of music and dancing, but unfortunately the traditional settings have been lost and cannot be reconstructed. Nonetheless rhythm as a matter of stress or emphasis based on significant words and the thought structure of the poetic line is still clearly discernible in the Hebrew texts of biblical poems, song, and proverbs. Unfortunately, the rhythmic character of the Hebrew text is not so readily recognized in English translations.

Another feature of Hebrew poetry is parallelism, the regular use of verses with two parts, or lines that have a definite relationship to each other. In some cases the relationship is a direct parallelism in thought between the first and second members.[19] This is called synonymous parallelism and is illustrated in Psalm 24:1:

> The earth is Yahweh's and all that is in it,
> the world, and those who live in it.

---

[19]Thus the term *Parallelismus membrorum*, which is applied to this characteristic of Hebrew poetry. It is not fully appropriate but is regularly used.

Or there can be an antithesis between the ideas expressed in the two lines, so that the contrast of the second line sharpens the emphasis of the first. An illustration of antithetical parallelism is Psalm 1:6:

> For Yahweh watches over the way of the righteous,
>> but the way of the wicked will perish.

Some parallelisms are often complex, as illustrated by Deuteronomy 32:1–2 where synonymous parallelisms are present in both the words and the meaning content of verse lines:

> Give ear, O heavens, and I will speak;
>> let the earth hear the words of my mouth.
> May my teaching drop like the rain,
>> my speech condense like the dew;
> like gentle rain on grass,
>> like showers on new growth.

Another variation occurs in Psalm 1:1–6 where both forms of parallelism are present in the lines of the two halves of the poem and where the second half is antithetical to the first:

> Happy are those
>> who do not follow the advice of the wicked,
> or take the path that sinners tread,
>> or sit in the seat of scoffers;
> but their delight is in the law of Yahweh,
>> and on his law they meditate day and night.
> They are like trees
>> planted by streams of water,
> which yield their fruit in its season,
>> and their leaves do not wither.
> In all that they do, they prosper.
>
> The wicked are not so,
>> but are like chaff that the wind drives away.
> Therefore the wicked will not stand in the judgment,
>> nor sinners in the congregation of the righteous;
> for Yahweh watches over the way of the righteous,
>> but the way of the wicked will perish.

Complementing the rhythmic and parallel structure of poetic verses is a wide range of sound repetition and sound patterns. This feature is discernible only in Hebrew, involving alliterations, repeated sounds, rhymes, and sound puns that cannot be easily translated. The following examples can partially illustrate this feature:

> I will riddle you a riddle. . . .
> Riddle your riddle and we will hear.
> [Judges 14:12a, 13b, our translation]

> he expected justice (*mishpat*),
> > but saw bloodshed (*misphach*),
> righteousness (*tsedakah*),
> > but heard a cry (*Tseakah*)!
> > > [Isaiah 5:7b]

The best way to understand the rich variety of Hebrew poetry is to read it. The following classification gives examples of the more important types of poetry.[20] Sample some of each group to get a feeling for and appreciation of the art of Israelite poets.

A. Sayings. Sayings represent attempts on occasions of almost every kind to express thoughts with solemnity, richness of expression, or exhilaration not common to everyday speech. Their range is extensive.
   1. Sayings from the life of an individual: Psalm 2:7, 23; 127:3; Genesis 2:23; 24:60; 35:17; Isaiah 9:5; Ruth 4:11; Hosea 2:4; Job 1:21.
   2. Sayings from the life of the community: 1 Samuel 10:24; 2 Samuel 10:12; 14:4; 15:10; Exodus 17:16; Numbers 10:35–36; 1 Kings 5:17; Genesis 9:6; Deuteronomy 25:9.
   3. Cultic sayings:
      a. Divine sayings (sayings where the speaker is understood to be God, although the spokesman is known to be a priest or prophet): Exodus 22:28; 33:19; Leviticus 11:44–45.
      b. Priestly sayings: Numbers 6:24–26; Zechariah 2:17.
   4. Prophetic sayings (here are included most oracles of the prophets, many of which are adaptations or utilizations of other literary forms). Typical examples: Jeremiah 2:1–3; 5–13; Amos 2:6–11; 4:1–3; 5:2–5.
   5. Wisdom sayings:
      a. Proverbs: Jeremiah 21:29; 23:28; 1 Kings 20:11; Proverbs 13:3; Isaiah 10:15.
      b. Riddles: Judges 14:14, 18.
      c. Wisdom sayings, practical wisdom for living: Proverbs 10.
B. Songs. Israel loved singing and its literature is filled with songs. Most of these are cultic, but some secular songs are also preserved.
   1. Secular songs: Numbers 21:17–18; Song of Solomon; 2 Samuel 1:19–27; 3:33–34.
   2. Cultic songs:
      a. Hymns: Psalms 8, 29, 47, 65, 87, 100, 105, 150.
      b. Communal laments: Psalms 44, 74, 79, 80, 85, 123.
      c. Individual laments: Psalms 3–7, 12, 25, 28, 140.
      d. Songs of thanksgiving: Psalms 30, 32, 41, 67, 124.

---

[20]The classification is based on that in Otto Eissfeldt, *Old Testament: An Introduction* (Harper & Row, 1965).

e. Songs associated with the life of the king: Psalms 2, 18, 20, 45, 72, 110.

f. Wisdom songs: Psalms 1, 37, 49, 73, 91.

In the poetry of Psalms, Proverbs, Lamentations, and prophetic oracles, it is obvious that theme, images, and literary mood are more important than is plot. The literary critic is interested in either the idea or the feeling, often both, conveyed by the poem. So this critic looks for the rhetorical devices in the poem that help convey its theme or mood. Psalm 23 is a fine example of a poem in which the symbolic use of words and images—"shepherd," "green pastures," "still waters," "rod and staff"—convey a feeling of security and contentment. And they do so much more effectively than would description in prose form. A different feeling is conveyed in the images of the following judgment oracle from Isaiah 1:10–20:

> Hear the word of Yahweh,
>> you rulers of Sodom!
> Listen to the teaching of our God,
>> you people of Gomorrah!
> What to me is the multitude of your sacrifices?
>> says Yahweh;
> I have had enough of burnt offerings of rams
>> and the fat of fed beasts;
> I do not delight in the blood of bulls,
>> or of lambs, or of goats.
>
> When you come to appear before me,
>> who asked this from your hand?
>> Trample my courts no more;
> bringing offerings is futile;
>> incense is an abomination to me.
> New moon and sabbath and calling of convocation—
>> I cannot endure solemn assemblies with iniquity.
> Your new moons and your appointed festivals
>> my soul hates;
> they have become a burden to me,
>> I am weary of bearing them.
> When you stretch out your hands,
>> I will hide my eyes from you;
> even though you make many prayers,
>> I will not listen;
>> your hands are full of blood.
> Wash yourselves; make yourselves clean;
>> remove the evil of your doings
>> from before my eyes;
> cease to do evil,
>> learn to do good;
> seek justice,
>> rescue the oppressed,
> defend the orphan,
>> plead for the widow.

Come now, let us argue it out, says Yahweh;
    though your sins are like sacrlet,
    they shall be like snow;
though they are red like crimson,
    they shall become like wool.
If you are willing and obedient,
    you shall eat the good of the land;
but if you refuse and rebel,
    you shall be devoured by the sword;
    for the mouth of Yahweh has spoken.

2. *Prose.* The stylistic characteristics of Hebrew prose are frequently the result of transmission and editing. Generally however, in prose narrative the language moves forward passionately from word to word and action to action. Numerous short sentences are linked by "and" with the effect of moving swiftly to a sudden conclusion. Character and situation are often revealed by dialogue/conversation rather than by description. Certain episodes are used more than once with slight variation. Other episodes are used frequently as type scenes—that is, the same events are repeated but the time, place, and characters are different.

A wide variety of prose forms was used in Israelite literature. Form critics have classified these into four comprehensive groups: speeches, records, laws, and narratives. Like Israelite poetry, Israelite prose can be appreciated best by examining some typical examples.

A. Speeches. Speeches include sermons and prayers, which also represent immediate contact between speaker and person or persons addressed.
    1. Speeches: Joshua 24; 1 Samuel 12; 1 Kings 2:1–9; 2 Kings 18:19–25; 28–35; Judges 9:7–20.
    2. Sermons: Deuteronomy 3:18–22; 7:1–26; Ezekiel 20.
    3. Prayers: Judges 10:10; 16:28; 1 Kings 3:6–9.
B. Records. Relatively few Israelite records have been preserved. Those available are particularly interesting.
    1. Contracts: Genesis 21:22–32; 31:44–54, 1 Kings 5:16–23.
    2. Lists: Genesis 10; 1 Chronicles 1–9; 2 Samuel 8:16–18; Exodus 35:21–29; Ezra 2:2–61; Nehemiah 7:7–63.
C. Laws. The Hebrew Bible contains laws regulating every aspect of Israel's life: Exodus 21:2–22; Deuteronomy 15:12–18.
D. Narratives. Narratives with poetic nonliteral character.
    1. These narratives represent popular comment on what has happened, kept alive by oral tradition.[21] Examples include: Genesis 2:4b–4:26; 16:4–14; 25:1–6, 21–26; Exodus 4:24–26.
    2. Historical narratives: Judges 2, 9; 2 Samuel 9–20; 1 Kings 1–2.

---

[21]All narrative types probably originated in storytelling.

3. Novellas or short stories of particular persons in their historical setting: Genesis 37; 39–48; 50; Ruth; Jonah.

Literary critics are concerned with the meaning of the text as it now stands. In interpreting it they consider the following literary features:[22]

1. Theme: the central dominating idea; sometimes stated but often the abstract concept made concrete through its representation in plot structure, character, action, and images. Theme is the central idea of a literary work; it enables readers to relate the work to their own world. It provides a point of contact between the text and the life of the reader.
2. Plot: the formulation about the relationships existing among the incidents of a narrative; a guiding principle for the author and an ordering control for the reader. Plot focuses life by selecting a few emotions, conflicts, characters, or episodes out of many and presenting them in an orderly way. Plot is the plan of the narrative that makes it interesting.
3. Climax: the point of highest interest, the point at which readers make their greatest emotional response, often a turning point in the action.
4. Denouement: the unraveling of the plot, the solution of the mystery, the explanation or outcome.
5. Interlude: episodes that interrupt the continuity of the main narrative, but often relate to and further the theme of the main narrative.
6. Characterization: the revelation of character by exposition—that is, identification, definition, classification, illustration, analysis; by presentation of the character in action; or by dialogue.
7. Symbol: something that suggests universal meaning; an image that goes beyond the reality it images to suggest other levels of meaning.

The literary critic takes the text of a narrative as it stands, analyzes the characters and the roles they play, and looks for the tensions and resolutions of the plot. Theme, image, metaphor, climax and anticlimax, and literary mood are of primary concern. A good plot entices the reader to read on to discover what happens, how the characters interact, what changes occur, and what the resolution is. Examples of biblical narrators' skillful use of plot are the stories of Abraham and Isaac (Genesis 12–22), Joseph and his brothers (Genesis 37–50), Moses and the Egyptian pharaoh (Exodus 1–15), Ruth, Jonah, and the court narrative of David's reign (2 Samuel–1 Kings 2).

> Select one of the passages and identify as many of the seven items above as appear in the materials.

A literary critical reading of the Hebrew biblical text discovers a skilled use of words to clarify theme and develop plot. Thematic and symbolic key words focus the historical, psychological, and theological meanings of these stories. In the patriarchal stories of Genesis the words "blessing" and "birthright" punctuate for the reader the idea of Israel's being born to fulfill a special his-

---

[22]These definitions are essentially taken from Holman, *Handbook*. Extensive illustrations are found in the discussions of the patriarchs/matriarchs in chap. 3 below.

toricaldestiny. In the Exodus narrative, "rod," a symbol of power, and "blood and water," a symbol of both death and life, point toward God's deliverance of a slave people from bondage in a life-and-death struggle with the ruling powers, human and divine, of Egypt. Other artful uses of words are contrasts between opposites like "light and darkness," "life and death," "heaven and earth"; the word puns, frequent in Hebrew but unfortunately obscured in translation; and the symbolic meaning of names, even the name of God.

These literary features are not, of course, equally present in all texts. Plot and characterization are common in narrative, but absent in proverbs, psalms, and most prophetic oracles, where theme, image, and metaphor are more widely present. Everywhere, except in law collections, boundary lists, and the like, literary skill is present, making the text alive and interesting. Thus the Hebrew Bible is in one sense a work of literary art. Biblical narrative is more than a cold and dry recording of events; it is the skilled use of literary devices to depict an intimate encounter between persons and their God. This story-telling art, poetry, and drama are reasons why much Hebrew literature has for centuries appealed to readers, who find in it meaning for their own age.

Structuralist and Reader Response Criticisms

Structuralist and reader response criticisms are variations of the more traditional literary criticism. Both are concerned with structures that influence the meaning of texts—structures inherent in the text but not immediately obvious, or structures the reader brings to a text out of the reader's own experience.

Structural Criticism. Structuralists relying on anthropological and sociological research and theory suggest that human existence is based on deep subliminal patterns of meaning that affect thought and action. All humanity shares the same mythic structures, and they are commonly expressed in a veiled way (encoded) in the stories, and so forth, that we all tell. These structures are not immediately apparent in all texts, but they do shape them. Therefore, similar themes, ideas, and issues are present in different contexts and are expressed in the patterns of society in worship and in ritual. These structures are composed of two elements (binary) that are in opposition or tension—life and death, order and disorder, chaos and creation, good and evil. Often a third element represents the reconciling of the binary opposites, bridging the gap or reconciling the opposition. If these structures encoded in texts are expressions of meaning at the deepest level, then decoding them enables an interpreter or reader of a text to discover and focus on fundamentally human patterns of thought and belief. Texts of all kinds from one tradition can be compared to and illuminated by texts of similar kinds from many traditions.

Reader Response Criticism. Reader response criticism focuses on a different kind of structure than those encoded in texts—the structure of the reader's context and thought. It differentiates between the interpreter/critic and the reader. The interpreter/critic in analyzing texts to a considerable extent views them as objects to be analyzed. The reader is captured by the text, to some extent subject to the text, that, however, each reader encounters in a unique context. Therefore, reader response critics distinguish between the real reader and the implied reader. The real reader is the actual person who reads the text; the implied reader is the reader the author has in mind when writing the text. There is also a real author who actually wrote the text and the implied author imaged by the reader. Further, there is more than one real reader of a biblical text—the ancient one who is close to the author's time and context and somewhat like the author's implied reader and the modern reader whose time and context is far removed from the real author. All interpreters work from the context of their own psychosocial world. This world may include deeply dynamic psychological and linguistic functions, but it also incorporates more immediate and observable features. Factors such as intellectual acumen, knowledge and information, inspiration and insight, imagination and creativity, religious background and affiliation, inevitably come into play. Interpretation of texts will be directly influenced by these and numerous other characteristics of the interpreter's world.

Although reader response critics put little emphasis on analyses like historical, source, and form criticisms, these methodologies are important to their aim of bridging the gap between the real author and the real reader by presenting texts in ways that address the reader in his or her own context or idiom. The various interpretations of texts are means by which the Hebrew scriptures help readers create contexts for understanding and acting in a "biblical way." The texts "make sense because there is some correlation of textual factors and factors in the reader's world. Characters, events, and situations in the text are not unlike those in the reader's world. But the text often challenges the conceptions and ideologies with which the reader begins, and the reader's world is modified or re-created ideologically. Since world and self do not exist in isolation, however, the reader's self is being redefined in the process. Experience with the text is an experience that alters needs and possibilities. The reader is then creating a world affectively in experience with the text."[23]

Feminine Hermeneutics

Feminine hermeneutics "refers to various methods of interpretation that are guided by an ideology that values the political, economical, and social equality of the sexes."[24] Feminist interpreters work with some or all of the above meth-

---

[23]McKnight, Edgar V., *Post-Modern Use of the Bible*, (Abingdon, 1988) pp. 176–77.
[24]Fewell, Donna N., "Feminist Hermeneutics," *Mercer Dictionary of the Bible*, p. 299.

odologies with the particular point of view that the western scholarly tradition has been dominated by patriarchal values and concerns.

History has been filled with prominent male figures who act in almost exclusively male events. This patriarchal orientation shapes the literature of Western society and is enforced, in turn, by that literature. These interpreters of the Hebrew Bible find it similarly patriarchal and perhaps the source of patriarchal domination of Western thought. This patriarchal bias, of course, was typical of the ancient world in which theHebrew scriptures originated, but its presence does not mean that it is a standard for the life of later religious communities. Feminist interpreters are quick to make this point. Then they move on in these texts, which, after all, informed and shaped the communities of faith to which they belong and have been determinations for their own lives. They read from their perspective and have presented interpretations that refreshingly enrich all interpretations of the Hebrew Bible. As women uncomfortable with and troubled by the male-centeredness of these religious texts, their study of the Hebrew Bible has resulted in new stimulating dimensions of meaning throughout the Hebrew scriptures. Their work has proceeded along a number of different lines:

1. *An emphasis on the concern throughout the Hebrew scriptures on human liberation.* Even though the Hebrew Bible does not oppose directly the oppression of women, it is filled with prophetic texts, with stories that condemn injustices of many kinds, and with prayers and hymns in which the oppressed cry out for help. Seeing these as analagous to women's concerns for liberation, feminist interpreters have found in them provocative new nuances of meaning.

2. *Interpretation of texts that portray women under oppression and texts that traditionally have been understood as negative evaluations of women.* Feminist interpreters admire the courage and determination shown by biblical women in oppressive circumstances, and sympathize with and grieve over their suffering. Their interpretations of "texts of terror," as some have called these stories of oppression, have a quality of sensitive sympathy often lacking in traditional readings of these stories.

3. *Interpretation of texts that portray women positively.* Over against texts that portray women as inferior to men are those that clearly intend a positive evaluation of women, and even some patriarchal texts, when read carefully, represent women more favorably than is at first apparent. Feminist interpreters focus on such texts. Some have, however, raised warning questions: Who defined the positive female qualities found in these texts? Was it the dominating patriarchal community? Are the values by which women are judged favorably the values that males desire them to have?

4. *Matriarchal reinterpretations of some patriarchal stories.* Feminists interpreters sometimes see a matriarchal storyteller behind some stories preserved in a patriarchal setting. In these cases there could be the possibility that a matriarchal retelling of the story might recapture some of its original feminine character and more realistically picture the importance and nobility of women about whom the story is told. This recovery would enrich all, female and male, who read and study the Hebrew scriptures.

5. *Cross-gender interpretation of patriarchy.* Feminist interpreters are beginning to consider how men are portrayed in biblical narratives. Are men also oppressed by patriarchal domination? Do men of patriarchal authority really treat other men any better than they treat women? How do women treat other women?

Canonical Criticism

The various ways of analyzing a Hebrew biblical text provide the interpreter different perspectives for looking at a biblical text. No one method is inherently superior to another. Rather, each complements the other, each adding to the overall understanding of the passage. However, the use of several methods often separates one text or passage from another or even leads to the conclusion that a text is a composite with early and late sections. Upon analysis, each text is part of a larger whole, a context that conditions the meaning of the various parts. So, a question that cannot be avoided by the biblical student is, What is the relationship between the text being studied and those around it? Or to phrase the question in other words, How does a particular text function in the *canonical whole* of which it is a part?

Consider the Abraham story in Genesis 12–25. This narrative can be studied in and of itself. It is a complete story with interesting plot, a theme and sub-themes, and clever use of symbols. Form criticism attempts to describe units in the story preserved in earlier oral form. Historical criticism looks for the historical context of its author and audience and raises questions about the various sources combined in the story as it now stands. Literary criticism looks at its theme, plot, and symbolisms. Sociological analysis looks for the cultural background of such a story and for the significance of the practices and institutions the story depicts. The final questions have to relate this story to its context as part of the canonical book of Genesis and as a part of the canonical Torah. What is the significance of this story in the longer narrative of Torah understood and revered as sacred scripture? Questions about authorship, date, historical setting, and original meaning are important questions. Finally, however, one must ask how the Abraham narrative relates to the preceding chapters of Genesis, to the remainder of the patriarchal narratives, and to the rest of the Hebrew Bible. Hence the materials may be understood to begin the resolution of the human predicament as presented in Genesis 1–11 by introducing the covenant theme depicted dramatically in a God who gives and protects a son of promise—a theme entwined in the remainder of the biblical story. In this sense canonical criticism is the final criticism: it places each part in the context of the whole so that each text is scripture as it stands in relationship to all other texts.

Thus, the interpreter has numerous interrelated methods available to search out the meaning of scripture. They are not all equally applicable to every text. The scholarly community in general has often emphasized one or two above the others, and individual scholars frequently work with a selected few or even a single methodology that suits their interest and interpretive goals. Scholars have used these various interpretive methods largely because for most of them the Hebrew scriptures are meaningful religious literature, and all the methodologies make significant contribution to contemporary understanding of the Bible. The more the data, the deeper and richer the understanding! This ought not to imply that scripture cannot be appreciated without the fruits of scholarly study. Obviously many pious folk, learned and unlearned, read the Hebrew Bible devotionally and derive considerable meaning, knowing little if anything about critical study. However, devotion could be greatly enhanced, and possible misinterpretation avoided, through careful critical analysis so that the Hebrew scriptures better reveal the ways of God and persons and significantly transform life and thought.

Reveal the ways of God and persons and significantly transform life and thought— this is what is meant when the biblical texts are designated as Holy Bible. For Jews, the Hebrew scriptures are *holy,* set apart from other books as the essential revelatory and redeeming texts; for Christians also, but with the addition of the Christian writings in the New Testament. For Muslims, the Hebrew scriptures and New Testament are secondary to the Koran, but also in their own right important religious documents. Three of the world's great religions believe the Hebrew scriptures were "inspired."

Perhaps the most significant factor that persons bring to the interpretive situation is their view of the authority of scripture. To what extent is the Bible a dependable source for religious belief and action? At one extreme a person may assume that the scriptures speak with absolute authority in all matters: science, politics, religion, ethics—whatever. At the other extreme the Bible may be seen as nothing more than a human attempt to solve human problems; accordingly anyone who sees it as more suffers from delusion.

Obviously what one believes about the authority of scripture determines how that person will approach biblical interpretation. Neither of the extremes does justice to materials that have become the "living word" for religious communities over many centuries.[25] For many ancient Hebrews, this "becoming a living word" was an immediate historical reality in their hearing, obeying, and preserving laws, prophetic oracles, and so forth. Therefore, giving divine sanction only to the present canonical form of the Bible shortchanges those devout figures involved long before canonical status was achieved. Can we assume

---

[25]Achtemeier, *Inspiration*, p. 13.

that the prophet Isaiah was inspired, but not those later editors and compilers who brought the present book to its final form? Or ought authority be vested in later redactors to the exclusion of the original "authors"? And what about the inspiration of countless readers who interpret on a variety of levels and find meaning, help, and direction from their interpretation?

These questions point toward a definition that locates inspiration in a process rather than a given moment.[26] The Hebrew Bible affirms Yahweh to be at work in the history of a covenant people, so the contemporary reader may affirm God to be authoritatively at work in the historical interplay of writers who produce, editors who rework, religious communities that canonize, and contemporary readers who find an authoritative word.

SUGGESTIONS FOR FURTHER STUDY

Be sure to become thoroughly acquainted with the skeleton history of Israel. The brief outline on page 6–7 is a good summary; this is the framework for the remainder of our study.

Use the Bible dictionaries listed in the General Bibliography to elaborate the meaning of several items mentioned in this chapter, such as canon and canonization, deuterocanonical, memory unit, covenant, Covenant Code, Decalogue, Sopherim and Masoretes, Septuagint, criticism, feminine hermeneutics, inspiration, Torah, Nevi'im, Kethu'bim, text. *The Anchor Bible Dictionary* will have the more extensive articles; *Harper's, Mercer, Interpreter's,* and the others listed have shorter but dependable entries.

The works on various types of criticism are extensive and a selected number of these are listed in the General Bibliography. At this point, the introductory titles may be more helpful, for example, Edgar McKnight, *The Bible and the Reader: An Introduction to Literary Criticism* (Westminster, 1985), and his earlier, *What Is Form Criticism?* (Fortress, 1969); John Barton, *Reading the Old Testament: Method in Biblical Study* (Westminster, 1984); Phyllis Trible, *Texts of Terror: Literary-Feminist Readings of the Biblical Narrative* (Fortress, 1984); Norman Perrin, *What Is Redaction Criticism?* (Fortress, 1969); Robert R. Wilson, *Sociological Approaches to the Old Testament* (Fortress, 1984); Jon Levenson, *The Hebrew Bible, The OldTestament, and Historical Criticism* (Westminster/ John Knox, 1993); Emanuel Tov, *Textual Criticism of the Hebrew Bible* (Fortress, 1992).

On understanding approaches to inspiration, Paul J. Achtemeier's *The Inspiration of Scripture: Problems and Proposals* (Westminster, 1980) is indispensible. James Barr, *Holy Scripture: Canon, Authority, Criticism* (Westminster,

---

[26]Ibid., pp. 105–36.

1983), is an important discussion of theological interpretation. Bernhard Anderson has edited *The Old Testament and the Christian Faith* (Harper, 1963) and Lawrence Boadt and associates have prepared *Biblical Studies: Meeting Ground of Jews and Christians* (Paulist, 1980), two works that help with understanding the relationship between the two traditions. A general work on the literary nature of the Hebrew Bible appears in the first part of Robert Alter and Frank Kermode, eds., *The Literary Guide to the Bible* (Harvard, 1987).

See the General Bibliography for an extensive listing on Canon, Text, and Versions.

2

Setting the Stage

The Hebrew Bible is a collection of literature from the Jewish community of the ancient Near Eastern world, a world different in kind from what most of us have experienced or even imagined. Like all important literary works, the materials in the Hebrew Bible transcend their ancient and disparate origin and setting, and address the modern reader with enduring literary and religious power. They can be read, appreciated, and responded to with little or no knowledge of the setting from which they came. Consider three texts. The first is the familiar Psalm 23 with its beautiful image of the divine shepherd:

> Yahweh is my shepherd, I shall not want;
> > he makes me lie down in green pastures.
> He leads me beside still waters,
> > he restores my soul.
> He leads me in right paths
> > for his name's sake.
>
> Even though I walk through the darkest valley,
> > I fear no evil;
> for you are with me;
> > your rod and your staff—
> > they comfort me.
>
> You prepare a table before me in the presence
> > of my enemies;
> you anoint my head with oil,
> > my cup overflows.
> Surely goodness and mercy shall follow me
> > all the days of my life;
> and I shall dwell in the house of Yahweh
> > my whole life long.

Of course, the meaning of this poem is clear. We have always understood it, even those of us who live in cities and seldom, if ever, see pastures, sheep, or shepherds. But our appreciation and understanding of the psalm's imagery is sharpened when we have some acquaintance with the character of Palestinian pastureland—the rugged nature of the terrain, the scarcity of water, the places where danger lurked for both sheep and shepherds.

The second example is the less familiar story in 2 Samuel 5:6–10 of King David's capture of Jerusalem from the Jebusites:

> The king and his men marched to Jerusalem against the Jebusites, the inhabitants of the land, who said to David, "You will not come in here, even the blind and the lame will turn you back"—thinking, "David cannot come in here." Nevertheless David took the stronghold of Zion, which is now the city of David. David had said on that day, "Whoever would strike down the Jebusites, let him get up the water shaft to attack the lame and the blind, those whom David hates." Therefore it is said, "The blind and the lame shall not come into the house." David occupied the stronghold, and named it the city of David. David built the city all around from the Millo inward. And David became greater and greater, for Yahweh, the God of hosts, was with him.

Again, we can generally understand the story without further information. However, answers to some questions would enhance our appreciation of David's achievement. What was the size of Jerusalem and how was it fortified? What was the water shaft and how did it provide access to the city? What did David build in Jerusalem? What about Jerusalem made it such an important and lasting center of Jewish life?

The third text is Genesis 12:1–9, the call to Abram to be the father of the future people of Israel—a call he obeyed by making a long journey from Haran to Canaan.

> Now Yahweh said to Abram, "Go from your country and your kindred and your father's house to the land that I will show you. I will make of you a great nation, and I will bless you, and make your name great, so that you will be a blessing. I will bless those who bless you, and the one who curses you I will curse; and in you all the families of the earth shall be blessed."
>
> So Abram went, as Yahweh had told him; and Lot went with him. Abram was seventy-five years old when he departed from Haran. Abram took his wife Sarai and his brother's son Lot, and all the possessions that they had gathered, and the persons whom they had acquired in Haran; and they set forth to go to the land of Canaan. When they had come to the land of Canaan, Abram passed through the land to the place at Shechem, to the oak of Moreh. At that time the Canaanites were in the land. Then Yahweh appeared to Abram, and said, "To your offspring I will give this land." So he built there an altar to Yahweh, who had appeared to him. From there he moved on to the hill country on the east of Bethel, and pitched his tent, with Bethel on the west and Ai on the east; and there he built an altar to Yahweh and invoked the name of Yahweh. And Abram journeyed on by stages toward the Negeb.

This text makes good sense as it stands without further data. It comes closer to life, however, when questions like the following are raised and answered. Where was Haran, Abram's country? Where was Canaan to which he journeyed? Where in Canaan were Shechem, Bethel, Ai, and the Negeb? Can we

place Abram and the other patriarchs in the context of the overall history of
the ancient Near East? What was life like then in Haran? In Canaan? To answer
these, if possible, gives some historical substance to Abram, a character who
otherwise would remain a shadowy figure in a story.

Background information about all three of these texts adds to our understanding of them. Their meaning is not dependent absolutely on such information, but the more one knows about the background of a text, the richer
that text becomes. Geography, archeology, and history expand our information
about the context and thereby enrich our understanding of the text. A geographical overview of the Near East will provide a better appreciation of the
physical, topographical setting of the Hebrew scriptures; archeology provides
historical, sociological, and cultural information. Knowledge of the overall historical context is necessary if we are to understand Israel's experience to be
that of real people in actual time and space. All help to bring the ancient
materials to life in a realistic setting.

GEOGRAPHY OF THE ANCIENT NEAR EAST

Israel's history and culture grew within a specific geography. Geography influences the large interactions of nations, the location of cities, the layout of roads,
the fields of battle, the nature of the economy, sometimes even the character
and forms of religious belief. Physical environment influences the circumstances of everyday life. Tools, houses, foodstuffs, the nature of agriculture,
and the character and extent of industry and trade are affected by the place
where human beings live. To understand the Hebrew Bible, then, one must
know something of the physical characteristics of the Near East. And because
the destiny of Israel was profoundly affected by the place Palestine occupied
in the total geographic picture of the Near East, our concern must encompass
Mesopotamia, Asia Minor, Armenia (today Iraq, Iran, and Turkey), Egypt,
and especially Palestine-Syria (modern Lebanon, Jordan, Syria, and Israel).
To most of us this is a strange and unfamiliar world, but it was the incubator
of biblical peoples and literature.

The "strange new world" of the Hebrew Bible is a little world of great contrasts. It contains fertile river valleys and vast reaches of desert; rugged, barren
mountain slopes; and inviting upland enclaves. It reaches to the heights in
Armenia and plunges to the depths in the Dead Sea. This area was a matrix
of humankind, with its lower mountain slopes, oases, and river valleys forming
a cradle of civilization. Within it some of the great states of the ancient world
developed, and out of its deserts and down from its mountains periodically
came human floods that brought an end to cultural epochs and a beginning to
others. Life was not always easy in the ancient Near East. Inhabitants there
had to face challenges hurled at them by the geographical conditions of their

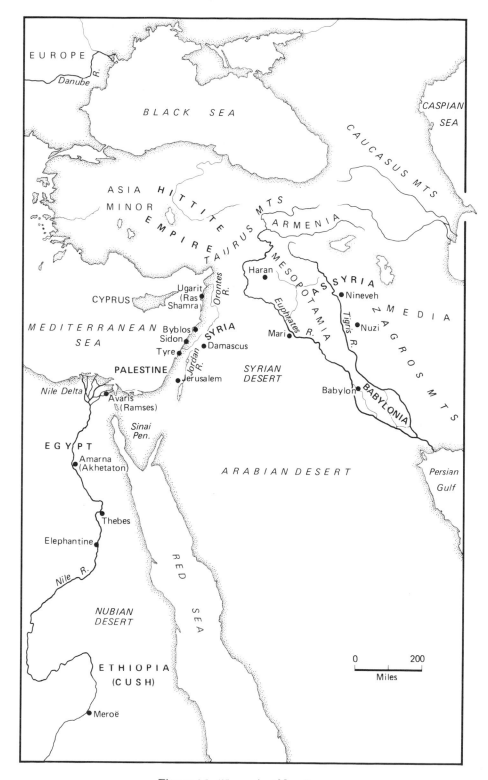

Figure 2.1. The ancient Near East

land. For some, the terror was drought and famine; for others, flood and de-struction; for others, the ordeal of eking out a living in areas where nature itself seemed opposed to survival. Nevertheless, their literature reflects their enthu-siasm for life, their love for their land and their nations, their hopes and dreams for the future. They were at home in the mountains, plains, river valleys, and even the deserts of the Near East and enjoyed life there.

The Fertile Crescent

The geographic world of the Hebrew scriptures is the area along the Tigris and Euphrates rivers (Mesopotamia), the Palestinian coastal plain and hill country, and the Nile River delta and valley in Egypt. This area is commonly called the Fertile Crescent, a name first used by the famous Egyptologist, James H. Breasted. One who is familiar with the green forests and rich agricultural lands of America or Europe might not think of Mesopotamia, Palestine, or Egypt as "fertile." This is a false perspective for judging it, however. To the ancients who lived there these lands watered by the rivers or by the rains blown in off the Mediterranean were good lands "flowing with milk and honey"—lands of pastoral and agricultural abundance.

The population of the ancient Middle East was concentrated in this relatively fertile area. Through it ran the most traveled roads or tracks. Great states were located here and they frequently waged war to control it. The major economic activity was agriculture, but trade and commerce were also common. Roads reached out in all directions, making some of the cities of the area hubs of commercial activity.

Unpromising terrain surrounded the Fertile Crescent. In Egypt the desert crowded the river bed. Its advance was halted only by the annual overflow of the Nile. Along the northern and eastern edges of the Asiatic segment of the Crescent, a series of mountain ranges and plateaus formed a semicircle. In Palestine the fertile areas were broken by low but rugged hills running from north to south through the center of the land.

Desert formed the inner perimeter of the Asiatic portion of the Fertile Cres-cent. This vast interior was partially uninhabitable desert and partially semi-wasteland capable of supporting only sparse nomadic life. In the wasteland, winter provided rain enough for pasture, and the nomad was free to roam with flocks. In summer, however, life was restricted to areas close to oases. The totally desert area, not blessed by winter rains, virtually precluded human use.

Egypt

Since the sixth century B.C.E., Egypt has been called "the gift of the Nile." The inhabited area was basically an oasis formed by the river. The Blue Nile and the White Nile, with sources in the interior of the African continent,

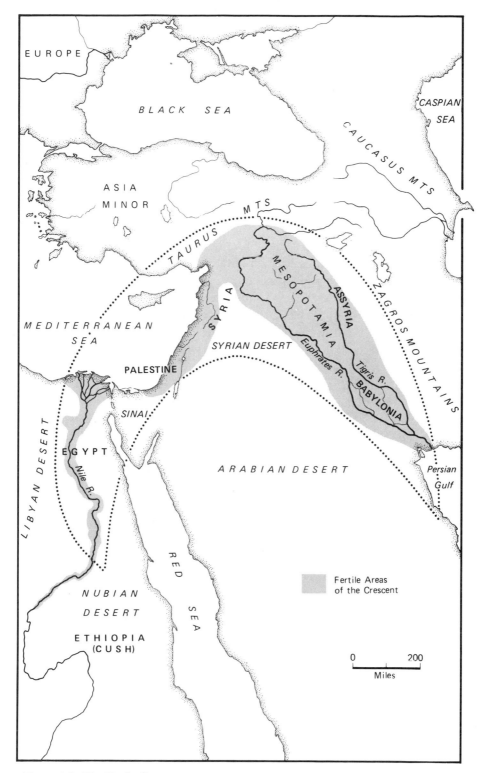

Figure 2.2. The Fertile Crescent

53

merged and flowed some nineteen hundred miles northward to the sea. For the last seven hundred fifty miles, north of six stretches of treacherous rapids or cataracts, the river traversed the territory of ancient Egypt. For the greater part of this distance the river flowed through a fertile valley with limestone cliffs or desert close on both sides. This narrow trough was known as Upper Egypt. At ancient Memphis, near modern Cairo, the Nile spread out into a delta forming a large fertile triangle crossed by many streams through which the river flows to the sea. This delta area constituted Lower Egypt. During the earliest times, Upper and Lower Egypt composed two separate and independent "kingdoms." For all practical purposes, however, the recorded history of Egypt opens at the time of their union.[1]

To all Egypt the annual Nile flood brought life-giving moisture and fertility. Even today, there is no measurable rainfall in Upper Egypt. In Lower Egypt it varies from eight inches in Alexandria to one inch in Cairo. It is no wonder that the ancient Egyptian looked to the Nile as a god. The water began to rise early in July, reached its peak in October, and began to recede early in November. Seed was planted in the still-moist refertilized soil. In the spring, if the floods had been good, there could be a harvest great enough for Egypt to serve as the granary for the ancient Near Eastern world. Egypt was so dependent on the Nile that the balance between prosperity and disaster was very delicate. The seven years of plenty and the seven years of famine known from the Joseph stories "was no fantasy for Egypt; it was always a threatening possibility."[2]

Egyptians have always been faced with the necessity of preserving and utilizing the water of their river so that the fertility of their soil would last more than just a few months. They early developed an extensive system of irrigation and spent a great deal of time and labor bringing water from the river to cultivated fields. Indeed, Egypt was a land "watered by the feet" of those who walked the treadmills of the ever-moving waterwheels that lifted precious water to the levels of irrigation canals by which it was conducted to the fields.

The Nile valley has been accurately called "a tube, loosely sealed against important outside contact."[3] To the west and east lay vast stretches of desert through which no enemy could easily move with force. To the northeast the Sinai region was less forbidding, but still furnished a formidable barrier to any would-be aggressor. To the north lay the treacherous waters of the Mediterranean Sea. To the south were the cataracts of the Nile and vast stretches of inhospitable land. None of these barriers prevented trade, and they contributed greatly to an Egyptian sense of self-sufficiency and independence. Shut up

---

[1]Around 3100 B.C.E. a ruling family from Upper Egypt united the two parts of the land and started a series of dynasties that lasted about three thousand years. Tradition assigns the leading role in this effort to Menes, who is pictured wearing a crown that combines the symbols of both Upper and Lower Egypt.

[2]John A. Wilson, *The Burden of Egypt* (University of Chicago, 1951), p. 10.

[3]Ibid., p. 11.

inside this tube, protected from enemies, the ancient Egyptians lavished attention on themselves. Their land was *the* land. They were *the* people. This intense sense of national pride fostered political stability. Apart from occasional moments when inner weakness and turmoil enabled Asiatics to invade and gain control over Egypt, the management of the country was in the hands of native Egyptian rulers. As a consequence, the civilization of ancient Egypt retained the same characteristics for more than twenty centuries, and the main outlines of its history are easy to follow.

Altogether, regularity of the Nile, security against outsiders, constancy of the sun, and stability of government gave Egyptians a sense of "essential optimism about [their] career in this world and the next."[4] Neither the world nor the gods acted capriciously or arbitrarily; they could be relied on. The Egyptian world was ordered and dependable.

Mesopotamia

At the tip of the Fertile Crescent opposite Egypt lay Mesopotamia. The name means "the area between the rivers"—the Tigris and Euphrates. Mountainous and hilly where the rivers rose in the north and northwest, the terrain of Mesopotamia gradually leveled into a great alluvial plain. In the north, along the mountain ranges, there was enough rain for good agriculture and abundant grazing land for nomadic herdsmen. The ancient alluvial plain in the south was formed over many centuries by the two great rivers on their way to the Persian Gulf. There was a gentle sloping of terrain away from the Euphrates, slightly higher in elevation than the Tigris. The rivers, therefore, could be connected by canals from which water was drawn to irrigate agricultural fields. Like Egypt, southern Mesopotamia was made fertile by the waters of its rivers. However, the Tigris and Euphrates were more capricious than the Nile. Their floods were sporadic and often highly destructive.

Unlike Egypt, Mesopotamia was exposed on every side to outside influences and invasion. From time to time marauding tribes descended from the mountains in the north and east, and from the endless steppes in the west. They sometimes laid waste the land and brought to sudden end the culture of centuries. Occasionally they brought new blood and vitality to a dying era and helped to birth a new civilization out of the dying agony of its predecessor.

Northwestern Mesopotamia was the land of Israel's origins. The homeland of its patriarchal ancestors was the area around Haran located on a northern tributary of the Euphrates River. From here Abraham began his journey to the land of promise; to Haran he sent for a wife for his son Isaac; here his grandson Jacob sojourned among Amorite kin and found wives and fortune.

[4]Ibid., p. 13.

Mesopotamia was also home for great empires that influenced Israel's life and thought, and, on occasion, posed serious threats to its security. The early cultures of Sumer and Akkad left their imprints on all the ancient Middle Eastern world. So did the later kingdoms of the Amorites, centered in Mari and Babylon, and the great Mittani or Hurrians, in which Amorite culture merged with that of the Indo-Aryans. Assyria centered in the highlands of Upper Mesopotamia; Babylonia radiated fabled splendor and power from its great city in the southern plain. Israel's destiny was inseparably bound to the desires and fortunes of these powerful states.

Asia Minor-Armenia

Asia Minor-Armenia lay north and northwest of the Fertile Crescent. The entire area was mountainous and suffered from inadequate rainfall. Here, as elsewhere in the ancient Near East, irrigation was necessary if there were to be strong states. The peoples who lived there were of hardy mountain stock and excellent fighters. Under proper conditions they established organized states second to none in the Fertile Crescent. In the second millennium B.C.E., Asia Minor was the home of the Hittites, an empire so powerful that it fought on even terms with Egypt at a time of Egyptian greatness. In the first part of the first millennium B.C.E., an energetic people known as the Urartu established a strong Armenian kingdom that nearly brought Assyria to its knees in the eighth century.

Palestine-Syria

The geographical focus of the Hebrew Bible lay along the Mediterranean seaboard in the area known as Palestine-Syria. Here Israel lived as a nation literally at the crossroads of the Near Eastern world. Palestine-Syria served as the land bridge between the continents of Asia and Africa, and more specifically between Egypt and Mesopotamia. The ports of Phoenicia along the northeastern coast of the Mediterranean provided access to the whole Mediterranean world. All the major land and sea routes converged on the small area where Israel lived. No wonder that ancient Israel thought of its land as the navel of the earth and that medieval geographers thought of Jerusalem as the center of the world.

Geographically, then, Palestine was the point of contact between the great Asiatic and Egyptian empires. The fate and destiny of its peoples were inevitably determined by international relationships between these centers of world power. More often than not, Palestine was within the sphere of influence of one or another of these empires. Only when Egypt and the Asian states were weak did Israel attain any real international stature. When Egypt, Assyria, or Babylon began to fade, Israel could blossom, but never for long and seldom to full flower before being overshadowed by another of its stronger neighbors.

Syria-Phoenicia

The northern part of the land bridge between Asia and Egypt was known as Syria-Phoenicia. From west to east this area was naturally divided into four regions. A narrow plain ran along the coast, quickly rising to a rugged mountain range. There were several good harbors along this coast; the Phoenicians who settled there turned to the sea and became the great seafaring people of the ancient Mediterranean world. The western mountain range, called the Lebanon range, fell away to the valley of the Leontes River. This valley then rose in the east to a second mountain range, the Anti-Lebanon range, capped by high snow-covered Mt. Hermon, the highest peak in the whole of Palestine-Syria. This range fell away to a high desertlike plateau. Located there in a wonderful oasis was Damascus, the capital of the kingdom of Syria, a major rival to the Israelite settlements on the Syrian border.

Palestine

This area derived its name from the Philistines, who settled along its southern coast in the twelfth century B.C.E.. The name given this local coastal area, Philistia, later in the Greek form, Palestine, came to be used for the entire region. An even older name was Canaan. This name originally meant "land of the purple" and probably had reference to the manufacture of purple dye from the murex shellfish found along the coast. Palestine was divided into four geographical zones, defined somewhat by topography.

Coastal Plain. The westernmost of these divisions was a maritime plain extending the entire length of the land, broken only at the point where the Carmel mountain range jutted into the sea. There were no natural harbors on this coast, so Israel did not turn to the sea like its Phoenician neighbors to the north, but lived landlocked in the hill country above the coast. This coastal area was subdivided into three plains—Acre in the north, Sharon in the center, and Philistia in the south.

The plain of Acre extended some twenty-five miles north from Mount Carmel and was from five to eight miles in width. It did not play an important part in Hebrew history, and it is doubtful that it ever really belonged to Israel,[5] being instead the possession of the Phoenician kingdom of Tyre.

The plain of Sharon lay between Carmel and Joppa. It was about fifty miles long and ten miles wide. During biblical times, the northern part of Sharon was largely wild wasteland and marsh. The hills along its eastern boundary were well watered and drained onto the plain, forming extensive marshes. The southern part of Sharon was covered by an impenetrable oak forest. This ex-

[5]Baly, *Geography*, p. 130.

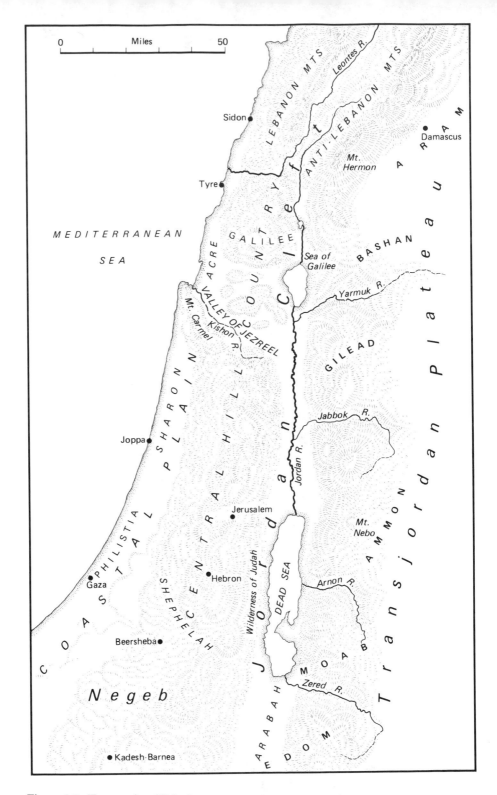

Figure 2.3. Topography of Palestine

plains why Israel never settled in the region, even though it was the only section of the coast over which it had effective control. Israelites thought of Sharon as "something extraordinary, rather exotic and outside their normal experience."[6]

South of the Sharon marshes and forests the character of the plain changed greatly. The land gradually rose to form gentle ranges up to three-hundred feet high. In ancient times this area, known as the plain of Philistia, was open country nearly all arable. It was dotted with grain fields and olive orchards.[7] The only threat to agriculture was the drifting sand, which created a "formidable barrier" along the entire coast, often extending beyond two miles inland.

The coastal plain was never a center of important Israelite settlement in biblical times. Israel never had effective control over any part of it, except the plain of Sharon. Its importance lay in the presence there of a major road from Mesopotamia to Egypt running along the coast, offering Israel opportunities for trade but also opening it to attacks by invading armies.

Central Hill Country. The chief centers of Israel's population and interest lay in the central hill country. An almost continuous range of rugged, rocky hills formed the "backbone" of western Palestine. It began in the Lebanon range in Syria and extended to the desert country in the extreme south of Palestine. Its entire length was broken solely by the Valley of Jezreel, which separated the Galilean hills from those of Samaria. The range was high only in Syria, where it rose at Mt. Hermon to about 6,000 feet. The highest point in Palestine was near Hebron in the south where the hills reached 3,370 feet above sea level. The lack of height in the central hill country, however, was more than offset by the steep and rugged character of the terrain. Although this range of hills was broken at only one place, for purposes of description it may be divided into three sections: Galilee, Samaria, and Judah.

Northern Galilee was a rugged plateau with windswept slopes, which in ancient times were, in all probability, heavily forested. This area was sparsely settled with small agricultural villages and was inconsequential in Israelite history: it often was not actually Israelite territory. Lower or southern Galilee was less hilly and much of its land was arable. Two level plains, one north of Nazareth and the other northwest of the Sea of Galilee, were intensively cultivated. There were numerous Israelite settlements in lower Galilee.

South of Galilee the central range was cut by a large plain that offered easy passage from the coast to the Jordan River valley. The name by which this plain was best known was the Valley of Jezreel (later known by the Greek name, Esdraelon). Jezreel was very fertile and was one of the best farming regions in Palestine. This area was of strategic military importance in ancient times and

[6]Ibid., p. 136; see Isaiah 65:10; 33:9; 35:2.
[7]Judges 15:5.

Figure 2.4. The rolling semidesert terrain of the central hill country near Hebron in the south, an area farmed with great difficulty. (*Illustrator* Photo/David Rogers)

was often the site of a decisive battleground. Within this valley almost every major power in the Near East fought at least one battle. The fame of the Valley of Jezreel as a battlefield with Megiddo as its dominant city provided the New Testament with a rich image for a final battle of Armageddon (Hill of Megiddo) between the forces of good and evil.[8] Of the many cities located there, Megiddo was the most important because it guarded the pass connecting the southern coastal plain with the valley of Jezreel.

At the geographical center of western Palestine were the hills of Samaria. From a watershed that averaged two thousand feet in elevation, these rocky hills descended toward the plain of Sharon, dotted by olive groves and fields. On the east the hills dropped more sharply to the Jordan valley. Viewed from a distance these hills gave the impression of a single massif. The two most conspicuous peaks were Ebal and Gerizim, in the heart of the district. They were significant militarily. Inasmuch as the main roads met near them, control of their slopes meant control of the country. They also had important religious significance for Israel. Between them the people gathered at the end of the war of conquest to ratify a covenant with God. Scattered throughout this mountainous region were numerous plains, meadows, and spacious vales, which created a sense of openness. The abundance of good land in these areas made

[8]See Revelation 16:12–16.

Samaria a fair place to live. It was firmly under Israel's control throughout most of its preexilic history.

South of Samaria lay the mountain fastness of Judah. Its heights formed an upland plateau bordered on the west by a series of low rolling foothills and on the east by the bleak and fearsome "Wilderness of Judah," which dropped off sharply to the Dead Sea. The plateau itself was moorland forested in ancient times with small trees. A prevailing impression was of stone: "The torrent-beds, the paths that are no better, the heaps and heaps of stones gathered from the fields, the fields as stony still, the moors strewn with boulders, the obtrusive scalps and ribs of the hills."[9]

In the brief rainy season, grain in the fields would hide the multitude of stones, and short-lived grass and flowers would clothe the naked hillsides; but soon the grass withered and the flowers faded.[10]

Figure 2.5. A wadi in the Negeb, typical of deep gorges cut by centuries of seasonal waters where there are dry beds most of the year. (Courtesy Israel Office of Information)

[9]G. A. Smith, *The Historical Geography of the Holy Land* (Hodder and Stoughton, 1894), p. 307.
[10]Isaiah 40:7.

Less than half of Judah was arable; the remainder was desert wilderness. Springs or pools were found only at Gibeon, Jerusalem, Bethlehem, and Hebron. There were no year-round streams and even in the rainy season only a few brooks. However, the area was well guarded and easy to defend. On the east were the steep ascent from the Jordan and the stern barrier of the Dead Sea. The western approaches to Judah were protected by low hills and a massive uplift of rock. The northern and southern sectors had less effective natural defenses. The north in particular afforded easy access to the plateau from either side. Nevertheless for the most part the inhabitants of Judah's heartland were insulated in a mountain stronghold. The terrain between this upland plateau and the Jordan cleft was tortuous in the extreme. Perhaps no landscape in the whole of Palestine was less inviting than the Wilderness of Judah. The barren slope plunged chaotically to the depths below. Here there were no cities, but the rugged terrain gave refuge to both monks and outcasts who shunned the towns.

Judah's western frontier was better favored. It was a region of low rolling hills separated from the plateau by a series of valleys that ran north and south.

Figure 2.6. The desolate Negeb south of Jerusalem was sometimes made moderately productive by terracing and irrigation. At about the time of Israel's settlement in Canaan, the technology of digging and waterproofing large cisterns had developed, making areas like this suitable for village settlement. (Courtesy Israel Office of Information)

Figure 2.7. The Sea of Galilee at its northern end with the hills of Transjordan in the background. (Courtesy Israel Government Tourist Office)

The Israelites called this territory the Shephelah or "lowlands." It was a thickly settled and fertile zone, rich in grain, vineyards, and olive groves. The area was important to Judah as a protective frontier. Unless it was in their control, the hill country was left exposed. The conquest of the Shephelah was a prerequisite to any conquest of the highlands.[11]

The narrow division between the Judean highlands and the Shephelah was marked by a line of fortified towns guarding the natural valleys across the region. In the south the Judean hills dropped abruptly into an area of broken and barren plains known in ancient times as the Negeb. This area was a sparsely-settled desert wilderness cut by countless dry valleys and dotted with sand dunes. There was little rainfall in the Negeb and it was continually swept by winds, hot and sand-laden in the summer, cold and cutting in the winter.

[11]Consider Joshua 10 and the campaigns of Sennacherib of Assyria and Nebuchadnezzar of Babylon. See Pritchard, *Texts*, pp. 287–88, and 2 Kings 18:13–19:37; 24:1–25:26.

Figure 2.8. The Jordan River as it exits the Sea of Galilee with Transjordan hills in the background. (*Illustrator* Photo/David Rogers)

The Jordan Cleft. A great geological rift split Palestine as if some giant of old had smitten the land with a battle-ax, leaving behind a gaping wound. The cleft began in Syria where it divided the Lebanon from the Anti-Lebanon range; it continued through Palestine as the Jordan River valley, and farther south it formed the Arabah, Gulf of Aqabah, and Red Sea.

The Jordan River rose on the western slopes of Mt. Hermon in the Anti-Lebanon range. For some distance the river ran above the level of the sea, but soon reached sea level near Lake Huleh.[12] Thence it dropped rapidly to the Sea of Galilee, approximately seven hundred feet below sea level. The "sea" was a beautiful freshwater lake surrounded on almost every side by hills descending gently to the shore. Leaving the Sea of Galilee, the river twisted its tortuous way down (the twisting course is three times the air miles) to the Dead Sea, 1,290 feet below the level of the Mediterranean. The Jordan valley

[12]The modern state of Israel rechanneled the waters of this lake; it no longer exists.

north and south of the Sea of Galilee was intensively cultivated during ancient times and its small tributary streams supplied networks of irrigation channels. Farther south, however, the valley was less inviting. The river ran through a narrow, junglelike depression where wild animals roamed. This southern portion of the valley was largely uninhabited except where major tributaries entered the Jordan from the east and at Jericho, where a great spring watered a lush oasis. Although never very wide except at flood and shallow enough for fording at a number of places, the Jordan and its valley, filled with thick undergrowth and lined with low, slippery, clay hills, was a natural barrier to communication between east and west Palestine. Hence, the Transjordan area was never as completely under the control of the Israelite nation as the territory on the western bank of the river.

The Jordan emptied into the Dead Sea. This sea has no outlet and as a consequence has about 25 percent salt content. Fish entering the sea from the river die in a matter of minutes. In ancient times the Dead Sea did not extend as far south as it does today. It ended opposite the peninsula presently extending from its eastern shore. The area around the sea was most desolate. On the east and the west were forbidding heights and in summer the heat was oppressive. Add to this the deadness of the sea and the area was foreboding. Below the Dead Sea the great rift continued in a dry riverbed known in the Hebrew Bible as the Arabah, an area similar to the Negeb region to the west.

Figure 2.9. Aerial view of the winding course of the Jordan River as it flows from the Sea of Galilee toward the Dead Sea. (Courtesy of Karen Haysod, Jerusalem)

The Transjordan Plateau. The whole of Transjordan was an upland plateau. Four streams, the Yarmuk, the Jabbok, the Arnon, and the Zered, flowed into the Jordan and divided Transjordan into five areas. North of the Yarmuk was the land of Bashan, a fertile area where agriculture was restricted only by inadequate rainfall. The area was noted for extensive grain production. Between the Yarmuk and the Jabbok was Gilead, a well-watered area capable of supporting a large population. In biblical times Gilead was more often directly associated with Israel than was any other area east of the Jordan River. The kingdom of Ammon was located between the Jabbok and Arnon rivers and was periodically controlled by the Israelite kingdoms west of the Jordan. South of the deep Arnon valley lay the kingdom of Moab, on a high and level plateau to which the Israelites rarely laid claim. The southernmost section of Transjordan, the area below the Zered, was Edom, a strong kingdom that controlled the desert trade as well as the copper and iron deposits found along the border of the Arabah.

Modern travelers to Israel and Jordan often wonder at the stark ruggedness of the hills and valleys of Palestine and are awed by its deserts. However, the ancient Israelites saw their land through different eyes, describing it as

> a good land, a land with flowing streams, with springs and underground waters welling up in valleys and hills, a land of wheat and barley, of vines and fig trees and pomegranites, a land of olive trees and honey, a land where you may eat bread without scarcity, where you will lack nothing, a land whose stones are iron, and from whose hills you can mine copper. [Deuteronomy 8:7–9].

Although this may be a somewhat idealized overstatement, by Near Eastern standards Palestine had a well-favored environment.

The territory controlled by Israel in Palestine was about ten thousand square miles, approximately the size of Vermont. The length from north to south was approximately one hundred fifty miles. The width in the north was about thirty-five miles, widening in the south to eighty-five.

The latitude of Palestine is that of the southern United States or southern Spain. It has two seasons, a rainy winter and a rainless, bright summer. The first rains come in September and October, and with them the agricultural year begins. Heavier rains fall from December through March, then come late rains in April and May, hastening the ripening of crops. These rains come from the west off the sea. The clouds drop most of their moisture on the coast and the western slopes of the central mountain range. The eastern slopes get little rain, but the fall increases over the plateaus and hills of Transjordan. The annual average rainfall varies from forty-seven inches in northern Galilee to twenty-five inches on the coast and the western slopes of the central mountains to twelve inches and less in the south of Judah.

The climate is comfortable year round. The summers are hot on the coast and in the lower Jordan valley, but they are pleasant in the highlands. The nights are cool. Winters are cool to moderately cold. There is occasional snow and frosts are common. The average temperature in Jersualem in the summer is about 70°F and in January about 50°F.

Compare the geography and topography of Palestine with that of your home state.

The plains provided good soil for crops of grain, and the mountain slopes were suited to the cultivation of olives, grapes, and vegetables. Farming was not easy and was somewhat risky, depending as it did on the sometimes fickle rainfall, but the agricultural economy was good. Even the deserts were useful. They too got some rainfall, and grasses that grew there were sought out by herders of sheep and goats. Sometimes desert streambeds were dammed and terraced to collect the waters of winter rains, which were used to irrigate fields to support small agricultural communities. The land was a good land, but to make it flow with milk and honey, produce wheat and barley, grow vines and pomegranates, ripen fig and olive trees, long and hard work was required. What life was like in this land for the ancient Israelite will become clearer as we read and interpret the Hebrew biblical materials themselves.

ARCHEOLOGY OF THE BIBLICAL WORLD

The Hebrew Bible also came from an ancient culture different in many ways from our own. The more we know about that culture, the whole way of life of the biblical Israelites, and of their Near Eastern neighbors, the better we shall be able to understand the rich legacy left us in their literature. Archeology of the biblical world has opened the past to us, providing masses of information of great value about "the strange world of the Bible." The information is incomplete, sometimes frustratingly so, is not easy to interpret, and often is not the information we expect or hope for. But archeologists who dig up the past of the Near Eastern world broaden our perspective of the life and culture of the peoples of the Hebrew scriptures and correct our misinformed distortions.

Most writings on archeology spell the word "archaeology." Notice that we are using "archeology," following the *Standard College Dictionary* (Harcourt, Brace and World).

Archeologists do "dig up the past," but the discipline of archeology entails more than just excavation. Archeology involves the recovery (usually, but not always, by excavation) and study of the material remains of past cultures from which conclusions can be drawn about the culture and history of the peoples who left the remains.

Some archeological discoveries have been dramatic and widely publicized. The late nineteenth and early twentieth century excavations at Nineveh, Babylon, and Persepolis uncovered the royal buildings of three great Mesopotamian empires: Assyria, Babylon, and Persia. Many artifacts from these cities were taken as treasures to Europe to be displayed in the British Museum (London), the Louvre (Paris), and the Pergamon (Berlin), where they can still be seen. (See Figs. 8.4, 6, 7 and 1.2, 5, 6.)

At Nineveh the excavations uncovered the library of the Assyrian king, Asshurbanipal, which contained thousands of cuneiform texts, ancient and contemporary, including Mesopotamian versions of creation and flood stories with many similarities to those in the Hebrew Bible. Specialists can read these and other cuneiform texts, thanks to the achievement of an English army officer, Henry Rawlinson, who transcribed and deciphered a mountainside royal inscription[13] of the Persian king, Darius I (522–486 B.C.E.). The scholars have been greatly helped by the work of this amateur.

In the 1960s another large collection of cuneiform texts was discovered in the royal archives of Ebla, the economic and political center of a previously unknown state in Syria. Some two thousand complete tablets and seventeen thousand fragments, making together approximately four thousand complete texts, include administrative texts, lexical texts for scribal references, religious and literary texts, and texts of routine daily correspondence.

A rather wonderful inscriptional find of a different kind was made in 1947 by a young Bedouin shepherd, who wandered into a cave near the shore of the Dead Sea to find a lost animal only to discover a collection of very old biblical scrolls. His discovery ignited an extensive cave hunt by archeologists, biblical scholars, and Bedouin resulting in the discovery by 1960 of scrolls in ten additional caves. There were texts of many kinds, but the most significant were biblical texts dating between 300 B.C.E. and 70 C.E.—the oldest manuscripts of Hebrew biblical texts of which we have knowledge.

The artifacts found in the tomb of the Egyptian Pharaoh Tutankamen are brilliant evidence of Egyptian aesthetics and artistic skills. They have been exhibited worldwide, but they are not as important for understanding the world of ancient Egypt and the role Egypt played in it as the hieroglyphic inscriptions found in tombs and on monuments and temples throughout Egypt. The key to deciphering these "picture writings" was the famous Rosetta Stone, a slab

[13]The Behistun inscription was found near the modern village of Behistun in Iran. The text is a trilingual cuneiform recounting of the military exploits of Darius. The languages are Old Persian, Akkadian, and Elamite. Beginning in 1835 Rawlinson copied the inscription and with his knowledge of local dialects painstakingly deciphered the Old Persian which he published in 1849. With help he deciphered the Akkadian, but due to the poor state of the Elamite version, it was not deciphered until 1951.

of black granite found in the Nile delta in 1798 C.E. by members of a Napoleonic military expedition.[14]

Dramatic in a different way were the discoveries of the water sources at Megiddo and Hazor, which demonstrated the large amount of labor and materials expended to enclose and protect these water supplies. Grimly dramatic and shocking was the evidence uncovered in Jerusalem of the fall of that city to Babylon in 587 B.C.—human remains in ruined and burned houses fallen where they were killed with the weapons that killed them still there with the bones.

For various reasons these and other archeological discoveries have been widely publicized and have captured the attention of the public, but of greater importance are the more routine results of numerous excavations in Syro-Palestine (modern Syria, Lebanon, Jordan, and Israel), the homeland of the ancient Israelites and their immediate neighbors. These excavations, beginning in the 1920s and continuing now at an increasing number each year, belong to two separate phases characterized by different emphases and somewhat different methodologies.

1. *1920–1960: Biblical Archeology.* Biblical Archeology is the designation given the work of a number of like-minded biblical scholars and archeologists (most were both, but biblical scholars first) who had studied with or had been strongly influenced by W. F. Albright, Director of The American School of Oriental Research in Jerusalem. Albright was an exceptionally gifted and learned man with incredible knowledge and expertise in all aspects of ancient Near Eastern studies. He saw archeology as a new tool for biblical studies, which could provide a historical framework "from the Stone Age to Christianity" (the title of one of his books). Consequently biblical characters and events could be given a new historical credibility over against the more negative conclusions of some historical, source, and form critics. To some extent all of the biblical scholar/archeologists in the so-called Albright School shared his concern to support the historicity of the Bible by more or less unquestionable archeological evidence. There was, of course, no intention to avoid negative evidence regarding the historicity of the biblical narrative.

To do this they needed a method that they could use to establish as precise a chronology as possible. Their methodology was sound and has been generally accepted by most archeologists, secular as well as religious. It consisted of *stratigraphy*, the reconstruction of the history of a site, period by period, by uncovering its occupational layers or strata one by one in the reverse order of their being deposited; and *ceramic typology/pottery chronology*, the skill of recognizing and charting changes in pottery styles and then correlating these styles

---

[14]The Rosetta Stone was covered with a trilingual inscription. It included the old hieroglyphic, an ordinary Egyptian script, and Greek. Starting with the Greek, a French scholar, Champollion, began deciphering the hieroglyphic and by 1822 C.E. was able to announce that he could read the language of ancient Egypt.

with similar styles from Egypt and Mesopotamia where ancient records had established fixed chronology points by astronomical references. Albright was *the* master of this skill and the biblical archeologists did establish a reliable and well-accepted fixed chronology for Syro-Palestine. They were not as successful in gaining acceptance for the correlations they made between this chronology and the biblical narratives.

2. *1960–Present: The New Archeology, or the New Biblical Archeology.* In the 1960s three factors contributed to the beginning of a rather revolutionary change in emphasis and some significant changes in archeological methods: (1) Biblical Archeology had not provided data that led to any consensus of scholarly opinion about certain key periods in biblical history—the date and setting of the patriarchal traditions and the date and nature of the "conquest of Canaan." (2) Biblical Archeology's emphasis on a chronological framework had focused on major events and on the excavation of public structures— palaces, fortifications, gateways, temples. Little attention was given to the living and work areas of average people who lived inside the walled town and almost no studies were made in the structures outside town walls. Much was learned about "officialdom" but little about how ordinary people lived. Little was learned about the economy, the environment, or climatic changes that would have affected both. Much that makes the lives of people what they fully are— diet, working conditions, class relationships, aesthetics, and so forth—had been largely ignored by the Biblical Archeologists. (3) More and more of the younger archeologists were accepting the more anthropological approach of New World (American) Archeology, particularly the idea that culture consists of a number of interrelated economic and social subsystems, which leave traces in the archeological record. Thus, the archeological artifacts recovered by excavation are clues to the human behavior of those who made and used them.

To learn more about these things, material remains of every kind have to be recovered and analyzed. Soil from the excavation is fine-sieved and then is put through froth flotation machines to recover seeds, grain, and other very small items. All bone fragments are saved. Pollen samples are taken and objects of material culture are submitted for laboratory analyses of various scientific kinds. This kind of careful recovery of data is also used on the non-tell structures that must have surrounded the walled sites. In addition, the New Archeology studies one-level occupational sites scattered here and there across the countryside. These sites can be identified by surface survey aided by new methods of aerial photography that exposes beneath the surface outlines of structures. The wider the area surveyed, the better the understanding of the relationship between urban and rural societies, the distribution and density of population, and the impact of changes in the climate.

The archeological staff now needs to be multidisciplinary. It will still include the traditional biblical scholars, historians, stratigraphers, and ceramic experts since the biblical archeologists' interest in the history of a site remains important. Now staffs may also include geologists, geomorphologists, climatologists, paleoethnobotanists, zoologists, cultural and physical anthropologists, ethnographers, and surely computer experts (considering the vast amounts of data to be analyzed). This is a formidable lineup to analyze a wide range of objects: remains of buildings, written materials, ritual objects, household objects, personal items, weapons, animal and human bones, weights, coins, even grains, seeds, and scraps of foods. The goal is to reconstruct, as far as possible, the day-to-day life of ancient peoples.

These new emphases and procedures do not negate the Biblical Archeologist's concern for relationship between the scriptures and archeological discoveries. The Bible is, after all, the one text, the use of which if ignored denies the archeologist an essential interpretive resource. Biblical scholarship, whatever its goals may be, cannot ignore the results of the careful and thorough investigative programs followed by the New Archeologists. The New Archeology—properly called the New Biblical Archeology—can tell us much about a biblical situation that the scriptures do not tell us: things, indeed, that to a considerable extent shaped the biblical situation.

Most Near Eastern excavations have been at tells, the sites of ancient towns, because they are the most obvious remains from ancient times. "Tell" is an Arabic word for a mound built up by many years of human occupation. Hundreds of tells are spread all over the Near East. Each tell is a low, flat-topped, human-made hill created by repeated occupation and abandonment of the same site over hundreds or even thousands of years. Early settlers would be attracted to a place because of certain natural advantages it offered: a good water supply, a level space for building, some elevation above the surrounding area so that it could be more easily defended, a strategic location for economic purposes such as the center of a rich agricultural area or the crossroads of trade routes. The settlers would build there, eventually surrounding their town with walls. As generations passed, the site would be rebuilt many times. Some of the changes would be relatively minor; others, after earthquakes or war, for instance, would be extensive. Gradually the debris of everyday life and the repeated building on the same site would grow into a tell built up by the many strata or layers of occupation. As in a great layer cake, successive centuries of life and culture lie in a tell waiting to be uncovered and interpreted. The most recent occupational level is near the surface of the tell; the most ancient is at the bottom just above virgin soil or bedrock.

Excavation is the process of carefully uncovering each successive layer of selected parts of a tell. Rarely has an entire tell been excavated because to do so destroys much of the evidence. Archeology is an inexact science and archeologists want to be able to return to a site for further study as methodologies are refined. Besides, total excavation of a tell of any size would be prohibitively expensive. The archeologist, therefore, chooses strategic parts of the tell suitable for his purposes and digs there. Biblical archeologists typically selected gateways, citadels, palaces, temples, and some living quarters. Practitioners of the New Archeology would not ignore these places, but would include more

(a)

(b)

Figure 2.10 a & b. The tell of Beersheba, considerably disturbed by excavations, but nonetheless illustrating that successive occupations built the site into a mound. The lower aerial photo shows the exposed results of the work of the archeologist on top of the tell. (Top photo courtesy *Illustrator* Photo/David Rogers; bottom photo courtesy Duby Tal/Albatross Aerial Photography, Jerusalem)

Figure 2.11. Archaeologists at work at Ai during the Callaway excavations in 1966. A worker in the foreground is seated by a crude wall; squares are separated by balks where the worker walks, carrying excess debris to the dump at the top right. A cobbled pavement is visible at center right.

of the homes of common people and might concentrate on shops, storehouses, and gathering places of the working classes. The results in either case are partial, telling us only about the areas the particular director of the excavation emphasized.

The usual procedure is to mark off areas in a grid system of five-meter squares separated from each other by a balk of soil one meter wide. Each square is then excavated, using small hand tools. All important objects found in the excavation are kept and carefully labeled. At regular periods a sketch is made of each square as viewed from above, providing a kind of rough architectural ground plan of buildings, pavements, walls, and so forth. The archeologists are in effect slicing off layers of the tell, carefully recording the contents and shape of each layer. The meter-wide balks are left standing as profile records of the stratigraphy of the tell. Viewed in good light, the balk pictures to the knowledgeable eye the various layers of the tell's occupation in profile, often with patterns of pavements and walls. Imaginatively using the ground plans and the profile in the balks, the archeologist can reconstruct to some extent the structures of the settlement at each major period of its occupation.

Archeological evidence falls into four categories: (1) written texts ranging from complete documents to broken fragments of a word or just a few letters,

(2) artifacts and all other objects of human manufacture or use, (3) strati-graphic evidence, and (4) ecological/environmental evidence.

1. *Written texts* of all kinds by the thousands have been discovered in Mesopotamia and Syria where the writing medium was clay tablets; when dried and baked, they are almost indestructible. In Egypt the medium was stone or papyrus (a paperlike substance), which, though perishable, survives in Egypt's dry desert sands. Among the written materials found throughout the ancient Near East are royal inscriptions and proclamations, court annals of various rulers, religious texts (creation stories, hymns, ritual texts, proverbs), codes of law, letters, and other documents of everyday common life (bills of sale, receipts, and so forth).

Occasionally some of these texts make specific reference to Israel, but their greatest importance is the information they provide for a reconstruction of the political, social, and religious context of the ancient Near East. The Hebrew scriptures are a major part of the vast literary heritage of Near Eastern peoples. When read in comparison with Mesopotamian, Egyptian, and Canaanite texts, the biblical materials take on new vitality and clarity as we see the many things Israel had in common with neighboring peoples and the many ways in which Israel was different.

Fewer lengthy inscriptional materials are found in Palestine because Israel's rulers did not often erect inscribed monuments to their achievements and because damp winters caused fragile papyrus and leather documents to decay. The texts most often found there were written on pieces of broken pottery, which were unaffected by the elements. Fortunately, the southern deserts of Judah are dry most of the year and rather significant inscriptional materials have been found there in recent years, including the Dead Sea Scrolls.

2. The *objects of many kinds* left by Near Eastern peoples in the strata of their cities, now tells, are rarely treasures of monetary value (movie and television representations of archeological adventures notwithstanding). They are, however, treasures to the knowledgeable interpreter who can "read" from these artifacts much about the life of the persons who used them. The remains of constructions reveal defense systems, sometimes with the evidence of their necessity and—alas—their inadequacy; administrative centers, occasionally with collections of official documents; places of worship, with altars and ritual objects; water systems, which reveal the extent to which a human grouping will go to have access to a good water supply; dwellings, with familiar objects of domestic life; pavements and stairs, which speak of city planning or its absence. Workshops indicate how ancient peoples threshed and stored grains and which grains were available (scales, weights, and measures tell of its distribution), how they pressed oil from olives and stored it in vats, how smiths forged metals into tools and weapons, how potters turned on their wheels the thousands of vessels of everyday use. In effect the various stages and activities of the ancient city take shape anew in the mind of the archeologist.

Ovens and the debris around them, small jars for oils and larger jars for grain, reveal something of an ancient people's diet. Pottery fragments tell us about the kinds of utensils they used and even something of their esthetic values—appreciation of shape, patterns, and color. Decorative items reveal their appreciation of both personal adornment and the things they kept around them. Their death is dramatically seen in the cave tombs in slopes near a tell, bodies laid out instate with treasured objects of life around them—not precious objects usually, but items of everyday use. Even in death they show us how they lived. The artifacts found in excavating a site index the life and culture of an ancient people.

The most common artifacts found in the excavation of a tell are pottery fragments. There are thousands of these fragments and they provide a reliable means of dating the strata in which they are found. Careful analysis of the changes in pottery styles, forms, glazes, and colors, and correlation of this analysis with datable inscriptional materials, has provided a reliable method of dating the pottery fragments, and occasionally whole pieces, found in excavations. When archeologists study the pottery found in the layers of a tell, the chronology of its occupation becomes discernible. Each occupational level can be dated with a fair degree of accuracy.

3. *Stratigraphic evidence* indicates when a site was first occupied, when it was finally abandoned, and much about its history. The various strata reveal the changes that took place; when and how a town grew larger; how defense and water systems were improved; in some cases how a large town declined, was destroyed, or even abandoned for a time to be rebuilt later. Strata also reflect economic growth or decline. Occasionally tentative but probable identification of structures with biblical persons or events is possible.

4. *Ecological/environmental evidence* like seeds, pollens, foodstuffs, remains of domestic animals, various indications of gradual or sudden changes in the climate, or the failure of the water supply help to complete the archeological reconstruction of the life of biblical people.

Many of the hundreds of tells in the Near East have been studied, but very little work has yet been done on the numerous small rural settlements and agricultural villages. Inasmuch as the majority of the population of countries like ancient Israel and Judah lived in these smaller places, we do not yet have a comprehensive picture of the social and religious culture of biblical times.[15]

Archeology is not a treasure hunt for museum objects, although museums are filled with wonderful things uncovered by archeologists. Neither is it a search for evidence to prove that biblical texts are true, although Biblical Archeology was interested in the historicity of biblical texts supported by archeo-

---

[15]Norman Gottwald's works, *The Hebrew Bible, A Socio-Literary Introduction* and *The Tribes of Yahweh*, are good examples of scholarly concerns for and attempts to reconstruct as comprehensive a view as possible.

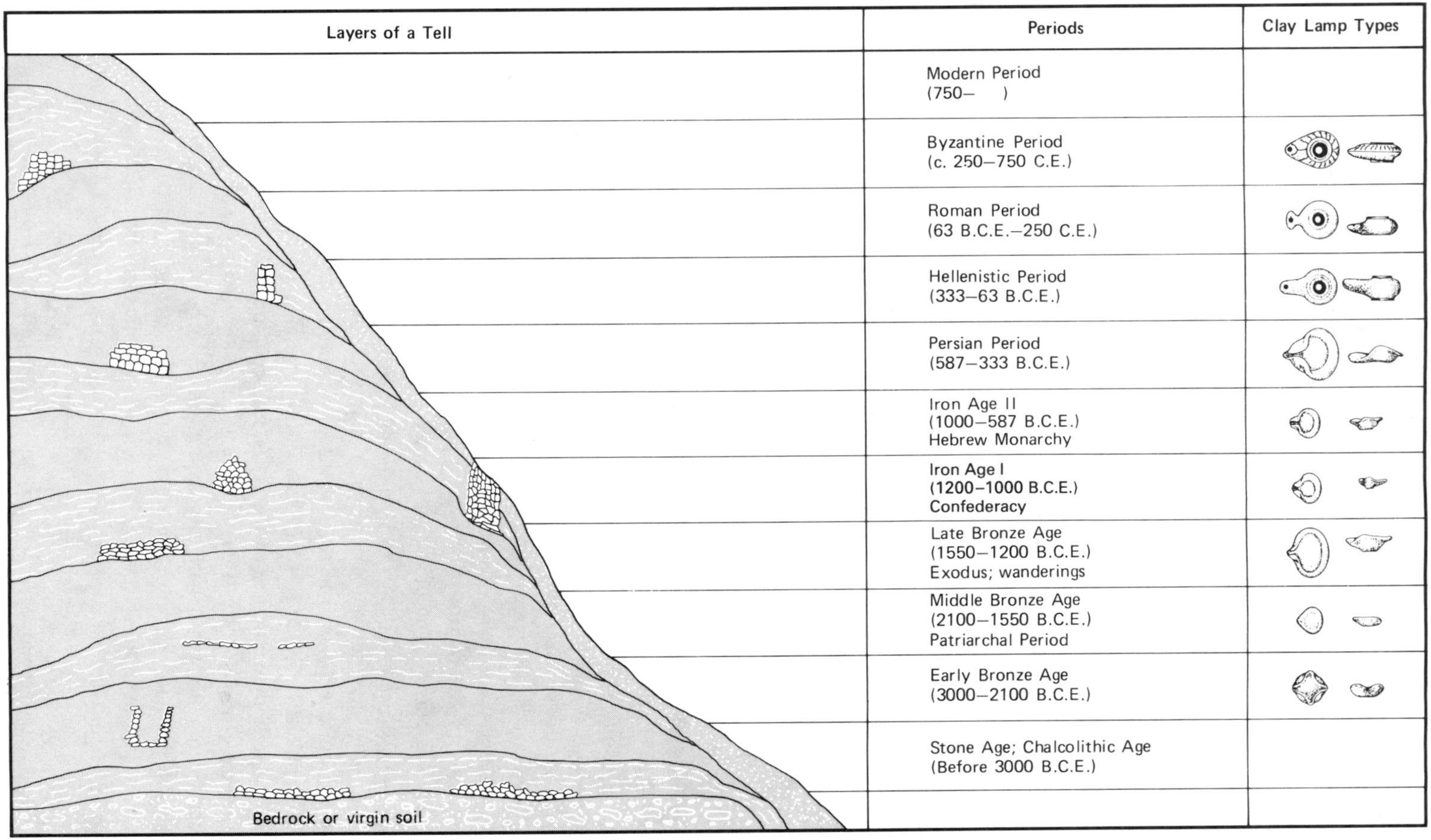

Layers of a Tell	Periods	Clay Lamp Types
	Modern Period (750—)	
	Byzantine Period (c. 250–750 C.E.)	
	Roman Period (63 B.C.E.–250 C.E.)	
	Hellenistic Period (333–63 B.C.E.)	
	Persian Period (587–333 B.C.E.)	
	Iron Age II (1000–587 B.C.E.) Hebrew Monarchy	
	Iron Age I (1200–1000 B.C.E.) Confederacy	
	Late Bronze Age (1550–1200 B.C.E.) Exodus; wanderings	
	Middle Bronze Age (2100–1550 B.C.E.) Patriarchal Period	
	Early Bronze Age (3000–2100 B.C.E.)	
	Stone Age; Chalcolithic Age (Before 3000 B.C.E.)	

Bedrock or virgin soil

Figure 2.12. Pottery types, as illustrated here with lamps, enable the archeologist to date specific layers of occupation of a tell.

Figure 2.13. The Rosetta Stone with trilingual inscription. The Greek text at the bottom was key to deciphering the hieroglyphic text at the top. The oval cartouche in the hieroglyphic text always contained a royal name and was crucial to decipherment. (Copyright British Museum)

logical data and has found in many cases archeological support for biblical stories. Obviously, archeology cannot prove the faith claims about God and persons that the Hebrew Bible makes. Archeological discoveries may sometimes authenticate the setting of certain stories; they cannot authenticate the stories themselves. In fact, as we shall see later in our discussion of biblical materials, archeological information affirms some points in the narratives of the Hebrew Bible, but raises serious questions about others. The Israelite "conquest" of Canaan is a good example of a narrative that must be reinterpreted in light of all the archeological evidence. On the other hand, Solomon's reputation as a builder and the account of the Babylonian destruction of Jerusalem late in the period are both graphically illustrated and confirmed by archeological evidence. What archeology should do best is help us recover much of the ancient life, culture, and history of the Near Eastern world in which the Israelites played an important role and to which they made the significant and lasting contribution represented by the literature of the Hebrew Bible.

Archeology is a rich and exciting field of study and work. We have not listed here the many important discoveries that have relevance to the study of the Hebrew Bible. The richness only hinted at here will be discussed later in detail in connection with our analysis of the places in the Hebrew Bible where archeological discoveries have a bearing on the interpretation of biblical materials.

THE ANCIENT NEAR EAST PRIOR TO THE TIME OF ABRAHAM

The Israelite's own account of their history begins with the migration of Abraham and his family from Mesopotamia to Canaan. The stories about these somewhat shadowy figures are set in the first half of the second millennium B.C.E., rather late in the history of the Near East. Abraham was not a simple primitive living at the dawn of human existence. Flint cultures of Paleolithic humans have been found in many places throughout the Near East dating back to perhaps two hundred thousand years ago. The story of the Stone Age is extremely interesting, but is not relevant to our study except as a reminder that before the earliest epoch of known human experience lie aeons of slow development and maturation of individuals and societies. For our purposes we begin with the first permanent settlements.

Permanent settlements with evidences of some civilized character were established throughout the Fertile Crescent as early as 8000 B.C.E. One of these was at Jericho, where a perennial spring provided an abundant water supply. The people of this "town" lived in mud brick huts protected by a surrounding wall. They had reed mats on their floors, made clay statues over reed frames (perhaps representations of their gods), modeled clay features with shells for eyes over human skulls (for reasons about which we can only make guesses—reverence for ancestors and the tribal way of life over which the ancestry were logical guardians?). They kept sheep, goats, pigs, dogs, and oxen, raised grain that they ground in mortars, and perhaps even irrigated their fields with water from Jericho's abundant spring. They had commerce with Anatolia (Asia Minor), the Sinai, and the Mediterranean coast from which they obtained obsidian tools (Anatolia), turquoise (the Sinai), and cowrie shells (the Mediterranean coast). These social, economic, and aesthetic achievements all occurred in the Neolithic (Old Stone Age) before pottery was made or metals were worked. These people were leading in the advance toward civilization, and they lived in Palestine five thousand years before Abraham.

The archeological evidence at Jericho, however, indicates that the march to civilization was not uniform and uninterrupted. The remarkable culture there ended, to be replaced after a long period during which Jericho was abandoned. The new culture had the skill of making pottery, but overall they were less advanced than their quite sophisticated predecessors. This kind of change of population characterized the whole ancient history of the Near East. This was a restless age with many different groups of wanderers beginning to settle down, often establishing new towns, but also occasionally taking over one that was already established. There is little doubt that the Israelite patriarchs were from one of these groups of restless, wandering, but also advancing people.

By the beginning of the third millennium B.C.E., throughout the Fertile Crescent the cultural advances had approached the age of "history." In fact, writing was known but the preserved texts available to us are too few and fragmentary to be deciphered. Pottery was common, and the widespread presence through the region of similar pottery styles and decorations indicates cultural exchange and communication. Houses were better constructed. Metalworking was known and artistic skills were even more refined. Cooperative efforts like irrigation projects and building of defenses were more common and more extensive. Great advances in agriculture made available many grains, fruits, and vegetables. Trade extended throughout the Fertile Crescent into Egypt and eastward toward India. Much of this reflects the beginnings of organized governments and civic action. History was at hand a thousand years before Abraham. Israel's ancestors were indeed quite late in entering the scene.

Early in the third millennium contemporary inscriptions, which modern scholars have deciphered, document affairs in the ancient Near East. The earliest of these ancient texts are still obscure and the best readings scholars make are uncertain, but from the second century of the third millennium abundant materials are intelligible to specialists. "History" in the Near East has dawned for us and immediately we encounter highly organized cultures already at the full blossom of their sophistication. It was an era of strong city-states and the first empires.

The Sumerians (c. 2850–2360 B.C.E.). Beginning around 3000 B.C.E., the Sumerians, a talented, literate people, entered parts of Mesopotamia. They built their cities near the "towns" of the earlier village settlers with whom they lived peacefully. These towns soon expanded into city-states, among the more important of which were Ur, Erech, Lagash, Eridu, and Larsa. The city-states were theocracies, ruled by god, and each city-state appeared to have a different name. The actual rule was administered by a *lugal*, "Great Man," or an *ensi*, "priest." The relation between these two offices is not clear, but it seems that the role of *lugal* developed when one city-state subjected others to its rule. That city's *ensi* would be *lugal* over all the cities together. This did not happen often, and there seems not to have been any occasion when all the city-states were brought together under any single leadership and authority. Both *ensi* and *lugal* were believed to represent god in their rule. The *ensi* was perhaps elected by a city assembly whose vote was considered evidence of divine sanction.

The city was god's home, its land his estate, the temple his palace. The people were his workers, who were treated with respect and protected by law. No code of their laws is known to us, but certain social reforms were carried out by the ruler of one of the city-states in accordance with "the righteous laws of Ningirsu." These cities and their administration were modeled after the heavenly city in which the gods lived, almost as an extension of the heavenly realm. This concept of city rests on a fundamental conviction shared by all early Mesopotamian societies and by the Egyptians. It is a cosmological conviction that "the meaning of life is rooted in an encompassing cosmic order in which man, society, and the gods all participate."[16]

At the center of some cities tall structures rose as temple towers toward the heavens. A sanctuary stood at the summit of these artificial mountains, intending to join Mother Earth with Father Sky. These were the site of a New Year's celebration of the primal union of the two, accounting for the creation of the world and all that fills it. The implication is that human beings, societies, and the gods all participate in a cosmic order assuring the good life. The creation myth, recited at the festival, was a confession that the gods created the cosmos as a place of meaning and value and that humans maintained such order by civil obedience, social morality, and religious ritual.

In the myths, Sumerian gods and goddesses filled the cosmos: An, god of the heavens; Enlil, god of the air; Enki, god of water; and Ninhurshag, earth mother. These deities represented sacred presence in the heavens, air, water, and earth. The entire cosmos was believed to be full of and controlled by their divine power. At times the power was described in sexual terms—the mating of the gods created a family of humanity, nature, and the sacred. At other times the sacred power of the gods was described with storm images. When things went well, the storm power was creative, refreshing, and life restoring. But when humans misbehaved, the storm power could be terrifying and destructive.

Several myths or mythlike stories expressed Sumerian distress over loss of stability in society and frightful outbreaks of nature. The Gilgamesh Epic (which will be discussed at length in Chapter 3) raised profound questions about human mortality and the loss of innocence. Like the biblical book of

[16]Loew, *Myth*, p. 5.

Job, the work raises questions about the cause of human suffering, but never doubts that it is deserved and has meaning in the larger cosmic order.

The Sumerians not only produced epic and mythic literature demonstrating the intellectual sophistication of their religion, they also enjoyed material and technological achievements: advanced methods of irrigation, excellence in metalworking and gem cutting, wheeled ox and ass-drawn vehicles, development of cuneiform writing, extended trade and cultural exchange. The architecture of their temples and other public buildings was monumental. They used a mathematical system based on 60 that standardized calculations of weight, measure, and time. All in all, the Sumerians represent a quite advanced culture for the daybreak of history in the Near East.

The Akkadians (c. 2360–2180 B.C.E.). Akkadians entered Mesopotamia from the northwest soon after the entry of the Sumerians. By the middle of the third millennium they were a sizable portion of the population in Sumer and were the majority in the northern part of the country. The Akkadians entered peacefully and adopted much of the Sumerian culture. Although their Semitic language differed from Sumerian, they adopted the Sumerian syllabic cuneiform script to write it. The two groups merged culturally to an extent that it is difficult to distinguish between them.

In the twenty-fourth century B.C.E. an Akkadian named Sargon accomplished what no Sumerian had been able to do; he seized power over all Sumer and established a dynasty of Semitic rulers. Sargon's origins are clouded in legend and myth. He is reported to have come to power in Kish, conquered Erech, and controlled Sumer as far south as the Persian Gulf. He made Akkad his capital, and by a series of legendary campaigns extended his control from the Mediterranean in the west to the Zagros mountains in the east.

Sargon established the first empire in history, but it was essentially Sumerian with modifications. Language was increasingly Akkadian, including the myths and speculative stories of the Sumerians. During his time, the palace replaced the temple as the center of political and economic life.

Ebla (2600–2250 B.C.E.). Prior to 1964 when excavations at Tell Mardikh in modern Syria began to uncover an ancient city of impressive size, Ebla was known only by references in scattered documents of the second and third millennia B.C.E. The city uncovered was Ebla and the excavations and studies of the material found there demonstrate that it was a Semitic state of considerable importance that for a time was a worthy rival of Sargon's Akkadian empire. The city was strategically located to control major east–west and north–south communication and trade routes. The population in the city, surrounding dependencies, and countryside was over 250,000. The city was well fortified. The palace was large and elaborate and contained, besides the collection of Ebla Tablets mentioned earlier, fine furnishings, sculptures, and seal impressions of excellent quality. The major industries were linen production and sheep raising. Trade was widespread and profitable. Ebla's period of relative greatness was cut short when the city was attacked and destroyed by Naram-sin of Akkad, a descendant of Sargon. Ebla was rebuilt, but on a much smaller scale.

The initial expectations and claims that the texts found in Ebla would shed considerable light on early biblical history have not been realized. Nevertheless, Ebla was a political and cultural center of considerable importance, demonstrating that centralized city-state governance was present in Palestine as early as in Mesopotamia.

Egypt's Old Kingdom (c. 2900–2400 B.C.E.). Around 2600 B.C.E., the Third Dynasty of Egyptian rulers[17] was on the scene. Here Egyptian history begins to claim our attention. By this time the northern and southern kingdoms had been united for more than three centuries and Egyptian culture had reached "classical" stages, that is, the forms and norms of later Egyptian culture had been established.

The Third Dynasty was the age of the pyramids, those great symbols of the primary importance of the pharaoh, the Divine King. The pyramids represent extraordinary precision in construction—the error of squareness in the Great Pyramid is approximately .09 percent and deviation from level is .004 percent. Precision in the construction of the pyramids testifies to the importance of the pharaoh. They were the tombs of the god-kings whose safe passage from earth back to the eternal realm of the gods guaranteed the peaceful continuity of every Egyptian's existence. Pyramids from the Fifth and Sixth Dynasties contain texts of spells and incantations designed to guarantee the pharaoh's safe passage from one realm to the other. These Pyramid Texts are the oldest Egyptian religious documents known to us.

Egypt was in regular contact with Asia, especially Palestine and Phoenicia. Copper was mined in the Sinai, timber was shipped from Byblos in Lebanon to Egypt, an almost treeless country. Various hieroglyphic inscriptions attest Egypt's important presence in Palestine throughout the Third through the Sixth Dynasties. Egypt's influence on life there was so pervasive that toward the end of the third millennium Semitic Canaanites in Byblos had developed a syllabic script based on Egyptian hieroglyphics.

A significant presence in Palestine and Phoenicia was always important to the Egyptians, who enjoyed a secure isolation in the delta and the long narrow valley of the Nile. Protected by virtually impassible deserts to the east and west, by miles of unnavigable river to the south, and by the Mediterranean to the

---

[17]Manetho, an Egyptian historian (c. 275 B.C.E.), established the dynastic division of Egypt's history. The dynastic designations, first, second, etc., are regularly used along with approximate dates in most references to Egyptian history.

immediate north, they were vulnerable only to the northeast by way of Phoenicia and Palestine down through the Sinai. To keep that area under their control provided a buffer between them and the Mesopotamian states who might threaten them.

End of the Third Millennium B.C.E. The centuries at the close of the third millennium were unsettled, sometimes chaotic. Disturbances troubled all areas of the Near East. Egypt's stability disintegrated into confusion, and in Palestine invading new peoples created chaos. In Mesopotamia the Akkadian empire collapsed before the onslaughts of aggressive mountain tribes.

For a brief period about 2180 B.C.E., the Sumerian empire flourished in a renaissance centered in Ur and Lagash. The Third Dynasty of Ur gained control of most of southern Mesopotamia under rulers who called themselves "Kings of Sumer and Akkad" and "Kings of the Four Parts of the World." Ur-nammu, founder of the Third Dynasty, is best remembered for his law code, the oldest so far known.

The Sumerian revival flourished and soon died. Sumerian culture was exhausted. Sumerians and Semites were thoroughly mixed by this time. Akkadian as the vernacular had replaced Sumerian, which lived on only as an antiquarian and liturgical language.

Egypt: The First Intermediate Period (c. 2100–2000 B.C.E.). Egypt's Sixth Dynasty was a dynasty of decline. The central power of the state gradually disintegrated to be replaced by less effective local rule. In the twenty-second century B.C.E., rival pharaohs claimed the throne, a strange phenomenon to be witnessed by people who believed pharaoh was their God-king and pharaonic dynasties represented the stability on which the good life depended. In some areas towns acted independently. Nomadic people moved into parts of the Nile delta. Law and order broke down and the result was chaos. The economy was endangered. Everything on which the Egyptians had come to depend seemed to be lost.

The literature of the time reflects a mood of deep and widespread anxiety and depression. They must have believed that civilization was at its end. Such pessimism is usually inappropriate and incorrect; it was in this case. In the twenty-first century B.C.E., a strong, capable pharaoh from Thebes ended the chaos and reunited Egypt. The Intermediate Period was only that—intermediate between periods of greatness.

Palestine just before the time of Abraham was in crisis. Its city-states had been overseen by a succession of nomadic invaders. This was possible because of the weakness of Egypt at this time. The archeological evidence suggests that almost all of the major cities were destroyed, many violently. The intruding nomads did not reoccupy these cities, preferring to live in the open for a time, eventually building villages on virgin soil. We cannot with certainty identify these nomads. They were probably Semites, perhaps the semitic people called Ammonites from the northwestern regions of the Fertile Crescent. Many scholars would place Abraham among them.

Before the time of Abraham, throughout the Fertile Crescent, civilizations had risen, had developed into empires, and had declined; entire cultural epochs had come into being, then in exhaustion had fallen into a sickness of laxity. But in all areas recovery was not far off.

SUGGESTIONS FOR FURTHER STUDY

Use the Bible dictionaries listed in the General Bibliography for further information on such terms as Fertile Crescent, topography, Behistun inscription, bedouin, and Rosetta Stone.

For the methods and findings of archeology for understanding the Hebrew Bible, consult E. M. Blaiklock and R. K. Harrison, eds., *The New International Dictionary of Biblical Archaeology* (Zondervan, 1983); A. Negev, ed., *The Archaeological Encyclopedia of the Holy Land* (Nelson, rev. ed. 1986); A. Mazzar, *Archaeology of the Land of the Bible: 1000–586 B.C.E.* (Doubleday, 1990). A four volume set edited by Ephraim Stern et al., *The New Encyclopedia of Archaeological Excavations in the Holy Land, I–IV* (Israel Exploration Society, 1993) is standard. An extensive bibliography is found in the General Bibliography; works on the Dead Sea Scrolls are also found there.

If you wish to pursue an investigation of the Ebla finds, begin with articles on these in H. Weiss, ed., *Ebla to Damascus* (1985); R. D. Briggs, "The Ebla Tablets," *Biblical Archaeologist*, 43 (1980) 76–87; and David Freedman, "The Real Story of the Ebla Tablets," *Biblical Archaeologist*, 41 (1978) 143–64.

Sources on Geography are listed under that category in the General Bibliography.

3

Israel's Theology of Beginnings

Beginning with Genesis and continuing through 2 Kings the orientation of the Hebrew Bible is "historical." These books tell the story of Israel from creation to Babylonian exile. The two books of Chronicles retell this story with variations and, combined with Ezra and Nehemiah, continue Israel's narrative through the return from exile and the reestablishing of Israelite life in and around Jerusalem. This "historical" orientation provides a framework in which to interpret other materials in the Hebrew Bible such as the collections of prophetic oracles (Isaiah, Jeremiah, Ezekiel, and the Book of the Twelve Prophets), the Psalms, the Wisdom writings (Job, Proverbs, and Ecclesiastes), the Apocalyptic book of Daniel, and the stories of Ruth, Esther, and Jonah.

We begin with Torah, which contains stories of beginnings—the beginning of the world and human life in the world, the beginning of sinfulness, the beginning of Israel, and the beginning of God's redemptive activity to set right the things that human sin has caused to go wrong.

THE STRUCTURE OF TORAH

The first five books of the Hebrew Bible are together called Torah or the Pentateuch.[1] Torah in the narrow meaning of the word is translated "law." Much of the material in Torah is legislative. Major collections or codes of law are in Exodus, Leviticus, and Deuteronomy. The larger part of the contents of the Torah books, however, is narrative: narratives of creation and fall, narratives of the patriarchs, narratives of the exodus, narratives of the covenant at Sinai, narratives of the wilderness wanderings. *Law*, therefore, is an inadequate

---

[1]Pentateuch is a scholarly designation used for Torah. The word is based on a Greek term, *he penetateuchos biblos*, "the book of the five scrolls."

translation of Torah. The word is better understood as *guidance* or *instruction*. Israel believed divine guidance was found in both laws and sacred stories. God's way in the world was made clear in codes; it was also known in experience. Both law codes and narratives were Torah to Israel.

The modern reader of Torah can pick up the narrative thread and recognize its continuity and organization, although the sequence is often interrupted by law codes. The story runs virtually uninterrupted through all of Genesis and the first fifteen chapters of Exodus, but is broken thereafter at places in Exodus, Leviticus, and Numbers by long lists of laws. Then in Deuteronomy part of the narrative story is repeated as introduction to another long and somewhat duplicated code of laws. The codes are often overlooked because the narrative is more interesting and the laws seem so culture-bound. Contemporary readers need to remember that both law and history were Yahweh's instruction to Israel.

The books of Torah were traditionally thought of as the "five books of Moses" and it was long assumed that he wrote them. Late books of the Hebrew Bible and the Apocrypha refer to Torah with phrases like "the law of Moses" and "the Book of Moses" (2 Chronicles 23:18; Ecclesiasticus 24:23), and the New Testament cites passages from "the law of Moses" and refers to the first two parts of the Hebrew canon as "Moses and the Prophets" (Matthew 19:8; Luke 24:27). This assumption that Moses was the author of Torah was doubtless based on the prominent place he has in the Torah narrative and the great respect in which he was held in late Jewish religion. But Mosaic authorship will not stand up to critical analysis. Internal Torah evidence for Mosaic authorship is limited to four references (Exodus 17:14, 24:4, 34:27–28; Numbers 33:2), each of which refer to Moses' recording something from the immediate context rather than to his authorship of any extended narrative. Even before modern biblical scholarship developed, rabbis questioned Moses giving an account of his own death (Deuteronomy 34:5–12). They also found it strange that Moses, who died before Israel crossed to the *west* bank of the Jordan River, should refer to the territory on the *east* bank as "beyond the Jordan" (Deuteronomy 1:1). Further, the insertion of law codes into a unified narrative framework, anachronistic references to the Hebrew monarchy and to peoples and places unknown in Moses' time, duplicated accounts of the same event, varied literary styles, and the use in Genesis of a name for God that Exodus insists was not known until the time of Moses indicate a more complex literary history than authorship by a single person.

The publication of Julius Wellhausen's *Prolegomena to the History of Israel* in 1885 established an approach to the materials in the Pentateuch that, with modifications, has become standard for biblical scholarship. Based on the matters listed above, Wellhausen argued that the books of the Torah were the combination of four "documents" labeled J for the Yahwist, who emphasizes Yahweh as the name for God; E for the Elohist, who preferred El/Elohim as the divine name; D for the Deuteronomist, whose document is essentially equal to the book of Deuteronomy, and P for a collection of materials that have characteristics typical of priestly thought and affairs. Wellhausen insisted that the chronological sequence of these documents was unquestionably from earliest to latest (JEDP) and that they reflected the evolutionary development of the faith and culture of Israel. He maintained that each document imposed on its sources the faith and customs of Israel at the time it was written—J the period of the early United Monarchy about 980 B.C.E., E about a century later. D was the distillation of seventh century prophetic ethics and religion, and P the fully developed Priestly/cultic religion of postexilic times. This analysis is called the *Documentary Hypothesis.*

Recent scholarship has significantly modified this hypothesis. The Wellhausen documents and their chronological sequence is generally accepted as established. His evolutionary suppositions have been largely rejected as has his supposition that the documents reflect more the times of their writing than the time they were writing about.

Careful study over many years has demonstrated that Torah is best understood as a composite work. The books contain major units with different interests and literary styles. For example, Deuteronomy is a preaching of law and an exhortation to Israel to be faithful to God in a literary style and vocabulary distinctive from the rest of Torah. Leviticus, large parts of Numbers, some parts of Exodus, and scattered sections elsewhere express the interests of the priestly community with religious rituals, institutions, and laws. The style of these materials is also distinctive—precise, legalistic, concerned with details. The remainder of Torah is an artistic narrative of Israel's origins from the creation of the world to the conquest of Canaan told by creative storytellers. The presence of such variation has led to the conclusion that the lively narrative forms a basic framework for Torah into which the law codes and the book of Deuteronomy have been inserted.

Behind the narrative as it now stands is a rich heritage of both oral and written stories of various kinds and diverse origins. Theological stories of beginnings, ancestral hero stories about Abraham, Jacob, Joseph, and Moses, and cultic narratives about altars, shrines, and rituals were remembered and told by Israelite tribes to help them understand who they were and how they were to live with God and with each other. Even in their oral preservation the materials were considered instructive "history."

Soon after the settlement in Canaan during the early Israelite confederacy, these resources began to take narrative shape. The Israelite storytellers were confessing that the God who had delivered them from bondage in Egypt and who had led them into Canaan (the freshest events in their memory) was also the God who had created the world and chosen their ancestors and hence themselves to be a blessing to all humankind. The narrative focused on themes of *creation and fall, covenant promise to the patriarchs, exodus from Egypt, covenant at Sinai, wandering in the wilderness,* and *entrance into the promised land.*

The Yahwistic Tradition (J)

Around the tenth century B.C.E. traditions of Israel's origins were shaped into
a grand epic narrative by a skilled theologian. This narrative is called "Yahwistic" because of the decided preference its author shows for the divine name
Yahweh as Israel's personal name for God. The anonymous author is called
the "Yahwist." Because this analysis was first worked out in German biblical
scholarship and the German spelling of Yahweh is Jahweh, the letter J has come
to be used to designate both the author of the epic and the narrative itself. J is
also an appropriate designation for the *Judah* version of Israel's beginnings.

The Yahwist shows a particular interest in the southern tribe of Judah. He
features Judean heroes and stresses Judah's central role among the tribes. He
thus provided a "national epic" to a young nation at a time when its power
and authority were being centralized in Jersualem under the leadership of Judean kings, David and Solomon. Although he wrote from a distinctly Judean
perspective, his primary purpose was theological, not political. The Yahwist
wrote as a man who believed that God's intentions for all humankind were
being fulfilled in the reigns of David and Solomon. Just as God had chosen
Abraham and his descendents to be servants through whom all humankind
would be blessed, so too in the new, strong, and unified Israelite state God
would bless all the families of the earth.[2]

The Elohistic Tradition (E)

The northern tribes also had their theologian[3] who, soon after the division of
the kingdom in 922 B.C.E., composed a second story of Israel's beginnings.
His story covered the same time as the Yahwistic story, with the exception of
the primeval traditions of creation and fall. This writer represents the perspective of those northern tribes that never felt fully united with tribes of the south
and who broke away after Solomon's death to found the northern state of
Israel. His epic is called "Elohistic" because its author uses the word *Elohim*
for God for the period before Moses, for he believed the name Yahweh was
first revealed to Moses (see Exodus 3:13–15; 6:2–4). The letter E for Elohim
is used to designate this account and the anonymous Elohist responsible for
it. E also conveniently stands for *Ephraim*, the most important of the northern
tribes.

The Ephraimite narrative was based either on the Yahwistic epic or on common earlier source materials perserved orally, probably the latter.[4] The E narrative is only partially preserved in the Torah because, after Israel fell to Assyria

[2]See von Rad, *O. T. Theology*, I:48–56, and "The Form-critical Problem of the Hexateuch,"
The Problem of the Hexateuch and Other Essays (McGraw-Hill, 1966).

[3]A number of scholars question the Elohist narrative as a separate source.

[4]Noth, *History of Israel*, pp. 33–41.

in 722 B.C.E., the narrative apparently was reshaped by Judean editors who gave preference to their own Yahwistic or Judean form of the Hebrew story. Enough of the Elohist tradition does remain for us to believe that it showed preference for "northern" heroes like Joseph and his son Ephraim, and for the covenant ways of the tribal confederacy over the monarchial ways of David and Solomon. For the Elohist God's purpose for Israel transcended the royal structures of the Judean monarchy. This, of course, was a natural position for a theologian from the north; the northern tribes had separated themselves from the Davidic dynasty, but not from the authority of Yahweh. Thus, the combined JE narrative retains both the political interests of the Yahwist in the Judah dynasty of David, and the Elohist's prophetic concerns for justice and righteousness.

The Yahwistic and Elohistic narratives have been so closely intertwined that they may be treated as one. The unified narrative included an important code of laws (Exodus 20:22–23:33) essentially intended to implement the basic principles of covenant law expressed in the Ten Commandments (Exodus 20:2–17). Both J and E originally contained a collection of laws attached to the narrative story at the point of covenant making at Sinai, but when the two were combined, these law codes were so conflated that they cannot now be distinguished from one another. Both narrators believed that the basic laws of Israelite society were part of God's divine guidance of the people and essential to maintain the covenant community.

The Deuteronomic Tradition (D)

The book of Deuteronomy was appended to the epic sometime after the seventh century B.C.E., but it is material of a very different kind. First, it subordinates narrative to law, and exhortation to ethical living. Second, although Deuteronomy has been incorporated into Torah, it stands alone as a complete and coherent text. Its removal from Torah would not alter the narrative, except for the description of the death and burial of Moses and Joshua's succession to leadership, which appears in the final chapter of the book. Third, Deuteronomy introduces and expresses the philosophical and theological presuppositions of a "history of Israel in the land of Canaan," which extends through Joshua, Judges, 1 and 2 Samuel and 1 and 2 Kings. This narrative is known as the deuteronomic history. Deuteronomy thus concludes Torah and introduces the deuteronomic history.

Deuteronomy is sermonic in style, organized around three "sermons" of Moses exhorting Israel to convenant faithfulness. There is no reason to doubt that, as his death approached, Moses formally challenged his followers with advice, admonition, and encouragement, all of which would have been given with references to the common historical experience they had shared. Moses reminded the people of their deliverance from Egypt, the hardships of wandering in the wilderness, their faithfulness and their unfaithfulness, and their initial victories in their conquest of the regions east of the Jordan. Such has been the responsibility in all traditional cultures for family and tribal leaders, chiefs, prophets, and so forth, to remind their successors of the values of their culture and the means by which these values are maintained. Anthropologist John Middleton tells of a deathbed speech by an African elder of the Lugbara tribe who began: "Now God has finished my days. Now I go. I leave you, my children. Later you must follow my words, to live quietly with people without quarrelling. Do not destroy our home, live in peace." He then spoke for two or three hours reminding his successors in very specific ways of their tribal/family responsibilities and specific measures they should undertake to preserve them.[5]

The Mosaic sermons as they are presented here, however, are filled with emphases and concerns that developed long after the time of Moses. They have affinities with periodic public ceremonies of covenant renewal held in the northern kingdom. At these ceremonies prophetic leaders strongly encouraged faithfulness to Yahweh and social justice, an emphasis often in tension with the political aspirations and actions of both Hebrew monarchies. The present book of Deuteronomy began to take shape in this context at about the same time that the Elohist was working on his narrative of Israel's beginnings. In a sense, then, Deuteronomy is prophetic encouragement to faithfulness, intended to supplement the Elohist's story of beginnings. It challenges each generation to be faithful to the principles of the founding ancestral community, principles that had their origin in God.

When Israel fell in 722 B.C.E., the deuteronomic exhortations were preserved by sympathetic circles in Judah where they came to light in 622 B.C.E. as a major factor in a reform movement led by King Josiah and supported in part by the prophetic community of Jerusalem (2 Kings 22–23; Jeremiah 11:1–13). Josiah's reform was clearly based on the law code found in Deuteronomy 12–26. The reform, however, failed and Judah soon fell to Babylon (587 B.C.E.). In exile the Deuteronomist, using the book of Deuteronomy as his theological introduction, composed an interpretation of the "history of Israel in the land of Canaan" in the light of Israel's and Judah's disobedience to Yahweh's covenant requirements: Obedience to Yahweh leads to welfare and peace; disobedience leads to hardship and defeat.

The Priestly Tradition (P)

Torah was completed during the late exilic period (c. 550 B.C.E.) by a priestly narrator. The priestly community assumed leadership in the conservation of

---

[5]John Middleton, *Lugbara Religion* (International African Institute, 1960), p. 197.

Israel's religious heritage during the trying circumstances of exile in a foreign land and in the restoration of the Israelite community in Judah once the exile was over. The priests felt that Israel could sustain its separation from other peoples as a unique religious community by faithfulness to priestly institutions and laws, thereby guaranteeing its survival. The priestly narrator, therefore, supplemented the JE narrative with ritual and cultic materials. These materials are found primarily in the cultic legislation in Exodus 25–31, 35–40, in Numbers 1–10, and in the laws on sacrifices, festivals, and ritual purity found throughout Leviticus. These laws doubtless gave formal shape to ritual practices that had grown up through the years. They reflect various dimensions and implications of Israel's belief that ritual was an essential process by which the religious community maintained its relationship to God and preserved the distinctions of its tradition. The creation account in Genesis 1 comes from the priestly narrator, as do the genealogical lists and chronological notations—all reflecting the priestly concern for order. By the priestly additions the JE narrative was divided into four broad areas: (1) from creation to the flood, (2) from the flood to Abraham, (3) from Abraham to Moses, and (4) Moses and the Sinai legislation. The priestly emphasis is on order in history maintained by a properly conducted ritual system. The order of society is maintained by proper worship of God.

It is important to remember that these four sources or strands of tradition (JEDP) have been carefully and artistically woven together. At times scholars have tended to pay more attention to their differences than to the skill that unifies them, even to the extent of dividing each of the sources into subsources so that J becomes J, J^1, J^2, J^3 and E, E^1, E^2, E^3, and so forth. Recent literary criticism has emphasized that the theologian/storytellers who combined these materials had "a faculty for molding disparate elements into an expressively unified whole not achieved outside of art." Literary critics emphasize unities rather than "discontinuities, contradictions, duplications, fissures." They accept the four-source hypothesis, but argue that scholarship too long has paid too much attention to the seams instead of being guided by the design of the whole. Their "goal is to lead us toward what the biblical authors and author-redactors surely aimed for—a continuous *reading* of the text instead of a nervous hovering over its various small components."[6]

As it now stands, then, Torah is a composite of Yahwistic, Elohistic, deuteronomic, and priestly materials, but it is in a sense incomplete. The narrative ends with the conquest of regions east of the Jordan River but with Israel still in the wilderness. It thus offers only a foretaste of the conclusion it anticipates. In spite of repeated emphases on God's promises to bless Israel's ancestors with the land of Canaan, Torah ends before these promises are fulfilled. The

---

[6]All quotations in this paragraph come from Robert Alter, "Introduction to the Old Testament," in *The Literary Guide to the Bible*, (Belknap, 1987) 25–26.

GENESIS	J — Most of the book with the exceptions of the E & P materials listed here E — Abraham and Sarah in Egypt, the birth of Isaac, the expulsion of Hagar and Ishmael, and the sacrifice of Isaac (chapters 20–22) P — The creation liturgy (1:1–2:4a); the genealogies (chapters 5, 10, 11:10–30, 36, 46:8–27); the flood story (chapters 6–9, J & P combined); the covenant with Abraham (chapter 17) and Abraham's purchase of a burial cave (chapter 23)
EXODUS	J — Combined with some E materials (chapters 1–24 and 32–34) P — Cultic regulations of various kinds (chapters 25–31 and 35–40)
LEVITICUS	P — The entire book
NUMBERS	JE — The unsuccessful attempt to enter Canaan (chapters 11–14), victories east of the Jordan, the incident of the poisonous serpents, and the Balak/Balaam stories (chapters 21–24) P — The rest of the book
DUETERONOMY	D — The entire book with some JE materials in chapters 27–34

Figure 3.1. JEDP Sources in the Pentateuch

completion of the story occurs in Joshua–Kings when land is conquered and nationhood is established. Thus Torah is closely connected to the books that follow. The nature of the relationship is an item of continuous debate among students of the Hebrew Bible.

1. Some consider the basic units to be Genesis–Deuteronomy (the traditional Jewish Torah designated as Pentateuch by modern scholarship) and Joshua–Kings (the traditional former prophets of Judaism).
2. Some trace the Yahwistic and Elohistic strata through Joshua and beyond, and designate Genesis–Joshua as Hexateuch (six writings).
3. Some accept the truncated form of the history of Israel's origins, Genesis–Numbers, and designate it as Tetrateuch (four writings) and consider Deuteronomy–Kings the deuteronomic history.

Deuteronomy belongs as much to the narrative that follows it, Joshua–Kings, as it does to the Torah narrative preceding it. It brings the Moses story to its conclusion and anticipates Israel's life in Canaan. It may well be that the Deuteronomist depends on the conquest narratives from the Yahwist and the Elohist for his treatment of Israel's entry into Canaan. He probably reshaped them for his own theological purposes. But in the Hebrew canon Joshua–Kings is separated from Torah, leaving Torah with a certain incompleteness. The priestly editor of Torah apparently intended that it end this way. Shaping Torah traditions for a community in exile, a community that had lost the land,

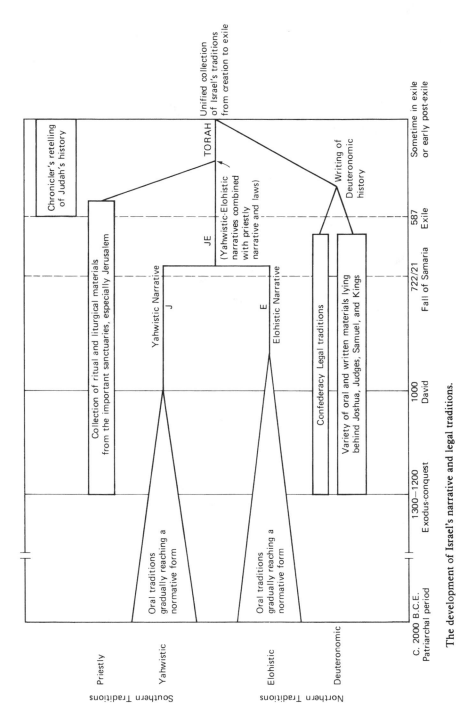

Figure 3.2. The development of Israel's narrative and legal traditions.

he stressed the very things the exiled community still possessed: the guidance and blessing of God preserved for them in Torah.[7] The God who had blessed the patriarchal ancestors while they were still aliens in Canaan would also bless those who were faithful to the covenant requirements in Babylon or any other foreign land.

Each stratum of Torah (J,E,D,P) represents an attempt to find in its rich stories and laws themes that met the needs of different generations of Israelites. Torah thus lays out the program for Israel's life in all periods and is for us "the primary key to understanding Israel's history, society, religion, and morality."[8]

THE STRUCTURE OF GENESIS

The first book of the Hebrew Bible is appropriately called Genesis, "beginning." Palestinian rabbis called the book *bereshith*, which is the opening word of the Hebrew Bible and means "in beginning." Later the Greek work *genesis*, "beginning," was used as the superscription for the book in the Septuagint. Subsequently, this word was carried over into the Vulgate and thence into English versions.

In Genesis the Israelite community expresses its faith in God as creator of the universe and of the people of Israel. The story is told in two parts, both of which introduce the narrative of God's work in Israel's history. Chapters 1–11 introduce the theological issues that make sense of God's selection and use of Israel to accomplish covenant purposes. Chapters 12–50 discuss the patriarchal forebears of the nation, moving the story toward the making of a covenant people. The division is reflected in an outline of the book:

A. Israel's primeval traditions. The theological need for the creation of Israel: chapters 1–11.
　　1. The creation of the world and all who inhabit it: 1:1–2:4a and 2:4b–25
　　2. The fall: chapters 3–11.
　　　　a. Rebellion and expulsion from Eden: chapters 3–4.
　　　　b. The flood: chapters 5–9.
　　　　c. The table of nations: chapter 10.
　　　　d. The tower of Babel and the confusion of languages: chapter 11.
B. Israel's patriarchal and matriarchal traditions. The beginning of the creation of Israel: chapters 12–50.
　　1. The Abraham, Sarah, and Hagar traditions: 12:1–25:18.
　　2. The Isaac and Rebekah traditions: 25:19–26:34.

---

[7]So Sanders, *Torah and Canon* (Fortress, 1972).

[8]Knight, "Pentateuch," in *The Hebrew Bible and Its Modern Interpreters* (Fortress, 1985), Knight and Gene M. Tucker, eds., p. 264.

3. The Jacob, Rachel, Leah, and Esau traditions: chapters 27–36.
4. The traditions of Jacob's family, largely the story of Joseph and the descent into Egypt: chapters 37–50.

This story of beginnings looks back from things as they are to things as they were understood to have been and interprets ancient traditions about primeval humankind and Israel's tribal ancestors. We must distinguish between the context of the final recorders of these stories and the settings of the stories themselves. The theologians who speak here of creation and fall, and of the patriarchal beginnings of Israel, are not news reporters on the scene. Much of the material is quite ancient, but it was given present shape and emphasis during the early Israelite monarchy (tenth–ninth centuries) and the Babylonian exile (sixth century).

Very old materials were collected and edited by a gifted theologian and storyteller to demonstrate a theological perspective on Israel's story. The primary character is Yahweh, the God of Israel; the primary concern is neither scientific nor historical, but religious. The primeval traditions in chapters 1–11 focus on the predicament of the creaturehood and sinfulness of humankind (chaps. 3–4). The human problem can neither be blamed on Yahweh, who has created all things good (chaps. 1–2), nor be resolved by wiping out humanity with a flood and starting again (chaps. 6–11). Rather, Yahweh has worked in Israel's history to achieve redemptive purposes. In chapters 12–50 the editor brings together ancient stories about Israel's ancestors to demonstrate Yahweh's beginning to make a nation, moving steadily toward the dramatic event of exodus from Egypt and the molding of a covenant nation.

The setting of the primeval traditions is the time before Abraham, the ancestor of the various tribes, which after the exodus and conquest, composed the community of Israel. Almost no historical detail appears in these materials, no concrete identification of historical persons, peoples, or places. The characters are representative of all humanity. The stories are literary and theological. They share with similar stories from other cultures concern with questions of primary significance about God, humanity, and the world—questions that cannot be answered adequately by scientific statement or historical chronicle. They are timeless statements about God as creator and human rebellion against the creator and, therefore, the need for redemption. They provide the theological introduction to the story of Israel.

These traditions represent attempts by persons of faith to answer fundamental questions about existence and meaning. Persons everywhere are concerned to know who they are and how they are related to the world, to each other, and to ultimate reality. The editor of Genesis 1–11 answered these questions in terms of human encounter with God as savior and ruler over life. Israel believed, therefore, that God is the creator and that humans are significantly responsible for their own life in the world, but they knew existentially that the present world was not ideal. Real persons are sinners in rebellion against the creator, and human culture is, in a sense, the consequence of egotistic denial of the sovereignty of God. Typically as illustrative, rather than literally as historical, the primeval traditions wrestle with ever-present realities of the human predicament and God's redemptive intention by telling stories set in the time before Abraham.

Genesis 1–11 stems from two sources, the Yahwistic and the priestly strata of Torah. A priestly liturgy can be clearly distinguished in 1:1–2:4 and there are priestly elements in the flood story. For interpretive purposes, however, these chapters should be treated as a unity. They have been woven together with considerable literary skill so that precise division into sources is not always possible or even necessary.

Although the stories of Genesis 1–11 come from different locales and from different periods, they are skillfully organized by an author concerned to show human dependence on a creating and redeeming God. These stories describe in theological terms the rebellious nature of humanity, which made the redemptive activity of God necessary. Materials from all over the ancient Near East were used by the authors of these stories, but the conception of God derived from the exodus deliverance—a God revealed as merciful and loving by redemptive action in Israel's history—is always imposed on them. The resultant account provides a religious orientation for persons struggling in a real world and a rationale for understanding the nature and meaning of life.

THE TRADITIONS OF THE CREATION OF THE WORLD
(GENESIS 1 AND 2)

Israel's Creation Faith

Israel believed in a God who both created the world and worked in the history of the nation. Israel's faith was nurtured by its speculation about the world and how it came into being, and by its historical experience. Its encounter with Yahweh had been direct at the exodus and in the wilderness of Sinai. And the God who delivered a slave people was the same God who made all things. Creation faith was, therefore, a corollary to historical faith. Israel's worship celebrated Yahweh, who was lord and controller of history, as the majestic creator of the world and all that it contains:

> Have you not known? Have you not heard?
> Yahweh is the everlasting God,
>   the Creator of the ends of the earth.
> He does not faint or grow weary,
>   his understanding is unsearchable.

> He gives power to the faint,
> 　　and strength to the powerless.
> 　　　　　[Isaiah 40:28–29; compare 45:18]

The God of Israel was creator and sustainer of creation. Yahweh had not withdrawn from creation to let it proceed on its own laws and regulation, but continued to be active in the world:

> O Yahweh, how manifold are your works?
> 　　In wisdom you have made them all;
> 　　the earth is full of your creatures . . . .
> These all look to you,
> 　　to give them their food in due season.
> When you give to them, they gather it up;
> 　　when you open your hand, they are filled with good things.
> When you hide your face, they are dismayed;
> 　　when you take away their breath, they die
> 　　and return to their dust.
> When you send forth your spirit, they are created;
> 　　and you renew the face of the ground.
> 　　　　　　　[Psalm 104:24, 27–30]

Two originally independent creation stories are utilized by the editors of Torah to express this mature faith in God as creator. The first of these, Genesis 1:1–2:4a, was given its form by the exilic compilers of the priestly history in the fifth century B.C.E. Showing traces of an earlier, less sophisticated form, it preserves preexilic ideas of creation. A second but older tradition,[9] Genesis 2:4b–25, comes from the tenth century B.C.E. in the Yahwistic story of Israel.

The Priestly Creation Liturgy (Genesis 1:1–2:4a)

The Hebrew Bible opens with a majestically simple declaration of Israel's creation faith: "In the beginning God created the heavens and the earth" (Genesis 1:1). The priestly narrative of creation, which begins with these words, was shaped distinctly and unmistakably by the character and mind of Israel. Although it is heavily dependent on ancient Near Eastern creation traditions, the emphasis on Yahweh's creative word, and therefore Yahweh's absolute sovereignty over nature and humankind, is characteristically Israelite. Written in final form during the Babylonian exile, it appropriately introduces Israel's scripture because it is a mature statement of the community's belief about God's relationship with the world and about the nature of persons as creatures of God. It also seems appropriate that Torah should begin with a poetical, liturgical proclamation of God's sovereignty.

---

[9]Remember that materials are not always arranged according to historical sequence. The Yahwistic story is probably placed here for the simple reason that the Yahwistic narrative continues in chapter 3.

The priestly account is prose, but in intention and character it is poetical, with poetic power excelled by few passages in the Hebrew scriptures. The rhythms and refrains reflect the cultic celebration of Yahweh as creator. This liturgical statement belongs to the worship of God in the Jerusalem temple. Praise of God as creator must have been a repeated emphasis in Israelite worship. Regular recitation of the creation stories would have been a reminder to worshipers that God intended men and women to live in an orderly world of meaning and values and to accept their responsibility for the maintenance of that kind of world.

In this "liturgy" God, by creative words, majestically calls into being everything that is. God speaks, and that which was not comes to be. Does this chapter teach *creatio ex nihilo*, "creation out of nothing"? Although not explicitly stated, something very near that is implied. The Hebrew word for "create" (*bara*) is used only of God and implies something beyond human imitation or comprehension. An absolute beginning is intended in Genesis 1:1, and at that beginning God was present to utter the creative word. The real intent and purpose is to say that whenever beginning occurred, God was there to begin it and is therefore worthy of praise and worship because God is lord over the world. Israel believed that the divinely spoken word was filled with power. When God said, "Let there be," *there would be* whatever God spoke into being. For Israel the word of Yahweh always accomplished its purpose and what it accomplished was good.

Here in the Genesis account we confront the concept of the creative word for the first time, already in a theologically developed form. The idea of the creative power of the divine word is familiar outside Israel in both Egyptian and Babylonian theology. In neither place, however, is it given fundamental significance as here. The speech/command structure of this liturgy focuses on the divine intention rather than on the technique of the creative process. The concern is not *how it happened*; science addresses that question with insights not known to ancient Israel. Israel is here confessing that the world was originally the world as conceived in the mind of God.

With great narrative artistry the liturgy divides creation into six orderly stages, each described with the same symmetrical structure:

> And God said, "Let there be. . ."
> And it was so. . .
> God saw that it was good. . .
> And there was evening and there was morning. . .

Each of these stages is represented as lasting one twenty-four-hour day. Any explanation of these days as indefinite in length goes against the ordinary meaning of the text. This creation statement is not scientific in nature, to be harmonized with modern geological estimates of the age of the universe. Nothing like that was in the mind of the ancient Israelite theologian. Consequently the faith statements of this chapter should not be placed in conflict with ideas about the origin of the universe offered by modern science. This "liturgy" *celebrates* creator and creation; it does not *describe* them. By refusing to describe them it avoids circumscribing and confining those realities whose full dimensions are ultimately beyond us.

The dark, formless, empty chaos was turned into a world of godly order and purpose by successive exclamations of the divine word. Each thing created had its divinely ordained purpose; each was subordinate to God. On the first day light was created; on the second, the heavens; on the third, land is separated from water, and vegetation is created. The elements of the world are there, "a primeval universe, with its lush forests and green valleys, blue skys and blue-black seas, but without anything in them—an empty magnificent vessel into which God . . . pours flying, swimming, walking, and creeping things."[10]

On the fourth day the creation of the heavenly bodies *parallels* the creation of light on the first day and assigns the lights roles as God's vice-regents to divide light from darkness. The ancients thought of the sun and moon as sources of light and made them objects of worship. The priestly author contradicts such beliefs by declaring light independent of sun and moon, and describing the heavenly bodies as mere instruments in the hands of the only true God. What a startling declaration that God, not sun, is the source of life! On the fifth day life is created in the air and water, *paralleling* the separation of the firmament on the second day. On the sixth day life is created on land, *paralleling* the creation of dry land on the third day. The world is thus set in motion and filled with life. Finally, on the seventh day God rested, thereby creating Sabbath, an emphasis distinctive to the priestly liturgy growing out of renewed concern with Sabbath observance during the Babylonian exile.

This symmetrical structure served two purposes. It emphasized that "the design of the world is not autonomous or accidental. It is based-on the will of God."[11] Also, as part of a poetic liturgy, it called for repeated congregational response. The worshipers response to the divine ordering of chaos by the creative command, "Let there be . . . ," must have been, "Amen," *may it be so!* So each recitation of this liturgy in Israelite worship was an act affirming order over chaos. Every repetition of the creation liturgy would thus be a celebration of the victory of the creator God over all forms a disorder, a victory in which the worshiping community participated.

On the sixth day humankind was created, subordinate to God but God's vice-regent over the natural order. This was a break in the symmetrical structure of the liturgy. The creation of humankind is set apart from all the rest as special by the structure of the liturgy itself. The creation of all else was prelude to the creation of humankind (*'adam*), an act in which God participates more

[10]Gros Louis, "Genesis I–II" in *Interpretation*, p. 43.
[11]Brueggemann, *Genesis*, p. 30.

intimately and intensively than in all other works of creation. The priestly writer
describes the creation of the human race:

> Then God said, "Let us make humankind in our image, according to our likeness;
> and let them have dominion over the fish of the sea, and over the birds of the air,
> and over the cattle, and over all the wild animals of the earth, and over every
> creeping thing that creeps upon the earth." So God created humankind in his
> image, in the image of God he created them; male and female he created them.
> [Genesis 1:26–27]

"Humankind" includes males and females "without establishing relative rank
or worth of the genders."[12] "Neither has power over the other; in fact, both
are given equal power."[13] Both are given dominion over all the earth, but
neither is given dominion over the other.

Created in the "image of God" human beings are not merely animals, but
enjoy distinction from all other created things. More important, however, is
the emphasis on the unique relationship of creature to creator. Persons are
distinctive from the rest of creation, but they are not equals with God. The
idea is expressed in Psalm 100:3:

> Know that Yahweh is God!
> It is he that made us and we are his;
> we are his people, and the sheep of his pasture.

Persons are essentially God's creatures and owe their existence to the creator. Like all else, they are created, but they are not at one with the rest of
creation. Persons share the natural limitations of creaturehood, but also may
rise above their creation. Like the animals, they are mortal, they cannot abide
in their pomp; like the beasts, they perish (Psalm 49:12); but they differ because of their capacity to respond to and communicate with God. They act as
responsible creatures beneath their creator, aware that they are in Yahweh's
presence and under Yahweh's judgment. Those who do not think of themselves
as creatures, but not just animal creatures—of God, but not a god—are in
some sense less than human. This Hebrew understanding of the dignity of
human creation was expressed later in Psalm 8:5–6:

> Yet you have made them a little lower than God,
> and crowned them with glory and honor.
> You have given them dominion over the works of your hands;
> you have put all things under their feet, . . .

Further, the concept of creation in the image and likeness of God included
dominion over the rest of creation. A person is a created being to whom all

---

[12]Sharon H. Ringe, "Genesis" in *The Women's Bible Commentary*, Newsome and Ringe, eds.,
p. 12.

[13]Trible, *God and the Rhetoric of Sexuality*, p. 18.

else is committed by the creator who commands: "Be fruitful and multiply, and fill the earth and subdue it; and have dominion. . . " (Genesis 1:28).

The mandate: to come to terms with the universe, to investigate its secrets, and to serve as its master under the overarching sovereignty of God. However, humankind is to remember "that he is lord over creation and ruler of nature not in his own right or to work his own will; he is God's vice-regent, charged with the working of God's will, responsible to God for his stewardship."[14]

Here the biblical idea of creation implicitly judges the abuse of nature. The Yahwistic description of humankind as *keeper* of the garden and the priestly emphasis on human dominion are ways of asserting responsibility to manage a creation whose maker, sustainer, and owner is God.

Thus far we have been concerned with the meaning of the phrase "image of God" when applied to humankind, male and female. The phrase also has implications for Israel's view of God. If humanity is made up of complementary interdependent qualities, must not these two qualities be shared by God? Even though God is regularly described as filling roles that are typically masculine (father, king, priest, judge), there are places where God's feelings and actions are more closely related to those typically thought of as female. These are not as common because of the patriarchal orientation of the biblical narratives, but those that are present are clear.

> But Zion said, "Yahweh has forsaken me,
>   my Lord has forgotten me."
> Can a woman forget her nursing child,
>   or show no compassion for the child of her womb?
> Even these may forget,
>   yet I will not forget you.
>
> [Isaiah 49:14–15]
>
> As a mother comforts her child,
>   so I will comfort you;
>   you shall be comforted in Jerusalem.
>
> [Isaiah 66:13]

There are also passages where the idea of God as parent "combines the protective power and the tender love which brings together both paternal and maternal qualities."[15]

Creation in the image of God was for Israel a matter of relationship between the divine and the human in which all humankind participated. Walter Brueggemann states it clearly:

> There is one way in which God is imaged in the world and only one: humanness!
> This is the only creature, the only part of creation, which discloses to us something

[14]Alan Richardson, *Genesis I–II* (S.C.M., 1953) p. 55. See also David Rutledge, *Humans and the Earth: Toward a Personal Ecology* (Peter Lang, 1993).

[15]Mason, *Old Testament Pictures of God*, p. 198.

about the reality of God. This God is not known through any cast or molten image. God is known peculiarly through this creature who exists in the realm of free history, where power is received, decisions are made, and commitments are honored. God is not imaged in anything fixed but in the freedom of human persons to be faithful and gracious.[16]

> Reflect on the relationship between this idea of God imaged in the world and in humanness and the New Testament idea of incarnation in Jesus of Nazareth. Is the New Testament heir to the Hebrew scriptures at this point?

Israel's sense of covenant responsibility to be God's servant community was, from the time of the giving of the law at Sinai, a particular expression of this image relationship. The Decalogue on which the law was based specifically forbade the making of images just because any images would detract from their responsibility to be the servants through whom God would accomplish his purposes; that is, Israel was to be the image of God.

The priestly liturgy affirms the goodness of creation with a sevenfold refrain, "God saw that it was good." This expression marked each work as one corresponding with God's intention, "perfect, as far as its nature required and permitted, complete, and the object of the creator's approving regard and satisfaction."[17] Israel, not an ascetic people, enjoyed the full richness of a good creation:

> You cause the grass to grow for the cattle,
>   and plants for people to use,
> to bring forth food from the earth,
>   and wine to gladden the human heart,
> oil to make the face shine,
>   and bread to strengthen the human heart. . . .
> When you open your hand,
>   they are filled with good things.
>   [Psalm 104:14–15, 28b]

The Yahwistic Creation Story (Genesis 2:4b–25)

The priestly creation liturgy appropriately opens Torah with praise of God as creator of a good creation and with affirmation of the dignity and responsibility of humankind. It is followed by a second and in many ways different creation account in 2:4b–25. This account is the beginning of the Yahwistic story of Israel's origins, which continues through much of the rest of Torah. The Yahwist's creation story is part of a theological analysis of the failure of human beings to be the responsible creatures God had created them to be. In this

---

[16]Brueggemann, *Genesis*, p. 32.
[17]S. R. Driver, *The Book of Genesis* (Metheun, 1904), p. 5.

treatment of the primeval age the Yahwist writes of both creation and fall, of Eden given and Eden lost. His characters are representative. Adam is every man; Eve is every woman. Cain who kills Abel is all of us. Abel who is killed is also all of us. The whole of humanity is in the waters of the flood and on Noah's ark. The entire human race knows alienation at the foot of the tower of Babel.

The Yahwistic creation story is simple and beautiful. The human race is personified in a man (*'adam*)[18] and a woman (*'ishshah*), Adam and Eve. God is described in anthropomorphic terms–that is, God is pictured as a human being. God *stooped* in the dust and out of it *molded* a man into whose nostrils God *breathed* the divine, life-giving breath. God *planted* a garden and *placed* man within it. *Working* in the garden, God grew all kinds of trees. God *walked* with the man in the garden and they conversed with one another. When the man found no companion among the beasts that he saw, Yahweh *put him to sleep* and, *performing surgery* on him, made woman. Of course, this does not mean that the ancient Israelites literally conceived of God as working with hands or having a human body. The language is figurative description. With such language finite beings attempt to describe the infinite. Even the most sophisticated theological and philosophical language about God is anthropomorphic because all language is of human creation and God is not. There is no reason, therefore, to assume that "storybook" language like that of the Yahwist is theologically less expressive than more sophisticated and less concrete theological and philosophical discourse. What is crucial for either is communication, and the Yahwist's story was heard and understood in old Israel.

The viewpoint of this early account is that of a Palestinian peasant. The man is the tiller of the soil and the garden is a fruitful place in a dry wilderness. Water is the source of life in this oasis and the chaos outside the garden is a waterless waste. The story obviously has as its background the land of Canaan, which the Israelites looked upon as a good land blessed by Yahweh and flowing with milk and honey. Notice how skillfully the story relates humanity to the physical environment best known to the Yahwist's contemporaries. Persons were created to live in their kind of world. The good earth of Canaan is the stage for life and its soil is for farming. Human existence is creaturely existence and in a real sense the world is the place intended for humankind. But human beings are not just a product of nature; they are animated by the breath of God. In this simple picture the Yahwist portrays something of the majesty of human existence. Man and woman are creatures of God and are dependent on God and ultimately responsible to God, not only for life but also for meaning and joy.

The order of creation in the Yahwistic account is: man, the garden, trees,

---

[18]The Hebrew word *'adam* is the same word used in 1:26 where God says, "Let us make man"; it means "humankind."

animals, and woman. The account begins and concludes with the creation of humankind, male and female, the focus of concern in the Yahwistic story. The man was created before plants and animals, and creation was not complete until woman was created to be his companion. With the bestowal of the divine breath, each became a living being (the Hebrew is *nephesh hayah*, "living breathing thing") different from all other creatures. The garden, plants, and animals were created for human use. Clearly the Yahwist tradition is more concerned with creation of persons than with creation of the world, although the latter is also extremely important.

In a profound way this tradition has depicted the reality of human existence. Humans are made from the ground[19] and the earth is our abode. That is, we are creatures and are mortal. But humans are not simply products of nature; they are creatures of God, the source of life. Humankind exists for God and is dependent on God. Yet, because God is graciously disposed toward Adam, Adam is a partner in creation. He approves and names every living creature, thus sharing to a degree in the creative act. In Semitic culture only one who has authority and power could bestow a name on anything.

Adam was placed in *'eden* "to till it and keep it." The Yahwist locates Eden to the east. This description is purposefully cryptic because the story is not concerned to locate geographically the primeval paradise. The Hebrew word *'eden* means "delight" or "enchantment," and the Israelites may have thought of the garden of Eden as a "delightful garden" or a "park of enchantment." Some scholars, however, suggest that the word *'eden* may be related to the Babylonian word *'edinu*, meaning "plain" or "desert," indicating that the garden was planted in a plain or like an oasis in a desert. It is also possible that Eden is intended only as a proper name, a place name.[20] In any case its location on a map is not intended.

The description of the garden is equally figurative, not geographical. A river flowed through Eden and, after leaving the garden, divided to become four rivers. This description roughly resembles a skeleton map of the earth's surface as the Babylonians conceived it. This map depicts the earth as centering in Babylon around which are certain towns and canals with the entire area encircled by the ocean. Finally, at the extreme outside are the most distant regions indicated by triangles. The similarity between Hebrew and Babylonian cartography reflects more a common worldview than any direct dependence of one on the other. Certainly the Babylonian worldview does not clarify the geography in the Genesis narrative. Any efforts to resolve the descriptions of the story are futile, because the Genesis tradition was not burdened with geograph-

---

[19]In Hebrew the words "man" and "ground" come from the same root. The verse, therefore, contains a play on words: "Then Yahweh formed *'adam* from the dust of *'adamah*."

[20]For defense of a geographical description, see E. A. Speiser, "Genesis," in *The Anchor Bible*, I:19–20.

ical concerns. Rather it says figuratively that "even the blessings of nature are ultimately derived from the grace of God in the creation."[21]

In the world known to ancient Israel, rivers were the great source of fertility; agriculture and civilization flourished only in the great river valleys. The picture, therefore, is of a life-giving river of such magnitude that, even after leaving the garden, it supplies four large streams. The writer's concern is with the sustaining abundance of God's original world. The tradition as developed in Israel had theological rather than geographical meaning. The life-giving powers of the great rivers known to Israel and the cultures that developed along them originated in the river that flowed from Eden.

Israel later replaced the "lost" Eden as the center of the world with Jerusalem, where Yahweh dwelt in the temple on Mt. Zion. Ezekiel draws on this imagery to describe a life-giving river that flowed from the altar in the Jerusalem temple, turning the desert waste of southern Palestine into a fruitful garden (Ezekiel 47). The sacred city was, therefore, the creative center from which life-giving powers extended into the chaos of the ungodly world of other nations, and at the end of history would become in some sense a new Eden.

The man was placed in the garden paradise to dress it and keep it. He was to work there. Paradise included honest and satisfying physical and productive activity. The ritual curse in 3:17–19 is on burdensome toil as evil, not on work itself. To work was the man's created destiny. If Yahweh worked as creator, why should the man not work as creature? "Then Yahweh God said, 'It is not good that man should be alone; I will make him a helper as his partner' " (Genesis 2:18). The man's paradise was not complete without companionship. At no point is the Yahwist's tradition more anthropomorphic than here. In an almost humorous way he depicts both God and the man seeking an animal mate for the man as if neither knew that only a creature of the man's own kind would be a suitable companion. Here at the beginning of the Hebrew Bible we become aware of a sense of humor, which, more often than is generally realized, characterizes biblical literature. The humor, however, introduces the serious creative work of God, without which all else would be incomplete. The man's hunger for fellowship was not satisfied by animals; woman was created. A deep sleep fell upon the man, and God made a woman from a part of the man's body. The creation of woman is the climax of the Yahwist's creation account. In contrast to the animals, inferior to the man, the woman is described as "a helper as his partner." "Helper" here has the sense of companion, not inferior assistant.[22] The woman is the man's equal, a partner rather than a creature to

---

[21]Richardson, *Genesis*, p. 65.

[22]Trible, *Good and the Rhetoric of Sexuality* (Fortress, 1978), p. 88, translates 2:18 thus: "And Yahweh God said,/ "It is not good for ha- 'adam to be alone/ I will make for it *a companion corresponding to it.*" She points out that the man being formed from the dust of the ground does not in any way imply that Adam is inferior to the dust of the ground. Therefore, the woman's being made from the rib of the man does not imply inferiority.

be dominated. The woman is God's free creation, without whom humanity is incomplete. Humanity is not sexless. We are male and female, and human sexuality is part of the goodness of creation. Our identities are interdependent and are to be experienced in "solidarity, mutuality, and equality"—a truth expressed in the poetry of Adam's response to the creation of the woman:

> This at last is bone of my bones
> and flesh of my flesh;
> this one shall be called Woman (*'ishah*),
> for out of Man this one was taken.
> [Genesis 2:23]

In this creation story the Yahwist places Adam in a social context of lasting relationships. God gives him a place to live with food to eat, relating man to his physical environment. Adam—that is, every Adam—is related to other living creatures, and accepts responsibility for them. But even more significant are relationships to other humans—in companionship, mutual responsibilities, and relationship to God, the source of every Adam's being, identity, and responsibilities. In the continuation of this story the Yahwist depicts the ways in which humankind responds to these relationships and how God reacts to human responsibility and irresponsibility.

Relationship of the Yahwistic and Priestly Stories

Two distinct traditions have been preserved by the editors of Genesis in the priestly and Yahwistic creation stories. The most conspicuous contrast is the fundamental structure of the stories:

Priestly	*Yahwistic*
Earth's original state a watery chaos	Earth's original state a waterless waste
The work of creation divided into six separate operations, each assigned to one day	No time reference
The order of creation:	The order of creation:
1. light	1. man formed from the dust
2. firmament	2. the garden
3. land, separation of earth from sky, vegetation	3. trees
4. heavenly bodies	4. animals
5. birds and fishes	5. woman, created out of man
6. animals and man, male and female together	

The two stories also have distinct styles and vocabularies, especially in the way they describe the creator God. In the priestly liturgy the language pictures a transcendent deity who creates by legislative command, a God whose word is law. This God *creates, says, sees, divides, calls, makes.* God is a God of order and pattern, majestic and distant. This picture of divine majesty reflects the sociological and theological context of the priestly author. In the Babylonian exile, there was concern for law and order and the restoration of Israelite sovereignty in Palestine. The priests looked to a transcendent God whose power to structure the universe could restructure human life in the world. Such a deity must be both joyfully praised and dutifully obeyed.

In contrast, the anthropomorphic God of the Yahwistic story *stoops, molds, breathes, plants, places, works, walks.* The deity here is the sympathetic, immanent helper of the man, a companion in a world in which they have common interests. They walk and talk together in the garden. The Yahwistic story thus complements the conception of God given in the priestly liturgy. The transcendent God of liturgical praise is also to be understood as a deity immanently active and continually concerned with the affairs of humankind in the maintenance of creation and history. This earlier view of God comes from a time in the early monarchy when rulers like David and Solomon seemed worthy companions for God in the enterprise of making Israel into a nation of the covenant.

These different views of God are not contradictory or incompatible. As one interpreter has noted: "It may be that individuals as well as epochs of man's history have vacillated between seeing God as the transcendent, all-powerful, distant deity of Chapter 1 [of Genesis] and as the personally concerned, sympathetic, merciful friend of mankind of Chapter 2."[23]

The two accounts express complementary perceptions of the nature of God, of personal relationships to deity, and the place of human beings in the world. Together they adequately reflect Israel's creation faith and its understanding of the essential nature of humans as creatures of God. In preserving them both, Israel was surely aware of their differences, but concerned with theological conceptualization, not scientific description. Hence both were treasured because each said something important. And together they express a perspective toward the relationship of natural reality and ultimate being that transcends any and all attempts to speak of creation in literal and historical terms.

Israel's Creation Stories and Other Views of Creation

Creation stories are not unique to Israel. Ancient peoples regularly attempted to account for the world by telling creation stories, often more than one. Although their content is imaginative and fanciful, certainly not scientific, these stories were believed to express lasting truth about deity, humanity, and the world. They often included descriptions about the origins of the structures and institutions that maintained social order. In fact, Israel's belief in creation in-

[23]Gros Louis, "Genesis I–II," p. 50.

cluded not only the "in beginning" creation of the universe, but also the "in history" creation of Israel as the servant people of God. In that sense the entire Torah is a "creation" narrative. In this and other ways Israel's creation stories may be compared to those of other peoples, especially those belonging to ancient Near Eastern culture.

The best-known extrabiblical story of creation is the Babylonian *Enuma Elish*. Recited on the fourth day of the Babylonian new year festival, Enuma Elish is a story of the birth of the gods and the creation of humankind in a well-ordered universe.[24] It begins with a picture of earliest primordial time when only the divine couple, Apsu (the fresh water) and Tiamat (the salt water), was existent:

> When on high the heaven had not been named,
> Firm ground below had not been called by name,
> Naught but primordial Apsu, their begetter,
> and Mummu-Tiamat, she who bore them all,
> Their waters comingling as a single body.

Many gods sprang from the first pair and eventually rebelled against their authority. Apsu was slain by the rebels, and Tiamat in revenge launched a well-planned attack on the younger gods. Marduk, the principal god of the city of Babylon, was made champion of the younger gods and entered into mortal combat with Tiamat. After a titanic struggle, Marduk triumphed, killed Tiamat, and from her body made the heavens and the earth:

> He split her like a shellfish into two parts:
> Half of her he set up and ceiled it as sky,
> Pulled down the bar and posted guards.
> He bade them to allow not her waters to escape.
> He crossed the heavens and surveyed the regions.
> He squared Apsu's quarter, the abode of Nudimmud,
> As the lord measured the dimensions of Apsu.
> The Great Abode, its likeness, he fixed as Esharra,
> The Great Abode, Esharra, which he made as the firmament.

Thus, order was established out of chaos. Thereafter, Marduk decided to make human beings to be workers for the gods:

> Blood I will mass and cause bones to be.
> I will establish a savage, "man" shall be his name.
> Verily, savage-man I will create.
> He shall be charged with the service of the gods
> That they might be at ease!

A god who had aided Tiamat in her battle with Marduk was used as material for the creation of humans.

---

[24]For a full text of the story, see Pritchard, *Texts*, pp. 60–72, from which the quotes are selected.

The priestly biblical and Babylonian Enuma Elish follow essentially the same order:

Enuma Elish	*Genesis 1*
1. Primordial water chaos—Apsu and Tiamat enveloped in darkness	1. Earth formless and void; the chaotic deep (*Tehom*) enveloped in darkness
2. Appearance of Marduk, "Sun of the Heavens"	2. The creation of light
3. Chaos overcome by Marduk in titanic battle with Tiamat; the sky fashioned from half of her body	3. The firmament of the heavens created
4. Earth formed	4. Waters gathered together; dry land appears
5. Constellations established	5. Light bodies created
6. Humankind made (as an afterthought) to serve the gods	6. Humankind created in God's image to have dominion over all creation
7. A banquet held by the gods	7. Seventh day, God rests

These stories also share the same cosmology (view of the structure of the world). It is a cosmology of sight experience—that is, the universe is described essentially as it appears to one who looks up and out at the sky and the world. One could not expect such a view to correspond to modern scientific conceptions of the universe.[25] The ancients divided the universe into three levels, as clearly stated in the familiar words of the second of the Ten Commandments: "You shall not make for yourself an idol, whether in the form of anything that is in heaven above, or that is on the earth beneath, or that is in the water under the earth" (Exodus 20:4).

The flat, circular earth occupied the center of the world. Over it stretched a solid dome, the firmament of Genesis 1 (literally "a beaten out place"), which rested on the mountains around the edge of the earth. Inside the dome the sun, moon, and stars moved in their proper courses, as if on tracks. Above the dome were the "waters above the firmament," originally part of the primeval ocean before it was divided at the creation of the world. Instead of flooding the earth these waters supplied rain, snow, and hail when God opened the "windows of heaven." Above the heavenly waters were the chambers of the deity. Beneath the earth was the great deep, a mighty ocean where all earthly waters, such as springs, or wells, had their source. The earth rested securely on great pillars sunk deep in the subterranean waters. Within this lower region was Sheol, the gloomy abode of the dead.

Other ancient conceptions of the world and its creation were similar to those of the Israelites. Egypt conceived of the earth as a flat platter with a corrugated rim. The bottom of the platter was the alluvial plain of Egypt; the rim was mountainous foreign lands. The platter of existence floated in abysmal waters

---

[25]One cannot be oversmug about contemporary scientific cosmology, for research continuously alters conceptualizations. Is the earth round or pear shaped?

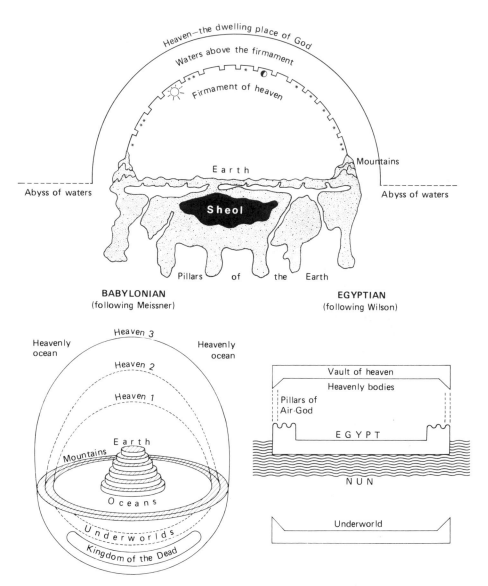

Figure 3.3. Ancient conceptions of the universe. (Sources: S. H. Hooke, *In the Beginning*, p. 20; B. Meissner, *Babylonien und Assyrien*, II, used by permission of Carl Winter, *Univeristätsvering.* Adapted from *The Intellectual Adventure of Ancient Man* by H. and H. Frankfort, John A. Wilson, Thorkild Jacobson, and William A. Irwin, by permission of the University of Chicago Press)

called Nun. Out of primordial Nun life first issued and still from it the sun rose daily. Nun fed the Nile and consequently sustained life. Above the earth was the sky, an inverted pan defining the outer limits of the universe. The underworld, the counterpart of the sky, bounded the limits below.

For the Egyptians, creation was related to the inundation of the Nile River. Annually they witnessed the re-creation that came as fertile mud appeared out of the waters of the receding Nile. Reason told them that what they saw every year must also have happened at the beginning. The world came into being as order was established out of the chaos of the primeval Nun. From the waters arose a hillock with a self-created god, Atum, squatting upon it. After the waters of the Abyss had receded, Atum continued creation by naming the parts of his body, and with each name called a pair of gods into being. Another version of the tradition records that Atum spat these lesser gods out of his mouth; still another indicates that they were the result of masturbation—an attempt to overcome the problem of generation by a god alone without a goddess. The gods so produced were the god of air and the goddess of moisture, the god of earth and the goddess of sky. Out of earth and sky came the creatures that populate the universe.

Other cultures had creation stories that at first glance seem quite different from the Near Eastern traditions. The Rig Veda contains a story from India:

Neither not-being nor being was there at that time; there was no air-filled space nor was there the sky which is beyond it. What enveloped all? And where? Under whose protection? What was the unfathomable deep water?

Neither was death there, nor even immortality at that time; there was no distinguishing mark of day and night. That One breathed without wind in its own special manner. Other than It, indeed, and beyond, there did not exist anything whatsoever. In the beginning there was darkness concealed in darkness; all this was an indistinguishable flood of water. That which, possessing life-force, was enclosed by the vacuum, the One, was born through the power of heat from its austerity.

Upon It rose up, in the beginning, desire, which was the mind's first seed. Having sought in their hearts, the wise ones discovered, through deliberation, the bond of being and nonbeing. Right across was their [i.e., the wise ones'] dividing line extended. Did the below exist then, was there the above? There were the seed-planters, there were the great forces of expansion. Below there was self-impulse, above active imparting.

Who knows it for certain; who can proclaim it here; namely, out of what it was born and wherefrom this creation issued? The gods appeared only later —after the creation of the world. Who knows, then, out of what it has evolved?

Wherefrom this creation has issued, whether he has made it or whether he has not—he who is the superintendent of this world in the highest heaven—he alone knows, or, perhaps, even he does not know.[26]

---

[26]Rig Veda 10.129, in W. T. deBary, *Sources of Indian Tradition* (Columbia University, 1958), pp. 17–18.

Or consider a Polynesian story:

> He existed, Taaroa was his name.
> In the immensity [space]
> There was no earth, there was no sky.
> There was no sea, there was no man.
> Above, Taaroa calls.
> Existing alone, he became the universe.
> Taaroa is the origin, the rocks,
> Taaroa is the sands,
> It is thus that he is named.
> Taaroa is the light;
> Taaroa is within;
> Taaroa is the germ.
> Taaroa is beneath;
> Taaroa is firm;
> Taaroa is wise.
> He created the land of Hawaii,
> Hawaii the great and sacred,
> As a body or shell for Taaroa.[27]

A Fulani creation story comes from Africa:

> At the beginning there was a huge drop of milk.
> Then Doondari came and he created the stone.
> Then the stone created iron;
> And iron created water,
> And water created air.
> Then Doondari descended the second time.
> And he took the five elements and he shaped them into man.
> But man was proud.
> Then Doondari created blindness and blindness defeated man.
> But when blindness became too proud,
> Doondari created sleep, and sleep defeated blindness;
> But when sleep became too proud,
> Doondari created worry, and worry defeated sleep;
> But when worry became too proud,
> Doondari created death, and death defeated worry.
> But when death became too proud,
> Doondari descended for the third time,
> And he came as Gueno the eternal one,
> And Gueno defeated death.[28]

These stories differ from each other and from the biblical and other Near Eastern creation stories, yet they all have much in common. They express the universal human concern for meaning and order. Such stories are told again and again, not primarily to describe the creation of the world, but to disclose

---

[27]Long, *Alpha*, p. 172.
[28]Ulli Beier, *Origin of Life and Death* (Hunemann, 1966), pp. 1–2.

that the world, humanity, and life have a divine origin and history.[29] Creation stories were repeated in ritual, providing worshipers knowledge of the community's belief in deity as creator and humankind as creature, reminding worshipers that life in a created order demanded that they live responsibly, and assuring them that chaos in all its forms could be overcome. Stories like these are the most important stories of all to the people who tell and retell them. They are important because they are sacred, exemplary, and significant. Sacred because they deal with ultimate values and concerns; they are always stories about the gods. Exemplary because they supply models for human behavior and the organization of society. Significant because they give value and meaning to life. They describe breakthroughs of the sacred into the world that serve as models for human activity, wisdom, and knowledge.

Israel's creation stories, with theological distinction, address the common human concern for life in an orderly world. Israel's conception of the character of God is unique. In contrast to the grossly polytheistic struggle of Enuma Elish, Genesis describes the creative activity of one sovereign god who, with a word, establishes order out of chaos. There is no implication of sexual union with a female consort. The creation is not the result of divine sex, but of divine thought expressed in creative command (Genesis 1) or creative work (Genesis 2). Israel believed that Yahweh, through whom the world came into being, was the omnipotent God, creator and redeemer of Israel. God who has called Israel into being had also spoken the world into existence. And for Israel Yahweh had no rival. Marduk and others to whom the role of creator had been assigned were nonentities, wholly unworthy of comparison with Yahweh. In the Genesis accounts other deities of the ancient world, the heavenly bodies, are stripped of their divine prerogatives, becoming mere instruments in the hand of Yahweh for delineating day and night.

The Rig Veda's affirmation is uncertain: "Wherefrom this creation has issued, whether he has made it or whether he has not . . . he alone knows, or, perhaps, even he does not know." But Israel declares, "In the beginning God created the heavens and the earth." And Israel means God as understood and experienced in its own ongoing historical experience. That God and no other is the creator God. *The creator is the redeemer* who moves history toward ultimate fulfillment. The creator God is the deity whose character has been revealed in Israel's experience as benevolent and without comparison.

Behind Enuma Elish and some other creation stories is the thought of a personal, chaotic force continually seeking to undo the work of the gods. The Hebrew Bible occasionally reflects this thought. The defeat of chaos is expressed as the conquering of the primordial sea (Psalm 104:9, 148:6) and as a terrible battle fought by Yahweh against a dragon called Rahab or Leviathan

---

[29]On the significance of creation stories in traditional religions, see Mircea Eliade, *The Sacred and the Profane* (Harper, 1961), pp. 68–113.

Figure 3.4. A cylinder seal (left) from c. 2000 B.C.E. and its impression (right) showing a woman and a man seated at a sacred tree, a common motif in ancient Near Eastern art. (Copyright British Museum)

(Psalm 74:13f; Job 26:12f; Isaiah 27:1; 51:9f). But always chaos is inferior to and powerless before Yahweh. Like the heavenly bodies, chaos is an instrument in Yahweh's hand.

The Genesis view of humankind as the climax of creation, made in the image and likeness of God, is further evidence of the theological genius of Israelite creation faith. Persons are made to have dominion over the world and to enjoy fellowship with its creator, not to be servants in the household of the gods, doing work they were reluctant to do for themselves. Placed in a good world human beings are intended to lead a good life, enjoying the blessings bestowed on them by a gracious God. They are free to work out their own destinies in cooperation with God and fellow humans. Compare the fatalistic view in another creation text from India where the caste social order is imposed on humanity by the creative act:

> His mouth became the priests; his two arms
> were made into the rulers and warriors;
> his two thighs the merchants and landowners;
> from his two feet the workers were born.[30]

Human life as Genesis understands it is responsible but not determined. The Yahwistic story makes this very clear as it continues beyond chapter 2.

Finally, the biblical creation faith affirms the goodness of creation. Humankind lives in a good world brought into existence by the sovereign power of the only God in whose hands it constantly remains. The earth stands firmly on its pillars, the mountains are steady, and chaotic waters do not return to cover the land. Day follows night and season follows season as God intends. Humankind, therefore, is secure because God protects the world against chaos.

[30]From Rig Veda 10.90.

In other words humans live in a world whose existence and meaning is derived from God and they are safe. For this they should be thankful. Any disruption in divine order and safety comes from some source other than God. How, then, do we account for a world where not everything is good? To this question the Yahwist turns in chapters 3 and 4.

The Genesis creation stories are different from understandings of creation in the modern natural sciences. What values do these stories have for a modern reader? Do they have to be reconciled with the theories of science? Why or why not? Can you think of similar nonliteral stories from which you have learned important lessons?

THE TRADITION OF THE FALL: REBELLION AND VIOLENCE
(GENESIS 3 AND 4)

The Yahwistic story of creation left humankind (Adam and Eve) in Eden's garden of paradise. Reality of life, however, is not Eden; humankind does not live in paradise. Genesis 3 and 4 give the Yahwist's explanation of what happened to the good creation. Contrary to divine intention, the good creation is corrupted by persons who distort God's purpose. Every imitator of Adam and Eve rebels against the sovereignty of their creator; violence in the human family results. The narrator describes the misconduct of men and women, continuing his story with an emphasis on human freedom and responsibility, and the consequences of irresponsibility. Persons as creatures are always in the position of both knowing creaturely limitations and imagining what it would be like to be without these limitations. Creatures can imagine that they are absolute—that is, that *they* are god. Entertaining the possibility of acting as if one controls one's own interests and destiny is rebellion and pride—a violation of the nature of personhood as created by God. Such rebellion and pride is in biblical theology called sin.

The Yahwist's story is set in the primeval past, but it is more than descriptive of what was; it describes what is. Here is the account of what is happening to Adam—that is, what characterizes the experience of every *'adam*. The story, therefore, is about typical, not causative, events. The fall is not everyone's experience *because* it was a primeval event that changed forever the human situation. The Hebrew Bible is not that fatalistic about humanity. The image of God was not tarnished in the remote past; it is tarnished a thousand ways each day. The fall is the experience of each man or woman who in his or her own way abuses freedom by acting irresponsibly toward God and fellow humans. Created in the image of God, persons are creatures of two-dimensional responsibility, one vertical and the other horizontal. This view of human responsibility is found throughout the Bible. For example, in the Ten Commandments (Exodus 20) four laws define responsibility toward God, and the remainder define responsibility toward neighbors. Hebrew prophets insist that protestations of one's fidelity to God be tested by social responsibility. And the New Testament summary of the law and prophets combines verses from Deuteronomy 6:5 and Leviticus 19:18:

> You shall love Yahweh your God with all your heart,
> and with all your soul, and with all your mind. . . .
> You shall love your neighbor as yourself.
> [Matthew 22:37, 39]

Persons are created to be responsible to god and to their fellow humans, but they act irresponsibly in both dimensions. Genesis 3 tells of irresponsibility toward God; Genesis 4 of irresponsibility toward fellow human beings.

Rebellion (Genesis 3)

With an exceptional dramatic gift for storytelling, the Yahwist mentions two trees in the midst of Eden, "the tree of life" and "the tree of the knowledge of good and evil." The significance of these trees is not clear. The "tree of life" perhaps represents the positive potential that the creator and the creation offer humankind, and the "tree of the knowledge of good and evil" those prerogatives that belong to God. But in the plot of the Yahwist's story "the tree of the knowledge" clearly represents a prohibition that is a challenge to the freedom of Adam and Eve. Prohibitions like this are common in these kinds of stories. They act as clues to the inevitable outcome. Adam and Eve are told that they *must not* eat of the fruit of this tree, not that they *cannot*. The reader or hearer of the story knows before being told that they will disobey and eat, and that the consequences will be disastrous. How it happens that they eat it and the nature of the consequences are issues the reader anticipates in the further unfolding of the story. And the reader is not disappointed. The Yahwist introduces the serpent, wise, mysterious, and crafty, perhaps even a force of dangerous evil. Later interpreters identify the serpent with Satan, but this identification is not made by the Yahwist. Satan as the personification of evil is a much later development in Jewish thought.

The peace of Eden is disturbed by the serpent's appeal to human senses; the forbidden tree is "good for food" and "a delight to the eyes." But more basically the serpent feeds human pride: "You will be like God, knowing good and evil." Before such enticement Eve and Adam are defenseless. The story moves swiftly to its point. First Eve and then Adam eat the fruit, yielding to the anticipation that they would become like God. In essence they are attempting to escape creaturehood, rebelling against God's control. The knowledge gained, however, proved to be quite different from that which the tempter had promised. Immediately they became aware of sin and guilt and found that their fellowship with God had been broken. When God called them, they sought to conceal themselves but found God's gaze inescapable. Their response, "I was afraid," represents their broken relationship with God. And it will be God who will seek to overcome it. Humanity is alienated from God, not God from humanity. The biblical response to humankind's cry of fear is, "Do not fear, I am with you" (Genesis 26:24).

But human rebellion brings judgment. The results of sin are described in terms of major disruptions in God's orderly creations:[31] First, the serpent is cursed to grovel in the dust, crawling on its belly. Just as the tempter serpent represents the element out of which sin arose, so the tempter's punishment demonstrates how God's curse rests on all evil. Second, the woman is sentenced to pain in childbirth. To the Hebrew the bearing of children was woman's greatest joy, a means for fulfilling her destiny. Now her greatest joy is to be marred by pain. Here again sin is depicted as disruptive of created order. Third, work is to be burdensome and accompanied by disappointments and vexations. In God's creation work was not a curse; it becomes a curse because of sin. The laborer's days would be filled with toil, and toil is irksome. Thus, the harsh and cruel realities of the world are described as direct results of sin. God intended neither that woman suffer as she brought children into the world nor that thorns and thistles of the ground turn human work into a burden. But sin as rebellion corrupted God's creation and humanity has to live with the consequences.

Even in the midst of pronouncement of judgment, the Yahwist includes an announcement of hope. The serpent is doomed to live in irreconcilable enmity with humanity. Therefore, humanity will always be threatened by evil. But ultimately victory will not belong to the tempter:

> I will put enmity between you and the woman,
>   and between your offspring and hers;
> he will strike your head,
>   and you will strike his heel.
>
> [3:15][32]

This story concludes with dramatic emphasis: Eden is closed to reentry. Man and woman are expelled from the garden and no longer have access to the tree of life. Their sin has alienated them from God. "Paradise is irreparably lost; what is left for man is a life of trouble in the shadow of a crushing riddle, a life entangled in an unbounded and completely hopeless struggle with the power of evil and in the end unavoidably subject to the majesty of death."[33] Cherubim and "a flaming sword which turned every way" guarded the tree of life. A

---

[31]The judgment pronouncements here use materials that earlier must have been etiological—that is, answering simple, childlike questions of origins: Why do snakes have no legs? Why pain in child birth? Why so much toil in tilling the soil?

[32]This verse is sometimes called the Protoevangelium or "first gospel."

[33]Von Rad, *Genesis*, p. 98.

cherub (plural, cherubim), a winged sphinx with a human head, familiar throughout the ancient Near East, protects the majestic presence of God. Thus God's decree of expulsion from paradise was enforced by power and majesty. The earthly garden of innocence, purity, and ideal happiness is no more. For Israel the real world was not Eden, but one populated with rebellious 'adam. The only hope for fullness of life rested in God. Renewed access to a tree of life would come only when God would act to remove the barriers. The Yahwistic story thus prepares the way for the drama in which Yahweh moves into Israel's history to do for it what it could not do for itself.

The Yahwist is convinced that even in judgment God reveals concern for creatures. Woman continues to bear children, though in pain; the farmer reaps a harvest from the earth, but with toil. When the man and the woman stand guilty and ashamed before God, God respects them in their shame and clothes them. And, driven from the garden, persons still can abide in the presence of God, who always seeks to restore the fellowship broken by human rebellion. Humankind is judged by God but not finally rejected. The creator who is judge is also redeemer.

Violence (Genesis 4)

Genesis 3 and Genesis 4 should be considered together not merely because they follow sequentially in the Yahwistic narrative, but because taken together they depict the Hebrew understanding of sin. The Yahwist portrays this conception of sin by following the Adam-Eve narrative with a story about two brothers, Cain and Abel. The agenda is the dilemma of living with brothers and sisters in human community. The Yahwist uses an ancient story about the conflict between shepherds and farmers, but reshapes it into a story about the brokenness of the human community. His story is about the self-will, jealousy, and pride with which humans assault one another by breaking human ties and affections.

Cain and Abel, the sons of Adam and Eve, offer their best as sacrifices to Yahweh. Cain, a farmer, offers the produce of the ground. Abel, a shepherd, brings the firstlings of his flock. Yahweh accepts the sacrifice of Abel and rejects that of Cain. Why Abel's sacrifice is accepted or Cain's rejected, the story does not tell. The narrative reflects traditional animosity between shepherd and farmer, but the text does not emphasize this and the Yahwist uses the story for other purposes. The story is not about sacrifice, but about fractured human society and the destiny of alienated humanity. Rejection of Cain's sacrifice presents the circumstances within which his jealous anger arises. It is essentially the occasion provided by the narrator for the crisis of his story. Cain, whose name implies "creativity" (from qanah, "to get," "to create"), murders his brother. Abel, whose name means "nothingness," is destroyed. Both the power and the fragility of human existence are brought together in a conflict in which human creativity is used for destruction.

Just as Adam is every person, so is Cain in his potential to promote or destroy human relationships. Created by God to live in social responsibility with neighbors, humankind in rebellious pride rejects brotherhood so that we all stand against one another, not as brother and sisters, but as aliens. This alienation is a recurring theme in the Hebrew Bible. Isaac and Ishmael are competing sons of Abraham (Genesis 21); Jacob steals his brother's birthright (Genesis 25); brothers are consumed with jealousy over their father's attention to Joseph (Genesis 37); the covenant nation Israel boasts of its superiority over other nations (Joshua–Kings); the privileged class exploits and oppresses the poor (Amos, Hosea). For Israel this is the reality of human existence. Human beings in rebellion against God violently abuse their neighbors.

Like Adam and Eve, Cain immediately hears the disturbing voice of God as both challenge and judgment, "Where is Abel, your brother?" Refusal to be his brother's keeper condemns Cain to life in the "land of wandering" (Nod). Alienation and fear come with rejection of one's brother or sister. Cain is now a fugitive at the mercy of both God and human beings. Other persons now become potential Cains to Cain who is now afraid of becoming Abel. That is a reality of life in the world of alienation. No less than the story of Adam and Eve, this is the story of every human being. The Yahwist writes about all humanity, not just about an ancient murderer.

Yet, is spite of his dastardly act, Cain the fugitive is "met with surprising grace."[34] God marks Cain as sinner, but also for protection. Cain's rejection of his brother cuts him off from God, "away from the presence of Yahweh," but does not cut God off from Cain. Even Cain's life belongs to God, who does not abandon him.[35] The divine punishment of Cain should not become "the occasion for barbarism among men."[36]

In concluding the story of Cain, the Yahwist describes the origins of civilization and, at the same time, passes judgment on culture. The first city was built by Cain, a murderer. Civilization began under the mark of Cain alienated from God, but an object of God's concern and grace. In such an environment sin intensified. Lamech boasted of his foul deeds:

> I have killed a man for wounding me,
> a young man for striking me.
> If Cain is avenged sevenfold,
> truly Lamech seventy-sevenfold.
> [Genesis 4:23b–24]

---

[34]Brueggemann, *Genesis*, p. 61.
[35]Von Rad, *Genesis*, p. 103.
[36]Ibid., p. 106.

Seventy-sevenfold means unlimited, rather like our term "to the nth de-gree." Life was cheap and vengeance gave way to endless vindictive retaliation. Of course, this judgment of culture should not be pressed too far. In fact, it betrays the peasant or nomadic background of its origin. On the other hand, no one who has lived in the midst of a developed but cruel and inhuman society would deny that the consequences of impersonal society are infinitely dangerous.

The Israelite Understanding of Persons as Sinners

Genesis 3 and 4 describe the reality of human existence. Created in the image of God, humankind was to have dominion over the earth and all that it con-tained. But human dominion was to be exercised under the overarching sov-ereignty of the creator. Created persons were to be Yahweh's representatives. The creator, not the creature, was supreme. The creature is "to image," not "to be," the creator. Persons made in the image of God enjoy a relationship with, and dependence on, the one who is represented. Their vocation is to reflect God's nature within that world over which they have been given do-minion. Therefore, a person must "maintain his relationship with God, he must remember that he is only an ambassador and his dominion over creation will be effective only in proportion as that relationship becomes more real."[37] In this sense dominion over creation is not so much authority as it is respon-sibility.

As representatives of a caring God, persons are responsible to care for their neighbors. They are commanded to "be fruitful and multiply and fill the earth"; that is, they are created to live in community. God intends that Cain be his brother's keeper, the object of his concern and love. Under God and in conformity with God's righteous will, the destiny of persons is to live in true community, with each concerned for the other.

However, the real is far from the ideal. Human relationships are marked by sin, which mars God's creation. The reality of life is quite different from Eden. Genesis 3 and 4 endeavor to explain the discrepancy between life as it is and life as it ought to be. They interpret sinfulness as rejection of responsibility toward both God and fellow humans. The attempt of Adam and Eve to be like God was a distortion of the dignity and holiness of their creation. Because they were created in the image of God, they were able to rebel against God. Sta-tioned above the animals and below God, Adam and Eve became enamoured, even intoxicated, with the idea that they could be God. They rebelliously de-nied their responsibility as God's representatives. The desire to be free from God caused them to reject the limitations set on their creatureliness. They

---

[37]Jacob, *Theology*, p. 171.

repudiated God in favor of their own powers and desires. The tragedy of human life is that men and women want to go their own way, to assert their independence, and to be free from obedience to God's law. They are proud and want equality with God. In effect, they wish to be God. This is the sin of Adam and Eve; it is the sin of every sinner and the reason why life is outside the garden. A theologian summarizes:

> It is revolt, it is creature's departure from the attitude which is the only possible attitude for him, it is the creature's becoming Creator, it is the destruction of creatureliness. It is defection, it is the fall from being held in creatureliness. This defection is a continual falling, a plunging into bottomless depths, a being relinquished, a withdrawal ever farther and deeper. And in all this it is not simply a moral lapse but the destruction of creation by the creature. The Fall affects the whole of the created world which is henceforth plundered of its creatureliness as it crashes blindly into infinite space, like a meteor which has torn away from its nucleus.[38]

The sequel to self-assertion and rebellion against God is irresponsibility toward humans. In short, persons live in a broken community. Their world is filled with murder, strife, hatred, and war; they are not their brothers' keepers. Such a broken community, according to the Yahwist, is not the intention of God or a part of God's good creation. Willful thwarting of God's creative purposes cannot be overlooked; its consequences are certain.

The condemnatory intent of these stories is fully realized, however, only when it is understood that they describe existential realities, not historical events. They condemn all sin by powerfully presenting the inevitable consequences of any and every human rejection of God and fellow humans, whether in the past, present, or future. But the judgment, although certain, is not vindictive. God's basic concern is redemption of the sinner. Hence chapters 3 and 4 are introductory to God's work through the nation Israel in two ways: (1) they present the human predicament that demands divine attention, and (2) they portray a God who maintains a gracious and redemptive concern in spite of human rebellion and violence.

THE TRADITION OF JUDGMENT
(GENESIS 5:5–8:20; 9:18–28; 11:1–9)

The Genesis narrative of human sin moves from climax to climax. Stories of rebellion and violence are followed by others of wantonness and destruction. The sequence is interrupted by a major attempt to blot out the problem and begin again, but the rebellion and violence remain. Finally, the Yahwist shows the human family at the tower of Babel, again declaring themselves indepen-

---

[38]Dietrich Bonhoffer, *Creation and Fall* (S. C. M., 1959), p. 77.

dent of the God they assume they no longer need. Consequently, humankind is portrayed as scattered abroad over the face of the earth—lost in a world without meaning.

From Adam to Noah (Genealogies)

Before telling the flood story, Genesis bridges the gap between Adam and Noah with two genealogies. The first of these (4:25–26) belongs to the Yahwistic tradition and traces the lineage of Israel through Seth, appointed by Yahweh to replace the rejected Cain. Here the Hebrew Bible begins to distinguish between Israel, the true people of God, and other nations. Cain and his descendents are cast aside and the true heritage is traced through Seth. This brief passage is the first of Yahweh's "beginnings again." Seth was in a sense a new creation, a fresh and new start. The Yahwist is convinced that, although humanity may rebel against God, God never absolutely rejects creation. One gets the impression from the narrative that persons continuously flaunt God by their rebellion, but God patiently and persistently begins anew. Sinful humanity for the Yahwist, and for biblical faith in general, is ever and again potentially redeemed humanity, a covenant people created by God's gracious redemption.

The second genealogy (5:1–32) is priestly and likewise connects creation and the flood. The priestly writer employs a scheme of ten traditional generations. Each individual in the catalog lived an extraordinarily long life, as if to say that it took a long time for the situation to get as bad as it was at flood time. The generations span 1,656 years in the Hebrew text, 1,307 years in the Samaritan Pentateuch, and 2,242 years in the Septuagint. The variance in the total figure indicates both that there was more than one tradition about the ages of these forebears and that the author's concern was not accurate calendar calculation. Israel, like other ancient peoples, preserved traditions about ancient heroes living to a fabulous age. The Sumerians, for example, had a tradition that calculated the time span between creation and flood as 241,200 years. A later form of the same tradition gives the astounding total of 432,000 years for the combined reigns of the ten kings who ruled between the creation and flood.[39] The total in the Genesis list is not as large, but a similar purpose is achieved. Both traditions express the belief that an extraordinarily long period elapsed; the desperate situation demanding flood did not develop overnight.

The function of these genealogies in the pattern of Genesis 1–11, then, is to indicate that humankind had populated the earth and that population growth only increased sinfulness. The point is emphasized by the special notation that

[39]See Pritchard, *Texts*, pp. 264–66.

Enoch "walked with God" as the singular exemplary figure during dark days when humankind was filling the earth with wickedness.

The Flood

One of the strangest stories in the entire Hebrew Bible introduces the story of the flood. "Sons of God" (semidivine beings from the heavenly court) married "daughters of men" and spawned a race of giants (Hebrew, "fallen ones"). Originally this must have been a popular etiological account of the origin of giants, but the biblical writer uses it for an entirely different purpose. How serious and extensive is human sin? The story addresses the thesis, "Sin has now so contaminated God's holy creation that the natural order is disrupted." Semidivine beings are entering marriage with human women. The increasing moral depravity has become so serious that God "regrets" creation.

The compiler of this material thus inserts an old fragmentary narrative into a rich theological context to suggest that human purposeful rebellion against the creator has contaminated nature itself. How far we are from the Eden of paradise! Human rebellion was cosmic in scope, affecting the whole creation. Corruption had seized the whole mind and purpose of humankind. It was complete and continuous. Could God ignore such flagrant wantonness? If not, what would the divine attitude be? Where does sinful humanity stand before God? These are major theological questions and the flood story addresses them. From the biblical perspective God attempts to correct a creation corrupted by human sin—destroy and start over. In this sense even the destructive flood is a comment on the intention of God to redeem.

The Genesis account of the flood preserves two versions of the tradition, originally separate but now interwoven. One version belongs to the Yahwistic stratum of materials, the other to the priestly. In both their separate and interwoven versions, Israel's account preserves a tradition of severe inundation common in the ancient world. The most famous nonbiblical flood story is part of a long Mesopotamian tale known as the Gilgamesh Epic. The tale deals with the quest for immortality. Gilgamesh was an honest and respected ruler of the Sumerian city-state of Uruk on the lower Euphrates river. Certain of his royal building projects, however, were opposed by the citizens of Uruk, who complained that their king was oppressing them. In response to their lament, the gods created a circumstance that would distract Gilgamesh from his building projects; they created Enkidu, a strong fighter who lived an innocent life with the animals in the wilds of nature. It was reported to Gilgamesh that this Enkidu was a threat to Uruk and plans were devised to capture him. They would send a love priestess into the wilderness to seduce him. She slept with him for six days and seven nights and taught him the ways of civilization and of the great power and strength of Gilgamesh. Enkidu boasted that in every

Figure 3.5. Clay tablet of the Gilgamesh epic, recording the Babylonian account of the flood. The epic dates to the third millennium B.C.E. (Copyright, British Museum)

way he was stronger than Gilgamesh, and he went to Uruk to confront him. The two men had a knock down-drag out fight, but neither could prevail. They suddenly became fast friends. Together they set out to destroy a forest demon, Humbaba. Although they both were afraid of Humbaba, they urged each other on, confronted the demon, and killed him. Later the two heroes fought against the Bull of Heaven who had been sent by the gods to keep Gilgamesh and Enkidu under control. Enkidu was blamed for the death of the Bull of Heaven and was condemned by the gods to die. In the midst of intense grief for his friend, who was in every way his equal, Gilgamesh realized that he too would have to die and began a search for the secret of immortality. Gilgamesh learned that one man, Utnapishtim, had been able to escape the common fate of humankind. After a long search, Gilgamesh found Utnapishtim, who told the following story:[40]

[40]Quotes are from Pritchard, *Texts*, pp. 93–97.

> I will reveal to thee, Gilgamesh, a hidden matter
> And a secret of the gods will I tell thee:
> Shuruppak—a city which thou knowest,
> And which on Euphrates' bank is situate—
> That city was ancient, as were the gods within it,
> When their heart led the great gods to produce the flood.

The gods intended to destroy all humankind, but one of them, Ea, warned Utnapishtim to heed the following advice:

> Man of Shuruppak, son of Ubar-Tutu,
> Tear down this house, build a ship!
> Give up possessions, seek thou life.
> Forswear worldly goods and keep the soul alive!
> Aboard the ship take thou the seed of all living things.

Utnapishtim was not to warn his neighbors of the coming deluge. In fact, he was to use deception, if necessary, to keep the plan of the gods from them. The ship was built and loaded, and then the flood came. From the ship Utnapishtim watched the storm reach such savage proportions that the gods themselves were frightened and regretted that they had decreed the flood:

> Shrinking back, they ascended to the
>   heaven of Anu.
> The gods cowered like dogs crouched against
>   the outer wall.
> Ishtar cried out like a woman in travail,
> The sweet-voiced mistress of the gods moans
>   aloud:
> "The olden days are alas turned to clay,
> Because I bespoke evil in the Assembly of the gods."

The deluge lasted six days and nights, but on the seventh day the storm subsided. Stillness set in and all humankind had returned to clay. The ship came to a halt on Mt. Nasir and Utnapishtim tried to find out if the waters were subsiding:

> I sent forth and set free a dove.
> The dove went forth, but came back;
> Since no resting-place for it was visible,
>   she turned round.
> Then I sent forth and set free a swallow.
> The swallow went forth, but came back;
> Since no resting-place for it was visible,
>   she turned round.
> Then I sent forth and set free a raven.
> The raven went forth and, seeing that the waters
>   had diminished,
> He eats, circles, caws, and turns not round.

> Then I let out all to the four winds
> > and offered a sacrifice. . . .
> The gods smelled the savor,
> The gods smelled the sweet savor,
> The gods crowded like flies about the sacrificer.

After the gods held a council, one of them went aboard the ship, touched the foreheads of Utnapishtim and his wife and blessed them thus:

> Hitherto Utnapishtim has been but human.
> Henceforth Utnapishtim and his wife shall be like
> > unto us gods.

After hearing this story, Gilgamesh concedes that Utnapishtim's immortality is unique and, therefore, unattainable to others. Utnapishtim comforts him by telling of a plant that will restore youth. Gilgamesh obtains this plant by diving to the bottom of the sea. Unfortunately he later loses it when he leaves it beside a pond while he bathes. A serpent eats it, sheds its skin, thus reviving its youth. Gilgamesh goes on his way sadly but reconciled to his mortality.

Compare the Genesis account of the flood with the one in Jubilees 4:28–10:17.

The similarity between this story and the Genesis account of the flood is obvious. The structure of the stories is the same, as are many of the details. Both are based on some known flood of impressive proportion. No physical evidence for a worldwide flood described in both Genesis and the Gilgamesh epic exists—nor is it needed to understand the materials. The Mesopotamian valley more than once was flooded by its great rivers. One of these cataclysms may have been accompanied by destruction on such a scale that it became the theme of an ancient tradition that lies behind both of these writings. However, the meaning of these stories is not dependent on the historicity of such a flood. Both stories are part of larger narratives dealing with the reality of sin and judgment—narratives that evidence early concerns with fundamental human questions to which no simple answers can be given.

Although both the Gilgamesh epic and Genesis speak to similar human issues, their approaches are distinctly different. In Genesis the coming flood was made known by God in advance, and humankind was granted time to repent and avert destruction; in the Gilgamesh epic, the disclosure was made on the sly by Ea contrary to the intentions of the other gods. Again, in Genesis God was in complete control of the natural elements—God was not surprised by the flood or its severity; in the Gilgamesh epic the storm got out of control and the gods fled to the highest part of heaven and cowered like dogs. The Gilgamesh picture of gods so dependent on Utnapishtim's sacrifice that they hover about him like flies was totally foreign to the Israelite conception of God, who exists independent of all creation. Finally, whereas Utnapishtim seeks immortality, Noah accepts mortality. The biblical story emphasizes judgment as a means to manage the sin problem, and ends in promise and covenant.

The real genius of the Genesis story is in the way it is told by the biblical narrator. It is first and foremost about God and the dilemma over what to do about human sinfulness. To be sure, the intensely anthropomorphic portrayal of deity slants the picture of God's character. God "was sorry that he had made man on the earth" and, almost with pique, decides to destroy. And certainly justice is not served by the death of everyone and everything in the waters of the flood, nor is there any mercy. This picture of God cannot be avoided in reading the story. But the larger context must also be kept in mind. The flood is redemptive in purpose even if the redemption is crudely conceived by the authors. A key phrase introduces God's action: "it grieved him to his heart" (6:6b). The willful rebellion and violence of humankind did not result in an *angry* but in a *grieved* God. And what should a grieved God do? Destroy the creation or redeem it? The Genesis writer understands that the answer is neither option exclusive of the other. In destruction there is an attempt to redeem. And remember where the story is going; redemption in God's calling a covenant people and working in its history.

The highly symbolic character of the story brings into focus the dilemma between destruction and redemption. Those who perish in the flood and the family of Noah who ride it out in the ark both represent the whole human race and both groups are victims of the destructiveness of sin. Even those who find favor with God, who are blameless and righteous, are victims of sin. Before the story is over, Noah and his sons are ensnared by their own desires. Thus the Genesis storyteller anticipates the psalmist (Psalms 14:1) and St. Paul (Romans 3:10), "None is righteous, no, not one." The problem that brings a flood is serious and God dares not treat it lightly. The flood story states it clearly: "the wickedness of man was great in the earth, and . . . every imagination of his heart was only evil continually" (6:5). The divine reaction at the beginning of the story is equally clear, "I will blot out . . . " (6:7), "I am going to destroy . . . " (6:13). Such drastic action illustrates the seriousness of sin, the alienation from God that it brings, and a God who acts to correct the situation decisively.

Punitive judgment, however, is not the primary thrust of the flood narrative. In a sense the flood fails to resolve the human predicament—Noah proves himself no less rebellious than Adam. The destruction of creation is never satisfactory if there are survivors. As John Calvin points out,[41] if such a solution to the sin problem were successful, God would need to punish with regular floods!

The narrative makes clear that deliverance is also part of the message. Humankind survives in the ark. God could destroy; God could save. Hence, the

---

[41]John Calvin, *Commentaries on the First Book of Moses Called Genesis* (Baker, 1984), p. 297.

divine attitude is also depicted at the conclusion of the story: "I will never again curse, . . . neither will I ever again destroy" (8:21), therefore "be fruitful and multiply" (9:7). These last words are reminiscent of the creation narrative in Genesis 1, as if to say that God's creative work continues.

And if floods do not succeed, how will God respond to insure God's creative purposes? The Hebrew Bible answers quite explicitly. God chooses Abraham, establishes covenant with him, and begins a solution far more difficult but also more redemptive than a flood. God chooses a covenant people and begins to work graciously in its history. Thus with Noah God starts over. The life of humankind is not extinguished, but is given a new beginning. Creation is restored and the original command to humankind is renewed:

> While the earth remains, seedtime and harvest, cold and heat, summer and winter, day and night, shall not cease. And God blessed Noah and his sons, and said to them, "Be fruitful and multiply, and fill the earth. The fear of you and the dread of you shall be upon every beast of the earth, ... Every moving thing that lives shall be food for you; and as I gave you the green plants, I give you everything" [8:22–9:2a, 3].

Thus alongside the theme of judgment in flood stands an emphasis on re-creation. God's lasting word in this story is a word of blessing and grace. In spite of profound disturbance, humankind may know in the continuity of life itself that God has not retreated in the face of rebellion and violence. God has not surrendered the sovereign claim over all creatures. Noah and his family are alive, and with them God makes covenant, promising divine presence and requiring of them the responsible allegiance originally demanded of them. The creator makes covenant with the creatures and promises constant care and protection, without which life could not continue:

> "As for me, I am establishing my covenant with you and your descendents after you, and with every living creature that is with you, the birds, the domestic animals, and every animal of the earth, as many as came out of the ark. I establish my covenant with you, that never again shall all flesh be cut off by the waters of a flood, and never again shall there be a flood to destroy the earth." God said, "This is the sign of the covenant that I make between me and you and every living creature that is with you, for all generations: I set my bow in the clouds, and it shall be a sign of the covenant between me and the earth. When I bring clouds over the earth and the bow is seen in the clouds, I will remember my covenant that is between me and you and every living creature of all flesh; and the waters shall never again become a flood to destroy all flesh. . . ." [9:9–15]

The idea of covenant, found here for the first time in the Hebrew Bible, became the basis of Israel's self-understanding and the key idea in defining its relationship to God. Covenant follows covenant. The peoples Moses led out of Egypt entered into covenant with Yahweh and were constituted as the "people of God." From the time of Moses on, the covenant became the basis for Israel's national life. Even when political and social forms changed, covenant remained. And when the nation seemed to be destroyed, the prophet Jeremiah expressed hope for the future restoration of an exiled nation in terms of a new covenant. So thoroughgoing was this idea that early Christians drew upon this familiar Hebrew idea to describe Jesus as the bringer of yet another new covenant.

The Nations and Abraham

Genesis 10 provides a transition between primeval history and Israel's specific development by setting the world stage with an array of peoples and nations. The Hebrew narrators trace all races to the three sons of Noah. Although not a scientific ethnology, the genealogy is an attempt to give rational explanation of the phenomena of race, language, and the dispersion of peoples. The persons mentioned are eponymous; that is, they represent peoples or countries. Ham, Shem, and Japheth, Noah's three sons, were represented as the eponymous ancestors of all nationalities known at the time the Hebrew traditions were taking shape. The arrangement is based on geographical proximity, not racial kinship. The Hamites were the peoples of southern Arabia, the Canaanites of Syria-Palestine, and those peoples belonging to the Egyptian sphere of influence: the Egyptians, Cushites, and other North Africans. The Japhethites occupied Armenia, much of Asia Minor, Greece, and the Mediterranean isles. The descendants of Shem, later called Semites, comprised virtually all the rest of the peoples of western Asia: the Assyrians, Aramaeans, Israelites, and Arabs.

The Tower of Babel

The Yahwist concludes the primeval narrative with the intriguing story of the Tower of Babel. The vignette is etiological, addressing the question of the origin of languages. It is also polemical, attacking things Babylonian. The sacred worship tower of Babylon is the site of human folly. And the relationship of the cryptic place name Babel to Babylon is not too camouflaged. But the story is also profoundly theological, a fitting summary of Genesis 1–11 and introduction to Genesis 12–50. Even after good creation, Eden, flood, and God's covenant promise, sin remains.

The background of the story is the early Sumerian settlement of southern Mesopotamia. The Sumerians organized themselves into powerful city-states and erected sacred towers, or ziggurats. One of these towers was at Babylon and was called Etemenanki, "House of the foundation of heaven and earth." The ziggurat was a sacred mountain where heaven and earth met, and those who lived around it thought they were secure because they had access to the gods. The sacred mountain in a sense allowed them to participate in the life of the gods and, therefore, to live in a meaningful world. The Yahwist has used these motifs to illustrate humankind's trust in its own power and efforts, even

Figure 3.6. The ruins of the ziggurat of ancient Ur built around 2100 B.C.E. The terraces of this multicolored temple-tower were planted with trees. Similar towers were built by a number of Babylonian city-states including Babylon and provide the context for the Tower of Babel story in Genesis. (Copyright, British Museum)

to the extent of attempting to scale heaven as if God did not exist. This attempt "to be like God" is no more successful than that made by Adam and Eve. God "confused the language of all the earth; and from there Yahweh scattered them abroad over the face of all the earth" (Genesis 11:9b). For the Yahwist the result of sin extends beyond mere inability to speak understandably. In the hands of the Yahwist this story is about a more fundamental problem of communication. In the broken and scattered human community, humans cannot understand one another. The collective human exaltation of self against God, the refusal to be creature, was for the Yahwist the explanation of humanity's broken community.

Thus in the tower of Babel story humankind is pictured in characteristic rebellion against creatureliness and under judgment. The primeval tradition, which opened with God's speaking the world into being and speaking with Adam and Eve in the garden, here concentrates on human beings unable to speak with one another. How can conversation begin again? The Yahwist ends the primeval narrative with a genealogy (Genesis 11:10–32) that focuses on one people chosen to be the agent of God's purposes for all humankind. The line of Shem gradually narrows to the family of Terah, father of Abram, who sired the covenant people and thus became a blessing to all humankind.

One point often overlooked in study of this passage is that, in spite of the brokenness of community, a unity prevails. God's purposes embrace all nations as objects of divine concern. God's interest in Israel has no meaning apart from Israel's role as the instrument by means of which redemption is made available to all peoples.

In the sketch of primeval history the biblical narrator has prepared the way for the history of the redemptive activity of God. The realistic pessimism of the description of the tragedy of human existence deepened as the narrative moved from the rebellion of Adam and Eve to the frustrated attempts at self-redemption at the tower of Babel. Humankind was alienated from God. But Genesis 1–11 is just the prologue; there follows the story of reconciliation.

SUGGESTIONS OF FURTHER STUDY

Additional reading in several of the Bible dictionaries listed in the General Bibliography will be helpful in understanding this chapter. Check these terms: etiology, liturgy, anthropomorphism, Enuma Elish, Gilgamesh Epic, genealogy, covenant, ziggurat, cosmology, the book of Genesis.

In addition to the dictionary articles on Genesis, see commentaries by Gerhard von Rad in *The Old Testament Library*; Walter Brueggemann in *Interpretation: A Commentary for Teaching and Preaching*; E. A. Speiser in The Anchor Bible; Bruce Vawter, *On Genesis: A New Reading*; Claus Westermann's three works, *Genesis 1–11, Genesis 12–36,* and *Genesis 37–50*. Full bibliographical information on these books and other sources for Genesis appear in the General Bibliography.

Summary studies of the structure of Torah are found in C. R. North in *The Old Testament and Modern Study* (ed. H. H. Rowley, Oxford University, 1951) and Douglas A. Knight in *The Hebrew Bible and its Modern Interpreters* (ed. Knight and Gene M. Tucker, Fortress, 1955). See also the General Bibliography under Book of Genesis and Pentateuchal Studies.

On the theology of creation, a collection of essays by various scholars appears in Bernhard Anderson, ed., *Creation in the Old Testament* and Anderson's book, *Creation and Chaos: The Reinterpretation of Mythical Symbolism in the Bible* (Association, 1967). A provocative study is Foster R. McCurley's *Ancient Myths and Biblical Faith: Scriptural Transformations* (Fortress, 1983). Other sources are in the General Bibliography under Creation and Theology and the Hebrew Bible.

The best collection of creation stories from various religions is Charles H. Long's *Alpha: The Myth of Creation* (George Braziller, 1963). See also Joan

O'Brien and Wilfred Major, *In the Beginning: Creation Myths from Ancient Mes-opotamia, Israel, and Greece* (Scholars, 1982), and Virginia Hamilton, *In the Beginning: Creation Stories from around the World* (Harcourt, Brace, Jovanovich, 1988). Also helpful is Lloyd R. Bailey, *Noah: The Person and the Story in History and Tradition* (South Carolina, 1989). For additional works consult the General Bibliography under Book of Genesis and Myth, Folklore.

4

Israel's Patriarchs and Matriarchs (Genesis 12–50)

All four strata of traditions in Torah (JEDP) and historical references in prophetic literature and the Psalms look back to the time of the Exodus, the covenant at Sinai, and the settlement in Canaan as the formative period in Israel's history and faith. To Israelite theologians and storytellers, however, these events were fulfillments of divine promises made to their patriarchal and matriarchal ancestors. They believed that in God's dealings with these ancient men and women an activity of redemption began, an activity that reached a climax in deliverance from Egypt and entrance into a land of promise. Israel's ultimate origins, therefore, belong to the patriarchal times. Unfortunately, Israel's patriarchal origins as history to a large extent are lost to us. We have only the delightful literary and significant theological stories about Abraham and Sarah, Isaac and Rebekah, Jacob and his wives, Leah and Rachel, and Joseph and his brothers. The writers of these stories were more concerned to express their postexodus belief that Israel's origins were rooted in a covenant promise than to write a history of their prenational origins.

THE SOCIOHISTORICAL CONTEXT OF PREEXODUS TRADITIONS

If it is important to reconstruct the history of Israel's ancestral times, the ancestral stories should be placed as precisely as possible in the context of ancient Near Eastern history. However, for a number of reasons, attempts to do this have not been consistent or satisfying.

First, chronological references in the Bible place the patriarchal age in the twenty-first or the nineteenth century B.C.E.1 Kings 6:1 states that Solomon began construction of the temple in Jerusalem in the fourth year of his reign and in the four hundred eightieth year after the exodus from Egypt. The fourth year of Solomon's reign was c. 960 B.C.E.[1] Using this rather certain date as

---

[1] The date 960 is approximate. Different chronologies vary by a few years for early dates in Israel's history. We use 960 as the nearest multiple of ten.

astarting point and working back with other chronological references, we can calculate as follows:

     960 B.C.E.   fourth year of Solomon's reign
+   480   1 Kings 6:1 reference
= 1440   exodus from Egypt
+   430   the number of years spent in Egypt according to Exodus 12:40
= 1870   entrance of the family of Jacob into Egypt
+   215   the number of years spent by the patriarchs and matriarchs in Canaan
= 2085   Abraham's journey from Haran to Canaan

Or we can calculate as follows:

     960 B.C.E.   fourth year of Solomon's reign
+   480   1 Kings 6:1 reference
= 1440   exodus from Egypt
+   400   the number of years spent in Egypt according to Genesis 15:13
= 1840   entrance of the family of Jacob into Egypt
+   215   the number of years spent by the patriarchs and matriarchs in Canaan
= 2055   Abraham's journey from Haran to Canaan

Or we can calculate as follows:

     960 B.C.E.   fourth year of Solomon's reign
+   480   1 Kings 6:1 reference
= 1440   exodus from Egypt
+   430   the number of years spent in Egypt *and* Canaan according to Exodus 12
             (Septuagint)
= 1870   Abraham's journey from Haran to Canaan

As can be seen from these calculations, biblical chronological references for these early narratives are clearly inconsistent. Furthermore they present a date for the exodus that does not match the Bible's own picture of the situation in Egypt at the time of the exodus—a situation that fits what we know of Egypt in the thirteenth century far better than the known situation there in the fifteenth century. If the exodus is dated to the thirteenth century and other biblical chronological references are considered, the entrance of Abraham into Canaan would be either in the nineteenth or seventeenth century B.C.E.

Second, these family stories about the patriarchs come from the Yahwistic and Elohistic strata in the Torah, which means there is a gap of at least a thousand years between the events in the stories and the time the stories were written. This time gap raises a question about how much the J and E writers could know about the actual events of the patriarchal age.

Third, the biblical patriarchal stories present only a small number of episodes from the private affairs of an individual family. There are few references to public events, none of which corresponds to a known event in general history. None are mentioned in external references. The biblical stories, therefore, provide no clues to their historical setting.

Fourth, there are no extrabiblical references of any kind to any of the patriarchs, and no person from general history is identified in the biblical stories. Certain kings are named, but these are not known from other sources. Pharaohs are mentioned, but they go unnamed. There are no extrabiblical references to Israel at all until long after the patriarchal times. The first is on the victory stele of the Egyptian pharaoh, Merneptah (c. 1224–1211 B.C.E.), celebrating a successful military campaign in Canaan. The inscription boasts, "Israel is laid waste, his seed is not."[2]

This reference is not the kind by which Israel would wish to be first recorded in general history. Indeed, it and the absence for so long a period of any other reference to the people of the covenant indicates that the Israelites were not among the important peoples of the ancient Near East. Events of major significance to Israel—the Exodus, the "conquest" of Canaan, the reigns of David and Solomon—are simply not mentioned in extrabiblical sources.

Relating the patriarchal stories to the external historical scene is clearly not possible from their contents alone. Any historical reconstruction of Israel's patriarchal origins, therefore, must be sought in the archeological record.

Let's begin with a brief description of the social and political situation in the early second millennium B.C.E. As we have already seen, by the time Abraham made his journey from Haran in Mesopotamia to Canaan, great civilizations had already risen, prospered, and decayed.[3] The world of Israel's ancestors was both old and confused. Established states were either being overthrown or experiencing the disturbance of dynastic changes. New peoples, from the mountains and the deserts, were entering the areas of civilization. Egypt was stable and loosely controlled Canaan.

The striking circumstance of the second millennium was widespread unrest and decline and the appearance throughout the entire Fertile Crescent of various wandering Semitic peoples. The unrest and decline were both economic and political. Many villages throughout the area were abandoned. Some of the inhabitants moved into the cities; others returned to the wandering life of pastoral nomads like those who had always been living alongside the established urban centers. Most of the peasant socieities of the time already, to some extent, practiced some form of pastoralism. Many apparently became *'Apiru*, that is, refugees who survived the unrest either by fleeing to other areas or by becoming outlaws in the mountains. The crisis was of such severity that it brought on widespread economic decline to which many of the towns succumbed. Some were actually destroyed. Ai, prominent in the Joshua account of Israel's conquest of Canaan (Joshua 7:1–8:29) was among them. This site was not reoccupied until about 1200 B.C.E. and then only as a village.[4]

---

[2]Pritchard, *Texts*, p. 378.

[3]See above, Chap. 2.

[4]Early second millennium is too early and 1200 is too late to fit the Joshua account. Ai was not occupied at all at the time usually given for Israel's entrance into Canaan. (See Chap. 6 for details.)

Among these people were the Amorites who have been described as moving on "toward the sea, like the mighty Euphrates itself, at times checked in its course but finally engulfing all before it."[5] They appeared in Mesopotamia, Syria, and Palestine. Their pressure, which reached its zenith around 2000 B.C.E., caused a progressive depopulation of Canaan. In Transjordan their movement terminated sedentary life for more than six hundred years, and the land east of the Jordan River became range country for seminomadic invaders.

From 2000 B.C.E. the Amorites or "Westerners," who were never true nomads, became more interested in settling down than in continuing endless raids through the countryside. A Mesopotamian hymn to the gods of the west reflects this transition. First, the hymn declares:

> For the Amorite the weapon is his champion—
> He knows no submission.
> He eats uncooked meat.
> Through his whole life he does not possess a house,
> His dead companion he does not bury.

Then, it marks gradual adaptation to sedentary life:

> Now Martu possesses a house . . .
> Now Martu possesses grain.[6]

During the two hundred years after 2000 B.C.E., practically every new dynasty of local princes throughout Mesopotamia was of Amorite origin. Shortly after 1800, two powerful Amorite states were established: one in Mari on the upper Euphrates and another at Babylon farther south. In Palestine and Syria a rapid recovery occurred as the seminomads began to settle down. Many new towns appeared, especially along the coastal plain and in the Jezreel and Jordan valleys, where city-state organizations developed, but large areas, particularly in the central mountains, remained sparsely settled. These mountainous regions at that time were still heavily forested. Therefore, they were not suitable as wandering range areas for peaceful nomads. They would, however, have provided hiding places for marauding outlaws.

A vivid and trustworthy impression of the appearance of one group of nomadic Amorites has been preserved. It is a scene from a large painting in the tomb of Khumhotep, an Egyptian noble who lived around 1900 B.C.E.[7] It portrays the family of a chieftain named Absha entering Egypt. The men are bearded and wear many-colored tunics or kilts, apparently of wool. The women are clothed in tunics very similar to those of the men; in their hair they have what appear to be ribbons. Some of the men wear sandals; the women

---

[5]R. T. O'Callaghan, *Aram Naharaim* (Pontificium Institutium Biblicum, 1948), p. 18.

[6]Quoted by P.K. Hitti, *History of Syria* (Macmillan, 1951), p. 66.

[7]Color reproductions of this painting may be found on the jacket of Heaton's *Everyday Life in Old Testament Times* (B. T. Batsford, 1956).

Figure 4.1. Amarna letter no. 49 from a ruler in Gezer acknowledging receipt of a message from the king and asking for assistance against the 'Apiru (Habiru). (Copyright, British Museum)

and children wear soft leather shoes. Two of the men carry water bags of skin slung over their shoulders. The males are armed with bows, javelins, and throw sticks. One man carries an ax, and another appears to be playing an eight-stringed lyre. Two pairs of bellows in the scene may indicate that there were metal workers in the entourage. Asses are the beasts of burden; one carries a load of implements, another a pack on which two children are riding.

Amorite nomads were dependent on pasturage for their herds of cattle, sheep, goats, and asses. Because such animals needed water at least every other day, the Amorites could not live in any part of the true desert except in late winter and early spring. Most of the year, they lived near oases or in the hill country of Palestine, Syria, and Mesopotamia, often on the outskirts of settlements. The difference in culture between settled Semites and nomadic Semites, who thus lived side by side, could not have been appreciable. The transition from nomadic to sedentary life was not very demanding, and many Amorites adapted to the more civilized environment and became tillers of the soil.

A later wave of migrations throughout Mesopotamia occurred between 1500 and 1000 B.C.E. when Aramaean peoples appeared in every corner of the Fertile Crescent. They established states in northwestern Mesopotamia, eventually settled among the Amorite population already in Syria and Palestine, and established a number of small states there.

A third group of wanderers who were present throughout the Near East during most of the second millennium was the Habiru/'Apiru.[8] Their disturbing presence is referred to repeatedly and widely through most of the second millennium. The term 'Apiru was used for over a thousand years to refer to wanderers of various ethnic backgrounds who threatened the established cultures. Careful study of the texts in which they are mentioned indicates that the term is derogatory and means "refugees," or "foreigners," or "outlaws." Their manner of life varied from place to place as they took advantage of the prevailing conditions. Some attained rank and status in the established communities, although these were exceptions to the rule. Others fought as mercenaries in the armies of various states. Most, however, remained wanderers and marauders. There seems to be an etymological relationship between the words 'Apiru and Hebrew, and it is probable that the Israelites were often considered to belong to the class of peoples to which the word applies, but obviously 'Apiru is used of a much larger group of people than Israel's ancestors.[9] The patriarchs cannot be identified with any specific group of 'Apiru.

It was assumed by many scholars that the unrest and decline was caused by the "invasion" of these nomadic people who were understood to have been marauders. The 'Apiru, many of whom were marauders, certainly contributed to the decline but could hardly have been its primary cause. The other wandering peoples were almost certainly not the cause but were among the victims. The best recent studies have rather convincingly shown that they were not typical nomads who were always on the move with little, if any, relationship to permanent villages. Instead, they practiced the "enclosed nomadism of dimorphic societies"; in other words, they practiced limited wandering as part of societies that were made up of two groups closely interrelated, one of which regularly wandered in the general vicinity of the permanent village of the other group. The nomadic groups' wandering was restricted, as is all nomadic wandering, to the semiarid steppe zone with limited rainfall of four to ten inches, suitable only for pastoralism. Throughout the Middle East the steppe area is partly surrounded by less arid agricultural areas in which there are permanent agricultural villages. The nomads were an integral part of the societies of the permanent villages of the areas in which they wandered. These nomads were, by no means, invading foreigners, and the unrest was not the result of conflicts between the peoples of the desert and the agricultural people of the villages and towns.

---

[8]Two thorough studies of this people are found in Greenberg, *The Hab/piru*, and Bottero, *Problème*.

[9]The first biblical use of "Hebrew" is in Genesis 14:13.

The conflicts that brought on the unrest and decline were between rural pastoral/village communities and states controlled by strong urban centers. Contributing factors may have been some forms of natural disaster, drought and famine or widespread disease. Such natural disasters could partially explain Egypt's lack of strong control of Canaan, which, in turn, would have contributed to the economic and political conflicts between the two societies living in close proximity to one another.

Does archeology provide evidence that enables us to place Israel's origins in this context of unrest and decline and supports the historicity of the patriarchs? Some leading biblical scholars, on the basis of the archeological evidence available to them, answered this question with a definite "yes," arguing that certain details in the patriarchal stories, including personal names, social and legal customs, and features of lifestyle parallel known features of early second millennium culture in Mesopotamia and Canaan.

First, they noted that the names in the patriarchal narratives belong to a class of Amorite names common in both Mesopotamia and Palestine in the early second millennium and only then. The names of the patriarchs, Abram and Jacob, and the names of other characters in the patriarchal narratives occur in a number of different extrabiblical texts. However, these names do not refer to any biblical persons. All that can be claimed from this is that the patriarchs have names that were typical of the times in which their stories are set.

Second, they found parallels to, and even explanation of, incidents in the patriarchal stories in customs referred to in extrabiblical texts from the second millennium, particularly texts from Nuzi in Mesopotamia dating from the fifteenth century B.C.E. For example, slave adoption practices parallel the relationship between Abraham and his slave-born son, Eliezer, and his son by Sarah, Isaac (Genesis 15:1–4). The practice at Nuzi of a childless woman providing her husband a concubine to bear a child, both of whom would remain members of the family, parallels the relationship between Sarah, Hagar, Ishmael, and Abraham (Genesis 16:1–4; 21:9–14). A number of the relationships between Jacob and Laban parallel Nuzi customs—Jacob's adoption by Laban perhaps implied in Genesis 31:43, Laban's insistence that Jacob take no other wives (Genesis 31:50), and Rachel's theft of Laban's gods (Genesis 31:19, 30–35).

Third, they claimed that the main Canaanite centers associated with the movements of the patriarchs—Shechem, Bethel, Hebron, Beersheba, Gerar, Dothan, Ai, and Jerusalem—were occupied and flourishing in the first few centuries of the second millennium.

Fourth, lacking the archeological and social anthropological understanding of the "enclosed nomadism of dimorphic societies," they argued that the area-wide collapse of urban culture that occurred late in the third millennium B.C.E. had been caused primarily by an invasion of nomadic peoples from the desert fringes of the region. They identified these people as the Amorites with whose movements the patriarchs could be associated on the basis of similarity of custom and lifestyle.

Considering all this, W. F. Albright boldly declared,

> As a whole, the picture in Genesis is historical, and there is no reason to doubt the general accuracy of the biographical details and the sketches of personality which makes the patriarchs come alive with a vividness unknown to a single extrabiblical character in the whole vast literature of the ancient Near East.[10]

Others were less positive, but did believe archeology had provided evidence that enabled the patriarchal stories to be placed in the historical context of the early second millennium B.C.E. G. Ernest Wright would not claim the certain historicity of Abraham as Albright had done, but was equally positive about the historical context of the stories. In widely used textbooks, he wrote,

> We shall probably never be able to prove that Abram really existed, that he did this or that, said thus and so, but what we can prove is that his life and times, as reflected in the stories about him, fit perfectly with the early second millennium, but imperfectly with any later period.[11]

In reference to the Khumhotep tomb painting, he wrote that it was the "best representation from antiquity of Asiatics, *probably Amorites of the time of Abraham.*"[12] More recently John Bright, who shared the same point of view as Albright and Wright, claimed from these arguments a considerably more cautious conclusion. He wrote,

> We know nothing of Abraham, Isaac, and Jacob save what the Bible tells us, and we have no means of controlling the details of its narrative; we cannot even fix the patriarchs in time with greater precision . . . . We may be quite sure that the actual events were vastly more complex than the Bible indicates . . . but such is the nature of the material, and such the limits of our knowledge, that to attempt a reconstruction would be profitless speculation. . . . The Bible's narrative accurately reflects the times to which it refers. But to what it tells us of the lives of the patriarchs we can add nothing.[13]

The close correlation between the patriarchal stories and the known history of the early second millennium B.C.E. seems to counter the argument first raised by Wellhausen that the patriarchal stories provided no authentic information about the patriarchal age, only information from the period in which they were written.

This reconstruction is attractive and has been widely accepted for decades. Recently, however, it has come under serious attacks in light of more recent and much more extensive archeological data. The names in the patriarchal

---

[10] *The Biblical Period from Abraham to Ezra* (Biblical Colloquium, 1950), p. 5.
[11] *Biblical Archaeology*, p. 40.
[12] Wright and Filson, *Atlas*, p. 23. Emphasis added.
[13] *History*, p. 93.

narratives that were also found in Mesopotamian and Palestinian texts are not limited to the early second millennium. They appear in a number of texts from later times. The supposed parallels between customs referred to in texts from Nuzi and Mari are not as close as they at first seemed, and similar parallels are mentioned in texts from times later than that supposed in this reconstruction. In almost every case, new archeological data demonstrate that the sites associated with the patriarchs in the Genesis stories were *unoccupied* in the early second millennium. Recent archeological evidence does not support their argument that the collapse of urban culture had been caused primarily by an *invasion* of nomadic peoples from the desert fringes of the region. Rather, it indicates that these wandering people had been on the scene for some time and remained on the scene until long after the date this reconstruction assigns to the patriarchs. The identification of the patriarchs and matriarchs with Amorite nomads ignores significant differences between Amorite nomadism and the Genesis picture of the nomadism of Israel's ancestors. The more recent and extensive archeological data and its interpretation has rather convincingly negated this reconstruction, but it has provided no evidence for the historical origins of patriarchal Israel.

Before stating conclusions about the history of the patriarchal period, we must consider the critical and history of traditions analysis of the patriarchal traditions undertaken by Martin Noth. Doubting that archeology could provide adequate data to place Israel's ancestors in historical context, he tried to discover an early stage of the patriarchal traditions by analyzing the biblical stories. Noth believed that the united twelve-tribe Israel of the early monarchy in which the Yahwistic writer essentially gave the patriarchal stories their present form had been formed by joining different tribal groups during the years of Israel's settlement in Canaan. Each of these tribes would have had its own independent tradition of origins. As the tribes united in the period of the settlement, these independent traditions would have been combined gradually into a common heritage. Noth noted that individual patriarchs had certain clear geographical connections, Abraham near Hebron (Genesis 13:18; 14:13; 18:1); Isaac at the oasis of Beersheba (Genesis 26:22–33) and at Beer-lahai-roi (Genesis 24:62; 25:11); Jacob near Shechem (Genesis 33:18–19), Bethel (Genesis 28:18–19; 35:1–8), and Gilead (Genesis 31:43–50; 32:2–3; 32:30; 33:17); the traditions about Abraham came from the Judean hill country, those about Isaac from southwestern Judah and the Negev, and those about Jacob from the central mountain country around Shechem. Since Jacob, whose name was also Israel, was the namegiving ancestor of the united Israelites and is associated with the heartland of the country in which the Israelites first settled, Noth concluded that his story was the oldest of the patriarchal traditions. The Abraham and Isaac traditions were added as Israel expanded southward absorbing the territories with which these patriarchs were associated. He explains the eventual priority of the Abraham stories on the basis of the southern Judean development of the tradition as presented by the Yahwist. His basic assumption was that small independent stories expanded into longer narratives. Therefore, simple units were early and stories with complex structures were late. Rather simple traditions about individual patriarchs were gradually combined in the long process of clan and tribal alliances into the united story of a twelve-tribe confederacy or nation. This means that the elaborate scheme of genealogical relationships that tie these stories together would have been a late literary creation to explain the combination of the stories.

Critics of Noth's analysis have pointed out that this assumption is contrary to what we know of the origin of oral literature. The Scandinavian sagas, Homer's *Iliad* and *Odyssey,* and, in the Middle East, myths and epics from the ancient city of Ugarit on the northern coast of Syria, were all early oral compositions and are all long narratives with very complex structures. Furthermore, recent studies of the tradition that underlies the present patriarchal narratives is an account of kinship relations expressed in terms of marriages and genealogies. Anthropological studies of traditional societies have demonstrated that patterns of kinship are fundamental to a society's definition and understanding of itself. Kinship patterns are often the basis of elaborate stories that describe the founding of a society and its understanding of itself. It is probable, therefore, that the genealogies in Genesis, rather than being late literary devices to tie independent stories together, are an early historical memory, which from the beginning shaped the telling of the stories. The genealogical description of kinship—linear, Abraham, Isaac, Jacob; laterally branched, the twelve sons of Jacob—defined from the beginning the ideal of Israel as a family.

What can we conclude about the historicity of Israel's patriarchs and matriarchs? Some claim that the patriarchal narratives originated in the time of the early monarchy and were given final shape in the postexilic period and have historical value only for these periods when they were composed and given final shape.[14] Clearly, we have no evidence that can add any details about the patriarchs that the biblical stories themselves do not contain; indeed, without the biblical stories we would know nothing about them. Every traditional (simple, undeveloped) culture tells stories about ancestral times when their ideals and values, their self-concepts, and their way of life were established, and there is no reason to doubt that there is a historical kernel in these stories. It would be surprising, indeed, if Israel did not from early times tell such stories. However, the biblical stories contain elements that enable them to be placed in a sociological context that is consistent with what we know about the Palestinian culture in the second and third quarters of the second millennium B.C.E. Their nomadism is typical of the "enclosed nomadism" of that time. The structure and character of their society and religion is clearly premonarchical, even

---

[14]Thompson, *The Historicity of the Patriarchal Narratives,* and Van Seters, *Abraham in History and Tradition.*

preexodus and covenant. It is very similar to the society and religion of simple, undeveloped cultures described in anthropological studies. The biblical descriptions of the family life and religion of the patriarchs show little, if any, influence of the later, developed monarchical structure of Israel and the postexodus covenant character of Yahwism. These descriptions must go back to very early forms of the narratives. The most important elements in these descriptions of patriarchal life are the importance of kinship and community and the belief that the character, ideals, and way of life of the community were revealed by God in the beginning to great ancestral figures.

Therefore, while we still know nothing additional about the lives of the patriarchs and matriarchs in particular, we can say that these ancestors of Israel were a family that moved about the Near East like many other peoples of the second millennium. Their socioeconomic situation is clearer in the biblical text than is their historical place. The patriarchs and matriarchs reside in the vicinity of major population centers as small clans not fully integrated into the established cultures. Their wanderings are described as "historically caused migrations for purposes of change of residence, religious pilgrimage, strife with outsiders, securing wives, escaping famine."[15] Attempts to relate them directly to any particular period or culture in the second millennium and then to construct a "history" of the age are more distracting than useful. They turn our attention away from the biblical stories themselves to uncertain historical constructions. We cannot satisfactorily write a protohistory of Israel because the patriarchs and matriarchs as presented to us in Genesis are more literary than historical figures. We cannot recover the history, but we do have the stories.

> Does the fact that it is not fully possible to construct a history of Israel's ancestral age make the stories of the patriarchs "less believable" as stories and as theological statements? Why or why not?

FROM STORIES TO STORY

One who reads the patriarchal stories should remember that the heroes are representative figures in two senses. First, Abraham, Isaac, and Jacob were not solitary individuals. They were chiefs of sizable clans and the simple stories about them conceal complex clan movements. "In them the individual belongs with the group, and his doings reflect those of the group."[16] In Israelite thought, individuals were important only to the extent that they were partici-

[15]Gottwald, *Bible: Socio-Literary Introduction*, p. 172.
[16]Bright, *History*, p. 93.

pants in the larger group of which they were a member.[17] They always looked on themselves as a part of a larger whole—the nation, the clan, the family. Therefore, narratives that seemingly describe the action of an individual often actually depict the action of the group of which the individual is a member. As a consequence, whether a certain narrative presents an interesting event in the life of its hero or portrays an interlude from the life of the clan of which the individual is the head cannot always be determined. When reading these narratives, therefore, it is well to remember that the memory reflected in them may be far more complex than the story would seem to indicate.

The patriarchs and matriarchs are also representative of the narrator's understanding of the character of the Israelite community of faith. The text intends its readers to see themselves in the actions and ideas of their ancestors. The "faith-doubt" relationship with God, prominent throughout the stories about Abraham, Jacob, and Joseph, represents the ambiguous relationship with God typical of Israel. The "friendly-quarrelsome" relationships between kin—husbands and wives, brothers and brothers, brothers and sisters, uncles and nephews, fathers and sons—represent the unity and divisiveness of the Israelite community. Uncertainty about the future represents the nature of Israel's pilgrimage of faith. Hence, to read these stories as simple history misses much of their didactic purpose.

Further, the way the stories are put together reflects Israel's faith and self-understanding. They are expressions of the national, racial, and religious spirit of the Israelite people. The Abraham and Isaac stories probably circulated first among the southern (Judean) tribes and the Joseph stories among the northern (Israelite) tribes. The Yahwist writer brings these stories together, skillfully uniting them by theme and plot into a unified story of the patriarchs and matriarchs. Even the interludes, stories that interrupt the main structure of the narrative, are linked to the larger narrative by key words and thematically contribute to its meaning. The final Genesis narratives present a unified story of Israel's origins brought together around the theme of covenant promise. No matter how diverse had been the memories of the pre-Exodus covenant experiences of the tribal confederacy of Israel, they shared faith that Yahweh, the God of the exodus and the covenant, had been the God who led their ancestors in earlier days to bring them together as a covenant people.

Even modern societies tell stories of their origins that reflect the ideals and values of the society, which they recall and celebrate on national occasions. How have we done this in the United States? Do you see any parallels to the way the Israelites told the stories of the patriarchs?

---

[17]See Johnson, *The Vitality of the Individual in the Thought of Ancient Israel* (University of Wales, 1949).

LITERARY ANALYSIS OF THE PATRIARCHAL STORIES

The artistic skill of the biblical storyteller is revealed in a literary analysis of the narratives. Like any good narration, the patriarchal stories contain theme, plot, climax, denouement, symbolism, and characterization.

The Theme of the Patriarchal Story

"God will keep the covenant with Israel and with humankind." This is one way of stating the theme of the patriarchal story. Another way to state it is, "God is working in history to accomplish redemption." This theme, underscoring God's faithfulness, appears at the very beginning of the Abraham story in God's promise to him:

> Go from your country and your kindred and your father's house to the land that I will show you. I will make of you a great nation, and I will bless you, and make your name great, so that you will be a blessing. I will bless those who bless you, and the one who curses you I will curse; and in you all the families of the earth shall be blessed [Genesis 12:1–3].

The essence of this promise is twice repeated to Abraham (18:18; 22:17–18) and is also made to Isaac (26:3–4) and to Jacob (28:13–14). It is echoed in repeated promises of many descendants. Two stories (chaps. 15, 17) sharply focus the theme in terms of a covenant between God and Abraham as the ancestor of Israel. And it is restated in a dramatically different way at the end of the Genesis narrative when Joseph assures his brothers that ultimately God is working in history even when it may not seem so: "Do not be afraid! Am I in the place of God? Even though you intended to do harm to me, God intended it for good, in order to preserve a numerous people, as he is doing today" (50:19–20).

This theme of God's covenant promise is dramatically focused, enforced, and illustrated by the subordinate themes, plot structures, symbolisms, and characterizations that make up Genesis 12–50.

Theme and Plot Structures

Abraham.   The Abraham story, a zigzag journey of faith and doubt, is contrasted with the determined movement of God toward covenant purposes. The story opens with God's promise to bless Abraham so that through him all the families of the earth would find blessing. The same promise is made near the end of the story on the basis of Abraham's faithfulness, "because you have obeyed my voice" (22:16–18). At the center of the narrative, structurally speaking, are two key stories of the covenant God makes with Abraham. In the first of these (chap. 15), in sacred ritual God makes a pledge to the patriarch and his descendents: "On that day Yahweh made a covenant with Abram, saying, "To your descendants I give this land, from the river of Egypt to the great river, the river Euphrates"(15:18).

According to an ancient custom, Abraham made preparation for a ritual of covenant making. Animals would be slain and divided; then all parties entering into covenant would pass into the sacred place between the parts, thereby taking upon themselves the stipulated responsibilities (cf. Jeremiah 34:18). In this story, however, Abraham watches an eerie scene in which "a smoking firepot and a flaming torch passed between these pieces." This must mean that Yahweh took the place of the subject people and gave a pledge to Abraham. Yahweh promised faithfulness. Also implied is the idea that what was to be done through Abraham was Yahweh's activity—an activity in which Yahweh permitted Abraham and his descendants to participate. The covenant is made with Abraham described as one who "believed Yahweh, and he reckoned it to him as righteousness"–a covenant with Abraham as a man of faith based on confidence in God. God would keep all promises made.

In the second covenant story (chap. 17) God makes covenant with Abraham and demands obedience to be symbolized by the rite of circumcision. This covenant pledge is accompanied by the promise of a son: "God said to Abraham, As for Sarah your wife, you shall not call her Sarai, but Sarah shall be her name. I will bless her, and moreover I will give you a son by her, and she shall give rise to nations; kings of peoples shall come from her'" (17:15–16).

This promise is so incredible that Abraham laughed and said: "Shall a child be born to a man who is an hundred years old?" (17:17). Here Abraham responds in doubt. Faith-doubt is the ambiguous stance of the patriarch. He believes and does not believe. In sharp contrast, God is described as steadfast, determined, and able to accomplish the divine will. The entire Abraham story emphasizes this contrast: God calls and promises; Abraham responds ambiguously.

The plot structure supports the theme. It centers on the questions raised by the childlessness of Abraham and Sarah. If they had no son, how could God's promise be fulfilled? How can a childless couple be parents of a great nation? The poignancy of these questions is acute in a culture where children, especially sons, are considered gifts from God and childlessness is looked on as a curse. Furthermore, the giving of the promise is repeatedly followed by some events that threaten its realization: famine in Canaan (12:10); the pharaoh's desire for Sarah, which threatens both her and Abraham, and of course the promise (12:11–16); contention between Abraham and Lot that results in a separation so that Abraham's family decreases rather than increases (13:1–12). The yes of God's promise is followed by the no of reality, so Abraham tries to hold things together and work things out. He struggles for Lot against raids by foreign kings (chap. 14) and against the wickedness of Sodom (18:16–19:29). He claims a servant as his heir (15:16) and he has a son, Ishmael, by Sarah's Egyptian maid Hagar (chap. 16), but neither is the legitimate heir through whom the promise can be realized.

And so the plot thickens as the suspense mounts. The two covenant chapters (15 and 17) focus the tensions sharply. In the first, God unequivocally pledges himself to Abraham in covenant faithfulness. In the second, Abraham is required to perform a ritual act as symbol of the acceptance of covenant faith and responsibility. Chapter 17 is filled with humorous irony. Abraham's name is interpreted as meaning "father of a multitude," but he has no son by Sarah. God promises that Sarah will have a son to be the true heir to the promise; Abraham's response is laughter and sarcasm: "O that Ishmael might live in your sight!" (17:18)—and irony: "Then Abraham took his son Ishmael and all the slaves born in his house or bought with his money, every male among the men of Abraham's house, and he circumcised the flesh of their foreskins that very day, as God had said to him" (17:23). He makes sure all the males bear the covenant sign, but none of them can be legitimate bearers of the covenant promise, blessing, and responsibilities. This is exceptional storytelling.

The narrative reaches its climax with the account of the birth of Isaac (21:1–7). The true heir of covenant promise is circumcised and the laughter of derision and doubt turns into laughter of joy and thanksgiving: "Now Sarah said, 'God has brought laughter for me; everyone who hears will laugh with me.' And she said, 'Who would ever have said to Abraham that Sarah would nurse children? Yet I have borne him a son to his old age' " (21:6–7).

The reader knows, though, that it is God who has given them the child in God's own mysterious way of keeping a promise, accomplishing the divine purposes. But notice how the narrator ties this story to the major episode that follows. The birth of Isaac leads to Abraham's loss of his son Ishmael. For Isaac to be the son of the covenant, Abraham had to give up Ishmael. However, Ishmael was not lost to God; "God was with the lad" (21:20). The choice of Isaac and his descendants is *not* a rejection of the rest of humankind. The narrator has obvious feelings for Ishmael and Hagar. The "other son" is not dismissed from God's family.

The tension of the story of "the two sons" is heightened in the story of "the sacrifice of Isaac" in chapter 22.[18] Climax follows climax and merges with denouement. The whole of the Abraham narrative is held in suspense and called into question by God's stark command: "Take your son, your only son Isaac, whom you love, and go to the land of Moriah, and offer him there as a burnt offering on one of the mountains that I shall show you" (22:2).[19]

This command is a dramatic counterpart to the command with which the Abraham narrative began, "Go from your country and your kindred and your father's house to the land I will show you," and brings the story of Abraham's zigzag pilgrimage of faith and doubt to resolution. The key to understanding the whole narrative must be here in this story; no other so captures readers'

---

[18]For a provocative, thorough interpretation of this story and for references to the vast literature about it, see Crenshaw, *A Whirlpool of Torment* (Fortress, 1984), pp. 9–29. The interpretation of Walter Brueggemann is also highly recommended. See his *Genesis*, pp. 185–94.

[19]Genesis 25:1–4 records that, after Sarah's death, Abraham took another wife named Keturah and had six more sons.

attention. This story is at once a story that repudiates the ancient custom of sacrificing the firstborn to the deity and a story of the testing and miracle of faithfulness—both Abraham's and God's. But most importantly it is an affirmation of the theme of all the patriarchal narratives—"God will keep the covenant with Israel and humankind." Filled with anxiety, fear, and pathos, the story affirms that "God will provide" (22:8, 14). In the final analysis this is what is important about the Abraham narrative. It affirms confidence in God's faithfulness.

Isaac.   With one exception, the stories about Isaac are essentially part of and subordinated to the stories about Abraham and the stories about Jacob. The exception (chap. 24) forms a connecting interlude between the stories about the other two patriarchs[20] and is more Rebekah's story than Isaac's. The apparent issue of the story is the attempt to find a proper wife for Isaac. The plot unfolds in four scenes. In the first, "Abraham and his servant" (24:1–9), the patriarch is again presented as a man of faith and of doubt, an "intensely determined and utterly believing man."[21] Abraham is concerned for the fulfillment of the covenant promise. Sarah is dead, Abraham is very old, perhaps on his deathbed,[22] and Isaac, the son of the promise, has no wife. This situation poses three threats to the possibility of the blessing. The first is obvious: a wifeless man cannot be father of the covenant people. The second and third are interrelated. If Isaac takes a Canaanite wife, the distinctiveness of the covenant people might be marred as they become like the Canaanites. However, if Isaac goes to Haran, the patriarchal homeland, for a wife, he would be making a journey into danger, one that reverses Abraham's journey of faith. Therefore, Abraham is depicted as taking "determined" action to safeguard the covenant promise. He gives a trusted servant specific instructions: "The servant said to him, 'Perhaps the woman may not be willing to follow me to this land; must I then take your son back to the land from which you came?' Abraham said to him, 'See to it that you do not take my son back there' " (24:5–6).

He provides the servant with rich bridal gifts (24:10) and makes him swear a solemn oath (24:2–4). Abraham himself will see to this guarantee of covenant fulfillment, but at the same time he expresses his faith that God will direct and provide: "Yahweh, the God of heaven, who took me from my father's house and from the land of my birth, and who spoke to me and swore to me, 'To your offspring I will give this land,' he will send his angel before you, and you shall take a wife for my son from there' "(24:7). These, significantly, are Abraham's final words. He is essentially a man of faith.

[20]Von Rad, *Genesis,* p. 254. Commenting on the structure and contents of the story itself, S. R Driver in his commentary on Genesis, p. 230, states that they "are all depicted with simple, yet perfect, literary skill, and with utmost truth to nature and life. Each successive scene, as it is drawn by the narrator, stands out before the reader in clear and vivid outline."

[21]Brueggemann, *Genesis,* p. 197.

[22]Von Rad, *Genesis,* p. 249.

The second scene, "the servant and Rebekah" (24:10–27), stresses God's "steadfast love" (vv. 12, 14) or "covenant faithfulness" by emphasizing the qualities of Rebekah, the wife whom God provides. She is helpful, kind, sympathetic to animals. She does not hesitate to invite Abraham's servant to lodge with her family. She also has beauty, proper genealogy, wealth, virginity. God has richly provided. God's steadfast love has been expressed in earthly ways, and the servant is grateful: "The man bowed his head and worshiped Yahweh and said, 'Blessed be Yahweh, the God of my master Abraham, who has not forsaken his steadfast love and his faithfulness toward my master. As for me, Yahweh has led me on the way to the house of my master's kin' " (24:26–27).

The third scene, "the servant at Laban's house" (24:28–61), also highlights divine providence. Rebekah's kinsmen confess that all that has happened between the servant and Rebekah has been God's doing: "Then Laban and Bethuel answered, "The thing comes from Yahweh; we cannot speak to you anything bad or good. Look, Rebekah is before you, take her and go, and let her be the wife of your master's son, as Yahweh has spoken' " (24:50–51).

The narrator notes with humor that Laban has seen the wealth Abraham has sent as bridal gifts and Laban (as we learn later in the Jacob stories) appreciates wealth. In this scene, too, Rebekah makes her own decision to return with Abraham's servant (24:58). She is no unwilling slave to either her male relatives or to God's covenant purposes. God has provided, but Rebekah must agree. When she does, she as future mother of another covenant generation receives a blessing reminiscent of those made to Abraham: "And they blessed Rebekah and said to her, 'May you, our sister, become thousands of myriads; may your offspring gain possession of the gates of their foes' " (24:60).

The closing scene, "Rebekah and Isaac" (24:62–67), unites wife with husband in a way that stresses Rebekah's importance, this time to Isaac: "Then Isaac brought her into his mother Sarah's tent. He took Rebekah, and she became his wife; and he loved her. So Isaac was comforted after his mother's death" (24:67).

Elsewhere (chap. 26) Isaac is described as a man of wealth and importance. Does the narrator here imply that to some significant extent Rebekah contributed to his success?

In this story themes of prosperity, blessing, and faithfulness work together to support the continuing theme of all the patriarchal stories. "God will keep the covenant with Israel and with humankind." Interestingly, there is something inscrutable about how the divine will is implemented. The narrator does not tell us of anything God has done directly. He does not say, "God did this or that." Rather, as von Rad has pointed out, in this narrative "the actual field of activity for this guidance is less the external, spatial world of things, but rather the realm of the human heart in which God works, mysteriously directing, evening, and removing resistance."[23]

---

[23]Ibid., p. 255.

Jacob.   The mysterious and unexpected way in which God works is even more dramatically illustrated in the Jacob and Joseph stories. They make it clear that the covenant purposes of God "are tangled in a web of self-interest and self-seeking."[24] Jacob is depicted as one whose selfish desire to receive God's blessing throws him into conflict with those around him, with God, and with himself. Jacob is clever, deceptive, and strong. He is not admirable. His behavior is shameful, if not offensive; yet through him God continues to work out the divine purposes in history. In these stories the narrator expresses Israel's belief that, in spite of its weaknesses and moral failures, it is "the people of covenant" through whom God's blessings are conveyed to others. God moves in mysterious ways and through unusual persons to accomplish the divine will.

The plot of the Jacob stories focuses on interwoven cycles of conflict and reconciliation. Jacob, whose name means "the supplanter," struggles with his twin Esau in the womb and at birth:

> The children struggled together within her; and she said, "If it is to be this way, why do I live?" So she went to inquire of Yahweh. And Yahweh said to her,
>
> > "Two nations are in your womb,
> > and two peoples born of you
> > shall be divided;
> > the one shall be stronger than the
> > other,
> > the elder shall serve the younger."
>
> When her time to give birth was at hand, there were twins in her womb. The first came out red, all his body like a hairy mantle; so they named him Esau. Afterward his brother came out, with his hand gripping Esau's heel; so he was named Jacob. [25:22–26]

The younger brother outwits Esau to gain the birthright of the firstborn son and with the cooperation of his mother Rebekah tricks Isaac into giving him the blessing of the firstborn (chap. 27). This blessing is the powerful extension of leadership and authority:

> > May God give you of the dew of heaven,
> > and of the fatness of the earth
> > and plenty of grain and wine.
> > Let peoples serve you,
> > and nations bow down to you.
> > Be lord over your brothers
> > and may your mother's sons bow down to you.
> > Cursed be every one who curses you,
> > and blessed be every one who blesses you!
> >   [27:28–29]

---

[24]Brueggemann, *Genesis*, p. 204.

This blessing concentrates on the things of the world: fertility, power, and prosperity. Jacob has struggled for and is given privilege and preeminence. In the conflict Esau is dominated by Jacob, portraying both the bitter struggle between two men and the intense rivalry between nations of which the two men are representative ancestors. This story and other stories about conflict between brothers (Ishmael and Isaac, Joseph and his brothers) serve as reminders of the grim conflict between Cain and Abel. They theologically connect the conflicts of history and story with the basic conflict of human pride and selfishness. Jacob is Israel; Esau is Edom. In a broader sense Israel is given preeminence over the nations. Israel is the "chosen people" of God's covenant. Abraham from among the nations, Isaac not Ishmael, Jacob not Esau—in each case God does the unexpected. The choice of Israel, however, is not rejection of the nations. Abraham and his descendants are to bless humankind; God promises to be with and bless Ishmael; the Jacob-Esau story is told with clear sympathy for Esau. Reading these stories Israel would recognize that its special place in God's purposes was not due to its merit but to what God could do through the covenant people in spite of all their human limitations.

Forced to flee the wrath of the brother he had wronged, Jacob began to struggle with God with whom he was also in conflict. At Bethel he dreams of God and the covenant promise (28:10–22). He acknowledges divine presence, but hisresponse is compromised by his attempt to bargain with God: "If God will be with me and will keep me in this way that I go, and will give me bread to eat and clothing to wear, so that I come again to my father's house in peace, then Yahweh shall be my God'" (28:20–21).

This reserved acceptance conflicts with God's demand for absolute obedience. If conditions are stated in the covenant, they can be stated only by God. Only deity can say "if." Throughout its history Israel failed to give God the unconditional obedience wanted of it. Like Jacob, Israel wanted privileged blessing. This story makes the important point that God, not the human being, establishes the terms of divine-human relationships. In the literary structure of the Jacob stories, the Bethel encounter with the sacred is a climax, a high point of the reader's interest. In the narrator's development of a theology of covenant, however, it is preliminary and inadequate. Jacob will continue to struggle with God.

But first he must struggle with Laban, the brother ofRebekah and, therefore, Jacob's uncle, whose trickery is equal to his own. The stories of the relationship between these men further illustrate Jacob's shrewdness. They must have been favorite and often-repeated tales among the Israelites. The victory in the first encounter went to Laban, who tricked Jacob into marrying his elder daughter, Leah, as well as his young daughter, Rachel, whom the young man loved. Laban's curt rejoinder to Jacob, after the deception in the marriage arrangements, makes Jacob appear as naive as Esau: "This is not done in our country— giving the younger before the firstborn. Complete the week of this one, and

Figure 4.2. The Jabbok River, setting for the Genesis story in which Jacob wrestles with a divine messenger. (*Illustrator* Photo/Ken Touchton)

we will give you the other also in return for serving me another seven years" (29:26–27).

In the end, however, it was Jacob, with Rachel's help, who "supplanted." His wives bore him many sons and he out-maneuvered Laban in "business matters," the breeding of goats. After many years in Haran, Jacob was a rich and successful man, largely at the expense of his relatives. Jacob's prosperity led Laban's sons to lament: "Jacob has taken all that was our father's; he has gained all this wealth from what belonged to our father" (31:1). Rachel participated in the supplanting by taking the household gods of Laban's family. These *teraphim* were probably representatives of the family's ancestors, and, in some way, guaranteed those who had them a place in the family's heritage, something that Laban and his sons would not have willingly granted Jacob.

Trickster deceives trickster and when they finally part, Jacob ready to return to Canaan, it is with a solemn pledge of distrust: "Yahweh watch between you and me, when we are absent one from the other. If you ill-treat my daughters, or if you take wives in addition to my daughters, though no one else is with us, remember that God is witness between you and me" (31:49–50).

And the boundary markers set between them symbolize the fragile character of human relationships founded on fear and suspicion:

> See this heap and see the pillar, which I have set between you and me. This heap is a witness, and the pillar is a witness, that I will not pass beyond this heap to

you, and you will not pass beyond this heap and this pillar to me, for harm. May the God of Abraham and the God of Nahor [The God of their father] judge between us. [31:51–53]

The narrator here raises a question of great theological importance. How can God bless the nations through Israel if Israel's self-interest alienates the covenant people from the nations? The brokenness of the human community (4:1–16; 11:1–10) continues to challenge Israel throughout the Hebrew Bible just because Israel like Jacob acted selfishly in ways that furthered rather than healed alienation.

Are the patriarchs and matriarchs admirable figures? Do biblical characters have to be admirable to serve as literary or theological figures? Who is your favorite patriarchal or matriarchal character? Why?

Jacob, who tricked his brother out of his rights, bargained with God for privileged blessings, and contrived to come out ahead of Laban, is now forced to come to terms with God and with his brother. Surely the narrator intends the story of the encounter at the Jabbok ford to represent Israel's continuing and reluctant struggle to yield to God's covenant requirements. In this encounter with God the story of Jacob comes to its real climax, one anticipated in the earlier story of divine-human encounter at Bethel (chap. 28). On his way home to meet his brother with whom he seeks reconciliation, he has to come to terms with God, who meets him as a mysterious, strong, hidden, and unknown power. The story is sketchy, leaving much to the imagination of the reader; but it is clear that the story reflects on the origin and character of Israel as the covenant people. Jacob becomes Israel through conflict with God—a conflict of discovery: "Please tell me your name" (32:29).

In Hebrew culture, this question asks about the essential identity of the other, "Who are you and what are you like?" It seeks some intimacy with the other—to give your name to another is an act of both revelation and relationship. This is also a story of new birth and transformation. Jacob, "the supplanter," becomes Israel, "he who strives with God." Israel is a people born out of struggle with God, a conflict in which it seeks to know God and its relationship to God. The struggle is demanding and continuous, but through it the community continually becomes something new. Israel's identity is not found in prestige or power but in an ongoing encounter with the holy. Israel *becomes* the blessed and blessing people in the repeated process of trying to know, understand, and respond to the "name"—that is, the character—of God.[25]

---

[25]The significance of the name of God will be discussed more fully in Chap. 5, below, in connection with the revelation to Moses of the name Yahweh.

Jacob's encounter with God anticipates and requires a meeting with Esau.[26] He might have avoided such a difficult confrontation, but he is now Israel and broken relationships must be mended. This is a natural consequence of true encounter with God. Love of God and love of brother belong together here and throughout the Bible. So with careful preparation and caution and with a certain obvious reluctance, Jacob/Israel goes to meet Esau/Edom. The narrator tells of their meeting with clear sympathy for Esau and with a certain hesitancy and suspicion about Jacob. Although it is not clear that Jacob has been genuinely changed, it is Israel who had seen God face to face (32:30), who tells Esau "truly to see your face is like seeing the face of God" (33:10). This is something Jacob had never sensed. With this scene the narrator unravels the account of Jacob's conflicts. This is the story's denouement, the crucial step in the process toward reconciliation.

The unraveling, however, is incomplete. The restoration of meaningful relationships remains partial and fragile. Jacob achieves only an uneasy truce with Laban. He has to struggle to understand and submit to God. He has seen God "face to face," but only begins to understand the significance of the encounter. Jacob and Esau have acknowledged each other as brothers, but real fellowship between them is not achieved. Jacob as Israel is a changed, but still greatly troubled man, a true representative of imperfections of understanding and response. Jacob is still badly flawed, but even so he is a useful person in the purposes of God.

Not only are the conflicts of Jacob's life only partially resolved, they also spill over into the lives of his sons. The narrator's description of Jacob's family depicts the complex origins of the tribes that later formed Israel and reflects their struggles with each other. Jacob had thirteen children, twelve sons and one daughter. Six sons were by his wife Leah; two by Leah's slave Zilpah; two by his second wife Rachel; and two more by Rachel's slave Bilhah. These represent twelve principal tribes (the sons) and one lesser tribe (the daughter). Their distribution as sons of wives or slaves reflects a national awareness of unequal degrees of kinship. The clans of which the future Israel was composed, while clearly cognizant of their varying backgrounds, also recognized a strong bond that brought them together. The common bond was the religious heritage of promise and covenant represented in the traditions about Jacob, grandson of Abraham. This was their heritage although their histories were not the same. They were in reality a "mixed multitude" bound together as recipients of the promise. These sons of different mothers but the same flawed father deceitfully struggle with the inhabitants of Canaan (chap. 34). Their actions in this story of gallows humor (tricking the men of Shechem into being circumcised and

---

[26]See Brueggemann, *Genesis*, pp. 266–74.

killing them while their wounds were still mending) offend Jacob, who says: "You have brought trouble on me by making me odious to the inhabitants of the land, the Canaanites and the Perizzites; my numbers are few, and if they gather themselves against me and attack me, I shall be destroyed, both I and my household" (34:30).

However, Jacob's sons are only acting in ways consistent with the actions of their father. And they continue to act that way in a struggle that again pits brother against brother and in some sense against the purposes of God.

Joseph. Yet in the tangled web of self-interest and self-seeking the purposes of God will not be frustrated. The Joseph story, long recognized as one of the great stories in literature, demonstrates this dramatically. In it the many themes, actions, characters, and the use of suspense focus "artfully on the major insight that God is acting in history, God is using events to his purpose and that the Israelites are somehow the primary means of carrying out his plans."[27] Themes of the eventual success of a promising hero in the face of great adversity, the lost son found, reconciliation of brothers, resistance to seduction, and the faithfulness of a servant have a universal appeal. However, the Joseph narratives culminate in the heroic ability of God to bring order out of apparent chaos, constructive ends out of destructive and devious actions, good out of evil.

The story is in three parts: Joseph and his brothers in Canaan, Joseph alone in Egypt, and Joseph in Egypt with his brothers. These parts are unified by the emphasis on God's continuing presence with Joseph for Joseph's good and the welfare of his whole family, the family of Israel. Each part is a conflict story, but the narrative as a whole is a story of reconciliation. In the first part Joseph is in conflict with his brothers. Younger but favored, he wears a patrician's coat and dreams of sovereignty over his brothers. They understandably resent his privileges and the flaunting of his dreams, and they plot to kill him. Reuben and Judah intervene. Instead of killing him outright, they put him in a pit, a prison alternative to death and eventually a means of directing Joseph to God's purpose for him in Egypt. His patrician's coat is bloodied, torn, and is presented to Jacob as evidence of Joseph's death. The son whose deceitful gain of blessing brought grief to Isaac, who loved Esau, is now the grieved father deceived by his own sons in conflict with one another. In both cases God uses the deceptive actions for constructive purposes. They intended it for evil; God used it for good.

---

[27]Duncan McArthur, unpublished lecture. We are much indebted to this colleague for insights used throughout this analysis of the Joseph story. We are equally indebted to Donald A. Seybold, "Paradox and Symmetry in the Joseph Narrative," in Gros Louis, et al. *Literary Interpretations of the Biblical Narratives* (Abingdon, 1974).

In the second part of the story Joseph in Egypt rises to favored position in Potiphar's household, a situation paralleling his favored status at home. The narrator tells us that Joseph was successful because God was with him:

> Yahweh was with Joseph, and he became a successful man; he was in the house of his Egyptian master. His master saw that Yahweh was with him, and that Yahweh caused all that he did to prosper in his hands. So Joseph found favor in his sight and attended him; he made him overseer of his house and put him in charge of all that he had. [39:2–4]

But when Joseph, faithful to both his Egyptian master and to God, resists the sexual advances of Potiphar's wife, his fortunes change. When he resists, she tears his coat from him and uses it as evidence that he tried to seduce her. Joseph's coat again becomes a symbol of a change in fortune. Again it is a message to the overlord, again it is a lie, and again it results in suffering for Joseph.[28] He is again cast into a "pit," the prison of the king. At this point the narrator significantly notes, "But Yahweh was with Joseph and showed him *steadfast love* [the Hebrew word here means something like "covenant faithfulness"], and gave him favor in the sight of the keeper of the prison" (39:21). As earlier, the "pit" proves to be an alternative to death–Potiphar could have executed Joseph–and a means of divine protection.[29] In prison Joseph, whose dreams had contributed to his misfortune, becomes an interpreter of dreams. He interprets the dreams of two fellow prisoners, a butler and a baker. One portends death, the other life and restoration. These dreams anticipate and parallel the later dreams of the pharaoh. This leads to his restoration and eventually to the salvation of his brothers, who had earlier turned against him because of his dreams. This is the climax of the story. When Joseph rightly interprets the pharaoh's dreams, he is appointed to high position in Egypt: "And Pharaoh said to Joseph, 'See, I have set you over all the land of Egypt.' Removing his signet ring from his hand, Pharaoh put it on Joseph's hand; he arrayed him in garments of fine linen, and put a gold chain around his neck" (41:41–42).

Joseph again wears the fine clothes of a patrician. Potiphar's wife had intended evil for Joseph. God had used it for Joseph's restoration and for the good of all Egypt.

The third part of the story centers again on Joseph's conflict with his brothers, but now the tables have turned. Joseph, who dreamed that he would exercise sovereignty over his brothers, is clearly an authority to which they must

---

[28]Duncan McArthur, unpublished lecture. This part of the Joseph story is similar to a number of Near Eastern stories. It is therefore part of the shared literary motifs of Israel's environment. See Thomas L. Thompson and Dorothy Irvine, "The Joseph and Moses Narratives," in *Israelite and Judean History*, Miller and Hayes, ed., (Westminster, 1977), pp. 149–212.

[29]Seybold, "Paradox," pp. 63–64.

submit. He who was formerly in their hands to be abused now has them at his mercy. Because of famine in Palestine, they have come into Egypt, for them a "pit" that can be either their destruction or the means to life. Joseph has the choice (prefigured in the dreams of the butler, the baker, and the pharaoh) to imprison, perhaps kill, or to preserve his brothers. So he tests them, and they show great affection for their father and one another (44:18–34). They have changed with time, a change that moves Joseph deeply and he forgives them. In two dramatic speeches, he reveals the paradoxical purposes of what has happened to him and them. Their attempt to bring him to "death" has been used by God to bring him and them to "life":

> And now do not be distressed, or angry with yourselves, because you sold me here; for God sent me before you to preserve life. For the famine has been in the land these two years; and there are five more years in which there will be neither plowing nor harvest. God sent me before you to preserve for you a remnant on earth, and to keep alive for you many survivors. So it was not you who sent me here, but God; he has made me a father to Pharaoh, and lord of all his house and ruler over all the land of Egypt. [45:5–8]

> But Joseph said to them, "Do not be afraid! Am I in the place of God? Even though you intended to do harm to me, God intended it for good, in order to preserve a numerous people, as he is doing today. [50:19–20]

These speeches clarify the meaning of the entire Joseph story. They partially answer the question raised about evil in the Genesis stories of the fall. Evil is evil, perhaps beyond understanding, but God can use it for good. They also remind the reader of something that is obvious throughout the patriarchal stories: God works through and in spite of the ambiguities of human responses. Although God's ways are sometimes inexplicable, God will keep the covenant purposes to bless all humankind through the community of Israel. Even though by the end of the Joseph story all of Israel has descended into the "pit/prison" of Egypt, all is not lost; God will create something good out of Israel's Egypt experience.

Symbolism

The use of symbols complements the theme and plot structure of the patriarchal story and enriches its theological meaning. Journeys are one of the most obvious and significant of these symbols.[30] Journeys are one of the recurrent symbols in all literature: Odysseus in the *Odyssey*, Aeneas in the *Aeneid*, Gulliver in *Gulliver's Travels* are ready examples. In each case the journey presents

---

[30]They continue so throughout the Bible: Israel's journey out of Egypt to Sinai, its journey from Sinai to wilderness wanderings, its entrance into Canaan, the exile journey to Babylon and return, Jesus' journey from Galilee to Jerusalem, the "missionary" journeys of Paul.

the threat of danger and hardship, but also the possibilities of self-discovery, understanding, and fulfillment of some important purpose or goal.

The story opens with Abraham's faith journey from Haran to Canaan: "Go from your country and your kindred and your father's house to the land I will show you . . . . So Abram went, as Yahweh had told him" (12:1, 4). He journeys throughout Canaan (12:4–9), into Egypt, and back to Canaan (12:10–13:8). Finally in the climactic scene he journeys with Isaac to Moriah (chap. 22). This probably was an actual journey, but more importantly in this narrative the journey is a move into theological understanding and obedience to the will of God. His whole life is described as a zigzag journey of faith and doubt and faith. Abraham sends his servant to Haran to find a wife for Isaac, a journey into danger that he did not want Isaac to make because it represented a threat to the covenant promise. Jacob later makes this journey, which for him is an inner journey to understanding. He begins it as Jacob the supplanter and ends it as Israel, the name-giving father of the covenant people.

Such stories about travel to and from Haran with the associated ideas of marriage and the enlargement of the patriarchal family may reflect the memory of the complex history of Israel's clan or tribal origins. They may have entered Canaan in different waves of tribal movements, associated with Amorites, Aramaeans, or 'Apiru, but the Genesis materials are more than descriptions of nomadic movements. The narrator uses the journey symbol to express theological ideas. Joseph journeys as captive to Egypt and later his family follows—movement that results in their salvation, but also leaves them exiles from the land of promise. Israel's early experience, and by inference the experience of later Israel and of all humanity, is depicted as a pilgrimage of attempting to understand and fulfill divine expectations. But God is not on pilgrimage. God's covenant purposes are certain, although they may not always be obvious.

Closely related to the symbol of journeys is the symbol of the pit, prison, and Egypt. All of these represent danger and the possibility of death—in other words, the frustration or negation of God's covenant blessings. Descent into danger, however, seems inevitable. Twice journeys to Egypt are forced by drought and famine (12:10–13:8; chaps. 42–46). Joseph is thrown into a pit, sold as a slave into Egypt, and there imprisoned. These descents into danger represent a setback or downturn in the fortunes of the persons involved, especially in the case of Joseph. Paradoxically, the dangerous place of imprisonment and exile is a place where God's presence preserves and eventually delivers. The pit and the prison are better alternatives for Joseph than death at the hands of his brother or Potiphar. "It is better to be the favored son than the favored slave, better to be the favored slave than the favored prisoner."[31] Exile in Egypt is better for Abraham and Jacob's family than is death by famine. The deliverance of Abraham from Egypt (12:17–13:1) and of Joseph from the

---

[31]Seybold, "Paradox," pp. 62–63.

pit and prison lead to better things. Humans meant it for evil; God used it for good:

> God spoke to Israel in visions of the night, and said, "Jacob, Jacob." And he said, "Here I am." Then he said, "I am God, the God of your father; do not be afraid to go down to Egypt, for I will make of you a great nation there. I myself will go down with you to Egypt, and I will also bring you up again; and Joseph's own hand shall close your eyes." [46:2–4]

Remember that the patriarchal narratives introduce the main Hebrew biblical story, which is set in motion by exodus from Egypt, the crucial moment when Israel is delivered from the "pit" to become the means for Yahweh's blessing all humankind. The pharaoh meant Israel's enslavement in Egypt for evil; God used it and Israel's deliverance for inestimable good.

One of the most obvious symbols in the patriarchal narratives is "name." The biblical narrative is filled with stories whose original purpose was to explain the names of persons and places. Many of these stories, however, have now become part of the literary art by which the narrator clarifies his theme and develops his plot. They have become part of the important theological information the narrator is conveying to the reader. In Israelite culture the name of a person represented the essence of the person. The giving of a name "was not merely for the purpose of providing a distinctive label for an individual, but was also commonly an occasion for expressing religious convictions associated with the birth of a child or its future."[32] A person is never merely a name, the combination of certain letters—Mary, John, David. "My *name* is David, but *I* am not just D-a-v-i-d." Those letters are just a sign or signal to identify the real person known to those who try to discover who one is. To name a person, therefore, is to designate character, and in a sense to determine the being of the one named. The names assigned certain patriarchal figures are particularly significant,[33] especially new names given them by God.

Abraham is first *Abram*, exalted father, a name of eminence and nobility. God changed it to *Abraham* and the narrator interpreted the new name in terms of the covenant promise: "No longer shall your name be Abram, but your name shall be Abraham; for I have made you the ancestor of a multitude of nations" (17:5).

On the same occasion the name of Abraham's wife was changed from Sarai to Sarah without explanation of the meaning of either name (17:15–16). As with the change of Abram's name, this change was associated with the blessing of many descendants. Jacob is at first appropriately named "he takes by the heel" (25:26) or "the supplanter," a name hinting at both his devious attempts to succeed and his successes by devious means. During the incident at the

---

[32]H. B. Huffman, "Names," in *The Interpreter's Dictionary of the Bible*, supp. vol., p. 619.
[33]Ishmael (Genesis 16:11) and Esau (Genesis 25:25).

Jabbok ford, God gave him the new name Israel,[34] "one who strives with God" (32:26–28). Israel is Israel only as the community struggles to know and obey God. In each of these cases the new name signified new status or new possibilities, a change in the fortune and future of these individuals in the purposes of God. Another name of particular symbolic significance is Ishmael. Ishmael was so named because "God has given heed" to his mother's cry (16:11). The rejected son of Abraham was thus represented as still the object of God's protection.

The narrator's interpretations of names and name changes are not always etymologically sound. Sometimes he may draw on popular folk meanings because these suit his plot and theme better than would linguistically correct ones. He uses them skillfully, to underscore God's ultimate intention to fulfill the covenant blessing. God is the one who changes a name to one of covenant significance and hence the name change says as much about God's intention as about the role of the person whose name is changed.

God's name, as well as those of humans, has symbolic meaning in the patriarchal narratives. One episode illustrates clearly the symbolic character of God's name for the narrator. In the incident at the Jabbok ford when Jacob was given the new name Israel, an interesting conversation over name occurs. Jacob wrestled with the divine stranger, but the struggle was also with himself and his relationship with God. The focus is name. Jacob/Israel asked, "Please tell me your name" (32:29). The query is an attempt to overcome the distance between Jacob/Israel and God.[35] To know God's name is to know God's being. If somehow name can be known, personality can be controlled. The response to the question is, "Why is it that you ask my name?"—as if to say, "How can you be so presumptuous?" Jacob/Israel is blessed, but the name is not revealed. The divine stranger of the night remains inscrutable! God's name will later be revealed to Moses (Exodus 3:14), but even then it is cryptic and mysterious. Later on, Israel preserved this symbolism by refusing to speak God's name, as if to say that human beings could never know or control the fullness of the divine character.

Closely related to symbolic name is symbolic place. For example, important stopping places on Jacob's religious pilgrimage are assigned symbolic names. Bethel is "house of God" and Peniel is "face of God," both reflecting a sense of divine presence. Even more regularly, places are given symbolic significance by the building of an altar or some other shrine object. Two examples illustrate the practice:

> Abram passed through the land to the place at Shechem, to the oak of Moreh.
> At that time the Canaanites were in the land. Then Yahweh appeared to Abram,

[34]The more likely correct etymological explanation of the name "Israel," which connects it with a root meaning "reliable," "happy," "successful," is not as suitable to the narrator's purpose as the meaning he assigns to the name. To try to explain the name with etymological exactness detracts from the meaning intended in the story.

[35]Brueggemann, *Genesis*, p. 269.

and said, "To your offspring I will give this land." So he built there an altar to Yahweh, who had appeared to him. From there he moved on to the hill country on the east of Bethel, and pitched his tent, with Bethel on the west and Ai on the east; and there he built an altar to Yahweh and invoked the name of Yahweh. [Genesis 12:6–8]

So Jacob rose early in the morning, and he took the stone that he had put under his head and set it up for a pillar and poured oil on the top of it. He called that place Bethel; but the name of the city was Luz at the first. [28:18–19]

To the patriarchs these altars and related structures probably had limited meaning; they were places to worship God and memorialize the divine presence on a specific occasion. But for later Israel and the Genesis narrator, they are something more. The building of altars represents the recognition and acceptance of divine presence and the intention to preserve that presence. Further, the action more broadly is similar to staking out a claim on a territory by making it God's territory.

For the narrator, then, the stories of the patriarchs present a saga of "taking possession of a land,"[36] which will be occupied later by the covenant community. Abraham, for example, possesses the new land and makes it habitable by consecrating places within it. In the description of the patriarch's initial movement into Canaan, we are told three times, "There he built an altar to Yahweh" (12:7, 8; 13:17). Further, the phrase in 13:17, "Rise up, walk through the length and breadth of the land," reflects a ritual act by which the sacred presence is extended to the limits of the territory. Thus Yahweh is understood to be the protector of the land, making it secure from all outside intrusion.[37]

Many sites of patriarchal shrines were already sacred places when the patriarchs entered Canaan. Roland de Vaux notes that "sanctuaries were erected where nature manifested the God of Abraham, Isaac, and Jacob—near a tree, for example, or on a natural height, or by a water source; but they were principally in places where God had shown himself in a theophany.[38] Before Abraham's encounter with Yahweh, Canaanites had sensed sacred presence in these places. Clearly there is continuity of the sense of sacredness between patriarchal experience and older traditions. The choice of place is not left to humans; gods choose the modes and places by which they reveal themselves. Persons recognize their presence and respond to it. Patriarchal worship lays claim to established Canaanite sacred places and thereby makes Canaan an Israelite cosmos by its recognition of sacred presence there. Around these sacred places Abraham and his people, and also later Israel, could live securely. But in foreign

---

[36]See the significance of Scandanavian sagas as intrepreted by Eliade, *Cosmos and History* (Harper, 1954), pp. 10–11.

[37]Kees Bolle describes an interesting village ritual in India, which he interprets as the extension of sacredness to the circumference, "Speaking of a Place," in *Myths and Symbols*, Kitagawa and Long, eds., pp. 131–32.

[38]De Vaux, *Israel*, p. 289.

lands—Egypt and Gerar—they were not at home (12:10–20; 20:1–18). When Lot chose to dwell in Sodom, he entered an insecure world, which all but destroyed him. Thus, erection of altars at places of revealed presence sacralized the limited world of the patriarchs and anticipated Israel's later occupation of Canaan. Beyond its perimeter, however, chaos pressed in as a threat to ordered and meaningful life.

Characterization

In spite of the highly symbolic nature of the ancestral stories, their actors come through to the reader as real persons. Although the Genesis narrative does not provide elaborate physical descriptions or analysis of motives, feelings, and intentions, it does give us a "sense of depth and complexity in its representation of character."[39] Abraham, Sarah, Hagar, Rebekah, Jacob, and Joseph seem real to us. Robert Alter attributes this descriptive transparency to several means by which character is delineated:

> Character can be revealed through the report of actions; through appearance, gestures, posture, costume; through one character's comments on another; through direct speech by the character; through inward speech, either summarized or quoted as interior monologue; or through statements by the narrator about the attitudes and intentions of the personages, which may come either as flat assertions or motivated explanations.[40]

These literary techniques must, however, be related to "the conception of human nature implicit in biblical monotheism: every person is created by an all-seeing God but abandoned to his own unfathomable freedom."[41] Persons are created in the image of God in potential, but not as accomplished ethical fact. Hence patriarchal and matriarchal figures are pictured with strengths and weaknesses, bundles of faith and frustrations, ambiguous and paradoxical in both beliefs and behavior. We have already discussed Abraham's ambiguity of faith and doubt. He is also portrayed as kindly and sensitive toward others, but not always sympathetic in how he treats them. His attitude toward Lot is generous and helpful (chaps. 13; 14; 18–19); toward Hagar and Ishmael he is sympathetic, but unable or unwilling to help (21:8–14). Jacob is deceitful and cunning, a take-charge man, but in his reunion with Esau he is uncertain, less in control of things than is Esau. Later he is genuinely distressed about Joseph's supposed death. Joseph is sometimes selfishly proud, arrogant, and prematurely confident (37:5–11); at other times he is shaken and afraid (39:7–18).

[39]Alter, *Art*, p. 114.
[40]Ibid., pp. 116–17.
[41]Ibid., p. 115.

In his later dealings with his brothers he shows the confidence of maturity and the genuine kindness of one who is in humble control of himself and his situation (chaps. 42–45). None of these characters are stiff or stylized, nor are they romanticized as perfect heroes.

Surprisingly, the character of the women in these stories is well defined. Sarah, Hagar, Rebekah, and Rachel are as interesting and as capable as their male counterparts. In patriarchal societies a female birth was less desirable than the birth of a male. A female would grow up close to her mother, but her life would be controlled to a large extent by her father and then her husband. If either abused her, she had to submit without recourse. She was to bear children, hopefully males. If she outlived her husband, an older male relative assumed authority over her.[42] In stories about such a society we would assume the female characters would be docile, dull, and colorless. Actually, in traditional societies like the enclosed nomad cultures with which the patriarchs can be identified, women played important roles and made significant contributions to the economy of the society.

In Genesis we encounter women who act with freedom, initiative, and insight equal to that of men. They have sometimes been characterized as being somewhat manipulative and deceitful, as if this is the only way they could accomplish their goals, but the men also are deceitful and manipulative at times. Sometimes an intention of a woman turns out to be the intention of God. When Sarah is quite old and has not conceived a son to be the heir of the promise, she encourages Abraham to take her servant, Hagar, as a wife to impregnate her. Her intention is closer to the purposes of God that she be the mother of the heir than that of Abraham to make his slave, Eliezer, his heir. When Sarah forces Abraham against his will to exile Hagar and her son, Ishmael, whom she saw as a competitor of her son, Isaac, Sarah is as strong willed as Abraham. Even Hagar is sketched briefly but boldly as capable of risking her life and the life of her son in the wilderness (16:7–14; 21:15–21), where she is equally as much an object of God's concern as any male character. Rebekah boldly deals forthrightly with Abraham's servant and has equal voice with her male relatives about going to Canaan to be Isaac's wife (chap. 24). She plots with Jacob to deceive old, feeble, and inept Isaac in the matter of birthright and blessing (27:5–28:5). Rebekah in fact dominates the Isaac stories. The competition between Rachel and Leah to bear sons to Jacob provides interesting counterpoint to the conflict between Jacob and Laban (29:31–

[42]Phyllis Trible, "Woman in the Old Testament," in *The Interpreter's Dictionary of the Bible*, supp. vol., p. 964. See also her article, "Depatriarchalizing in Biblical Interpretation," *Journal of the American Academy of Religion*, (1973) 30–48. For a more comprehensive study of the role of women in the Bible, see her book, *God and the Rhetoric of Sexuality*. See also John H. Otwell, *And Sarah Laughed*; Phyllis Bird, "Images of Women in the Old Testament" in Ruether, *Religion*, pp 41–88.

30:24). Both women encourage Jacob when he seizes goods from Laban and flees with them, including the household gods that Rachel steals and cleverly conceals (31:14–20; chaps. 33–35). Laban was no match for Jacob and his two scheming wives. The women in these stories are clearly drawn and well-developed characters who play important roles essential to the unfolding plots and are indispensable to fulfilling God's purposes.

We may conclude, then, that the narrator of the patriarchal stories portrays God as working not with angels or human puppets, but with believable human persons, female and male, whose lives and actions reflect the conflicting dimensions of free personhood. The characters change; they are both strong and weak, faithful and doubting, loyal and disloyal to each other and to God. One of the reasons why the human players are so described is that the chief actor in all these stories is God.

What can be said about the characterization of God in the patriarchal/matriarchal materials? God is spoken of anthropomorphically and appears regularly as an ordinary person with one exception (15:17), where God is represented by fire in the midst of a sacrifice. God is not always recognized immediately as God (18:1–15). God as God is not fully described in the Hebrew Bible until late in the preexilic period and then in a grandiose manner that conceals as much as it discloses. The elaborate opening vision of Ezekiel tells us that what he describes is "the appearance of the likeness of the glory of Yahweh" (Ezekiel 1:28). In the patriarchal stories, God appears in visions (15:1), in dreams (28:10–17), through an angel or messenger (16:7), or as a mysterious wrestler in the night (32:24–32). However he appears, God is always intimately related to the patriarchal families, knowing and caring for their every need. Throughout these stories God's character is best known through speech, through commands and conversations with men and women of the patriarchial families, and through the claims made for and about God by human characters. These divine speeches and human claims portray God as the directing character in the stories, doing things God's own way. Yahweh rejects the inheritance principle of primogeniture by choosing younger sons like Jacob, but does not abandon older sons like Ishmael and Esau. Yahweh has great power and authority, but is strangely dependent on men and women to carry out the divine purposes. God's ways mystify humans; even their weak and devious actions are used to accomplish the divine will.

Genesis 12–50, then, is masterful storytelling. Using material that had come to be treasured by Israel, the narrator has woven together stories about its heroes. Skillful use of plot and theme, climax and denouement, symbolism and characterization make them delightful reading. But the concerns of the Genesis writer go beyond the telling of interesting tales. The materials are preparing the way for the more dramatic story of exodus and covenant making in which Yahweh's purposes become clearer and clearer.

THE SOCIETY AND RELIGION OF THE PATRIARCHS AND MATRIARCHS

The Yahwistic narrator of the ancestral stories wrote after Israel's exodus from Egypt and the making of the covenant at Sinai, but his descriptions of the patriarchs' way of life and religion are little influenced by the exodus and Sinai experience. He wrote with some real feeling for Israel's past and the different way of life of Israel's patriarchal and matriarchal ancestors. The way he tells the stories provides some real insight into the social structures within which the patriarchs lived and the general character of their religion.

Patriarchal and Matriarchal Society

Patriarchal and matriarchal society was what we might call a "traditional society"[43] characterized by corporate solidarity and conservatism.

Corporate Solidarity. Every person in such a society had a strong sense of his or her relationship to all others in the community. They were bound together by strong kinship ties. They lived together in compounds. This is demonstrated by recent archeological study of some early Israelite villages, which indicated that related families lived together in a cluster of houses. The corporateness of the society included the living humans, the ancestors, and the divine beings. Classes in a traditional society were more determined by roles than by wealth. There was relatively little inequity of wealth. Everyone in the society—man, woman, and child—participated in its economic enterprise. Division of labor was equally distributed between males and females. Carol Meyers[44] summarizes the division of labor in tribal Israel as follows: food preparation was largely the responsibility of women; plow agriculture, cistern digging, land clearing, and terrace building were male responsibilities; horticulture and animal husbandry were shared by males, females, adults, and children. Crafts were likely performed exclusively by either males or females. Metallurgy was a man's job; weaving and pottery were likely done by women. Males and females alike felt that the obligation to do their part was a primary responsibility of kinship.

In such a society an individual understood oneself in terms of all these relationships and responsibilities and had virtually no real identity apart from them. Johannes Pedersen summed this up:

> Life is not something individual, to be shaped according to the needs of each individual. Man is only what he is as a link in the family. He derives his life from the family, shares it with the family and leaves it to be continued in posterity, though not as an impersonal force. It is a definitely shaped life which man takes

---

[43]Other designations less desirable because they are pejorative, are tribal, clan, undeveloped.
[44]Meyers, *Discovering Eve*, p. 148.

over, distinctive, great or small; his task is to renew it and to hand it over to those who come after him, as rich as he received it or, if possible, still richer.[45]

Conservatism.   A traditional society is conservative in that tradition dictates ends and means. The way a society is structured and the way it acts are determined by traditional patterns of life that were revealed by God in the past to the ancestors. Therefore, the present community has great reverence and respect for the ancestors who were thought to have continuing influence on the living community. The way to show this respect was to maintain the traditional patterns of life that would please the ancestors and please God, the original ancestor. This concern for the ways of the past is paralleled by a strong attachment to or nostalgia for original place, their homeland; for the patriarchs and matriarchs, Haran was the homeland, even if they had lived elsewhere for many years.

Patriarchal and Matriarchal Religion

The religion of the patriarchs and matriarchs was simple family piety, the calm, confident trust that God was with them and that he would help them meet every need. There was no need for priests or other representatives to intervene between them and God. The father, as head of the family, was the priest, but it was not necessary to approach God through the father. All members of the family had access to the God who was near. God did not make himself known exclusively through the father. He appeared to young and old, men and women, and all to whom he appeared were comfortable in his presence. They had no sense of the numinous danger of the cultic nearness of God. When God appeared before Abraham's tent, Abraham invited him in as he would any visitor. When Sarah overheard God's promise to Abraham that she would bear a son, she laughed without embarrassment. More than once when God appeared to Jacob in dreams and as a mysterious wrestler in the night, Jacob felt free to bargain with God.

   Relationship with God was part of the family's tradition and structure that was passed on from generation to generation. God is often called "God of my father," indicating his close relationship to the family. God was the original father who continues to be present with every generation.

   Each family worshipped God as the occasion dictated. There was no formal cult that all families followed, no common theology or ritual. The religious experiences and ideas were primarily determined by the needs of each family. There was no need for religious symbols and practices to be identical with those of society as a whole. This is quite different from the religion of the later tribal confederacy and monarchy. This family religion was characterized by

[45]Johannes Pedersen, *Israel: Its Life and Culture* (Branner Og Korch, 1940), p. 259.

tolerance with almost total absence of dogmatism and polemic. Apparently, the different families thought of themselves as worshiping the same god as other families, but they felt no need for everybody to understand God in the same way. This simple piety was not directed to "one eternal God, creator of heaven and earth," to whom everyone was responsible, but to the God who was immediately present with their family to meet their everyday needs. This God was a God that one could meet in everyday human circumstances.

Obviously, in the brief accounts of these patriarchal families, there is no complete description of their worship experiences. Those that are described indicate that God appeared at important or critical moments in the family's life. One of these moments is the occasion of the promise of a son, significant for a family. It was important for the economic and future well-being of the family that children should be born, especially sons. They would keep the workforce of the family's occupation going. They guaranteed the survival of the family. They would take care of the parents in their old age and give them a proper burial. All traditional societies surrounded the birth of children, especially sons, with rituals that would insure the safe delivery and growth of the child. Everyone was aware of divine presence at such times.

God also appeared when an important member of the family was beginning a venture that might determine the family's destiny, as to Abraham when Lot moved to Sodom (18:16–33) and to Jacob at Bethel and at the Jabbok ford (28:10–22; 32:22–32). God also appeared when the family was threatened by superior human powers, as when the Egyptian pharaoh added Sarah to his harem (12:10–20) and when Isaac's sheepherders were denied water rights by the sheepherders of Gerar (26:17–35). In such cases God's intervention is not militaristic; rather, God shapes the circumstances that result in a resolution of the problem by sending plagues on pharaoh and helping Isaac find other sources of water. The patriarchal families did not understand God as a warrior god who, in the later conquest stories and in many stories during the period of the monarchy, led Israel in battle and fought for them against their enemies.

Finally, the patriarch's sense of living in God's presence is demonstrated by their regular building of altars at the site of already established shrines or to establish new shrines. In the first case, they visited the shrines because they could expect God to appear there. In the second case, God appeared to them, and they felt it appropriate to establish a shrine. The already established shrines were probably shrines to El, the great creator god of Canaan, "a king living in a palace and surrounded by a court of other Gods, the master of the world who never intervened in human history."[46] Although the patriarchs recognized El's sacred power, they interpreted the Canaanite god in terms of their understanding of the God of the father. For them, El was not a cosmic deity who lived above and beyond human experience, but the friend and relative who

---

[46]Roland DeVaux, *The Early History of Israel* (Westminster, 1961), pp. 281–82.

had always been with their family to provide security, health, shelter, food, and children.

In postpatriarchal times, Israel established an elaborate cultic system and priesthood to ritually guarantee harmony among human beings, between human beings and nature, and between the believing community and God. This system itself, at times, seemed to be more important than either the God who was worshiped through it or the people who through it sought to experience God. Always, however, at the level of the average Israelite family something like patriarchal religion was present.

SUGGESTIONS FOR FURTHER STUDY

For varying perspectives on the patriarchs, consult the *Harper's Bible Dictionary* and *The Mercer Dictionary of the Bible* on patriarch, Amorites, 'Apiru, Aramaean, Hebrew.

The commentaries of Gerhard von Rad in *The Old Testament Library* and Walter Brueggemann in *Interpretation: A Biblical Commentary for Teaching and Preaching* contain helpful but differing interpretations of the patriarchal stories.

The literature on the "history" of the patriarchal period is extensive and scattered throughout many books and articles in professional journals. The best summaries of the various opinions are found in John Bright, *A History of Israel* (3d ed., Westminster, 1981); Roland DeVaux, *The Early History of Israel* (Westminster, 1978); and P. Kyle McCarter, Jr.'s chapter on "The Patriarchal Age" in Hershel Shanks, ed., *Ancient Israel* (Prentice-Hall, 1988). Robert Alter's *The Art of Biblical Narrative* (Basic Books, 1981) is a provocative general study of Hebrew narrative style and J. P. Fokkelman's chapter on "Genesis" in Robert Alter and Frank Kermode, eds., *The Literary Guide to the Bible* (Harvard, 1987), is an extremely helpful supplement to the literary analysis of the patriarchal stories in this chapter.

Carol Meyers, *Discovering Eve: Ancient Israelite Women in Context* (Oxford University, 1988), is an outstanding example of both feminine hermeneutics and the sociological study of biblical materials. A very useful analysis of the patriarchal stories from a feminist perspective is found in Susan Niditch's chapter on "Genesis" in Newsome and Ringe, eds., *The Women's Bible Commentary* (Westminster/John Knox, 1992).

5

The Exodus and the
Sinai Covenant

The book of Exodus unfolds a drama central to the understanding of the entire
Hebrew Bible. The drama was Yahweh's action in the emancipation of the
people of Israel from Egyptian slavery. Israel's belief that the exodus events
were the activity of redemption gave meaning and value to all that the nation
remembered. To Israel it was the crux of history in a way similar to the event
of the incarnation to Christianity. All that preceded and all that followed were
interpreted against the background of what God did for the people on that
occasion. The story is filled with miracles to an extent unparalleled elsewhere
in the Hebrew scriptures[1] to demonstrate that the exodus was an act of divine
deliverance. Themes of disobedience and judgment are intertwined with
themes of deliverance to demonstrate that nothing can hinder Yahweh's purposes. Israel's disobedience may delay but cannot deny God's purposes (Exodus 32:35). The nation's theology developed out of what was made known
about God in this signal event. The exodus was *the* mighty act of Yahweh.

THE PERIOD OF THE SOJOURN

The Hebrew Bible tells us that the family of Jacob sojourned in Egypt for
approximately four hundred years. Not all of Israel's ancestors were in Egypt
throughout this period. Some probably came and went at will; others never
left Canaan. Some of Israel's ancestors probably migrated from Mesopotamia
to Canaan during this period when others of them were in Egypt. Describing
only the beginning (the Joseph stories) and the ending (the exodus story) of

---

[1]Although miracles in the Hebrew scriptures are not confined to specific sections, they tend to
be gathered around the Exodus narrative and the stories of Elijah and Elisha. See J. B. Polhill,
"Perspectives on the Miracle Stories," *Review and Expositor*, 74 (1977) 389–400.

the story of the sojourn in Egypt, the biblical account only hints at momentous changes that occurred in both Egypt and Canaan in the second quarter of the second millennium B.C.E.

The Hyksos Occupation of Egypt and Canaan

The tribal movements with which we have associated the patriarchal migrations to Canaan continued and both Canaan and Egypt were invaded by an Asiatic people whom the Egyptians named Hyksos, "rulers of foreign lands." The Hyksos swept into Egypt during a time of Egyptian political instability. Aided by advanced weapons (the war chariot and the laminated bow) they overthrew the native Egyptian dynasty around 1710 B.C.E. and hastened to build a great state of their own, which included Canaan and southern Syria. They were able to maintain absolute control of Egypt over only its northern half, where they established their capital in the Nile delta at Avaris.

The Hyksos dominated northern Egypt and Canaan for a century and a half before an Egyptian revolution in 1570 B.C.E., headed by Ahmose I, brought their regime to an end. Avaris was captured and the Hyksos fled to Canaan, pursued with vengeance by Egyptian forces. Several Palestinian cities, Shechem among them, were destroyed as the Egyptians sought to recover their former Asiatic empire.

The stories of Joseph's experiences in Egypt and the settlement there of Jacob's family may be linked with the Hyksos period. Egyptian officials often allowed bedouins from stricken areas to enter Egypt and live in the delta. An Egyptian frontier officer in about 1350 B.C.E. wrote the pharaoh that such a group "who knew not how they should live, have come begging a home in the

Figure 5.1. Backgrounds of national formation, c. 1700–1020 B.C.E.

Israel	Egypt		
	1710	Hyksos domination of Egypt	
Sojourn in Egypt, *c.* 1700–1300 (Migrations into and out of Egypt occurred throughout this period)	1570	18th Dynasty, independence won by: Ahmose I	1570–1546
		Egyptian strength at peak Thutmose III	1490–1435
		Religious revolution, unrest, weakness in Amarna period Amenhotep IV	1370–1353
Oppression of the Hebrews	1310	19th Dynasty, building and strength, establishment of Delta capital	
Exodus from Egypt *c.* 1280 (Moses)		Seti I	1308–1290
Conquest of Canaan, *c.* 1250–1200 (Joshua)		Ramses II	1290–1224
	1200	20th Dynasty Ramses III	1175–1144
Tribal Confederacy, *c.* 1200–1020 (Struggle with Canaanites and Philistines)		Defeat of sea peoples resulting in settlement of Philistines in Canaan	
	1065	End of Egyptian Empire	

Backgrounds of national formation, c. 1700–1020 B.C.E.

Figure 5.2. Relief depicting Amenhotep IV, pharaoh of the Amarna age who called himself Akhnaton, Splendor of Aton. (Copyright, British Museum)

domain of Pharaoh . . . *after the manner of your fathers' father since the beginning.*"[2] Such migrations would have been particularly plausible during the time of Hyksos control of the delta of Egypt.[3]

---

[2]Wright, *Archaeology*, p. 56; emphasis added.

[3]Grollenberg, *Atlas*, p. 40. Many of the names associated with the Hyksos are Semitic, lending some support to the hypothesis that some ancestors of the Israelites may have been associated with the Hyksos. H. H. Rowley, however, argues that Joseph went into Egypt in the Amarna Age. See his *From Joseph to Joshua* (Oxford University, 1950), pp. 110ff. His argument is worthy of consideration.

According to the biblical narratives, the Israelite settlement in Goshen was near the pharaoh's court (Genesis 46:28ff.). Before the Hyksos invasion, the Egyptian capital had been at Thebes in Upper Egypt, over three hundred fifty miles from the land of Goshen. The Hyksos capital at Avaris was in the very area where the Israelites were reported to have lived. When the Hyksos were expelled, Avaris was destroyed and the capital was returned to Thebes, where it remained until after 1300 B.C.E. The Hyksos period, when Egypt was under Semitic rule, would also have been a time when conditions were propitious for the rise of a Semite like Joseph to the position of prime minister in the pharaoh's court. The probability, therefore, is that Israel's ancestors entered Egypt sometime during the period of Hyksos domination. The Hyksos period is the likely setting of the Joseph story.

Egyptian Revival Under the Eighteenth Dynasty

After the expulsion of the Hyksos, the new Egyptian dynasty (the eighteenth according to the reckoning of the third century B.C.E. Egyptian historian Manetho) was ambitious, aggressive, and able. Egypt's strength was recovered and its empire was restored. Egypt once again ruled the East. Its pharaohs were men of energy and ability who sought to extend the frontiers of Egypt as deep into Asia as possible. Their armies were strong and soon Egypt's empire stretched northward through Canaan and Syria. Swiftly Egypt had been brought to the zenith of power. This period of dominance lasted until early in the fourteenth century when signs of impending trouble appeared. An erratic pharaoh came to the throne, and a calamity of major proportions arose.

The Age of Akhnatan (Amarna Age)

The ninth king of the eighteenth dynasty, Amenhotep IV (1370–1353), was an eccentrically religious man who began a revolution that shook Egypt to its foundations. He was a proponent of the cult of the Sun God, Aton, whom he declared to be the sole god and in whose honor he changed his own name to Akhnaton (Splendor of Aton). Open conflict developed between this heretical king and the powerful Theban priests of Amon, the traditional high god of Egypt. As a result Akhnaton withdrew to a new capital city, which had been built to his order. He named the city Akhetaton (Place of the Effective-Glory of the Aton). The religion of Akhnaton was not pure monotheism: the pharaoh was still regarded as a god and the status of other gods was never clarified. Any relationship between the supposed monotheism of Akhnaton and the fully developed monotheism of later Israel goes far beyond the evidence.[4]

[4]See Wilson, *Burden*, pp. 221–18.

The Aton cult was opposed by the established priesthood and was too refined for the majority of conservative Egyptians. But the Aton revolution caused such internal dissension that the empire began to crumble away. Conditions became especially chaotic in Canaan where prince after prince pleaded in vain with the pharaoh to concern himself with this Asiatic province and send them aid. This correspondence was found at Tell el-Amarna, the modern name for the site of Akhetaton, and supplies a dramatic picture of conditions in Canaan in the mid-fourteenth century B.C.E.

Akhnaton himself was tragically affected by these chaotic circumstances. He broke with his queen and perhaps with the Aton religion, but was unable to restore order. His successors were two sons-in-law, neither of whom was a particularly effective ruler. With them the once great eighteenth dynasty came to a dismal end. Thus it was that this very early religion of monotheistic character brought dissension to its land, ruin to its founder, and death to many of its adherents.

Restoration of Order

Standing in the gap between the eighteenth dynasty and the nineteenth was Haremhab, once a faithful general of Akhnaton and now the savior of Egypt. This forceful and able man purged Egypt of the Aton heresy and its destructive side effects and inaugurated at the close of the fourteenth century B.C.E. Egypt's final period of greatness.

The biblical narrative makes almost no reference to these momentous years. The descendants of Jacob continued to live in the Goshen area of the delta. Their situation probably changed somewhat when the Hyksos were expelled; they and others like them must have remained where they were rather than cast their lot with the defeated Hyksos. They may have remained almost unnoticed in the territory that had been assigned to them, following their old ways of life, drawing their livelihood from their flocks and agriculture. The biblical narratives silently pass over this period. The silence has been explained by the assumption that "nothing occurred in which the people recognized the special providence of God, or which led to a significant enrichment of the spiritual heritage of Israel." [5]

Eventually many foreigners were forced to become workmen for the pharaoh on royal building projects. The Israelites would have been one small group among these workers. But as a people of promise, they were destined for deliverance by an act of Yahweh, their God.

---

[5]Grollenberg, *Atlas*, p. 41.

THE BOOK OF EXODUS

The book of Exodus must be understood as a part of the larger epiclike collection of Israel's historical and legal traditions beginning with the stories about Abraham (the primeval materials were added as prologue) and continuing through the wilderness wanderings and conquest of Canaan. That Exodus exists now as a separate and named entity is due to the simple fact that the great literary history of Israel's origins had to be apportioned among five separate scrolls, each of which was named for convenience of reference. There is no meaningful break between Genesis and Exodus. The materials in Exodus relate to the Genesis traditions as fulfillment of promise:

A. Traditions of the exodus: 1:1–15:21
    1. Moses: 1:1–7:7
    2. Signs and wonders: 7:8–10:29
    3. Passover and exodus: 11:1–13:16
    4. Miracle at the sea: 13:17–14:31
    5. Praise to Yahweh for deliverance: 15:1–21
B. Wilderness traditions: 15:22–18:27
C. Covenant traditions: 19:1–24:11
    1. Theophany on Sinai and the decalogue: 19:1–20:21
    2. The book of the covenant: 20:22–23:33
    3. The covenant: 24:1–11
D. Covenant cultic legislation: 24:12–31:17
E. Miscellaneous: 31:18–40:38

The events in Exodus are the heart of Israel's theological traditions. *Yahweh brought up Israel out of the land of Egypt*—this was always a fundamental expression of Israelite faith. The covenant community believed that in the exodus-covenant events "Yahweh had by a decisive act demonstrated for Israel that he was at work in history and at the same time clearly took Israel to himself."[6] Perhaps, therefore, the title given this book in the Hebrew text, "These are the names," is a more appropriate designation than the more familiar "Exodus" applied by the Septuagint. The Hebrew title is taken from the book's opening words: "These are the names of the sons of Israel who came to Egypt." More than just a narrative about the "way out" of Egypt, Exodus is a confession of faith about the origins of Israel.

The interrelated themes of *exodus from Egypt* and *covenant at Sinai* fill the book of Exodus and form the heart of the narratives of Israel's origins and of all Israelite faith. The exodus and covenant traditions are inseparably intertwined in Israelite theological and cultic attempts at national understanding.

---

[6]Noth, *Exodus* (Westminster, 1962), p. 10.

The dramatic narratives of the exodus are climaxed in the covenant. In fact, the book might easily be divided into two parts indicating intimate connection between the two themes: what God has done (chaps. 1–19) and how Israel should respond (chaps. 20–40). Israel was delivered from Egypt to enter into covenant with Yahweh at Sinai. The covenant traditions are always the traditions of the delivered people. The fundamental unity of the two themes is clearly expressed in the religious confession with which the covenant ceremony opens: "I am Yahweh your God, who brought you out of the land of Egypt, out of the house of slavery" (20:2). Together, therefore, the themes of exodus and covenant represent the inseparable union of Yahweh's revelation of the divine nature in the saving acts in history and Yahweh's revelation of the divine will in covenant.[7]

THE EXODUS: YAHWEH'S MIGHTY ACT
(EXODUS 1:1–15:21)

The Historical Setting

Although the narratives in the Hebrew Bible speak eloquently of the significance of the exodus, they say almost nothing about the historical context in which it occurred. No specific dates are given and the Egyptian pharaohs who play a large part in the story go unnamed. The biblical narrator is much more interested in the theological drama of his story than in historical detail. He so focused his attention upon Yahweh, the chief character in this story of redemption, that he omitted distracting details about Yahweh's Egyptian opponents. Egyptian records make no mention of the flight of any Semitic slaves to escape forced labor in the service of the pharaohs. To the Egyptians such an escape, in spite of all that is made of it in the biblical narrative, would have been "an insignificant episode, too small and lacking in glory to find any place in the accounts of the Pharaoh, whom the Egyptian chroniclers had to immortalize."[8]

The Egyptian Coloration of the Narrative.   The biblical narrative of the exodus reflects an accurate picture of the life of Asiatics in the Egyptian delta. The entrance of the Hebrews into Egypt to find relief from famine seems to have been typical of the migratory patterns of seminomads, as illustrated by the report of an Egyptian border official in the thirteenth century B.C.E. In a report to his superior, he recorded that Edomite nomads had been given permission

---

[7]So, essentially, Artur Weiser as against Gerhard von Rad and Martin Noth.
[8]De Vaux, *History*, p. 390.

to move past a border fortress into the Egyptian delta "to keep them alive and to keep their cattle alive."[9]

The process of brick making described in Exodus 1:13–14 and 5:15–21 is documented in Egyptian texts and art. A wall painting in the the tomb of the vizier Rekhmire (c. 1460 B.C.E.) pictures the various chores involved in brick making, and a leather scroll from the fifth year of the reign of Ramses II (1290–1224 B.C.E.) mentions a quota of 2,000 bricks from each of forty workmen. An exceptional number of bricks were needed for the extraordinary number of construction projects Ramses undertook in the delta. Completely new cities were established and long abandoned cities were rebuilt. These cities were surrounded by brick walls approximately sixty feet high and fifty feet wide. The enlistment of Israelites as brick makers is typical of the corvée system used in all periods of Egyptian history and particularly typical of Ramses II, who exploited the foreign population in the country. Moses' request to Pharaoh that the Israelites be given time off for a religious observance is similar to an account from the time of Ramses II, which mentions that on the feast day of a certain goddess the corvée laborers would not be required to work.

The account of the ten plagues reflects an understanding of Egyptian religion. To a large extent they are described as judgments on Egyptian gods. The Nile and the sun were major representations to the Egyptians of divine creative and sustaining power. The transformation of the life giving water of the Nile into "blood" represents the victory of chaos over order. Three days of darkness would have meant to the Egyptians the defeat of the sun god who was the greatest of the Egyptian deities. Nothing in Egyptian experience was as reliable as the daily appearance of the sun bringing light and life and the annual flooding of the Nile bringing sustaining water for crops and people.

This Egyptian coloring of the narrative, however, provides no basis for putting the biblical story into historical context.

The Date.   Evidence both within and without the Hebrew Bible suggests a thirteenth-century date for the events that became so important for Israel's theological self-understanding.

1. Exodus 1:11 states that the Israelites worked on the construction of the store-cities of Raamses and Pithom. To have done so, they must have been in Egypt during the reigns of Seti I (1308–1290) and Ramses II (1290–1224), the pharaohs who built these cities. In addition the events of the first few chapters of Exodus represent the Israelites as living near the Egyptian court. The Egyptian court was in the delta region of Egypt—where the Israelites were settled—in the time of Seti I and Ramses II. The latter made Raamses his capital.

---

[9]Pritchard, *Texts*, p. 259.

Figure 5.3. Seated statue of Ramses II of the Egyptian nineteenth dynasty. Ramses, builder of the store cities mentioned in the book of Exodus, is the most probable pharaoh of the Hebrew exodus from Egypt. The granite statue original represented Amenhotep III, but Ramses "slenderized" the torso and arms, recarved the face, cut back the throne, and reinscribed the piece with his own cartouche on the right side of the statue. This appropriation of an important predecessor is illustrative of Ramses' sense of power. (Courtesy Museum of Fine Arts, Boston)

2. Archeological evidence of warlike destructions of several Canaanite cities in the late thirteenth century may be related to Israel's entrance into Canaan under Joshua, although destruction of most cities in the Joshua campaigns is not supported by archeological evidence.

3. An inscription from the fifth year of Pharaoh Merneptah (1224–1216) celebrates an Egyptian campaign into Canaan. It mentions Israel among the peoples encountered there. A group of persons, then, known as Israel had settled in Canaan by 1220.

Such evidence does not confirm the exodus as a historical event. The only "evidence" we have for such an event is the biblical narrative itself. What this other evidence means is that the exodus story best fits into the Egyptian and Canaanite milieus of the thirteenth century.

The Route of the Exodus and the Location of Sinai.   The fleeing Israelites did not take the most direct route from Egypt to Canaan. They avoided frontier fortifications and the heavily guarded commercial and military highway. "God did not lead them by way of the land of the Philistines, although that was nearer" (Exodus 13:17).[10] The narrative is more concerned with their movement toward the holy mountain of Sinai where God had appeared to Moses than with clarifying the route they took. So they moved toward the marshes that covered the area now crossed by the Suez Canal. Here they crossed a "sea of reeds" or "papyrus lake" in which the pursuing Egyptian chariots bogged down and were destroyed (the "sea of reeds" or "papyrus lake" are both literal translations of *yam suph,* the Hebrew words for this body of water. In the Septuagint *yam suph* was mistranslated "Red Sea"). From this "sea" they moved toward Sinai.

Since the sixth century C.E., tradition has located Sinai in a range on the southern tip of the Sinai peninsula, identifying it with a mountain now called Jebel Musa. With this site for Sinai in mind, it has been assumed that the Israelites traveled from Egypt down the west coast of the peninsula and that the oases and sites mentioned in the Exodus account were along this route. Exploration has been of little help in locating either Sinai or the oases, but a number of reasons have called the traditional view into question. First, in the scriptural account there is no mention that the Israelites encountered Egyptians at any point along the route. This is somewhat surprising if they traveled southward along the eastern shores of the present Gulf of Suez where they would have passed Egyptian mines heavily guarded by troops. It is doubtful that the Egyptian troops would have allowed them to pass uncontested. Again, the peninsula of Sinai is about two hundred fifty miles long from the Mediterranean to the southern tip. This line of flight would certainly have been out of the way that led to Canaan. Further, Kadesh, a site that repeatedly occurs in the biblical story dealing with the wilderness period, was located in the Negeb, far north of the traditional Sinai. In the general area of Kadesh are springs sufficient to support several thousand migrants. Also, some poetic expressions designate Seir and Paran in the northern part of the Sinai peninsula as the point of origin of Israel's religion. These and other reasons have led many contemporary scholars to lean toward a location for Sinai somewhere in the Mount Seir range, the general area around Kadesh.

The traditional Jebel Musa site, however, will not be readily surrendered. A

---

[10]The early Hebrews believed implicitly in Yahweh as sovereign. The question of a good God causing evil was not a problem to them. Later, under the influence of late Babylonian and Persian thought, patterns of dualism in thinking about good and evil became evident.

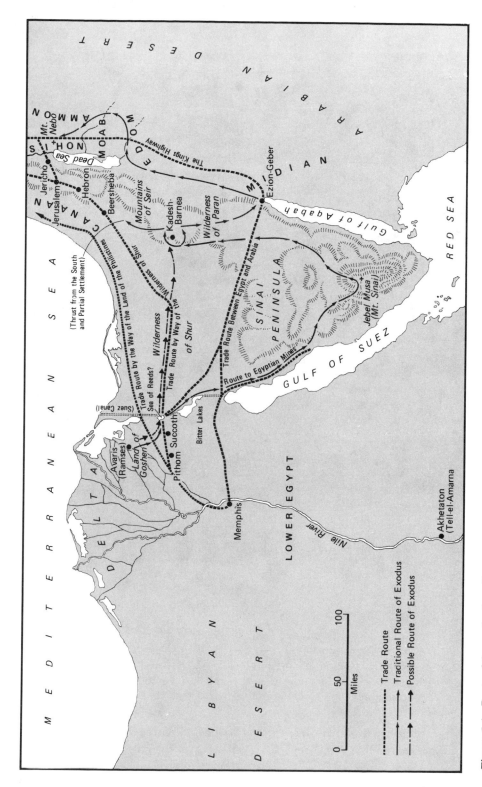

Figure 5.4. Route of the exodus from Egypt

Figure 5.5. The biblical world as seen from space. The Sinai Peninsula is in the center with Palestine in upper left-hand area and Egypt in lower part of photo. Dark areas are waterways. The traditional site of Sinai is at the southern tip of Sinai at the throat of the "Y" made by the arms of the Red Sea. (Courtesy of NASA)

foremost archeologist, G. Ernest Wright, holds that a few of the stations along the route to Jebel Musa can be identified with some degree of probability:

> [I find it] extremely difficult to understand why the early church would have located the sacred spot in the most inaccessible and dangerous area imaginable for pilgrims, especially at a time when the tendency was to do just the opposite, unless the tradition was so old and firmly fixed that no debate was permitted about it.[11]

The conclusion is that Sinai cannot be located with certainty. Wherever it was located, the narrative represents Moses as returning to an area he had

---

[11]Wright, *Archaeology*, p. 64.

Figure 5.6. Jebel Musa, "the mountain of Moses," the traditional location of Mt. Sinai. (Courtesy of the Scofield Collection/DarganResearch Library, Nashville, Tennessee)

already been when shepherding the flocks of his father-in-law and where God revealed to him the divine concern for the enslaved Israelites in Egypt. Now the holy place was to become the locus for a new manifestation of Yahweh's presence.

The Number of Israelites Who Fled from Egypt. Exodus 12:38 calls the people Moses led out of Egypt "a mixed crowd," indicating that other descendants of Jacob were in the company. Later in Canaan the mixed company would be joined by others of kindred origins. The number involved in the migration is difficult to determine. The reference in Exodus 12:37 to six hundred thousand males of fighting age, a number of warriors that indicates the total population would have been about two and a half million, must surely be an exaggeration. The departure from Egypt of that many slaves would have been a major event, which would not have gone unnoticed in Egyptian records. Further, it's impossible to imagine such a large caravan of people and their animals surviving in the hostile wilderness of Sinai. In fact, a population of that size is incompatible with several features of the biblical story itself where two midwives served the childbearing needs of the entire community (1:15–20) and, when they approached Canaan, the Israelites are described as too few to engage the Canaanites in battle (23:29ff). This reference to six hundred thousand fighting men is more a part of the biblical narrator's storytelling than a census count.[12]

The Exodus and Covenant Event in Story

The narrative of the exodus is more firmly set in history than are the patriarchal narratives, but like them has all the characteristics of a skillfully and dramatically told story. Because the story was about their freedom and redemption, it must have been a favorite story of the early Israelites. As such it was associated with the celebration of Passover, the most important religious festival in the Israelite cult. At Passover they told the story as the explanation of their very existence as a people and of their special sense of being the people of God. In the same way that the early chapters of Genesis are stories about the creation of the world, the exodus and covenant narrative is a story about the creation of a religious community, about the definition of its place in the purposes of God, and about the structuring of its way of life.

Major Literary Strands in Exodus, Leviticus, and Numbers.   In Exodus the Yahwistic and Elohistic strands are prominent with some additions of priestly character, especially in the cultic legislation in chapters 25–31 and 35–40. Most of Numbers is priestly material, as is all of Leviticus. The narrative throughout Exodus is skillfully woven into a literary whole so that distinction of sources is not helpful except in the story of the revelation of the name Yahweh to Moses and in the story of the plagues. More important is the way that the motifs of exodus from Egypt, covenant at Sinai, and guidance in the wilderness are used to support the overall theme of Yahweh's deliverance of the people.

The Dramatic Character of the Story.   Reading this story as a straightforward historical narrative misses much of its power. This is a story of cosmic significance, like all creation stories, with implications for the whole of humankind. The characters, especially Moses and the pharaoh, are bold and bigger than life and their actions have far-reaching implications. In many ways the story is like a classic comedy that deals with human nature in its human condition, restrained and often made ridiculous by its limitations, faults, and animal nature. Comedy brings laughter and satire from the spectacle of these human limitations and failures. It juxtaposes appearance and reality, deflates pretense, and mocks excesses. In the exodus and covenant story the pharaoh is the arrogant human boaster who claims more knowledge and power than he really

---

[12]Some scholars reduce the high figure by suggesting that the Hebrew term *'elph*, translated "thousand" should be translated as "family" or "fighting unit." Others suggest that a later census figure has been read into the earlier story.

has and who, therefore, is bound to fall—and the reader or hearer knows this from the outset. Moses is the hero whose destruction is sought by the arrogant boaster, but a hero who cleverly leads the boaster to destruction. The story moves to an inevitable happy ending because God is in control. Part of the dramatic attraction of the story lies in this certainty of its outcome. Even though there are suspenseful moments when the fate of Israel, or even of all humanity, seems to hang in the balance, the hearer or reader of this story knows that in the end all will be well.

Theme and Subtheme. The theme of the Exodus covenant story is stated in the scene in which God speaks to Moses out of a burning bush:

> I have observed the misery of my people who are in Egypt; I have heard their cry on account of their taskmasters. Indeed, I know their sufferings, and I have come down to deliver them from the Egyptians, and to bring them up out of that land to a good and broad land flowing with milk and honey . . . [Exodus 3:7–8a].

Put in other words, the theme is that Yahweh is a powerful and loving God who will deliver the Israelites from bondage and will bind them to God in covenant.

Related inseparably to this main theme is the subtheme of Israel's responsibility to accept God's deliverance and commit itself in covenant to be God's servant people. Israel must choose between the powers of bondage and death represented by Egypt and the pharaoh, and the opportunities of responsible freedom present in exodus and covenant with God. A second subtheme is that of the chosen one, a recurring motif in Genesis and Exodus. Moses is a chosen individual; Israel is a chosen people. Neither choice at first glance seems logical. Moses is hesitant and complains that he is not a good speaker. Moses is also a younger brother and the elder would ordinarily be the leader. Israel is not the most powerful or culturally advanced people. But here, as in Genesis with Jacob and Joseph, God chooses against normal patterns and expectations. This motif affirms God as a deity who must be trusted even though God's actions are often inscrutable.

Plot, Characterization, and Interpretation. The exodus and covenant narrative is in six episodes: the situation of Israel, preparation of the hero deliverer, revelation at Sinai, conflict with the pharaoh, the victory at and over the sea, and covenant at Sinai.

THE SITUATION OF ISRAEL (1:1–14). The story opens with a section that serves as a transition from the story of Joseph and his brothers to the story of the Israelites in Egyptian bondage (1:1–7). Considerable time has passed and the twelve sons of Israel who migrated to Egypt (1:1) have become the Israelite people (1:7), *fruitful* and *increasing greatly, multiplying,* and *growing increasingly strong.* This stately, deliberate, repetitive language underscores the cosmic significance of what is about to happen. Israel in Egypt is "portrayed as the microcosm of the macrocosm—the fulfillers of the divinely ordained destiny of man laid out following the creation and flood":[13] "Be fruitful and multiply, and fill the earth and subdue it; and have dominion over the fish of the sea and over the birds of the air and over every living thing that moves upon the earth" (Genesis 1:28; cf. 9:1–2).

The sequel to the creation story is the failure of humankind and expulsion from Eden. Noah's descendants multiply and are scattered abroad in alienation and confusion, which cannot be overcome by building the tower of Babel. Now the descendants of Jacob, exiled in Egypt and building a new Babel for the pharaoh, are nevertheless fulfilling the creative intention of God. In what follows God will be performing a re-creation of the human community that offers "man the hope of overcoming the broken relationships which had been part of his condition since primeval times."[14]

To their own grievous loss, the pharaohs are described as unknowingly standing in the way of God's creative purposes. One pharaoh does not know Joseph (1:8) and his successor does not know Yahweh (5:2). In the ancient world Egypt was renowned for the wisdom of its court and the pharaohs represented the epitome of human wisdom. Ironically, however, they are portrayed in Exodus as wicked fools whose attempts to destroy or limit Israel bring about events that lead to their own destruction.[15] Israelites must have laughed as stories of duped pharaohs were told. One pharaoh increases the labor burdens of the Israelites, but they continue to multiply. He commands that the newborn male Israelites be killed, but one child who escapes eventually becomes instrumental in plaguing Egypt, in killing a pharaoh's firstborn son, and destroying his armies in the sea. Nothing can deter what Israel's God is doing.

PREPARATION OF THE HERO DELIVERER (2:1–4:31). Death is threatening life. The pharaoh will destroy Israel; all its male infants will be thrown into the Nile. Strangely but appropriately, at this point the story changes its focus from the public story of Israel to the private story of one Israelite, who will be instrumental in the rescue of the many. The theme is that of "the chosen one," a familiar theme in ancient Near Eastern literature. A story similar to that of Moses' birth and rescue from the Nile was told about Sargon of Akkad (c. 2300 B.C.E.)[16] and there are several stories of the sending of the hero deliverer from various Near Eastern cultures. How closely these stories are related to the Moses story cannot be determined, but it is possible that the biblical narrator borrowed motifs from them. Regularly in the Hebrew Bible the birth of special sons (Isaac) and hero-deliverers (Moses, Samson, Samuel) is described as un-

---

[13]James S. Ackerman, "The Literary Context of the Moses Birth Story (Exodus 1–2)" in *Gros Louis*, p. 78.

[14]Ibid, p. 79.

[15]Childs, *Exodus*, pp. 13–17.

[16]Pritchard, *Texts*, pp. 119ff.

usual. They are God-given sons and God is instrumental in preparing them for their task, a motif similar to other Near Eastern stories.

In the exodus story of the birth of Moses and his rescue from the Nile, the waters of death are transformed into the waters of life. Then when the child becomes a man, he will see that life prevails for Israel over the powers of bondage and death. As a child adopted and named by a pharaoh's daughter, he will grow up aware of things Egyptian. Nursed and, we assume, taught by his mother, he will also be an Israelite.

With an economy of words–nothing is said of his childhood and youth–the story next tells of Moses the man. Prepared in Egypt for position and authority, he will now enter the wilderness, both a place of threatening danger and a secluded retreat for preparation. There he will learn the way of his ancestors and encounter the God who will deliver Israel from bondage. Seeing the oppression of an Israelite, he will take the initiative and smite the oppressor (2:12) just as God will later take the initiative to smite the oppressor of all the Israelites (13:15). Moses' action seems to endanger his mission of destiny, but the reader is continuously reminded that the enterprise is in God's hands. Neither the cunning pharaoh nor the impetuous Moses can change the outcome. Even Moses' flight to Midian is part of his preparation for God's mission. In the wilderness "Moses came back to his forefathers. . . . A man of the enslaved nation, but the only one not enslaved together with them, had returned to the free and clean air of his forebears."[17]

Notice now how Moses is characterized as the hero-deliverer. Several times Moses is referred to simply as "Moses the man" (Exodus 32:1, 23; Numbers 12:3). This is a strangely simple way to speak of one who according to later traditions combined in his own person almost all the possible honors and powers of religious and political leadership. He became priest, leader, prophet, lawgiver, and commander of his people. Yet he was only "Moses the man," a human being, not a saint, or an ascetic, nor even a hero in the ordinary sense of that word. How did he become what he became?[18] Was it primarily because of his preparation? He was born during dangerous times. He grew to maturity in a pharaoh's household. He was able to maintain his sense of being an Israelite, and that must have been difficult to do. In defense of one of his own people, angered, he rashly killed an Egyptian. Thus he lost his privileged position and had to flee. In Midian he became a shepherd like his ancestors. There is nothing unusual in all of this; similar things could easily have happened to other men with no significant consequences.

Perhaps the answer lay in his character. Moses was surely related empathetically with his Israelite heritage and from that background came a keen sense of justice. He was courageous but with a rashness that needed to be

[17]Buber, *Moses*, p. 38.
[18]Von Rad, *Moses*, pp. 10–11.

tempered with sense and purpose. He was a man of decisive action, but not always clear thought. He was also fearful and insecure and perhaps, in a genuine way, humble. His reluctance to confront the pharaoh was not just fear. There is really nothing unusual in this either. In other words Moses is described as a real man, flesh and blood. Yet in both his preparation and character, God is depicted as working in a mysterious way to perform wonders through "this man Moses." This seems to be the key to the narrative. Moses is the hero, but not really. God is the hero; the cause was God's and the outcome belonged to God. Only as "this man Moses" responded to God's call would he be able to do what he would do, or rather what God would do through him.

Moses' call came on a sacred mountain through a phenomenon described in unexplainable mystery. A bush burning but not consumed signals sacred presence, a theophany of first magnitude. Often in the Hebrew Bible God is described as appearing in fire (Genesis 15:17; Exodus 19:18; Psalm 104:3–4; Ezekiel 1:27). The vision occurs at a place already considered holy (3:1). Probably the site was a sacred place of the Midianites where Moses had worshiped earlier. On sacred ground he might have even expected to hear a voice from God. The vision of the call is understood as the real presence of Israel's eternal God. God's initial command calls for reverence and attention (3:5), and God's subsequent command is a call to service (3:10). Moses is warned that the task will not be easy (4:21), but also is assured of divine presence (3:12)—awesome, challenging, comforting, and enabling. To this call "the man Moses" responds as a man, with a mixture of fear, doubt, confused faith, and genuine humility. He says, "Who am I?" (3:11) "What is your name?" (3:13) "I am slow of speech" (4:10). "Please send somebody else" (4:13). Then hesitancy and doubt gave way to confident and subdued faith in the God who here on this mountain grants self-disclosure to Moses the man. The reader or hearer of this story would be confident that the cause and outcome belonged to God.

REVELATION AT SINAI (3:1–21).[19] This episode completes the call of Moses to be the deliverer and as such belongs to or continues the episode of his preparation. But because of its unique revelatory context, it represents a significant crisis in the larger narrative of exodus and conquest.

The dramatic presentation of the encounter at the holy mountain emphasizes the significant meaning of the experience for Moses. His attention is focused on that awesome voice, which identifies itself: "I am the God of your father, the God of Abraham, the God of Isaac, and the God of Jacob" (3:6). This is no alien deity "discovered" by Moses on the mountain; it is the God of his fathers, before whose presence Moses hides his face. This is also the God of those who tell the story and who believe that God in seeking Moses seeks them and in redeeming Israelite slaves also sets them free.

---

[19]A full treatment of the archeology of Sinai may be found in Stern et al., *New Encyclopedia*, IV, 1384–1403.

Through this theophany Moses becomes intently aware of God's purpose to deliver the enslaved Israelites from Egypt and surrenders to an overwhelming assignment in the drama. Moses is to return to the pharaoh and lead his kin to freedom. Moses' initial protest, "Who am I that I should go to Pharaoh and bring the Israelites out of Egypt?" (3:11) is dismissed by God's assurance: "I will be with you; and this shall be the sign for you that it is I who sent you: when you have brought the people out of Egypt, you shall worship God on this mountain" (3:12).

God's reply thus changes the question. It is not a matter of Who is Moses? but Who is God? and What does God intend? The adequacy of the prophet is dependent on the adequacy of God, who both commissions him and promises to accompany him. The success of the venture is not dependent on Moses' resources, but is guaranteed by God. Further, this sense of dependence on God represents a fundamental affirmation of Israelite faith. The genius of Israel was never its own worth or accomplishments, but its sense of and response to the creative and redemptive presence of Yahweh.

Identify at least three names (other than "Yahweh") used for God in the Hebrew Bible. Use a Bible dictionary to state the essential meaning of each and illustrate that meaning in a specific passage.

Primary in the revelation on the holy mountain was the disclosure of God's name. The narrator presents it as a response to a practical question about authority raised by Moses: "If I come to the Israelites and say to them, 'The God of your ancestors has sent me to you,' and they ask me, 'What is his name?' what shall I say to them?" (3:13). How could he convince the Israelites that God had actually spoken to him? Part of the answer to this question is presupposed in it. This God is the God of Abraham, Isaac, and Jacob, known by past deeds and promises, promises God is now about to fulfill. But Moses wants to know more. To go to his fellow Israelites in Egypt and tell them of his experience at the mountain, he would have to know God's name. To be believed, the new revelation had to be accompanied by a new name.

Of greater importance, Moses wants to know the mystery of the divine nature, the secret of the being of his God. In Semitic thought the character or identity of a being, human or divine, was expressed in name. Much more than a combination of letters used to distinguish one being from another, a name represented the total being of the one who bore it. To know a name was to know the essential self or identity of a person. The answer that God gives to Moses, then, is at once both cryptic and satisfactory, both concealing and revealing. God says, "*I am who I am* .... Thus you shall say to the Israelites. *I am* has sent me to you' " (Exodus 3:14). The exact meaning of the sentence name, *I am who I am,* is ambiguous, perhaps intentionally so. The fullness of the mystery of God is not to be known through God's name. Whatever the exact meaning of the name, in knowing it Moses is given confidence. At the same time he should understand that God is never given away, to be known and controlled. The name of God does not provide the one who knows it with power over God.

Here is the only place in the Hebrew scriptures where the first-person form *'ehyeh* of the divine name is used. Elsewhere it is always in the third person. God could indeed say *I am* or *I will be*; Moses and Israel, however, could only say *he is* or *he will be*. In both cases the Hebrew verb involved is "h-y-h." When vocalized, the third-person form "Y-H-W-H" becomes "Yahweh," the peculiarly Israelite personal name for God. The disclosure of God's name is intended as a revelation of God's character. What, then, about God is being revealed? We cannot be certain, but there are clues in the meaning of the phrase, *I am who I am*. The original Hebrew *'ehyeh 'asher 'ehyeh* can be translated in different ways. If read to mean "I am who I am," the emphasis is on the mystery of divine "being." God, then, is the eternal one. Alone, such an emphasis on "being" is more characteristic of Greek philosophy than of Israelite thought. If this is the meaning, it is God's "being there" for Israel in the ongoing affairs of historical experience that is intended. A similar meaning is extracted if the sentence name is understood in the future tense, "I will be who I will be," an acceptable reading of the verb form *'ehyeh*. In general the meaning would then be that this God is God of the present and the future, a deity adequate for all future needs. That is, "Trust me, Moses, and wait and see what I can do for those who have faith in me." In the immediate context God says to Moses, "I will be with you" (3:12), "I will be with your mouth" (4:12), and "I will be your God" (6:7). Yahweh also instructs Moses to speak on Yahweh's behalf to the enslaved Israelites:

> I am Yahweh, and *I will* free you from the burdens of the Egyptians, and deliver you from slavery to them, and *I will redeem* you with an outstretched arm and with mighty acts of judgment. *I will* take you as my people, and *I will be your God*. You shall know that I am Yahweh your God, who has freed you from the burdens of the Egyptians [6:6–7].

Moses' question Who is God? will be answered in God's acts of grace and in the covenant requirements to be placed upon Israel.

The divine reply, therefore, did not end with this veiled and intentionally ambiguous revelation of God's name. The secret of God's being was not to be discovered in the divine name alone, or even primarily, but rather in what God was about to do. Yahweh was to be known, not in static being, but in the redemptive confrontation of his people. The question Who is God? would be answered in time through events about to take place:

> Go and assemble the elders of Israel, and say to them, "Yahweh, the God of your ancestors, the God of Abraham, of Isaac, and of Jacob, has appeared to me, saying, "I have given heed to you and what has been done to you in Egypt. I

declare that I will bring you up out of the misery of Egypt, to the land of the Canaanites, the Hittites, and Amorites, the Perizzites, the Hivites, and the Jebusites, a land flowing with milk and honey [3:16–17].

The ultimate question for Israel, therefore, was not just Who is God? but also What had God done? In presenting Yahweh, the Hebrew Bible does not focus on the philosophical nature of the divine being, but on the redemptive quality of divine activity.[20]

Further, the God who here revealed a new name also revealed identification with the God of Abraham, the God of Isaac, and the God of Jacob. The new name is evidence of both new revelation and additional understanding of the same God who had directed the fortunes of Israel's forefathers. Under this new name, *Yahweh*, God was about to be made known to the enslaved Israelites, whose cries had been heard and whose cause would be championed. The might of El Shaddai, "God the Mountain One" of the patriarchs, would be revealed in an act of redemption as Yahweh.

When was the name Yahweh first known in the Israelite tradition? From the story in Exodus 3 it appears that the name is first revealed to Moses at Sinai. The alternate account in chapter 6 claims this emphatically: "I am Yahweh, I appeared to Abraham, to Isaac, and to Jacob, as God Almighty, but by my name Yahweh I did not make myself known to them" (6:3). However, the Yahwistic narrative traces the name back to ancient times, the period before the flood: "At that time men began to call upon the name of Yahweh" (Genesis 4:26).

The Yahwistic narrative uses the name Yahweh throughout Genesis. This use is perhaps based on a tradition that the name Yahweh was actually known in the pre-Mosaic period by some patriarchal clans.[21] It may be, though, that the Yahwistic use of Yahweh is theologically anachronistic—that is, the Yahwist was so convinced of Yahweh's lordship over both creation and history that he used the name from the beginning of his story. The weight of the evidence is that the name came into common use only at the time of Moses. After that time, parents often gave their children names compounded with a short form of the name Yahweh. This was not the case earlier. Whenever the name was first used, the revelation at Sinai was a new and exciting understanding of God as the redeemer of those who are oppressed.

With this revelation Moses' preparation as the hero-deliverer is complete and victory over the pharaoh is assured, but this is only the first crisis. All is not yet resolved; Israel is still in Egyptian bondage and the pharaoh does not

---

[20]With a slight alteration the word *'ehyeh* can be read to mean "I cause." The emphasis then would be on God in whose will all natural phenomena and historical events have their origin. Because this meaning is based on an alteration of the phrase in question, it is less satisfactory than the others.

[21]Harrelson, *Interpreting*, p. 79.

yet know the power that will confront and defeat him. Moses must return to Egypt.

THE MIGHTY ACT OF YAHWEH: THE CONTEST WITH THE PHARAOH. The narrative concerning Moses' encounter with the pharaoh is charged with dramatic suspense from beginning to end. Step by step the account unfolds the contest with sustained interest until Yahweh through Moses becomes victor over the powers of Egypt. In Moses' return to Egypt Yahweh seems to risk everything, entering as it were the very territory of Egyptian gods.

From the beginning Yahweh's victory and the freeing of the Israelites has been anticipated. At Sinai Yahweh commissions Moses: "So come, I will send you to Pharaoh to bring my people, the Israelites, out of Egypt" (Exodus 3:10). Moses then returns to Egypt as Yahweh's messenger or prophet[22] to announce to the pharaoh: "Thus says Yahweh, Israel is my firstborn son . . . . Let my son go that he may worship me. But if you refuse to let him go; now I will kill your firstborn son" (Exodus 4:22–23).

But first the Israelites had to be persuaded that Yahweh had appeared to Moses and would act to deliver them. They had to be led to faith:

> Then Moses and Aaron went and assembled all the elders of the Israelites. Aaron spoke all the words that Yahweh had spoken to Moses, and performed the signs in the sight of the people. The people believed; and when they heard that Yahweh had given heed to the Israelites and that he had seen their misery, they bowed down and worshiped. [Exodus 4:29–31]

Yahweh is presented to the Israelites as a sovereign superior to the pharaoh. Now the contest is on; issue could be drawn with the pharaoh. Moses requests permission for the Israelites to worship Yahweh in the wilderness. The pharaoh interprets the request as evidence of both idle time on the part of the slaves and labor agitation on the part of Moses. He reacts by increasing the work load of the slaves, a reprisal so effective that the Israelite foremen accuse Moses and Aaron of making the life of the people more difficult. Moses in turn protests to Yahweh. His faith waivers (5:22–23). In this way the Hebrew scriptures heighten the drama by magnifying the obstacles to Yahweh's victory. In the face of the obstacles, the people and Moses waver; Yahweh's hand remains firm and deliverance is sure.

The contest with the pharaoh is presented as a cosmic struggle between Yahweh and the dark forces of chaos. It is like the great struggles depicted in the creation myths of the ancient world. Order, meaning, and the stability of society are forever threatened by chaotic forces beyond human control. These forces can be overcome only by the creative activity of the sacred. In this light the exodus-covenant story should be read as a creation story, the story of Yahweh's creation of that servant community through whom Yahweh will work to

---

[22]In the Hebrew Bible a prophet's primary function is to speak for God.

dispel the pernicious powers that threaten all humankind. The creation of Israel as "God's holy nation" (19:6) is as important as the creative act told of in Genesis 1. Indeed, primeval creation is incomplete without the creative act of the exodus. So Yahweh is described as joining battle with the pharaoh and the outcome will be universal in scope.[23]

With increasing tension the narrative indicates that the initial efforts of Moses and Aaron before the pharaoh prove abortive. A magical act of turning a rod into a serpent is duplicated by the Egyptian magicians. This "magical" action is reminiscent of an Egyptian text for the exorcism of serpents: "A face has fallen against a face; a face has seen a face. The mottled knife, black and green, goes forth against it. It has swallowed for itself that which it tasted."[24]

Although some hint of victory is present in the devouring of the serpents of the Egyptians by the serpent of Aaron, the pharaoh is not impressed. Greater powers of Yahweh will be mustered against the pharaoh.

With artistic appropriateness, the battle between Yahweh, God revealed on the mountain, and the pharaoh is set on the banks of the Nile, where the Egyptian gods should have been supreme. Against them Yahweh will now perform great wonders to give freedom to the Israelites. With preliminary skirmishes indecisive, a series of ten major engagements are listed in Exodus as coming in successive order. In each engagement Yahweh's wonders plague Egypt. None of the Torah sources mention all ten plagues. The Yahwist epic describes eight, as does Psalm 78. The priestly source adds two, the plagues of gnats and boils. The total of ten is probably an idealization of the completeness of the divine signs and wonders Yahweh brought against Egypt. Psalm 105 also lists this completeness of wonders but in a different order. Whatever their number, the account of the plagues maintains suspense in the narrative, but still the reader knows the final outcome.

With dramatic fullness, the narrative pictures Yahweh's total victory over the pharaoh and Egypt. Yahweh's victory is won through "signs and wonders." Most of the plagues parallel natural phenomena common in Egypt. Seven of the ten plagues can be related to phenomena associated with the annual rise of the Nile. A reddening of the Nile is caused by minute organic life when the river nears its crest in August. Great numbers of frogs prevail in the autumn, usually in September. G. E. Wright notes that plagues would occur more often were it not for the ibis, a bird that feeds on vermin. Decomposing dead frogs suggest lice and flies, followed in turn by pestilence suffered by cattle and humans. Natural explanations have also been suggested for other of the "wonders." Thunderstorms, although not common, occasionally do great damage

---

[23]Mircea Eliade has written much about the distinctions between "cosmos," the ordered and meaning-filled world, and "chaos," the nonworld of emptiness, disorder, and no meaning. See his *The Sacred and the Profane* and *Cosmos and History*.

[24]Pritchard, *Texts*, p. 326.

in the region, as do plagues of locusts. The *khamsin*, a hot, spring wind, resembles the dust or sandstorm in the "darkness to be felt" (10:21). The connection between "wonders" and natural events is the key to the meaning of the contest. If Egyptian gods are superior anywhere, would it not be in the control of the annual Nile overflow? No, even here Israel's God is supreme.

Here and elsewhere in the Hebrew Bible miracle is not necessarily "supernatural."[25] It is erroneous to transpose the twentieth-century mind-set, which confines miracle to the realm of the supernatural, to the Hebrew mind-set. In the Hebrew Bible, miracle refers to the marvel of Yahweh's power in pursuit of the cause of the Israelite people. Inasmuch as both nature and history are the domain of Yahweh's mighty deeds, miracle does not require the breaking of natural law. Miracle is Yahweh's continual working in the history of the people, apprehended by faith:

> I hereby make a covenant. Before all your people I will perform *marvels*, such as have not been performed in all the earth or in any nation; and all the people among whom you live shall see the work of Yahweh; for it is an awesome thing that I will do with you. [Exodus 34:10]

With this orientation the mind of faith could see in even ordinary events the hand of Yahweh. Interpretation given by faith could lift such events out of the realm of the commonplace and see them as the redemptive deeds of Yahweh. Indeed, faith itself is the fundamental miracle. The Hebrew Bible relates miracles especially to those periods of crisis when Israel was intently aware of God's action in its behalf. Such times were the exodus, the period of the dawn of the prophetic movement, the age of intense conflict with Canaanite religion, and the Babylonian exile. In all events the mark of the miracle was not its "miraculous" character, but its revelation of Yahweh, who wondrously and intently worked with the people.

This granted, that the plagues had natural parallels was not foremost in the mind of the narrator, or the minds of the hearers or readers of his story. For them these wonders were unquestionably the extraordinary acts of Yahweh in overcoming Egyptian gods in their own territory. Other ancient literature of the Near East and the epics of Greece and Rome, such as the Iliad, Odyssey and Aeneid, describe gods as acting similarly. Natural explanation of the divine acts interprets them in a way that is foreign to the ancient writers and readers. Notice that the narrator attributes each event not to a causal sequence but to Yahweh's action. The natural parallels underscore the magnificence of Yahweh's wonders; Yahweh controls the divine forces of nature. Yahweh also controls the pharaoh's reluctance to allow the Israelites to leave Egypt: "When you go back to Egypt, see that you perform before Pharaoh all the wonders

---

[25]See Harold Songer's article on "Miracle" in the *Mercer Dictionary of the Bible*, 577–79. Also note the bibliography on miracle in Suggestions for Further Study at the end of this chapter.

that I have put in your power; but I will harden his heart, so that he will not let the people go" (4:21; cf. 7:3; 14:4; 17).

The pharaoh's divine powers are so under Yahweh's control that he is not even responsible for his own stubborn resistance. Although awed by the first nine plagues, he refuses to release the Israelites. Only the terrible plague of death of the firstborn children of the Egyptians, including the pharaoh's son, persuades the Egyptians to let Israel go.

The story of the plagues, especially the last one, is inseparably connected with Israel's observance of Passover. This feast, originally a spring nature festival related to the birth of the new flocks of sheep and goats, was transformed into a holy remembrance of Israel's redemption by Yahweh. The exodus traditions, as already noted, were shaped and passed on in the context of this important festival. The symbolism and story of the feast recalled the ominous last night in Egypt, the visit of the angel of death, and the crossing of the Sea of Reeds. The exciting and terrible story of the plagues was recited "repeatedly in the households of the Israelites, used in instructing the young . . . and in the songs and prayers and lamentations of individuals, groups, and the whole community."[26] In this sense it was a true "folktale" expressing faith in Yahweh the redeemer:

> And you shall tell your child on that day, "It is because of what Yahweh did for me when I came out of Egypt." It shall serve for you as a sign on your hand and as a reminder on your forehead, so that the teaching of Yahweh may be on your lips; for with a strong hand Yahweh has brought you out of Egypt. You shall keep this ordinance at its proper time from year to year [13:8–10].

When the Passover meal was eaten, it was explained to the young as "the passover sacrifice to Yahweh, for he passed over the houses of the people of Israel in Egypt, when he struck down the Egyptians but spared our houses" (12:27). The festival of unleavened bread, which is closely associated with the Passover, is traced back to the time when the Israelites hurriedly left Egypt without time for their dough to be leavened (12:34, 39). They explained this custom to their children, saying: "It is because of what Yahweh did *for me* when I came out of Egypt" (13:8).

THE VICTORY AT AND OVER THE SEA (14:1–15:21). The story of exodus and covenant moves from crisis to crisis. When Yahweh's victory seemed certain and Israel's deliverance sure, a new danger appeared. The pharaoh changed his mind and sent chariots to recapture his slaves; and the fleeing Israelites were cut off by the sea. The waters involved were probably the marshy lakes in the area through which the Suez Canal now passes, rather than the Gulf of Suez, the northwestern arm of the Red Sea. As we have earlier noted, in the Hebrew text the "sea" is called *yam suph*, which translated literally

---

[26]Harrelson, *Interpreting*, p. 83.

means "sea of reeds." Moses certainly would not have led Israel across the Gulf of Suez; the danger in the marshy lakes was real enough. The Israelites panic and complain:

> Was it because there were no graves in Egypt that you have taken us away to die in the wilderness? What have you done to us, bringing us out of Egypt? Is this not the very thing I told you in Egypt, "Let us alone and let us serve the Egyptians." For it would have been better for us to serve the Egyptians than to die in the wilderness [14:11–12].

This is the first of many complaints the Israelites will make during their time in the wilderness. Moses reassures them and Yahweh leads them safely through the waters that engulf the pursuing Egyptian chariots. The description of the waters driven back by an east wind and piled up like a wall on either side of the Israelites is often interpreted as evidence here of two sources, the latter description being attributed to the priestly tradition. This explanation overlooks the narrative's enthusiasm for Yahweh's miraculous play with the pharaoh.

With literary excess, the storyteller writes of a wind unlike any other wind. In Homer's *Odyssey* when the winds captured in a bag given to Odysseus by Aiolos are freed, they drive Odysseus's ships into danger. Here, too, the description of winds is not intended to be logical, but poetically powerful. What seems to Israel to be a grave danger is only a stratagem used by Yahweh to make sport of the pharaoh. Yahweh tells Moses to lead the Israelites to encamp by the sea (14:2) so that the pharaoh will believe them trapped, and when he follows them Yahweh will act: "I will harden Pharaoh's heart, and he will pursue them, so that I will gain glory for myself over Pharaoh and all his army; and the Egyptians shall know that I am Yahweh" (14:4). The pharaoh who claimed not to know Yahweh learns who Yahweh is in the terrible events of the plagues and in the destructive wonder of the sea. The divine king of Egypt who toyed with Israel and made them slaves is finally now a toy in Yahweh's victorious hands.

This victory is also a victory *over the sea* and, as such, is also a cosmic victory. The sea is symbolic of the sinister, threatening, primordial waters of chaos— the foreboding, covered deep of Genesis 1:2. The sea thus represents a threat to Yahweh's creative and redemptive purposes for and through the people of Israel. However, Yahweh overcomes it here as in the beginning, using it now to destroy the other forces of chaos threatening the people. The pharaoh's powers, by which he intended to swallow up Israel in Egyptian slavery, are swallowed up in the sea. Neither the pharaoh nor cosmic sea can stay what Yahweh is doing. We hear no more of the pharaoh, and Israel sings of Yahweh's victory: "Sing to Yahweh, for he has triumphed gloriously; horse and rider he has thrown into the sea" (15:21).

The longer triumph song in 15:1–18, which presupposes the later entrance of Israel into Canaan (15:13–15), is a later cultic hymn based on the earlier song of Miriam. With songs like this Israel in worship celebrated its deliverance from Egyptian bondage.[27] In the centuries following their emancipation, the Israelites looked back on the exodus and conquest as Yahweh's doing. Yahweh was operative in the entire event and associated with its every particular. Although Moses and Aaron were attendants, Yahweh gave birth to the nation. No moment in all the nation's history was to be compared to that moment and this mighty act of Yahweh was the dramatic proclamation of concern for Israel. The Babylonian Talmud emphasized the continuing meaning of the event: "In every generation a man is bound to regard himself as though he personally had gone forth from Egypt."[28]

THE COVENANT AT SINAI. The narrative of Yahweh's redeeming wonders reaches its climax and denouement at Sinai in an awesome ceremony. The holy mountain is surrounded with thick clouds and smoke, resounds with thunder and trumpet blasts, and is illuminated by flashes of lightning. Together these represent the powerful presence of Yahweh, who will now make known to Israel what is the appropriate response for a redeemed people. In this impressive setting Israel, led and represented by Moses, accepts a covenant relationship with God. Yahweh here repeats the promise made to the patriarchs that Israel will be a blessing people, but here the promise is made more explicit: "You shall be my treasured possession out of all peoples. Indeed the whole earth is mine, and you shall be for me a priestly kingdom and a holy nation" (19:5b–6a).

This, in a way, says it all. Israel is to be Yahweh's personal property with a vocation to reveal Yahweh to the nations. Yahweh's sovereignty is universal, "the whole earth is mine." Yahweh's covenant with Israel will make it a servant people, "a priestly kingdom"—that is, a community that both speaks for humankind to God and for God to humankind. Acceptance of Yahweh's covenant will bind Israel to God for both blessing and terrible responsibility.

The ceremony of covenant making is a ceremony of awesome splendor and utmost seriousness. As Moses earlier had approached the burning bush with shoes removed, now all Israel gathers at the foot of the moving and shaking mountain of Yahweh's presence with reverence, respect, and awesome wonder, with a sense of holy fear. The Israelites dare not come casually into the presence of the holy and majestic God. They come to worship Yahweh, an attitude characteristically expressed by a Hebrew word that means "to bow down in the presence of."

Before the actual ceremony of covenant making, Yahweh recalls the saving deeds of the past, and summons Israel to obedience: "You have seen what I did to the Egyptians, and how I bore you on eagles' wings and brought you to

---

[27]Cf. Psalm 78.
[28]Epstein, "Seder Mo'ed, Paschim," *Talmud*, p. 595.

myself. Now therefore, if you will obey my voice and keep my covenant . . . ."
(19:4–5a).

In this awesome setting Yahweh's covenant requirements are clearly stated
in ten absolute commandments stating human responsibility to God and to
other humans. Israel agrees to obey these commandments and the covenant is
sealed by solemn symbolic actions. Sacrifices bind the people to Yahweh in
communion, and blood is poured on the altar and on the people. This blood
symbolizes life, the life of God pledged to Israel and the life of Israel pledged
to God. Israel thus has been created as God's new humanity that understands
human freedom as a divine gift, enabling it to be God's servant people with a
redemptive mission to all humankind.

Symbolism in the Exodus and Covenant Story.   Several things in this narrative
can profitably be understood as symbols enriching its theological meanings.
Together these symbols focus readers' attention on the alternative possibilities
open to the Israelites and by extension to all humanity. First, consider Egypt
itself. As in the Joseph story, Egypt is a place of danger and exile, a chaos in
which Israel's very being may be destroyed by death. The Israelites there seem
to be subject to hostile divine powers before whom they are helpless slaves.
Yet clever midwives outsmart the divine pharaoh and Moses' mother challenges the divine river by trusting her son to its waters in a fragile basket-boat.
From this danger Moses is rescued by the pharaoh's daughter to be raised as
her son, a status that will put him in position to champion the cause of his
people and lead it to freedom. Therefore, instead of being the place of Israel's
death, Egypt becomes a place of its discovery of God's character as Yahweh,
the God of the oppressed. Egypt is the chaotic womb into which young, im-
mature Israel descends to emerge as an adult community reborn to a clearer
understanding of God and God's purposes for Israel.

Similarly the wilderness is a place of danger, but also of Moses' maturation.
After killing the Egyptian, he flees to an alien land. How many exiles are lost
forever in the dangerous wilderness? Yet, there Moses meets God as Yahweh
to discover his own true role in life not as an Egyptian prince, but as the
spokesman of Yahweh who will challenge the oppressor of his people and eventually lead it to freedom. Egypt and wilderness, both places of chaotic danger,
are instead places where the possibilities of God's future are recognized and
accepted.

Consider also Moses' rod. We are told that this rod is a sign of God's presence and power (4:1–8). The rod is a traditional symbol of power as in Psalm
23, "Your rod and your staff—they comfort me." The rod represents two
universal figures, the shepherd and the wizard who controls natural forces for
his own ends. Because Moses is acting as God's representative, these dual roles
suggest "a certain doubleness in the Israelites' perception of God. God is a
shepherd as in the reassuring Psalm; but he is also mysterious and inscrutable

in his ways and fearsome in his power."[29] The author of this story is suggesting that the God who protects and delivers Israel is a great and fearsome deity, both to the Egyptians and to Israel.

A more complex pattern of literary and theological symbolism is the symbolism of water and blood. Water as a symbol is often associated with birth. In the exodus story water is associated with two symbolic births. Moses is taken out of the Nile waters by the pharaoh's daughter, and this represents a new birth for him. The pharaoh had threatened his life, along with those of other young male Israelites: "Every boy that is born to the Hebrews you shall throw into the Nile" (1:22). For Moses though—and the reader would have understood that this was through divine providence—the waters of death become the waters of new life. Moses will survive to adulthood. Later, in a parallel passage, all Israel is driven by the pharaoh into the deadly waters of the sea from which Yahweh delivers it as a great and free people; and, in a great reversal, those who would have destroyed Israel perish in the same waters.

Like water, blood symbolizes both death and life in the exodus story. When Moses turns the water of the Nile into blood, the blood represents destruction and death. This plague "seems to be an indication that where men resist God, water loses its proper function of cleansing and restoring. . . . Water that represents the principle of life is corrupted and becomes an emblem of death."[30] Blood also represents deliverance and life. By the blood of the passover sacrifice, Israel is protected from the plague of death, and blood poured on the altar at Sinai and over the people assembled there binds Yahweh and Israel in covenant commitment. This commitment is the guarantee of Israel's future life.

The name of Moses is also symbolic. As an Egyptian name, which it must have been originally, it means "son" and was sometimes joined with names of deities, as in the names of the pharaohs Ahmose and Thutmose. The author of Exodus, however, was an Israelite and has the pharaoh's daughter give an incorrect Hebrew explanation of the name, "She named him Moses (*Mosheh*), because," she said, "I drew (*Masheh*) him out of the water" (2:10b). *Mosheh* is not the passive participle of the verb "to draw out." It is the active participle, "the one who draws out." Thus with a certain humorous irony, the pharaoh's daughter unwittingly anticipates the child's destiny. He becomes the man who will draw his people out of bondage.[31]

These symbols, of universal character, support the theme of Yahweh's powerful deliverance of Israel as a creative act. With skillful literary artistry the Hebrew story preserves the basic conviction that Yahweh is the primary actor in exodus and that Israel must respond to Yahweh's mighty deed with gratitude and responsibility.

---

[29]William E. Rogers, unpublished lecture. The whole discussion of symbolism here is influenced by the provocative interpretations of Professor Rogers, as are other parts of our literary analysis.

[30]Ibid.

[31]Ackerman, "Literary Context," in Gros Louis, *Interpretation*, p. 78.

Figure 5.7. Sandstone relief from Kumma Fort along the Nile depicting Thutmose II of the eighteenth Egyptian dynasty making offerings to the god Knum, lord of the cataracts. The name "Moses" is sometimes associated with the pharoahs named "Thutmose" and "Ahmose," names meaning son of Thut or Ah. The omission of the deity prefix is then taken to separate Moses the man from the Egyptian divinity tradition. (Courtesy Fine Arts Museum, Boston)

COVENANT AT SINAI: ISRAEL'S APPROPRIATE RESPONSE
(EXODUS 19:1–25:31; LEVITICUS 1–5, 23)

The covenant expressed at Sinai is the foundational bond between Yahweh and Israel. In the Sinai commitment the people responded to Yahweh's initiative by forming a covenant community. Loyalty to Sinai covenant was not always universal and, during the Hebrew monarchy, did not enjoy primary status. Nonetheless the covenant established at Sinai became the norm by which Israel defined itself. In affirming the covenant Israel began to move toward the theocratic nation that Yahweh intended. This was indeed its appropriate response to what Yahweh had done in leading the people out of Egypt.

The Sinai Covenant In Near Eastern Context

The form of the Sinai covenant as it appears in the Deuteronomic story resembles Hittite suzerainty-vassal treaties of the fourteenth and thirteenth centuries

B.C.E. and Assyrian treaties of the seventh and sixth centuries B.C.E.[32] There were six essential elements in the Hittite treaties imposed by great Hittite kings (suzerains) on vassal states:

1. Preamble. The great king gives his name and the titles of his sovereignty.
2. Historical prologue. The suzerian rehearses the historical basis for the treaty, especially deeds of benevolence on behalf of the vassal. Thus the vassal's motive for obligation is gratitude.
3. Stipulations imposed on the vassal. The vassal must take a loyalty oath, vowing to come to the aid of the king in time of war.
4. Preservation and public proclamation of the covenant. Copies of the treaty are to be preserved in the temples of both countries, and it is to be read publicly in the vassal state once a year.
5. Witnesses to the treaty. Gods of both countries are invoked as witnesses with precedence given to the Hittite gods. Other witnesses are natural powers such as heaven and earth, winds and clouds, mountains and rivers.
6. Sanctions. Blessings will result from obedience to the treaty, but curses will fall upon the vassal if it is unfaithful.

The Sinai covenant has a preamble, "I am Yahweh your God," without titles. Israel is usually restrained in its references to God; it is enough to say that its God is Yahweh. The historical prologue is equally brief and to the point, "who brought you out of the land of Egypt, out of the house of slavery." That alone merited Israel's gratitude and justified the covenant stipulations stated in the decalogue. The stipulations were preserved and read publicly to the people. Other elements of suzerainty treaties are absent from the Sinai covenant, and the latter contains some additional features: the dramatic disclosure of Yahweh in the cloud, smoke, thunder, and trumpet blasts and the bloody ceremony of the sealing of the covenant. Hence, direct relationship between Israel's covenant and Hittite treaties cannot be proven, but they do belong to the same general pattern of covenant making. Yahweh, therefore, may be understood as bestowing self-revelation on Israel in patterns with which it may have been familiar.

The Yahweh of Israel's covenant is its great king and more. This covenant was not a covenant of equals. The atmosphere of Sinai indicates a clear distinction between the people and its God. The people could come into Yahweh's presence only after acts of purification. Smoke, noise, and quakings like a volcanic eruption, accompanied by an earthquake, symbolized Yahweh's otherness, holiness, and revelation. Such a deity rightly demanded obedience. The Yahweh of Israel's covenant is also the great king and *less*. This great king, with more power than Pharaoh, is the helping, saving father. The Israelites are God's children (Deuteronomy 14:1; 32:9–12, 18). Israel is God's firstborn son (Exodus 4:22). The stipulations of the covenant are Torah, fatherly instruction

---

[32]See G. E. Mendenhall, *Law and Covenant* and McCarthy, *Covenant*. For a critique of Mendenhall's view, see Gottwald, *Bible*, pp. 202–7.

(Deuteronomy 31:25–26). The patriarchal sense of family piety is here still influential on the fundamental charter of Israel's religious faith.

If Israel was to be Yahweh's people, it had to take upon itself the sacred obligations of covenant. As Yahweh's people, it correctly responded to divine redemptive activity by pledging obedience to Yahweh's covenant and law. Thus the tensions inherent throughout the story of the exodus are resolved in a covenant agreement between Yahweh and the people Yahweh had rescued from bondage. Such a resolution by its very nature, however, created new dimensions of responsibility in the ongoing life of the Israelite community. To be responsible to the great king of power is awesome, and to be a member of the family of God is a demanding privilege. Like primeval stories of the creation of the world, this story of the creation of Israel is followed by accounts of human failures and divine acts of deliverance.

The Meaning of the Covenant

Yahweh's covenant with Israel included both what Yahweh had done and Israel's appropriate response. It had been initiated by Yahweh's mighty act of deliverance, and Yahweh provided covenant law, the vehicle for faithfulness. But Israel was not forced to agree to the covenant. Its proper response would be an act of gratitude and faith. Covenant was sustained by Yahweh's continuing actions on behalf of the people, and each generation was to renew its grateful response to covenant demands.

The essence of Yahweh's covenant demands on Israel is found in the Ten Commandments or, as the Hebrews called them, "the Ten Words" (in Greek, *dekalogos*). The Ten Commandments, or decalogue, are the basic statements of Mosaic law.[33] Here are found the ethical claims that Yahweh as a God of holiness makes on the chosen people. The covenant relationship was grounded in ethical obedience to Yahweh. The first four commandments clarify specific obligations of the covenanter toward Yahweh. The last six deal with responsibility toward other persons.

The commandments concerned with Israel's relationship with God focus on the responsibilities of human beings to a deity who is believed to be both creator and redeemer.

1. *"You shall have no other Gods before me."* Yahweh here makes an absolute claim on Israel. Yahweh is a God without limits and therefore without rivals. This is not a formal monotheistic claim; there may be other Gods, but not for Israel. Israel's experience has not yet stripped its world of all deities, but it understands clearly that Yahweh alone is its covenant God. Later it will learn to call all other gods no gods at all.

---

[33]The basic decalogue is found in Exodus 20:1–17 and Deuteronomy 5:6–21. There is also a ritual decalogue in Exodus 34.

2. *"You shall not make for yourself an idol."* This commandment points up the inherent risk involved in using images to think of deity. God cannot readily be conceived as a pure abstraction; for us, God is always imaged in some way. Even the word "God" is an image and for most persons triggers mental pictures, such as a bearded old man, which may be made into an object of worship. Whatever the image, it can never encompass the full meaning of deity. Even the use of "he" limits God to specific times and cultures. The commandment is a reminder that images, as necessary as they may be, are not divine in themselves. They are only "mirrors" in which the sacred is revealed "through a glass darkly." Israel is to avoid idol making, choosing rather to comprehend God through God's own self-disclosure in nature, God's actions in history as in the exodus, and significantly in Israel itself.[34] Israel, therefore, must be an image of God rather than a maker of idols.

3. *"You shall not make wrongful use of the name of Yahweh your God."* Because "name" represents the essence of God's being, as discussed earlier, the commandment here has to do with God's personhood, not words that are taboo. "In vain" here means "for nothingness," "for any trivial purpose." This commandment prohibits treating God as unimportant and insignificant by using the divine name as a magic power for any purpose, by blasphemous usage, or by taking God lightly in any way.

4. *"Remember the Sabbath Day, and keep it holy."* A holy day is a day "set apart." The basic meaning of "holy," in biblical language, is "to be different from." The Sabbath day is to be "set apart" to God in worship and rest.

The decalogue also addresses the second "table" of Israel's ethical concerns—namely, relationships between persons. For Israel the testing ground for one's relationship with God was one's relationship to neighbors. Hence its legal system addressed matters basic to individual and social responsibility.

5. *"Honor your father and your mother."* Here the concern includes but reaches beyond honor for parents as beloved relatives. Respect for authority is necessary for the stability of society, "that your days may be long in the land." The survival of both the individual and the community requires order and respect. Further, honor for parents is honor for God and God's commandments. Parents are those who transmit God's gifts of life and law. Thus, when persons honor their parents, they honor God as parent, both father and mother. Yahweh is not just sovereign deliverer and judge; Yahweh is also the loving parent.

6. *"You shall not murder."* Life is given by God, belongs to God, and is therefore sacred. Israel did not apply this restriction to the slaying of animals, capital punishment, or killing in war. Nonetheless, the commandment itself implies a broad reverence for life itself. Although humans, both ancient and modern, may have difficulty with its broader implementation, the law serves

---

[34]Harrelson, *Commandments*, p. 66.

as a standard by which any act of killing is to be called into question and judged.[35]

7. *"You shall not commit adultery."* Here, too, the practice of Israel limited the application of this commandment. An engaged or married woman committed adultery if she had sexual relations with anyone except her husband-to-be or her husband. A man committed adultery only if he had relations with the betrothed or wife of another man. In practice, men, therefore, had more sexual freedom than did women. But the principle is broader than the application Israel made of it. The marital relationship is sacred and this sacredness is threatened by sexual promiscuity.

8. *"You shall not steal"* is a direct prohibition of theft. Goods are an extension of one's self, of one's family. In a poor and often marginal economy like that of ancient Israel, property virtually amounted to life itself and hence had to be respected. Yet persons are always to be put ahead of property; the commandment must not be used to justify a particular economic system.

9. *"You shall not bear false witness against your neighbor"* is a commandment that protects the basic right of a member of the covenant community against false accusation. Specifically, lying in public testimony in court, and in social and commercial situations, is prohibited. The commandment forbids lies that threaten the integrity of any fellow human being.

10. *"You shall not covet."* The final commandment forbids the attitude that lies behind lust, theft, defamation, and murder. Covetousness is an expression of pride that gives rise to both rebellion against God and violence against one's neighbor. Basically, sin is a selfish focusing on oneself. Covenant law requires that we respect and love both God and our fellow human beings.

These two "tables" of concern in Israel's earliest ethical formulations are typical of biblical religion throughout. To Israel and later to Jesus the twofold obligation to love God with all one's being (Deuteronomy 6:5) and to love one's neighbor as oneself (Leviticus 19:18) remained the summary of the law.

Clearly, then, covenant bound the chosen people to Yahweh in a solemn relationship of obligation and obedience. It was Israel's pledge of loyalty to the one who had first chosen and saved it. The covenant was based on what Yahweh had already done. No obligation was placed on Yahweh, who was already pledged to Israel. The initiative in the covenant was Yahweh's, and Israel had the opportunity to accept or reject Yahweh's overture. If it accepted the covenant, it bound itself to the covenant demands. If it repudiated the requirements of covenant, it in reality denied Yahweh and thereby thwarted covenant. If Israel was not obedient to the divine will that ruled it, no real covenant relationship could exist.

Israel's initial response to Yahweh's demands was dramatic and enthusiastic: "Moses came and told the people all the words of Yahweh and all the ordi-

---

[35]Ibid. p. 115.

nances; and all the people answered with one voice, and said, 'All the words which Yahweh has spoken we will do' '' (Exodus 24:3). The people were ritually bound to this response in an awesome ceremony of sacrifices and sprinkling of blood. Blood as a symbol of life was sprinkled on the altar and over the people, an act to be experienced with utmost solemnity and dedication. This awesome ritual was followed by another ceremony in which Moses and Aaron and other leaders of the people approached the holy place and "saw the God of Israel" as an approachable deity with whom "they ate and drank" (Exodus 24:9–11). The ratification ceremony thus ends in a ritual of family fellowship. Yahweh and the people of Israel are bound together by blood, life is given to life, and Israel is now the people of Yahweh, the great God of power who is also the loving, helping father.

Of course, such serious commitments cannot be fully sustained by initial emotional enthusiasms, no matter how moving and sincere they may be. Obedience and loyalty to Yahweh could not automatically pass from father to son, and so the covenant had to be renewed by each generation. Successive covenant renewals, however, were not completely new beginnings. Every generation inherited the religious traditions and blessings that covenantal claims imposed on it. Consequently, Israel was under solemn moral obligation to renew the covenant. Not to renew would be apostasy.

History demonstrates the failure of Israel to keep the covenant and much of its later literature centers around Yahweh's attempts to win Israel back and renew Yahweh's claim on its loyalty. Again and again, Israel's story was one of judgment and salvation. Yahweh was always ready to abide by the covenant when Israel turned from evil ways, renewed its vows, and became again Yahweh's servant. Israel's response to covenant, therefore, had to be structured for its long pilgrimage as Yahweh's people. These obligations were formulated in the corpus of Israelite law and in the forms of cultic (worship) life.

Common Law

Laws governing daily life and covenant were inseparably intertwined. Such broad application indicates the seriousness with which Israel took covenant. Every member of the community was a covenant person and no activity was exempt from covenant responsibility. The nature of this responsibility was clarified by Israel in the covenant code, Exodus 20:22–23:23, a succinct ethical elaboration of the decalogue. The covenant code is an application of the fundamental principles of the Ten Commandments to specific matters of daily conduct. Each commandment is a comprehensive base on which is built a fitting superstructure of specific legislation. For example, the commandment "You shall not murder" embraces the principle of basic respect for human life. The covenant code seeks to make the principle practical by distinguishing situations in which a life is taken:

Whoever strikes a person mortally shall be put to death. If it is not premeditated, but came about by an act of God, then I will appoint for you a place to which the killer may flee. But if someone willfully attacks and kills another by treachery, you shall take the killer from my altar for execution [21:12–14].

Whereas the Ten Commandments probably came from Moses himself, the covenant code represents an accumulation of laws coming from various periods in Israel's history. Certainly parts of the covenant code suggest a later, more settled life than that of the wandering in the wilderness. Included in its instruction is legislation on altars, sacrifices, slaves, capital and noncapital crimes, property rights, social morals, the Sabbath, and feasts. The code closes with Yahweh's exhortation that Israel remain obedient.

The Israelite covenant code is young among ancient codes of law. The codes of Ur-Nammu (c. 2060 B.C.E.), Eshnunna (c. 2000 B.C.E.), Lipit Ishtar (nineteenth century B.C.E.), Hammurabi (c. 1700 B.C.E.), and the Assyrian code from the time of Tiglath-pileser I (twelfth century B.C.E.) are all older.[36] These codes, like that of Israel, ascribe their origin to the deity worshiped by the people among whom they were formulated. There probably were indirect ties between the biblical codes and their ancient Near Eastern counterparts. Israel must have utilized a common legal heritage, but no example of direct borrowing can be demonstrated. The religious concerns of the extrabiblical codes clearly are not so pronounced as those of Israel's law.

One distinction of the Israelite code is to be found in the form given to its basic laws. In the Torah two general types of law are found: conditional (or case) law, and absolute or apodictic law. Conditional law had a characteristic formula: "If . . . happens, then . . . will be the legal consequence." This type of law was found everywhere in the ancient world and was typical of all the ancient codes. Absolute law, on the other hand, was more characteristically Israelite and expressed unconditional covenant demands. There were no "ifs" involved. It was absolute and stated in categorical language. The best examples of absolute law are, of course, the individual commandments of the decalogue. Further examples are found in Deuteronomy 27 where curses are pronounced upon twelve types of violators of the covenant.

For Israel all law was rooted in the grace of God and was conceived as a special revelation, an expression of Yahweh's will. It was a Yahweh-given source of justice and security, binding on community and individual alike. Although the covenant law had been given to the community as a whole, it singled out the individual and addressed the individual directly with the divine "you shall . . . ." As a result, life in Israel assumed a meaning and dignity seldom known elsewhere in the ancient world.

[36]See Pritchard, *Archaeology*, pp. 206–27. Translations of these codes may be found in Pritchard, *Texts*.

Figure 5.8. The stele of Hammurabi inscribed with a law code dating to c. 1700 B.C.E. The scene crowning the eight-foot stele shows the Babylonian king, Hammurabi, receiving the symbols of authority from the sun god Shamash. (Courtesy, The Louvre)

Cultic Legislation

A religion may be understood on the basis of its teachings, the behavior of its adherents, and the symbols used in its worship. The decalogue expresses succinctly the foundational ethic of Israel's faith. The covenant code is concerned with justice in the practical application of this ethic in the daily behavior of the Israelite. Levitical law, so called because the Levites were the designated priests, defines the ritual practice of the worshiping community. Israel's ritual laws are found primarily in Exodus 25–31 and in the book of Leviticus, named by Israel "Yahweh called," the opening words of the book. These laws are concerned with the following issues:

In Exodus:
1. The ark and the tabernacle: chapters 25–27
2. Priestly vestments: chapter 28
3. Ordination of priests and other priestly matters: chapters 29–31

In Leviticus:
1. Laws dealing with sacrifices: chapters 1–7
2. Consecration of the priesthood: chapters 8–10
3. Distinctions between clean and unclean: chapters 11–15
4. The Day of Atonement: chapter 16
5. Laws on Israel's holiness: chapters 17–26
6. Religious vows: chapter 27

Like its judicial covenant code, Israel's ceremonial legislation emerged over a period of centuries, not attaining the form described in the final chapters of Exodus and the book of Leviticus until the time of the priestly writing in the sixth century B.C.E. Moses must have established Israel's cultic life but, at its best, worship is also characterized by spontaneity, creativity, and relevance. In coming before God Israel both repeated what was old and did new things. Therefore, a presentation of Israel's worship cannot be exhaustive or even typical of Israelite worship at any given moment in its history. Rather, it suggests certain fundamental emphases and actions.

Symbols of the Sacred: The Ordering of Space.   Worship is entering into the presence of and responding to *the sacred*. Israel believed profoundly in the sacred presence of Yahweh, the Holy One, and found security and responsibilities in Yahweh's *being with* them. The presence of Yahweh was symbolized by the ark, the tabernacle, and the temple.

THE ARK. The ark, called "the ark of Yahweh," "the ark of the covenant with Yahweh," or "the ark of the testimony," was an oblong wooden box, three and three-fourths feet long, two and one-fourth feet wide, either open or closed at the top. To the outer four corners, near the top, four rings were attached through which two shafts were passed, one on either side. Thus, the ark could be carried by two priests, one before and one behind, with the shafts resting on their shoulders. This apparatus was Yahweh's portable throne. Two cherubim, winged mythical creatures with the body of an animal and head of a man, were positioned on the top of the ark, as symbolic guardians of Yahweh's presence.

The ark symbolized the immanence of Yahweh. The holy deity, who could not be represented by a physical image, was symbolized as present with the people. Yahweh was not remote and disinterested, but near and involved. An ancient song about the ark reminded the people that the ark represented the presence of deity: "Whenever the ark set out, Moses would say, 'Arise, O Yahweh, and let your enemies be scattered; and your foes flee before you.' And when it rested, he said, 'Return, O Yahweh of the ten thousand thousands of Israel' " (Numbers 10:35–36).

Yahweh's abiding presence with the people anywhere it might go was symbolized by the prohibition against removing the carrying poles from the ark (Exodus 25:15). Wherever Israel was, there Yahweh would be also.

The ark first served as a religious symbol in the life of Israel during its wilderness days and continued to play an important role in its life during the time of the monarchy, when from David's time on it was housed in the Jerusalem sanctuary. However, its influence seems to have waned as the nation abandoned nomadic life. After the destruction of Solomon's temple in 587 B.C.E., the ark was lost from Israel's history. In postexilic synagogue worship the symbol of divine presence was the scroll of the Torah that was kept in an "ark" or sacred cabinet.

THE TABERNACLE AND TEMPLES. The ark was first kept in a "tent of meeting," or tabernacle. The tabernacle was a movable "dwelling" where Yahweh met the people. It belonged to the wilderness period, although its description probably is an elaboration from later times. It was Yahweh's tent in the center of the camp, wherever the wanderers stayed. Encamped around it, they felt the security of dwelling in a holy place. As Israel passed to the more settled conditions of postnomadic days, the mobile sanctuary became less and less meaningful. It may have been destroyed by the Philistines during the late years of the tribal confederacy, for David had to build temporary housing when he brought the ark to Jerusalem.[37] The tabernacle was later replaced by the more elaborate and imposing temple of Solomon.

The architecture of these sanctuaries focused on the presence of Yahweh, who symbolically dwelled in the Holy of Holies, the innermost part of the sanctuary. This symbolism continued that of the ark, conveying the immanence of the transcendent deity. Yahweh is present in the midst of Israel and moves with Israel wherever it goes. Josephus, the first-century C.E. Jewish historian, considered the entire sacred area to portray the earth (the court), heaven (the Holy Place), and the innermost heaven (the Holy of Holies), as interpreted from the Solomonic statement on the dedication of the temple: "But will God indeed dwell on the earth? Even heaven and the highest heaven cannot contain you, much less this house that I have built!" (1 Kings 8:27).[38] This may well also represent the ancient Israelite understanding of the sanctuary as the extension of the heavenly realm into the earthly realm for the blessing and governance of Israel.

---

[37]Cf. 2 Samuel 6:17.

[38]Josephus, *Antiquities*, III, vi, 4.

Ancient Israel wanted to live in the presence of God, in sacred space. It felt that there was a real difference between sacred space and ordinary space. Meaningful existence is possible only in sacred space, in the presence of God. Value and purpose, apart from sacred presence, are lost in disordered, unstructured chaos. Israel's concern for sacred space is clear from the beginning of Genesis with the distinction between creation (cosmos) and chaos. God intended that human beings would live in God's presence in paradise, but paradise is lost when humankind rejects God and has to survive in the chaos of broken relationships with God and with each other.

Israel's sanctuaries of every kind (simple altars, portable thrones of God, elaborate mobile tabernacles, or permanent temples) reestablished sacred space by representing divine presence. They were sacred centers where righteousness and peace reigned, and they were sources of salvation and justice. Responses to God's presence in these places guaranteed for Israel God's presence in their lives. Such places, therefore, were places of awesome wonder, profound blessing, and serious moral challenge. They were special places that helped Israel live in a "real" world of meaning and power rather than in empty chaos.

During the Israelite monarchy, the tabernacle was replaced as a symbol of Yahweh's presence by permanent cultic centers at Jerusalem in Judah, and at Dan and Bethel in Israel. In the northern sanctuaries the ark was replaced by golden calves intended as Yahweh's throne. The Israelites, however, did not restrict Yahweh's habitation to any of these sanctuaries. Yahweh dwelled among them as a creative and redeeming presence, but did not dwell in the sanctuaries as human beings "live" in one place or another. Both Yahweh's otherness and approachableness were preserved.

Sacred Days and Seasons: The Ordering of Time.	Worship in Israel was not restricted to any certain days. Burnt offerings were presented at the sanctuary daily, and the individual worshiper could present a thanksgiving offering or gift offering on any occasion. Yet there were particular times, when Israelites felt the need to approach Yahweh with special earnestness, supplication, or thanksgiving. Certain days and periods were set apart from all the rest by their holiness. These were the festival days, the fast days, and days of commemorative significance.

ANNUAL FESTIVALS. Three annual feasts are prescribed in the liturgical calendar in Exodus 23:14–17. These festivals were Passover-unleavened bread (*Pesach-Mazzoth*), the feast of weeks or firstfruits (*Shabhouth*), and the feast of ingathering or tabernacles (*Succoth*). All three were originally connected with the agricultural year. As practiced by the nations surrounding Israel, agricultural feasts recognized the manifestations of divine power in nature or the divine powers of nature itself. Behind the major festivals of the pagan world lay the conception of sympathetic magic. By imitative action persons thought they could become identified with powers of nature and thus make the powers available to meet their needs.

Two of the three major feasts of Israel early became both celebration of Yahweh's gifts in nature and anniversaries of events in which Yahweh's power in history had been manifested. In them the great events of Israel's history were brought to life in the experience of worshipers. This does not mean that history repeated itself, but that the basic historical facts of religion were experienced as real, as if worshipers were themselves present and taking part in them. In the festival they relived Yahweh's redemption revealed in historical events.

The Passover-unleavened bread festival, described in Leviticus 23:5–8, was understood as a reenactment of deliverance from Egypt. Passover itself was a one-day feast, but it came to be closely associated with a seven-day festival of unleavened bread that followed it immediately. Thus Passover was an exalted initiatory day of an eight-day celebration of deliverance from the misery of Egyptian bondage. As a whole the festival was a meaningful re-creation of that momentous night when the angel of death "passed over" the dwellings of the Israelites and Yahweh delivered them from bondage, when they "passed over" out of Egypt. This feast came to enjoy first place among the annual celebrations. Its drama, along with its warm ritual, kept alive the memory of Yahweh's supreme act in behalf of the people. In later centuries it came to have great significance for the Christian community, for during its celebration Jesus, understood by Christian believers as the Lamb of God, was crucified and later resurrected. Through these events Christians also celebrate Yahweh as redeemer.

The feast of ingathering or tabernacles (Leviticus 23:33–44) also celebrated the redemptive activity of Yahweh. During this festival, the Israelites lived in booths for seven days, rekindling the memory of their living in booths when Yahweh brought them out of the land of Egypt. This festival was a great day of thanksgiving, when the fruits of the year had been gathered, especially the harvest of the vineyards. It was also the celebration of the New Year, when, according to many scholars, Israel renewed the covenant of Sinai, reminding itself of Yahweh's goodness and its responsibilities to Yahweh.

In all primitive societies the New Year was a time of renewal when persons at worship participated in the moment of creation and in the transformation, cleansing, and renewal of their natural and social world. For Israel the New Year was this and more because not only was natural creation to be celebrated, but also Israel's own redemptive creation in exodus and covenant. As scholars reconstruct its ritual, two features dominated Israel's observance. First, Israel was to rejoice in Yahweh's presence at the sanctuary, presence as creator, victory over Israel's enemies, and judgment over the nations (see Psalms 18, 50, 68, 77, 97). Second, divine law was ceremonially presented (Deuteronomy 27). The requirements of law were proclaimed in the form of curse ritual. Those who disobeyed Yahweh's law would be judged by that law and by Israel.

In response to the presence of Yahweh, ceremonially represented, and in obedience to Yahweh's law, Israel thus renewed its pledge to deity in covenant allegiance.

The feast of weeks (Leviticus 23:15–21; also called Pentecost, for it was observed fifty days from the sheaf-waving ceremony that opened the feast of unleavened bread) was celebrated at the completion of the barley harvest. It remained an agricultural festival throughout biblical times, intended in part to ensure fertility of the soil in the year to come. This aspect of nature worship common in surrounding cultures, however, played a less significant part in Israelite worship. In the feast of weeks Israel expressed gratitude to Yahweh for the abundance of good things poured out upon it. In later Judaism the festival was made an anniversary of the giving of the law at Sinai.

FAST DAY. The Israelite ecclesiastical year also included one scheduled fast day, the Day of Atonement (Leviticus 23:26–32; Yom Kippur). Its central concern was to make atonement for the pollution of the temple and for the sin of the nation. In early Israel it was probably observed from time to time but, with the postexilic concern for sin and its removal, this day was given a fixed place in the liturgical calendar. Elaborate rituals were used to make atonement for the high priest (who officiated at the ceremonies of the day), his family, and all the people of Israel. Then the sins of the community were symbolically laid upon a goat, which was led into the wilderness, representing the removal of sin.

> In contemporary Jewish circles "Kol Nidrei," Opus 47, an 1881 composition by Bruch, is used in connection with the observance of Yom Kippur. Listen to the work to hear how the composer captures the sense of contrition. Do you hear anything of confession or forgiveness?

THE SABBATH. The Sabbath was observed from earliest times in Israel as a special day of religious, historical, and moral meaning. Exodus 20:11 gives a theological explanation for Sabbath observance by describing it as a memorial of Yahweh's rest at the completion of creation: "For in six days Yahweh made heaven and earth, the sea and all that is in them, and rested on the seventh day; therefore Yahweh blessed the seventh day and consecrated it." A historical explanation of the Sabbath is found in Deuteronomy 5:15: "Remember that you were a slave in the land of Egypt, and Yahweh your God brought you out from there with a mighty hand and an outstretched arm; therefore, Yahweh your God commanded you to keep the sabbath day." A third interpretation, in reality a corollary to the other two, is also found in Deuteronomy (5:14). The Sabbath is to be observed for humanitarian reasons: "But the seventh day is a sabbath to Yahweh your God; you shall not do any work—you, or your son, or your daughter, or your male or female slave . . . so that your male and female slave may rest as well as you." In Israel, therefore, the Sabbath was a day of profound religious and social significance.

The way the Sabbath was observed changed over the years. Throughout, however, it was a day of rejoicing in Yahweh. On this day Israelites rested from customary pursuits and celebrated Yahweh as creator in a day of joy and gladness.

The giving of historical meaning to these days of religious observance is an expression of Israel's desire to live in sacred time, by participating in sacred events. Its belief that God acted in history was not just the occasion for pious remembering of sacred times in the past. Those acts of God worth remembering were to be represented as meaningful for the present. Therefore, the rituals of the festivals, fasts, and the Sabbath enabled the worshiper *to be present at* and *to participate in* the creative and redemptive acts of Yahweh. Thus at the feast of ingathering Israel participated in God's creative time, both the time in the beginning when order was established over primeval chaos and the time of the covenant at Sinai when Yahweh created Israel as the servant people. At Passover the Israelites participated in God's redemptive time when Yahweh overcame the historical forces of chaos that threatened their lives with bondage. Every Sabbath Israel came into Yahweh's presence on a "holy day" set apart from other days. Participation in this day helped make all days sacred. Abraham Heschel says of the Sabbath that it is "the day on which we are called upon to share what is eternal in time, to turn from the world of creation to the creation of the world." He describes Israelite worship as "a religion of time aiming at the sanctification of time, [it] teaches us to be attached to holiness in time, to learn how to be attached to sacred events."[39]

Mediations of the Sacred

Priesthood. Any Israelite could commune with God. Formal worship, however, was led by priests. In the patriarchal times the head of a family or clan exercised priestly functions, as Abraham did when he built altars and offered sacrifices. As late as the time of the settlement in Canaan, ordinary Israelites still offered sacrifices at altars or high places (Judges 13:19–20), but in the central sanctuaries (all Israel sanctuaries) like Shiloh, only "levitical priests" performed the ritual. From the time of the Sinai covenant the levitical priesthood was a formal, inherited office associated with Aaron. These priests are regularly called "Levites" or "levitical priests." The word *levite* is derived from a verb meaning "to join" and is used of the priestly community as a group joined together in their concern for service to God and his causes for which they were ordained (Exodus 32:29). This priestly group is probably not to be identified with the tribe of Levi, descendants of one of Jacob's twelve sons, which for reasons we cannot determine, received no inheritance in Canaan but disappeared from history.

The levitical priests directed the worship at the central sanctuaries down to

[39]*Sabbath*, pp. 8, 10.

the time of David who, without replacing them, introduced a new priestly line originating with Zadok, who had been a priest in Jerusalem before David conquered the city. David's successor Solomon made Zadok the chief priest, and from then until the beginning of the Babylonian exile in 587 B.C.E., Zadok's line was responsible for worship in the Jerusalem temple, the most important Israelite sanctuary. The levitical priests throughout this period apparently were permitted to direct worship at local sanctuaries. Certain cities were even designated as "levitical cities," in which these priests directed the worship and were supported by the state. Late in the preexilic period Levites served in the Jerusalem temple but not as priests. They maintained order, acted as doorkeepers, and were responsible for slaying the sacrificial animals. After the exile, the Aaronic family of priests began to function alongside the Zadokites as full priests and, for all practical purposes, the two lines were united. However, by this time the two lines of priestly families had become so numerous that there was no need for them all to serve as priests at the same time, so the priests would be called on to officiate for only a short period of time each. The various responsibilities were divided so that each household had opportunity to serve in some capacity.

Late in the pre-Christian period the priesthood represented the Jerusalem aristocracy and leadership community. The high priest was, in effect, the head of government in Judea and dealt with foreign ruling powers.[40] The priests were leaders of the Sadducees, the religious "party" who controlled the Sanhedrin, a powerful religious and political council in Judea.

Although the personnel of the priesthood varied with time and circumstances, the role priests played in the worship life of Israel was vital and their influence in directing the course of Israel's history was immeasurable. No other group wielded a comparable influence. They were primarily responsible for conserving the cherished religious traditions of the nation. They provided the materials that ultimately comprised a large part of Torah. Even though they were involved in institutional forms that could easily have become devoid of significant religious content and they often received scathing denunciations from the prophets, they played a vital role in the development and preservation of Israel's faith.

Priests performed four essential services in the Israelite cultus. They were keepers of the various sanctuaries; they delivered oracles from God; they preserved, interpreted, and taught the sacred tradition; and they offered sacrifices. Priests were, therefore, mediators through whom Yahweh made the divine will known to Israel and through whom Israel approached Yahweh. They were especially set apart to represent the people before Yahweh and to minister Yahweh's demands. The priests instructed the people in "the way" (Torah) of Yahweh and tried to help the people make proper response to God's will.

---

[40]There is no certain preexilic mention of the office of high priest. If there were such an office before the exile, it was not as important as it obviously was in the later times.

Sacrifice. The most obvious means by which the Israelites worshiped Yahweh was sacrifice. The priestly writers have written in great detail about the sacrificial rites, how they were to be performed, how the cultus was organized, the proper animals to be sacrificed, and so forth. Nowhere, however, have they presented a theology of sacrifice. Although exactly what sacrifice meant to the worshiper is difficult to determine, essentially it must have represented Israel's attempt to respond to the holiness of Yahweh. There seem to have been three fundamental purposes for offering sacrifice: (1) to make a gift to Yahweh, (2) to enhance communion with Yahweh, (3) to atone for sin. No one of these ideas explains all the sacrifices and their ritual. Primitive notions may have sometimes been blended with refined religious feeling, and prescribed sacrificial customs were often followed, not because they were filled with theological meaning, but simply because they belonged to immemorial tradition. In any event, sacrifice remained the expression of Israel's response to Yahweh because it was believed to be a means of bridging the distance between sinful people and holy God.

Sacrifice, then, was the divinely given traditional mode for expressing religious sentiments. The sacrificial system in priestly theology was Yahweh's revelation, Yahweh's gift to Israel. As such it was the "prescribed form of worship, of praise, thanksgiving, communion, and especially of atonement for sin,"[41] which Yahweh accepted when performed in the proper manner and with the proper attitude. In Israel sacrifice was valid when properly performed with the proper spirit. Not sacrifice itself, but obedience in life mediated blessing and renewal to humankind. The ritual was potent only when accompanied by genuine penitence and submission. On the other hand, penitence and submission alone were not enough if sacrifice was prescribed. The faithful act of offering a sacrifice was important. Israelites could not save themselves by either penitence or sacrifice. It was Yahweh's divine power that reached down to save them at the moment when they offered themselves with their sacrifice.[42]

Several types of sacrifice were expressions of Israel's ritual approach to Yahweh.

1. *The burnt offering* (Leviticus 1:1–17; 6:8–13) was an animal sacrifice in which a whole animal was burned on the altar as "a pleasing odor to Yahweh." Before sacrificing the animal, offerers placed their hand on its head to identify themselves with it, thus symbolizing their own full consecration to Yahweh in praise and love.

2. *The peace offering* (Leviticus 3:1–17; 7:11–21) was the most common type of sacrifice. An expression of thanks for deliverance, it was consummated by a covenant meal in which the worshipers shared fellowship with one another and with Yahweh. The blood, fat parts, and internal organs of the sacrificial animal

---

[41]G. Ernest Wright, *The Old Testament Against Its Environment* (S.C.M., 1950) p. 104.

[42]The substance of this paragraph comes from H. H. Rowley, *The Rediscovery of the Old Testament* (Westminister, 1946), pp. 161–63.

(symbolizing its life) were burned on the altar to Yahweh. The remainder of the animal was eaten by the worshipers who thus felt that they were guests at Yahweh's table, or better, that Yahweh was a guest at theirs.

3. *The sin offering* (Leviticus 4:1–5:13; 6:24) and the guilt offering (Leviticus 5:15–6:7; 7:1–10) were sacrifices made for unintentional or inadvertent violations of the holiness of Yahweh. Deliberate sin was not covered by the sacrificial system at all. It is a mistake, therefore, to suppose that Israel made light of sin, imagining that it could be counteracted by sacrifice. In the sin and guilt sacrifices there was an emphasis on the blood, the life of the sacrificed animal (Genesis 9:4). This release of life was the necessary condition for forgiveness of sin, but only if it truly symbolized the dedication and renewal of the worshiper's own life.

4. *The tribute or gift offering* (Leviticus 2:1–16; 6:14–23) was a cereal offering, which normally accompanied a burnt offering or a peace offering. Cereal was offered cooked without incense or uncooked with incense. Thus it was presented as a sweet savor to Yahweh, a "memorial" that represented the offering of worshipers themselves. As they presented their cereal offering, Israelites gave themselves to Yahweh.

Many other kinds of sacrifices were offered in ancient Israel, as well as other means of worship, such as private prayer and liturgical participation in song. These occupied a more definite place in worship in the later history of Israel than in the early days, but they played some role from the very beginning. Many of the psalms were sung in connection with worship and others were originally private prayers of individual worshipers, adopted as prayers for public use.

Significance of the Cultus

The cultus is to be appreciated for what it represented to Israel. The ceremonials of the people were art forms of worship and, as such, embodied the basic religious values of the worshiping community. Contemporary readers may discount the crude and unsophisticated nature of some of these early cultic patterns, but the real meaning they had for those who practiced them must be acknowledged.

The attraction and heart of the Israelite cultus was the holiness of Yahweh. When Israelites spoke of worship, they used words expressive of their attitude toward such a God. They "presented themselves" before the Holy One; they "bowed down" in God's presence; they entered into God's service. Yahweh, the awe-inspiring, unapproachable God of Israel, could be approached in acceptable worship. Acceptable worship and life is defined in Leviticus 17–26, the code of holiness. Even as Yahweh is holy, Israel must be a holy people. "You shall be holy to me; for I Yahweh am holy, and I have separated you from the other peoples to be mine." (Leviticus 20:26). To Israel, then, cultus expressed its "set-apartness" to the holy Yahweh. In ceremonial practice Israel maintained the covenant responsibilities to the *sacred* who had selected it.

Israelite worship reflects a number of motifs. The memory of momentous events recalled the might of Yahweh and Yahweh's works. The sense of sin and personal responsibility for it was expressed in actions of cleansing. Contrition and confession were epitomized in tangible petitions for Yahweh's forgiveness. There was joy and thanksgiving because of the goodness of Yahweh, who had been gracious to Israel in history and in nature. Israel's worship, therefore, was the covenant people's celebration of Yahweh as the redeemer and sustainer of those who had been chosen to be members of God's people. Consequently, even though cultus was often far from pure and was sometimes abused, it was an effective means of worshiping God.

OTHER THEOLOGICAL CONCERNS IN THE EXODUS AND COVENANT NARRATIVES

As we have noted, much of the theological emphasis in the exodus and covenant materials is woven into the literary character of the narrative. The idea of Yahweh as the champion of Israel's cause and the maker of covenant relationships is basic to the materials. Israel's solemn obligation is to respond, in faith and grateful obedience, to Yahweh's mighty deeds. However, additional theological themes undergird the narrative and demand the reader's attention.

Yahweh, the God of the Oppressed

In the exodus story Yahweh identifies with enslaved Israelites. Their God had seen their misery and *knew* their suffering. Accordingly, he had delivered them from Egyptian taskmasters (Exodus 3:7–8).

The Hebrew verb "to know" implies an intimate relationship with the object of the knowledge. Yahweh feels empathy with the people. Yahweh takes the side of the poor Israelites in bondage against the prominent, prosperous, and powerful Egyptians. This experience of God's concern for their cause lay the foundation of Israel's ethics of justice and mercy. It lies behind the Ten Commandments. In one version of the commandment to keep the Sabbath holy Israelites are admonished to remember that they were slaves in the land of Egypt (Deuteronomy 5:15) and, in remembering, identify with others, who were to be objects of their humane action.

Faith in Yahweh as the deliverer from oppression became part of the classic Israelite confession of faith:

> When the Egyptians treated us harshly and afflicted us, by imposing hard labor on us, we cried to Yahweh the God of our ancestors; and Yahweh heard our

voice, and saw our affliction, our toil, and our oppression. Yahweh brought us out of Egypt with a mighty hand and an outstretched arm, with a terrifying display of power, and with signs and wonders [Deuteronomy 26:6–8].

The protection of the underprivileged is the inspiration behind Nathan's judgment of David in the Bathsheba and Uriah incidents (2 Samuel 12:1–24) and also Elijah's brave stand against Ahab and Jezebel in the cause of poor, betrayed Naboth (1 Kings 21:1–29) and his kind help to the poor widow of Zarephath (outside Israel) who had no food for herself and her son (1 Kings 17:8–16). The great prophets Amos, Hosea, Micah, Isaiah, and Jeremiah repeatedly champion the cause of the needy, condemning social injustice with scathing words:

> Thus says Yahweh:
> "For three transgressions of Israel,
>   and for four, I will not revoke the punishment;
> Because they sell the righteous for silver,
>   and the needy for a pair of sandals—
> they who trample the head of the poor
>   into the dust of the earth,
> and push the afflicted out of the way; . . ."
>   [Amos 2:6–7a]

Yahweh's concern for the oppressed, finally, is in the background of Israel's finest sense of its mission in history:

> Here is my servant, whom I uphold,
>   my chosen, in whom my soul delights;
> I have put my spirit upon him;
>   he will bring forth justice to the nations.
> He will not cry or lift up his voice,
>   or make it heard in the street;
> a bruised reed he will not break,
>   and a dimly burning wick he will not quench;
>   he will faithfully bring forth justice.
> He will not grow faint or be crushed
>   until he has established justice in the earth;
>   and the coastlands wait for his teaching.
>   [Isaiah 42:1–4]

Israel as God's people in the world must share God's feelings for and mission to the oppressed. A twentieth-century C.E. rabbi sums up brilliantly the attitude in its extension to contemporary humankind:

God is the Power working within individuals and peoples that will not permit them to acquiesce in servitude, their own or that of others. He is the spark that kindles them into rebellion and the iron that makes them stubborn for freedom's sake. And simultaneously He hardens the heart of tyrants, until lost to reason, incapable of either learning or forgetting, they destroy themselves.

Of God's emancipations all peoples have had experience, but Israel especially, most particularly when it was brought forth from Egypt by a mighty hand and an outstretched arm. Wherefore the Exodus is to Jews, as indeed to much of mankind, the classic instance of liberation; a proof that, since God *is*, every bondage, political, economic, or spiritual, can be and someday will be broken.[43]

Election to Service

For Israelite faith, the covenant at Sinai brought to a climax the selective activity of God that Israel traced back to the call of Abraham. In its patriarchal ancestors Israel believed it had been chosen to be Yahweh's peculiar people through whom God would bless all humankind:

> But you, Israel, my servant,
>> Jacob, whom I have chosen,
>> the offspring of Abraham, my friend;
> You whom I took from the ends of the earth,
>> and called from its farthest corners,
> saying to you, "You are my servant,
>> I have chosen you and not cast you off; . . ."
>> [Isaiah 41:8–9]

Deliverence from Egyptian bondage was understood as the wonder-filled fulfillment of promises made to Abraham, Isaac, and Jacob: "It was because Yahweh loved you and kept the oath that he swore to your ancestors, that Yahweh has brought you out with a mighty hand, and redeemed you from the house of slavery, from the hand of Pharaoh king of Egypt" (Deuteronomy 7:8). At Sinai Israel accepted the responsibilities of being the people of Yahweh, a most serious commitment.

This sense of election lay at the heart of Israel's self-understanding. It existed only because Yahweh had chosen it from among the nations and had redeemed it from Egyptian bondage. In itself it was nothing, but through elective grace became a special people. This relationship was expressed in later literature by the figures of Yahweh's wife (Hosea 2:19–20; Jeremiah 2:1–7; Ezekiel 16 and 23), Yahweh's firstborn son (Exodus 4:22), and Yahweh's inheritance (Exodus 34:9; 1 Samuel 10:1; Psalm 28:9). Israel had no inherent greatness that caused Yahweh to choose it; its greatness lay only in the fact that Yahweh had chosen it. Both existence and worth were owed to the redemptive activity of a sovereign God, who made Israel God's own people.

Israel often forgot that Yahweh had chosen it for service and not for privilege. Its only privilege was to serve Yahweh. It had been singled out not just to receive a blessing, but also to be one, and failure to do so would necessitate its rejection.

---

[43]Steinberg, *Judaism*, pp. 48 49.

IN THE WILDERNESS
(EXODUS 16:22–18:27; NUMBERS 11–14; 20–24; 27)

The tradition about Israel's stay in the wilderness is an interesting one although it is not as dramatic as the traditions about exodus and covenant. It represents more the hard and tedious process of maturation than the exciting events of deliverance from bondage and covenant encounter with God. The events in the wilderness are narrated in Exodus 16:22–18:27 and throughout the book of Numbers. The designation "Numbers" comes from the Septuagint, referring only to the account of a census of Israel that opens the book. The Hebrew title, "In the Wilderness," is more appropriate. The book contains three major narrative sections into which are incorporated various legal and cultic materials similar to those found in Exodus and Leviticus:

1. Preparations for departure from Sinai: 1:1–10:10
2. Journey to Kadesh and attack on southern Canaan: 10:11–21:13
3. Journey from Kadesh through Transjordan: 21:14–36:13

In these wilderness traditions Israel is portrayed as faithless, rebellious, and complaining. The enthusiasm generated by the experience at the Sea of Reeds rapidly dissipated as the Israelites faced the rigors of wilderness life. Food and water were seldom adequate. Dangers surrounded them and enemies opposed their advance. Argument, strife, and discontent broke out on many occasions. Complaining became so exaggerated that the Israelites even longed to return to bondage in Egypt, where at least they "sat by the fleshpots and ate our fill of bread" (Exodus 16:3). Even Moses, Aaron, and Miriam are said to have shamefully stumbled.

The most forceful presentation of Israel's weakness and lack of faith is the story of the "spies from Kadesh" (Numbers 13–14). When the Israelites arrived at Kadesh, an oasis on the southern edge of Canaan, spies were sent into Canaan. They were to gather data about the productivity of the land, the strength of its cities, the nature of its inhabitants, and other information important to prospective settlers. They reported on the fruitfulness of the land, the strength of the Canaanites, and the fortifications of the cities. Two spies, Joshua[44] and Caleb, advocated that Israel proceed to take the land, but the others disagreed. They referred to some of the Canaanites as *nephilim*, giants, and saw the taking of the land as impossible. Two reports about Canaan's productivity seem contradictory: Numbers (13:27,32) says that the land "flows with milk and honey," but also that "the land that we have gone through as spies is a land that devours its inhabitants." The Deuteronomist clearly aims to depict Israel's faithlessness in spite of encouragement from Joshua and Caleb.

---

[44]Joshua's name may be a later insertion.

Faced with the pessimistic report of the majority, the Israelites were on the verge of returning to Egypt. When Joshua and Caleb suggested that they could conquer Canaan by the power of Yahweh, they were stoned. This display of faithless ingratitude angered Yahweh, who was ready to disinherit the chosen people and begin again with the descendants of Moses and Aaron. In words strikingly reminiscent of the promises made to the patriarchs, Moses is described as father of a great nation:

> How long will this people despise me? And how long will they refuse to believe in me, in spite of all the signs that I have done among them? I will strike them with pestilence and disinherit them, and I will make of you a nation greater and mightier than they. [Numbers 14:11–12]

Nowhere else is Moses better depicted as a representative and leader of his people. He interceded on Israel's behalf and Yahweh substituted a stalemate of one generation for the immediate execution of the people. None of the rebellious generation, except Joshua and Caleb, were permitted to enter Canaan. The remainder were doomed to wander in the wilderness until they died. Rebellion, even when forgiven through prophetic intercession, has serious consequences.

When the spies who had made the unfavorable report about Israel's chances against Canaan died in a plague, the Israelites immediately reversed their decision. Against the advice of Moses they attacked the Canaanites at Hormah in southern Canaan without divine sanction (Moses and the ark remained back at camp) and were soundly defeated. The Canaanites drove the majority of the tribes back into the southern Negeb. Portions of Judah and Simeon, however, probably remained in the area around Hormah. This story explains the later presence in this area of tribal groups sympathetic with Israelites who were settling in other parts of Canaan. The tribes that fell back from Hormah returned to the area around Kadesh where they continued to wander.

Then their leaders decided to move into Transjordan before again attempting to enter Canaan proper. The king of Edom was asked for permission to pass through his land. The request, however, was denied, illustrating the longstanding enmity between Israel and the Edomites. Denied passage through Edomite territory, Israel moved eastward along Edom's northern border and thence northward into Transjordan. Moab was also bypassed along its eastern side until the river Arnon was reached. At this point the Amorite kingdom of Sihon stood in Israel's path. When passage through his land was denied, Sihon was engaged in battle at Jahaz and the Israelites defeated him. This victory gave them territory from the Arnon to the Jabbok rivers. The territory north of the Jabbok belonged to the kingdom of Bashan, whose king was Og. At Edrei, the capital of Bashan, Israel again was successful in battle.

In connection with these struggles for territory east of the Jordan, the narrator illustrates Yahweh's faithful care of the people by telling the humorous but serious story of Balaam.[45] It illustrates the foolishness of attempting to interfere with the will of Yahweh, or even thinking about doing so.

Balak, king of Moab, greatly concerned about the victories won by the Israelites, summoned Balaam, an eastern diviner of highest reputation. Balaam was a typical diviner, possessing the powers believed by the ancients to be divine gifts to prophets. He was brought from a town on the upper Euphrates to curse the invading Israelites so that Balak might be successful against them in battle. Balaam is portrayed as a true prophet who, although greatly tempted by promises of exalted status and wealth, could not proclaim any oracles except those given him by Yahweh.

As Balaam comes to Moab he is met by the angel of Yahweh (Yahweh's messenger), who is seen and recognized by the ass on which the prophet rides, but not by the prophet. Wise ass, unseeing prophet—with such images the story makes sport of all attempts to use divine powers against the people blessed by Yahweh. This episode of the insightful and talking animal is probably a popular folk story used here to ridicule all efforts to thwart Yahweh's purposes for Israel. As the story of Balaam continues, Balak makes ample if not perfect (seven altars) preparation for a ritual of cursing, but Balaam can only pronounce blessings on Israel to the misfortune of Moab and others who stand in Israel's way.

When the conquest of the Transjordan was near completion, Moses delivered his farewell address to Israel. Soon thereafter, on Mt. Nebo, he died. He was buried, but the thrust of his life reaches far beyond the grave. The name of Moses is found in any list of those who have most influenced the history of humankind. Besides his gift of the decalogue, his influence on Torah, his role as an emancipator, three of the major living religions (Judaism, Islam, and Christianity) are to be directly or indirectly traced to him. Men of such long shadows rarely pass across the world scene.

Joshua, one of the two spies who had encouraged the taking of Canaan, was chosen as Moses' successor. As he took office, he made preparations for the conquest of Canaan itself. The tribes of Reuben and Gad and half of Manasseh were assigned territory in Transjordan with the understanding that they would settle there only after assisting in the conquest of Canaan. Thus, with Transjordan under control and a new leader in command, Israel stood poised to enter the land of promise.

SUGGESTIONS FOR FURTHER STUDY

Use the Bible dictionaries listed in the General Bibliography to elaborate on Hyksos, Amarna Age, Aton cult, Jebel Musa, Sinai covenant, Yahweh, miracle, suzerainty treaty, decalogue, Covenant Code, cultus, fasting, festivals.

---

[45]Similar popular stories are used elsewhere. Among them are the stories about Samson, the story of Ruth, and the stories in the book of Daniel.

For further study, consult the commentaries on the Book of Exodus by Martin Noth and Brevard S. Childs in *The Old Testament Library* and by J. C. Rylaarsdam in *The Interpreter's Bible*. Good studies of Moses are Martin Buber, *Moses: The Revelation and the Covenant* (Harper Torchbooks, 1958), and Gerhard von Rad, *Moses* (Lutterworth, 1960).

On Israelite worship, the studies of Walter Harrelson, *From Fertility Cult to Worship* (Scholars, 1980); Hans-Joachim Kraus, *Worship in Israel: A Cultic History of the Old Testament* (John Knox, 1966); and H. H. Rowley, *Worship in Ancient Israel: Its Forms and Meanings* (S. P. C. K., 1967), are especially helpful. Additional works are listed in the General Bibliography under Worship.

For help with the legal materials in Exodus, see the General Bibliography on Law in the Hebrew Bible. Two works consider the continuing relevance of the Ten Commandments: the indispensible work by Walter Harrelson, *The Ten Commandments and Human Rights* (Fortress, 1981); and Joy Davidson, *Smoke on the Mountain: An Interpretation of the Ten Commandments* (Westminster, 1985).

Further reading on miracles can be found in J. V. McCasland, "Signs and Wonders," *Journal of Biblical Literature*, 76 (1957) 149–52; J. L. McKenzie, "God and Nature in the Old Testament," *Catholic Biblical Quarterly*, 14 (1952) 18–39, 124–45; J. B. Polhill, "Perspectives on the Miracle Stories," *Review and Expositor*, 74 (1977) 389–400; James Pritchard, "Motifs of Old Testament Miracles," *Crozier Quarterly*, 27 (1950) 79–109; and Bible dictionary articles on the subject.

Two specialized studies of interest are G. H. Parke-Taylor, *Yahweh: The Divine Name in the Bible* (Wilfred Laurier University, 1975), and Karen R. Joines, *Serpent Symbolism in the Old Testament: A Linguistic, Archaeological, and Literary Study* (Haddonfield, 1974).

See also the General Bibliography on Covenant; Themes in the Hebrew Bible; and Pentateuchal Studies.

6

Possessing the Land

The biblical narratives depict the period between the wilderness wanderings and monarchy as a time when Hebrews entered what would gradually become their holy land and when rudimentary, centralized religio-political structures began to emerge. How does a "no-people" become a nation? That is the question being unraveled during the two centuries prior to the establishment of Hebrew monarchy.

These are indeed times of dramatic change as tribal elements are finding their place in a new land, altering their lifestyle, and seeking, as it were, a sense of unity and identity. A portion of the community is moving in from the perimeters of the Fertile Crescent. Their story is thus subtle transition from nomadic society to a farming culture. Life and institutions during this period are fluid to say the least. Israelites have been emancipated and possess the core of a religious code but taking the land and forming organized life there move forward in fits and spurts not always amenable to precise description.

THE DEVELOPMENT OF ISRAEL'S DEUTERONOMIC TRADITIONS

The Deuteronomic History

The biblical narration of Israel's movement into Canaan and its premonarchical experience there is part of an extensive collection of literature commonly referred to as the deuteronomic telling of Israel's story. The collection includes five books of the Hebrew Bible. Deuteronomy serves as an introduction to this narrative and connects it with the earlier Genesis–Numbers. Joshua describes the conquest of Canaan and the division of its territory among Israelite tribes; Judges deals with life in the early Israelite confederacy; Samuel continues the story of the confederacy, depicts struggles with the Philistines, and describes the establishment of monarchy under Saul and David; and Kings continues the story of monarchy until its disastrous end in Babylonian exile in 587 B.C.E. These materials came to their final form during and after the Babylonian exile and, therefore, express many concerns of this later period. The telling of Hebrew history attempts to make sense of the trauma of exile.

In the Hebrew Bible the books of the deuteronomic historical narrative appear as individual and independent works: Deuteronomy, Joshua, Judges, Samuel, and Kings. Closer examination, however, reveals that the materials form an ideological and literary unit. Deuteronomy introduces the corpus and throughout the other books there are materials of diverse types and origins (hero tales, tribal traditions, royal records, prophetic traditions, popular stories, and so on), which do not correspond to the fivefold canonical structure. Actually, the canonical divisions are both artificial and arbitrary. Between Joshua and Judges no real division exists. Judges opens with materials that largely parallel the content of Joshua 1–12 and, unlike the rest of Judges, deals with the conquest, not the defense, of the land. The books of Judges and Samuel are joined by two links: first, the Samuel for whom the latter book is named appears as the last of the judges. Second, the appendices to Judges in chapters 17–21 prepare for the emergence of the monarchy by their repeated mention of disasters that occurred *before Israel had a king*. Finally, 1 Kings 1–2 forms a direct sequel to 2 Samuel 13–20; hence the break between the books of Samuel and Kings separates material that belongs together. Equally supportive for the unity of these materials is the pervading presence of editorial influences reminiscent of the book of Deuteronomy. In fact, editorial sections tie originally divergent materials together. The conclusion, therefore, is that the books of Deuteronomy, Joshua, Judges, Samuel, and Kings in their present form comprise a literary unit.

How did these materials come to be a unit? Some claim that their unity is the result of an editorial interweaving of source strata. According to this analysis, the Yahwistic and Elohistic strata of the Pentateuch or Hexateuch can be traced through the books of Judges and Samuel and even into Kings.[1] For the period of Israel's life in Canaan these strata were edited from the perspective of the book of Deuteronomy and were bound together with deuteronomic additions. However, no attempt to trace the materials in Judges–Kings to narrative strata has been very successful.

Another suggestion is that the books from Deuteronomy through Kings form a single historical work. The author of this history is thought to have worked in Judah during the exile and combined into a single unit originally independent materials—hero tales, tribal traditions, royal records, and so on. His own contribution was editorial and expository, reflecting always his particular interpretation of the disastrous course of Israel's life in Canaan. This analysis

---

[1]See above, pp. 85–94.

provides a reasonable explanation, both for the gathering of the various materials preserved in Joshua–Kings and for the obvious deuteronomic tone pervading them. There are, however, some objections. Editorial perspective seems
to change from section to section. For example, Judges reflects a cyclic interpretation of history with the frequently repeated sequence of apostasy-punish-
ment-repentance-deliverance, whereas Kings presents "a course of history that
leads downward in a straight line to destruction."[2] Again, the book of Samuel
shows almost no evidence of deuteronomic influence. Nevertheless, the idea
of a deuteronomic historian who intentionally set out to provide an interpretation of Israel's road to tragedy best accounts for the form and tone of the
books Joshua–Kings.

That these materials were originally prefaced by the book of Deuteronomy
also makes sense: that work lays the theological groundwork for the interpretation of history that follows. Deuteronomy had at one time existed independent of the other strata of the Torah and was later combined with them. Conceivably it was at some time separated from the larger deuteronomic history
and added to Genesis–Numbers, perhaps without an intention that the following history be considered a separate and different work. Neither Torah nor
deuteronomic history is complete without the other. Separated, the former has
no conclusion and the latter no beginning. In effect, if not by original intention,
Deuteronomy successfully ties the two together.

Our interpretation of Joshua–Kings assumes their place in a unified deuteronomic telling of Israel's story. In each section the "historian" used his sources
to further his theological purpose. With an understanding of the perspective
from which these materials were brought together, we can properly evaluate
the Deuteronomist's contribution to Israelite theology and history. For him
Israel's relationship to Yahweh entailed dimensions not expressed in the old
narrative materials. How could a covenant people understand Yahweh's presence at a time of traumatic crisis? He wrote at a time "when the saving history
over Israel was at a standstill and when . . . the question which had to be answered was, how had all this come about and how could it have been possible
for Yahweh to reject his people?"[3] Therefore, he tried to supply the reader
with special theological ideas for sustaining the people of the covenant during
trying times. From the crisis of Babylonian exile the deuteronomic historian
applied some of these ideals to his interpretation of Israel's history. In this
sense his work is homiletic.

Above all, the Deuteronomist was convinced that the nation's sin had
brought Israel to a tragic end. Its sin was the rejection of Yahweh for gods of
Canaan, combined with acts of social injustice. Israel had had to choose between worship of the Lord of history and the Baal nature cults. To its shame
and sorrow, it had chosen the latter. Thus, the work of the Deuteronomist is

---

[2]Georg Fohrer, *Introduction to the Old Testament* (Abingdon, 1965), p. 194.
[3]Von Rad, *Old Testament*, I: 342.

"a comprehensive confession of Israel's guilt."[4] He wrote, therefore, of Yahweh's *judgment word* in Israel's history, exercised again and again in a measured way, but finally and all but irreversibly in the catastrophe of national destruction and exile. At the same time, however, he wrote of Yahweh's word of promise. For him this was not so much the promise to the patriarchal ancestors as it was the covenant with David. This was a promise of salvation. The judges saved Israel from chaos, but not permanently. Israel's kings had had the potential of being Yahweh's representative to bring the people to the full and good life, but none, not even David, actualized that potential. The possibilities of the covenant had repeatedly gone unrealized.

Promise and salvation, however, were still offered and must be grasped by the faithful. Even though the Deuteronomist was preoccupied with Israel's guilt, he offered his interpretation of Israel's history as a kind of national confession and hinted throughout that forgiveness was available and redemption possible. By implication he anticipated the ideal one who would come to Israel to serve "his people as deliverer not merely on one occasion alone,"[5] who would be king and would do all that the nation had failed to do. Thus he interpreted Israel's history as guilt and judgment within which was offered messianic promise. Admittedly the latter was only an undercurrent and was never prominently exploited. To a people in chaos, and Israel's exile was chaos, the word of salvation came as a whisper in the deuteronomic history, to be amplified only later.

The Book of Deuteronomy

The book of Deuteronomy stands as a conclusion to Torah and as an introduction to the deuteronomic history work to which it gives direction and theological perspective. As with the other books of Torah, this scroll was known in Israel by its opening words, "these are the words" or "the words." The Septuagint translators rendered a phrase in 8:18 and 17:18, "a copy of this law," as *deuteronomion*, "second (or repeated) law," and this term became the title of the book.

Deuteronomy is essentially a resumé of Israel's religion posited within a sermonic framework. It is an expansion of the Mosaic law code arranged so that its public proclamation might be effective. The literary structure around three "sermons" of Moses is reflected in the outline:

A. First address: chapters 1–4
   1. Historical review: 1:1–3:29
   2. Appeal for faithful obedience: 4:1–40

---

[4]Ibid., p. 337.
[5]Ibid., p. 329.

B. Second address: chapters 5–28
    1. Law and its meaning: chapters 5–26
    2. Curses of disobedience: chapter 27
    3. Blessings of obedience and curses of disobedience: chapter 28
C. Third address—exhortation to renew covenant: chapters 29–30
D. Concluding passages on Moses: chapters 31–34

The first sermon (1–4) recounts the acts of Yahweh, closing with an exhortation to obedience and absolute fidelity. Infidelity and disobedience will result in the dissipation of the nation.

The second sermon (5–28) is the longest and forms the core of the book. It is a presentation of Yahweh's law. The first part of the discourse (5–11) begins by citing the decalogue and continues with an elaboration on the first commandment. It sets forth the fundamental principles that undergird all particular legislation. Disobedience is an invitation to catastrophe; the wilderness experience corroborates the fact. The second part of the discourse (12–28) contains the laws themselves. The code relates to all phases of Israelite life—civil, moral, ceremonial. It closes with an appeal for obedience—with its promised reward, as opposed to the curse to be merited by disobedience. Chapter 27 seems to be an interpolation dealing with the preparation for a covenant ceremony at Shechem, perhaps the one observed at the end of the conquest.

The third sermon (29–30) exhorts Israel to keep the covenant and presents the alternative of life or death to the covenant community. The blessings and curses of chapter 28 are the ceremonial expressions of these alternatives. The choice belongs to the nation and repentance is an ever-present recourse for apostasy.

Compare the law code of Deuteronomy 5–28 with the code found in Exodus 20–23; Leviticus 17–26; or Leviticus 1–7; 11–15.

There follow additional words of encouragement and exhortation, and Moses' parting blessing on the individual tribes. The book closes with the account of Moses' death (possibly transfered from the end of Numbers) and an evaluation of his work.

The structure of the book fits well with the liturgical progression of the ceremony of covenant making.[6] Deuteronomy, therefore, may be an expanded commentary on the Sinai experience formulated as three sermons attributed to Moses. Thus the laws of Deuteronomy represent a later development on Israel's earlier law code.[7] The codes on which deuteronomic sermons are based were compiled at religious shrines, such as Shechem and Shiloh, organized in

---

[6]G. E. Wright, "Cult and History," *Interpretation*, 16 (1962) 10.
[7]Deuteronomy should be studied with other legal codes in the Hebrew Bible: covenant code (Exodus 20:23–23:19), holiness code (Leviticus 17–26), and priestly code (Leviticus 1–7, 11–15).

the days following the conquest of Canaan. These were sanctuaries where covenant must have been celebrated with some regularity, and thus served as bonds of unity during this period of change and uncertainty. The climax of these covenant ceremonies was the reading and acceptance of the law of Yahweh. The homiletical presentation of law in Deuteronomy seems to have grown out of the law read on such occasions. To this corpus of ancient cultic tradition were added later refinements and interpretations until Deuteronomy appeared in its present form. As it now stands in the canon, Deuteronomy is "a finished, mature, beautifully proportioned and theologically clear work."[8] Its audience is a community widely separated from the wilderness and conquest experiences. As Moses addressed those who stood across the Jordan from the land of promise, so the book proclaims without equivocation that throughout its history Israel remained the object of Yahweh's election and salvation. In this sense the book is a profound theology of the exodus.

Although Deuteronomy reaches superlative moral heights, it also advocates ruthless treatment of Israel's enemies and worshipers of other gods. Further, the book reduces the problems of suffering and adversity to a simple equation—pain and penalty to the disobedient; pleasure and prosperity to the obedient. In spite of these liabilities, however, the book links Israel with its founding days and encourages it to the best of the covenant faith. It proclaims the message of the redeeming God, who established a covenant with the people emancipated from slavery. Yahweh loved Israel when Israel had not merited it, and Yahweh ever remained faithful to divine commitments made to Israel. Israel is to respond by a loving obedience in the acknowledgment that its security is found in Yahweh alone. Israel is Yahweh's people and must give witness to Yahweh by its conduct. This calls for integrity and justice. As Yahweh's people, Israel has a destiny ensured by faithfulness to Yahweh. Apart from this, Israel has no future, only death.

It is not surprising that the code of Deuteronomy played an important role in later Israelite history when proclamation of the law was highly desirable. In the midst of a political and religious reform during the reign of King Josiah (640–609) of Judah, a law book, probably Deuteronomy, was found in the temple. It was read publicly and became the basis for national religious revival.

Deuteronomy was a favorite of New Testament writers. Jesus replied to his wilderness temptation by quoting from three places in the book;[9] and for the first part of his answer concerning the first and great commandment,[10] he cited Deuteronomy 6:5, one of Israel's great confessions of faith. His teachings in the Sermon on the Mount may have had in mind Deuteronomy 18:13. Altogether more than eighty quotations from Deuteronomy occur in the New Tes-

[8]Von Rad, *Studies in Deuteronomy* (S.C.M., 1953), p. 37. See also pp. 70ff.
[9]Matthew 4.
[10]Matthew 22:37.

tament. The reasons for this attraction to the book are obvious. Here is found an exalted summary of the religion of Israel. Like few other portions of the Hebrew Bible, it soars beyond the expected and grasps the concern of Yahweh for Israel and calls for its response in love.

TAKING THE LAND: CONQUEST AND INFILTRATION
(JOSHUA 1–12; JUDGES 1:1–2)

For the deuteronomic historian Israel's settlement in Canaan was a fulfillment of Yahweh's promise to Abraham that he would become the father of a great nation (Genesis 12:2), that he and his offspring would be given "all the land of Canaan for a perpetual holding" (Genesis 17:8), and that Israel's taking possession of the land was a sign of Yahweh's continuing faithfulness to those he had delivered from Egyptian bondage. This theological interpretation of Israel's settlement in Canaan is clear; the accounts of the taking of the land, however, are ambiguous, even confusing. The early chapters of Joshua describe a military effort of sweeping proportions in which the land was swiftly overrun in three lightning campaigns, while Judges 1 and 2 suggest a more gradual infiltration of the land over considerable time and still incomplete at the beginning of the monarchy and "even to this day" (1:21). Archeology has not clarified the picture, so historical reconstruction of the settlement is quite difficult.

Canaan in the Last Quarter of the Second Millennium

Canaan[11] was a land occupied by many peoples. "Canaanite" seems to have been a term covering various peoples living in the area between Gaza and Hamath, a territory including both Palestine and a part of Syria. The first of these peoples may have migrated into the land from the Arabian desert. By 3000 B.C.E. cities such as Jebus (Jerusalem), Megiddo, Byblos, Ai, Jericho, Gezer, Hamath, and Beth-shan had been established. Some of these cities yield evidence of occupation hundreds to several thousand years before this date.

The peoples of Canaan distinguished themselves by several cultural achievements. If they were not responsible for the invention of the alphabet, they were responsible for its improvement and dissemination across the Mediterranean world. Most of the Western world uses alphabets based on the Canaanite or Phoenician. Some were prominent seafarers who laced together in a loose fash-

---

[11]"Canaan" probably first meant "land of the purple." This title referred to the dye industries for which the area was noted. The coloring was derived from a shellfish, *murex mollusca*, widely found along the Palestinian coast. The Greeks later called the area Phoenicia from a Greek word also meaning "purple."

ion of communication the diverse corners of the Mediterranean. Consequently, they were themselves taught by these contacts. Whether by caravan or by ship, they were in the path of the movements and ideas of the world around them. Their architecture, musical instruments, ceramics, and early use of copper and iron established them as an advanced people for the age.

The deuteronomic historian accurately reflects that at the time of Israel's settlement "the people who live in the land are strong and the towns are fortified and very large" (Numbers 13:28). Had the Canaanites been unified, the story would have had to be written differently. But that never happened. The terrain of Canaan was rugged and natural elements tended to separate communities. Instead of consolidating their strength into a great nation, they narrowly crystallized their life around city or town centers. They developed city-states similar to those of the Greeks. A city with its neighboring countryside considered itself a unit for purposes of government and defense. Each had its own king and administered its own affairs. Occasionally two or more would join to meet a common enemy (Joshua 10:12), but most often each went its own way. Most of these city-states were in the desirable lowlands and the plains, which were suitable for agriculture and grazing. Only a few, such as Jebus, Hebron, Luz, and Shechem, were in the highlands or mountains where the water supply was meager and the slopes were steep and heavily wooded, therefore, not suitable for agriculture.

Throughout the second millennium Canaan was largely under Egyptian influence, but control was rarely overt. Fortification outposts were sometimes maintained and Egyptian vassals controlled some cities. During the Amarna period (the early 14th century), Egyptian influence was only nominal. Because Akhnaton was primarily interested in his experiments with religion, his leadership in administering the affairs of state was uncertain. Consequently, vassals, city kings, and Egyptian officials did largely as they pleased. Some of Israel's ancestors were among the 'Apiru who took advantage of this situation to gain a foothold in the land of Canaan. Settling down around Shechem, they waited for the proper time to assert themselves more strongly.

Other peoples were also moving into the land of Canaan. Amorite relatives of Israel's ancestors had been entering the land from the time of Abraham on. Some had settled down and established city-states of their own. Some, like the Israelites, were still living the life of enclosed nomadism. The Hittites, remnants of outposts of the Hittite empire of central Asia Minor, settled in isolated pockets here and there in Canaan. The Jebusites were those Canaanites who lived at the city of Jebus. The Horites were Hurrians, whose origin was Mitanni in northern Mesopotamia. Some Horites may have resided in Edom or Seir. Late in the second millennium the Philistines settled on the southern coast and gradually pushed the other unestablished peoples into the hills and mountains.

From around 1300 to 1000 B.C.E. the entire Mediterranean world experi-

Figure 6.1. Amarna letters nos. 61 and 68 from princes in Shechem and Hebron discussing military actions regarding invaders (Habiru). (Copyright, British Museum)

enced extensive decline. These were years of unrest and uncertainty. The cause of this decline is not known to us, but its evidence appears everywhere. Important states declined, the population dropped, many cities were destroyed— some more than once, many communities were forced to leave long-settled areas to try to find "living room" elsewhere. In Canaan many of the diverse groups who had not yet established themselves there, Israel among them, must have taken this opportunity to do so. Some of these peoples were related to Israel's ancestors and with them the newly arrived former slaves from Egypt found some ties and allegiances. For years Hebrews or Amorites of one description or another had been entering the land. Although they had been to varying degrees "outsiders" and had not become part of Canaanite communities, they were there and were related to Israel. As Israel moved into the land, many of these disenfranchised groups were ready and willing to identify their cause with Israel and become part of the covenant community.[12] But others saw the newcomers as competitors for the land, resisted their entry, and hence became "the enemy."

The Book of Joshua

The most extensive, and the most dramatic, biblical account of entry into Canaan appears in the book of Joshua. The book, as a part of the deuteronomic

---

[12]This doubtlessly casts some light on the question of why the writer of the "conquest narrative" in Joshua gives no account of military activity in central Canaan.

narrative, obviously tells the story from the perspective of the themes of the larger work. It reflects a religio-military interpretation of conquest, idealizing Yahweh as the military champion of Israel. Yahweh's cause cannot be held back by anything other than Israel's unfaithfulness. Like a mighty army with Yahweh leading against the foe,[13] Israel marches into battle, and its enemies

> From a contemporary hymnal select other hymns with war imagery and compare them with imagery in the book of Joshua.

do not stand a chance. It was Yahweh's cause, Yahweh's fight, Yahweh's victory. The land is occupied in three sweeping campaigns, then allocated to various tribal groups. Victory is celebrated by solemn affirmation of covenant. The book's outline reflects the story's organization:

A. The conquest of Canaan: chapters 1–12
  1. Crossing the Jordan: 1:1–5:15
  2. Campaign into central Canaan: 6:1–10:27
  3. Campaign into southern Canaan: 10:28–43
  4. Campaign into northern Canaan: 11:1–15
  5. Summary of conquest: 11:16–12:24
B. Allocation of land and cities among the tribes: chapters 13–21
C. Concluding materials: chapters 22–24
  1. Departure of Transjordan tribes: 22:1–34
  2. Joshua's farewell address: 23:1–16
  3. Covenant ceremony at Shechem: 24:1–28
  4. Death and burial of Joshua: 24:29–31
  5. Burials of Joseph's bones and Eleazer: 24:32–33

The Joshua Account of Conquest

Joshua 1–12 leaves the impression that all the land fell into Israelite hands under Joshua and all Israel's prominent enemies were resoundingly defeated or otherwise immobilized. The peoples of Canaan were utterly destroyed, "both men and women, young and old, oxen, sheep, and donkeys" (Joshua 6:21; cf. 8:24; 10:28–39; 11:10–22).

Thrust into the Central Highlands. The Joshua narrative of conquest depicts three highly successful military operations. First, Jericho was overrun and a thrust was made into the central highlands at Ai. The siege of Jericho is pictured as a ritual act. Priests and their sacerdotal functions were integral to the entire affair. Soldiers, as a consequence of their purifications, became "holy men" for the duration of the engagement. The order of march to Jericho was

---

[13]The language similar to "Onward, Christian Soldiers" is not accidental.

Figure 6.2. The military conquest of Canaan as depicted in the book of Joshua.

Figure 6.3. An orthodox Jew blowing the shophar, a ram's horn used on ritual occasions. This is the type of instrument described in the ritual conquest of Jericho. (Courtesy of the Israel Office of Information)

a vanguard, seven priests blowing ram's horns, the ark, and a rear guard. The religious nature of the endeavor is evident in every way. The march to war was a procession. Six days of marching in silence were followed by a seventh day on which six circlings around the city were followed by a seventh when the signal was given by the ram's horns, whose sounds may have symbolized the voice of Yahweh,[14] and the marchers burst forth in shouting. The walls of the city were leveled and the entire city was sacrificed to Yahweh. Included in the destruction was every living thing: men and women, young and old, even the animals. The single exception was the harlot Rahab, whose speech clearly echoes deuteronomic themes. The riches of the city—silver, gold, vessels of bronze and iron—were placed in a treasury for Yahweh; then the city was burned.

---

[14]Cf. Numbers 10:10.

Figure 6.4. The tell of Jericho has been extensively excavated over many seasons without demonstrating a destruction of the city during Joshua's day. (*Illustrator* Photo/Ken Touchton)

It is quite possible that later at Gilgal or Shechem a cultic procession like that described in Joshua 6 was combined with a ceremonial crossing of the Jordan into a great celebration of conquest victory.[15] Such a celebration may have influenced the way the Deuteronomist tells this story.

The account of the conquest of Ai is also dominated by ritual concerns, defeat there explained by ritual disobedience of the rules of holy war. Everything captured in the Israelite attack on Jericho was supposed to have been dedicated to God as his possession. When a soldier kept some of the booty for himself, the entire army was penalized for this man's violation of the rules and suffered a decisive defeat at Ai. To remove the penalty of defeat, the cause had to be identified and the culprit had to be punished along with all his family and possessions (Joshua 7:24–26). After this was done, Israel moved on to victory at Ai.

The account of Israel's initial thrust into Canaan is throughout more concerned to emphasize Yahweh's sovereignty over Israel and the Canaanites than

---

[15]Hans-Joachim Kraus, "Gilgal; Ein Beitrag zur Kultusgeschichte Israels," *Vetus Testamentum*, 1 (1951) 181–99.

to describe details of battles. This concern to show that Israel's settlement in Canaan was fundamentally a cultic achievement accounts for the insertion of a covenant ceremony at this point in the narrative (8:30–35). The setting is Shechem, where kindred people already settled in central Canaan were incorporated into the community of Israel.

The story of the covenant with a league of Gibeonite cities (chap. 9) serves the same purpose. These cities by deception entered into covenant with Israel. Clearly the book of Joshua indicates that even the deception of Israel's enemies was turned to the advantage of the covenant people. Yahweh's victory could not be turned aside. Cities of the league became Israel's allies and therefore under protection of the holy war. Leaders in the deception became "hewers of wood" and "drawers of water"—that is, slaves to the cause of Yahweh.

Defeat of the Southern League. Joshua's "southern campaign" is not described in detail as are the battles against Jericho and Ai, but nonetheless the defeat of cities in the south is described as decisive. An Amorite coalition of Hebron, Jarmuth, Lachish, Eglon, and Jebus was formed to oppose Israel, but to no avail. "Yahweh fought with Israel" (10:14), even causing the sun to stand still. The Israelites routed the coalition; the Amorites retreated, but there was no escape. The kings hid in a cave at Makkedah until they were found and killed. Joshua then moved to lay siege to their cities. Libnah, and then in succession, Lachish, Eglon, Hebron, and Debir or Kirjath-sepher fell to him. The Joshua account of this phase cryptically concludes: "So Joshua defeated the whole land, the hill country and the Negeb and the lowland and the slopes, and all their kings; he left none remaining, but utterly destroyed all that breathed, as Yahweh, God of Israel, commanded" (10:40).

Conquest in the North. The third phase of the military conquest, according to the book of Joshua, was against a group of northern kings who allied themselves under Jabin, king of Hazor, the largest city of the region and probably one the largest cities of Palestine and head of one of the strongest city-states. Joshua met and defeated the coalition at its rallying place near the Waters of Merom. Hazor was attacked and both the city and the coalition were totally destroyed.

For the Deuteronomist the Joshua campaigns concluded a major chapter in the Hebrew story. Israel was in full possession of the land. All that remained to be done was to divide the land among the tribes that had not yet received their allotment and for them to settle there. A crucial issue had been settled. Joshua's victories assured the fulfillment of the promise to Abraham; the land of Canaan was now in the hands of his heirs. Yahweh's promise had been fulfilled with the fall of Hazor.

So closes a chapter begun with Abraham. Yahweh had used Joshua as a "second Moses." To fulfill the nation's hopes and dreams, Yahweh had taken a no-people and placed them in a land they could call their own.

> Trace how the biblical presentation of Joshua demonstrates that he is a "new Moses."

The Judges Account of Israel's Settlement in Canaan

The "holy war" conquest account in Joshua overshadows a different view of Israel's settlement found in the book of Judges. The events in Judges are represented as coming "after the death of Joshua" (Judges 1:1), but they are not at all consistent with the account given in Joshua 1–11. The opening question of the book, "Who shall go up first for us against the Canaanites, to fight against them?" (Judges 1:1), comes as a surprise. Joshua was said to have completely destroyed the Canaanites and then to have allotted their lands to the tribes of Israel. In Judges the land still occupied by the Canaanites is allotted to the tribes, and they are left in various ways to occupy their territory. Judges 1 describes various struggles by individual tribes or family groups of tribes trying to gain living room in the Canaanite hill country. There is no unified effort of all Israel to possess the land. Judah and Simeon fight together in small military operations to gain control of their territory. The Kenites, descendants of Moses' father-in-law and now part of the Israelite community, settle in the south peacefully (Judges 1:16). The bold claims in Joshua that Israel wiped out the inhabitants of Canaan are quite different from the statement in Judges that there were twenty cities from which the Canaanites were not driven out by newcomers (Judges 1:21, 27–33). Among these cities are Jerusalem, Gezer, Taanach, Megiddo, and Dor, all cited in Joshua 12:7–24 as defeated by Joshua and the Israelites. These cities are some of the most strategically located cities in all of Canaan and would be very influential in the later history of Israel. Judges, therefore, presents a view of Israel's settlement that differs significantly from the conquest narrative of Joshua.

The Archeology of the Conquest/Settlement

Archeology has focused more on the period of the settlement, perhaps, than on any other period of Israel's history. Early excavations at a number of the cities that Joshua is said to have conquered and destroyed led Albright and many others to conclude that the conquest narrative was essentially verified. They pointed out that the sequence and strategies of the conquest were consistent with good military procedure and that the cities destroyed were reoccupied by newcomers of discernible cultural difference, building different style houses and making different styles of pottery. There seemed to be discontinuity with the previous culture, exactly what you would expect if new arriving nomads had conquered and resettled these cities.

From the beginning, however, this conclusion had to be made over against negative archeological evidence at the key sites of Jericho and Ai, neither of which was occupied at the time of Joshua. Both had been abandoned for centuries. This was explained in a number of ways.

1. *Jericho.* The absence of protecting walls and major structures at Jericho dating from the time of Joshua was explained either by the claim that all these structures had eroded away over the centuries during which the city destroyed by Joshua was abandoned, or that the Jericho of Joshua's time had made use of the walls of an earlier occupation of the site. Neither explanation is satisfactory. The tell of Jericho had been completely abandoned for a century or more prior to the time of Joshua. Nothing from the thirteenth century was found: no walls, structures, foundations, pottery, or tombs. The complete removal by erosion of all the contents of a sizable city would be a singular incident and virtually impossible. Recognizing this, some have suggested that the attack at Jericho was made on a military outpost established in the ruins of the abandoned city. The biblical story, however, is about an attack on a large, well-fortified city.

2. *Ai.* Albright suggested that the Ai story in Joshua 8 originally referred to the capture of nearby Bethel, which was destroyed and reoccupied at the time of Joshua. The story came to be told instead with reference to the very impressive ruins at Ai. However, the description of the attack in Joshua 8 much better fits the topography of Ai than that of Bethel. Some believe that the site excavated as Ai is not Ai. No satisfactory alternate site has been found. The suggestion about Ai, which was also made about Jericho, that the Israelites attacked a military outpost on the ruins of the abandoned city is also in conflict with the biblical story about an attack on a well-fortified city.

Although the problems of Jericho and Ai remained, there still seemed to be adequate evidence to support the Joshua account of a major military conquest of the Canaanites. More recent and more extensive archeological investigations suggest a very different picture than a unified conquering and destruction and resettlement of a large number of Canaanite cities. Cities were destroyed, some more than once. Only two, Bethel and Hazor, are among those that the biblical writers describe as forcibly taken by the Israelites under Joshua or his successors. The archeological evidence relevant to these cities is summed up in the following chart:[16]

---

[16]This chart, with some modifications and rearrangement, is based on Table 1 in William G. Dever's, *Recent Discoveries and Research*, pp. 56–57.

Site	Biblical Reference	Biblical Description	Archeological Evidence
		East of the Jordan	
Heshbon	Num 21:25–30	Destroyed	Not occupied at the time of Joshua
Dibon	Num 21:30	Implied destruction	Not occupied at the time of Joshua
Zephath	Num 21:1–3; Judg 1:17	Destroyed by Judah and Simeon	Probable site not occupied at time of Joshua
Medeba	Num 21:30	Destruction implied	No evidence of destruction
		West of the Jordan	
Bethel	Josh 8:17; Judg 1:22–28	Destroyed	Destroyed
Hazor	Josh 11:10–13	Destroyed	Destroyed
Jericho	Josh 6:1–21	Destroyed	Not occupied at the time of Joshua
Ai	Josh 8:24–28	Destroyed	Not occupied at the time of Joshua
Hebron	Josh 14:13–15; 15:13–14; Judg 1:10	Captured but no destruction described	No evidence
Lachish	Josh 10:31–32	Destroyed	Destroyed after the time of Joshua
Dan/Laish	Judg 18:11–28	Destroyed	Evidence unclear
Gaza, Ekron, Ashkelon	Judg 1:18	Taken by Judah and Simeon	No evidence
Jerusalem	Josh 10:1–27; Judg 1:8, 21	Texts contradictory	No evidence of destruction
Debir	Josh 10:38–39; 15:15–17; Judg 1:11–13	Texts contradictory; destroyed by either Joshua or Judah	Site disputed; one shows destruction evidence, other does not
Eglon	Josh 10:34–35	Destroyed	Probable site—no evidence of destruction
Makkedah	Josh 10:28	Destroyed	Probable site—no evidence of destruction
Libnah	Josh 10:29–31	Destroyed	Probable site—no evidence of destruction

Clearly, there is not adequate archeological evidence to support a military conquest of Canaan in which cities were captured, destroyed, and their inhabitants exterminated, to be replaced by newcomers who settled in the destroyed cities bringing new material cultures. The pottery, houses, and other items of material culture of the people who rebuilt the destroyed cities were less skillfully made, but not different from that of the previous inhabitants, indicating continuity rather than discontinuity of culture.

The Judges' picture, therefore, is probably a more accurate representation of Israel's settlement in Canaan—a gradual infiltration over a long period of time by various related groups of people who peacefully moved in to live alongside the Canaanites, only occasionally engaging in military conquest. This kind of settlement is demonstrated by the most recent archeological discoveries. Report after report from archeologists mention the amazing number of new villages established in the hill country between about 1200 B.C.E. and the time of David and Solomon about 1000 B.C.E. These villages were small and unfortified and seemed to spring up everywhere. Before 1300 this kind of village was practically unknown; then suddenly they appeared by the hundreds. The villagers were farmers and herders of sheep and goats who were already well acquainted with the culture of enclosed nomadism. They seemed to have entered the highlands from all directions to settle in the more or less uninhabited mountain areas. Two subsistence technologies made this possible. One, they carved cisterns out of solid rock using iron tools. Every village had a number of these cisterns. Two, they terraced the steep hillsides to provide level land for agriculture.

Many archeologists and biblical scholars see the establishment of these villages as the first phase of Israel's settlement, which continued throughout the period of the Judges. The second phase, not completed until the time of the early monarchy, was one of expansion into the lower hills and the plains, which had long been occupied by Canaanites. This expansion must have required some military activity, probably by individual tribes or groups of related tribes. This settlement was part of a larger cultural transition, ". . . a gradual, exceedingly complex process, involving social, economic, and political—as well as religious—change, with many regional variations."[17]

If Israel's settlement in Canaan and its emergence as an important state there was not the result of military conquest, how did it come about? In contrast to the once widely accepted theory of Albright—that the military conquest was archeologically supported—Alt and Noth argued that the Israelites were

> land hungry semi-nomads [who] probably first set foot on land in the process of changing pastures and in the end . . . began to settle for good in the sparsely populated parts of the country and then extended their territory from the original domains as occasion offered, the whole process being carried through, to begin with, by peaceful means and without the use of force.[18]

In their view the stories of military conquest were etiological legends to explain certain phenomena (for example, the ruins of Ai). Some did settle peacefully and the settlement went on for a long period of time, but as we have already seen, the new villages were not established by newly arrived nomads.

---

[17]Dever, *Recent Discoveries and Research*, p. 79.
[18]Noth, *History of Israel*, p. 68.

George Mendenhall and Norman Gottwald[19] also reject an all-Israel invasion under Joshua and agree that the people who made up the later community
of Israel had moved into Palestine over a long period of time, settling wherever
they could without use of force. Their major emphasis, however, is on the
circumstances that resulted in the union of these peoples as a confederacy of
tribes with a common sense of identity and purpose. Peasants suffering intol-
erable conditions were inspired to revolt by the introduction into Canaanite
society of a new religion with a new view of the human community—the Yahwism of the Israelites of the exodus and covenant. The result of the rebellion
was a tribal community bound as equals under the Yahwistic covenant.

This view of Mendenhall and Gottwald best satisfies all the evidence, explaining as it does how peoples of diverse origins could identify with each other
by participating in a common cause and begin to develop an all-Israel sense of
identity and history. The British settlement of North America and the establishment of thirteen colonies with very different perspectives and interests
joined in revolution to become the United States of America. The absence of
Canadian colonies in this union is paralleled in the Israelite experience by the
fact that all Canaanites did not become Israelites.

HOLY WAR AND CHEREM. What then can we conclude about the Joshua
conquest narrative? Obviously, it is a simplified and idealized account of holy
war. The story is told with dramatic stress to emphasize Yahweh's role. Event
is piled on event to create a mood of certain victory that can be stopped by
nothing except breach of Yahweh's battle instructions. The army was called
the *'Am Yahweh* ("the people of Yahweh") and was under strict sacral regu-
lations. The warriors were "holy." Preparations for battle included elaborate
cultic acts to ensure that the will and direction of Yahweh be known and
obeyed. In preparation for the holy war males born in the wilderness were
circumcised. Those who had earlier received an Egyptian-style circumcision
were probably recircumcised with flint knives in the same fashion as Moses.
In Yahweh's war all participants had to demonstrate their singular commitment to Yahweh's leadership. Priests carrying the ark of the covenant led the
procession across the Jordan, marking the beginning of conquest. Just as Yahweh took Moses across the Sea of Reeds, so Yahweh led Joshua across the
Jordan. At Gilgal Joshua set up an altar, a cultic act establishing Yahweh's
claim to the land, a ritual probably celebrated at the Gilgal shrine during the
period of tribal confederation. Victories won in such a war were credited to
Yahweh and the spoil of battle belonged to Yahweh. The capture of Canaan
was a sacral act and all the booty and prisoners taken were to be *cherem*, usually
translated as "utterly destroyed." The *cherem* indicated Yahweh's ownership
of the land and all that it contained. In this account of holy war Yahweh enables
Israel to possess the land in which the patriarchs had lived as strang-

[19]G. Mendenhall, "The Hebrew Conquest of Palestine," *Biblical Archaeology*, 25 (1962) 66–
87; and Gottwald, *Tribes of Yahweh*, pp. 191–233.

ers.[20] Only in the burial cave had they found a place that really belonged to them.[21] But during the time of Joshua, Yahweh gave the land to Israel as evidence of divine mercy, grace, and sovereignty. The conquest was interpreted as a sacral act by which the promise to the patriarchs became a reality.

Although it existed in earlier form, probably from the time of David, the Joshua conquest narrative was given its final shape in the Babylonian exile by the Deuteronomist, who was convinced that obedience of Yahweh and purity of worship were essential if Jewish religion and national life were to continue. Memory of past greatness achieved by obedience, especially when idealized, was one means of challenging the exiles who were to return to "Canaan" to meet these divine requirements and thus assure their future. Perhaps the Deuteronomist even had Nehemiah and Ezra in mind as great leaders who, like Joshua, the hero of old, would stand to say: "Now therefore revere Yahweh, and serve him in sincerity and faithfulness. . . . If you are unwilling to serve Yahweh, choose this day whom you will serve . . . but as for me and my household, we will serve Yahweh" (Joshua 24:14–15). If so, he would have hoped that the generation of the exile would respond as had the generation of the settlement: "Yahweh our God we will serve, and him we will obey" (24:24).

The conquest narrative, then, is a piece of religious and national patriotic idealism that came to be accepted as the official view of the Israelite settlement in Canaan. Only the most conservative scholars today would agree that it, in its full claims, was the most historically accurate account.

Holy War and *Cherem*: A Moral Critique

Sensitive readers of the Joshua narrative will be offended by the moral stance of the materials. Brutality and savage conquest is not only condoned, but even sanctioned as the will of Yahweh (see 6:16–21). The book portrays war as an instrument of deity in the hands of an elect people. All who oppose it do so at the risk of their lives, including the infant and the woman. The book of Joshua demanded that the inhabitants of Canaan be *cherem*, usually translated "utterly destroyed," but probably better translated "placed under the ban" or "devoted" in the sense of an offering to God. Because Yahweh was the protagonist and the real victor in battles, Israel felt that spoils belonged to Yahweh. The *cherem* indicated this ownership and recognized the divine prerogative to do with the booty as Yahweh wished, and according to Joshua, Yahweh wished the extermination of the Canaanites. Therefore, the conquest narrative considered the accomplishment of the *cherem* a religious act to be performed with complete faithfulness and devotion. Sometimes "utter destruction" was en-

---

[20]Gerhard von Rad, "Verheissenes Land und Jahwes Land im Hexateuch," *Zeitschrift des Deutschen Palastine-Vereins*, 66 (1943), is an able presentation of the whole idea here under discussion.

[21]Genesis 23; 25:7–10; 50:13.

forced as sacrifice to God. At other times the enemy was simply enlisted in the service of Yahweh.

The conquest narratives' sanction of cruelty as the will of God illustrates the limited perspective that even a religious community might have at any given moment. Throughout the Hebrew Bible some individuals perceive Yahweh with greater clarity than do their contemporaries, but most are caught up in the thought forms that are a part of their culture. Some even revert to primitive morality. A graph of religious understanding in the Hebrew Bible would be irregular, but generally upward. Israel could openly and honestly reflect on days when it served Yahweh unworthily because of its confidence that Yahweh did not wait for the nation to be worthy of Yahweh. Israel understood that its God was not small, capricious, and slow; it was Israel who moved tardily and unsteadily toward maturity of both faith and understanding.

Modern generations can hardly boast of moral superiority over ancient cultures. Persons still kill their neighbors in the name of God or good or a way of life. Whatever the situation or the century, persons often enter battle feeling that they are on the side of God or the gods or at least the "right." Such a mentality both promotes the idea that whatever they do is in some fashion an act of God and rationalizes a multitude of sins as vindicated by the cause. In this context, modern humankind can understand, but not excuse, the early Israelites, for on this point the twentieth century C.E. is not so far separated from the thirteenth B.C.E.

The brutality of the conquest, then, is the story of warfare, and Israel's perception of *cherem* was more the result of its limited grasp of the nature of Yahweh than of Yahweh's purpose. Although the savagery of Israel cannot be excused, it can be understood as an act of misguided faith and obedience. It could be hoped that later generations would act with more light, but the shutters of understanding are always conditioned by the environment. God remains the same; persons change as God's revelation breaks upon them.

Holy Land and Covenant People

However the land of Canaan became the land of Israel, a widespread scriptural tradition emphasizes that the land was actually Yahweh's land,[22] or Yahweh's heritage.[23] This concept was supremely important for the life and worship of Israel. It could never look upon the land as totally its possession. Although it had been given Israel in the conquest, it remained Yahweh's land and accordingly remained a land of promise.

Because Canaan continued to be Yahweh's heritage, Israel interpreted its role to be that of proving itself worthy of dwelling in Yahweh's land. If it were to enjoy a long and happy possession of the land, it had to obey Yahweh's law.

---

[22]Leviticus 25:23; Joshua 22:19; Jeremiah 2:7; 16:18.
[23]1 Samuel 26:19; 2 Samuel 14:16; Jeremiah 50:11; Psalms 68:9; 79:1.

The virtual paradise of Canaan, tended by Yahweh, would be Israel's only so long as it remained faithful to its covenant obligations. If Israel failed to live by covenant law, Yahweh would forsake the land and paradise would turn to chaos.

To keep the land holy, Israel had to be particularly careful to avoid defilement by sins characteristic of the Canaanites.[24] Israel had to abstain from the offensive fertility customs of these people lest it, like they, defile the land and be driven from it. In its later history the nation did defile Yahweh's land and made Yahweh's heritage an abomination. In the face of such corruption the eighth-century prophets warned Israel that such unfaithfulness would result in its expulsion from Canaan to die in an "unclean" land.[25] The prophet Ezekiel (chap. 10) in Babylonian exile envisioned even Yahweh driven from Jerusalem because of abominations practiced there. To abide in Yahweh's land, Yahweh's heritage, Israel had to be holy because the land was holy.

Such thinking about the land influenced Israel's legal code. Numerous laws were oriented around the agricultural experience as a way to confess the holiness of the land. Laws pertaining to firstfruits,[26] the tithe,[27] and gleaning[28] were closely tied to the idea that the Israelites lived as strangers and sojourners in Yahweh's land. The first gatherings of a harvest were brought to the sanctuary as an offering because the Israelites considered themselves serfs or tenants on the property of their God. Similarly, the tithe was an instrument for sharing the bounty of the land with the priests, strangers, orphans, and widows. Sheaves were to be left in the fields for the poor to gather. In these ways the Israelites, themselves sojourners and strangers in a holy land, shared with the less fortunate among them. In doing so they brought blessings on themselves and the land where they lived.

THE TRIBAL CONFEDERACY
(JOSHUA 23, 24; JUDGES 2:5–16:31)

Affirming Sinai Covenant: Shechem

Joshua 24 brings the book of Joshua to a fitting theological climax. At Shechem "Joshua gathered all the tribes of Israel . . . and they presented themselves before God" (24:1).[29] There follows a recounting of Yahweh's deeds in Israel's history (strangely omitting events of Joshua 1–12) and an appeal to "fear Yahweh and serve him in sincerity and in faithfulness" (24:14). Clearly the Deu-

---

[24]Leviticus 18:25–29; 20:22–24; Deuteronomy 21:22ff.

[25]Amos 7:17; Hosea 9:3.

[26]Exodus 23:19; 34:26; Leviticus 19:23; 23:10; Deuteronomy 26:1.

[27]Leviticus 27:30; Deuteronomy 14:22ff.

[28]Leviticus 19:9–10.

[29]The verb "to present oneself" used here is the same verb used in Joshua 1–12 of the assembling of troops for battle.

Figure 6.5. The ruins of ancient Shechem, site of the convocation described in Joshua 23–24. (*Illustrator* Photo/Ken Touchton)

teronomist intends to affirm that the basis of Hebrew unity was to be covenant faithfulness. Although settlement in the land was as separated tribes and each tribe would largely operate its own affairs, the diverse groups were joined by their commitment to Yahweh. This idea lay at the heart of tribal confederacy that preceded the Hebrew monarchy. In solemn ceremony Joshua celebrated the affirmation of covenant earlier established at Sinai (24:25–28).

The Shechem convocation thus brought together tribal groups that stood together in their allegiance to Yahweh, but they were neither a "nation" nor a homogeneous unit. Although they were kindred folk, many had entered Canaan at different times and under different circumstances. Now a lasting bond was necessary. At Shechem their pledge of allegiance provided them with a common bond—participation in all the saving deeds of the covenant God.

Three groups "presented themselves before Yahweh" at Shechem: (1) the tribal elements that had not been in Egypt and were not worshipers of Yahweh, at least not of Yahweh as the covenant God, but recognized their relationship to the tribes that had been led into Canaan by Joshua (24:2–15); (2) those who were more fully identified with Canaanite culture and religion (24:15); and (3) the tribes that had entered Canaan with Joshua and were descended from those who had been at Sinai (24:5–9). Those in the first group, now worshipers of the patriarchal deities, were summoned to acknowledge Yahweh as Lord and to receive the story of Yahweh's dealings with the tribes that had left Egypt as their own story of faith. They were asked to recognize that the God of Abraham was the same God who had delivered Israel from Egypt and who had given them the good land of Canaan. The second group was challenged to abandon Canaanite religion in favor of covenant faith. It was imperative that they be made aware of the obligations and responsibilities that union with Israel placed on them. If they were to share in the deeds of the covenant God, they must also share in worship of the covenant God. Worship of the deities of a land implied submission to the people of that land; therefore, all allegiance to the gods of Canaan had to be forsaken in favor of allegiance to Yahweh, to whom the land belonged. The third group, those led out of Egypt by Moses and into Canaan by Joshua, reaffirmed its allegiance to the God who had delivered it from Egypt, protected it in the wilderness, and given it a new land. It also was to recognize that all the tribes represented at Shechem were recipients of the patriarchal promise.

Thus the entity "Israel" emerged from the mass of kindred 'Apiru who had for centuries been entering Canaan. The people of Yahweh had a common religious tie. Israel was identified by its covenantal relationship with Yahweh and consequently began its life in the land of promise as a religious confederacy in which Yahweh was supreme.

Life in the Confederacy

Reconstruction of Israel's organization in the period of tribal confederacy is difficult. Martin Noth[30] has put forward the thesis that Israel was an amphictyony, using a term describing later Greek amphictyonies like the Delphic league. If so, the Hebrews possessed a central religious sanctuary around which the various tribes organized themselves. Annually each tribe sent representatives to the sanctuary for the observance of a ceremony of covenant renewal presided over by an amphictyonic leader, "the judge of Israel." The man who held this office (Samuel, for example) was responsible for the preservation and interpretation of divine law to which Israel was subject. Such law had been promulgated at the Shechem convocation and was regularly proclaimed anew at covenant renewal. Its main concern was to preserve intact Israel's relationship to Yahweh and to prevent disturbance of the relationship by unlawful acts.

The Noth thesis has come in for vigorous criticism on grounds that it is anachronistic but, more significantly, assumes an organization not revealed in the evidence. Roland De Vaux reviews the evidence and concludes, "The use of the word 'amphictyony' in connection with Israel can only cause confusion and give a wrong impression of the mutual relationships between the different

---

[30]Noth, *Das System der Zwölf Stämme Israels* (W. Kohlhammer, 1950). See also Walter Harrelson, "Worship in Early Israel," *Biblical Research*, 3 (1958) 1–14.

tribes. It should be abandoned."[31] John Bright, on the other hand, is willing to preserve the term but relativize its meaning.[32] Whatever the vocabulary, one thing is clear. Tribal confederacy was held together by a religious confession. If the word "amphictyony" is used, therefore, it should designate the willingness of diverse tribal elements to act independently while confessing that they belonged to the same covenant community, affirming their belief in Yahweh as maker and sustainer of the relationship.

Membership in Israel's confederacy varied from time to time. The numbers may not have remained constant through the period; it became a twelve-tribe confederacy gradually, probably related to monthly or bimonthly service at a cultic shrine. But the number twelve eventually became sacrosanct for Israel, even when the existence of twelve Israelite tribes was not a historical reality. Although some tribes faded from the historical scene and some prominent subtribes made their appearance, Israel all the while preserved the tradition of twelve tribes descended from Jacob's sons.

The confederacy gave Israel a political life that lasted for around two hundred years. This commitment provided a unity that enabled a people who had not known sedentary existence since departing from Egypt to adjust to the soil, weather, and terrain for survival and prosperity. Through "trial and error" the Israelites learned from their neighbors to build cities marked by advances in tastes, technological skill, defenses, and productivity. Later the kingship, which replaced confederal organization, was possible only because in confederacy the tribes had already been rather loosely, but significantly, united as one people under one God, Yahweh, with "the judge" as the symbol of unity.

Religion in the Confederacy

Although we cannot describe the religio-political structures of tribal confederacy with certainty, some features are clearly evident. Shechem, the locale where confederacy was established, became a shrine center symbolizing Israel's tribal unity. Other cities, such as Shiloh, were places where the ark and tabernacle were located and hence preserved "amphictyonic" heritage.

At these shrine centers tribal groups would have gathered regularly to celebrate their unity under Yahweh. Here the ancient festivals, Passover-unleavened bread, weeks, and tabernacles, were observed. All celebrated Yahweh's acts in behalf of the people. The most important of these was the feast of tabernacles, at which there was a ceremony of covenant renewal,[33] a repetition of the type of ritual described in Joshua 24. The decisive meaning of this ceremony was the reaffirmation of allegiance to Yahweh. The recitation of Yah-

---

[31] De Vaux, *History*, p. 715.
[32] Bright, *History*, p. 163.
[33] Cf. Deuteronomy 31:9–13.

weh's deeds of salvation was a part of the observance, which brought the history of Israel to life. Sacred history was reenacted, relived, and made equally binding on every generation to which it was presented. This is clear in the deuteronomic introduction to the decalogue: "Yahweh our God made a covenant with us at Horeb. Not with our ancestors did Yahweh make this covenant, but with us, who are all of us here alive today" (Deuteronomy 5:2–3).

These sacral festivities accentuated the uniqueness of Israel's God. Yahweh was the God who had chosen the Israelites, delivered them, and watched over them in memorable fashion until they were guided by Yahweh into possession of the land. They worshiped Yahweh as sovereign and sought to obey Yahweh's bidding. Yahweh was king over their theocratic nation and, because theirs was a covenant relationship, Yahweh's demands had to be met for the covenant to be maintained.

The central figure at the central shrine city (whether Shechem, Shiloh, or Gilgal) was a "judge of Israel."[34] Like the shrines and festivals, this charismatic person symbolized tribal unity and served across tribal lines (1 Samuel 7:15f). Yahweh was the head of the confederacy, but the judge was Yahweh's representative before the people. The biblical materials tell us about at least one person who served this function, Samuel. Although Samuel functioned in many capacities, as judge he was to preserve and interpret divine law to which Israel was subject. This law had been promulgated at the ceremony by which confederacy had been organized and was regularly proclaimed anew at covenant renewal. Its main concern was to preserve intact Israel's relationship with Yahweh and to prevent disturbance of this relationship by antisocial acts. At times certain judicial responsibilities, such as settling intertribal disputes, may have also belonged to the judge.

Israel symbolized its religious life in sanctuary, ceremony, and judge. Select a contemporary religious group and indicate how it symbolizes basic religious commitments.

Yahweh versus Baal.   In sanctuary, ceremony, and judge, Israel's tribes affirmed their unity around covenant commitments. Yet the ideal was not always realized. Throughout the period true worship of Yahweh struggled against native Canaanite religions. A great deal about Canaanite religions has been learned from the Ras Shamra cultic texts. These tablets were discovered in 1929 at Ras Shamra, the site of an old Canaanite city named Ugarit on the coast of northern Syria. They can be dated roughly to the middle of the fourteenth century B.C.E., or earlier. These discoveries show that Canaanite reli-

---

[34]Samuel is the only one about whom we have detailed information. These judges are not to be confused with the military heroes of the day who were also called judges. See Noth, "Das Amt des Richters Israels," *Festschrift für Alfred Bertholet* (J. C. B. Mohr, 1950), pp. 404ff.

gion centered on fertility cults. A pantheon of deities was headed by an inactive but powerful god named El, who was the creator of earth and human beings and the begetter of all other gods. He was known as "the King, Father of Years," that is, he was the primeval father noted for wisdom, kindness, and benevolence. Although he was inactive, El controlled the universe through the gods, all of whose powers were derived from him. El's female counterpart was named Asherah, symbolized by a wooden pole.

The most active of the gods was Baal, the bringer of rain on which the fertility of the soil depended. He was the thunderer who announced his coming as rain in the lightning and thunder of storm. He was portrayed as a bull and represented by a standing stone (*massebah*). His female counterpart was his companion sister, Anath, revered as a goddess of war, bloodthirsty and passionately sexual.

The religion emphasized a myth reenacted annually by its devotees. The drama rehearsed a death and resurrection of Baal. Reenactment of the myth was believed to continue the rhythmic cycle of nature. The Canaanites sought thereby both to control the order of nature and to be associated with their deity. Among the practices of the worshipers were rituals involving sex in several forms. By means of "sympathetic magic" they attempted to induce fertility. Many types of images related to the worship were believed to possess magic powers of fertility.

The Israelites essentially identified El with Yahweh. His attributes are like those of "God, the Father," the deity of patriarchal family piety. There are no negative comments about El anywhere in the Hebrew scriptures. There are many, however, against Baal worship, which was attractive to the Israelites as agriculturalists. Why not honor the god of rain without forsaking Yahweh?

Many Israelites named their children after Baal and frequented the Baal shrines. They did not think of forsaking Yahweh; they only added the fertility practices of the native farmers. The struggle for pure religion continued long into the period of the monarchy. Although in time Yahweh, a "jealous" God, won out, the contest was long and the ordeal of purging sometimes approached catastrophe. The strength of Israel's confederacy largely accounts for the survival of its faith during this period.

Confederacy was a transitional age for the Israelites. Yahweh had been their God from Egyptian servitude to settlement in Canaan. Yahweh had been victorious in battle and adequate to their needs as a people on the move. Changes in theological concepts were called for by their new status as a "landed" people. Theological questions, however, were inseparably bound to practical questions of when to plow, plant, weed, and harvest. Countless lessons had to be learned if Israelites were to be as successful in the field as they had been as nomads and holy warriors. Skills had to be acquired from their enemies, the Canaanites and others who had lived long on the soil. In an age when deities were aligned

Figure 6.6. A "baal of lightning" from Ras Shamra, dated to the first half of the second millennium B.C.E. A fertility deity towers over a smaller figure, either a lesser deity or a subject of the god. (Courtesy, The Louvre)

with the cycles of the seasons and other elements basic to agriculture, the Israelites faced an almost impossible assignment of separating Canaanite farming techniques from Canaanite religion. The deuteronomic writer emphasizes repeatedly the infidelity of the Israelite tribes to Yahweh in favor of pagan deities. But the primary relationship between Yahweh and the people during this most difficult era was kept alive by telling stories about the heroics of military "judges" who opportunely appear to deliver groups of Yahweh's people from oppressors.

Shophets and the Book of Judges

The book of Judges is a deuteronomic interpretation of Israel's history during the days of confederacy. The historian uses stories about the heroism of various local military leaders to emphasize Yahweh as the deliverer of Israel during times of distress. The deeds of these heroes are told through the literary device of a cycle that reflects the Deuteronomist's understanding of Israel's judgment based on infidelity to Yahweh and Israel's blessing based on Yahweh's faithfulness. The cycle: the Israelites fall away from Yahweh (apostasy); Yahweh permits enemies to fall upon them (oppression); under oppression they repent and call upon Yahweh (repentance); Yahweh calls out a leader and delivers them (deliverance). Then the cycle would begin again. The repetitive cycle forms the heart of the book of Judges:

A. Conquests by various Israelite tribes: chapter 1
B. Introduction to the stories of the judges: 2:1–3:6
    1. Death of Joshua and the rise of a postconquest generation: 2:1–10
    2. Israel's cycle of apostasy, oppression, divine deliverance: 2:11–16
    3. Israel's unrepentance and peril before its enemies: 2:17–3:6
C. The age of Judges: 3:7–16:31
    1. Othniel vs. Cushan-rishathaim: 3:7–11
    2. Ehud vs. the Moabites: 3:12–30
    3. Shamgar vs. the Philistines: 3:31
    4. Deborah and Barak vs. the Canaanites: 4:1–5:31
    5. Gideon vs. the Midianites: 6:1–8:35
       (story of Abimelech, son of Gideon: 9:1–57)
       (Tola and Jair: 10:1–5)
    6. Jephthah vs. the Ammonites: 10:6–11:40
       (jealousy of the Ephraimites: 12:1–7)
       (Ibzan, Elon, and Abdon: 12:8–15)
    7. Samson vs. the Philistines: 13:1–16:31
D. Appendices: chapters 17–21
    1. Micah and the relocation of the Danites: 17:1–18:31
    2. A Levite and the Benjaminites of Gibeah: 19:1–21:25

The length of time covered by Judges and the confederacy must be determined by data found outside the book. If it is assumed that each judge immediately followed his predecessor, the period would have covered four hundred ten years. However, the judges were largely local and some were contemporaneous. The time of the judges probably lasted through most of the two centuries just prior to the days of the monarchy—that is, from about 1200 to 1020 B.C.E.

The Shophet. The name "judge" as used for these temporary leaders is something of a misnomer. The term designates in contemporary English "one who decides" or "one who renders a verdict." However, the Hebrew term *shophet*, translated "judge," means "deliverer" or "one who sets things right" or even "one who rules."

Although not elected, the *shophetim* of Israel were both civil and military rulers over those who acknowledged their leadership. They should not be confused with "the judge of Israel," who was a sanctuary official. The *shophets* were military heroes. Their status was temporary and not subject to inheritance. They acquired and held their position by virtue of the fact that "the spirit of Yahweh was upon them"—that is, they were charismatics. Apparently the prestige and following of a local *shophet* might grow as he was proven to possess extraordinary powers, attributable to Yahweh. Thus, occasionally a *shophet* might lead a coalition of two or more tribes when danger was present, but once the danger had passed, the *shophet* no longer functioned. Twelve of these *shophets* are mentioned in the book of Judges, but of six of them we know only their names.

Accounts of the feats and foibles of the judges provide some of the best examples of storytelling in Hebrew literature. Some of the stories appear to have been relatively unchanged by their incorporation into the large saga of the deuteronomic historian. The basic cycle is preserved, but with numerous variations in detail: dire oppression of sinful Israel by a non-Israelite foe, a commoner appears endowed with the spirit of Yahweh, the charismatic leader summons one or more tribes in Yahweh's battle, and Yahweh delivers the Israelites from their oppression. The final proof of the *shophet*'s charisma is Yahweh's act of victory in battle.

The book of Judges illustrates the ongoing process of conquest. The era was one of continuing tension. Israel was largely restricted to the mountains of Canaan; its enemies controlled the plains. In spite of confederacy it was fragmented according to tribes and divided by natural boundaries—rivers and mountains. Consequently, it often fell prey to its cultured and better equipped neighbors. Many towns were destroyed; some of them more than once. The non-Israelite inhabitants of Canaan evidently capitalized on Israel's weakness and used it largely at will to their own advantage and profit. These oppressors were strong enough to overpower a single tribe. At crucial times *shophets* arose against these threats. Their morality often was not exemplary, but they nonetheless championed Israel against its enemies.

Deborah and Barak. The story of Deborah and Barak is one of the most intriguing traditions in the book and illustrates the ancient character of materials that form the book of Judges. Judges 4 and 5 present two versions of the same story; chapter 4 in prose, chapter 5 in poetry. The setting is the area surrounding the Plain of Esdraelon. The occasion was a revival of strength by the Canaanites after their defeat at Hazor by Joshua. The leaders of the Canaanites were Jabin, king of Hazor, and Sisera, commander of the military forces.

Deborah was both a prophetess and a *shophet* in Ephraim when she summoned Barak to lead an army of Yahweh against the Canaanites. Assured of her support, he accepted the mission. In the prose account, ten thousand men from Zebulun and Naphtali responded to his call; in the poem, men from Ephraim, Benjamin, Issachar, and Machir (a portion of Manasseh) were also involved. All of the responding tribes were located in the north and bordered the plain that had been ruled by the Canaanites.

The important battle took place on the Plain of Esdraelon about 1125 B.C.E. and was decisive. A torrential storm assisted the Israelites by overflowing the stream Kishon and rendering the chariots of the Canaanites useless in the mud. The enemy was overwhelmed. Although Israel did not control Esdraelon after the battle, free access to the strategic area was achieved, bringing tribes in the area closer together.

The role of women in this story is significant. How surprising that a male-dominated culture would preserve such dramatic feminine heroism!! Deborah is prominent throughout and the prose account with no little humor closes with a story of a second heroine. Sisera escaped the battle and fled for sanctuary at the tent of a certain Heber. Jael, Heber's wife, received Sisera, gave him milk to drink, and hid him under a rug. Instead of standing guard as instructed, Jael took a hammer and drove a tent peg through Sisera's temple. The poetic account differs in details, but preserves the memory of Jael's heroism.

Contemporary interpreters, both male and female, have become increasingly concerned that biblical literature, obviously written and nurtured in patriarchal terms, be interpreted to enlarge its relevance for both men and women. Works focusing on this point of view may be gathered under the heading of *Feminine Hermeneutics*. A list of writings on this subject appears in the General Bibliography. Look particularly at the work of Phyllis Trible, L. M. Russell, and J. R. Mollenkott. An excellent summary article appears in the *Anchor Bible Dictionary*; examples of the approach are in *The Women's Bible Commentary*.

Deborah's song of victory in chapter 5, dated about 1100 B.C.E., is one of the oldest poems in the Hebrew Bible. The song praises the victory at Esdraelon as a mighty act of Yahweh over the Canaanites. Israelites who responded to the call to holy war are praised and blessed; those who refused to join the battle are scornfully rebuked. Yahweh is poetically described as coming on the clouds from Mount Sinai and Edom to deliver the people.[35] This imagery and

---

[35]W. F. Albright, "The Song of Deborah in the Light of Archaeology," *Bulletin of the American School of Oriental Research*, 62 (1936) 26–31.

other stylistic elements in the poem resemble Canaanite-Phoenician models, but here clearly aim to show that Yahweh controls mountain and plain.

The poem fixed in Israel's memory the great day:

> The stars fought from heaven,
> > from their courses they fought against Sisera.
> The torrent Kishon swept them away,
> > the onrushing torrent, the torrent Kishon.
> March on, my soul with might!
> > > [5:20–21]

And the hope is expressed:

> So perish all your enemies,
> > O Lord!
> But may your friends be like the sun
> > as it rises in its might.
> > > [5:31]

Samson, the Hero. The Judges story of Samson is unlike the report on the other *shophet*s. Rather than a cycle ending in Yahweh's victory, here are episodes of heroic, though finally unsuccessful, exploits of a man of deep passion and wild appetites. The enemy is the Philistines, hardly mentioned earlier but now a formidable foe of Israel. Samson, mighty in muscle, continuously embarrasses the enemy. Independent stories are strung together[36] to glamorize a hero who kills Philistines with a donkey's jawbone (15:10–17) and burns their fields with the help of foxes (15:4–5). But the giant is also vulnerable to Philistine women (chap. 16) and finally dies as a Philistine hall is pulled down around his head (16:29–30).

The Samson narrative, drawing heavily on Hebrew folk tradition, contains, for one of the few times in Hebrew scripture, sexual humor. On an occasion when Samson visited a prostitute, Gazites lay in wait for him, expecting him to be exhausted from his exploit. Rather, Samson emerged invigorated and not only escaped the plot, but also pulled down the city gates, leaving Gaza defenseless (Judges 16:1–4).

Thus the Samson narrative is not of a *shophet* who rallies tribes to fight an enemy, but stories of personal vendetta against an opponent still around at the end. The Samson materials reflect a growing animosity between Philistines and Hebrews. Does the Deuteronomist intend to prepare the way for his chief hero, David? Samson may have won a few skirmishes, but final victory would belong to David.

The Appendices. Two stories of unknown origin are appended to the book of Judges (chaps. 17–21), probably included here merely because they are

---

[36]See Blenkinsopp, "Structure," pp. 65–76. Crenshaw (*Samson*) speaks of his approach to these materials as esthetic criticism.

about two of the tribes, Dan and Benjamin. The first story (chaps. 17–18) relates the migration of a portion of Dan from central to northern Canaan. Presumably the Philistines had taken over most of their original land and forced them to move. The story tells of a Levite who accepts employment as family priest for Micah, an Ephraimite, only to be persuaded by the migrating Danites to become their priest. Together with the Danites, he steals Micah's valuable religious images and later places them at a shrine at Dan. The story probably was preserved to account for a shrine at Dan prior to its later use during the monarchy.

The second appendix (chaps. 19–21) centers on the tribe of Benjamin. It is an example of intertribal friction, and even skirmish war, which often blunted the religious confession of tribal unity (cf. 12:1–6). The story may have been preserved by Judeans to tarnish Saul's reputation and the fame of the Benjaminites as fearless warriors. It concerns a wandering Levite who was dishonored by men of Gibeah, the Benjaminite town that was to be Saul's first capital. Men of Israel were assembled at Mizpah to hear the Levite's complaint. The assembly demanded unsuccessfully that the wrongdoers of Gibeah be surrendered for violation of the covenant. War ensued, Benjaminite men were practically wiped out, and a ban against marriage to Benjaminites was introduced. The story ends with an ingenious plan to preserve the tribe by providing virgins from Jabesh-Gilead for men of Benjamin. The tribe survives, not by its own ability, but by the patronage of other Israelites.

The Theology of Judges. The book of Judges contains little high religion, but it does reflect Israelite life during the period of confederacy. The stories reflect the sinister and brutal side of life when covenant responsibilities are neglected. Hostility between Israel and neighboring tribes and the open friction among Israelite tribes themselves is clearly pictured. Temporary charismatic leaders, not always admirable, dominate the scene and, insofar as possible, are interpreted as instruments of Yahweh's providence. Remember that the book makes its point in its literary structure, not in the character of its heroes.

In the way the materials are used in Judges, the deuteronomic historian at times seems to be critical of certain features of the confederacy, but for him these are illustrative of the relationships between Yahweh and Israel in any age. Israel's faithlessness brings Yahweh's punishment; only its repentance leads to deliverance. The religious center is not a pillar of strength, nor assurance of Yahweh's presence. Israel's leadership is hardly to be applauded. Even some of the heroes appear in caricature. Samson is a lusty bully. A depraved son of Gideon murdered seventy brothers in a fool's try at kingship. Jephthah offered human sacrifice in the person of his own daughter, extraordinary in Hebrew history. Generally the deliverers show little or no knowledge of Moses' teachings or the religious traditions of Israel.

Why was there not intervention to save Jephthah's daughter as with Abraham's son (Genesis 22:11–12) or Jonathan (1 Samuel 14:44–45)?

The Jephthah story is particularly tragic and disturbing. Jephthah, who was abused as a child, as a man becomes an abuser. When he bargained with God and made his tragic vow, he abuses the tradition and law of Israel because human sacrifice was prohibited (Leviticus 18:21; Deuteronomy 18:10). Yahweh himself is abused by the implied belief that Yahweh was a deity who would be party to such an arrangement. Jephthah's daughter was abused when he sacrificed her as a payment of his vow to Yahweh. The integrity of the Israelite community was abused by the failure of anyone to protest or even question Jephthah's action. The failure to question applies not only to the persons in the story, but also to the editor or redactor who included it in Judges. The action of both Jephthah and his daughter abused all the women of the Israelite community by implying that women should willingly accept such treatment from both men and God. Phyllis Trible[37] writes of this story as a "text of terror."

Yet the book is not completely without religious value. Although the leaders are military heroes, their imperfections are not praised. The book seems to say, "This is the best that Yahweh had to work with at this time." Yahweh, even through weak *shophet*s, remains the covenant God. The book closes with these words, "In those days there was no king in the land; all the people did what was right in their own eyes" (21:25). Although the Deuteronomist records the foibles of later kings, the condemnation of confederacy leaders prepares for a better day. Yet neither judge nor king—only Yahweh—could be Israel's hope.

Weak confederal leadership and the attractiveness of many features of Canaanite religion make it little short of amazing that Hebrew religion survived during confederacy. However, threatened as it was, Yahweh worship did survive until a better day.

SUGGESTIONS FOR FURTHER STUDY

For further clarification consult the *Harper's Bible Dictionary, Mercer Dictionary of the Bible*, and the *Anchor Bible Dictionary* on these terms: amphictyony, tribal confederacy, settlement in Canaan, covenant ceremony, Deuteronomist, holy war, Baal, fertility cult, *shophet*, Canaanites, Shechem convocation, *cherem*, syncretism, charismatic leadership.

For further study of the literature of this period, read introductions to Deuteronomy, Joshua, and Judges in the standard commentary series, especially

[37]Trible, *Texts of Terror*, chap. 4.

Interpreter's Bible and *Anchor Bible*. Martin Noth, *The Deuteronomic History* (a supplement to the *Journal for the Study of the Old Testament*), is a basic study of the deuteronomic history. Consult the General Bibliography on social scientific approaches to the period (especially the works of Norman Gottwald).

Detailed technical histories of the period may be found in the works of John Bright and Roland De Vaux. Millard Lind, *Yahweh Is a Warrior: The Theology of Warfare in Ancient Israel* (Herald, 1980), treats the warrior God issue; Manfred Weippert, *The Settlement of the Israelite Tribes in Palestine*, emphasizes the peaceful entry of Hebrews into Canaan.

Archeological studies of the period are numerous; Kathleen Kenyon's reports on Jericho, Joseph Callaway's on Ai, and Yigael Yadin's on Hazor are good examples found in the journals *Biblical Archaeology* and *Biblical Archaeology Review*. A summary of all the issues related to conquest and settlement is Callaway's, "The Settlement in Canaan: The Period of the Judges" in Shanks, ed., *Ancient Israel* (chap. 3). A more comprehensive summary is in Dever's article, "Israel, History of (Archaeology and the 'Conquest')" in the *Anchor Bible Dictionary*. Also see Israel Finkelstein, *The Archaeology of Israelite Settlement*, and Weinfeld's article, "Historical Facts Behind the Israelite Settlement Pattern," *Vetus Testamentum*, 38 (1988) 324–36.

7

United Monarchy: Rise of Davidic Covenant

The latter years of the eleventh century were indeed perilous times for the Israelites. Both the end of the book of Judges and the early chapters of Samuel make it clear that the loosely constructed confederacy was no match for contemporary problems. Heroic exploits by the *shophet* Samson ended in his own death and even Samuel, the greatest of confederacy judges, could not muster sufficient strength to overcome a formidable enemy, the Philistines. The political and military environment demanded a new order for Israel to preserve its life as the people of the covenant.

From the biblical point of view, the period was more than a time of political and military crisis. Israel's religious ideas and sentiments had been closely linked to the forms and practices of confederacy. Judge, sanctuary, and cultic ceremony were sacralized vehicles by which a people had come to express religious commitments. If these structures were surrendered, what would happen to covenant? Could Israel distinguish between form and substance, organism and organization, enough to sacralize new structures? What happens when established ways of "doing religion" are no longer possible? Are there other options besides merely wishing nostalgically for the "good old days" or giving up on Yahweh? These were the questions faced by Israel as it moved toward the first millennium B.C.E., seeking to preserve its religious commitment amid the dramatic shift from confederacy to monarchy.

BACKGROUND OF THE MONARCHY
(1 SAMUEL 1–7)

The Book of Samuel

With the rise of monarchy Israel's history becomes more focused. The age of David and Solomon gave political, economic, and social form to an identifiable nation with past and future. David's monarchy in particular was radical innovation that transformed an informal and somewhat isolated community into a power among powers.[1] Because Israel's faith had been tied to passing forms, the religious task facing David was to create a "theological empire." Old ideologies had to be cast in the new molds of a royal religion. Jesse's son was able to accomplish such a transition and thus merited a status comparable to that of Abraham and Moses as a maker and preserver of Hebrew religion.[2]

Israel's change from a tribal confederacy, with loose, inadequate ties, to a strong, centralized government under a monarch is the story contained in the book of Samuel in which the chief characters are Samuel, Saul, and David. Although concerned primarily with events in the lives of Saul and David, the book carries the name Samuel, the singular religious leader who formed the major link between the judges and the kings. He was the last of Israel's judges and anointed its first two monarchs. Samuel's genius influenced the entire period and the book therefore bears his name. The book of Samuel may be outlined according to the dominance and interplay of its principal characters:

A. Samuel: 1 Samuel 1–7
B. Samuel and Saul: 1 Samuel 8–15
C. Saul and David: 1 Samuel 16 to 2 Samuel 1
D. David, king at Hebron: 2 Samuel 2–4
E. David, king at Jerusalem: 2 Samuel 5–20
F. Appendices: 2 Samuel 21–24

The book of Samuel recounts the transition from confederacy to monarchy with a sense of historical continuity, hence reconstruction of the story is not too difficult. Yet these materials have many characteristics of a historical novel to the extent that fact is not easily distinguished from the Deuteronomist's skill as a storyteller. The hero is obviously David and the counter hero is Saul— and to some extent Solomon. The supporting cast includes a variety of characters: Samuel, whose role is minimally supportive; wives from Saul's household; brigands who accept David as champion; Jonathan, an intimate friend.

David's rise to power is told with suspense often missed by readers familiar

---

[1] See Walter Brueggemann, "The Trusted Creature," *Catholic Biblical Quarterly*, 31 (1969) 484–98. In another place Brueggemann forcefully argues that the Yahwist in Genesis 2–11 intended to legitimate David's reign as the fulfillment of Yahweh's promise. Hence the Genesis narrative is neither statements about historical beginnings, nor a collection of ancient myths but extremely sophisticated theological statements dependent on the David story. See Brueggemann, "David and His Theologian," *Catholic Biblical Quarterly*, 30 (1968) 156–81; and *David's Truth in Israel's Imagination and Memory*.

[2] The separation of Samuel (as well as Kings) into two books is somewhat artificial. When the Hebrew text was translated into Greek, vowels were added nearly doubling the size of each book. So Samuel and Kings were each divided into two scrolls for ease of handling. Both books are integral parts of the deuteronomic history. The book of Ruth, found between Judges and Samuel in most Bibles, belongs among the Writings, the third division of Hebrew scripture. Although the setting of Ruth is the period of confederacy, and the story of Ruth itself is probably very ancient, the book in its present form was probably written centuries later.

with the story and fully aware of the ending. But success is not self-evident at the outset. Not only are dual accounts of the young man's selection woven together to question the value of kingship itself, but also David's status seems to be in jeopardy, first from Saul's threats and subsequently from opposition within his own family.

The story moves through the suspense to a fitting climax when David overcomes obstacle after obstacle, becomes king, nurtures growing support, and unifies a nation under ruler and capital city—all because he is Yahweh's chosen one. Denouement is reenforced by the report of Solomon's rule. With all the veneer of success, Solomon is no David. Yahweh's covenant is with Jesse's son, a commitment that continues even when signs of decay appear in the fledgling kingdom.

Although the novel characteristics of the narrative give a general sense of continuity, the story is not of one piece. Repetitions, opposing accounts, telescoped stories, narratives in tension with one another—all indicate the loose compilation of heterogeneous literary traditions. A number of ancient sources originating during the times of David and Solomon are discernible: a narrative concerning the ark, a story of Saul's rise, another of David's rise, and a narrative of David's reign. In the strongly nationalistic and historically conscious period after David's reign, these traditions were brought together into an interpretation of the course of events beginning with the Philistine troubles and consummating in the establishment of the Davidic state. The narrative as we have it is an artistic and interpretive chronicle, rather than straightforward historical narrative. It contains all the literary features characteristic of the stories in Genesis and Exodus, but in this narrative the "history" lies closer to the surface so that we are able to trace the course of events with some certainty.

However, we should not forget that the narratives of the book of Samuel are not "history" in the modern sense of the word, but are stories emphasizing developments that demonstrate Yahweh's making the nation and continuing the covenant relationship as that development occurs. Leadership of the covenant community moves from charismatic to dynastic, Samuel the judge representing the former and David the king the latter. Amid these changes, however, Yahweh remains the same covenant God, ever faithful to the Abrahamic promise.

Although the narratives of Samuel generally follow historical structures, they may be analyzed according to literary structures. Look at these materials with a literary eye and isolate plot themes, primary and secondary characters, devices used by the writers to make their point, and climax and denouement. For guidelines refer to the discussion of the literary analysis of the patriarchal-matriarchal narratives in Chapter 4 above.

In the Samuel story of the rise of monarchy, kingship is given only qualified praise. David himself is a tainted hero, demonstrating more often than might be expected that he has feet of clay. Further, the narrative has been overlaid with supplementary material about Samuel and Saul that indicates limits in kingship. The deuteronomic historian, writing after Israel had witnessed degenerate "sons of David," fitted earlier materials into the scheme of the deuteronomic telling of Israel's story. For him some kings failed to realize the purpose of their rule, both in themselves and in their style of leadership—namely, that by character and religious practice they demonstrate the nation's faithfulness to Yahweh. Their reigns represented the downside of monarchy. In this context the appointment of Israel's king is viewed as Yahweh's compromise with the insistent demand of a stubborn people. As prophet, Samuel voiced concern that the nation risked forsaking Yahweh by becoming overly dependent on the monarchy. Hence, the Deuteronomist's view of Israel's history emphasizes the conflict between earthly power politics and divine power available through faith in Yahweh. His was a prophetic attempt to come to grips with the early history of monarchy and its significance for later Israelite history and faith.

The combination of early promonarchical traditions and later antimonarchical materials[3] is seen clearly in 1 Samuel 7–12:

Antimonarchial	*Promonarchial*
7:3–8:22 Samuel leads Israel to victory over the Philistines; he opposes kingship and warns of the implicit evil of monarchy	
	9:1–10:16 Saul appointed king by Samuel, the seer, with Yahweh's approval and confirmatory signs
10:17–27 Repeated warning from Samuel and choosing Saul by lot	
	11:1–15 Saul proves himself in battle and is made king publicly
12:1–15 Samuel's "farewell address" with deuteronomic emphasis (vv. 14, 15)	

The combination represents more than weaving together material with different points of view; it reflects the Deuteronomist's judgment on Israel's monarchy. As long as centralized organization preserved the religious emphasis of the confederacy, it was a blessing; when confidence in political structure replaced dependence on Yahweh, it was a curse. Samuel's fear that the people of Israel would forsake Yahweh in reliance on monarchy was a real threat. He

---

[3]The two views of monarchy in Samuel have often been reduced to two sources: an early, promonarchy source favoring Saul (including 1 Samuel 4–6; 9:1–10:16; 11:1–11; 24 (or 26); 25; 27–31; 2 Samuel 2–7; 9–21) and a late, antimonarchy source favoring Samuel (including 1 Samuel 1–3; 7–8; 10:17–27; 12; 26 (or 24); 2 Samuel 1. See George B. Caird, "The First and Second Book of Samuel," *Interpreter's Bible*, II:855–61.

and religious leaders after him were perpetual prodders of national conscience, reminding Israel that it belonged to Yahweh in fact as well as in name.

The Coming of the Philistines

Although the Deuteronomist has reservations about the rise of monarchy, changes in Israel's political, social, and religious structures were inevitable. Simply the passing of time encouraged movement toward more formal organization.[4] But a primary factor in the rise of monarchy was the coming of the Philistines, a people who appeared in Canaan early in the confederacy period.[5] The Philistines were one of many "sea peoples" who moved out of areas around the Aegean Sea and settled along the eastern shores of the Mediterranean from Ugarit in the north to Ashkelon in the southwest of Canaan. Some of these "sea peoples" attacked Egypt as early as Merneptah and were driven back at great cost. Soon after 1200 B.C.E., they pressed to the borders of Egypt and were repelled by Ramses III in a great sea and land battle. Thwarted in their attempt to enter Egypt, they occupied the coast of Canaan.

Along the southern coastal plain the Philistines settled in five major centers:[6] Gaza, Ashkelon, Ashdod, Ekron, and Gath. Each city with its surrounding area was ruled over by a "lord." Because there were close fraternal ties among the lords, the Philistines were sufficiently united to constitute a major threat to the Israelites. Their appearance in Canaan, coupled with the fact that they had an almost monopolistic control over the iron coming into the land, made them a formidable enemy. Iron weapons gave them an advantage over their neighbors, which was not to be broken until Israel came into free use of the metal. So strong were the Philistines that, although they were unsuccessful in invading Egypt, they with other "sea peoples" thwarted the dream of Ramses III to establish an empire across the East. Egypt's last hope for renewed imperial glory vanished with the settlement of Philistines along Canaan's shores and Israel's loose confederacy soon suffered from Philistine pressure. After their occupation of the coastal plain, the Philistines somewhat adapted themselves to Canaanite culture, language, and religion. They grew in prowess and influence, and gradually began to dominate Israel. No *shophet* came forward in Israel to deliver it from Philistine oppression. Samson's personal grudge fight against them was singularly dramatic but unsuccessful. Israel's confederacy with religious identity but little military muscle was simply inadequate to deal with a threat of such dimensions. Under the pressure the tribes turned toward

---

[4]Cf. James W. Flanagan, "Chiefs in Israel," *Journal for the Study of the Old Testament*, 20 (1981), 47–75.

[5]See Neal Bierling, *Giving Goliath His Due: New Archaeological Light on the Philistines* (Baker, 1992), and Edward Hindson, *The Philistines and the Old Testament* (Baker, 1972).

[6]For examples of archeological work at these sites see Stern, *New Encyclopedia*: Moshe Dothan, "Ashdod," I, 93–102, and Lawrence Stagner on "Ashkelon," I, 103–12.

centralized political organization. Religious syncretism had weakened confederacy ties, but the military strength of the Philistines brought the old order into serious jeopardy.

Culturally the Philistines far surpassed their inland Israelite neighbors. As a maritime people their commercial contact with other peoples gave them a cosmopolitan outlook; Israel was isolated in the hills. Philistines worked and fought with iron tools and weapons; Israel had only flint and soft copper. The Philistines had a monopoly on the available iron and carefully withheld the technique of its production from Israel.[7] Even the ceramics of Israel were inferior. Hence, political dominance of the Philistines during the days prior to the monarchy was only one of many aspects of Philistine supremacy over the less accomplished Israelites.

Breakdown of Confederacy

The Philistines, who eventually gave their name to Canaan for centuries to come,[8] thus provided the occasion for the establishment of monarchy. Their growth in power and insatiable demand for additional territory were directly related to the confederacy's collapse. Informal Israelite armies were no match for the efficient Philistine machine. As the Philistines increased in numbers and power, they moved inland and Israelite tribal groups along the border felt their presence. This pressure is preserved in the Judges story (18:1–31) of the migration of a sizable portion of the tribe of Dan to a new land in northern Canaan, forced by the Philistine appetite for land. Although Israel had other enemies, none compared with the Philistines. Only when a leader arose who could break the power of Philistia would the fortunes of Israel improve. To the Israelites, such a leader would have to be a king. To the Deuteronomist, confederacy embodied the religious ideal for Israel and the move to a monarch was a major threat to covenant as it had been preserved through tribal confederacy.

The Philistine crisis reached a critical stage when the cultic center at Shiloh fell. The deuteronomic story focuses on Eli, the "judge of Israel," and his two sons. Eli was faithful, but Hophni and Phinehas were selfish and corrupt men who used the sanctuary and its sacrificial system for personal gain and sensual gratification. The Philistines won a devastating victory at Aphek (or Ebenezer) near the Philistine coast.[9] The Israelites were defeated; Hophni and Phinehas

---

[7]The first datable iron agricultural implement discovered in Israel by archeologists is a plowpoint coming from Saul's capital, Gibeah. See Wright, *Archaeology*, p. 120.

[8]The name "Palestine" derives from "Philistine."

[9]1 Samuel 4. This event probably occurred between 1050 and 1030 B.C.E. Archeological data on Aphek may be found in the summary by Pirhiya Beck and Moshe Kochavi in Stern, *New Encyclopedia*, I, 62–72.

were killed; the ark of the covenant, symbol of Yahweh's presence and Israelite unity, was captured; and Eli, the judge, died. In one swift stroke the Israelites sustained both military collapse and spiritual demoralization. Israel's low morale was dramatically epitomized by the name given to the child of Phinehas born at the time of the defeat: "Ichabod" meaning "no glory." The evaluation of the narrator is succinct: "The glory has departed from Israel; for the ark of God has been captured" (1Samuel 4:22).

Archeological evidence indicates that the Philistines followed their victory at Aphek with a march on Shiloh.[10] The religious capital of Israel was burned to the ground. The captured ark made a plaguing round of the Philistine cities before it was finally returned to Israel.[11] With the sanctuary at Shiloh gone and the ark out of the public eye, order was shattered. Although Shiloh's fall seemed to be utter catastrophe for Israel's religious life, the people actually stood on the threshold of a new day. Israel was forced to reexamine values preserved in the old confederacy to seek new ways to sustain covenant with Yahweh. With Shiloh in ruins and the Philistines pressing inland for their territory, something had to be done. The expected sociological transformation from tribal/clan through chiefdom toward kingship was undoubtedly part of the breakdown of confederacy, but the major factor was the increasing threat of the Philistines. Stronger political and military organization was demanded; but more necessary from the point of view of the Deuteronomist was preserving cherished religious principles by associating them with emerging political structures. Survival of Israel's religion demanded it!

Standing in the breach between the old and new order are Samuel and Saul, for whom the times must have been as personally confusing as they were for the nation. Samuel appears as seer, priest, and prophet. He served as "the judge of Israel," frequenting the important shrines at Bethel, Gilgal, and Mizpah.[12] At times he resembled the charismatic military *shophets*, leading Israel into battle against the Philistines. Certainly he performed priestly functions in anointing kings and blessing troops. As spokesman for Yahweh, he preached as a prophet. His multiple roles may be partially explained by the conflation of literary traditions, but even the combination demonstrates Samuel's uniqueness in Israel's memory. As diverse roles converged in him, so the hopes for a new day of unity and identity centered in him. What Moses had been to the exodus and Joshua to conquest, Samuel was to become for the monarchy.

---

[10]Israel Finkelstein, "Shiloh," in Stern, *New Encyclopedia*, IV, 1364–70.

[11]1 Samuel 5:2–5. Notice how the ancient tradition of the ark plays up the malevolent presence of the sacred by emphasizing that plague followed it through Philistia and Philistine gods were powerless in its presence.

[12]1 Samuel 7:15–17.

SAMUEL AND SAUL
(1 SAMUEL 8–31)

Selection and Anointing of Saul

Reconstructing the history of transition to monarchy faces some problems. The Deuteronomist obviously possessed more materials about monarchy than about confederacy, but details are scarce. Theological and prophetic concerns color the way independent cycles of stories about Samuel, Saul, and David are woven together. Yahweh's judgment on the kings for their failure to realize covenant promise and blessings is stressed; all subsequent kings are measured against the ideal sovereign, David, whom the Deuteronomist presents not as perfect, but as the noblest expression of kingship under Yahweh's sovereignty. The Deuteronomist is vitally concerned with the worship of Yahweh at the Jerusalem sanctuary because such centralization demonstrates Israel's choice of Yahweh over the Baals of Canaan.

The book of Samuel portrays tribal leaders asking Samuel to anoint a king for them. The establishment of a monarchy seemed the only hope for survival. A king would provide the authoritative leadership necessary in the crisis. A strong centralized government would surpass the city-state system of the Philistines and assure ultimate victory.

As noted above, the selection of Israel's first king is presented from two points of view. The promonarchy tradition[13] makes Saul the central figure and the favored of Yahweh, whereas the antimonarchy tradition[14] glorifies Samuel and describes Saul as rejected by Yahweh. The earlier story tells of the tall handsome Benjaminite coming to the seer, Samuel, seeking information about some lost asses of his father. Under Yahweh's authority Samuel anointed Saul as king. A successful campaign against the Ammonites satisfactorily demonstrated that the spirit of Yahweh was upon Saul, and subsequently "all Israel" recognized him as Yahweh's anointed sovereign and at Gilgal publicly installed him as king.

In the other tradition Samuel resisted the idea of kingship and reluctantly anointed Saul after insistent demands for a king by the people. In effect these demands were tantamount to rejection of Yahweh, as well as Samuel and his sons, in order to gain a king "like all the nations." Samuel interpreted this demand as apostasy. In this tradition political unity threatened unity by religious commitments. So Samuel reluctantly yielded only at Yahweh's command: "Listen to the voice of the people in all that they say to you; for they have not rejected you, but they have rejected me from being king over them" (1 Samuel 8:7). After a severe warning to Israel about what it could expect

---

[13]Ibid., 9:1–10; 11; 13:3b–15.
[14]Ibid., 7:3–8:22; 10:17–27; 12.

Contemporary Events	Israel	
	United Monarchy	1020–922
Philistine threat continued through Saul's reign	Saul	1020–1000
	David	1000–961
Defeat of Philistines by David	Hebron reign	
	Jerusalem reign	
Shechem convocation, 922 (Revolt of the North)	Solomon	961–922
	Divided Monarchy	922–587
	Judah	Israel
	922–587	922–722

Figure 7.1. The Hebrew monarchies, c. 1020–587 B.C.E.

from a king,[15] Samuel cast lots that fell upon Saul, and at Mizpah Saul was proclaimed king of Israel.

These dual perspectives may well reflect the selective process whereby Saul became the fully recognized ruler over Israel. During the unstable period of transition from the loosely organized tribal confederacy to the more stabilized monarchy, a certain amount of vacillation must have occurred. Through several convocations the tribal units gradually came to agree on their new way of life. The ambiguities of the period are typified in Samuel, who is entwined in all the events with oddly ambivalent emotions, given the degree of his personal involvement. As the story is told, Samuel represents the past and the future. Clearly he was being asked to take a secondary role. Throughout Saul's reign, Samuel must have found himself strangely torn between support of and opposition to the whole idea of monarchy. One can wonder if Saul's outcome would have been different had he enjoyed the enthusiastic support of the chief religious leader of Israel.

Do you admire Samuel as a leader? Why or why not? If you could be Samuel with benefit of hindsight, how might you have acted differently?

On the other hand, Samuel's suspicion of the monarchy served Israel creatively. His fear that Israel would forsake Yahweh in its dependence on a king was a real possibility. When Saul violated covenant, Samuel's role was clear. His voice again became a cry of Yahweh's judgment. This was Samuel's primary role in Israel's history. He was Yahweh's agent for preserving Israel's basic covenant identity as tribal groups moved toward monarchy. To the Deu-

---

[15]Ibid., 8:10–18. The present wording is clearly deuteronomic.

teronomist, Samuel's judgment on Saul pointed up demands made on Yahweh's anointed king: that out of personal closeness to Yahweh he lead the people in faithful and obedient adherence to covenant.

Saul as King

The book of Samuel first focuses on Saul's selection as king, his early demonstrations of Yahweh's victorious power, and the slow deterioration of the new king. Then, though the story of Saul continues, the emphasis shifts to David's rise to kingship, the real heart of the deuteronomic account of the early monarchy. Saul's story is a sad one of brilliance diminishing toward murkiness, of the awful journey from God-anointed to God-forsaken, of glory departed. For the Deuteronomist, Saul is both a historical and literary example of the promises and failures of kingship. But remember that in the story he is not the chief character. Saul's failure to be the ideal king serves only to enhance the introduction of the more successful hero, David.

Saul began his reign in approximately 1020 B.C.E. as a charismatic judge. Samuel recognized the young man as one on whom the spirit of Yahweh rested. Anointing by Samuel was official religious endorsement of Saul. However, popular acceptance by the people was also necessary to make him king. A convocation in which Samuel openly declared his support won considerable following for Saul, but what really thrust him into the public eye was a military campaign against the Ammonites.

The town of Jabesh-Gilead in Transjordan had been attacked by the Ammonites, who demanded the right eye of all inhabitants as the terms of surrender. Jabesh-Gilead appealed to Saul for help and "the spirit of God came mightily upon Saul."[16] He killed one of the oxen with which he was plowing, cut it into twelve pieces and sent the parts to the twelve tribes, threatening to act similarly with any tribe that failed to join in a holy war to relieve Jabesh-Gilead. The response was unanimous and the military effort decisively victorious. At Gilgal, following this victory, the people gave Saul its enthusiastic endorsement. He became king in fact. As a bonus he gained the unfailing devotion of Jabesh-Gilead.

Although similar to that of Edom and Moab,[17] early kingship in Israel was unique in form. In some ways it attempted to give a permanent structure to charismatic judgeship. Saul came to the kingship primarily as a charismatic warrior and continued as Yahweh's designated leader because of the perennial Philistine threat. Installed as king at the sanctuary at Gilgal, Saul made little discernible change in the nature of the tribal organization. In short his reign was marked by no clean break with Israel's old order.

[16]Ibid., 11:6.
[17]See Noth, *History*, p. 171.

The pomp, splendor, and ornateness often associated with eastern rulers were absent from the reign of Saul. He established no royal court. A large part of the army came from his own tribe of Benjamin and headquarters remained at his hometown, Gibeah. Saul had no harem, levied no regular taxes, conscripted no troops. What could be called his palace was more like a rustic fortress than the luxurious dwelling of an eastern monarch. Located on a prominent hill about three miles north of Jerusalem, the Gibeah residence was strongly fortified. At each corner was a protective tower. Indeed this palace-fortress was formidable and adequate, but without splendor.[18] The unadorned exterior of the building and its ordinary contents reflect the simplicity of the life of Israel's first monarch. Saul remained more akin to his *shophet* predecessors than to wealthy and cosmopolitan potentates.

Saul's Early Success

Like the earlier *shophet*s, Saul was a warrior. He did what he could do best; he waged holy war for Yahweh. On the battlefield the king performed brilliantly during the early part of his reign. By military exploits he maintained the allegiance of all the tribes, which was in itself an accomplishment. Saul's personal magnetism caught the imagination of his soldiers so that they followed him with pride. Thus, he laid a foundational esprit de corps, which was to live after him and be utilized by his more glamorous and better-endowed successor.

Saul's military success against the Philistines[19] is related by the Deuteronomist to underscore the heroics of Saul's son Jonathan and at the same time indicate that the son failed the test for kingship by violating the *cherem* of holy war. Israel won a successful skirmish with a Philistine garrison, but the enemy amassed a retaliatory attack. When Israelite defeat seemed imminent, Jonathan recklessly plunged into the Philistine camp at Michmash, creating chaos. The Philistines were routed, their garrisons were driven from the central hill country, and Israel enjoyed greater freedom of movement in their own territory.

But victory almost cost Jonathan his life. Saul had proclaimed all food taboo during the day of battle. Jonathan, unaware of his father's prohibition, ate some honey and Saul ordered his execution for violating the *cherem*. Only intervention by the people, who pleaded that the victory proved Yahweh's presence, saved Jonathan. Nonetheless, the biblical writer sees this as a failure of Jonathan to qualify for kingship.

The defeat of the Philistines was followed by successful campaigns[20] against

---

[18]For a brief summary of recent archeological studies of Gibeah, see the article by C. Graesser, Jr., in *Interpreter's Dictionary: Supp. Vol.* pp. 363–64.

[19]1 Samuel 13.1–14:46.

[20]Ibid., 14:47–15:9.

Moabites, Edomites, and the Aramean kingdoms of Zobah. The Amalekites, who from their home in the desert around Kadesh had continued to harass Israel, were so subdued that they ceased to be an enemy. Yet sweeping military success did not assure religious support for Saul.

Saul Without Samuel

Two stories in the book of Samuel focus on the rejection of Saul's kingship. In these episodes Samuel withdrew whatever support he had given the king. The first story condemns Saul for performing a priestly function.[21] During the Philistine campaign, Samuel failed to appear at Gilgal in time to bless the army for holy battle. Saul offered sacrifices and was vigorously denounced by Samuel as presumptuous. The seer announced that Saul's house would not continue to rule over Israel.

In the early source[22] Saul performs such functions without condemnation and later both David and Solomon do the same.[23] David is even praised for his behavior. Although these stories may reflect that roles for priest and king have not yet been specifically defined, the point of the Deuteronomist is clearly in another direction. The materials are antimonarchy and anti-Saul. In a way the theme is a question, Is Saul the man after God's heart? The answer both in the ancient traditions and in the deuteronomic use of them is No, unfortunately, he is not.[24]

A second story about Saul's rejection appears in the later source of Samuel.[25] Here, although Saul wins a military victory, he is portrayed as disobedient to Yahweh and unworthy of kingship. After victory over the Amalekites, Saul violated *cherem* by sparing Agag, the Amalekite king, and saving the best of the spoils. Although Saul explains that these had been preserved for a special sacrifice at Gilgal, Samuel's response is condemnation without mercy:

> Surely, to obey is better than sacrifice,
>   and to heed than the fat of rams. . . .
> Because you have rejected the word of Yahweh,
>   he has also rejected you from being king.
>   [1 Samuel 15:22–23]

Samuel personally slaughtered Agag by cutting him to pieces, a forceful and gruesome act of primitive religious behavior. Saul is closer to moral responsibility than Samuel, but the storyteller is not really concerned with the ethics of dealing with enemies. The Deuteronomist condemns Saul, the political and military leader, for usurping the religious authority of Samuel. In the revised

---

[21]Ibid., 13:7b–15a.
[22]Ibid., 14:31–35.
[23]2 Samuel 6:12–19; 24:25.
[24]Hans W. Hertzberg, *I and II Samuel* (Westminster, 1964), pp. 118, 123.
[25]1 Samuel 15:1–35.

theocracy, this was unacceptable. Kingship had not yet been vested with such religious authority and would not be until Samuel passed from the scene and David as king became Yahweh's emissary. So Saul had violated Israel's covenant character; he had to go. Samuel the king-maker is pictured as Samuel the king-breaker.

Saul without Samuel became increasingly tragic. The situation was worsened by the maneuvering of an aging Samuel, who not only withdrew his support, but began to arrange for the next king to move into place. A stronger person might have withstood the pressure, but not Saul. He perceptibly disintegrated, becoming depressed to moroseness. Physically every inch a man, he often acted like a child, fleeing from even the imaginary. Without Samuel, Saul was a man without Yahweh. Without a sense of divine destiny, he trembled before his responsibilities.

Separated from Samuel, Saul's problems continued and multiplied and mounted. The Philistines continued to press their advantage. The tribes retained too much autonomy and independence—a weaker person could hardly have held them together. Mental depression tormented the king; his charisma was departing. Jealousy grew to unnatural proportions. In such a portrayal is the Deuteronomist preparing for his hero David? Saul becomes increasingly tragic, almost a caricature of what Israel's king should be.

Having removed his endorsement from one king, Samuel selected another.[26] The narrative describing this is strikingly similar to the story of Saul's anointing and is told with exceptional drama. Under pretext of offering sacrifices in the village, Samuel went to Bethlehem in Judah to the house of Jesse. During the oblations required as preparation for sacrifice, each member of the family came before Samuel. Finally David, the youngest son, was brought in from the fields and, to the surprise of his family, was selected as Saul's successor. David, in contrast to Saul, was not selected because of his physical stature. Samuel was restrained from anointing the more imposing Eliab, the elder brother, by the words of Yahweh, "Do not look on his appearance or on the height of his stature . . . for Yahweh does not see as mortals see; they look on the outward appearance, but Yahweh looks on the heart" (1 Samuel 16:7).

Samuel anointed the handsome, ruddy lad, and "the spirit of Yahweh came mightily upon David." Saul's successor had been chosen and now the narrative moved to the chief character.

Saul and David

The book of Samuel has been put together to legitimate David's reign. The materials underscore that David succeeds Saul because he is Yahweh's choice, not only over his brothers but also over Saul's dynasty. This is affirmed by his

---

[26]Ibid., 16:1–13.

marriage into the house of Saul, his military prowess over the enemies of Yahweh's people, and popular affirmation by both southerners and northerners. The theological point is clear: David is Yahweh's elect, selected to replace one from whom Yahweh's presence has departed. Saul's declining influence and the rise of David to popular acclaim are parts of the same story. In the deuteronomic account,[27] obviously colored by the bias of later evaluation, the lives of Saul and David are interwoven. Saul lived out a dreary existence as a rejected man—abandoned by Samuel and forsaken by Yahweh to struggle with the isolation of his own confusion. Compounding Saul's travail was the growing popularity of a young national hero who ironically came to the public eye through the palace of Saul.

In Saul's House.   Two stories of David's introduction to Saul are preserved. One reports his selection as the king's musician and armor-bearer. His music stilled the rage of the agitated, depressed king, and in this role he won royal affection and favor. The other account reports that David came to Saul's attention through the well-known Goliath incident. After the shepherd youth had met successfully the taunting challenge of the giant Philistine, killing Goliath with his own sword, Saul inquired about the hero's name.[28]

Both accounts reflect a pleasant relationship between Saul and David at the outset. David became part of palace life and enjoyed the favor of the king. Mutual devotion developed between David and Jonathan. Although David's popularity and later his marriage into the royal family made him a logical threat to whatever aspirations Jonathan might have had to the throne, the two remained steadfast friends,[29] even establishing a covenant recognizing David as king-elect.

David's early days in Saul's palace were also times of growing popularity with the masses. His military prowess not only won him rapid promotion in the army and the loyalty of soldiers who fought under him, but also captured the public imagination. Soon women in the streets, welcoming home the soldiers, chanted:

> Saul has killed his thousands,
> and David his ten thousands.
> [1 Samuel 18:7]

Initially David's rise to power seemed meteoric and certain, but then the theme is reversed. His success and popularity bred uneasiness and distrust in

[27]Ibid., 16:14–31:13.

[28]2 Samuel 21:19 credits Elhanan with Goliath's death and 1 Chronicles 10:5, obviously trying to reconcile the two traditions, says that Elhanan killed Goliath's brother. The interpretation that Elhanan and David refer to the same man, David being simply a throne name, is improbable. See Bright, *History*, p. 192.

[29]Cf. 1 Samuel 20:42.

the troubled mind of the rejected Saul. The king, already personally on the defensive because of his separation from Samuel and his fear that his own charisma had also departed, saw in David the aspirant to the throne. Possibly rumors of David's anointing ran through the palace. Apprehension mounted to jealousy and jealousy to a rage, which culminated in Saul's decision to kill the young commander in his army.

An early attempt to slay David with a spear as he played for the depressed Saul was the temperamental action of an agitated king, but soon Saul overtly attempted either to mar David's hero image or to kill him. Saul reneged on his promise to give his daughter Merab as wife to the slayer of Goliath. [30] Again, when he discovered that his younger daughter Michal was in love with David, Saul maneuvered the situation, hoping for David's death. Saul set the price for marriage to his daughter at one hundred Philistine foreskins. David brought two hundred and Michal became his wife. Another royal plan was thwarted.

Eventually the efforts of Saul became cool, calculated attempts to kill an opponent. Jonathan and his servants were instructed to slay David. Soldiers were sent to arrest David at his residence, but Michal delayed the pursuers and her husband escaped. Saul's plans to kill the young aspirant failed, but David's flight appeared to short-circuit his claim to kingship.

David, the Fugitive.   In spite of several efforts by Jonathan to reconcile the two, Saul's hostility was too deep for David to remain in Gibeah without endangering his life. Therefore, David left the palace and spent the next several years as a fugitive from the king. The Deuteronomist underscores that David never wavered in his respect for Saul as Yahweh's anointed king even when Saul acted so inconsistently with Israel's religious heritage. Saul is the villain; David, the hero. [31]

David first sought sanctuary with religious leaders. He went to Samuel in Ramah and was delivered from the pursuing Saul only when the king was caught up in the religious fervor of a band of ecstatic prophets. David fled to Nob where he received help from a group of priests led by Ahimelech. He was given the holy bread and Goliath's sword, which had evidently been brought to Nob as a religious trophy. Saul continued his pursuit and David had to leave for Philistia. For assisting David, eighty-five priests of Nob, including Ahimelech, were ruthlessly murdered. Saul's Israelite warriors would not lay sword to the priests, and so an Edomite mercenary, Doeg, did the work of execution. Of the priests, only Abiathar, a son of Ahimelech, managed to survive the bloody purge and escape to David's camp.

---

[30]Ibid., 17:25.
[31]Consider episodes with the Ziphites (1 Samuel 23.14–24), at Engedi (1 Samuel 24), and at Ziph (1 Samuel 26), where David had opportunity but refused to slay Saul.

From Nob David fled to Gath and sought refuge with the Philistine king there. However, the Philistines became suspicious and David escaped Gath only by feigning madness. He returned to the hill country of Judah and made his hideout near the cave of Adullam in the Shephelah southwest of Bethlehem.[32] There David became the leader of an "outlaw" band as debtors, fugitives, and political malcontents joined him. Abiathar, the priest of Nob, also joined the group. Like the outlaws of the early American West who moved from one hideout to another to elude arrest, these men of Israel with prices on their head ranged across the wilderness. The group was organized around David and maintained itself by selling protection to wealthy men along the borders of Judah.

A characteristic story of the period is about the ill-natured Nabal,[33] a "churlish and ill-behaved" Calebite who refused to return a favor from David. Only a secretive large gift by Nabal's beautiful wife, Abigail, diverted the impulsive wrath of the fugitives. David's eventual marriage to Abigail made all Nabal's property the possession of his soldiers. The episode undoubtedly reveals not only the means by which David's group maintained itself, but also how they assured friendship of persons of Judah living along the border under constant threat from marauders.

During his exile from the palace, David also befriended Philistines without tying his cause to theirs. When the fugitives were driven into Philistine territory, David shrewdly played both ends to accomplish his own purposes. Sometimes he sided with Israelites against the Philistines;[34] at other times he joined Philistines to fight common enemies. On one occasion he took his soldiers to Gath where he was accepted as vassal and given the village of Ziklag, whence David's brigands made strategic raids against Israel's enemies in the Negeb. David so distributed the spoils of battle between Gath and Judah that both assumed he was on their side. Thus, the period is strategic for David's rise to power. When Saul dies, David already has a base of support in Judah where his loyalty to his own people is established.[35] Further, Philistine attitudes are likely to be tolerant toward David, who from their perspective is Saul's enemy and therefore their friend. Both factors contribute to a lull in the struggle between David and Saul, which enabled David to solidify his position.

The Battle of Gilboa.   The controversy between David and Saul was resolved with dramatic suddenness on the plain of Esdraelon at Mt. Gilboa. Here the Philistines marshaled for attack on the Israelite forces. David and his men were among the Philistines and might have been in the battle against their own people but for Philistine fears that they might defect to Israel. David's men were released to return to Ziklag.

---

[32] 1 Samuel 22:3–4 suggests that David took his parents to Moab for protection.
[33] 1 Samuel 25.
[34] Ibid., 23:1–13.
[35] Ibid., chap. 27.

On the eve of the battle Saul was a pitiable sight. A source replete with legendary materials conveys the depths of the king's despondence. The tragic king made every effort to find some religious reassurance of victory. Dreams, oracles, and prophets failed him. Finally, he resorted to a measure exceptional for an Israelite, particularly a king. Magic was forbidden by law and, although Israelites were tempted to consult with the dead as did their neighbors, necromancy and mediums were specifically forbidden by Saul himself. Out of desperation Saul disguised himself, sought out a witch at Endor, and had her summon the dead Samuel. Even from the dead Samuel contributed to Saul's downfall. He reminded Saul of his rejection by Yahweh and predicted defeat for Israel and death for Saul and his sons. The king was left to face the enemy with simply his own resources. The medium showed more kindness toward Saul than did the Deuteronomist. She prepared a meal, fed Saul and his servants, and sent them into the night. With this strange story the Deuteronomist describes Yahweh as in control over the occult.

The Philistines won decisively. Saul and his sons, Jonathan, Abinadab, and Malchishua,[36] died. The Philistines found the corpses, cut off Saul's head, displayed his armor in a temple of Ashtaroth, and hanged the bodies on the walls of Bethshan. Friends from Jabesh-Gilead, which Saul had delivered early in his reign, took the bodies from Bethshan and buried them at Jabesh. Israel's first king had come to an inglorious end.

The tragic narrative about Saul is shaped by the deuteronomic presupposition that faithfulness to Yahweh brings success and unfaithfulness brings failure. The story is filled with themes reminiscent of earlier narratives. Saul's turning against David is like Cain's rejection of Abel. Like Jacob he is a flawed "prince of God." As king he represented Yahweh to Israel and Israel to Yahweh. As a character in this tragic story he represents both his own successes and failures and those of the whole nation of Israel. The genius of the Israelite narrator lies precisely in this ability to recount "history" in a way that fills it with relevant theological meaning.

Israel's losses at Gilboa were devastating and demoralizing. Its king and most of its choicest fighting men were killed. Israel was in dire straits; Philistines controlled the heart of western Canaan. But a better day was about to dawn under the leadership of David.

THE REIGN OF DAVID
(2 SAMUEL)

By any measure, the outstanding figure of Israelite monarchy was David. His rule was so successful that Israel's covenant traditions came to be associated

---

[36]Ibid., 31:2; cf. 14:49, where a son named Ishri is listed but not Abinadab.

with his reign and Davidic traditions became symbols of covenant long after his death.

Introduced into palace life at the court of Saul and disciplined by the rigors of survival in the rugged terrain of southern Judah, David came to the kingdom at an opportune time. No strong empire dominated the Near East. The Hittite empire had been destroyed, Egypt was no threat, and Assyria had not yet matured. Saul had borne the weight of an awkward confederacy and softened the fall of outmoded political forms. The time was right for establishing a stabilized government. Building a strong and respected Israelite state was primarily the accomplishment of one man—David.

Davidic kingship falls into three distinct periods. For two years after the death of Saul he reigned in Hebron over Judah alone.[37] Then he ruled in Hebron for an additional five and a half years over all of Israel. The longest period of his reign came after the transfer of the capital to Jerusalem, where for thirty-three years David remained in control.[38] During his reign of approximately forty years, Israel became a recognized power among the states of the Near East.

King of Judah

After Gilboa, Israel's experiment with monarchy appeared to have ended in failure. The venture had begun well with the cautious sanction of Samuel. Saul's initial forays against the Philistines had been successful. Trouble began with Samuel's early disenchantment with the anointed king and ended with Israel's devastating defeat at Gilboa. Now the Philistines controlled interior western Palestine. At this point the story turns directly to David, the fugitive who, although Yahweh's anointed successor to the throne, seemed out of the picture.

Circumstances were peculiarly propitious for the rise of David, and he was patiently willing to avail himself of the opportunities. As we have noted, David was on quasi-friendly terms with the Philistines. They considered him Saul's enemy and were willing to support David in order to keep the Israelites divided in loyalty. Most certainly it was with Philistine consent that David became ruler in Hebron,[39] a town in Judah in southern Canaan.

Remember also that David and his soldiers had protected outlying areas of Judah from marauding enemies, making lasting friends there. But more than that, David was himself a Judean. As a native of Bethlehem he was a tribal hero who had established himself as a seasoned military campaigner. Hence after the battle at Mt. Gilboa, Judah independently acclaimed David king of

---

[37]Cf. 2 Samuel 2:10.
[38]See ibid., 5:5.
[39]Avi Ofer, "Hebron," in Stern, *New Encyclopedia*, II, 606–9.

Hebron, the chief Judean city. Judah had always been one of Israel's strongest tribes, tending largely to go its own way. Its action not only commenced the reign of Israel's most illustrious monarch, but also gave Judah "an enduring political form. A state of Judah emerged as a separate entity."[40]

After his acclamation as king in Hebron, David gradually gained support from outside Judah, undoubtedly enhanced by his generous attitude toward the house of Saul. Who can tell what motivated him? Was his a genuine appreciation for "Yahweh's anointed," or a calculating desire to maneuver Saul's followers into his camp? Whatever his purpose, David's personal warmth toward Saul's family, especially Jonathan, is beyond question. The passionate lament over Saul and Jonathan in 2 Samuel 1:19–27 reflects in haunting beauty the sincere emotion of David in grief:

> Your glory, O Israel, lies slain upon your high places!
>> How the mighty have fallen!
> Tell it not in Gath,
>> Proclaim it not in the streets of Ashkelon;
> or the daughters of the Philistines will rejoice,
>> the daughters of the uncircumcised exult.
>
> You mountains of Gilboa,
>> Let there be no dew or rain upon you,
>> nor bounteous fields!
> For there the shield of the mighty was defiled,
>> the shield of Saul, anointed with oil no more.
>
> From the blood of the slain,
>> from the fat of the mighty,
> the bow of Jonathan did not turn back,
>> nor the sword of Saul return empty.
>
> Saul and Jonathan, beloved and lovely!
>> In life and in death they were not divided;
> they were swifter than eagles,
>> they were stronger than lions.
>
> O daughters of Israel, weep over Saul,
>> who clothed you with crimson,
>> who put ornaments of gold on your apparel.
>
> How the mighty have fallen
>> in the midst of battle!
>
> Jonathan lies slain upon your high places.
>> I am distressed for you, my brother Jonathan;
> greatly beloved were you to me;
>> your love to me was wonderful,
>> passing the love of women.
> How the mighty have fallen,
>> and the weapons of war perished!

---

[40]Bright, *History*, p. 196.

David brought swift retribution to one who brought the news of Saul's death[41] and sent a message of gratitude to those of Jabesh-Gilead who had given decent burial to Saul and his sons.[42] Whatever their motivation, these deeds won the loyalty of many who followed Saul.

David's wise policy toward Saul's house is seen further in his attitude toward the civil struggle that developed soon after his accession at Hebron. A surviving son of Saul, Ishbosheth,[43] with the help of Abner, captain of Israel's army, claimed the crown. At best Abner's monarch was a pretender. Inasmuch as dynastic rule was not accepted in Israel, Ishbosheth could claim little loyalty as Saul's son. Further, he did not have military force either to expel the Philistines or to challenge David. One gets the impression that Ishbosheth was a weak pawn in the hands of the ambitious Abner.

David chose to wait out the situation. Skirmishes between the forces of David and Abner occurred, but the conflict was resolved when Ishbosheth and Abner quarreled over the possession of one of Saul's concubines. The rift resulted in Abner's offer to transfer his allegiance to David. Abner came to Hebron with a large group of supporters and David welcomed them with amnesty. But the presence of a second military leader was too much a threat to Joab, David's commander, and he took the first opportunity to murder his rival.[44] Soon thereafter Ishbosheth was assassinated by two of his officers who then came to David seeking reward. Joab was publicly reprimanded for killing Abner and the two officers executed for the murder of Ishbosheth, but David's grief at the passing of the opposition must not have been very deep. With brevity and lack of emotion David lamented Abner:

> Should Abner die as a fool dies?
> Your hands were not bound,
>   your feet were not fettered;
> as one falls before the wicked
>   you have fallen.
>   [2 Samuel 3:33b–34]

King of All Israel

Like the *shophet*s and Saul before him, David gradually achieved acceptance as king because of his gifts—that is, he was a charismatic leader; "Yahweh's spirit rested upon him." From the beginning of his Hebron reign, he won increasing loyalty from other parts of the "nation." At the death of Ishbosheth the growing shift in allegiance became a landslide. The Deuteronomist de-

[41]2 Samuel 1:2–16; 4:10.
[42]Ibid., 2:4–7.
[43]Called "Eshbaal" in 1 Chronicles 8:33.
[44]2 Samuel 3:22–39.

scribes the result: "So all the elders of Israel came to the king at Hebron; and King David made a covenant with them at Hebron before Yahweh, and they anointed David king over Israel" (2 Samuel 5:3).

Securing the Land. After his accession as king over all Israel, David confronted two major problems. Internally, the tribes remained divided in spirit with Judah in the south and Ephraim in the north being especially competitive. Externally the perennial Philistine threat plagued Israel. To the latter and more pressing problem David gave his immediate attention.

The unification of monarchy under David agitated the Philistines, who had remained calm as long as their "friend" David ruled over Hebron. Now they were threatened and set out to destroy the rival nation. The details of the subsequent struggle between Philistia and the new Davidic kingdom are obscure; the encounter is sketchily preserved in 2 Samuel 5:17–25. Possibly the materials in chapters 21 and 22 also relate to these campaigns.[45] Although no detailed account has been preserved, David's forces clearly defeated the Philistines and shut them up in a small coastal cage; never again were they a serious threat to Israel. The Philistine control over iron was broken and the introduction of its common use among the Israelites brought economic revolution to the country. David was free to give attention to the consolidation of the state.

Following defeat of the Philistines David moved toward consolidating Israel's borders to include all of Palestine, thereby securing an area that could be called home by the young nation. Because the Hittites were weak and both Assyria and Egypt were concerned with problems elsewhere, Israel's foes were the small neighboring states easily overcome by David's superior forces. Ammon, Edom, and Moab were overrun. With Philistia confined to a small area in the southern maritime plain and Phoenicia made a friend through alliance with Hiram of Tyre, David pushed Israel's boundaries to their greatest extremity. For the first time in its history, "Israel," formerly a tribal confederacy whose members occupied only parts of Palestine, now designated a geographical unit encompassing the whole of the land of promise, from the Gulf of Aqabah in the south to southern Syria in the north, from the Mediterranean in the west to the Arabian Desert in the east. Israel indeed began to look like a nation.

The sweeping military success of David was made possible largely by his personal army, composed of professional soldiers assembled during his outlaw days rather than men levied from the Israelite tribes. Foreign mercenaries, including Philistines,[46] were also included in the fighting forces. Deeds of outstanding courage seem to have been rewarded with a place in the king's special

---

[45]H. Wheeler Robinson, *The History of Israel* (Duckworth, 1957), p. 62.

[46]"Cherethites and Plethites" refer to "Cretans and Philistines." According to 2 Samuel 15:18, six hundred warriors from the Philistine city of Gath followed David.

Figure 7.2. The kingdom of David and Solomon. The empire extended southward to the north-ern tip of the Gulf of Aqabah.

honor guard, a legion of merit known as "The Thirty."[47] The exploits of this special unit largely accounted for the fact that David's Israel became the most powerful of the small states between Mesopotamia and Egypt. This indeed was Israel's political golden age.

Jerusalem. With the Philistines and lesser enemies subdued, David directed his attention to the second problem—unifying a divided people. Undoubtedly the most important political and religious step in this direction was choosing a new capital. To avoid an impression that his reign was no more than an expansion of his reign over Judah, he moved the capital to Jerusalem, a Jebusite city in the territory of Benjamin associated with neither Judah nor the northern tribes.

By the time of David, Jerusalem was already an old city. The site had been occupied as early as 3000 B.C.E. and was actually called "Jerusalem" as early as 1900 B.C.E. The city was located on the easily fortified hill of Ophel surrounded by three valleys. Joshua had been unable to take it from the Jebusites in the conquest of Canaan, and heretofore Jerusalem had neither political nor religious connotations for Israel. The city occupied a small area, probably no more than about eleven acres, but was supplied with excellent water from the Gihon spring. The Jebusites had protected the water supply by a hidden shaft that brought water inside the city walls.[48] Using his personal troops rather than levied forces, David captured the city and made it his private holding, the "city of David." Israelites began to flock to the new capital and rapidly it became the center of Israelite life.

The astute David was keenly aware of the importance of the religious ties that had bound the diverse tribal groups in the old confederacy. The ark narratives[49] in 1 Samuel 4–6 and 2 Samuel 6, materials closely associated with the later Jerusalem temple, underscore David's move to preserve old religious feeling by making his new capital the center of Israelite cult. He transferred the ark of the covenant, Israel's most sacred cult object, from Kirjath-jearim to Jerusalem. A tent was erected for housing the ark and, amid pageantry and rejoicing in which David openly participated, the symbol of Israel's unity was transferred to its new home. The king purchased a site for the erection of a more permanent temple, but abandoned the plan, probably because of oppo-

[47]Cf. 2 Samuel 23:13, 24.

[48]Archeological excavations on Ophel and the slopes of the Kidron valley have been extensive over many years. Kathleen Kenyon, who has also done extensive work at Jericho, is to be credited with much of this work. See her *Digging Up Jerusalem*, pp. 76–106. See also Shanks, *City*, pp. 15–37; Yadin, *Jerusalem Revealed*; Mazar, *Mountain*, pp. 153–74; Shiloh, "City," pp. 165–71. An excellent summary of Jerusalem archeology appears in Hillel Giva, "Jerusalem," in Stern, *New Encyclopedia*, II, 698–804.

[49]See references at end of this chapter for further reading on the ark narrative.

Figure 7.3. Jerusalem with the old city encompassed in a wall and dominated by the golden-domed Muslim mosque. The modern city is in the background. The Davidic city lay to the left of the old wall and on the slope of the Kidron Valley in the foreground. (*Illustrator* Photo/David Rogers)

sition from those concerned to preserve the wilderness tradition of Yahweh's "tenting" with the people. Nevertheless the selection of neutral Jerusalem and the transfer of the ark, establishing the city as Israel's cultic center, were major steps in unifying the tribes. In these acts David brought in a new day in Israel's religious story and bound the new era to ancient traditions. Henceforth, Jerusalem, previously without Israelite religious associations, would become the religious capital of Israel and remain so, with some interruptions, even to this day. It was actually the "city of David" and would be ruled over by his dynasty until 587 B.C.E. Both its religious and political significance were enormous.

David's arsenal for challenging divisiveness in the new state also included skillful staff organization. Following either Egyptian or Canaanite models, the king appointed officials who were assigned specific administrative tasks. The king himself remained in command, but the involvement of others must have contributed a sense of broad participation in government.

Court History of David's Reign

Although the David materials in Samuel and Kings are better thought of as historical novel than pure history, they contain outstanding examples of ancient Near Eastern historiography. The writer of 1 Samuel 16:14–2 Samuel 5 and

2 Samuel 8:1–15 uses early and late materials to weave the story of David's rise to power with exceptional artistic skill. And the so-called "court history of David" (2 Samuel 9–20 and 1 Kings 1–2) not only provides the most important materials concerning David's rule, but also brings together smaller narrative units to form one of the finest pieces of historical storytelling preserved from the ancient world. The court history "is, in view of its superb literary style and sober objectivity, the prose masterpiece of the Old Testament."[50] It suggests an eyewitness as the source of much of the material, perhaps someone in the royal court of David who continued through the early years of Solomon's reign. The narrative is realistic, presenting life as lived in conversations and episodes, but at the same time skillfully framed so as to sustain drama for its readers.

> Analyze the Court History of David from a literary point of view: What are its plot, themes, chief and secondary characters, climax, denouement? The discussion of the literary nature of the patriarchal-matriarchal materials in Chapter 4 will give you guidance.

In candor the court history[51] reports the serious shortcomings, the family disruptions, bitterness and revolt, and ignominious deeds that marked the closing years of David's reign. Utter frankness with no attempt to gloss over the king's weakness characterizes the stories. Event piles on event: sin with Bathsheba, Uriah's death, rape of Tamar, murder of Amnon, rebellion of Absalom and his subsequent execution, rebellion of Sheba.

The incident with Bathsheba occurred during the Ammonite war while Uriah, Bathsheba's husband, was with the army in Transjordan. David yielded to lust, appropriated Bathsheba as his own, and soon learned that she was pregnant. Afraid of being found out, the king attempted to cover his deed by having Uriah return from the battlefront. When Uriah refused to violate his soldier's ban by sleeping with his wife, David "arranged" for the brave warrior's death in battle and married Bathsheba. For the Deuteronomist David's sin was not his lust for Bathsheba but its distortion of kingship—the assumption that the king could have anything he wanted. "The disgrace in the whole affair lay in the fact that Uriah, by his devotion to the cause of Yahweh, proved himself to be a better 'Israelite' than the king."[52]

The Hebrew Bible condemns David's sin with the same clarity that it praises his valor. Because Yahweh is Israel's king, it is unnecessary to idealize Yahweh's earthly representative. David, like the Israelite man-in-the-street, is Yah-

---

[50]W. F. Stinespring, "Annotations on I and II Samuel," in *The New Oxford Annotated Bible with the Apocrypha*, H. G. May and B. M. Metzger, eds., p. 386. For a summary of scholarly views, see John H. Hayes and J. Maxwell Miller, eds. *Israelite and Judean History* pp. 337–38.

[51]The court history is also called the succession narrative. See Whybray, *Succession*. The narrative of David's reign in 1 Chronicles omits most of these materials.

[52]F. E. Eakin, Jr., *The Religion and Culture of Israel* (Allyn and Bacon, 1971), p. 18.

weh's subject and obligated to covenant demands. Nathan, the prophet of Yahweh, to the king's face protrayed him as one who had stolen the "one little ewe lamb" owned by a poor man.[53] The prophet's ingenious use of an imaginary court case so affected David that he immediately accepted responsibility for his deeds and in remorse confessed his sin to Yahweh. Although his confession brought Yahweh's forgiveness, David was unable to escape the results of his folly. He became an overindulgent parent who thoroughly spoiled his sons[54] and a pampering husband who could not resist the desires of his wife.[55] The uneasiness of David's family life, coupled with the people's ambiguous ideas about how his successor was to be chosen, contributed to restlessness in the kingdom during the closing years of his reign.

The most tragic consequence of all was the rebellion of Absalom, David's son by an Aramean princess. David's oldest son and possible claimant to the throne, Amnon, seduced Tamar, the sister of Absalom. After two years in which Amnon went unpunished, Absalom coolly murdered his half-brother and fled. After three years in exile, Absalom was allowed to return to Jerusalem and later was restored to the good graces of his father. Yet he secretly plotted David's overthrow. Gradually winning the ear of many with various grievances against the throne, Absalom was finally proclaimed king in, of all places, Hebron! He obviously hoped thereby to insure Judah's support. The insurrectionists marched on Jerusalem and David had to flee. David's personal army remained loyal; forces were recouped and the rebellion quelled. Absalom, to the deep grief of his father, was slain by Joab. The elders of Judah, fearful of possible retribution for their actions, reluctantly approached David for reconciliation. David accepted them into his camp and even promised that the rebel general, Amasa, would replace Joab as captain of the army. Peace was brought to this quarter, but rebellion broke out in another.

A group from the northern tribes, embittered by David's kind treatment of the Judeans who had joined in Absalom's rebellion, was led in revolt by Sheba of Benjamin. With David looking the other way, Joab killed Amasa and again assumed uncontested command of David's professional army. The brief rebellion was then put down as rapidly as it had begun. Sheba was assassinated and David was again without opposition.

David's Significance for Israel

In spite of domestic troubles and political disturbances during the last years of his reign, David stands with Abraham and Moses as a major figure in Hebrew history. Building on the transitional accomplishments of Saul, David firmly

---

[53] 2 Samuel 12.
[54] See 1 Kings 1:6.
[55] See ibid., 1:15ff.

established monarchy as a pattern for Israel's government. He overcame the military opponents of Israel, extended its boundaries to embrace all of Palestine, and created in the minds of divergent peoples some sense of national identity. Apparently David governed directly, with no prime minister and few cabinet officials of real authority. In his own person David symbolized political unity.

Moreover, David preserved a fundamental religious identity in both his personal and national commitments. David greatly loved Yahweh and this influenced all his actions. Jerusalem became both the political and religious capital, and in a sense, David served as both king and priest. Many loyalties previously centered in Samuel passed to David when the aged seer died.

Covenant with David.　By the conclusion of David's reign, it was evidently assumed that a son would succeed him. Charismatic selection of the leader had given way to dynastic rule. In time the personal weaknesses of David became less important to the people, and much of its theology and national hopes became centered on its great hero. In the deuteronomic tradition David became the primary figure for accomplishing God's purpose in history. He was remembered as one selected by Yahweh to administer "justice and equity to all his people."[56] So definite was this selection that not only David, but also his dynasty, was established in Jerusalem, where a theology of "covenant with David" developed. David himself was remembered as saying:

> Is not my house like this with God?
> 　For he has made with me an everlasting covenant,
> 　ordered in all things and secure.
> 　　　　　　　　　　　　[2 Samuel 23:5a]

This theology of unbreakable covenant with the Davidic house forced the Sinai covenant into the background in the Davidic state until the seventh century B.C.E., when a rediscovery of Mosaic Torah once again placed before Israel its obligation to serve the Sinai covenant. Historical and prophetic traditions originating in the south reflect the supremacy of the bond with David. Neither the Yahwistic history nor the Judean prophets, Isaiah and Micah, emphasize the Sinai event. Isaiah, in particular, makes much of the covenant with David and its promise of Jerusalem's inviolability. Thus David's covenant and David's city became central to subsequent religion, literature, and even the later messianic hope.

For Israel, David's reign had brought to fulfillment Yahweh's covenant commitments traced to Abraham. A nation had been promised and now Israel dwelled in a land with defined boundaries and relative security. Jerusalem symbolized Yahweh's faithfulness to the divine promises and hence must be

---

[56] 2 Samuel 8:15.

guarded as Yahweh's dwelling place. Even after its destruction, Israel will yearn for its restoration and the prophet Ezekiel will look toward its reconstruction from which will spring waters that freshen the world.[57] Centuries later a Christian writer will express his utopian hope for "new Jerusalem" adorned as a bride for her husband.[58]

Further, kingship itself was becoming a holy office, replacing confederal judgeship as Yahweh's covenant office. Some confusion regarding distinction between priest and king still existed, but Samuel was gone and David in spite of his weakness understood that the king was no oriental despot. Like all other members of the covenant community, the king was Yahweh's subject.

> The shift from confederacy to monarchy necessitated dramatic changes in the religious structures of the Hebrews. Can you draw parallels between this process and personal growth from childhood to adolescence to adulthood? Do such changes teach us anything about denominational and sectarian religious groups?

In this fashion the Davidic tradition gave the nation a means for maintaining its relationship to covenant. The death of confederacy did not mean the death of God. Old religious sentiments came to be attached to new forms. For over three hundred years the idea of "covenant with David" gave the nation ruled by his dynasty both political and religious stability. Remaining faithful meant keeping David's descendants on the throne and giving due honor to Yahweh's sanctuary in Jerusalem. Furthermore, when the Davidic political structure was destroyed, Israel's later dreams of Yahweh's rule were decidedly Davidic. Out of the "house of Jesse" would come "David's son" as Yahweh's anointed one to bring in a new "kingdom." The deuteronomic historian believed that Yahweh had indeed made "an everlasting covenant" with David.

SOLOMON
(1 KINGS 1–11)

The accession and reign of Solomon is reported in the first book of Kings,[59] the concluding section of the deuteronomic history work. In Kings the Deu-

---

[57]Ezekiel 40–48.

[58]Revelation 21.

[59]The books of Chronicles give an account of monarchy that in many ways parallels Kings. However, because Chronicles dwells on the history of Judah and mentions Israel only incidentally, only the account in Kings is listed here as primary source material. David's reign is covered in 1 Chronicles, Solomon's in 2 Chronicles 1–9.

teronomist uses a number of sources,[60] which he edits and places in his typical deutcronomic framework. Here the theme is the same: obedience brings blessing; disobedience, chaos. For the Deuteronomist[61] obedience to Yahweh means following the Davidic covenant. Solomon gets "a mixed press." He is David's son and builds Yahweh's temple in Jerusalem, but he also introduces foreign worship in the shadow of the temple and aspires to royal designs foreign to Israel's traditional covenant. The result is a rift in the covenant community. The subsequent story of revolt and division provides the Deuteronomist an explicit demonstration of his theme: the northern kingdom rejects Jerusalem and David's heirs, rejects the covenant with David. In sharp contrast the southern kingdom has kings who are David's heirs and worships in Zion. The south therefore is Yahweh's favored people, clearly to be preferred over the north. After the fall of the north, however, the south is not treated so kindly. Its national sin brings God's judgment and ultimately punishment. These events in Kings may be outlined as follows:

A. Solomon's accession: 1 Kings 1–2
B. Solomon's reign: 1 Kings 3–11
C. The two kingdoms: 1 Kings 12 to 2 Kings 17
D. Judah until its fall: 2 Kings 18–25

Solomon's Accession

The account of Solomon's accession justified his claim to the throne by depicting him as victorious in an unsavory struggle for power among David's sons. Although dynastic rather than charismatic selection seems to have been established by the achievements of David, clear patterns for selecting the new king had not developed. The result was palace intrigue. As David neared death and his grasp on the kingdom weakened, two parties began to vie for control. One group was led by Joab, long David's strong-arm deputy, and Abiathar, the priest who had been David's counsel since his fugitive days. Seemingly without protest from the king, this party supported Adonijah, David's oldest son and logical successor had primogeniture been accepted.

A second party was organized by Nathan, David's prophetic critic in the Bathsheba incident. Nathan had the support of Bathsheba in winning David's favor for her son Solomon. One can only surmise what part David's guilt may

---

[60]These include the ending of the Court History (1 Kings 1–2), a book of the acts of Solomon (1 Kings 11:41), a book of the chronicles of the kings of Israel (1 Kings 14:19 and other places), a book of the chronicles of the kings of Judah (1 Kings 14:29 and other places), and other historical and archival records.

[61]Some scholars see evidence of two Deuteronomists compiling these materials: one writing before the fall of Jerusalem in 587 B.C.E. and the other after that event.

have played in leading him to accede to Bathsheba's request. Probably Solomon received support more because he was the son of David's most influential wife than because of his personal qualifications for the kingship. One wonders at Nathan's involvement here.

With David's announced support, Solomon was publicly proclaimed "ruler over Israel and over Judah."[62] Soon after David's death, he secured his rule in forceful and drastic fashion. A gossipy little tale preserves the story of Adonijah's end. In his dying days David had been provided a concubine named Abishag, a maiden very beautiful, who "became the king's attendant and served him, but the king did not know her sexually" (1 Kings 1:4). After David's death, Adonijah requested that Abishag be given to him, an act interpreted by Solomon as pretension to regal power and used as an excuse to eliminate Adonijah. The priest Abiathar was banished and Joab was slain even as he clung to the horns of the altar, traditionally a place of safety.

"So the kingdom was established in the hand of Solomon" (1 Kings 2:46). The faction with the power to enforce its rule won the contest. David's support carried some weight, but the cheering of the populace was only ex post facto approval of what had been done by force. The day of selecting a king of Israel on the basis of charismatic gifts was over, and Samuel must have moved a little in his grave.

Accomplishments of Solomon's Reign

Solomon's reign, as the biblical report reflects, is a study in contrasts. With David he shared a desire to make Israel a glorious nation. The newly crowned king was consumed by a passion for Israel's splendor, and against the backdrop of extended boundaries and increasing national prowess, Solomon envisioned a land of oriental opulence.

With the opposition eliminated early in his reign, Solomon proceeded to fulfill his dream. Little challenge came from outside Palestine. Egypt was too weak to interfere. The fall of the Hittite kingdom had left Asia Minor without a strong power. Syria was not yet a major threat, although the action of Rezon in having himself proclaimed king in Damascus[63] might well have been taken as an ominous sign. The only political force of any consequence on the scene at the time of Solomon's accession was Phoenicia. The new king took immediate steps to continue his father's treaty arrangements with this neighbor to the northwest.

Trade.   Hiram, king of the Phoenician city of Tyre, became Solomon's primary accessory in accomplishing the material advancement of Israel. Phoenicia

[62]1 Kings 1:38–40; cf. v. 35.
[63]Ibid., 11:23–25.

provided both skilled craftsmen and unskilled labor for Solomon's construction projects. The maritime skills of this seafaring people also enabled Solomon to extend his commercial activities through Phoenician ports to Sicily, Sardinia, North Africa, and even Spain. Phoenician sailors also advised and assisted a novice Israelite merchant fleet, which sailed to the south and east from the Israelite port at Ezion-geber on the Gulf of Aqabah. With the direct help of these neighbors Israel's natural resources were tapped for the first time as building materials and as export commodities. In every possible way Solomon used agreements with Phoenicia to Israel's advantage.

Solomon's construction of a seaport at Ezion-geber is a remarkable innovation in Israel's history.[64] Although mines and smelters in the area, often popularly known as "King Solomon's mines," have been shown by archeology to date two centuries before Solomon,[65] maritime activity was a significant factor in Solomon's economy. The Palestine coast had no natural harbors and, hence, the Israelites were rarely a seafaring folk. Now, however, ships manned by Phoenician sailors and Israelite novices sailed from Ezion-geber on voyages lasting more than a year. Far ports of the East became accessible to Israel through the Red Sea. Imports must have included gold, silver, ivory, and jewels, as well as tales of distant peoples spun by returning sailors.

Trade in horses and chariots provided another significant aspect of Solomon's commercial activity:

> Solomon's import of horses was from Egypt and Kue. . . . A chariot could be imported from Egypt for six hundred shekels of silver, and a horse for one hundred and fifty; so through the king's traders they were exported to all the kings of the Hittites and the kings of Aram. [1 Kings 10:28–29][66]

Evidently Solomon seized the opportunity to serve as middleman in a lucrative exchange of horses and chariots. Strategically located between Egypt and the kings of the north, his "agency" became the only avenue of exchange for these important implements of warfare. This extensive commercial activity brought much wealth to the coffers of Israel. Undoubtedly, Solomon and Israel became wealthy.

Building. Trade income partially underwrote Solomon's ambitious construction program. Throughout the empire, buildings were refurbished, cities fortified, and trade facilities constructed. But clearly the Deuteronomist was most impressed with the building of the Jerusalem temple. Three full chapters (1 Kings 5, 6, 8) detail the preparation for, building of, and dedication of the sanctuary crucial to maintaining the Davidic covenant.

---

[64]Beno Rothenberg, *Timna: Valley of the Biblical Copper Mines* (Thomas and Hudson, 1972).
[65]Ibid.
[66]"Kue" was most likely Cilicia in Asia Minor.

Solomon's temple combined the splendor of Phoenician architecture[67] with traditional symbols of Hebrew worship. An outer vestibule was entered through large ornate doors standing between two bronze pillars. The main sanctuary held the sacred furnishings: the golden candlesticks, the table of shewbread, and the altar of incense. The Holy of Holies was reached by a flight of stairs leading up from the main sanctuary. In this cube was Yahweh's throne, the ark of the covenant. The temple, therefore, represented Yahweh's presence. Although patterned by Phoenician architects following Phoenician design, the temple and its cult remained thoroughly Yahwistic.[68]

Solomon's construction of the Jerusalem temple consolidated the relationship between Israel's political forms and its cult. The temple was Israel's central shrine and the king as Yahweh's vice-regent was its chief officer. The transition from confederal to monarchial forms insured under David had now been given specific symbolic structure.

The temple was splendidly ornate, making ample use of copper and Lebanon cedar, but it was probably no more elaborate than other of Solomon's buildings. The king's palace built near the temple must have been costly: its construction lasted thirteen years, whereas seven years had sufficed for the temple. The palace complex was fronted by massive cedar pillars cut from the forests of Lebanon. It served as treasury, armory, and courtroom, as well as residence for the regal harem.

Other construction works took place throughout Palestine. Hardly a site was not enlarged. Recent studies suggest that the so-called "Solomon's stables" at Megiddo belong to the later Ahab period, but some of the construction at this site is Solomonic. Archeology has also revealed a distinctive city gateway at Hazor and Gezer coming from Solomon's time.[69] All of these illustrate the king's passion to bring strength to a fledgling nation and represent a glory unknown in any other period of Hebrew history.

Literature.   Although the major growth during Solomon's day was material, there were also significant literary and cultural achievements of greater importance for Israelite religion. Contact with neighbors opened the door for cosmopolitan attitudes; peace and prosperity promoted cultural development. Lit-

---

[67]See Wright, *Archaeology*, pp. 136–40.

[68]For a good brief discussion of the temple and its role in Israelite life, see G. E. Wright, "The Temple in Palestine and Syria," in *The Biblical Archaeologist Reader*, I:169–84. See also Yohanan Aharoni's report on a similar Hebrew temple at Arad in his "Arad: Its Inscriptions and Temple," *Biblical Archaeologist*, 31 (1968) 2–32.

[69]See Yigael Yadin, *Hazor: The Rediscovery of a Great Citadel of the Bible* (Weidenfeld and Nicolson, 1975) pp. 187–231. See also his "Solomon's City Wall and Gate at Gezer," *Israel Exploration Journal*, 8 (1958) 80–86; and "Megiddo of the Kings of Israel," *Biblical Archaeologist*, 33 (1970) 65–96; and his chapter on Hazor is Stern, *New Encyclopedia*, II, 594–606. Also Yigal Shiloh, "Megiddo," in Stern, *New Encyclopedia*, III, 1003–24.

erature flourished. Writings of the period reflect the continuing interests of Israel in its historical heritage. The court history of David came from Solomon's reign, as did the Yahwist's great epic of Israel's beginnings, written as a national epic inculcating the basic values of the covenant people in the hope that they would be preserved and cherished by the new monarchial nation. There was no greater literary achievement in Israel's history.

Wisdom literature also flourished. The King's account describes Solomon as one who "composed three thousand proverbs and his songs numbered a thousand and five" (1 Kings 4:32). Even allowing for later editorial additions, the king's contributions to the wisdom materials must have been significant. His wisdom teachings seem to have been deductions about human behavior made from observations of nature. "He spoke of trees . . . , of animals, of birds, and of reptiles, and of fish" (4:33). The later tradition attributing the book of Proverbs to Solomon is an idealization. Some of his sayings may be incorporated in that collection, but most of it is material of a different kind. The wisdom tradition that Proverbs represents was certainly already in the making in Solomon's time. His primary support of wisdom was probably more by his patronage of scribes than by his own writings. This connection, nonetheless, illustrates the cultural sophistication of Solomon's reign.

Weaknesses

The literary, cultural, and economic advances of Solomon's era made this one of Israel's finest ages. Commercial potential had been realized, provincialism had given way to international contact, the land was secure and at peace, and Yahweh's cult was firmly established. Transition from tribal organization to monarchial stability had largely come to pass. Following David, Solomon was in the right place at the right time to reap the benefits of Israel's social development.

Yet the story has another side. Solomon's visions of Israel's splendor were tempered neither by religious values rooted deeply in Israel's past nor by sensitivity to ordinary Israelites. He represented a growing elite aristocracy widely separated from the less fortunate person in the street. Born in purple, Solomon knew only the protected life of the palace. He had been spared the austerity of survival in the Negeb and endurance on the battlefield. He knew nothing of life in the street or the plight of common citizenry. The king's achievements and wealth were shared by the elite populace, but to the vast majority the glory itself became a burden. Many saw Solomon as an ostentatious monarch concerned only with his own grandeur and void of consideration for the welfare of his people.

Taxation.   Solomon's ambitious building projects were partially financed by income from commercial activities, but in no way were those funds adequate to pay the entire bill. Solomon attempted to make up the difference through taxation. The land was divided into twelve administrative districts, each supervised by an officer responsible to the king. Each district was to supply one month's provisions for the king; and (if the list in 1 Kings 4:22f. is not exaggerated) this was quite an order. Such taxation undoubtedly became a heavy burden to the Hebrew commoner. More seriously, the revised administrative organization, disregarding the old tribal lines guaranteed during the confederacy, weakened tribal sovereignty, incorporated non-Israelites into the state system, and consolidated power in the hands of the king. Those committed to old Sinai traditions, and not yet convinced that "new" Davidic traditions should supplant them, must have been more than irritated by Solomon's policies.

To the tax burden was added a distasteful practice of forced labor battalions, the corvée. Israelites were forced to work alongside Canaanite slaves. One month of every three was to be given in the service of the king. The hated labor force of Israelite workers as coolies and quarry workers further illustrates the deepening divisions in Hebrew society.

Solomon was burning the taxation candle at both ends. Not only did taxes become heavier and heavier, but also the productive ability of the masses was decreased as large segments of the populace were forced into the corvée. For many, therefore, material progress became not so much a source of pride in the prosperity of their land as a striking symbol of the extensive sacrifice extracted from them to humor the insatiable desires of a pompous king.

The King's Harem.   Even memory of beloved David would not enable overburdened Israelites to tolerate for long such disregard for the covenant community. The growing unrest of Israel's masses over exorbitant taxes was encouraged by the lax religious behavior of the king. As contacts with outside peoples became commonplace, Solomon became more cosmopolitan in his outlook. The Deuteronomist cites the king's harem as an obvious example of his liberal attitude toward non-Israelite culture, including foreign religions, lamenting that Solomon had "seven hundred princesses and three hundred concubines; and his wives turned away his heart" (1 Kings 11:3).

Such a harem was created more for political purposes than to satisfy Solomon's sensual pleasure. Political treaty sealed with marriage was Solomon's stratagem to secure the boundaries of Israel and to strengthen ties with neighboring peoples. The importance of such alliances is seen in his marriage with the daughter of a pharaoh (1 Kings 3:1f.), by which he received Gezer, one of the most important city-states of southern Palestine (1 Kings 9:16) and the gateway to the pass leading from Joppa to Jerusalem. Other marriages were contracted with the Moabites, Ammonites, Edomites, Phoenicians, and Hittites.

Such marriages represented legitimate political process in the East and, had all else been right, might have gone unnoticed by Israel's religious leaders. But the harem became another focus of criticism. Solomon permitted the worship of his wives' deities. In Jerusalem near the sanctuary of Yahweh, shrines to foreign deities were constructed. Solomon's toleration of outside religions was more than Yahwistic religious leadership could endure. His "wives had turned away his heart after other gods, and his heart was not wholly true to Yahweh his God, as was the heart of David" (1 Kings 11:4). Solomon's religious tolerance had contaminated the pure faith of Israel by allowing the encroachments of outside faiths. The religious leadership of Israel must have remembered the admonition of Samuel that the selection of a king carried the inherent danger of forgetting dependence on Yahweh. In fact, Solomon was surely the model for the deuteronomic warning about selecting a king:

> Even so, he must not acquire many horses for himself, or return to Egypt in order to acquire more horses, since Yahweh has said to you, "You shall never return that way again." And he must not acquire many wives for himself, or else his heart will turn away; also silver and gold he must not acquire in great quantities for himself [Deuteronomy 17:16–17].

So, Solomon can be given only qualified praise. His reputation as "wiser than all other men" is supported by Israel's arrival at a time of unprecedented prosperity. Boundaries won in David's battles had been secured, and cultural exchanges with neighbors near and far were promoted. Natural resources were developed on an extensive scale. However, these achievements came at enormous costs. Class divisions began to appear in Israelite culture with luxuries bought for the royal "haves" at the expense of lasting prosperity for the "have nots." Religious laxity allowed pagan religion to creep into official practices authenticated by the king's cultic support. Developing urbanization, weakening tribal lines, and incorporation of Canaanites eroded traditional covenant definitions of Yahweh's people before monarchy was firmly established as Yahweh's community. Power was increasingly focused in the king, more typical of an Eastern potentate than the older ideal of Yahweh's vice-regent. Israel was now a long way from Shechem, even more from Sinai! Solomon had lost touch with his people and become callous to national religious ideals.

> If you were a Hebrew in Palestine when Solomon died, what would be your political and religious alignments? Defend them to someone whose loyalties differ.

Although Solomon was able to maintain tight control on the kingdom during his lifetime, beneath the placid surface a storm was brewing. Signs of eroding control were already evident. The king had been forced to give twenty Galilean towns to Hiram of Tyre to satisfy his debts. Edom, Damascus, and Aram revolted. The alarm had been sounded and the king's death was the occasion for the eruption of internal dissatisfaction and the dissolution of "united" monarchy.

SUGGESTIONS FOR FURTHER STUDY

Elaboration of many points in this chapter may be made by consulting Bible dictionaries on the following terms: temple, Philistines, Davidic covenant, Court History of David, Wisdom, historiography.

Additional treatments of Samuel and Kings as biblical literature may be found in appropriate volumes of commentaries, such as *The Interpreter's Bible*, *The Old Testament Library*, and *Anchor Bible*. Walter Brueggemann, *First and Second Samuel*, Interpretation: A Bible commentary for Teaching and Preaching (Westminster, 1990), ought not be missed. Bible dictionaries as listed in the General Bibliography also contain extensive articles on Samuel and Kings.

For important studies of kingship, see Baruch Halpern, *The Constitution of Monarchy in Israel*, Harvard Semitic Monograph 25 (Scholars, 1981); S. H. Hooke, ed., *Myth, Ritual and Kingship* (Clarendon, 1958); A. C. Welch, *Kings and Prophets of Israel* (Lutterworth, 1952); T. Ishida, ed., *Studies in the Period of David and Solomon* (Eisenbaums, 1982); and E. W. Heaton, *Solomon's New Men: The Emergence of Ancient Israel as a National State* (Thames & Hudson, 1974). A. R. Johnson, *Sacral Kingship in Ancient Israel* (University of Wales, 1967, 2d ed.), emphasizes the cultic role of Judah's kings and Sigmund Mowinckel, *The Psalms in Israel's Worship, I–II* (Abingdon, 1962), discusses the relationship of certain psalms to kingship.

Useful studies centering on David include Walter Brueggemann, *David's Truth in Israel's Imagination and Memory* (Westminster, 1985), and his article, "David and His Theologian," *Catholic Biblical Quarterly*, 30 (1968) 156–81; David M. Gunn, "David and the Gift of the Kingdom," *Semeia*, 3 (1975) 14–45; and J. J. M. Roberts, "The Davidic Origins of the Zion Tradition" *Journal of Biblical Literature*, 92 (1973) 329–44. Specific treatments of the court history of David include Leonard Rast, *The Succession to the Throne of David* (Almond, 1982); Roger N. Whybray, *The Succession to the Throne of David* (Alec R. Allenson, 1968); Gerhard von Rad, *Old Testament Theology*, I, 1962, 1965, pp. 312ff.; and J. S. Ackerman, "Knowing Good and Evil: A Literary Analysis of the Court History of 2 Samuel 9–20 and 1 Kings 1–2," *Journal of Biblical Literature*, 109 (1990) 41–60.

The "Ark Narrative" is the focus of Patrick D. Miller and J. J. M. Roberts, *The Hand of the Lord: A Reassessment of the "Ark Narrative" of I Samuel* (Johns Hopkins, 1977); and A. F. Campbell, *The Ark Narrative (I Samuel 4–6; II Samuel 6): A Form-Critical and Traditio-Historical Study*, Society of Biblical Literature dissertation series, 16 (Scholars, 1981).

For archeological materials related to this period, consult Ephraim Stern et

al., eds., *The New Encyclopedia of Archaeological Excavations in the Holy Land,
I–IV* (Israel Exploration Society, 1993). Also see M. Kochavi, "The History
and Archaeology of Aphek-Antipatris," *Biblical Archaeologist,* 44/2 (Spring,
1981) 75–86; Nelson Glueck, "Ezion-geber," *Biblical Archaeologist,* 28 (1965)
70–87; and three articles by Yigael Yadin: "Solomon's City Wall and Gate at
Gezer," *Israel Exploration Journal,* 8 (1958) 80–86; "New Light on Solomon's
Megiddo," *Biblical Archaeologist,* 23 (1960) 62–68; and "Megiddo of the Kings
of Israel," *Biblical Archaeologist,* 33 (1970) 66–96.

An extensive bibliography on Jerusalem is found in the General Bibliography.

8

Divided Monarchy: Zion vs. Sinai

The Hebrew Bible contains two reports of the divided monarchy, 922–722 B.C.E. The primary account of the two kingdoms appears in 1 Kings 12-2 Kings 17—part of the deuteronomic interpretation of Hebrew history. These materials see divided monarchy from the perspective of Babylonian exile after Jerusalem's fall in 587 B.C.E. and underscore the apostasy of Yahweh's covenant people, which explains both the destruction of the northern kingdom and the devastation of the south's temple city and the deportations of its populace. For the Deuteronomist the breakup of the united monarchy was itself evidence of the rebellious will of the covenant people. He draws on several sources, primarily chronicles of the kings of both Israel[1] and Judah and stories about prophets, to evaluate the kings of Israel and Judah. His norms are the ideal sovereign David and Zion theology. Good kings are those in David's line who support Jerusalem as the acceptable place of worship. Bad kings (primarily those of the north, of course) do not measure up to these criteria.

The Deuteronomist follows a stylized pattern, moving from Judah to Israel and then back to Judah to present his subjects. The introduction of each king of Israel includes:

1. the dating of the king's reign in terms of Judah's reigning monarch,
2. the name of the capital,
3. the duration of the reign, and
4. a brief and condemning characterization of the king (except for Shallum, whose reign lasted only one month).

Four items also appear in the introduction of Judah's kings:

1. the date of accession in terms of who is king of Israel,
2. the age at which the king came to the throne,
3. the name of the queen mother, and
4. a comparison of the king with David.

---

[1]"Israel" now refers to the northern kingdom rather than to all of Jacob's descendants.

The pro-David and therefore prosouthern bias of the interpreter is clear. Israel's revolt and history illustrates a breach of Yahweh's covenant with David, and Israel's death in 722 vindicates that judgment.

The second biblical description of divided monarchy belongs to the priestly tradition and is part of a larger literary work including the books of Chronicles,[2] Ezra, and Nehemiah. These works are generally referred to as the "Chronicler's history" and, when taken together, survey the whole period of Israelite history from Genesis through the reforms of Ezra and Nehemiah. The priestly Chronicler emphasizes the religious life of Judah. Overall the work can be outlined:

A. Genealogical survey from Adam to Saul: 1 Chronicles 1–9
B. The united monarchy (Saul, David, and Solomon): 1 Chronicles 10–2 Chronicles 9
C. From the division of the kingdom through the exile: 2 Chronicles 10–36
D. Return from exile and restoration of the temple: Ezra 1–6
E. The work of Ezra: Ezra 7–10
F. Rebuilding Jerusalem's wall: Nehemiah 1–7
G. Reading the book of law under Ezra and further reforms: Nehemiah 8–13

Because the Chronicler wrote many years after the destruction of the northern kingdom, the northern kings are hardly mentioned. The material comes from the postexilic period, when the continuity of covenant through Judah had been demonstrated, and hence northern history is hardly relevant to covenant faith. The writer intends to support the priestly faith of the restored nation built around Judah and northerners who repented and acknowledged the Jerusalem sanctuary. In pursuit of this religious bias, the writer included and excluded items at his discretion. For example, his primary interest in David was as a religious leader. Military accomplishments are mentioned, but only as something incidental to the picture of the religious patriot who built Jerusalem as the holy shrine and whose line was continued by covenant. David's outlaw career and his behavior with Bathsheba have no place in the Chronicler's account.

In places the Chronicler quotes his Samuel-Kings source word for word. At others, he alters details to illustrate his point, as when he describes Satan's provoking David to number Israel (1 Chronicles 21:1). On other occasions he adds to the Samuel–Kings story events taken from other sources. Both Chronicles and Ezra–Nehemiah are the result of this process of adding and editing, subtracting and modifying—all for the purpose of supporting the Hebrew faith of the postexilic period.

Because of this bias, the Chronicler's account is not the best source for the

---

[2]The two books of Chronicles, like Samuel and Kings, were originally a single book.

period of the divided monarchy. For this reason, the deuteronomic source will be given primary consideration in this chapter, with Chronicles serving as an additional or auxiliary source.

THE SCHISM
(1 KINGS 12:1–13:34)[3]

Reopening Old Conflicts

Resentment over Solomon's fiscal excesses and religious compromises was ready to erupt by the time of the king's death. The trouble, however, was not entirely Solomon's making. Long-standing and intense tribal differences lay barely beneath the surface, only needing an occasion to emerge. The competition between Ephraim and Judah was particularly intense.

Ephraim vs. Judah.   Israel's memory treated the Joseph tribes (Ephraim and Manasseh) as superior over other northern tribes, a status traced back to the day when Joseph dreamed of his superiority over his brothers and openly boasted of his dreams. Further, Hebrew tradition counted Ephraim greater than Manasseh. Ephraim's preeminence is explained in a fascinating tale of patriarchal blessing[4] where Ephraim is regarded first although Manasseh was the older son. Joseph says: " '[Manasseh] shall also become a people, and he also shall be great. Nevertheless his younger brother shall be greater than he, and his offspring shall become a multitude of nations' . . . . Thus he put Ephraim before Manasseh" (Genesis 48:19–20).

Likewise Judah is praised in Hebrew memory. A series of blessings on all tribes reported in Genesis 49 includes comments about Judah that are extravagantly laudatory.[5] It is a young lion, conqueror of enemies, and therefore honored by other tribes:

> The scepter shall not depart from Judah,
>   nor the ruler's staff from between his feet,
> until he comes to him
>   and the obedience of the peoples is his.
>   [Genesis 49:10]

The dominance of both Judah and Ephraim encouraged a competitive spirit reflected in the biblical record. After Gideon's sweeping conquest of the Mid-

---

[3]Also 2 Chronicles 10:1–19.
[4]Genesis 48:8–22.
[5]See Gerhard von Rad's discussion in his *Genesis*, pp. 406–23.

ianites in the time of the *shophet*s, Ephraim complained that it had not been called to the battlefield to share the victory. During the leadership of Jephthah, the tribe again protested that it had not been called to champion the cause of Israel. Nor had Judah been modest about its relationship to other tribes. Before tribes led by Joshua entered Canaan from the Transjordan, a major segment of Judah had come into the land from the south. Around Hebron it had formed religious order of its own prior to the creation of the confederacy at Shechem. Later Judah had separately acclaimed David king and also supported the Absalom rebellion. Ephraim and Judah each had often acted independently of one another and without consideration for the other tribes. The deep-seated division of even David's kingdom is attested when Solomon was selected as king "over Israel and over Judah"(1 Kings 1:38–40).

The competition between Judah and Ephraim inevitably led to antagonism, a major factor in the split of the kingdom. Solomon encouraged the rift by preferential treatment of Judah. Not only did his administrative districts for taxation not coincide with old tribal boundaries, but also Judah seems to have been exempt from taxation (1 Kings 4). If this were the case, jealousy of the other tribal groups is certainly understandable.

Geography. The spirit of divisiveness and tribal independence that outlasted David's united monarchy was aided by Palestinian geography. No feature of the topography of this region is more outstanding than the central ridge of mountains that runs the length of the land and occupies the larger part of the area between the Jordan and the Mediterranean. This rugged terrain was better suited to local than to strong, centralized government.

Judah was isolated in the heart of the mountain heights. Between Jerusalem and Jericho is an area so rugged that it has become proverbial. On Judah's east was the Dead Sea, which separated it from Reuben and Gad. With the Mediterranean to the west and the wilderness of the Negeb on the south, Judah was almost an island. Geography tended to isolate it from caravan routes passing outside its borders. By way of contrast, the terrain of the Joseph tribes to the north was exposed to the trade lines that connected Damascus as a hub with other points in the Near East. The roads running along the Mediterranean coast turned eastward through the plain of Esdraelon, which served as an important pass through the mountains of western Palestine and made Phoenicia accessible to the north. Whereas Judah remained largely isolated from outside contact and influence, the northern Joseph tribes were largely open to cosmopolitan influences. Thus, geography contributed to the rift that had been developing between north and south for a long while. Nature as well as history seemed to work against union. Add the excesses of Solomon, and anyone who succeeded him was in trouble from the outset.

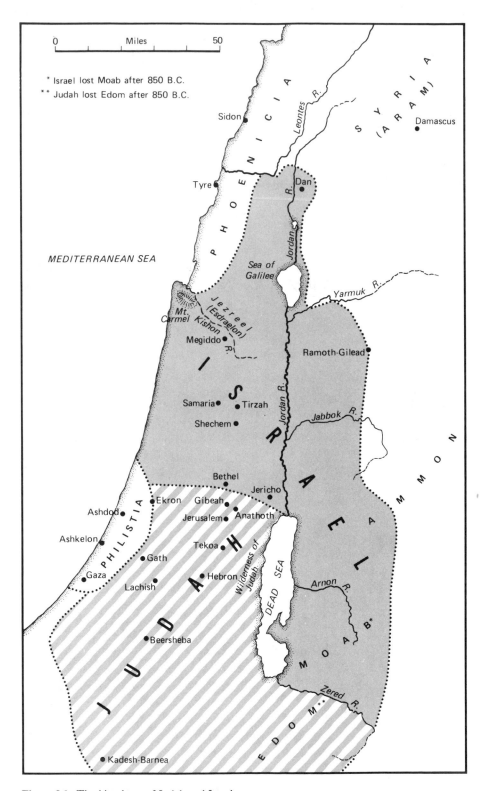

Figure 8.1. The kingdoms of Judah and Israel.

298

The Revolt (922 B.C.E.)

During Solomon's final days, signs of trouble appeared. Ahijah, a prophet of Shiloh, organized religious opposition to the royal house. The prophet put forward as leader Jeroboam, one of Solomon's construction foremen, and announced that he would become king. The rumor spread rapidly. When the word reached Solomon, Jeroboam was forced to "resign" and flee the king's anger. He found refuge with the pharaoh of Egypt, Shishak, who was anxious to make friends with anyone of prominence in Israel. Although Solomon rid the country of Jeroboam and squelched an early uprising, discontent continued to grow and at Solomon's death was ready to explode. Only by "personal courage and shrewd policy"[6] had David been able to win the affection of the people and amalgamate these tribal groups into a nation. Now unity, so difficultly and tenuously achieved, was in danger of disintegrating. Perhaps a person more sensitive to traditional divisions and more immediate dissatisfactions might have avoided open rebellion, but Solomon's son was not that person.

The Shechem Convocation.   On Solomon's death, 922 B.C.E., his son Rehoboam was accepted as king by the southern tribes of Judah and Benjamin.

Figure 8.2. The ruins of Shechem where the revolt of the northern kingdom began in the encounter between Jeroboam I and Rehoboam. The area shown is the city gate. (*Illustrator* Photo/ Ken Touchton)

[6]H. Wheeler Robinson, *The History of Israel* (Duckworth, 1957), p. 70.

Strong supporters of David, they were willing to accept Rehoboam by right of dynasty. The northern tribes, however, were not so closely tied to David's house that they felt bound to his lineage. Tradition dating from the ascension of David himself to the throne of all Israel required that the northern tribes ratify the kingship.[7] Anointing by a prophet of Yahweh was an important step in the process. Inasmuch as Ahijah was a recognized prophet, his earlier anointing of Jeroboam could not be disregarded merely because Jeroboam had been politically exiled to Egypt. The northern tribes, therefore, reserved judgment on accepting Rehoboam until they had opportunity to question him. At Shechem, the sacred place of covenant renewal, the tribes assembled to make a decision on Solomon's successor.

When Rehoboam arrived at Shechem, the seething caldron spilled over. Jeroboam I, recalled from political exile, led the delegation of northern tribes to approach the incoming monarch with a direct request for relaxation of Solomon's heavy burdens in return for allegiance. The older advisors of Rehoboam suggested that he take advantage of this opportunity to gain support by making concessions, but the young men who had grown up with Rehoboam and probably envisioned a more splendid state than Solomon's advised that this was the time to assert authority. Rehoboam followed the advice of the young men, declaring: "My little finger is thicker than my father's loins. Now, whereas my father laid on you a heavy yoke, I will add to your yoke. My father disciplined you with whips, but I will discipline you with scorpions" (1 Kings 12:10b–11).

The response of the northern tribes was decisive:

> What share do we have in David?
>   We have no inheritance in the son of Jesse.
> To your tents, O Israel!
>   Look now to your own house, O David.
>   [1 Kings 12:16b]

Their decision was final. The north wanted nothing to do with a continuation of Solomon's policies. Jeroboam offered hope for reform. When Adoram, Rehoboam's labor captain, set out to collect the hated corvée, the people killed him. Fearing for his own life, Rehoboam retreated to Jerusalem, and Jeroboam was proclaimed king of the north.

Lines between north and south were now clearly drawn. The northern boundary of the tribe of Benjamin, about ten miles north of Jerusalem, became the dividing point. The major portion of Benjamin remained loyal to the house of David and joined Judah to form a political entity that bore the name of its major tribal group, "Judah."[8] The remainder of the tribes retained the name

---

[7]2 Samuel 5:1–3; 1 Kings 121.

[8]The tribe of Simeon had been absorbed into Judah sometime during the confederacy, if not before.

"Israel." Following Shechem the latter group of tribes struggled unsuccessfully to recapture the ideal of charismatic rule, while the southern tribes strengthened the rule of David's dynasty. Thus, north and south went their separate ways. Although the prophets continued to think of Yahweh's people as an essential whole, the political unity so arduously achieved and difficultly maintained under Saul, David, and Solomon was gone forever.

Davidic/Zion Theology vs. Sinai Covenant

Ironically, Israel's revolt motivated in large measure by *religion* is thoroughly condemned by the Deuteronomist *on religious grounds*. Northern leaders saw in Solomon's policies, particularly in his conception of kingship, a contamination of the noblest Israelite religious tradition. Ahijah, the prophet who prompted Jeroboam, stood unquestionably in the tradition that favored Samuel over Saul when he encouraged Jeroboam to act in response to Yahweh's will.[9] For Ahijah, the claim of the Davidic house to rule in perpetuity was not an adequate guideline for selecting a new king. Rather aspirants to the throne should be tested by their commitment to Israel's longstanding loyalty to Yahweh. In this sense Israel's covenant with Yahweh secured at Sinai took precedence over the more recent covenant with the house of David. Thus those who stood with Ahijah were willing to attempt the restoration of an idealistic confederacy in which religious devotion was a unifying bond to be preserved through charismatic leadership. This action indicates that part of the religious leadership still stood in the tradition of Samuel, who saw in kingship a violation of Yahweh's covenant with the people. For them the cold and worldly Solomon had violated the very heart of covenant and could not be tolerated. The deep dissatisfaction of responsible religious leaders with the monarchy as typified by Solomon led them to press for a return to confederacy and charismatic leadership.

Jeroboam's early actions represent his attempt to give northern Israel religious identity, as well as stability. His decisions have a decidedly confederal flavor. Shechem, the locale of covenant renewal ceremonies, was selected as the new "capital." The city was fortified, as demonstrated by archeological excavations,[10] and served until the capital was moved to Tirzah.

More significantly Jeroboam erected shrines for Yahweh worship at Dan and Bethel. The schism had left Israel without the primary religious symbols of faith: the temple and the Jerusalem priesthood. To allow Israelites to return to

---

[9] 1 Kings 11:29–39.

[10] See G. E. Wright, "Shechem: The Archaeology of the City," *The Biblical Archaeologist*, 20 (January 1957) 19–32; James F. Ross and Lawrence E. Toombs, "Three Campaigns at Biblical Shechem," *Archaeology*, 14 (September, 1961) 171–79. Also see Itzhak Magen, "Shechem," in Stern, *New Encyclopedia*, IV, 1345–59.

Jerusalem for religious observances was to risk the loss of their allegiance to the north. Jeroboam's solution was to construct sanctuaries at Dan in the northern part of Israel and at Bethel in the south. These centers were nearer than Jerusalem and more convenient to the Israelites. Golden calves at each site were the primary cult symbols. Also, new priests (volunteers from the tribes) were provided to replace Levites who had migrated to Jerusalem at the time of the separation.

Some reasonable questions arise at this point. What was the meaning of the golden calves? Was this direct apostasy on the part of Jeroboam? Did Jeroboam intend to replace Yahweh worship with some native cultic practice? The move had obvious political overtones, but the new king was also attempting to preserve Israel's faith. In fact Jeroboam, himself designated to the throne by God's prophet, was a thorough Yahwist. He gave his sons names that bespoke loyalty to Yahweh. Shrines at Dan and Bethel were for worship of Yahweh, not pagan deities.

The form of Jeroboam's cultic symbols may have been influenced by the practice of neighboring peoples who often represented their gods (visible or invisible) as standing or riding on animals.[11] For example, the storm god of Syria was pictured as riding on a bull calf. Like the cherubim in Solomon's temple, the golden calves were symbolic of the presence of the invisible Yahweh.

Uncritical masses, perhaps, might not make clear distinctions between calves as symbols and calves as objects of worship. Consequently, syncretism with native Canaanite practice, which used bulls in the worship of El and Baal, was encouraged by the introduction of the calf symbol. To this syncretism the later Israelite reformers reacted violently. Their condemnation of the "sin of Jeroboam" may account for the story about Aaron's golden calves (Genesis 32). The account, set in the Mosaic era, served as a polemic against the shrines at Bethel and Dan.

Hence Jeroboam attempted to lead Israel to be Yahweh's people in traditional ways, but his effort at religious reformation is seen by the Deuteronomist from a quite different perspective. The historian writes from the Babylonian exile or later, long after the northern kingdom had met its tragic destiny in 722 B.C.E. The destruction of Israel is for him a classic example of the deuteronomic premise: infidelity to Yahweh brings sure judgment. The historian therefore uniformly condemns northern kings; neither Jeroboam nor Israelite kings after him receive the wholehearted endorsement of the Deuteronomist. A recurring condemnation of each king knelled Israel's doom: "He did what was evil in the sight of Yahweh, and walking in the way of Jeroboam and in the sin that he caused Israel to commit."[12]

---

[11]See L. R. Bailey, "The Golden Calf," *Hebrew Union College Annual,* 42 (1971) 97–115; also Wright, *Archaeology,* pp. 147–48.

[12]Cf. 1 Kings 15:34.

And what was Jeroboam's sin? Certainly not the denial of Yahwism. In the judgment of the historian, Jeroboam is condemned not because he built idols to false gods, but because he established Israel's worship to rival Jerusalem. For the Deuteronomist, pure Yahwism was to be preserved in Davidic forms. Israel's infidelity was its rebellious rejection of the Jerusalem-controlled Yahweh cult. Further, its kings were not in David's line. The destruction of Israel in 722 B.C.E. vindicated his opinion that Yahweh's judgment was severe against those who violated covenant with David.

The stern rejection of Israel by the Deuteronomist does not mean that Judah was treated without judgment. Solomon had been condemned for condoning the worship of foreign deities, and kings of Judah are denounced when they do not promote the Jerusalem cult wholeheartedly.[13] Nevertheless Judah more than Israel fits the deuteronomic bias. Just as the destruction of Israel illustrates the depth of the north's apostasy, so the survival of Judah through Babylonian exile demonstrates that the south, though sometimes under Yahweh's judgment, benefits from Yahweh's reward because it has been more faithful to covenant. For the Deuteronomist Zion is more important than Sinai.

TWO CENTURIES OF COEXISTENCE
(1 KINGS 14:1–2 KINGS 16:20)[14]

For two centuries after the schism, Judah and Israel coexisted until the northern kingdom was destroyed in 722 by Assyria. During this period, it would be difficult to determine which of the kingdoms was the stronger. Neither north nor south could boast of moral superiority. Apostasy and immorality permeated Judah as thoroughly as they did Israel. In an imaginary contest to do evil, Manasseh of Judah might hold his own with any of Israel's kings. To choose between Jezebel of the north and Athaliah of the south for bloodletting would be difficult. Certainly Judah cannot claim Yahweh's preference on the basis of moral superiority.

Militarily and politically Israel exceeded Judah. At some points Judah was little more than a vassal to Israel. In the alliance of Jehoshaphat of Judah with Ahab of Israel, the northerner was clearly in control. Israel's military resistance to both Syrian and Assyrian aggression had no counterparts in Judah, largely due to Judah's isolation.

Further, cultural and economic progress was more pronounced in the north than in the south. The economic resources of Phoenicia, the cultural initiative of liberal attitudes, and the trade potential offered across the Plain of Esdraelon all belonged to Israel. Judah, on the other hand, was financially crippled by Shishak of Egypt during the reign of Rehoboam. Recovery came slowly and

[13]Cf. 2 Kings 15:4–5.
[14]See also 2 Chronicles 11–28.

Near Eastern Power of Influence in Palestine		Israel		Judah	
Egypt					
918—Shishak invaded Judah		Jeroboam I	922–901	922–915	Rehoboam
				915–913	Abijah
Syria		Nadab	901–900	913–873	Asa
Benhadad I	c. 880–842	Baasha	900–877		
		Elah	877–876		
		Zimri	876		
		Tibni	876–?		
		Omri	876–869	873–849	Jehoshaphat
(853—Battle of Karkar)		Ahab	869–850		
		Ahaziah	850–849		
Hazael	c. 842–806	Jehoram	849–842	849–842	Jeroham or Joram
				842	Ahaziah
		Jehu	842–815	842–837	Athaliah
		Jehoahaz	815–801	837–800	Joash or Jehoash
		Joash	801–786	800–783	Amaziah
		Jeroboam II	786–746	783–742	Uzziah
Rezon	c. 740–732	Zechariah	746–745	750–735	Jotham
(732–Fall of Damascus to Assyria)		Shallum	745		
		Menahem	745–736		
Assyria		Pekahiah	736–735		
Tiglath-pileser	745–727	Pekah	735–732	735–715	Ahaz
		Hoshea	732–722		
Shalmaneser V	727–722				
Sargon II	722–705				
(722–Fall of Samaria)					

Israel and Judah, 922–722 B.C.E.

Figure 8.3. Israel and Judah, 922–722 B.C.E.

Judah remained conservative, much more reluctant to accommodate to Canaanite innovations. Moreover, isolated as it was, its recovery from the trauma of tribal revolution was much slower.

During the two centuries of coexistence, Israel remained the stronger, wealthier, and more progressive of the two kingdoms. However, there were two features of Judah's history that made it attractive to the biblical writer. First, Jerusalem was the center of the southern kingdom. Benjamin, on whose border lay the city of David, may originally have been more sympathetic to the north, but Rehoboam was able to secure Judah's boundaries to include Benjamin. Consequently, the temple in Jerusalem remained the seat of religion for Judah and carried a religious significance far deeper in meaning than did the shrines of Jeroboam, at least for those who preserved the tradition. For the deuteronomic historian, worship of Yahweh at sacred centers other than Jerusalem endangered what was distinctive in Yahwism by mixture with the fertility cult of Baal. His narrative about Elijah presents the issue in unequivocable terms: "How long will you go limping with two different opinions? If Yahweh is God, follow him; but if Baal, then follow him" (1 Kings 18:21).

Israel may on that occasion have chosen Yahweh, but that the issue was raised at all was for the Deuteronomist's evidence of Israel's grave error. It sought to keep covenant without the cultic context in which Yahweh came to the people and made the divine will known. Consequently, although it did not often openly choose Baal, it did regularly confuse Yahweh with that fertility deity. The concern was not primarily with sacredness of place, but with purity of faith. The Jerusalem cultus was for him the best protector of the Sinai covenant.

Second, the kings of Judah were of the line of David. In contrast to the nineteen kings of nine dynasties who ruled Israel for two hundred years, twenty kings of one dynasty[15] controlled Judah for more than three hundred thirty years. This firm entrenchment of the Davidic dynasty was providential for Judah. Whereas hopeful usurpers in Israel could take advantage of choosing rulers charismatically, the populace of the south learned to depend on the Davidic dynasty. In this context there was a degree of fulfillment of the prophetic word: "He shall build a house for my name, and I will establish the throne of his kingdom forever" (2 Samuel 7:13).

These two features receive the endorsement of the biblical writers, the first primarily of the Deuteronomist and the second of the Chronicler. However, the importance of these features reflects more than simply the biases of the biblical historians. They are facts about Judah's life that not only provided a more consistent leadership, but also enlisted a stronger identification of the populace with their nation's destiny. The temple at Jerusalem and the house of David became foci around which developed a strong sense of unity. Without prominent centers of traditional loyalty comparable to these, Israel was threatened by native Canaanite and Phoenician influence and also lost its identity when subjected to the dispersal and mixture policies of Assyria. In possession of centers of national consciousness, Judah was able to endure a national disaster similar to that confronted by Israel without final loss of faith, tradition, and identity.

Jeroboam I of Israel/Rehoboam of Judah

Throughout the reigns of Jeroboam I of Israel (922–901) and Rehoboam of Judah (922–915) hostility between the two kingdoms continued, restrained only by circumstances. Immediately after the Shechem convocation, Rehoboam's first inclination was to gather an army and bring the rebellious Jeroboam into line. Except for the intervention of Shemaiah, the Hebrew prophet, and Shishak, the Egyptian pharaoh, there might have occurred a bloody civil war from which neither Judah nor Israel could have recovered.

The chief deterent here was Shishak, the same pharaoh who had earlier offered sanctuary to Jeroboam. This founder of the twenty-second dynasty of

---

[15]For the brief period 842–837, Judah's throne was controlled by Athaliah, who was non-Davidic.

Figure 8.4. Massive winged bull with man's head. It marked the entrance to the palace of the Assyrian King Asshurnasirpal, c. 885–860 B.C.E. (Copyright, British Museum)

Egypt moved as far north as Megiddo on an expedition to extend his control into Syria-Palestine.[16] In 918 B.C.E. Jerusalem was saved from the strong force of Lybians and Nubians under Shishak by payment of extensive tribute, including much of the wealth that Solomon had accumulated in his temple and palace.[17] The damage in Judah was lasting. Crippled economically, its inferiority to Israel became more pronounced. Judah did little more than survive under the shadow of a flowering Israel.

[16]An inscription on the temple of Karnak in upper Egypt depicts this as a campaign that brought a host of Palestinian towns into subjection.

[17]Pritchard, *Texts*, pp. 263–64, 242–43. Because of the exaggerated nature of the claims, the inscription cannot be taken as an accurate historical account of the campaign.

In spite of its military weakness following the Shishak invasion, Judah's hostility with Israel endured. After Rehoboam and Jeroboam I, tension between the two thrones continued. Border towns in the north and south were fortified. Gibeah, Saul's old capital, in Judah and Bethel in Israel were reinforced as defensive measures. The clearest evidence of rivalry is seen at a place seven miles north of Jerusalem, known today as Tel en-Nasbeh. Here excavators have uncovered the most formidable of Judah's fortifications.[18] The wall around this city was twenty feet thick. A heavy coat of plaster on the lower part of the wall made it almost impossible for an enemy to scale. The fortification of Tel en-Nasbeh was probably the doing of Asa (913–873) and remains "eloquent testimony to the ill-feeling and civil war between Judah and Israel."[19]

Surprisingly, these feelings erupted into open conflict only rarely. Such fighting as did occur was sporadic and mostly concerned with the rectification of borders between the two states. This seems to be the situation described in 2 Chronicles 13 where Abijah (915–913) is described as defeating rather convincingly the forces of Jeroboam I. At best such a victory could only have been temporary, for shortly thereafter the two states were again warring over border fortifications.

A greater success was Judah's resistance to "Zerah the Ethiopian."[20] Zerah may have been an ambitious commander left by Shishak to protect Egyptian interests on Judah's southern border. Asa met and defeated him, and Judah was free to continue its bickering with Israel.

The Omrids of Israel/Jehoshaphat of Judah

Israel could not have endured much longer the political instability of its first fifty years. Following the reign of Jeroboam I, there were abbreviated reigns, assassinations, and bloody attempts to secure the throne. Not a single king was able to maintain charismatic leadership. Also the political complexion of the Near East changed to the disadvantage of the loose confederal structure of the north. By the second quarter of the ninth century, the northern and eastern borders of Israel were threatened by both Syria and Assyria. If Israel was to survive in the power struggles of the Near East, the conflict between charismatic ideal and dynastic continuity had to be resolved.

Omri of Israel (876–869).   The hero of Israel in this situation was Omri, an army commander who led a successful coup and placed himself on the throne. The deuteronomic historian dismisses Omri with a brief discussion of eight

---

[18]See Wright, *Archaeology*, p. 150; and Jeffrey R. Zorn, "Tel en-Nasbeh," in Stern, *New Encyclopedia*, IV, 1098–1102.

[19]Wright, *Archaeology*, p. 151.

[20]2 Chronicles 14:9–14.

verses,[21] evidently considering his reign to have contributed little to the religious history of Israel. With the conventional format Omri is condemned as provoking Yahweh to anger by following the ways of Jeroboam, who caused Israel to sin—that is, he did not destroy the shrines at Bethel and Dan, restore proper respect for the Jerusalem sanctuary, and acknowledge the authority of David's dynasty. Nevertheless, Omri was undoubtedly a king of superior ability. His reign was brief and much of it was spent in securing the throne from his competitor, Tibni. But he restored so much stability to Israel's throne that long after his death, the Assyrians referred to Israel as "the land of the house of Omri."

Soon after consolidating his position, Omri exercised a foreign policy resembling that of David and Solomon. His objective was to establish strong relationships with close neighbors like Phoenicia and Judah. An alliance with Phoenicia was sealed by the marriage of Omri's son, Ahab, to Jezebel, the royal princess of Tyre. Although this alliance was to bear undesirable fruit in the religious history of Israel, its immediate result was valuable both politically and commercially. Phoenicia, long a prosperous and faithful ally, strengthened Israel against the rising threats of Syria and Assyria in the east. Further, Phoenician trade with northern Africa was at its peak. The alliance provided once again, as in the days of Solomon, expanded trade, which brought considerable wealth to Israel's treasury. There may even have been an effort to rebuild the old and profitable port of Ezion-geber in the south.[22]

Although separation was now so well settled that reunification was practically impossible, Omri advocated cooperation between Judah and Israel. This desire was later implemented by the marriage of Athaliah, the daughter of Ahab (or his sister),[23] to Jehoram, a Judean prince.

Omri also had military success. An inscription on the Moabite Stone suggests a successful campaign in Transjordan by which Moab was subjected. This inscription from Mesha, king of Moab, contemporary with Ahab, states that "Omri, king of Israel, he humbled Moab many years. . . . Omri had occupied the land of Medeba, and [Israel] had dwelt there in his time."[24] The Kings account elaborates that Mesha of Moab "had to deliver annually to the king of Israel a hundred thousand lambs, and the wool of a hundred thousand rams."[25] This is only one illustration of the strength with which Omri expanded the influence of Israel.

---

[21]1 Kings 16:21–28.

[22]Ibid., 22:48.

[23]2 Kings 8:18 and 2 Chronicles 21:6 list Athaliah as the daughter of Ahab; 2 Kings 8:26 and 2 Chronicles 22:2 have her as the daughter of Omri (NRSV, granddaughter). The birth of her son around 864 B.C.E. indicates that she was not the daughter of Ahab and Jezebel, who had themselves been married only ten years at the time. She may have been a daughter of Ahab by an earlier wife than Jezebel.

[24]Pritchard, *Texts*, p. 320.

[25]2 Kings 3:4.

Figure 8.5. The Moabite Stone, discovered at Dibon in Transjordan, describing the victory of Mesha, the Moabite king, over Israel after the death of Ahab. The inscription refers to Moab's earlier subjection to Omri. (Courtesy, The Louvre)

The primary monument to Omri's successful administration was his transfer of the capital to Samaria.[26] Although Shechem was the natural capital of the north because of its religious associations, the town could not be easily defended. Even before the days of Omri, Tirzah had been utilized as capital by some of the minor kings of Israel. Now Omri chose to build a new city better situated for his relationships with Phoenicia. Lying seven miles northwest of Shechem, it was the gateway to the commanding plain of Esdraelon and consequently to Phoenicia. The strategic significance of the city is confirmed by

[26]Samaria has been extensively excavated. See the summary in Stern, *New Encyclopedia*, IV, 1300–11.

the extensive use of the site during the Greek and Roman periods. Its location on the summit of a gently sloping hill made it almost impregnable to standard tactical assault. Three walls around the hill begun by Omri and completed by Ahab provided a formidable defense against outside invaders. A century later mighty Assyria could capture the capital only after extended siege.[27] Samaria remained the capital throughout the rest of Israel's history. Like Jerusalem it became a hub of life in Palestine. As a place of "strength, fertility, and beauty combined" its equal in all Palestine would be difficult to find.[28]

Undoubtedly the strength brought to Israel's throne by Omri prolonged its life and restored something of the splendor of Solomon's reign. But also like that of Solomon, Omri's prosperity was accompanied by an internal moral deterioration later to be denounced vehemently by Amos and Hosea. To these prophets, Omri's Samaria became a symbol of the idolatrous sin of the northern kingdom.

Ahab (869–850).   Ahab receives a more negative evaluation from the Deuteronomist than was given his father, primarily because of his wife Jezebel. Politically Ahab was an able leader. During his reign, the fortification of Samaria was completed and adornments of elaborate ivory work were added to its buildings. The "pool of Samaria"[29] may have been built by him. He also built at Megiddo and in Transjordan.[30] Friendly arrangements with neighboring nations were continued. Jezebel assured Phoenicia's friendship and events during the early days of Ahab's reign indicated his willingness to be friendly to both Judah and Syria, even entering an alliance with Judah.

The decisive factor in a coalition with Jehoshaphat of Judah (873–849) was the common threat of Syria. In many ways Jehoshaphat was an idealist. He envisioned Israel and Judah reunited under common rule with the glory of Yahweh's people reestablished. This explains his willingness to join Ahab of Israel, although Judah's role would approximate that of a vassal. Ahab's concern was resistance to Syria, whereas Jehoshaphat also desired to reunify the covenant community. But Jehoshaphat was more successful at home than with

---

[27]Although the hill of Samaria was greatly disturbed by Greek and Roman builders, it has been extensively excavated. Here George A. Reisner and Clarence S. Fisher, working in 1908–10, developed their now famous stratigraphical method of digging. Instead of cutting trenches across the mound, they excavated small areas, carefully recording all findings so as to be able to reconstruct on paper the entire site. This procedure has contributed greatly to the gigantic strides taken by archeology during the last half-century.

[28]Edward Robinson, *Biblical Researches in Palestine*, vol. 2 (1941), pp. 307–9, as quoted in Wright, *Archaeology*, p. 151.

[29]1 Kings 22:38.

[30]See Wright, *Archaeology*, p. 153. Construction at Megiddo previously credited to Solomon have been demonstrated to belong to Ahab; see Yadin, "Light," pp. 62–68, and "Megiddo," pp. 66–96.

Israel. In Judah he defended Yahweh against Baalism[31] and accomplished important judicial reforms. His dream of reunion, however, went unrealized.

Ahab's success as a military commander was remarkable. He defeated Benhadad of Syria and enlisted him against the increasing threat of Assyria. Since Assyria's early westward movement around the turn of the eleventh century, its imperialistic designs had become increasingly feared by Phoenicia, Syria, and Israel. The brutal Asshurnasirpal II (883–859) had renewed the Assyrian drive toward the Mediterranean, and his successor, Shalmaneser III (859–824), actually reached for the whole Fertile Crescent. Undoubtedly this mounting Assyrian threat influenced Ahab to act kindly toward Benhadad. Half a friend with military strength was better than none in such days.

The annals of the conquests of Shalmaneser[32] provide ample and reliable information about the struggle between Assyria and the smaller and weaker states near the Mediterranean. Benhadad of Syria organized a coalition of resistance composed of twelve kings of the Syria-Palestine region. "Ahab the Israelite" was one of the three key leaders of the coalition. Ahab contributed a major force of ten thousand foot soldiers and two thousand chariots. Battle was joined in the vicinity of Qarqar on the Orontes. Shalmaneser claimed an overwhelming victory, but if there was a victory, it was not complete enough to allow him either to take Damascus or to march into Israel.

The Bible does not mention the battle of Qarqar. However, the fact that the annals of Shalmaneser date the battle precisely to the sixth year of his reign (853 B.C.E.) makes this a pivot event for biblical chronology. Because the battle of Qarqar can be placed with some accuracy in Ahab's reign, it provides a point of reference for calculating the dates of surrounding events.

Jezebel and Elijah. For the Deuteronomist the military success of Ahab could not offset his tolerance of the Canaanite cult of Baal. The king's wife, Jezebel of Tyre, was an ardent devotee of her native Baal Melkart and also a strong believer in the absolute powers of the king. In telling and preserving the stories of contest between Jezebel and Elijah the Tishbite, Israel confessed its faith in pure Yahwism and its belief that the king had special responsibility to preserve covenant community.

The stories are told with dramatic seriousness. Jezebel became queen with a consuming passion to make her god the god of Israel. The Canaanite fertility religion, of which the worship of Melkart was only one expression,[33] had been a major threat to Yahweh worship since Israel's arrival in Canaan. But now

---

[31]1 Kings 22:41–46; 2 Chronicles 19:1–3.

[32]See Pritchard, *Texts*, pp. 276–77.

[33]Excavations at Ras Shamra in northern Syria have uncovered numerous Canaanite religious texts. From these we have learned a great deal about the fertility religion of the Baalim.

this particular cult had an ardent missionary. Ahab, following the earlier pattern of Solomon, constructed a temple of Baal in Samaria for Jezebel's benefit.[34] Jezebel, apparently with the king's approval, began an enthusiastic effort to make the Phoenician Baal the only god of Israel. Against her missionary efforts stood the prophetic community's allegiance to Yahweh. Consequently, Jezebel created a conflict between the two rival state cults, each of which tended to be mutually exclusive of the other.

The ardor with which Jezebel promoted Baalism was met with an equally vigorous defense of Yahwism. The champion of Yahweh in this situation was Elijah, a prophet in the tradition of Moses. Elijah appears in the narrative as a man of enormous powers; unapproachable, unpredictable, often hated but ever faithful to Yahweh, and always someone to be reckoned with. At a time when Jezebel and the cause of Baal were evidently gaining a foothold in the northern kingdom,[35] Elijah sought to show Baal to be no god at all. He was little concerned with promoting the Jerusalem sanctuary and undisturbed by the shrines of Jeroboam;[36] his Yahwism was in the tradition of Moses. Elijah came from Gilead east of the Jordan where Yahwism would have more likely preserved its separation from other cults. West of the river, however, contact with Baal cults was more immediate and hence maintaining purity of faith was more difficult. Elijah was horrified at the syncretism he encountered in Israel when he crossed the river and set out to rally decadent forces of prophetism in allegiance to historic faith. He proclaimed that Yahweh would tolerate no other gods and that Israel could no longer go halting between two opinions. Like Samuel, he interpreted the state as Yahweh's enemy if pure Yahwism was compromised at any level. Jezebel, as perpetrator of the compromise, was anathema to Yahweh. The only solution to Elijah was holy war to purge the land of Baalism.

The struggle between the two faiths is epitomized in a story full of drama and subtle humor.[37] Elijah challenged four hundred fifty prophets of Baal to a contest at Mt. Carmel to determine the true God, Yahweh or Baal. The contest was conducted in a sphere where Baal was supposed to be supreme—the fertility of the land. Famine had devastated the country. Even the king was forced to scour the land for small pools of water and patches of grass to keep animals alive. The cause of the drought was clear to the prophet: Ahab had forsaken Yahweh by following the Baalim. Here was the source of the problem and here would be found its solution. Elijah challenged the Baal prophets to demonstrate that Baal could break the drought by bringing rain. Sacrifices were

---

[34]1 Kings 16:32.

[35]Ibid., 18:4f.

[36]He built an altar on Mt. Carmel apparently independent of both cultic systems; see 1 Kings 18:30.

[37]1 Kings 18:17–40. The account as it presently appears probably weaves together two ancient stories, one embodying acts to bring about an end to the drought and another describing the production of fire as evidence of Yahweh's supremacy.

prepared and the frenzied ecstatics went into action, crying out for Baal to hear, doing their limping dances around the altar, even cutting themselves with swords and lances. Elijah satirically taunted their efforts: "Cry aloud! Surely he is a god; either he is meditating, or he has wandered away, or he is on a journey, or perhaps he is asleep and must be awakened" (1 Kings 18:27). Their rantings ended in nothing: ". . . there was no voice, no answer, no response" (1 Kings 18:29).

Then the real drama began. After the Baal ecstatics had failed, Elijah went quietly into his ritual. An altar to Yahweh, previously torn down, was restored. Sacrifice was prepared. The breaking of the drought was symbolized by pouring water on the altar until trenches around it were filled. In response to Elijah's prayer, the "fire of Yahweh fell," consuming the sacrifice, even lapping the water from the trenches. The prophets of Baal were slain. The drought was broken, proof that Yahweh, not Baal, controlled the productivity of the land and merited full allegiance from the people.

Jezebel would not tolerate such an enthusiast and determined to kill Elijah, as she had other prophets of Yahweh.[38] Fearing for his life, Elijah fled to the sacred mountain of Horeb (Sinai). After experiencing the traditional manifestations of Yahweh's revelation in earthquake, wind, and fire, there came in an awesome stillness the reassurance that the cause of Yahweh would prevail. The house of Ahab would be overthrown and Yahweh's faithful would be preserved.

Jezebel's effort to establish Baal worship was only one point of concern to Elijah. Perhaps equally threatening was her conception of the role of king. She viewed the king in typical oriental fashion as an absolute despot. To her, he ruled with unlimited privilege with his subjects as pawns to his desires. Jezebel's interpretation of the monarchy and Elijah's reaction to it are reflected in the story of Naboth's vineyard.[39] Ahab wanted a tract of land belonging to Naboth, but the peasant farmer refused to surrender his land to the king under any circumstance. To Naboth the land was not his to sell. It had been passed down within his family as a sacred trust from Yahweh. Although sulking in despair, Ahab evidently accepted Naboth's right of refusal. But not Jezebel. The king was king with rights to take what he wanted. If Ahab wanted the land, it belonged to him. Ahab would not assert himself, and so the queen manipulated the "courts of justice" to have Naboth condemned for treason and blasphemy, and then executed.

Elijah's reaction was again immediate and forthright. Confronting Ahab in the vineyard, he called Naboth's stoning a murder demanding blood revenge. Because no kin of Naboth remained, Yahweh himself would see that justice was done. Jezebel had triggered an explosion that would eventually destroy Ahab's house.

---

[38]Ibid., 18:4, 13; 19:10, 14.
[39]Ibid., chap. 21.

Elijah's opposition to Ahab, Jezebel, and Baalism differs from the typical deuteronomic denunciation of the northern kings.[40] Not the covenant with David, but traditional Mosaic faith was his consuming passion. Imagery in the narrative clearly depicts Elijah as a second Moses—defying national power, journeying to Horeb, commissioning his successor, and challenging people to avoid apostasy. For him Sinai superceded Zion. As Yahweh's spokesman he firmly opposed a monarchy that tried either overtly to introduce a foreign cult or covertly to usurp Yahweh's role. Energetically he proclaimed a covenant Yahweh who both contests with Baal on Mt. Carmel and champions the cause of the underprivileged in social relationships. These themes of Yahweh's sovereignty and Israel's ethical responsibility will be more fully developed by later Hebrew prophets.

The Jehu Dynasty

Elisha and the End of the Omrids.   Although Elijah was a lonely and isolated individual, his passion for pure Yahwism found many sympathizers among religiously sensitive Israelites. Many of the prophetic communities were intolerant of the Melkart cults and vast segments of the populace had been offended by Queen Jezebel's concern for the "divine rights" of the kings. Hence, Elisha, the successor of Elijah, had a sympathetic following that could be rallied to bring down Ahab's house. Elisha's personality was very different from Elijah's, but he shared with his predecessor an intense loyalty to the Sinai tradition and forthrightly criticized the royal household for its disloyalty to the Yahweh covenant. Elisha was one of a withdrawn and unusual company of persons called *beni hanebi'im*, "sons of the prophets." They were probably poor and without status, but they represented "pure uncontaminated Yahwism and its divine law."[41] This is the man who was the chief actor in the overthrow of Ahab.

The details of Elisha's political activity are difficult to recover, partially because the narrative is interspersed with numerous miracle stories. Nowhere else in the Hebrew scriptures are so many miracles crowded into so small a space. Elsewhere in the Hebrew Bible miracles occur to arouse awe for and to compel devotion to Yahweh. In the Elisha cycle, however, miracles such as a floating ax head,[42] the tearing of cursing boys by bears,[43] and the purifying of pottage[44] are reported seemingly to express "sheer delight . . . at the repeated and astonishing proofs of the prophet's charisma."[45] That miracles in the He-

---

[40]Interestingly the Elijah stories come from northern sources, brought to Judah after the end of the northern kingdom in 722. Hence they are not so focused on Davidic covenant.

[41]Von Rad, *Old Testament*, II:28.

[42]2 Kings 6:1–7.

[43]Ibid., 2:23–25.

[44]Ibid., 4:38–41.

[45]Von Rad, *Old Testament*, II:27.

brew scriptures are clustered around the exodus narrative and around the tales
of Elijah and Elisha suggests that they are used here to authenticate these men
as prophets in the Mosaic tradition.

Elisha was more than the interesting hero of fascinating tales. The zealous
character of the devout community to which he belonged left him with a consummate passion for purging Israel of the evil house of Ahab. Unwilling simply
to let time take its course, he became active in marshaling political means to
the end of accomplishing his religious purpose. The tool in his hand was a
captain in Israel's army, Jehu.

The backdrop for the overthrow of the Omri dynasty was the longstanding
struggle between Syria and Israel for the prize of Ramoth-Gilead. Hazael, with
the undisguised encouragement of Elisha,[46] had murdered his predecessor and
usurped the throne of Syria. Jehoram, Ahab's son and successor, interpreted
this as an opportune time to recover Ramoth-Gilead and with the aid of Ahaziah of Judah sought to do so. The initial battle went against Israel; Jehoram
was wounded and retired to Jezreel to recover.

When Jehu was left in charge, Elisha seized the moment. He commissioned
a prophet to go to Ramoth-Gilead and anoint Jehu as king. The army backed
the newly anointed king and a revolution was on. A blood purge of the house
of Ahab followed, related in all its gory details in 2 Kings 9. Following Jehu's
hurried chariot ride from Ramoth-Gilead to Jezreel, the blood of the Omrids
flowed freely until "Jehu killed all who were left of the house of Ahab in Jezreel,
all his leaders, close friends, and priest, until he left him no survivors."[47]
Jehoram was killed and his corpse thrown into the vineyard of Naboth—with
dramatic fitness illustrating that the blood-revenge law had been satisfied. The
hated Jezebel was thrown from an open window and ignominiously trampled.
The orgy of reprisals extended even to the worshipers of Baal.[48] Although the
Kings writer praised the revolutionist, Hosea a century later declared Yahweh's
judgment because of the bloody execution of the Omrids: "I will punish the
house of Jehu for the blood of Jezreel" (Hosea 1:4).

Jehu (842–815). For all its religious overtones the revolution led by Jehu
was a political disaster. It is true that he established a dynasty of some stability.
Jehu himself ruled Israel for twenty-seven years, and four kings of his house
extended his dynasty for almost a hundred years, the longest in Israel's history.
And yet Israel was set on a course leading to political and religious ruin.

For one thing, the alliance with Phoenicia present since the days of David
was now forever broken. The profitable exchange through the ports of its seafaring neighbor was lost to Israel. And Jehu's reprisals had damaging reper-

[46]See 2 Kings 8:7–15.
[47]Ibid., 10:11.
[48]Ibid., 10:18–27.

Figure 8.6. The description in the lower right hand corner reads, "The Black Obelisk of Shalmaneser III, King of Assyria, 858–824 B.C.E. The five rows of reliefs depict various conquered peoples bringing tribute, each one being identified by the caption above the reliefs. In the second row down, Jehu, King of Israel, or his ambassador, does obeisance to Shalmaneser and is followed by a line of 13 Israelites carrying his tribute. The inscription at the top and bottom of the obelisk describes events from the beginning of his reign until his 31st year. From Nimrud, c. 825 B.C.E." (Copyright, British Museum)

cussions in Judah. Whereas Omri and Ahab had encouraged friendly relationships with Judah, Jehu's purge included Ahaziah of Judah, whose wife was also of the house of Omri. This action extended the revolution to the royal house of Judah and widened the chasm separating the two kingdoms.

Further, whatever had remained of the western coalition against Assyria was erased. Rather than unite with his neighbors to resist the growing power of Assyria, Jehu chose concession. Soon after the revolution, Assyria under the aggressive Shalmaneser III again began moving westward toward the Mediterranean. Instead of rallying to the support of Israel's only buffer against Assyria, as Ahab had done at Qarqar, Jehu purchased protection from Shalmaneser with tribute. The black obelisk of Shalmaneser depicts the scene of Jehu's humiliation. He is portrayed as prostrate before Shalmaneser, forehead to the ground, acknowledging the sovereignty of Assyria. This expedient compromise led Hazael of Syria to take devastating retaliation on Jehu. When Shalmaneser had returned to Assyria, Hazael launched a campaign against Israel that "threshed Gilead with threshing sledges of iron" (Amos 1:3) and brought Israel very near extermination.

Thus Jehu, although praised by the Deuteronomist for his struggle against the Baal cult (1 Kings 19:15–18) brought Israel to humiliation. He was succeeded by his weak son Jehoahaz (815–801), and all during these years "the anger of Yahweh was kindled against Israel" (2 Kings 13:3). Israel's military strength was reduced to a mere fifty horsemen, ten chariots, and ten thousand footmen.[49] Thus, during the last quarter of the ninth century, Israel was little more than a dependency of Syria.

Jeroboam II of Israel (786–746)/Uzziah of Judah (783–742). The difficult days of Jehu's reign in Israel were paralleled by political confusion in Judah, although problems in Judah were milder and briefer. The culprit was Athaliah, a non-Davidic claimant who seized the throne of Judah and put to death any

Figure 8.7. Closeup of panel of Black Obelisk showing "Jehu, son of Omri" bowed before Shalmaneser. This is the only contemporary representation of an Israelite king. Jehu brought tribute of "silver, gold, a golden bowl, a golden vase with painted bottom, golden tumbler, golden buckets, tin, a staff for a king . . .". (Copyright, British Museum)

[49]Ibid., 13:7.

who opposed her. Although Athaliah was able to maintain control of Judah for several years (842–837), the people did not support her. They had little sympathy with her Baal worship and less with her non-Davidic background. Consequently, when the priest Jehoiada set forth Joash, a son of Ahaziah who had been saved from execution and protected in the temple, the people immediately rallied to his side. Athaliah was executed, and the house of David was restored.

These difficult times in both Israel and Judah might have spelled the end of the two kingdoms had political fortunes of the Near East not turned to their favor. Another of the frequent revivals of Assyria abruptly broke the superiority of Syria. A campaign of Assyria crushed Damascus (in 802) and threatened Israel. Internal dissensions, however, prohibited Assyria's further move westward, and once again Israel and Judah enjoyed peace because of the preoccupation of their powerful neighbors. Into this circumstance came Jeroboam II of Israel and Uzziah of Judah.

The stellar gem in the Jehu dynasty was Jeroboam II. Although the Kings narrative dismisses him as continuing the apostasy of the north, Jeroboam was an important leader. His contemporary in Judah was Uzziah. Both men were capable rulers, and under their leadership the territories of Israel and Judah were extended "from Lebo-hamath as far as the sea of Arabah" (2 Kings 14:25), the limits of the old Davidic kingdom. Geographical expansion was accompanied by tremendous and sudden internal prosperity. With both Syria and Assyria preoccupied with difficulties, control of the great trade routes fell once again to Israel. In a span of a quarter-century Jeroboam II was able to bring a tottering nation to glory unknown since the days of Solomon. Excavations at Samaria have brought to light ostraca from this period reflecting an extensive fiscal organization that surely brought wealth into the coffers of Jeroboam II.[50]

In the south Judah also took advantage of international politics. Uzziah came to the throne when he was sixteen years old and began a long and able rule that restored Judah militarily and politically. Fortifications of Jerusalem were restored. The army was reorganized and reequipped; siege engines of warfare were introduced. Uzziah continued Edom's subjugation, and the Philistine and Negeb areas remained secure. The Ezion-geber port was repaired, and nearby copper smelteries were restored.[51] "During this period Judah was the most stable state in Palestine and probably in all Syria."[52] The high regard with which the people held Uzziah is attested by the fact that he remained the real ruler even after he was stricken with leprosy and forced to yield the public exercise of his office to his co-regent, Jotham (750–735).

[50]Wright, *Archaeology*, p. 158.

[51]A seal of Jotham unearthed in this area probably belonged to Uzziah's son and co-regent; it attests to the activity of the king in developing the Negeb regions. See Diringer, "The Seal of Jotham," in Thomas, ed., *Documents*, pp. 224–25.

[52]W. F. Albright, *The Biblical Period* (Biblical Colloquium, 1950), p. 40.

The prosperity that typified Judah and Israel in the mid-eighth century was not without its problems, however. Empty rituals and social injustice characterized the growing decay rapidly eclipsing the external prosperity achieved under Jeroboam and Uzziah. Two prophets in the north, Amos and Hosea, and slightly later, Micah and Isaiah in the south, sought courageously to correct the moral and religious course the nations had taken. But Yahweh's prophetic word went essentially unheeded, and with the revival of Assyria, the future became increasingly ominous.

Israel's Covenant with Death

Jeroboam's death was followed by twenty-four years of continued degeneration of the social structure and unstable leadership. In the decade following Jeroboam's death, Israel had five kings, none of whom could provide able leadership. Zechariah (746–745) had been in power only six months when he was assassinated by Shallum (745). After only a month's rule, the latter was liquidated by Menahem (745–736). Such anarchy and instability, coupled with the internal sickness decried by the prophets, made Israel's resistance to Assyria only nominal. Destruction of the nation was at hand. "Her ship of state, leaking at every seam, without compass or competent helmsmen and with its crew demoralized, was sinking."[53]

The major political factor in the downfall of the northern kingdom was the restoration of Assyria. No name of this era is comparable to that of Tiglath-pileser III (designated in the biblical account as Pul), who came to the Assyrian throne about the time of Jeroboam II's death around 746 B.C.E. Tiglath-pileser was an extremely capable and energetic ruler. After securing the Assyrian neighborhood, he directed his ambitions toward the west. Although Syria and Egypt were his primary targets, Israel's strategic position as the bridge of the Fertile Crescent made its involvement a foregone conclusion. Tiglath-pileser marched westward and soon was receiving tribute from most of the states of Syria and northern Palestine. In 732 B.C.E. Damascus fell to him, and Israel's buffer was gone; part of Israel was also overrun and the rest stood naked before Assyria.

Tiglath-pileser's control of the west lasted until his death in 727 B.C.E. Hoshea (732–722), who followed Pekah to Israel's throne, took Pul's death as a signal for revolt. Hoshea refused to pay tribute to the new Assyrian monarch, Shalmaneser V, who consequently moved against Israel. Samaria managed to withstand a three-year siege, thus validating Omri's choice of the city as an easily defendable capital. However, Shalmaneser's successor, Sargon II, was able to destroy both the city and nation in 722 B.C.E.

---

[53]Bright, *History*, p. 272.

Transcolonization.   Instead of the usual procedure of exacting tribute and demanding allegiance, Sargon deported and dispersed many of the Israelites across his vast empire. According to Assyrian records, 27,290 Israelites were resettled beyond Mesopotamia. These deportees were replaced by displaced persons from other areas of the Assyrian empire. The amalgamation of these imports with the remaining natives resulted in a half-breed folk referred to in the New Testament as Samaritans. As far as the Deuteronomist was concerned, the tribes of the north were lost to the elect nation of Israel. The prophets would plead for a reidentification of the north with the "new Israel," but the fall of Samaria marked for the Deuteronomist the natural end for revolt against Yahweh, born and bred in the spirit of apostasy.

The march toward destruction, presaged by the prophets Amos and Hosea, moved forward as though no recourse was available. Without repentance and return to covenant fidelity, Israel as a nation was doomed. Outside the covenant, it was not Yahweh's people and Yahweh was not its God. Yahweh had "sent her away with a decree of divorce" (Jeremiah 3:8). A covenant broken was no longer a covenant. Having turned from Yahweh to the world, Israel was now what it had chosen. There was hope for its return and salvation, but for the moment only Judah remained to face the choice between covenant fidelity or a destiny like that of Israel.

SUGGESTIONS FOR FURTHER STUDY

Using Bible dictionaries as listed in the General Bibliography (especially Anchor, Harper, and Mercer) expand you understanding of Zion theology, Omri dynasty, Qarqar, fertility religion, Shechem convocation, transcolonization, and stratigraphy. *The Anchor Bible Dictionary* article on Baal is especially helpful.

Pursue your study of the books of Kings and Chronicles by consulting the standard commentary series. A useful, nontechnical treatment of Chronicles is the volume in the Daily Bible Study series. John Gray has written a helpful book, *I and II Kings,* in *The Old Testament Library* series (Westminster, 1963), and an insightful article is J. D. Newsome, "Toward a New Understanding of the Chronicler and His Purposes," *Journal of Biblical Literature,* 94 (1975) 201–17.

Additional study of archeological excavations at sites related to this chapter should begin with summary chapters in Ephrain Stern et al., eds., *The New Encyclopedia of Archaeological Excavations in the Holy Land, I–IV* (Israel Exploration Society, 1993). Two articles elaborate on work at Shechem: G. Ernest Wright, "Shechem: The Archaeology of the City," *The Biblical Archaeologist Reader,* 20 (1957) 19–32; and Lawrence Toombs, "Three Campaigns at Shechem," *Archaeology,* 14 (1961) 171–79. Yigael Yadin's articles on Megiddo in *Biblical Archaeologist*—33 (1970) 66–96 and 23 (1960) 62–68—are important. See also other general works under Archeology in the General Bibliography.

Works on specific topics related to this period include E. T. Mullen, "The Sins of Jeroboam," *Catholic Biblical Quarterly*, 49 (1987) 212–32; J. M. Miller, "The Fall of the House of Ahab," *Vetus Testamentum*, 17 (1967) 307–24; S. B. Frost, "Judgment on Jezebel, or a Woman Wronged," *Theology Today*, 20 (1964) 305–17; Lelia Bronner, *The Stories of Elijah and Elisha as Polemics Against Baal Worship* (Brill, 1968); and Jon D. Levenson, *Sinai and Zion: An Entry into the Jewish Bible* (Winston, 1985).

A brief bibliography on Miracles is on page 221.

9

The Prophetic Word

The movement of the Hebrews from the deserts of Sinai and Kadesh-Barnea to settlement in Palestine is in one sense an experience in altered self-conception. In the wilderness nomadism fostered expectancy for change. Although the Hebrews during this period were not constantly on the move, their life was characterized by only brief settlement and frequent uprooting.[1] There were no permanent houses, no capital cities, no localized temple, no libraries or books. Tents typified a fluid culture. Peoples who move from camp to camp, from waterhole to waterhole, focus on the present, with each day's harsh realities enough to occupy their attention. This mind-set concentrates on the present without much concern for past or future. Sacred tradition is preserved in stories told around the campfire. Society is largely egalitarian because everyone faces the difficult task of daily survival. There is little or no concern with status, rank, and privilege. Unwritten, but clearly understood, standards of morality and justice protect a life that is at best tenuous.

Settlement, an agrarian mode of life, and finally a measure of urbanization present in monarchy produced other ways of thinking and living. Life gradually became more "settled" and organized; smaller social groups began to be identified with larger units. Ultimately a sense of national consciousness eroded individuality and began to rank persons in terms of their contribution to or profit from the larger body. Self-identity increasingly came to be preserved through "our nation" as much as through "my family" or "my clan." The rise of villages created a new society whose members had more specialized functions. Classes emerged with standards of morality influenced by ideas of responsibility within one's group. Permanence outweighed change. Preserving an efficient order in which persons do their duty in their place became the

---

[1]See Exodus 13:13, 34:20, references that suggest Hebrew dependence on the ass rather than the camel, the animal of the pure nomad.

agenda. Stability was more expected than change, class structure more than unidimensional society, nation more than family. The past gained its attention as the way the nation had been brought to its present station, and the future was anticipated as the time for even greater accomplishments for the community.

In this context of changing structures and self-understanding, Yahweh's covenant people constructed specific leadership roles designed to preserve the sacralized order interpreted as the deity's gift to the nation. The change was gradual and often painful, but by the time of Hebrew monarchies, united and divided, religious institutions had begun to take definitive shape. An established cult demanded a priesthood to maintain proper worship. Although differing considerably over whether it was necessary to preserve David's line, both north and south revered the king as the preserver of Yahweh's holy nation. Both king and priest were granted authority as Yahweh's representatives to maintain Yahweh's relationship to the covenant community.

Thus, in transition from seminomadism to monarchy the Hebrews experienced patterns of social and political growth that dramatically influenced the shape of their religion. Generally, movement was from transiency to stability and conservation. Religious structures, as culture itself, became established and sacralized. Stories earlier told around campfires to preserve sacred tradition began to take written form carrying their own authority. Religious practices were legitimated as holy instruments for relating to deity. Cult, scripture, and religious leadership were given normative status. In short, religion, like the people, became "settled" and organized. Preserving the legitimated forms was understood as the heart of faithfulness with responsibility vested in both priest and king. Obedience and loyalty to established religion became the cardinal virtue, and disobedience or eccentric behavior that threatened the ordered establishment was the cardinal sin. In such circumstances the Hebrews might easily have protected the legitimated forms as if they were the very heart of faith. How could religious vitality be maintained if religious structures were not made normative?

In such a matrix the Hebrew prophetic movement was born. At times when religious structures were becoming set and endowed with power to act on Yahweh's behalf, how could the system be protected from possible abuses? How could the religious establishment, bent on preservation of the sacred, maintain a critical attitude toward holy injunctions to avoid crystallization of forms? How was Israel to revere the past without being tied to it? How was it to honor David or Jerusalem without their usurping honor due only to Yahweh? The Hebrews attempted to respond to such questions through the office of the prophet. In the process of consolidating establishment, and often faced with abuses associated with the protection of such order, the prophet aimed to maintain religious vitality. The great prophets intended to preserve virtues in a context where loyalty to forms and structures threatened to undermine loyalty to Yahweh's covenant.

PROPHET, PRIEST, KING

Hebrew prophecy in a sense may be traced to earliest biblical history. Abraham, Moses, and other early figures are referred to as prophets, although such references are probably more honorary than descriptive of religious office. Properly speaking, Hebrew prophecy belongs to the monarchial period. By the mid-eighth century, shortly before the end of the northern kingdom, the phenomenon had reached definitive form and the prophet had taken his place alongside the priest and the king as one of the three chief religious functionaries of Hebrew religion.

These three offices were not entirely independent of each other and certainly were not always antagonistic. There were cultic prophets and prophetic priests. Both prophets and priests sometimes functioned within the court; Jeremiah and Isaiah served as counselors to the king. Nathan seems to have been court prophet to David, and Ezekiel is expressly described as a priest (Ezekiel 1:3). Clearly functions often overlapped. Nor were prophets the only social critics or lone individuals isolated from the social mainstream. They shared society's ills with their neighbors and hoped to work with and through king and priest to preserve basic covenant commitments.

Nevertheless, the Hebrew community perceived the functionaries differently. Priests were expected to conserve cultic order. Because materials of the Hebrew Bible are influenced measurably by the prophetic viewpoint, priests are sometimes given a bad report, but they were usually faithful to Yahweh. Their religious devotion focused on serving proper cultic forms. Priests were protectors of the sanctuaries and the holy vessels housed therein. Their "ministry" was concerned to preserve the established Torah. They presided over sacrifices presumed to be vehicles for religious faithfulness. Transmission of the sacred tradition was their responsibility. Although priests "often failed to emphasize motivation as opposed to mechanism, they pivot at the core of Israel's traditions. Much of Israel's faith was preserved because of the often tenacious obduracy of the priests."[2] In short, priests were guardians of cultic purity and served to stabilize Hebrew society and religion.

Also during the monarchy, the Hebrew king became a conserver of religion. Israelite kingship may have been patterned after that of the Canaanites and other ancient Near Eastern peoples,[3] but the role of the Hebrew king bore the

---

[2]Frank E. Eakin, Jr., *The Religion and Culture of Israel*, pp. 139–40. See Eakin's discussion of the role and function of the priest, pp. 128–163.

[3]Cf. 1 Samuel 8:5. See also Mowinckel, *He That Cometh*, (Abingdon, 1954), p. 21.

distinctive mark of preserving religion. The earthly king served properly only when he remembered "that there was a heavenly king to whom he was ultimately responsible."[4] Through his rule the vice-regent was to promote and protect Yahweh's righteousness and peace. Because Yahweh was the *real* king, Israel felt no compulsion to make its king divine. The king, like everyone else, was subject to covenant restrictions. He functioned not as divinity, but as a man through whose reign Yahweh could work.[5] The stability given Israel by kingship has led one observer to conclude that the introduction of kingship, along with the establishment of the Jerusalem capital and the construction of Solomon's temple, put a new stamp on Israelite religion.[6]

The Hebrew prophet in a sense stood over against both priest and king not as their enemy, but as their critic. He was expected to remain free and independent of both regal and cultic establishment. Personal encounter with Yahweh, unhindered by static structures or institutional commitments, stimulated his message. Prophets were not expected to be bound by correctness or purity of ritual, nor could they be obligated to the king. Their message was to be unhindered by intimidation or reward. Such freedom, of course, risked the appearance of the false prophet who would indulge his own eccentricity and challenge or support the establishment with various motives, but the risk of a false prophecy was the price paid to assure that Yahweh's word not be confined to establishment structures. In developing prophecy, Israel intended to destroy neither priesthood nor kingship, but to maintain vitality in both. Hence, prophecy kept Israel's institutional life under the vigorous scrutiny of moral and ethical criteria enhanced by an atmosphere of inspiration and urgency.

> Indicate how the distinctive function of prophet, priest, and king is served by contemporary social, political, and religious figures.

THE FUNCTION OF ISRAEL'S PROPHETS

Not all Hebrew prophets were cut from the same pattern and consequently their work is marked by distinctiveness often attributable to their unique personalities. Amos was an indignant herdsman; Hosea, the husband of an unfaithful wife; Isaiah, a man of station in Jerusalem; Jeremiah, a descendant of a line of outcast priests; Ezekiel, a priest in exile. Such diversity could not be expected to yield identical expressions. The mission and message of each prophet was colored by his distinctive circumstances and personal outlook. Yet as individual as they were, the prophets shared a common function and com-

---

[4]Aubrey R. Johnson, *Sacral Kingship in Ancient Israel* (University of Wales, 2d ed., 1967), p. 35.
[5]Yehezhel Kaufmann, *The Religion of Israel* (Allen & Unwin, 1961), p. 266; and Walther Eichrodt, *Theology of the Old Testament*, I (Westminster, 1961) p. 440.
[6]Helmer Ringgren, *Israelite Religion* (Fortress, 1966), pp. 58–63.

mitment to Yahweh. The religious community expected each to remain independent and to speak Yahweh's word as it was given to him.

Prophetic Terminology

The function of the prophet is reflected in several terms used in the Hebrew scriptures to refer to this role. The most important of these is *ro'eh,* "seer"; *hozeh,* "seer" or "visionary"; and *nab'i,* "spokesman." The first two of these words reflect the divinatory side of early Israelite prophecy and are often used in a verbal form in introductions to prophetic oracles. The book of Amos opens, "The words of Amos, who was among the shepherds of Tekoa, which he saw *(hozeh)* . . ." (1:1). The books of Nahum and Obadiah are described as visions *(hazon* from *hozeh)* of the prophet (1:1 and 1:1). The precise meaning of these two words should not be overstressed, however; they are roughly synonymous with the more widely used and more inclusive term *nab'i.*

The word *nab'i* is the most important of the prophetic words, but its precise meaning cannot by etymologically unraveled.[7] Among the many suggestions that have been made, the most attractive trace the word to an Akkadian root *nabu,* "to announce," "to call." If the word is taken in the active sense, the prophet *(nab'i)* is "one who announces" or, if the form is taken as passive, "one who has been called." In a real sense both are true. The prophets of Israel were "called" of Yahweh to "announce" Yahweh's word. They spoke for Yahweh and their message carried the authority of the one who had given them the message.[8] The clearest illustration of what the Hebrew Bible means by *nab'i* is found in Exodus 7:1: "And Yahweh said to Moses, 'See, I have made you like God to Pharaoh; And Aaron your brother shall be your prophet *(nab'i).'* "

The English word "prophet" preserves the spokesman idea. It derives from the Greek word *prophetes,* "one who speaks for another." Hence the popular association of the prophet with prediction is a misunderstanding of the original meaning of the word and certainly a distortion of the work of the prophet. The Hebrew prophet was no crystal-ball gazer, simply using intuition or magic to predict coming events. Nor was he the medium through whom God revealed the long-range future. The prophet did anticipate the future, but saw tomorrow primarily as the outgrowth of today. "If what I observe today continues, then the result will be . . . ." The future is seen in terms of the present, evaluated by Yahweh's covenant requirements. Even when the *nab'i* spoke about the future, his primary concern was the application of Yahweh's word to the present life of Israel.

[7]A good resumé of the literature on the word *nab'i* is found in H. H. Rowley, "Old Testament Prophecy and Recent Study," in his *Servant,* pp. 96ff.

[8]See James F. Ross, "The Prophet as Yahweh's Messenger," in Anderson and Harrelson, *Heritage,* pp. 98–107.

Prophetic Consciousness[9]

In the Spirit.   Prophets could speak Yahweh's word because they had been filled by the spirit of Yahweh. In the Samuel accounts of the beginning of Israelite prophecy, persons began to play the *nab'i* when "the spirit of God came mightily upon them." The same is true of the later classic prophets, although they spoke more often of possession by God's word than of possession by God's spirit. What sort of phenomenon was this spirit possession? It was the Israelite equivalent of the ecstatic experience of the prophets in the remainder of the ancient world—and more.

In the wilderness of Sinai, the "spirit of Yahweh" filled the artisans who designed and made the ornamentation for the tabernacle (Exodus 35:30–35). By the power of the "spirit" that came upon them, the military judges defeated the enemies of Yahweh's people (Judges 3:10; 11:29). When the "spirit of Yahweh" came mightily upon Samson, he killed Philistines and took their property to pay a bet (Judges 14:19). "In the spirit," he slew the Philistine host with the jawbone of an ass (Judges 15:14, 15). And the "spirit of Yahweh" fell upon the ecstatics in Samuel's day and caused them to play the *nab'i*. This invasive power of presence, then, performed a variety of tasks in the course of the biblical narrative, coming upon persons and inspiring them to the extraordinary. In a more refined way the great prophets of Israel felt themselves captured by the divine spirit, and in them the spirit of Yahweh did its noblest work.

Prophecy and God's Word.   In what sense were the prophets aware of this divine presence? Doubtless both ecstasy and divination were media of revelation, but they were by no means the only ways by which Yahweh was known by the prophets. Visions or dreams, and ordinary events and sights, became instruments that reminded a prophet of the divine will for a particular moment or situation. The very diversity of prophetic personalities and backgrounds indicates that no one means could sufficiently explain their inspiration. All, however, were persons in communication with Yahweh.

The prophet was first and foremost someone caught up by Yahweh, whatever the means—someone into whom the very personality of God had been extended. When the prophet spoke, it was as if, or it was, Yahweh who spoke. In the symbolic acts of the prophets it was Yahweh who acted. The totality of the prophetic being was lifted up into the "spirit of Yahweh" and Yahweh's personality was extended into that person, who thereby became an instrument of the divine will.

---

[9]The authors are dependent on the work of A. R. Johnson for much of the material in this section. The University of Wales published his *The Cultic Prophet in Ancient Israel* (1944), *The One and the Many in the Israelite Conception of God* (1942), and *The Vitality of the Individual in the Thought of Ancient Israel* (1949).

Israelites believed that a person was a center of vital power and personality that extended beyond the body into all that the person has and even beyond that. It could be imparted to others. The spoken word was for them an objective thing, carrying with it the personality of the person who uttered it. Thus, both blessing and curse had power and, once uttered, could not be changed. Words could not be retracted until they had accomplished their purpose. The one cursed was cursed; the one blessed was blessed. Remember Isaac's word to Esau when he discovered that he mistakenly had given Jacob the blessing intended for the older Esau: "Who was it then that hunted game and brought it to me, and I ate it all before you came and I blessed him? . . . yes, and blessed he shall be" (Genesis 27:33).

In a similar way, one's personality extended into one's name. As long, therefore, as the name continued, the personality remained. Hence, the birth of a male heir who would preserve the family name created excitement (Deuteronomy 25:5f.). The personality also extended into one's household and even into one's servants.

In a higher sense this also was true of Yahweh. Even more than humans, deity was a center of vitality that could be extended into the created world. Name was presence. When the name was uttered, Yahweh was presented in the midst of the covenant people. In this light the familiar priestly benediction takes on new depths of meaning: "Yahweh bless you and keep you: Yahweh make his face to shine upon you, and be gracious to you: Yahweh lift up his countenance upon you, and give you peace. 'So shall they put my name on the Israelites, and I will bless them' " (Numbers 6:24–27).

More important for an understanding of prophecy is the extension of the divine personality through spirit and word. Through spirit Yahweh was with persons, divine personality entering into them to make them covenant persons. The prophetic ideal was to be in accord with the spirit of Yahweh that had entered into the spokesman:

> Create in me a clean heart, O God,
>   and put a new and right spirit within me.
> Do not cast me away from your presence,
>   and do not take your holy Spirit from me.
> Restore to me the joy of your salvation,
>   and sustain me with a willing spirit.
>   [Psalm 51:10–12]

When the prophet was in accord with the spirit of Yahweh, he was the temporary extension of Yahweh's personality. Although the *nab'i* remained himself, Yahweh had taken abode in the human personality. Yahweh's spirit had entered, transforming him into a man of God. When he spoke, he spoke the words of Yahweh. Something of God was present in the prophetic word and extended into history not to return until it accomplished its purpose (Isaiah

55:10–11). The word was uttered and the situation changed—made different by the word that was in some sense creative of the event about which it was spoken.

True and False Prophets. Israel's prophets were not merely frenzied ecstatics, like some of their ancient Near Eastern counterparts. Although for some of them ecstasy did occur, their certainty that they were commissioned by Yahweh did not rest on ecstatic experiences, but on the conviction that they had received Yahweh's clear, intelligible word, filled with moral and religious content.[10] The prophet in Israel was one who had a sense of audition and vocation. He was a prophet because he had stood in the presence of Yahweh and could do no other than speak.

Such an assurance was a personal thing. There was no objective way to prove the experience. The true prophets of Israel were, consequently, faced again and again with the soul-rending question as to the validity of their prophetic word—a question forced on them by the presence in Israel of other prophets whose messages did not coincide with those proclaimed by the true prophets. These other prophets also claimed the presence of Yahweh's spirit. How, then, could an Amos or a Jeremiah be certain that he was right and those who disagreed with him wrong? How did they know that their message came from Yahweh and was not merely the projection of their own views and desires?

Answers to these questions were difficult for the prophets themselves, and persons such as Jeremiah seem sometimes consumed by loneliness and uncertainty. The religious community often misunderstood and rejected the true prophet because of the strangeness of his message. Often only the passing of time would validate the prophet's message as true.

Some immediate guidelines, however, were available. Some prophets could be judged false because they were men of immoral life whose messages corresponded to their character. They were "professionals" who prophesied for hire and consequently spoke what their employers wanted to hear. This caused them to be dishonest in their claims of prophetic revelation. They lacked originality, mimicked genuine prophetic oracles, and passed off lying dreams as real prophetic visions.[11]

The true prophet was not validated, however, simply through judgment on his opponents. His message could be distinguished as genuine in and of itself. Certainly the true prophet spoke not for hire, but because of an impulse to speak independent of, and often contrary to, his own volition. He felt a com-

---

[10]Sigmund Mowinckel, "Ecstatic Experience and Rational Elaboration in Old Testament Prophecy," *Acta Orientalia*, 13 (1935) 287, as quoted by O. Eissfeldt in "The Prophetic Literature," *Old Testament: An Introduction* (Harper & Row, 1965), p. 140.

[11]These criticisms are delineated by John Skinner in his *Prophecy and Religion*, (Cambridge University, 1922), pp. 191–94.

pulsion to utter words that were like "fire in his bones." The power of the prophet's word came from Yahweh. The prophetic oracle had a rational content consistent with Yahweh's will as known in history and could thus stand the test of time. What the true prophet said had moral worth and immediate relevance, although often contrary to what his audience wanted to hear. Consequently, in the last analysis the real proof of the prophet's message lay deep in the prophetic personality. He knew he was a true prophet standing in personal relationship to Yahweh. This immediate consciousness of having the mind of Yahweh was the ultimate secret of prophetic inspiration. H. H. Rowley has summed it up well:

> What is really vital is the relation of the prophet and his word to God. The prophet who is properly so-called was a man who knew God in the immediacy of experience, who felt an inescapable constraint to utter what he was profoundly convinced was the word of God, and whose word was at bottom a revelation of the nature of God no less than of His will, who saw the life of men in the light of vision of God, and who saw the inevitable issue of that life, who therefore declared that issue and pleaded with men to avoid it by cleansing and renewing their lives. He was a true prophet in the measure of his experience of God, and the measure of his experience was the measure of his receptiveness and of his response to it.[12]

DEVELOPMENT OF PROPHECY IN ISRAEL

The prophetic movement in Israel came into prominence during the period of monarchy and lasted into the early postexilic period. Its fullest development came during the eighth, seventh, and sixth centuries B.C.E. The movement emerged as something distinctively Israelite when men like Amos and Hosea spoke "the word of Yahweh" to communities confronted with critical situations, but its origins were related to the traditions of Israel's neighbors, especially those in Canaan.

Prophecy in the Ancient Near East

Prophetic figures of many types were found throughout the Mediterranean world. Sacred texts from Mesopotamia mention an important class of divinatory priests whose function was the pronouncement of oracular words from the deity.[13] By divination of various omens they discovered and proclaimed

---

[12]H. H. Rowley, "The Nature of Prophecy in the Light of Recent Study," in his *The Servant of the Lord and Other Essays on the Old Testament* (Lutterworth, 1952), p. 128.

[13]The Akkadian word is *baru*, "to behold" and refers to ritual divination. See Haldar, *Association*, for a good study of pre-Israel prophetic groups. See also Heschel, *Prophets*, pp. 447f.; Lindblom, *Prophecy*.

the divine answer to perplexing questions.[14] Their oracles were considered "messages from the gods" and were recorded as "omen texts" to be consulted whenever a similar omen should occur.

Working alongside these divinatory priests was another group characterized by ecstatic trance.[15] Their function was to receive oracles through a trance state in which their minds had gone forth to be replaced by the breath (spirit) of God. The trance was induced by raving frenzy, and oracles spoken from this ecstatic state were considered the very word of the deity. These divinatory ecstatics were organized into prophetic guilds, whose members were called "sons." Such prophetic bands were not unlike bands of ecstatic prophets found in Israel in the closing days of confederacy.

Prophetic guilds also operated in Canaan. In fact, ecstatic prophecy is more characteristic of Canaanite religion than of any other. The Egyptian Wen-Amon's account of his travels in the Canaanite city of Byblos is especially illuminating:

> While he [the prince of Byblos] was making offering to his gods, the god seized one of his youths and made him possessed. . . . And while the possessed youth was having his frenzy on this night, I had already found a ship headed for Egypt and had loaded everything I had into it.[16]

That this type of ecstasy was also characteristic of the prophets of Baal we know from the Hebrew Bible itself, where their orgiastic frenzy is well attested (2 Kings 18:28–29).

Texts from Mari, the great Amorite city of the second millennium B.C.E., speak of the "man of Dagan" who was a messenger with a divine commission to fulfill. He appeared "unasked and unbidden with a definite divine charge." As proof of his prophetic authority, he introduced himself with the words, "The God Dagan has sent me." The similarity to the Hebrew description of the prophets of Israel is unmistakable and cannot be accidental. Some roots, then, of Israelite prophecy go back to the Amorite heritage from which Israel sprang.[17]

Hebrew prophets shared the ecstatic tradition with their eastern counterparts, and even after prophecy had come into its own in Israelite life, touches of ecstasy were preserved in persons such as Ezekiel. However, the Hebrews

---

[14]Among the many kinds of omens, the following were most common: observation of oil and water in a cup, observation of entrails (especially the liver) of sacrificial animals, observation of celestial phenomena (astrology), birth omens, physiognomical omens, observation of the flight of birds, interpretation of dreams of others, dream vision experienced by the priests themselves.

[15]Akkadian *mahhu*, "to rave," or Sumerian *uddu*, "to go forth." The reference clearly is to ecstasy.

[16]Pritchard, *Texts*, p. 26.

[17]A thorough analysis of the relationship between the prophets of Mari and those of Israel and the meaning of this relationship for our understanding of the Hebrew Bible may be found in Noth, *History of Israel*, pp. 194–206.

did not look to psychic phenomena as validation of the prophetic message. Rather, as we have noted, the moral and religious content of the message affirmed the prophet as a true spokesman of Yahweh.

Beginnings of the Prophetic Movement in Israel

The Ecstatic Tradition.   Among the Israelites, Yahweh had always had "spokesmen" who interpreted history in terms of the divine will and who saw Israel as a people peculiarly responsible to the sovereign God. Not, however, until the crisis days of the disappearing confederacy does the Hebrew Bible mention prophetic bands similar to those of Canaan and the rest of the ancient Near East. The spirit of Yahweh that had rested upon the judges in times of trouble, empowering them to defeat enemies, now came to rest on the prophets, filling them with the irrepressible word of Yahweh. In 1 Samuel 9–10 there is a vivid picture of Samuel as a seer or diviner who was associated with a group of roving ecstatics. Saul, the young Israelite king-to-be, seeking information about the lost asses of his father, came to Samuel, an old and respected diviner who on payment of a price would consult the oracle of Yahweh. After supplying information about the whereabouts of the lost animals, Samuel went further and arranged for Saul to meet a band of ecstatic prophets who roamed in the vicinity. Saul did as instructed and encountered a strange group "playing the prophet" to the accompaniment of harp, tambourine, flute, and lyre. Clearly these were ecstatics. When Saul met the prophetic band, "the spirit of Yahweh possessed him, and he fell into a prophetic frenzy with them" (I Samuel 10:10). Infected by the ecstasy of this strange group, Saul himself became ecstatic and played the *nab'i*.

Later in the story Samuel is associated directly with the ecstatic bands. Always, however, Samuel as the man of Yahweh stands above the group. We are told that he was a man held in honor because "all that he says comes true" (1 Samuel 9:6). This indeed was one of the tests of true prophecy in later Israelite tradition.[18] In Samuel, then, there is the merger of two functions, divination and ecstasy, both to obtain a word (oracle) from God. Also we see in Samuel the beginnings of Israelite prophecy as it transcended the milieu that gave it birth. The prophetic movement in Israel, at least as represented by the prophets at its spiritual center, appears as a radical and enhancing transformation and refinement of ancient Near Eastern prophetism. The Israelite called by Yahweh to be spokesman confronted his people with a message of ethical and moral integrity unmatched in the ancient world. Like his Near Eastern counterparts, he at times was a diviner. He might even (and often did) obtain his "word from Yahweh" in an ecstatic trance, but the content of his message set him

---

[18]See Deuteronomy 18:21–22. For an able investigation of the complexities of distinguishing the "true" from the "false" prophet, see Crenshaw, *Prophetic Conflict*.

apart. The Israelite prophets were distinguished from those of other cultures because they stood in the council of Yahweh, whom they believed to be righteous, holy, and sovereign.

The Prophetic Pioneers.   We could hope that the picture of the emergence of prophecy out of the early ecstatic tradition was clearer. Unfortunately, data are scarce and much is left to inference and conjecture. Certainly, during the early monarchy, Israel had prophetic guilds, largely resembling other Near Eastern ecstatic groups. But by the time of David, prophets independent of the guilds and operating in independence of cult and palace began to appear. They dart onto the scene and disappear without the preservation of their message in a canonical book, but nonetheless these pioneers contributed significantly to the later full development of prophetic faith. These early prophets were not of a single type, and generalities about them would be misleading. In fact, the prophetic movement was never a singular homogeneous movement apart from the conviction characteristic of every true prophet that he spoke Yahweh's word in his own particular context.

Some of these precursors of classical prophecy are already familiar from earlier discussions. Samuel's many roles include that of prophet.[19] As "seer" Samuel assists Saul in finding asses and is instrumental in Saul's becoming associated with an ecstatic guild. Saul himself participates in the ecstatic rituals, stripping off his clothes and being overcome by trance, giving rise to the proverb, "Is Saul also among the prophets?" (1 Samuel 10:9–13).

Gad and Nathan illustrate prophets brought into the royal court but without the obligation to preach what the king wanted to hear. Both appear in the traditions about David. Gad is a seer who acts as a herald and minister of the will of Yahweh, supplying the king with oracular words from the deity. He also rebuked the king for action that he thought inappropriate. Nothing else about Gad is told. Nathan, however, is distinctly represented as divinatory prophet and court politician. He was influential in the intrigue through which Solomon's succession to the throne was achieved and participated in Solomon's coronation. He was not, however, in the strictest sense a court functionary; at least, he does not appear as such in the court lists of David or Solomon.[20] Nathan was active in religious matters and influenced to some degree the construction of the Jerusalem temple. Of greater importance, however, for the later character of prophecy is the fact that he applied moral sanctions to the king. With typical prophetic utterance he judged David with the parable of the ewe lamb. This belongs to that grand tradition of prophecy that leads through Elijah to the classic prophets.

---

[19]See W.F. Albright, "Samuel and the Beginnings of the Prophetic Movement," in Orlinsky, *Tradition*, pp. 151–76.

[20]2 Samuel 8:15–18; 1 Kings 4:1–6.

That prophets were not typically spokesmen for the court or the establishment is further illustrated in the story of Micaiah ben Imlah. He predicted tragedy for Ahab at Ramoth-Gilead and provides an interesting insight into the nature of prophetism in the early divided monarchy. During the reign of Ahab, a staff of "official" prophets had been maintained about the court at court expense. Jezebel maintained a force of prophets of her own, estimated by the historian to number four hundred fifty. They functioned as formal consultants to the king and queen. The gregarious nature of the ecstatics simply enhanced this function.

Micaiah and his contemporary Elijah appeared in marked contrast to these official prophets. They stood alone and spoke on the impulse of their own experience with Yahweh. Micaiah, in opposition to both the desires of the king and the views of the majority of the prophets, presented the word of Yahweh as he understood it. His message did not support the throne; it spelled out doom and disaster. Micaiah, then, stood outside the ranks of official prophetism. For the first time, prophet of woe stood opposed to prophet of weal, expressing both an idea and an attitude that would characterize prophecy for the next several centuries. Prophetic independence of the throne was established, and oracles of denunciation were often directed toward the king. In prophetic thought following Micaiah and Elijah, the maintenance of the monarchy was unnecessary to the preservation of the best of Israelite faith.

Probably the best known of the ninth century B.C.E. "nonwriting" prophets are Elijah and Elisha. In his opposition to Ahab and Jezebel, "Elijah appears to have been the first prophetic champion for Yahweh faith against its pagan rivals, in this case Baalism."[21] The details of Elijah's struggle with Jezebel and the court prophets supporting Baalism have already been reviewed. Clearly this prophet stands alone in his willingness to oppose officialdom and to remain loyal to pure Yahwism. The exclusive commitment demanded in Elijah's proclamation will have fuller development in later prophets, but Elijah emphatically calls for allegiance to a God who tolerates no other gods. No "limping with two different opinions" (1 Kings 18:21) would be tolerated. Either Yahweh or Baal is God, not both. When the sacrifice is consumed, the eyewitnesses shout, "Yahweh, he is God."[22]

The Elijah narrative is replete with an emphasis on Yahweh as the primary actor. The miracle belongs to Yahweh; Yahweh's word is the potent force of presence.[23] Yahweh's word, not the prophet's office, achieves divine purpose and authenticates the message. So revered is Elijah as Yahweh's messenger that his passing is described in a legend of being taken up in a whirlwind.

---

[21]James K. West, *Introduction to the Old Testament*, (Macmillan, 1981), p. 278.

[22]1 Kings 18:39. The similarity between the shout and the meaning of Elijah's name ("Yahweh is my God") is probably not accidental.

[23]B. D. Napier, "Prophet, Prophetism," *Interpreter's Dictionary*, III:910.

No ordinary man who died as others, he was translated into heaven (2 Kings 2:11–12).

The mantle of Elijah fell on Elisha, the prophet active in bringing the Omri dynasty to conclusion. He supported a bloody coup led by Jehu, a purge that even by ancient laws of blood revenge was merciless and inhumane. Elisha was very different from his prophetic "father" (2 Kings 2:12). Elijah operated alone; Elisha worked in close harmony with prophetic guilds. Elijah sneered at the court; Elisha worked through the palace to achieve his ends. Yet the two men shared the prophetic mentality, intensely committed to Yahweh's word without regard to power structures.

Jehu also had the prophet Jehonadab as an ally in revolt. This son of Rechab[24] opposed the cultural development of Israel and, as a descendant of the Kenites, piously advocated a conservative interpretation of Israel's faith. Jehonadab evidently saw in the revolution an opportunity to express his zealous opposition to the agrarian culture of Israel and was all too anxious to support Jehu. How disillusioned he must have been in the later developments of the Jehu dynasty!

Hebrew religious life inherited a great deal from these early prophetic figures. Their insistence on untainted loyalty to covenant demands on the part of both king and common folk, their uncompromising allegiance to the word of Yahweh known "like fire in the bones," and their urgent demand that arrogant claims of unscrupulous kings be checked by a theocratic understanding of monarchy are legacies that left a permanent mark on Hebrew faith. Refinements and implications of these concepts provide much of the agenda of the classic prophets.

THE SOCIOLOGICAL STUDY OF BIBLICAL PROPHECY

Recent cross-cultural studies of prophecy comparing Israelite prophecy with a variety of prophetic activity recorded in anthropological studies have provided further understandings of the roles performed by Israelite prophets. A brief summary of the major emphases of Robert Wilson's *Prophecy and Society in Ancient Israel* and Thomas W. Overholt's *Channels of Prophecy: The Social Dynamics of Prophetic Activity* will indicate the importance of this relatively new but very significant methodology.[25]

---

[24]Those with similar ideas in later times were known as Rechabites, named after the illustrious opponent of things cultural.

[25]One reviewer of Overholt's book, Bernhard Lang, considers this methodology a revolution in biblical scholarship. Another reviewer, Gene M. Tucker, said, ". . . his use of anthropological tools and cross-cultural data . . . brings fresh, interesting, thoughtful, and important insight to bear on the question of prophecy." See dust jacket of Overholt, *Channels of Prophecy.*

Utilizing anthropological/ethnological studies of religious specialists, Wilson examines the ways that prophets interact with their societies and concludes that social support is necessary for the success of prophets in all societies, including ancient Israel. On the basis of the type of support group with which prophets are associated, he identifies two types of prophets. *Central prophets* belong to the social center of power and customarily enjoy social prestige and political power. They tend to be concerned with the preservation of the status quo. Since central intermediaries belong to the established social structure, they can be controlled by their support groups who expect them to follow closely established social and religious practices. *Peripheral prophets* belong to the fringes of society and lack social prestige and power deriving their authority only from the marginal groups to which they belong. These prophets emphasize social change to improve the situations of their marginal support groups.

Wilson suggests that prophets in the south—Gad (2 Samuel 24:10–25), Nathan (2 Samuel 12:1–24), Amos, Isaiah, Micah, Nahum, Habakkuk, Zephaniah, and Ezekiel—were central prophets rooted to the Jerusalem traditions, Davidic monarchy, and Jerusalem temple and cult. They preserved these ancient traditions, reinterpreting them "to bring about control, social change."[26] They delivered judgment oracles against Judah's enemies whenever one or another of these enemies threatened Judah's traditions in any way. Isaiah's initial offer of support to Ahaz at the time of the Syro-Ephraimitic crisis (Isaiah 7:1–9) and his support of Hezekiah in the Sennacherib crisis (2 Kings 19:32–34 and Isaiah 37:33–35) are good examples of the stance of a central prophet.

Prophets in the northern tradition—Samuel, Ahijah (1 Kings 11:29–39; 14:1–18), the "man of God" from Judah and the "old prophet" from Bethel (1 Kings 13:1–32), Jehu (the son of Hanani) (1 Kings 16:1–4, 11–14), Elijah, Elisha, Micaiah ben Imla (1 Kings 22:1–38), Jonah, the prophetess Huldah (2 Kings 22:8–23:3), Hosea, and Jeremiah—were peripheral prophets who conflicted with the central institutions of society, the patterns of central authority, and the actions of central leaders. The story of Elijah's opposition to Ahab and Jezebel in defense of Naboth is an excellent example of the stance of a marginal prophet (1 Kings 21).

Central prophets under certain circumstances became peripheral prophets. Isaiah's ultimate condemnation of Ahaz in the Syro-Ephraimitic crisis, the symbolic naming of his children as living oracles of judgment, and his temporary withdrawal from prophetic activity (Isaiah 7:10–8:22) clearly are the actions of a peripheral prophet.

Using prophetic materials in the Hebrew Bible, anthropological tribal traditions from the American Indians, and from New Guinea, Siberia, and Africa, Overholt emphasizes the social dynamics of prophecy and divination as an interaction between the supernatural (God), the prophet, and the pro-

---

[26]Wilson, *Prophecy and Society*, p. 286.

phet's audience. He acknowledges certain differences between prophets and diviners: prophets initiate their activity, diviners respond to requests from their clients/patients; prophecy is essentially a public action, divination is essentially private/family. But Overholt argues convincingly that both prophecy and divination involve God, the intermediary, and the audience. Focusing on the interrelationship of these three, he suggests that the following components are typical of all prophetic activity:

1. revelation from God, in some cases involving unusual behavior understood by his audience as confirmation of the revelation;
2. a pronouncement based on the revelation, generally concerned with present needs rather than long-term future predictions;
3. audience reaction, positive, negative, or indifferent, but always affecting the prophet's subsequent pronouncements;
4. the prophet's feedback to the source of revelation, essential to continuing communication between God, the prophet, and the audience;
5. additional revelations and proclamations;
6. supernatural confirmations, miracles and unusual actions that persuade the audience to take the prophetic message seriously (seeing is believing); and
7. disciples, mediators between the prophet and the audience who help preserve the teachings of the prophet.

Wilson's and Overholt's use of anthropological materials provides fresh new means of understanding biblical prophecy. The important role they assign to the audience has previously been largely ignored, even to some considerable extent in the biblical materials themselves, which emphasize the content of the prophets' oracles. Although content is largely ignored in anthropological analyses of prophetic behavior, such analyses provide new bases for interpreting and understanding the content. Understanding anthropologically the dynamics of the prophetic situation is essential to theological interpretation of the prophetic message. Their work and that of others who are using the relatively new methodology of cross-cultural comparison promises much for future understanding of the religion of the Hebrew Bible and its place in and relation with other religious traditions, both ancient and modern.

SUGGESTIONS FOR FURTHER STUDY

The Anchor Bible Dictionary gives the most extensive treatment of the following terms; shorter, more introductory discussions appear in *Harper's*; the *Mercer Dictionary* is quite dependable and up-to-date: prophecy in the Hebrew Bible, nab'i, ro'eh, hozek, spirit of Yahweh, divination, omen, ecstasy, Mari, court prophet, seer, Rechabites.

The bibliography on the nature of Israel's prophetic movement and its relation to the life of the ancient Near East is quite extensive. A selection of some important works will be found in the General Bibliography. Works that will clarify the role of the Hebrew prophet include: Bernhard W. Anderson and Walter Harrelson, eds., *Israel's Prophetic Heritage* (Harper, 1962); Walter Brueggemann, *The Prophetic Imagination* (Fortress, 1978); James Crenshaw, *Prophetic Conflict and Its Effect upon Israelite Religion* (Walter de Gruyter, 1971); William McKane, *Prophets and Wise Men* (S. C. M., 1965); Thomas W. Overholt, *Channels of Prophecy: The Social Dynamics of Prophetic Activity* (Fortress, 1989), and *Prophecy in Cross-Cultural Perspective: A Sourcebook for Biblical Researchers* (Scholars Press, 1986); D. L. Peterson, ed., *Prophecy in Israel* (Fortress, 1987); and Robert R. Wilson, *Prophecy and Society in Ancient Israel* (Fortress, 1980).

10

Israel's Eighth-Century Prophets

The narrative accounts of Israel's prophetic pioneers (such as Elijah and Elisha) is contained in the canonical materials usually designated the Former Prophets, especially the books of Samuel and Kings. No collections of the proclamations of these significant individuals have been preserved. Whether this means that procedures for preserving their sayings had not emerged or that these early materials were lost is uncertain. Perhaps their highly individualistic behavior kept them so socially marginal that a group of disciples to preserve their work did not gather around them. However, by the eighth century B.C.E. the messages of several prophets began to be preserved and come to us as the Latter Prophets, books bearing the names of Israel's major "writing prophets."

The "Writing" Prophets. The primary literary unit of these great prophetic collections is the oracle, a terse poetic statement, sometimes stylized in form, and set off by formulas such as, "Thus says Yahweh" or "Says Yahweh." The writings of the later prophets, as we have them, are primarily collections of these poetic units, although large bodies of prose materials—discourses, biography, historical narratives—sometimes hold the materials together. Biographical or autobiographical materials, as well as historical narratives, are used to enhance the prophet's message and give information about the prophet's life and times. Much of the life of each prophet, however, remains a mystery.

The prophetic books were for the most part put together by disciples concerned to preserve the prophet's message. Remember that the prophets were first and foremost spokesmen. Some of the materials may have originated with written records kept by the prophets themselves. Jeremiah actually dictated portions of his message to his scribe Baruch, but this does not seem to be the typical pattern. More often most of the material was initially preserved orally by disciples. The poetic style of the oracles would have assisted their memory.

339

Eventually the remembered speeches and narrative statements from the prophet himself formed the nucleus of each book. Quite often the disciples then added oracles of their own as well as interpretations of the prophet's own teachings. Thus, the final compilation often occurred over several centuries. Ultimately the finished products were preserved as four prophetic scrolls: Isaiah, Jeremiah, Ezekiel, and the Book of the Twelve.

The Eighth-Century Prophets	
In Israel:	In Judah:
Amos (c. 750)	Isaiah (c. 742)
Hosea (c. 745)	Micah (c. 730)

THE FIRST OF THE CLASSIC PROPHETS

By mid-eighth century B.C.E. the great period of classic Hebrew prophecy had arrived. At this time four dominant figures appear: Amos, Hosea, Micah, and Isaiah. The earliest of the classic prophets were Amos and Hosea, both of whom preached in the northern kingdom in the mid-eighth century. By this time prophecy seems to have its own institutional identity, having "achieved enough institutional and ideological independence to stand on its own."[1] Israel had come to expect systematic criticism of the establishment. Hence both Amos and Hosea enjoyed some public support even when their preaching ran counter to much popular opinion. Their work was done against the backdrop of Jeroboam II's reign, a period of prosperity, expansion, and national confidence accompanied by widespread religious enthusiasm. The festivals were popular and the sanctuaries of the northern kingdom were thronged. Yahweh's great deeds were remembered, and the covenant was renewed as a guarantee of Yahweh's protection of the nation in the years to come.

However, if we read the situation from the writings of Amos and Hosea, religion, though flourishing, was decadent. Ethical obligations were largely forgotten as covenant came to be considered fulfilled by elaborate ritual and lavish support of the national shrines. The heart of Israel's religion had been replaced by the ceremonial means intended to keep it alive. Sacrifice, ritual, even prayer ceased to be means and became ends in themselves. Yahweh was personally unknown to those most involved in ceremonial worship. Yahwism in a pure form was no longer maintained. Numerous local shrines became openly pagan as the Canaanite fertility cult was practiced everywhere. Baal had become as important as Yahweh. Yahweh worship, which laid stern ethical and moral requirements on its followers, was losing to the sensual excesses of Baal worship, which appealed to the base instincts of the average Israelite. Some Samaria ostraca indicate that almost as many Israelites had names compounded

[1]Gottwald, *Hebrew Bible: Socio-Literary Introduction,* p. 306.

with Baal as with Yahweh. Yahwism so diluted could not maintain the covenant law. The priests were part of the system and would not speak out against
it, and no effective rebuke came from the cultic and court prophets. The syncretism so abhorrent to Elijah had spread to an extent that even he might not
have anticipated.

The distinctive desert social structure of Israel based on covenant brotherhood had lost its character. A class of newly rich had arisen, and exploitation
of the poor was commonplace. In every way Israel had ceased to be a covenant
people. Basic covenant law had no meaning to many Israelites, and the faith
of Mosaic days was neglected. Yahweh was not God to them, but a talisman
to be kept against possible days of trouble. In the peaceful interim of Jeroboam
II's reign, the Baals were gods enough for Israel. In light of such circumstances,
Yahweh's voice had to be heard; Amos and Hosea became Yahweh's spokesmen.

Amos

> You only have I known
>   of all the families of the earth;
> therefore I will punish you
>   for all your iniquities.
>   [Amos 3:2]

In this incisive judgment on the covenant people, the prophet Amos thun-
dered forth "in a moment, the explosion and discharge of the full storm of
prophecy."[2] All that we know about the man who uttered this short oracle are
the few facts given in the book called by his name; it is more concerned with
the "words of Yahweh" than with biographical details of his life. He was a
herdsman or sheepmaster from Tekoa, a Judean village lying a few miles south
of Jerusalem in the rugged wilderness of Judah. The severity of life in this
barren region contributed to the simplicity and devastating power with which
he proclaimed the word of Yahweh.

Amos was not, however, merely a rustic shepherd. He probably owned his
own flocks and in addition grew sycamore fruit. Of course, he was not
wealthy—he cared for his own flock, perhaps sold his own wool, and tended
his sycamore trees—but he was a man of some substance. He knew much about
conditions throughout Israel and Judah and was aware of what was going on
in other countries. He may have traveled widely as a wool merchant. Certainly
in this capacity he visited Israelite trade fairs at Bethel and other shrine cities.
There he broke forth in the fury of prophetic anger against the injustices so
characteristic of the prosperous but decadent state of Israel.

---

[2]George A. Smith, *The Book of the Twelve Prophets*, I (Harper & Row, 1928), p. 145.

The Word of Yahweh.   Like other prophets, Amos felt grasped by the word of Yahweh. When Amaziah, priest at Bethel, demanded that Amos cease prophesying and leave Israel, the prophet insisted that he did not belong to the popular guilds that prophesied for pay and, therefore, was not obligated to heed priestly commands. He was responsible only to Yahweh and spoke only because Yahweh compelled him to speak. Thus, he was a prophet by divine calling, not a professional representative of the state religion (7:10–17).

In a series of autobiographical visions Amos portrayed the temporal and psychological developments leading to his becoming a prophet. An examination of these visions provides a point of departure for understanding other oracles contained in his book. The basis of each of the visions is an event or situation visible to everyone. For the prophet, however, these situations became media of divine revelation. The first vision occurred in early spring:

> This is what Yahweh showed me: he was forming locusts at the time the latter growth began to sprout out (it was the latter growth after the king's mowings). When they had finished eating the grass of the land, I said,
>
>> "O Yahweh God, forgive, I beg you!
>> How can Jacob stand?
>> He is so small!"
>> Yahweh relented concerning this;
>>> "It shall not be," said Yahweh.
>>>   [7:1–3]

Locust plague, the dread of agriculturalists, devastated the Tekoa region, devouring the second crop so that there was no hope for recovery. This meant trouble for all and perhaps even disaster, but for Amos it was a sign that Yahweh was determined to call Israel to account for its sins and punish it in divine wrath. Amos's plaintive prayer, however, was heard and Yahweh withheld the punishment.

But soon a different and more terrible vision indicative of Yahweh's impending judgment appeared to the Tekoan herdsman: "Thus Yahweh God showed me: behold, Yahweh God was calling for a judgment by fire, and it devoured the great deep and was eating up the land" (7:4). Was this the searing of the earth by drought, or the scorched earth policy of invading Assyrian troops? It mattered not, because either would be symbolic of the wrathful judgment of a God angry because of Israel's gross sinfulness. As before, the disaster was forestalled by the prayer of Amos:

>> O Yahweh God, cease, I beg you!
>> How can Jacob stand?
>> He is so small!
>>   [7:5]

In these prayers for his people, Amos became a prophet.

Later at Bethel other visions clearly revealed to Amos the true condition of Israel, a sinful nation deserving Yahweh's judgment:

> This is what he showed me: Yahweh was standing beside a wall built with a plumb line, with a plumb line in his hand. And Yahweh said to me, "Amos, what do you see?" And I said, "A plumb line." Then Yahweh said, "See, I am setting a plumb line in the midst of my people Israel; and I will never again pass them by, the high places of Isaac shall be made desolate, and the sanctuaries of Israel shall be laid waste, and I will rise against the house of Jeroboam with the sword" [7:7–9].

Like a wall out of plumb, Israel did not deserve to stand. For Amos the wall under construction had become Israel, and the workman with the plumb line, Yahweh.

Swiftly the visions moved to a climax as a basket of summer fruit (*qayits*) by word association became a sign that the end (*qets*) was at hand. Then the last and most terrible vision convinced Amos that he must take up his prophetic word:

> I saw Yahweh standing beside the alter, and he said:
> "Strike the capitals until the thresholds shake,
>   and shatter them on the heads of all the people;
> and those who are left I will kill with the sword,
>   not one of them shall flee away,
>   not one of them shall escape.
>
> [9:1]

Yahweh was to be found at the accustomed place, but not to bless, redeem, or forgive. Sacrifices would not be received; prayers would not be heard. Yahweh stood by the altar in judgment with the sword of Israel's doom in hand. Aware of this and compelled by the God whose call he had heard, Amos began to prophesy.

The Prophecies of Amos. The book of Amos may be concisely outlined as follows:

A. Editorial introduction: 1:1–2
B. Oracles against the nations and Israel: 1:3–2:16
C. Oracles of doom: 3:1–6:14
D. Visions of the end: 7:1–9; 8:1–3; 9:1–4
E. Amos and Amaziah: 7:10–17
F. More oracles of doom: 8:4–14; 9:5–10
G. Epilogue—hope for eventual restoration: 9:11–15

The book contains some fairly extended sermons delivered on single occasions, plus shorter oracles from other occasions. Most of them came from Amos himself and were remembered and recorded by his followers. Certain of the oracles, however, may have been added by later editors of the prophetic literature. Fragments of a hymn are found in 4:13, 5:8–9, and 9:5–6; these complement the speeches to which they are connected. Although its precise origin cannot be determined, this hymn may be from the Jerusalem cultus. The oracle in 9:11–12 about the restoration of Judah and Jerusalem could hardly be from Amos: it presupposes the Babylonian exile. The concluding oracle of restoration, however, belongs to the popular eschatological expectation of the eighth century. Its hope for the triumph of Yahweh's purpose in the future is not incompatible with Amos's view that the end for Israel was imminent.

The Motto of the Book: Doom! Doom! Doom! When Amos began to speak Yahweh's words that had come to him,[3] Israel's doom was already close at hand. The inevitable punishment was already in progress and could not be turned back:

> Yahweh roars from Zion,
>   and utters his voice from Jerusalem;
> the pastures of the shepherds wither,
>   And the top of Carmel dries up.
> > [1:2]

Yahweh was moving upon the land to devastate a sinful people. There would be no escape: even the fertile Carmel range, where the rains most often fell, was to wither in the blast of war.

Yahweh, God of the Nations. In an electrifying series of oracles, Amos portrayed a world in moral chaos. Its nations were guilty before a sovereign God. There was no loyalty or honor among the peoples. Not only the covenant people, but all humankind stood under Yahweh's righteous judgment. Israel and its neighbors had disobeyed a law that members of the human race must acknowledge, a law "bound up with the very constitution of this world."[4]

Using the imprecatory oracular form common to the cult of his day, Amos pronounced judgments on enemy peoples in the name of Israel's God. Syria, Philistia, Phoenicia, Edom, Ammon, and Moab in turn were damned "for three transgressions, and for four." Of these denunciations his listeners approved. Then the prophet turned his wrathful words on Judah, and still his listeners approved. That nation, although kin to Israel, was guilty like the rest. The final and most severe castigation of all, however, was reserved for Israel, unfaithful to its covenant responsibilities. That nation, with a sacred history behind it, was guilty of social injustice and cruelty. In the face of Yahweh's gracious action and the warnings of the past, Israel was ungrateful. Its cultic

---

[3]1:1—"words . . . which he saw."
[4]A. C. Welch, *Kings and Prophets of Israel* (Lutterworth, 1952), pp. 125–26.

religion was empty, bereft of social justice. As elsewhere in the Hebrew Bible, pure religion required both love of God and love of fellow human beings. Amos denounces Israel's religion not because it fails to worship Yahweh, but because it oppresses the poor and weak. It permits ruthless and cruel power to crush the rights of the needy in the rampaging corruption of both secular and religious life. On such a people judgment had to come, and Amos was its herald:

> "Flight shall perish from the swift,
>> and the strong shall not retain their strength,
>> nor shall the mighty save their lives;
> those who handle the bow shall not stand,
>> and those who are swift of foot shall not save themselves,
>> nor shall those who ride horses save their lives;
> and those who are stout of heart among the mighty
>> shall flee away naked in that day,"
>
>> says Yahweh.
>> [2:14–16]

Monotheism. Amos clearly believed that Yahweh was sovereign in judgment over the foreign nations. Indeed, Yahweh was concerned for all peoples and kingdoms far and near in every dimension of their activity:

> "Are you not like the Ethiopians to me,
>> O people of Israel?" says Yahweh.
> "Did I not bring Israel up from the land
>> of Egypt,
> and the Philistines from Caphtor and the
>> Arameans from Kir?"
>
>> [9:7]

Yahweh was sovereign, too, in the realm of nature. Rain came or was withheld according to Yahweh's pleasure (4:7). At Yahweh's command the great sea would dry up and the lands be burned with drought (7:4). Blight and pestilence were instruments of Yahweh's purpose (4:9–10). In all the world Yahweh alone was God.

This was practical monotheism born not of speculation, but of religious faith that saw history as the great arena of divine activity. In the preaching of Amos, thoughts begun with Abraham and Moses took explicit form as Israel's Yahweh was described as God of all humanity.

Election, Privilege, and Service. Although Amos believed Yahweh to be the God of all nations, he recognized a special relationship between Yahweh and Israel—a relationship of Yahweh's own making, not of Israel's choosing. In stating this, the prophet echoed the popular nationalistic theology of his day, "You only have I known of all the families of the earth." But his conclusion was not the expected word of assurance, "Therefore I will forgive your sins and bless you." Instead Yahweh said, "Therefore, I will punish you for all your iniquities" (3:2). Thus the prophet exploded the popular, easy, superficial optimism of the official priests and prophets. To know Yahweh was a deadly serious thing. To be Yahweh's covenant nation meant great responsibility. Israel had been elected for service, and when it entered into covenant, it bound itself to Yahweh with cords of responsibility. It could cast aside those bonds, but not with impunity. Rebellion against Yahweh was a capital offense. Because it was the chosen people, Yahweh would punish Israel all the more severely.

Death of a Nation.   In poignant lamentation Amos depicted Israel as a nation already as good as dead:

> "Fallen, no more to rise,
>   is maiden Israel;
> forsaken on her land,
>   with none to raise her up . . . ."
>
> Therefore, thus says Yahweh, the God of hosts, the Lord:
>   "In all the squares there shall be wailing;
>   and in all the streets they shall say,
>   'Alas! alas!' . . .
>   for I will pass through the midst of you,"
>
> says Yahweh.
[5:2; 16–17]

But even though the prophet was sure of doom, he still called Israel to repentance. As its "covenant conscience" he pleaded with Israel to turn from its evil ways. "Seek Yahweh and live." "Seek good and not evil, that you may live." If Israel would turn to Yahweh, its devastation might yet be turned aside. But Israel had to seek Yahweh in truth and justice, not by false pretentious cult that merely added to the enormity of the people's corruption.

Anything less than true righteousness would not suffice, and Israel had forgotten how to do right (3:10). History's lessons had gone unheeded as again and again Israel ignored the signs of Yahweh's dissatisfaction. Famine and drought, blight and pestilence, and finally war had been sent upon the land; yet Israel did not return to Yahweh (4:6–11). Therefore, Israel was doomed to meet Yahweh on the great and terrible "day of Yahweh." In popular theology this day was the future day of blessing, but Amos saw no blessing for a sinful, degenerate people. To wish for the day of Yahweh was to wish for woe, for that day would be devastation:

> It is darkness, and not light;
>   as if someone fled from a lion,
>   and was met by a bear;
> or went into the house and rested
>   a hand against the wall,
>   and was bitten by a snake.

> Is not the day of Yahweh darkness,
> not light,
> and gloom with no brightness in it?
>
> [5:18b–20]

With this bitter humor Amos spoke of the doom about to befall a nation already dying.

Escape from Divine Wrath.   Amos, incensed as he was by the gross injustice and oppression of callous and recalcitrant Israel, held some hope that from the maelstrom of Yahweh's vengeful wrath some Israelites could escape or be rescued. Not everyone was evil and surely some deserved mercy. A remnant would be saved and perhaps the prophet hoped that with them Yahweh could begin again to shape a covenant people. This remnant, however, would be small and saved from the very depths of death itself: "Thus says Yahweh: 'As the shepherd rescues from the mouth of the lion two legs, or a piece of an ear, so shall the people of Israel who dwell in Samaria be rescued, with the corner of a couch and part of a bed' " (3:12).

This ominous picture may have been what the prophet had in mind when he said more in hope than in belief:

> "Behold, the eyes of Yahweh are upon
> the sinful kingdom,
> and I will destroy it from the
> face of the ground;
> —except that I will not utterly destroy the
> house of Jacob,"
>
> says Yahweh.
>
> [9:8]

Hosea

Hosea's prophecy belongs to the same general period as that of Amos, though some few years later. His earliest preaching occurred during the last days of Jeroboam II, but unlike that of Amos, Hosea's ministry continued into the hard times following the destruction of the Jehu dynasty and preceding the fall of Samaria.

Read Hosea 10–11 in the KJV, NRSV, and AS versions and note variations in translation. Use footnotes in NRSV to account for these variations.

The collection of Hosea's oracles is badly preserved. The text can be restored in many places only with the help of the Septuagint and other versions, and sometimes only by conjecture.[5] Matters of interpretation are as difficult as the text, for the book is filled with perplexing exegetical problems. Nevertheless, although detailed outlining is extremely difficult, the general structure of the book is plain:

A. Editorial introduction: 1:1
B. Hosea's domestic biography parallels Yahweh's experience with Israel: 1:2–3:5
　　1. Hosea and Gomer: 1:2–9 and 3:1–5
　　2. Yahweh and Israel: 1:10–2:23
C. Yahweh's indictment of Israel: 4:1–9:9
D. The lesson of history—Yahweh's grace and Israel's apostasy: 9:10–13:16
E. Israel's future hope: 14:1–9

There is little doubt that most of this book came from Hosea. The only passages about which there is real question are those that refer to Judah.[6] These may have been additions made after the fall of the northern kingdom when Hosea's teachings circulated in the south. However, some of these references to Judah may have come from Hosea himself.[7]

The oracles in this book are the expressions of a compassionate man in love with his people, but aware of its sin. Like Amos he was sensitive to Yahweh's judgment and denounced Israel's social injustice, but through personal tragedy he had come to know God's heart and there he found *chesed*, covenant love. Therefore, he couched his message in tenderness, which stands in dramatic contrast to the tone of Amos.

Hosea and Gomer: Yahweh and Israel.　The book of Hosea opens with strange words from Yahweh to the prophet: "Go, take for yourself a wife of whoredom, and have children of whoredom, for the land commits great whoredom by forsaking Yahweh" (1:2).

This verse and those connected with it present one of the most difficult problems in biblical studies. To complicate the problem Hosea later records another similarly startling divine word: "Go, love a woman who has a lover and is an adulteress, just as Yahweh loves the people of Israel, though they turn to other gods and love raisin cakes" (3:1).

Although there is some difference of opinion about the identity of these women, it is generally agreed that they are one and the same, and that the latter verse is a reference to Hosea's later experience with the woman mentioned in chapter 1. But even so, what does this mean? How are we to interpret the initial command for the prophet to marry a harlot? The contemporary interpreter

---

[5]The many footnotes in the NRSV give ample evidence of this fact.
[6]1:10–2:1; 3:4ff.; etc.
[7]See John Mauchline, "The Book of Hosea," in *The Interpreter's Bible*, VI:563f.

must guard against imposing modern Western concepts of monogamous marriage on the ancient texts and reading the story with undue romanticism. At least three alternatives are possible:

1. The whole account of the prophet's marriage relations is imaginary and symbolic—an allegory of Yahweh's experience with Israel as bride.

2. Gomer, the woman involved, was chaste when Hosea married her. She may or may not have had tendencies toward harlotry before the marriage, but afterward she was unfaithful. The words of chapter 1, therefore, are judgments after the event: the prophet describes her as a harlot from the beginning.

3. The literal interpretation says Hosea loved Gomer, even though she was a harlot, perhaps a Baal temple prostitute, and married her in obedience to what he conceived to be Yahweh's command. She remained after the marriage what she had always been, proving unfaithful to Hosea by going back to her former ways.

The allegorical interpretation seems quite improbable; the materials are bathed in too much personal sentiment to be merely a literary invention. The decision between the other two alternatives is not as easy to make. This is not surprising, for Hosea's intention was not to give a detailed account of his domestic tragedy, but to tell only what was necessary in order to symbolize the story of Yahweh's relationship to Israel.[8]

The prophet's experience may be reconstructed somewhat as follows. He loved and married Gomer, whatever her character may have been (we have to remember the power of love). She bore three children to whom the prophet gave names symbolic of Yahweh's word to Israel. The first he called "Jezreel," because at Jezreel Jehu had been established on the throne by excessive bloodshed.[9] The name as borne by Hosea's child was a reminder of this bloodshed for which punishment must come and an announcement of the place at which the judgment would fall. That historic battlefield was thought by Hosea to be the place where the whole fate and future would be decided. Hosea named the second child "Not Pitied," for Yahweh's pity was at an end and nothing could turn away divine judgment. "Not My People," the pathetic name given the third child symbolized the rejection of the nation that had broken its covenant bond. From the time of Moses Israel had been taught that it was Yahweh's people,[10] but now it had forfeited the privileges it had so flagrantly neglected and was in danger of rejection.

Evidently, after the birth of these children, Gomer left her husband to pursue her lovers. She may even have become a prostitute of the streets. Nevertheless, love prevailed. Hosea bought the degraded woman, either repaying her paramour for the loss of his mistress, or perhaps (if she had become a slave) her

---

[8]For an able and thoroughly documented discussion of this entire problem, see H. H. Rowley, "The Marriage of Hosea," *Bulletin of the John Rylands Library*, 39 (1946) 200–233.

[9]See 2 Kings 10.

[10]See Exodus 3:7; 5:1; 7:16.

master for the loss of his slave. Then after a period of discipline, he restored his beloved as his wife.

Whatever the status of his marriage, Hosea clearly saw in Gomer's relationship to him an analogy of Israel's relationship to Yahweh. Like the other prophets, Hosea glamorized the wilderness period as a time of a pristine covenant faith. At that time Israel, Yahweh's bride, had been faithful, but Israel, like Gomer, had become a wanton harlot, giving itself to the Canaanite Baals. Israel said:

> I will go after my lovers,
> they give me my bread and my water,
> my wool and my flax, my oil and my drink.
> [2:5b]

The nation had become insensitive to Yahweh's love and grace. Lewd and naked it had gone after lovers, utterly corrupted by the fertility cults of Canaan.

The transition from nomadism to agriculture was completed when the nomads accepted the farmers' gods. Israel had not completely denied Yahweh; it had merely added gods associated with things of the soil—wine, grain, oil. Such syncretism, however, was totally destructive to the true nature of Yahwism. Yahweh alone was God of both the nomad and the farmer:

> She did not know
> that it was I who gave her
> the grain, the wine, and the oil.
> [2:8]

For gods who were no gods and for worship of the basest sort, Israel had pushed Yahweh and the covenant demands into the background. On such a nation divine judgment had to fall.

Sin, Sin, Sin. Like Amos before him, Hosea took seriously the social evils of the day, but he was more inclined to interpret these ills as a breach of Yahweh's covenant love (*chesed*) than as a breach of Mosaic law. Yahweh's controversy with the people was because there was "no knowledge of Yahweh in the land" (4:1). This lack of knowledge was not so much intellectual misunderstanding as it was a breakdown of the covenant relationship.[11] The "spirit of harlotry was within Israel" (5:4). Chapter 4 of Hosea shows the extent of its corruption and 6:1–13:16 reads like a catalog of sin. The decalogue, the basis of all Israel's law, had no meaning:

> Swearing, lying, and murder, and stealing
> and adultery break out,
> bloodshed follows bloodshed.
> [4:2]

---

[11]The Hebrew word translated "knowledge" is used of the most intimate relationships.

This collapse of law and order had created anarchy in which life was no longer safe.[12] Hosea doubtless had in mind the chaotic years following the death of Jeroboam II.

The heart had gone out of religious life and moral decay was complete. Religious leaders were in the vanguard of corruption. Priests fed on the sins of the people, speaking out against sin just enough to keep sacrifices and offerings flowing in. They wanted the people to be iniquitous, for this would fill their larder. Little wonder that idolatry and Baals were so important. Pagan poison filled the vacuum of empty Yahwism:

> My people consult a piece of wood,
>   and their divining rod gives them oracles . . .
> They sacrifice on the tops of the mountains,
>   and make offerings upon the hills,
> under oak, poplar, and terebinth,
>   because their shade is good.
>
> [4:12–13a]

What little worship of Yahweh remained was meaningless, for it was devoid of real faith and mercy, and unsupported by social justice. Trouble, however, still brought the usual claim on the traditional hope that Yahweh was bound to help the covenant people:

> "Come, let us return to Yahweh;
>   for it is he that has torn, and he will heal us;
>   he has struck down, and he will bind us up.
> After two days he will revive us;
>   on the third day he will raise us up,
>   that we may live before him.
> Let us know, let us press on to know Yahweh;
>   his appearing is as sure as the dawn;
> he will come to us like the showers,
>   like the spring rains that water the earth."
>
> [6:1–3]

But prayer without repentance is not prayer, and persons who have transgressed the covenant cannot be redeemed by sacrifice:

> Though they offer choice sacrifices,
>   though they eat flesh,
>   Yahweh does not accept them.
> Now he will remember their iniquity,
>   and punish their sins;
>   they shall return to Egypt.
>
> [8:13]

---

[12]Hosea 4:1–2; 7:1–7; 8:4.

When help from Yahweh was not forthcoming, the Israelites turned to the nations, trimming "their foreign policy to every political wind that blew,"[13] but they were always wrong:

> Ephraim has become like a dove,
>   silly and without sense,
>   they call upon Egypt, they go to Assyria.
> As they go, I will cast my net over them;
>   I will bring them down like the birds of the air;
>   I will discipline them according to the report made
>   to their assembly.
> Woe to them for they have strayed from me!
>
> $\qquad\qquad\qquad\qquad\qquad\qquad$ [7:11–13a]

They indeed had strayed from Yahweh, who alone could help, and the nation was in ruin. To all this the prophet voiced Yahweh's disheartened cry:

> What shall I do with you, O Ephraim?
>   What shall I do with you, O Judah?
> Your love is like a morning cloud,
>   like the dew that goes away early.
> Therefore I have hewn them by the prophets,
>   I have killed them by the words of my mouth,
>   and my judgment goes forth as the light.
> For I desire steadfast love and not sacrifice,
>   the knowledge of God, rather than burnt offerings.
>
> $\qquad\qquad\qquad\qquad\qquad\qquad$ [6:4–6]

To this sinful people destruction would come, and soon. Harlotry had to be punished and the judgment was about to fall:

> Egypt shall gather them,
> Memphis shall bury them.
> Nettles shall possess their precious things
>   of silver;
>   thorns shall be in their tents . . . .
>
> Ephraim's glory shall fly away like a bird—
>   no birth, no pregnancy, no conception!
> Even if they bring up children,
>   I will bereave them until none is left.
> Woe to them indeed
>   when I depart from them! . . .
>
> Ephraim is striken,
>   their root is dried up,
>   they shall bear no fruit.
> Even though they give birth,
>   I will kill the cherished offspring of their womb,

[13]Bright, *The Kingdom of God* (Abingdon, 1953), p. 73.

Because they have not listened to him,
  my God will reject them;
  they shall become wanderers among the nations.
               [9:6, 11–12, 16–17]

Yahweh and Israel Again. But Hosea, who as a man had so loved wayward Gomer, knew that Yahweh could not give Israel up. The sensitive prophet plaintively characterized Yahweh's desire:

How can I give you up, O Ephraim!
How can I hand you over, O Israel! . . .
My heart recoils within me,
    my compassion grows warm and tender.
               [11:8]

Yahweh must punish but could not utterly destroy. Had not Israel been called as a child to be Yahweh's son, leading him from Egypt and teaching him to walk? Was Israel not Yahweh's beloved people? Yahweh was God, not man, the Holy One in the midst of the people, and Yahweh's compassion was warm and tender. God would not utterly destroy. God could forgive. The divine love for Israel was greater than Hosea's human love for Gomer.

In the prophecy of Hosea, we have an epochal combination of the wrath and love of Yahweh. Hosea said to Israel that Yahweh had not forsaken the apostate nation and that Yahweh's judgment was redemptive. From the consequent wilderness, Israel could, even as in the days of the exodus, respond to Yahweh's "overture of love." Then the "not-pitied" would obtain pity, "not-my-people" would become "sons of the living God," and great would be the day of Jezreel.

The final chapter brings the book to a fitting conclusion as a chastened and

Figure 10.1. The Hebrew "Writing" Prophets.

Century	Israel—North	Judah—South	Exile	Post-exile
8th	Amos Hosea	Isaiah of Jerusalem Micah		
7th		Zephaniah Jeremiah Nahum Habakkuk		
6th		Ezekiel	Ezekiel Obadiah Deutero-Isaiah	
5th			(Trito-Isaiah)	Haggai Zechariah Joel Malachi Jonah

repentant Israel brings Yahweh "words," not sacrifices, pleading that iniquity be taken away. Unable to help itself and aware of the futility of seeking aid elsewhere, it could only appeal for help. Then help would come.

SUGGESTIONS FOR FURTHER STUDY

Use *The Anchor Bible Dictionary* to elaborate the meaning of prophetic vision, day of Yahweh, and oracle.

Those interested in further study of Amos and Hosea should first consult articles in *The Anchor Bible Dictionary* and the *Mercer Dictionary of the Bible*. Then use the commentaries for additional elaboration.

On Amos: Hans Wolff's volume in the Hermenia series, *Joel and Amos* (Fortress/Augsburg, 1973); Gerhard Hasel, *Understanding the Book of Amos* (Baker, 1991); John H. Hayes, *Amos: The Eighth Century Prophet* (Abingdon, 1988); R. B. Coote, *Amos Among the Prophets* (Fortress, 1981); James M. Ward, *Amos and Isaiah: Prophets of the Word of God* (Harper, 1966); Hans Wolff, *Amos the Prophet: The Man and His Background* (Fortress, 1973); the article by D. L. Williams, "The Theology of Amos," *Review and Expositor*, 63 (1966) 393–404; and M. Paul Shalom, *Amos: A Commentary* (Fortress, 1991).

On Hosea: Walter Brueggeman, *Tradition for Crisis: A Study in Hosea* (John Knox, 1968); James L. Mays, *Hosea: A Commentary* (Westminster, 1969); James M. Ward, *Hosea: A Theological Commentary* (Harper, 1966); and the article by H. H. Rowley, "The Marriage of Hosea," *Bulletin of the John Rylands Library*, 39 (1956) 200–33. H. Wheeler Robinson, *The Cross in the Old Testament* (S. C. M., 1955), discusses Hosea and others; William H. Bellinger, *Hosea: A Study Guide* (Smith & Helwys, 1993), is introductory and helpful.

11

Judah's Struggle for Survival

The concluding portion of the deuteronomic history relates the story of Judah's struggle to survive the onslaught of Assyria, which overran Israel in 722, and the resurgence of Babylon resulting in several invasions and finally the fall of Jerusalem in 587. For the Deuteronomist, northern Israel's sojourn from its revolt to its destruction was a prime example of the fate of an apostate people. Judah, on the other hand, was the nation through which covenant was to be continued. The southern kingdom had no reason to boast of moral superiority; like Israel, it stood under Yahweh's judgment for unfaithfulness to covenant. Nevertheless, Davidic heritage, including the Jerusalem sanctuary, gave it enough stability to endure the ordeals of Near Eastern politics longer than Israel. Further, because the Deuteronomist wrote from a perspective that included Babylonian exile, it was obvious that any hope for preserving covenant lay in preserving and reestablishing Judah's heritage.

UNDER THE ASSYRIAN SHADOW
(2 KINGS 18–20)[1]

Mid-eighth century was for Judah, as it was for Israel, a prosperous time. Judah's stellar king at this time was Uzziah (783–742). During his long and able rule, the southern kingdom reached a zenith comparable to that of Solomon. Both he and his contemporary in Israel, Jeroboam II, capitalized on Assyrian weakness to strengthen their kingdoms. Uzziah restored the fortifications of Jerusalem destroyed during his father's day. He reorganized and reequipped the army, introducing siege engines of warfare. Edom's subjugation was continued, and the Philistine and Negeb areas were secured. Further, the

---

[1]See also 2 Chronicles 29–32.

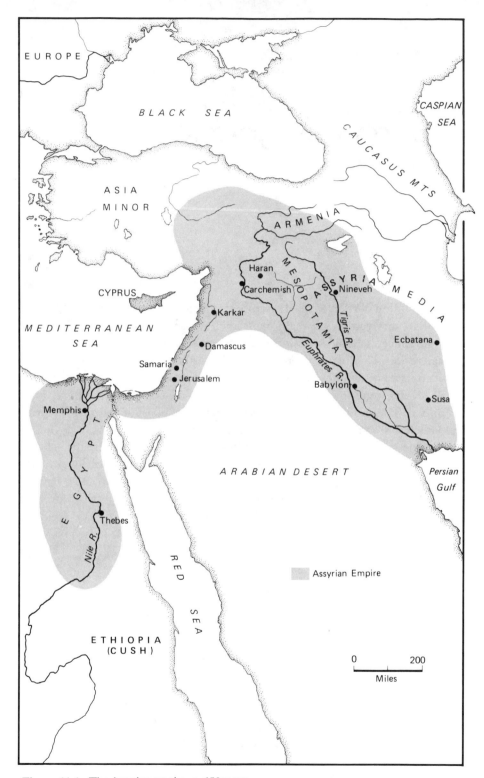

Figure 11.1. The Assyrian empire, c. 650 B.C.E.

356

Figure 11.2. Phoenician merchants bringing monkeys to the Assyrian king, Asshurnasipal II, suggesting the practice of Ahaz in relation to Tiglath-pileser of Assyria. (Copyright, British Museum)

port of Ezion-geber, renamed Elath, was repaired and the nearby copper smelteries were restored.

Judah shared with Israel a prosperity unknown since the days of the united kingdom. "During this period Judah was the most stable state in Palestine and probably in all Syria."[2]

Ahaz and Appeasement

As we already know, the prosperous and peaceful interlude in north and south came to an end with the revival of Assyrian strength under Tiglath-pileser III

[2]Albright, *Period*, p. 40.

Near Eastern Power of Influence in Palestine		Judah	
Assyria			
Tiglath-pileser	745–727	Ahaz	735–715
Shalmaneser V	727–722	(734 Syro-Ephraimitic War)	
(724–22 Siege of Samaria)			
Sargon II	722–705	Hezekiah	715–687
(722 Fall of Samaria)		(714–711 Ashdod Rebellion)	
Sennacherib	705–681	Manasseh	687–642
(701 Siege of Jerusalem)			
Esarhaddon	681–669		
Asshurbanapal	669–633?		
Assuretililani	633–629?	Amon	642–640
Sinsharishkun	?629–612	Josiah	640–609
(612 Fall of Nineveh to Babylon)			
Egypt			
Necho	609–593	(609 Battle at Megiddo)	
		Jehoahaz	609
Babylon			
Nabopolassar	626–605	Jehoiakim	609–598
Nebuchadnezzar	605–562		
(605 Battle of Carchemish)			
(597 First expedition to Exile)		Jehoiachin	598–597
(587 Fall of Jerusalem,			
second group to Exile)		Zedekiah	597–587
(582 Third expedition to Exile)			

Judah, 722–582 B.C.E.

Figure 11.3. Judah, 722–582 B.C.E.

(Pul). The certain onslaught on the western states included Israel, and after a courageous defense, Samaria fell, bringing death to the northern kingdom. Judah and King Ahaz (735–715) stood next in the path of Assyria's wrath.

How did Judah escape the same fate as Israel? Coalition and resistance were certainly a possibility. Even before 722 Pekah of Israel and Rezin of Damascus had led in forming a coalition to halt oncoming Assyria. Judah was invited to join, but for some reason both Jotham and Ahaz refused to become party to the resistance. When Pekah and Rezin invaded Judah "to bring her into line" and when Edom took this as an occasion to revolt, Ahaz appealed to Tiglath-pileser for aid and accentuated his plea with an enormous gift.[3] Through such appeasement with Assyria, he hoped for Judah's survival.

This foreign policy of Ahaz was vehemently opposed by the prophet Isaiah (Isaiah 7). He chided Judah because its heart "shook as the trees of the forest shake before the wind" when it heard of the league between Syria and Ephraim.

[3]See 2 Kings 16:5–8. Cf. Fig. 11.2.

In his famous Immanuel sign the prophet announced the ultimate fate of Judah's compromise with Assyria:

> For before the child knows how to refuse the evil and choose the good, the land before whose kings you are in dread will be deserted. Yahweh will bring on you and on your people and on your ancestral house such days as have not come since the day that Ephraim departed from Judah, the king of Assyria (Isaiah 7:16–17).

In spite of this objection from Isaiah, however, the policy probably saved Judah from Israel's fate. Tiglath-pileser moved decisively to destroy the Syro-Ephraimitic coalition; Damascus fell in 732. Ten years later Samaria met a similar fate, and Judah was left alone. Ahaz had made Judah a vassal of Assyria, but it survived.

Although Ahaz's decision spared the nation's life, his transforming of Judah into a vassal state came at great price. Tribute to Assyria drained it of considerable wealth and the temple had to be stripped to pay the bill. The territory lost to the Pekah-Rezin coalition was not recovered, and the profitable industries of Ezion-geber lost to Edom were not regained. Judah's economy remained depressed throughout the days of Ahaz.

Further, the reign of Ahaz was marked by one of Judah's most exaggerated periods of idolatry. Political subservience to Assyria was accompanied by recognition of its gods. Alongside the great altar in the temple, Ahaz constructed a bronze altar for worship of Assyrian deities. Also, high places to other gods were provided "in every city in Judah." Such apostasy led Isaiah to say:

> Their land is filled with idols;
>> they bow down to the work of their hands,
>> to what their own fingers have made.
>> [2:8]

The apostasy was so complete that Ahaz, on an unidentified occasion, offered his son as a sacrifice to Moloch according to Syrian custom.[4]

The two features of political subservience and rank paganism characterized the reign of Ahaz and were inseparably intertwined. Paganism entered a door set ajar by political acquiescence, and the faithful person in the street met agony from two directions. On the one hand, the heavy taxes paid to Assyria testified to political dependence. On the other hand, idols to Assyrian gods symbolized religious contamination.

Both religious apostasy and political servitude met strong opposition within Judah. This is understandable: devotion to Yahweh and national self-determination were deep-seated in the traditions of the covenant people.[5] Although

---

[4] 2 Kings 16:3.
[5] See Bright, *History*, pp. 272–73.

a blind and foolhardy reaction by secular standards, many began to support certain religious and religio-political enthusiasts who defied the policy of compromise with Assyria. Standouts among these leaders of discontent were the son of Ahaz, Hezekiah, and the prophets Isaiah and Micah.

Reforms of Hezekiah (715–687 B.C.E.)

Hezekiah succeeded his father to the throne when times were ripe for reform. The converging of religious devotion and political enthusiasm made "reform" almost equivalent to "revolt." Should these be considered two motivations rather than one, a question might be raised concerning the depth of Hezekiah's religious concern: Was he primarily concerned with purifying Judah's religion or did he use religious reform simply as an instrument for expressing political resistance to Assyria? But such a question would have been only academic for Judah: neither Hezekiah nor his contemporaries would have made such categorical distinctions between religious reform and political independence. Identifying the two objectives, Hezekiah took advantage of the international scene and launched an internal reform that a decade later erupted into open rebellion against Assyria.

Immediately after Samaria's fall in 722, Sargon was greeted with dissension elsewhere in his Assyrian empire. Merodach-baladan of Babylon successfully rebelled and other vassal states followed suit. With Sargon's attention diverted from Palestine, Hezekiah was free to proceed with internal innovations that were clearly anti-Assyrian.

Spell out the U.S. constitutional view of separation of church and state relationships and compare this with the stance of Hezekiah.

Initially Hezekiah began to purify Judah's religious practices. Rather than throwing off the Assyrian yoke immediately, he began to reemphasize the centralization of Yahweh worship in Jerusalem. Local shrines where pagan practices had prevailed were torn down. A bronze serpent associated with Moses was removed from the temple. Assyrian elements introduced by Ahaz were withdrawn. Although this was tantamount to repudiation of Assyria, Sargon was too preoccupied with rebellion by Babylon and others to give much attention to Judah.

In his desire to enlist the support of all the people for the shrine at Jerusalem, Hezekiah sent couriers throughout the land, including regions of defunct Israel, urging the people to "come to the house of Yahweh at Jerusalem to keep the Passover."[6] The Chronicler indicates that some success was achieved in Gal-

---

[6] 2 Chronicles 30:1.

Figure 11.4. The Siloam Inscription describing Hezekiah's project to bring water inside the city to protect against enemy attack. (Courtesy Istanbul Archeology Museum)

ilee, but Ephraimites were cool in their reception of Hezekiah's program. Although not universally accepted or permanently successful, the reforms prepared the way for the similar work of Josiah a century later.

Inasmuch as Hezekiah's religious actions carried specific anti-Assyrian implications and prepared the way for open rebellion, the king took steps to better Jerusalem's military position. The walls of the city were strengthened, several Judean cities were fortified, the army was reorganized, and diplomatic relationships with neighbors were restored. The most dramatic evidence of Hezekiah's military plan was his step to secure the city's water supply. An unreliable water supply had been a major weakness in Jerusalem's defense since the time of David. Except for a perennial fountain called Gihon, a spring just outside Jerusalem, the city had to depend on rain-filled reservoirs. A successful siege of Jerusalem could easily cut off access to Gihon and thereby place the defenders of the city in dire circumstances.[7]

Hezekiah undertook to bring water from Gihon into Jerusalem in such a way that concealed it from an enemy. In an amazing engineering feat, the king's workmen cut an aqueduct almost a third of a mile long through the solid rock beneath Jerusalem. The diggers began at both ends and with only slight miscalculation joined the excavated channels, known now as the Siloam tunnel. The Gihon spring was so sealed and camouflaged that it could not be observed from the outside and its water was conducted through the tunnel into the city to form the "pool of Siloam." An inscription found near the Siloam end of the tunnel "has for many years been the most important monumental piece of

[7]Cf. 2 Kings 20:20.

writing in Israelite Palestine, and other Hebrew inscriptions have been dated by comparing the shapes of the letters with it."[8]

Revolt Against Assyria.   Although the internal policies of Judah implied discontent with Assyrian domination and Sargon continued to be harassed by Merodach-baladan, Hezekiah refrained from open revolt. Assyrian records suggest that Hezekiah was related to a rebellion by Ashdod of Philistia;[9] but if he actually joined the revolt, he was able to withdraw in time to avoid Assyrian reprisals. Jerusalem was untouched and for a while Hezekiah seems to have been content to follow his father's policy of submission.

Sargon's death in 705 B.C.E., however, evoked a dramatic change in Hezekiah's attitude. As usual, the change in Assyrian administration created a moment of instability throughout the east. Troublesome Merodach-baladan saw in the uneasy transition to the new king, Sennacherib, an opportunity for organizing resistance to Assyria. He immediately enlisted support for a general revolt not only in the nearby areas of Mesopotamia, but also in the west. Judah had an important place in his plans. On pretext of congratulating Hezekiah upon his recovery from a serious illness, Merodach-baladan sent messengers to Palestine. Hezekiah received the messengers cordially, opened for their review the resources of Judah, and identified Judah with the conspiracy (2 Kings 20). Because of its advantageous military position, Jerusalem as the capital of the strongest state in southern Palestine was made a primary center of the rebellion. The small western states joined the league of resistance.

The die was cast. Although the policy of Hezekiah was strongly criticized by Isaiah (Isaiah 39), the long simmering discontent erupted into overt resistance from which there was no turning back. Sennacherib and Assyria now stood as Judah's enemy.

Sennacherib's reaction to the conspiracy is recounted in both Assyrian and Hebrew records[10] with vivid, though somewhat confusing, details. After Merodach-baladan had been subdued in the east, Sennacherib moved freely against the rebelling western coalition. His arrival in the west heralded an early collapse of the coalition. Tyre fell, marking the end of her commercial preeminence on the Mediterranean. In rapid succession king after king gave in, rushing to Sennacherib with tribute in hand. Cities of the Philistine plain fell before the crushing power of Assyrian armies. Forty-six fortified cities of Judah, by Sennacherib's counting, were reduced to submission.[11] Hezekiah soon was shut up "like a bird in a cage in the midst of Jerusalem."[12]

---

[8]Wright, *Archaeology*, p. 169. cf. Fig. 11.4.

[9]See the broken prism A published by Winckler and reproduced in Pritchard, *Texts*, p. 287.

[10]The cylinder of Sennacherib, a hexagon prism containing an account of his westward expedition, augments the biblical description of Sennacherib's invasion of Palestine in 701 B.C.E.

[11]The swift Assyrian march through Judah is vividly portrayed in Micah 1.

[12]See the text of the cylinder of Sennacherib, Pritchard, *Texts*, pp. 287ff.

With the coalition destroyed, Hezekiah saw little hope in further resistance and yielded. Vast areas of Judah were stripped from his control. Tribute was increased to such an extent that Hezekiah was forced to deplete his royal treasury and remove adornments from the temple to meet the assessment (2 Kings 18:14–16).

Apparently Sennacherib soon left Palestine because of renewed trouble at home (2 Kings 19:7) only to return later to deal with another rebellion by Hezekiah.[13] About 691 B.C.E. Sennacherib, confronted by further revolt in Baylonia, suffered serious defeat. Conceivably this defeat encouraged Hezekiah to hazard a second revolt, which recalled Sennacherib to Judah sometime during the closing days of the Judean king, 689–687 B.C.E. Jerusalem was spared by the intervention of an epidemic that crippled Sennacherib's army. Herodotus says that the Assyrian army was struck down by a plague of mice, possibly suggesting bubonic plague. Whatever the means, both the biblical historian and the prophet Isaiah saw Yahweh acting to redeem the people. Jerusalem was delivered, but Judah remained under an Assyrian cloud.

With strength derived from the prophetic support of Isaiah and Micah, Hezekiah was able to resist idolatrous encroachments by his Assyrian overlord. The extent of his religious reforms is open to some question, and as we shall see, they were not continuously effective. However, a reform party was established, which, though early quiescent, would resist paganism and provide a milieu out of which a resurgent and thorough deuteronomic reform would come during the days of King Josiah.

JUDAH'S EIGHTH-CENTURY PROPHETS
(ISAIAH 1–39; MICAH)

During the chaotic latter half of the eighth century B.C.E., when Israel to the north was moving through its final days, two prophets were active in Judah. Isaiah of Jerusalem and Micah followed in the tradition established by Amos and Hosea in Israel. In fact, they were in some ways dependent on the religious concepts enunciated by their Israelite counterparts. Both Isaiah and Micah had extensive prophetic missions during the period when Judah's chief problem was reconciliation with Assyrian power.[14]

Isaiah of Jerusalem

The prophet Isaiah was called to his mission in 742 B.C.E., "the year that King Uzziah died,"[15] and was still active during Sennacherib's siege of Jerusalem in

---

[13]Bright, *History*, pp. 287–88.
[14]See Brevard S. Childs, *Isaiah and the Assyrian Crisis* (Alec R. Allenson, 1967).
[15]The date of Uzziah's death is debated, ranging from 746 to 742 B.C.E.

Figure 11.5. Hexagonal prism of Sennacherib recording details of his campaigns, 705–681 B.C.E. Hezekiah is described as "a prisoner in Jerusalem, his royal residence like a bird in a cage." (Copyright, British Museum)

Figure 11.6 a & b. Above, part of a limestone relief from the palace of Sennacherib at Nineveh, Mesopotamia (modern Iraq), depicting the conquering of the Jewish fortress at Lachish about 700 B.C.E. At the left Sennacherib's battering rams attack the fortress wall, and in the closeup (below) Assyrian warriors impale Jewish prisoners on stakes. (Top: copyright, British Museum; bottom: Erich Lessing/Art Resource NY)

701 B.C.E. His wife was called a "prophetess" (8:3) and two sons bore names symbolic of important themes in his preaching. It is certain that he was city-bred, if not city-born. He knew Jerusalem well. Its streets, defenses (towers, wall, and water supply), and temple were all familiar places to him. He may have come from the Jerusalem aristocracy; at least he moved freely in circles of royalty and nobility. Whether he was an aristocrat or not, something aristocratic, if not regal, characterized his prophetic manner and his literary style.

Isaiah was unofficially court prophet to both Ahaz and Hezekiah, though not departing from the independent prophetic tradition begun by Amos and Hosea. He was no hireling of the court paid to predict good for kings on whom he was dependent for support. Rather, he was Yahweh's representative before rulers and his counsel was heard, though not always heeded.

The Book of Isaiah

The message of the prophet is contained in the first part of our canonical book of Isaiah. Although Isaiah appears in the Bible as a single unit of sixty-six chapters, its material is neither the work of a single author nor from the same historical period. Chapters 1–39 differ dramatically from chapters 40–66. For example: (1) the background of 1–39 is the Assyrian crisis, that of 40–66 is the exile and after; (2) the former part develops the idea of Yahweh's holiness, the latter emphasizes Yahweh's infinity; (3) 1–39 are concerned with a messianic king, 40–66 propose the idea of a "suffering servant;" (4) the atmosphere of the first part of the book is one of rebuke, in the latter part the writer's desire is to encourage and comfort Yahweh's people. These and many other reasons have led to the widely accepted conclusion that chapters 40–66 were written sometime after the fall of Jerusalem and are related to the captivity and return from exile.[16] They are usually designated as Deutero-Isaiah. Some further divide 40–66 into two parts (40–55, 56–66) and talk about Trito-Isaiah as the author of the last section of the book. However the division is made, our canonical book is clearly an anthology of materials arising across many years, while also an anthology with a unity of prophetic emphases and concerns.

The message of Isaiah of Jerusalem is confined, therefore, to chapters 1–39 of the book that bears his name. However, not all of these chapters are his. The oracles of the eighth-century prophet are found primarily in chapters 1–12, 13–23, and 28–31. The remainder of the material comes from prophetic sources of other times. An annotated outline may clarify the complex structure of the prophetic anthology found in this first half of the book of Isaiah:

[16]Jerusalem has been destroyed and the exile is a present fact (42:22; 49:14–21). Babylon is mentioned as a place of exile (47:1–5; 48:14) and Babylon's conqueror Cyrus is even mentioned by name (44:28).

A. Editorial introduction: 1:1.
B. Early oracles against Israel and Judah: 1:2–12:6. These oracles are the core of Isaiah's message, containing words of doom and hope. Most of this material came from Isaiah of Jerusalem although there are a few minor additions throughout.
C. Oracles against foreign nations: 13–23.[17] The oracles against Assyria, Philistia, the Syro-Ephraimitic coalition, and Arabia are from Isaiah. Those against Egypt and Tyre may be from him. The others all appear to be later additions.
D. The "Little Apocalypse": 24–27. A picture of Yahweh's cosmic judgment, followed by full restoration. Similar to material from exilic and postexilic times. These chapters may be as late as the fifth century or even later; we cannot be sure. They contain the first clear references to the resurrection of the dead (25:8 and 26:19).
E. Six woes: 28–32. Primarily from the time of the Sennacherib crises, 705–701. Appeals for dependence on Yahweh's power to save, followed by the promise of a king who would rule in righteousness. Most of this material comes from Isaiah of Jerusalem.
F. A prophetic liturgy: 33. Probably belongs to the Isaian tradition, but not from Isaiah himself.
G. Oracles of doom and salvation: 34–35. The situation presupposed here is that of the exile or later, and the style is similar to that of chapters 40–66 with which the chapters should be associated.
H. Historical narratives: 36–39. Almost identical with 2 Kings 18:13–20:19, from which it was taken.

How did it come about that all these materials plus the prophecies in chapters 40–66 were gathered into one unit linked with the name of Isaiah of Jerusalem? The answer seems to be that Isaiah's words and deeds were remembered, recorded, and elaborated by a circle of disciples (8:16f.). An Isaiah tradition developed, based on the teachings of the great prophet, and was passed on and continued to influence Israelite life and faith. Gradually oracles consistent with Isaiah's teachings and originating among his followers were added to the original core of genuine Isaian material. Most of chapters 1–39 had thus been shaped by the time of the exile. During and after the exile, the Isaiah tradition influenced other prophets who produced the majestic materials of 40–66. When the exile was over, the several blocks of material were placed together as a great presentation of Isaian prophetic faith. Isaiah of Jerusalem

---

[17]This section is similar to collections of oracles on foreign nations found in Jeremiah and Ezekiel (cf. Amos 1:1–2:8), indicating that the oracle of judgment on Israel's enemies was a popular literary type among the prophetic group.

was, therefore, a man whose vision and spirit impressed those about him to the degree that his influence lived on long after his death.[18]

The Crises of Isaiah's Ministry.   The oracles of Isaiah of Jerusalem can be gathered around three major crises in Judah's history:

1. *The Syro-Ephraimitic war, 734* B.C.E. In general, chapters 1–12 belong to the period between the prophet's call in 742 and the Syro-Ephraimitic conflict, which led to the preservation among his followers of the message so curtly rejected by King Ahaz.

2. *The Ashdod rebellion, 714–711* B.C.E. When Sargon II marched through Syria, Israel, and Judah to capture Ashdod, Isaiah warned Hezekiah that he should not take part in the Egyptian-inspired intrigue against Assyria. The prophet went naked for three years during the Assyrian threat as a reminder that those who trusted Egypt rather than Yahweh would suffer similar fate as Assyrian prisoners of war. Apparently Isaiah's "prophetic symbolism" had the desired effect because Hezekiah was not attacked by Assyria.

3. *The revolt of the western coalition and the Sennacherib invasion, 705–701* B.C.E. Hezekiah participated in this rebellion bringing the Assyrian armies to Jerusalem. The prophetic faith of Isaiah, inspiring both king and people, saved the day.

A glimpse at oracles selected from these periods of Isaiah's ministry gives us some idea of the spiritual depth and political insight characteristic of the man.

Called by the Holy One: Chapter 6.   During the Syro-Ephraimitic crisis, Isaiah wrote an account of his call as he had come to understand it through the years. Although written in retrospect, this is an authentic account of the determinative vocational moment in his life, the time when he became a prophet. The chapter describes the important psychological and spiritual experience through which Isaiah passed in the year King Uzziah died. The exact occasion is not mentioned, but in the background are the dramatic events connected with the death of one king and the coronation of another. The prophet was tragically disturbed because the long and prosperous reign of Uzziah had ended. The immediate situation was critical; the future ominous. The life of the people of Judah centered on its king,[19] and grief was great at the death of a good one. How could Judah face the increasing Assyrian menace under the leadership of Uzziah's weak and ineffectual son Jotham? Out of disheartening sorrow at such an hour, Isaiah became a prophet when he saw *the King*, Yahweh, the real ruler of Israel, seated on his throne. The prophet then realized that whereas kings on David's throne might come and go, Yah-

---

[18]The kinship of these materials was firmly established very early; the Isaiah scroll in the Dead Sea Scrolls contains the entire book.

[19]Pedersen, *Israel*, p. 275.

weh was Judah's everlasting king and on Yahweh the security of the Davidic state depended.

Discuss the call of Isaiah as an experience of worship.

The place of his inaugural vision was the Jerusalem temple and its form that of a cleansing ritual. The prophet stood in the temple where he may have served in some official capacity as a priest or, more likely, a temple prophet.[20] At a moment in the ritual in which kingship of Yahweh was celebrated, he gained a new and deeper understanding of what it meant for Holy Yahweh to be king over Judah. He saw Yahweh seated in council with the heavenly court in judgment over the nation:

> In the year that King Uzziah died, I saw Yahweh sitting on a throne, high and lofty, and the hem of his robe filled the temple. Seraphims were in attendance above him; each had six wings; with two they covered their faces, and with two they covered their feet, and with two they flew. And one called to another and said:
>
> > "Holy, holy, holy is Yahweh of hosts;
> > the whole earth is full of his glory."
> > [6:1–3]

His response was a confession of sin and unworthiness: "Woe is me! I am lost; for I am a man of unclean lips, and I live among a people of unclean lips, for my eyes have seen the King, Yahweh of hosts" (6:5).

After being symbolically cleansed, the prophet responded to the divine call, "Whom shall I send and who will go for us?" A positive affirmation of his dedication followed: "Here I am! Send me." He was then presented with a dreadful commission. He was to declare Yahweh's will even though Judah's failure to respond would develop into stubborn opposition making response impossible. Isaiah protested: "How long, O Lord?" And he was told:

> Until cities lie waste without inhabitant,
> and houses without people,
> > and the land is utterly desolate;
> until Yahweh sends everyone far away,
> > and vast is the emptiness
> > in the midst of the land.
> > [6:11b–12]

But he was also given a glimmer of hope. Yahweh might build up a new Israel from the ruins of the faithless people:

> Even if a tenth part remain in it,
> > it will be burned again,

---

[20]See R. B. Y. Scott. "Isaiah" in *Interpreter's Bible*, V:207–8.

> like a terebinth or an oak
>   whose stump remains standing
>   when it is felled.
> The holy seed is its stump.
>
>   [6:13]

Isaiah developed this glimmer into a doctrine of a purged and purified remnant in whom the nation survived as the people of God.

Faith (Isaiah) and Expediency (King Ahaz): The Syro-Ephraimitic Crisis. When Ahaz was faced with war against Israel and Syria (Damascus), his heart "and the heart of his people shook as the trees of the forest shake before the wind" (7:2b). With confident faith, Isaiah encouraged the king to trust Yahweh for deliverance. Israel and Syria were only smoking firebrands about to burn out, and Yahweh would render them totally incapable of harming Judah (7:3–9).

Construct a conversation between Ahaz and Isaiah on foreign policy.

Ahaz refused to listen to Isaiah and out of expediency appealed for Assyrian help. To Isaiah this was unfaithfulness. Yahweh alone could deliver; alliance with Assyria was a covenant with death. To become debtor to that empire was to become its slave. Ahaz was opening the door of Judah's doom. When the king refused to heed the prophetic advice, Isaiah pronounced the famous sign of the royal child Immanuel, meaning "God with us": "Therefore the Lord himself will give you a sign. Look, the young woman is with child and shall bear a son, and shall name him Immanuel" (7:14).

The symbolic name given this child is intriguing because it may mean at once both judgment and promise. God's presence with the people can be the devastating divine presence acting in wrath against sin. Clearly Immanuel does have that significance. The child would see tragic days of Assyrian invasion of the land:

> Therefore, Yahweh is bringing up against it the mighty flood waters of the River, the king of Assyria and all his glory; it will rise above all its channels and overflow all its banks; it will sweep on into Judah as a flood, and, pouring over, it will reach up to the neck; and its outspread wings will fill the breadth of your land, O Immanuel. [8:7–8]

The name "God with us" is also intended to be a sign of promise. The child would live through the disaster as a reminder of Yahweh's presence to redeem a remnant through which the nation would be saved.

The Song of the Vineyard: Summary of Isaiah's Early Ministry. When Ahaz refused to accept Isaiah's admonition to trust Yahweh, the prophet committed his teaching to his disciples for preservation until a time when they would be heeded: "Bind up the testimony, seal the teaching among my disciples" (8:16).

The testimony book must have included much of chapters 1–11, upbraiding the people for its sinful ways. Judah like Israel stood under Yahweh's judgment. More dumb than oxen and with less insight than asses, they had been rebellious sons and now were utterly estranged (1:2–4). The prophet's thoughts on the sins of the people are climaxed by the minstral song of the vineyard in which Isaiah sings of a farmer who bestowed tender and loving care on a vineyard on a fertile hill. He dug, cleared, and planted it with choice vines. He guarded its plants and made preparation to enjoy their wine. Then harvest came and the vines yielded wild, inedible grapes. In judgment he destroyed the vines and made the field a waste, forbidding the clouds to rain on it. Then to climax the song and make his point quite clear, Isaiah explained:

> For the vineyard of Yahweh of hosts
> is the house of Israel,
> and the people of Judah
> are his pleasant planting;
> he expected justice [*mishpat*],
> but saw bloodshed [*mispach*];
> righteousness [*tsdakah*],
> but heard a cry [*ts'akah*]!
>
> [5:7]

Quiet and Confident Faith: Isaiah and the Sennacherib Crisis. When Sargon of Assyria died in 705 B.C.E., the western states raised the signal for revolt, hoping that troubles at home would detain the new Assyrian monarch from putting down the rebellions. Encouraged by a promise of Egyptian and Babylonian help, Judah's leaders made what Isaiah termed a "covenant with death" (28:18). They joined the coalition against Assyria. Sargon's successor, Sennacherib, quickly squelched the opposition to his sovereignty in Assyria and moved to deal with the western rebels.

Isaiah proclaimed that only a covenant faith could annul the covenant Judah had made with death. Alliance with Egypt, an unreliable source of help, was useless:

> For Egypt's help is worthless and empty,
> therefore, I have called her
> "Rahab (great dragon) who sits still" . . . .
> The Egyptians are human, and not God:
> and their horses are flesh, and not spirit.
>
> [30:7; 31:3]

Then in a word that sounded the ruling principle of his statesmanship, he told Judah of the hope for salvation: "In returning and rest you shall be saved; In quietness and in trust shall be your strength" [30:15].

Repentance and faith in Yahweh, not political alliance and intrigue, was the solution to Judah's insecurity. Quiet faith, without anxiety or fear, and trust in sovereign Yahweh was Isaiah's formula for deliverance.

For a while Judah would have none of this advice, trusting instead in military and political alliances. Soon, however, it felt the fierce wrath of Assyrian might as Sennacherib swept through the countryside leaving fields, towns, and walled cities in ruins. From Jerusalem Isaiah looked out upon his land and lamented:

> From the sole of the foot even to the head,
>   there is no soundness in it,
> but bruises and sores and bleeding
>   wounds;
> they have not been drained or bound up,
>   or softened with oil.
>
> Your country lies desolate,
>   your cities are burned with fire;
> in your very presence
>   aliens devour your land;
> it is desolate, as overthrown by foreigners.
>   [1:6–7]

Jerusalem alone was left to Judah, a "lodge in a cucumber field."

With the holy city itself threatened with destruction, Hezekiah and his "faithful remnant" repented in sackcloth and ashes. Then Isaiah declared that Jerusalem would not fall. Yahweh would protect the city of divine habitation, the seat of David's line, from the anger of the haughty Assyrian who dared to question the power of Judah's God (36–38).

Emerging Messianic Expectations.   Prominent among Isaiah's sermons are oracles of messianic character. These oracles proclaim a coming Messiah, or "Anointed One," an ideal king from David's line who will establish the wholeness of life for which Israel's faithful yearn. Beyond judgment on the sinful nation, Yahweh would reestablish the Davidic rule through a newborn child destined for the throne:

> For a child has been born for us,
>   a son given to us;
>   authority rests upon his shoulder,
>   and he is named
> Wonderful Counselor, Mighty God,
>   Everlasting Father, Prince of Peace.
> His authority shall grow continually,
>   and there shall be endless peace
> for the throne of David, and his kingdom,
>   He will establish it, and uphold it
> with justice and righteousness
>   from this time and forevermore.
>   [9:6–7]

The destruction pictured by Isaiah was redemptive in its character. From the ruins of the Davidic dynasty, a king would rise as Yahweh began again to establish a covenant people. Also a remnant would emerge, purged of evil ways and anxious to be led by Yahweh's representative:

> A shoot shall come out
>> from the stump of Jesse,
>> and a branch shall grow out of his roots.
> The spirit of Yahweh shall rest upon him,
>> the spirit of wisdom and understanding,
>> the spirit of counsel and might,
>> the spirit of knowledge and the fear of Yahweh.
> His delight shall be in the fear of Yahweh.
>
> [11:1–3a]

With such a king to rule over it, Judah would fare well and fulfill its place in Yahweh's plan for humankind.

Contact a rabbi and discuss views of messiah in contemporary Judaism. Compare these with Isaiah's approach.

Did Isaiah have in mind a specific person when he painted these messianic portraits? If so, of whom was he thinking? And did he expect them to be fulfilled immediately or in the distant future? If the poems are related to the Immanuel sign of chapter 7 (and they may well be), the prophet felt that fulfillment was imminent. They probably were coronation hymns for Hezekiah. At any rate, the prophet looked forward to a king from David's line who would embody what Yahweh intended kings to be, ruling the people with justice and equity and establishing for it "peace," which meant everything necessary for the good life. John Bright sums it up well:

> The messianic hope of Israel was thus tied firmly to the line of David, to Jerusalem and the temple, and given a form which it would never lose. A mighty faith was therewith created which nothing could shatter. Indeed, the darker the days, the brighter its flame. For Messiah does not come to a proud nation glorying in its strength, but to a beaten nation, a cut-down stump of a nation, a nation tried in the furnace of affliction. No humiliation could be so abject, no torment so brutally severe, but that faith might whisper: Who knows but that this suffering is the purge that is even now producing the pure Remnant; who knows but that tomorrow Messiah, the Prince of David's line, may come?[21]

There was in this prophetic hope, however, real danger. Israel did make the mistake of confusing the hope with a particular form of its expression, and dared to believe that Jerusalem and the Davidic state could never be destroyed.

---

[21]Bright, *Kingdom*, p. 93.

Later it even attached messianic expectations to unlikely pretenders from David's line and denied others who served as Yahweh's messengers because they were unlike kings. Nonetheless Isaiah provided Yahweh's people an enduring image by which it maintained hope. No matter how desperate the circumstances, the people looked to the coming of Yahweh's deliverers, messiahs, who kept hope alive.

Summary of Isaiah's Faith.   Through these crises Isaiah's message contains certain key concepts that influenced the specific advice he gave to king and people. First, the idea of Yahweh's holiness was pivotal in his thinking. As a devoted Yahwist, Isaiah denounced the efforts of the people to shun the ethical responsibilities consequent to its relationship to Yahweh. Yahweh was of a majesty that was severe. Yahweh's holiness was both sublimely above humanity and pure above human sinfulness. So vividly did Isaiah believe this that his sense of mission centered around it. His call to prophetic ministry, as recounted in Isaiah 6, was essentially his reaction to the presence of the holy Yahweh (thrice holy for emphasis), who knows no comparison. In the presence of this Holy One the prophet immediately began with prayer for himself.

The holiness of Yahweh also brought national sin into focus. Yahweh of Hosts was the "Holy One of Israel" (1:4). In the same way that Amos had assailed the northern kingdom, Isaiah denounced the south for immoral conduct that violated the very character of Yahweh. Outward displays of religion without corresponding moral standards were sacrilege to Yahweh. The decadent upper class meant that the nation was crumbling from within (chap. 3), and the Day of Yahweh was to be a day of judgment. Against the background of the holy character of Yahweh, the prophet painted his portrait of national catastrophe.

A second determinative concern of Isaiah was what Martin Buber calls his "theo-politics."[22] That is, Isaiah believed that Judah owed allegiance only to a sovereign God. He opposed all entangling alliances with foreign powers on the basis that such relationships violated complete dependence on Yahweh. Judah's real salvation rested in its confident trust in the rule of Yahweh.

This basic concept charted Isaiah's advice to the king (whether Ahaz or Hezekiah) on matters of foreign policy. He opposed joining the Syro-Ephraimitic coalition against Assyria; he also opposed appealing to Assyria for help (chap. 7). Dependence on Yahweh assured deliverance. The same premise lies in the background of Isaiah's directive to Hezekiah. Redemption from the scourge of Assyria would come solely from the Holy One of Israel. Dependence on "the shadow of Egypt" would only end in Judah's humiliation (30:1–5). Isaiah would have agreed with the general of Sennacherib that dependence on

---

[22]See Buber, *Faith*, pp. 135ff.

Egypt was like leaning on a broken staff (36:6). But neither was Judah to submit quietly to Assyrian dominion. When Sennacherib laid siege to Jerusalem, Isaiah was confident that Yahweh would deliver the people (37:5–7). Yahweh was Judah's sovereign, and its destiny was directly correlated to its reliance on Yahweh's promises. This Isaian emphasis became the basis for an optimism in the religious thinking of Judah out of which would emerge the definite structure of hope expressed in Deutero-Isaiah.

A third idea is closely associated with "theo-politics:" Isaiah's emphasis on the continuity of the Davidic monarchy. We have already seen how in Judah the "covenant with David" virtually replaced the Moses-Sinai covenant. Isaiah's hope for a continued relationship between Yahweh and Israel was not based on a return to the principles of the covenant of Sinai, but on the conviction that Yahweh would be faithful to the covenant with David and through his line establish peace and prosperity for the nation. Isaiah was from Jerusalem, David's city, "where the 'David idea' lived with tenacious power."[23] He naturally, therefore, associated Yahweh's redemptive activity with the promise made to Israel's greatest king. His faith in Yahweh was the basis of his hope, and his associations with Jerusalem and its kings prompted the expectations of the way that hope would be realized. When the ideal age dawned after the purging of the nation, the messianic king would come in Yahweh's redemptive activity. He would come from David's line (9:7), a shoot from Jesse's stump to stand as an ensign to all peoples (11:1, 10), reigning over the redeemed faithful remnant of the people of God.

The final dominant concept is Isaiah's "doctrine of the remnant." Yahweh's purpose in history would be realized through the faithful few who remained loyal. Isaiah, therefore, distinguished between "Israel according to the flesh" and "Israel according to the spirit." Now with the northern state gone, Yahweh would work out salvation in Judah, never as guilty as its northern relative. But Isaiah was realistic enough to know that such a distinction could not be so precisely drawn. Judah was not blameless; in fact, most of its people were as rebellious as their kin in the north had been. Further, some from Israel now scattered among the nations had been faithful. The remnant, therefore, of which Isaiah had much to say was the remnant of Yahweh's faithful, whether from Israel or Judah (Isaiah perhaps believed more from Judah than from Israel, which is understandable).

The judgment that had fallen on Israel and would soon fall on Judah was a purge out of which the remnant of God's people would emerge:

> I will turn my hand against you;
> > I will smelt away your dross as with lye
> > and remove all your alloy.
>
> > > > [1.25]

---

[23]Bright, *Kingdom*, p. 91.

Whoever is left in Zion and remains in Jerusalem will be called holy, everyone
who has been recorded for life in Jerusalem, . . . [4:3]

The prophet named one of his sons Maher-shalal-hash-baz, "The spoil
speeds, the prey hastens," symbolic of the fiery trial to befall the nation; and
the other son he called Shear-jashub, "A remnant shall return," symbolic of
the hope that from the purge would come forth the true people of God. The
prophet left this idea with his disciples among whom it developed along the
lines expressed by the Isaian prophet of the exile in the portrait of the "Suffering Servant."

Micah

The prophet Micah was a contemporary of Isaiah and consequently addressed
the same situation. Unlike Isaiah, Micah was a man "of the people." He was
from a peasant background, a native of Moresheth in the Shephelah. But like
Isaiah, he was not deceived by the pretentious facade of Judah's culture. He
scathingly denounced the rich who exploited the small farmer (2:1–5), prophets who divined for money (3:11), and politicians who "tear the skin from off"
the people (3:1–3). Micah knew firsthand the sufferings of the poor and proclaimed his message in keeping with traditions common in the prophetic movement.

The superscription of his book relates his work to the kingship of Jotham
(750–735), Ahaz (735–715), and Hezekiah (715–687), but the Micah oracles
contained in the book belong generally to the time of Hezekiah. The activity
of the prophet was primarily concerned with crises of the Ashdod rebellion of
714–711 and Sennacherib's invasion of Judah in 701. In both of these situations Micah saw the possibility of Jerusalem's destruction and may have been
discredited when this did not come to pass. However, Jeremiah validates the
work of Micah, indicating the effect his preaching had on Hezekiah: "Did he
[Hezekiah] not fear Yahweh and entreat the favor of Yahweh, and did not
Yahweh change his mind about the disaster that he had pronounced against
them?" (26:19)

The book containing the preaching of Micah is a composite of doom and
hope. Micah in its present form preserves a balanced message of judgment and
promise. The prophet himself may have given greater stress to disaster that
was about to befall Judah and left largely to disciples the addition of oracles of
hope. The final editor of the book has balanced the prophet's message by
including both stern pronouncements of doom and oracles of comfort and
consolation.

Most of chapters 1–3 come from the prophet himself. Of these materials
only the oracle in 2:12–13 is seriously questioned as coming from Micah.

Chapters 4–7 seem to be composed of two anthologies (4–5 and 6–7) interspersed with materials of later date, but certainly containing materials from the
eighth-century prophet. Chapter 4:1–5 is the same oracle preserved in Isaiah
2:2–4 and is probably included in Micah to bring hope to the grim despair
portrayed in chapter 3. The liturgy with which the book ends (7:8–20) could
come from Micah's time but is usually considered postexilic. In spite of diversity in origin, however, the book of Micah is unified by its message and may
be outlined:

A. Superscription: 1:1
B. Oracles against Samaria and Jerusalem: 1:2–3:12
   1. Against Samaria: 1:2–7
   2. A lament over Jerusalem: 1:8–16
   3. Woe to Jerusalem: 2:1–11
   4. Interlude of hope: 2:12–13
   5. Appeal to Jerusalem leaders: 3:1–12
C. Oracles of hope and restoration: 4:1–5:15
   1. Visions of universal religion and peace: 4:1–8
   2. Visions of a restored kingdom: 4:9–5:15
D. Oracles of judgment, liturgy, and promise: 6:1–7:20

Micah shared with Amos an intense moral realism that issued in a stern
message of rebuke of social injustice. The first three chapters, interrupted only
by 2:12–13, carry through this attitude:

> Alas for those who devise wickedness
>   and evil deeds on their beds!
> When the morning dawns, they perform it,
>   because it is in their power.
> They covet fields, and seize them;
>   houses, and take them away;
> They oppress householder and house,
>   people and their inheritance.
>
> [2:1–2]

These circumstances spelled disaster for the covenant people and would
bring Yahweh's judgment on them: "Zion shall be plowed as a field; Jerusalem
shall become a heap of ruins" (3:12).

Over against the irresponsibility of the people, Micah saw Yahweh's basic
requirements centering on social justice:

> "With what shall I come before Yahweh,
>   and bow myself before God on high?" . . .
> He has told you, O mortal, what is good;
>   and what does Yahweh require of you
> But to do justice, and to love kindness,
>   and to walk humbly with your God?
>
> [6:6, 8]

Some of Micah's oracles were directed toward Samaria, but most of his preaching was to Judah. His rural background sensitized the prophet to the problems immediately around him. He saw the failure of spiritual and political leaders in terms of internal moral decay more than entangling political alliances. He condemned priest and prophet for manipulating Yahweh's word for material gain and civil officials for profiteering from the poor. The Yahweh of social justice overshadowed the Yahweh of international sovereignty. The nation's base morality caused the prophet to repeatedly sound Judah's doom.

The book of Micah is not without its word of hope. For example, oracles in the second half of the book envision a day when the nation would attain a place of leadership and other peoples will say:

> Come, let us go up to the mountain of Yahweh,
>   to the house of the God of Jacob;
> that he may teach us his ways
>   and that we may walk in his paths.
>
> [4:2b]

This particular oracle belonged to the Jerusalem cultic tradition and was also used by Isaiah (2:2–5) to declare his hope of Yahweh's redemption even of the nations. Like Isaiah, Micah also emphasizes the ideal ruler who would deliver Israel from injustice and oppression. He would be raised up like the judges of confederacy to establish "peace," the full presence of all that life and joy means:

> But you, O Bethlehem of Ephrathah,
>   who are one of the little clans of Judah,
> from you shall come forth for me
>   one who is to be ruler in Israel,
> whose origin is from of old,
>   from ancient days. . . .
> And he shall stand and feed his flock
>   in the strength of Yahweh,
>   in the majesty of the name of Yahweh his God.
> And they shall live secure, for now he shall be great
>   to the ends of the earth,
> and he shall be one of peace, . . .
>
> [5:2, 4–5a]

Oracles like these are often denied to Micah by scholars, but such oracles represent a genuine dimension of his thought. Judgments of the eighth-century prophets were not without hope; they were rather the basis of hope. To deny positive oracles to men like Amos and Micah simply because they are positive would be to question their belief in the redeeming sovereignty of the covenant God.

Generally, however, Micah emphasizes less hope for Judah than the high optimism for the nation's restoration expressed by Isaiah. Although they preached at the same time, their perspective on the situation differs. Neither prophet mentions the other, so the probability of their acquaintance with each other is remote. However, moving in different circles of Judah, their messages must have complemented each other to give strength to the reforms of Hezekiah, an initial step in deuteronomic reformation coming in full fruition almost a century later.

SUGGESTIONS FOR FURTHER STUDY

Items that may be further clarified with the use of Bible dictionaries include messiah and messianism, the Ashdod rebellion, holiness, theo-politics, and Syro-Ephraimitic coalition.

Useful background material on social, political, and religious life of the period is found in Georges Contenau, *Everyday Life in Babylon and Assyria* (Edward Arnold, 1954), and relevant sections of John Bright, *A History of Israel* (3d ed., Westminster, 1981), and J. Maxwell Miller and John H. Hayes, *A History of Ancient Israel and Judah* (Westminster, 1986).

On Isaiah of Jerusalem, see the basic commentaries and William J. Doorly, *Isaiah of Jerusalem: An Introduction* (Paulist, 1992); Sheldon Blank, *Prophetic Faith in Isaiah* (Harper, 1958); James M. Ward, *Amos and Isaiah: Prophets of the Word of God* (Harper, 1966); Elmer A. Leslie, *Isaiah* (Abingdon, 1963); J. William Whedbee, *Isaiah and Wisdom* (Abingdon, 1971); and Otto Kaiser's two volumes, *Isaiah 1–12: A Commentary* (Westminster, 1972) and *Isaiah 13–39: A Commentary* (Westminster, 1974). Two articles on special issues are important: David J. Clark, "The Influence of the Dead Sea Scrolls on Modern Translations of Isaiah," *Biblical Translator*, 35 (1984) 122–30, and Walter Brueggemann, "Unity and Dynamics in the Isaiah Tradition," *Journal for the Study of the Old Testament*, 29 (1984) 89–107.

On Micah, see the basic commentaries and Delbert R. Hillers, *Micah* (Hermeneia series, Fortress, 1984); James L. Mayes, *Micah: A Commentary* (Westminster, 1976); Hans W. Wolff, *Micah the Prophet* (Fortress, 1981); and L. C. Allen, *The Books of Joel, Obadiah, Jonah, and Micah* (Eerdmans, 1976).

References on Messianism are included in the General Bibliography.

12

Judah's Last Days:
From Heights to Depths
(2 Kings 21–25)[1]

The hundred years prior to Jerusalem's fall were undoubtedly the most tu-
multuous times of Judah's life. Struggles between Assyria, Egypt, and Babylon
for the control of the eastern world reached alarming proportions. As usual,
the fate of Palestinian peoples was intimately entwined with these struggles.
During these days, Judah both soared to glory on the tide of Josiah's deuteronomic reform and also prostrated itself in the dust of departed glory. So
compact were the events of the period that one man, the prophet Jeremiah,
could live to know a people who at one time sought "the fountain of living
waters" and shortly thereafter "hewed out cisterns for themselves, broken cisterns, that can hold no water" (Jeremiah 2:13).

This is one of the better documented periods of Hebrew history. Although
the Kings and Chronicles accounts devote most of their space to Josiah's reform, they are supplemented by the extensive prophetic writing of Zephaniah,
Jeremiah, Ezekiel, Nahum, and Habakkuk. Additionally, Babylonian sources
are very helpful in reconstructing the circumstances leading to the fall of Jerusalem. Especially informative is the Babylonian Chronicle, a document giving a detailed summary of Assyria's fall to Babylon. Altogether, these sources
enable us to reconstruct in some detail the several decades prior to 587 B.C.E.,
the year of the destruction of the Judean state.

JOSIAH'S REFORMS

Manasseh (687–642).   In spite of the immense struggle by Judah's religious
leadership during the last half of the eighth century, Hezekiah's reforms were
short-lived. Along with the passing of Hezekiah, Micah, and Isaiah went the

---

[1]See also 2 Chronicles 33–36.

gains of reform. With no outstanding prophetic voice to champion the cause of Yahwism, resistance to popular cults diminished. When Manasseh followed his father to the throne in 687 B.C.E., a general regression from the high level of Isaian faith set in with no opposition from the new king.

Politically, Manasseh returned to the foreign policy of Ahaz. Throughout his long and infamous reign, the nation remained a vassal to Assyria. No other choice was left him, for Assyria under Esarhaddon was at the zenith of its power, even controlling Egypt. Manasseh's submission, therefore, is understandable, but not his enthusiasm for things Assyrian. Such an attitude of submission bore the same religious fruit under Manasseh as it had under Ahaz. Adoration of the gods of the foreign suzerain became part of Judah's worship. Worship of Yahweh was not destroyed; Yahweh simply became one among other deities. This widespread downplay of Yahwism enabled old Canaanite fertility cults to be revived. Their local sanctuaries were rebuilt and their barbaric sacrifices of children as burnt offerings reappeared. All in all, the reforms of Hezekiah were, at least temporarily, swallowed up by spreading religious deterioration.

Such thorough idolatry was not without opposition. Quite likely it was ardent Yahwists whose blood "filled Jerusalem from one end to another" (2 Kings 21:16). Religious enthusiasts in the tradition of Isaiah could neither easily nor completely be silenced, and by the middle of the seventh century, Judah once again needed and desired drastic and major religious reformation. At Manassah's death, Amon became king but was soon assassinated, and the young child Josiah was put forth as hope for a new day.

Josiah (640–609).   By the time of the accession of Josiah, world politics had developed to Judah's favor. During the closing decade of Manasseh's reign, Assyrian control over the eastern world began to waver. Although it was rivaled by no major world power, Assyria was torn by revolts within and continuing raids by barbarian tribes on its northern borders. Under Asshurbanapal (669–633?) it was barely able to maintain its equilibrium. By the time that Josiah came to manhood, Asshurbanapal had passed from the scene and Assyria had lost effective control of its empire. Consequently, independence came to Judah in the 620s by default. Its severance of vassal ties with Assyria brought discredit to its former master's gods. Now political independence could merge with enthusiastic Yahwism to provide fertile ground for Josiah's plans.

Finding the Book.   The early years of Josiah's reign are quite obscure. When he was still a child, the affairs of state were in other hands. Whether or not Yahwists were involved in the assassination of Amon, they certainly were advisors to the new young king. Also the prophet Zephaniah was probably active inside the palace during the reforms of the 620s, and it may be that he was among the young king's advisors.

Figure 12.1. Depiction of Asshur-banapal, Asssyrian king about 669–633 B.C.E., carrying a basket on his head. The king was known for ghastly treatment of enemies, including such things as flaying with knives and tearing out the tongue. Toward the end of his reign Asshurbanapal lost effective control over Syria-Palestine and Egypt. Here he is represented as a basket carrier at the rebuilding of the temple of the god Marduk in 668 B.C.E. (Copyright, British Museum)

Josiah's reform began around 626 when he came of age and began to assert himself as ruler of Judah. The event that seems to have ignited religious fervor was the finding of "the book [scroll] of the law" in the temple. This discovery came in 622 when the temple was undergoing repair. What was found was probably the major corpus of the book of Deuteronomy, a resumé of Mosaic faith. Hilkiah, the priest, took the work to the king's secretary, who in turn delivered it to Josiah. Josiah was deeply moved by the radical contrast between the syncretism of contemporary religion in Judah and the lofty ideal of Mosaic faith (2 Kings 22:11–20). His reaction enlarged the discovery of the law book into the most epochal of Judah's many religious reformations. What had been promoted for a long while behind the scenes by enthusiastic Yahwists now found energetic leadership.

Josiah set out to establish religion of the character reflected in the book of Deuteronomy. Primary among the objectives was the elimination of adulterated cultic practices prevalent since the days of Manasseh. Josiah took this to mean centralization of worship in Jerusalem. Calling a convocation of the people, he read to them the newly discovered scroll and decreed its prescriptions the law of the land (2 Chronicles 34:29–33). This convocation took the form of a ceremony of covenant renewal, indicating that Josiah sought to incorporate certain confederacy ideals in the reform movement. The temple was cleansed of furnishings for the worship of Canaanite and Assyrian gods. Astral worship, cult prostitution, child sacrifice to Moloch, mediums, and wizardry were all "outlawed." High places and altars outside Jerusalem were destroyed. Included was that perpetual anathema in the deuteronomic tradition, an altar at Bethel. To the extent of Josiah's ability, worship was concentrated in Jerusalem.

Cultic reform under Josiah had both political and religious implications. As had been the case with Hezekiah, purification of the cult was a graphic expression of Judah's independence from Assyria. And, because his reforms extended into the regions of the defunct northern kingdom,[2] it seems clear that Josiah's desire was to reestablish a united monarchy with a central religious shrine at Jerusalem. Further, the reclamation of the deuteronomic idea of centralized worship in Jerusalem tangibly expressed the uniqueness of Judah's God. The pointed words of Deuteronomy 6:4–5[3] summarized the nation's understanding of its God: "Hear, O Israel: Yahweh our God is One Lord; and you shall love Yahweh your God with all your heart, and with all your soul, and with all your might." The policies of Josiah affirmed this exclusiveness of Yahweh and undergirded the strong sense of nationalism that accompanied the rediscovery of the faith of the Sinai covenant.

Externally, the Josianic reforms may be called successful. However, Judah's course was essentially unaltered. Outer change was accompanied by little inner commitment. The populace learned to trust the deceptive words, "the temple of Yahweh," without amending its ways and its doings (Jeremiah 7:3, 4). Jeremiah, whose call came during the early days of the reform, reminded the people of Judah of the fallacy of simple cultic reform without inward renewal and social justice: "Here you are, trusting in deceptive words to no avail . . . . Obey my voice, and I will be your God and you shall be my people; and walk only in the way that I commanded you, so that it may be well with you" (7:8, 23).

CHANGING POLITICAL SCENERY AND JUDAH'S FALL

The final decade of Josiah's reign witnessed a rapid and dramatic change in the political scenery of the east. Assyria's mid-century superiority declined with the death of Asshurbanapal, but it disappeared only after great struggle. As

---

[2] 2 Kings 23:19 speaks of the enforcement of his religious program in "all the cities of Samaria."

[3] These words open the Shema, the confession of faith that occupied a central place in the ritual of later Judaism.

late as 616 and 615, Nabopolassar of Babylon (626–605) failed in campaigns against it. In 614, however, the Medes joined forces with the Babylonians and the fate of Assyria became certain. Finally in 612 B.C.E., after an extended siege, Nineveh, the proud capital of Assyria, fell to Medo-Babylonian power. Remnants of the Assyrian army led by a pretender king fled to Haran where they made a final stand, but Assyria was ended.

The fall of Nineveh inflamed the growing anxiety of Egypt. Now only Palestine lay between it and the mounting force of the Babylonians and Medes. Consequently, Pharaoh Necho determined to take aggressive steps to halt the advance. He began to march northward through Palestine to support the pretender Assyrian king in his attempt to regain Haran from the coalition of Babylonians and others. Josiah, long committed to an anti-Assyrian policy, elected to oppose Necho and intercepted him on the famed battleground of Esdraelon at Megiddo. In the ensuing battle Josiah was tragically killed, or captured and executed, and his army fled. This battle at Megiddo occurred in 609 and marked the end of Judah's brief excursion in independence.

For a brief period after the battle at Megiddo, Judah fell under Egyptian control. A son of Josiah, Jehoahaz (609), was chosen by "the people of the land" to be the new king. But Jehoahaz, evidently not sympathetic enough with the conqueror, was deposed by Necho and taken to Egypt as prisoner. He was replaced by his brother, Jehoiakim (also known as Eliakim), who was more inclined to submit to Egypt.[4] A heavy tribute was laid on Judah, insuring its vassalage to Necho.

Egyptian control of Palestine, however, was temporary. For several years the struggle between Egypt and Babylon was a standoff, but eventually the balance of world power shifted to Babylon. In 605 B.C.E. Necho was decisively defeated at Carchemish by the Babylonian Nebuchadnezzar (605–562). After this, Egypt rapidly deteriorated as a power. Soon after his victory at Carchemish, Nebuchadnezzar marched to the very edge of Egypt, asserting his control over Judah. Jehoiakim (609–598), who owed his kingship to Necho's patronage, encountered no problem in switching allegiance to Nebuchadnezzar and Babylon. It was the same policy, only a new overlord. Judah became a vassal of Babylon, and factors leading to its ultimate destruction began to fall into place.

While Jehoiakim overtly paid homage to Babylon, he looked for an opportunity to improve Judah's fortunes. In a further conflict between Egypt and Babylon in 601, Jehoiakim thought he saw Judah's hope. He rebelled and immediately found himself in difficulty with Nebuchadnezzar. By the time Nebuchadnezzar arrived in Palestine to crush the rebellion, Jehoiakim had died and been replaced by his son, Jehoiachin (598, three months). The defense of Jerusalem was less than enthusiastic, and after only three months, the city was open to the invader.

---

[4]By selecting the leader, Necho asserted his full authority over Judah.

Nebuchadnezzar was surprisingly lenient with Judah on this occasion. Captives were taken to Babylon,[5] although most of the populace remained around Jerusalem. Included among the deportees were the king, his royal family, and a major segment of Jerusalem's intelligentsia. The prophet Ezekiel and others of religious and political prominence were among the captives. Evidently, by diminishing Judah's leadership Nebuchadnezzar hoped to preclude further revolt. The Holy City itself was spared, but it suffered heavy loss. The deportation of 597 began an economic and political trauma from which Jerusalem and Judah never recovered.[6]

Although in exile, Jehoiachin was still considered king of Judah by both the people at home and the Babylonians.[7] The practical affairs of state, however, were conducted in Jerusalem by his uncle Zedekiah (597–587), a good man, but weak and uncertain, who could provide little of the much-needed stability in such times of crisis. Although Zedekiah must have sworn allegiance to Babylon to receive Nebuchadnezzar's support (Ezekiel 17:13f.), he was continually enamored by ideas of rebellion. His vacillation between submission and independence caused Babylon to be suspicious and incurred the opposition of Jeremiah (21:3–7). As early as 594 Zedekiah began to toy with the idea of revolt. Conferences were held with ambassadors from the neighboring states of Edom, Moab, Tyre, and Sidon. Some prophets encouraged the idea, actually predicting the return of the captives within two years. Jeremiah, however, supported submission and continually denounced the palace for every notion of rebellion. The yoke of Babylon was to be borne as the will of Yahweh (Jeremiah 27–28). He went so far as to write the captives that they should make themselves at home in Babylon and plan for an extended stay (chap. 29). This position of apparent appeasement and collaboration brought the hatred of the populace on the prophet. The man in the street considered him a traitor who advocated selling out to the enemy.

For some reason Zedekiah's plan for revolt came to naught, and he sent envoys to Babylon to make peace with Nebuchadnezzar. The tide of patriotism, however, was not held back for long. The "patriotic party" began to pressure Zedekiah to bid for Egyptian support and rebel. The king repeatedly consulted with Jeremiah, who resolutely advised submission to Babylon. Zedekiah, without clear conviction himself and unable to control his nobles, finally yielded to the voices of revolution. Judah bolted in 589.

Nebuchadnezzar reacted with dispatch and ferocity. He marched into Palestine, overran outlying areas, and laid siege to Jerusalem. The defense of the

---

[5]See 2 Kings 24:14, 16; Jeremiah 52:28.

[6]This date, long a subject of scholarly debate, was supplied in 1956 with the publication of a tablet of the Babylonian Chronicles in Wiseman, *Chronicles*.

[7]See G. Ernest Wright, *Biblical Archaeology* (Westminster, 1957), pp. 177–78. Also W. F. Albright, "King Jehoichin In Exile," *The Biblical Archaeologist Reader*, I, Wright and Freedman, eds., (Doubleday, 1961), pp. 106–12.

city was noble, but futile. Token help from Egypt brought only temporary relief (Jeremiah 37). Inside the city Jeremiah advised capitulation and almost lost his life (Jeremiah 38). Famine became a major problem. Morale sank to the bottom and pitiable Zedekiah ran continually to Jeremiah hoping for some word of optimism. Finally, in July of 587 after an eighteen-month siege, the city fell. The date of the fall may now be established with relative precision on the basis of calculation from the 597 date clarified by the Babylonian Chronicle.[8]

Zedekiah fled the city, but was captured and brought before Nebuchadnezzar at Riblah. After compelling him to witness the execution of his sons, Zedekiah's eyes were put out and he was led away in chains to Babylon. The captain of Nebuchadnezzar's guard was dispatched to Jerusalem to level the walls and burn the city. Many leading citizens were slain. The remainder of the inhabitants, save those who fled Jerusalem and some of the poorest vine-dressers and plowmen, were carried captive to Babylon. This deportation left Jerusalem's political and economic life at a standstill and ended the southern kingdom. Jeremiah, given his choice of going to Babylon or remaining in Judah, chose to stay in the land with the peasantry.

The thankless task of trying to bring some order out of the chaos in and around Jerusalem fell to Gedaliah, a former palace official who was appointed governor by Nebuchadnezzar. With Jerusalem in ruins, the seat of government was transferred to Mizpah. Gedaliah began wooing the confidence of certain captains of the army who had escaped the Babylonian sword. Before any ordered structure could be achieved, however, the new governor was assassinated by a group of overzealous patriots. The army captains, fearing further reprisals from Babylon, fled to Egypt, taking the prophet Jeremiah with them. After the assassination of Gedaliah, a third deportation to Babylon occurred, probably around 582 B.C.E. Here the covenant story shifts to Babylon and the new community that would arise out of the trauma of exile.

THE PROPHETS OF JUDAH'S DECLINE

The last half of the seventh century produced four prophets whose preaching has been preserved in the biblical canon. Zephaniah, Habakkuk, and Nahum are generally associated with the period of Assyria's decline and Babylon's rise to a dominant role in the Near East, although details of their lives are lost to history and precise description of their prophetic ministry is impossible. Jeremiah lived and preached over the last several decades of the seventh century,

---

[8]A summary discussion of this calculation may be found in Freedman, "The Babylonian Chronicle," *Biblical Archaeologist Reader*, I, Wright and Freedman, eds. (Doubleday, 1961), pp. 119–24.

Figure 12.2. One of the Babylonian Chronicles, numerous tablets that record historic events in the reigns of Babylonian kings. The chronicle on this side recounts among other events Babylon's defeat of the Egyptian army at Carchemish in 605 B.C.E. On the other side it is reported that Nebuchadnezzar mustered an army to march into Syro-Palestine and on the second day of Addar (16 March 597 B.C.E.) captured Jerusalem and seized Jehoiachin. From this dating of the first deportation, the final fall of Jerusalem in 587 B.C.E. can be calculated. (Copyright, British Museum)

continuing beyond the destruction of Jerusalem in 587. These men, chiefly Jeremiah, represent another era of spiritual strength in Israel's prophetic tradition. They were thoroughly involved in affairs that spelled disaster for Judah, witnessing the flow of international circumstances that culminated in the fall of Jerusalem. They were men of their own times, interpreting current events as Yahweh's judgment on a wayward people. Yet they were also men of the future, refusing to give in to despair and attempting to arouse a new religious awareness among God's covenant people. In a sense the seventh-century prophets represent a powerful loyalty to Yahwism during a period when covenant, so long identified with monarchy, was threatened with death in the ashes of Jerusalem. In quite different ways each contributes to the survival of covenant faith when Judah, like its northern counterpart, might have been lost to history.

Zephaniah

In the superscription of his book Zephaniah is described as a descendant of Hezekiah and as prophet during Josiah's reign. The Hezekiah to whom reference is made could be the good king who ruled Judah, but the superscription does not specifically call Hezekiah "king." Reliance on this datum for interpreting Zephaniah's ministry would, therefore, be precarious.

Whether Zephaniah preached before or after Josiah's reforms cannot be decided with certainty. The book does portray the kind and depth of religious decline that immediately preceded Josianic reform. In an age that had lapsed into syncretism, Zephaniah attacked the adoption of foreign customs (1:4–9), including in his denunciation the Canaanite Baal, the Ammonite Milcom, and Assyrian astral worship. With vehemence he decried violence, fraud, idolatry, pride. Judah was thoroughly corrupt:

> The officials within her
> > are roaring lions;
> its judges are evening wolves
> > that leave nothing until the morning.
> Its prophets are reckless,
> > faithless persons;
> its priests have profaned what is sacred,
> > they have done violence to the law.
> > > [3:3–4]

Probably, therefore, the time is fairly early in the reign of Josiah, before the reforms of 621.

The book containing Zephaniah's oracles includes the basic emphases found in other prophetic collections: judgment on Yahweh's people, judgment on the nations, and promise of restoration. This pattern is clearly determinative in the collection and editing of the prophetic literature and is evident in its literary arrangement:

A. Superscription: 1:1
B. The Day of Yahweh against Judah: 1:2–2:3 and 3:1–7
C. Oracles against the nations: 2:4–15
D. Proclamation of salvation: 3:8–13
E. Eschatological hymn of salvation: 3:14–20

Zephaniah saw the Day of Yahweh in which judgment would fall upon "those who do not seek the Lord or inquire of him" (1:6). Yahweh's "jealous wrath" would erupt against Judah in a day of distress and anguish, ruin and devastation, darkness and gloom, clouds and thick darkness (1:14–18). God's own people stand under the threat of a great cult day when they themselves will be the sacrifice (1:7)!

> Compare the purposes of judgment in Zephaniah and Nahum and support your interpretation with specific references to the two books.

The nations, too, stand under the sovereign judgment of Yahweh, who will hold them responsible (2:4–15). The purpose of judgment, however, is not destruction of either Judah or the nations but redemption of both. Judah and the nations are judged so that Yahweh may gather a remnant of the "humble and lowly" who will "call on the name of Yahweh and serve him with one accord" (3:9). The oracles and hymn of salvation bear the mark of postexilic editing, but the vision of a redeemed and restored people is consistent with the prophetic hope that Yahweh's wrath accompanies the purpose of salvation.

Nahum

Nahum is quite unlike Zephaniah in religious outlook, choosing to focus exclusively on an outside people rather than Yahweh's people. Nothing is known about the prophet, except that he was a native of Elkosh, a village whose location is unknown. Probably he was from Judah.

The short book that bears his name celebrates the destruction of Nineveh, capital city of the hated Assyrian empire. Some place the writing soon after the fall of the Egyptian city Thebes (663 B.C.E.) to which reference is made (3:8–10). Others see Nahum's words as description, not threat, and so date the work soon after 612 B.C.E., the date of Nineveh's fall. Probably the threatening elements should be taken seriously and the book dated shortly before 612.[9]

The book portrays the destruction of proud Nineveh with brilliant metaphors and description. It consists of a brief and incomplete acrostic[10] poem (1:1–10), whose authorship is the subject of much debate, and a longer poem (1:11–3:19) of superior quality. The following outline suggests its basic theme:

A. Title: 1:1
B. Yahweh's vengeance on enemies: 1:2–11
C. Judah called to celebrate Nineveh's fall: 1:12–15
D. An oracle on Nineveh's distress: 2:1–12
E. Nineveh cannot recover: 2:13–3:19

The caustic hatred and vengeance that animate the book belie the prophet's name, which means "comfort," "consolation." To Nahum Yahweh intended

---

[9] A full treatment of the dating problem appears in Maier, *Nahum*.

[10] An acrostic is a poem in which successive verses begin with sets of letters in order.

Nineveh's destruction in blood because of the city's gross immorality. The prophet spells out the reason for Yahweh's judgment in unmistakable terms. God is punishing a brutal and unscrupulous nation:

> The lion has torn enough for his whelps
> > and strangled prey for his lionesses;
> He has filled his caves with prey
> > and his dens with torn flesh.

See, I am against you, says Yahweh of hosts, and I will burn your chariots in smoke.

[2:12–13a]

The brutality of Assyria is well attested in the literature and art of the Near East and the prophet commendably understands that God's control extends to the nations. But he has nothing to say about Judah also standing under divine judgment and thus his work illustrates the unfortunate linking of religion too closely to a nationalistic outlook. The prophet understands that Nineveh comes to its end tragically with none to mourn its passing. But can God's people "clap hands" with no assuaging of pain (3:19), even when destruction is deserved?

Habakkuk

The intriguing prophet Habakkuk also belongs to the period encompassing the fall of Assyria and the rise of Babylon. Nothing is known of the prophet's life or ministry. The story of Bel and the Dragon, an apocryphal addition to the book of Daniel, tells of Habakkuk's carrying food to Daniel in the lion's den in Babylon, but the story is legendary. Liturgical materials in the book suggest that the prophet was linked to the priesthood, probably in Judah.

Scholars have long debated whether such diverse materials as are found in the book could have come from a single hand. The commentary on Habakkuk found in the Dead Sea Scrolls, obviously a complete scroll, contains only the first two chapters, suggesting that chapter 3 may have been a later addition. Chapter 3 is a magnificent poem, praising Yahweh's salvation of his people. The poem was probably taken, either by Habakkuk or by disciples, from an existing collection of hymns and used here because of its appropriateness for a prophetic liturgy. Hence a certain wholeness marks the diverse materials:

A. Superscription: 1:1
B. Dialogue of complaint and answer: 1:2–2:5
C. Woes against various groups: 2:6–20
D. Habakkuk's prayer: 3:1–19

Habakkuk, like Nahum, interpreted international events toward the end of the seventh century[11] in the light of his understanding of Yahweh. Although the two viewed the same circumstances, their perspective was quite different. Nahum reveled in the pronouncement of disaster on Judah's enemy, but Habakkuk saw the havoc wrought in the world by mighty nations as Yahweh's scourge, which ought to be instructive for the people of Judah:

> Look to the nations and see!
> Be astonished! Be astounded!
> For a work is being done in your days
> that you would not believe if told.
> [1:5]

Some think that Habakkuk's reflection on the international scene is "only a cloak for the prophet's real thought. He is indirectly attacking the cruel and merciless rule of Jehoiakim."[12] Certainly, unlike Nahum, he takes Assyrian oppression as the occasion to reflect on Yahweh's relationship to the covenant people.

The book of Habakkuk is a pioneer writing in Jewish speculation. It raises a profound question about the righteous character of Yahweh and stands as a challenge against any simple view of divine justice. Like Jeremiah, Job, and some of the psalms, the prophet engaged in an honest "struggle in depth" with God. In light of the world situation, belief in Yahweh's righteousness raised two questions. "How can righteous Yahweh tolerate a covenant people as unrighteous as Judah?" Yahweh's answer was that the wickedness of Judah would cause its fall to Babylon, but this only raised a second question: "Why would Yahweh select a nation more evil than Judah as the instrument of its punishment?" How can a just God remain "silent when the wicked swallows up the man more righteous than he?" (1:13). To this question Habakkuk knew no

---

What are possible answers to the Habakkuk questions?

---

satisfying reply. The prophet could only continue his search for insight. His unwavering conviction was that he should remain steadfastly faithful to the righteous Yahweh, who was in command and whose righteousness would prevail:

> Look at the proud!
> Their spirit is not right in them,
> but the righteous live by their faith.
> [2:4]

---

[11]Some relate the book specifically to the reign of Jehoiakim (609–598 B.C.E.). See Harrelson, *Interpreting*, p. 375.

[12]Ibid., p. 374.

Jeremiah

The life of Jeremiah paralleled Judah's changing fortunes during the last half of the seventh century. Born near the close of the infamous reign of Manasseh, his public ministry extended from his call in 626 past the fall of Jerusalem in 587 B.C.E. He witnessed the nation's most extensive revival of faith, yet pronounced on it some of the strongest prophetic judgments. During his lifetime, his nation came under the dominion of Assyria, then Egypt, then Babylon. To his own people, whom he dearly loved, he was compelled to preach an unpopular and troublesome message.

Jeremiah was from Anathoth, a small village just north of Jerusalem. His family was of the priestly line of Abiathar, who had been removed from authority in Jerusalem by Solomon (1 Kings 1:28–2:26). The prophet himself may have been a priest who served at the Anathoth shrine. His destiny, however, was not to be fulfilled in the simple rural atmosphere of the village of his birth. He was torn from this place while still a young man by a call to be Yahweh's prophet to the nations. His early ministry was spent prior to the reforms of Josiah in both Anathoth and Jerusalem. During Josiah's reform, Jeremiah was in Jerusalem, but seems to have been relatively inactive during this period. Certainly, the most significant period of his work began with Josiah's death in 609 and continued until Jeremiah's deportation to Egypt around 582. During these catastrophic days for Judah, Jeremiah faithfully spoke his understanding of Yahweh's intention for the covenant people. Consistently he advised Judah to yield without rebellion to new Babylonian power, which had wrested the east from Assyria. His advice, however, went unheeded, Judah felt the full and crushing weight of Babylon, and Jeremiah concluded his prophetic mission in exile in Egypt.

Composition of the Book of Jeremiah.   The record of Jeremiah's life and oracles is found in an anthology made up of three major types of material.

1. Prophetic oracles against Jerusalem and Judah, from Jeremiah himself (most of chapters 1–25).
2. Biographical narratives about Jeremiah, presumably from Baruch, the prophet's scribe and friend (most of chapters 26–45).
3. Oracles against the foreign nations and certain biographical stories, all in a style similar to that of the deuteronomic historian. These materials probably came from a "school" of Jeremiah's followers (most of chapters 46–51).

The complex process by which these materials were organized into their present form is open to considerable conjecture and is a matter on which no one should speak dogmatically. Obviously, Jeremiah, his scribe Baruch, and disciples who followed the great prophet all had a hand in bringing the book to its final structure.

Any attempt to discover the various streams that gradually coalesce to give us the present book should begin with the scroll the prophet dictated to Baruch in 605. This document contained a select group of oracles Jeremiah remembered out of the first twenty-two years of his ministry. At the prophet's request Baruch delivered this summary of Jeremiah's thought to King Jehoiakim, who, finding the contents to his disliking, cut to pieces and burned the scroll as it was read to him. Having thus angered the king, Jeremiah went into hiding and redictated the scroll with many additions (36:32). At this time historical or "biographical" sections and prayers (i.e., expressions of Jeremiah's inner feelings) were added, plus some strong words against Jehoiakim. Later Jeremiah himself made scattered additions to the scroll.

To this expanded scroll, roughly equivalent to chapters 1–25 of the present book, were added the extensive biographical sections from the pen of Baruch (chap. 26–45) and Jeremiah's oracles against the nations (46–51). Later the Jeremiah "school" added other information about its prophetic master and additional oracles against the nations, bringing the book of Jeremiah to something quite like its present form. Finally, chapter 52, taken from 2 Kings 24:18–25:30, describing the fall of Jerusalem, was appended as a historical conclusion.

A completely systematic outline of Jeremiah is impossible, but a survey of its contents, indicating their general character, is useful:

A. Editorial introduction and account of his call: chapter 1
B. The scroll of 605—judgments against Judah and Jerusalem: 2:1–25:14
   1. Oracles from Josiah's time: chapters 2–6
   2. Oracles and biographical information from the time of Jehoiakim: chapters 7–24
   3. Summation: 25:1–14
C. Oracles against foreign nations: 25:15–38 and chapters 46–51. A mixture of genuine oracles from Jeremiah and those of the Jeremiah "school."
D. Biographical materials from Baruch plus oracles of judgment and hope, the latter predominating: chapters 26–35. Some of the oracles are from Jeremiah; others, in the deuteronomic style, probably came from the Jeremiah "school."
E. Jeremiah's passion—biographical narratives from Baruch: chapters 36–45. These chapters for the most part came from the period during and after the siege and destruction of Jerusalem.
F. Historical appendix: chapter 52.

In reading the book of Jeremiah we meet an extremely sensitive spokesman of Yahweh's message to Judah. The prophet moved in the tragic circumstances of a lonely life, torn between love for his people and hatred of its sins. Glimpses of his inmost thoughts trumpet the deep feeling of his mind and heart. His courage and strength induce admiration. If he were "the weeping prophet," as he has often been called, his tears were for his nation, his people, whom he loved: "O that my head were waters, and my eyes a fountain of tears, that I might weep day and night for the slain of the daughter of my people!" (9:1).

His love for Judah made Jeremiah's prophetic burden all the more difficult to bear because his message was a forecast of its doom. How distasteful this condemnation was to the prophet is echoed in his empathetic words:

> My joy is gone, grief is upon me,
>   my heart is sick,
> Hark, the cry of my poor people
>   from far and wide in the land. . . .
> "The harvest is past, the summer is ended,
>   and we are not saved."
>   [8:18, 20]

When Jeremiah warned his people of its imminent doom, Judah turned in derision on him because his oracles were not immediately fulfilled, and they denounced him because they disliked the tenor of his words:

> For I hear many whispering:
>   "Terror is all around!
> Denounce him! Let us denounce him!"
>   All my familiar friends are
>   watching for me to stumble.
> "Perhaps he can be enticed,
>   and we can prevail against him,
>   and take our revenge on him."
>   [20:10]

The Judeans preferred the falsely optimistic words of the professional prophets who proclaimed peace, even when there was no peace (23:17). Therefore Jeremiah's ministry seemed doomed to failure and to many, even to himself, it appeared that it did fail; but "some men's failures are eternities beyond other men's successes."[13] It was so with Jeremiah.

Call and Inaugural Visions.   The work of Jeremiah began in the thirteenth year of Josiah's reign (626) with a call, succinct and vivid, to the prophet. The divine summons came in an ordinary way, not in temple splendor as had Isaiah's. The experience was an intimate confrontation between a young man and the God whom he already had come to know in a deep personal faith. The call was the consummation of a lifelong relationship with God rooted in the pieties of home and early training. A growing knowledge of God had ripened into the awareness of a special mission.

The call took the form of a dialogue between Yahweh and Jeremiah in which the divine commission and the prophet's answer stand over against one an-

---

[13]George Macdonald as quoted by H. W. Robinson, in *The Old Testament: Its Meaning and Message* (Hodder and Stoughton, 1937), p. 121.

other, like challenge and response. There is much similarity to the call of Moses in Exodus 3. The youth was told that he had been ordained to be a prophet even before his conception in the womb. Yahweh put Jeremiah on notice that the prophet had a role to play in the divine plan and purpose. In spite of evil filling the land during the reign of Manasseh, Yahweh had not forsaken the covenant intention and was preparing a spokesman to summon the nation back to worship and faithfulness. Jeremiah described his sense of urgency to prophesy as "a burning fire shut up in my bones, and I am weary with holding it in, and I cannot" (20:9). His task was to be "prophet to the nations" in troubled days when national prophecy was no longer possible. Yahweh's purposes operative on the international level called for prophecy to the world situation.

Jeremiah's natural response was to cringe in a manner reminiscent of Moses. His cry, "Ah, Lord God! Behold, I do not know how to speak, for I am only a youth," was swept aside by the promise that Yahweh would be present to give him words to say. Yahweh would provide the oracles; the prophet would only speak Yahweh's word, which would accomplish its purpose (1:7–9). Then Yahweh told him the frightful nature of his task:

> See, today I appoint you
> > over nations and over kingdoms,
> to pluck up and to pull down,
> to destroy and to overthrow,
> to build and to plant.
> > > [1:10]

Jeremiah sometimes concluded that destruction was to be his only message. His word was to be a fire to devour the people (5:14) or like a hammer smashing rock (23:29), so that once again Yahweh might build and plant a people to do the divine will. Upon the destruction of what stands in the way, Yahweh would construct a work suitable to the divine will (18:1–11). Faithfulness to such a message would separate the prophet from family and friends—even from public worship—but he would not be alone nor need he be discouraged. Jeremiah is in Yahweh's service and can be assured of Yahweh's continuing presence (1:17–19). This presence remained disturbing to Jeremiah throughout his troubled life.

Two "visions"[14] were directly associated with Jeremiah's call. The prophet saw in the shoots of an almond tree (*shaqed*), the first tree to blossom in spring, a reminder that Yahweh was watching (*shoqed*) over the divine, spoken word to perform it, a revelation that came by means of word association. Yahweh is "watching" over the word to bring it to pass (1:11). Yahweh's judgment on the people is certain and Jeremiah must sound the alarm.

---

[14]Visions here may not be the right word for it is probable that Jeremiah actually saw the objects concerned. Here and elsewhere in the prophetic books, ordinary sight becomes a means of revelation to the prophet with insight. Cf. Jeremiah 24:3; Amos 7:7–9; 8:1–2.

The prophet looked again and saw a boiling pot, perhaps the cooking pot in his home, tilted toward the south so that its contents were about to spill out from a northerly direction. As a complement to the "vision" of the *shaqed*, the boiling pot signified that an enemy was about to attack Judah from the north. Precise identity of this enemy is impossible. The Scythians in upper Mesopotamia were a real threat to Israel, but never wrought havoc to the extent envisioned by Jeremiah. If the Scythians provided the stimulus for Jeremiah's descriptions, the Babylonians later fulfilled his fears.[15] Invasions traditionally came from the north. Quite clearly the prophet's main concern was not to identify the enemy, but to assert that Yahweh's judgment is about to come upon a people that had rejected covenant. Both visions underscore the depth of the nation's sin and the destiny of Jeremiah as Yahweh's spokesman.

Jeremiah and the Josianic Reformation.   Jeremiah's earliest oracles, found in chapters 2–6, encouraged reformation and undoubtedly helped gain support for Josiah's program. In these oracles the prophet dealt with the religious conditions resulting from Manasseh's syncretistic policy. Using imagery like that of Hosea, Amos, and Isaiah, he pleaded for national repentance. Judah is likened to Yahweh's bride and entreated to remember past favors and return to its youthful devotion and bridal love. Yahweh's people, however, did a strange thing, something that even the heathen would never do, something at which heavens themselves would be shocked: the people committed flagrant and inexcusable apostasy:

> For my people have committed two evils:
>   they have forsaken me,
> the fountains of living waters,
>   and dug out cisterns for themselves,
> cracked cisterns
>   that can hold no water.
>   [2:13]

A robust and dynamic Yahweh faith had been replaced with a syncretistic faith. The true and living God had been rejected in favor of false gods.

Using oracles from the Josiah period, show Jeremiah's attitude toward the reforms of Josiah.

Judah may have protested that it had been led astray by the wickedness of the Manasseh administration, but in two vivid pictures Jeremiah reminded the Judeans of their wickedness and obstinacy. The guilt was theirs because they were like wild beasts unable to restrain their lust, or like harlots of the streets

---

[15]See H. H. Rowley, "The Early Prophecies of Jeremiah in Their Setting," *Bulletin of the John Rylands Library*, 45 (1962) 198–234.

with many lovers who were brazenly unashamed of their immoral actions (2:23–25). But even though these sins were grievous, forgiveness was possible if they would only repent:

> Return, faithless Israel,
>> says Yahweh.
> I will not look on you in anger,
>> for I am merciful,
>>> says Yahweh;
> I will not be angry for ever.
>> [3:12b]

Then, as though this were too good to be true, Jeremiah sounded a note of doom in a series of oracles found in chapters 4–6:

> My anguish, my anguish! I writhe in pain!
>> Oh, the walls of my heart!
> My heart is beating wildly:
>> I cannot keep silent;
> for I hear the sound of the trumpet,
>> the alarm of war.
>> [4:19]

These early oracles end with a clear picture of judgment on the sinful nation. The enemy is vividly described as if already in the land, raging, killing, ravaging, destroying. These oracles anticipating a coming destruction must have encouraged an initial preparation for the cultic reform of 621.

Jeremiah supported reform because he was in general sympathy with its objectives. In fact, while the Josianic ceremony of covenant renewal was in progress, he openly advocated the acceptance of "the words of this covenant" (11:1–5). Such strong support created opposition to Jeremiah. Because the reform had as one of its tenets the unification of worship in Jerusalem, it did not attract enthusiastic promotion from many religious leaders in outlying areas. Jeremiah's friends and relatives at Anathoth even made an attempt on his life:

> But I was like a gentle lamb
>> led to the slaughter.
> I did not know it was against me
>> that they devise schemes, saying,
> "Let us destroy the tree with its fruit,
>> let us cut him off from the land of the living,
> so that his name will no longer be remembered."
>> [11:19]

Jeremiah nevertheless continued to support the reform and even went on a preaching tour of Judah to remind the people of the solemn responsibility placed on it by covenant with Yahweh (11:6–8).

Apparently Jeremiah was less active during the Josianic reformation, from about 621 to 609, than after the death of Josiah. Perhaps reforms may have led the prophet to believe that Judah had heeded the warnings of his early preaching and would be spared. If he had predicted a Scythian invasion that did not come to pass, he may have been discredited for a while. More likely the Josianic reforms made the prophet's preaching less necessary for a time, and Jeremiah simply withdrew from the public eye only to be summoned again by Yahweh when the good king came to his untimely death.

For a number of years Jeremiah remained optimistic about the prospects of a people led by a model king who sought to purify Judah's religion and reestablish the Davidic kingdom. During this optimistic period, there were no words of judgment from the prophet, who perhaps thought that divine punishment was turned aside. Before long, however, the defects of the reform became obvious, and Jeremiah saw how shallow and artificial it was. More than a cultic reform was needed to make Judah the people of Yahweh. In his famous "temple sermon" (7:1–8:3), Jeremiah decried dependence on the presence of the temple as an assurance of God's presence. In an acidic oracle delivered in disappointment over Josiah's death and the collapse of his reform, perhaps on the day of Jehoiakim's enthronement, the prophet denounced pride in the temple while sin swept through the land (7:8–9). Further, he denounced sacrifice as insignificant and irrelevant to the demands of true religion (7:21–24) and predicted the destruction of the temple (7:8–15). Consistent with the view of genuine religion in Hebrew scripture, Jeremiah knew that love of God must be paralleled with love of neighbor; worship without social responsibility was no religion at all (7:5–11).

Moreover, the prophet saw the impotence of the legal method of dealing with sin and spoke out against the new–found law in blistering words:

> How can you say, "We are wise,
> and the law of Yahweh is with us,"
> When, in fact, the false pen of the scribes
> has made it into a lie?
>
> [8:8]

His later emphasis on rejuvenated religion embodied in a new covenant is probably a lesson drawn from the failure of the external effort under Josiah. The covenant could not be restored by external means, no matter how thorough their extent and sincere their intent.

The Crisis with Jehoiakim.   Hope for better things through Josiah came to bitter end at Megiddo when the good king was slain by Pharaoh Necho. Jeremiah mourned his sovereign and confessed real sympathy for Josiah's young successor, Jehoahaz, who was doomed to Egyptian exile:

> Do not weep for him who is dead,
>   nor bemoan him;
> weep rather for him who goes away,
>   for he shall return no more
>   to see his native land.
>
> [22:10]

Then the prophet turned his attention to King Jehoiakim. At first Jeremiah pleaded with the new monarch to fulfill the expectation of both Yahweh and Judah, lest he be destroyed and his people with him: "Act with justice and righteousness, and deliver from the hand of the oppressor anyone who has been robbed. And do no wrong or violence to the alien, the orphan, and the widow, or shed innocent blood in this place" (22:3).

When it became clear that Jehoiakim was a vain and pretentious king, Jeremiah unleashed the full force of his righteous wrath against him as one for whom he had lost all respect:

> Woe to him who builds his house in unrighteousness,
>   and his upper rooms by injustice;
> who makes his neighbors work for nothing,
>   and does not give them their wages;
> who says, "I will build myself a spacious house
>   with large upper rooms," . . .
> They shall not lament for him, saying,
>   "Alas, my brother!" or "Alas, sister!"
> They shall not lament for him, saying,
>   "Alas, lord!" or "Alas, his majesty!"
> With the burial of a donkey he shall be buried,
>   dragged off and thrown out beyond the gates
>   of Jerusalem.
>
> [22:13–14, 18b–19]

Such vigorous and open insult could not go unnoticed by the king and actually jeopardized the prophet's life. A mob, led by priests and temple prophets, was about to put Jeremiah to death (26:7–11), but he was saved by the intervention of the princes and "elders" of the land, perhaps conservative Judean landowners. Jeremiah was set free, but Jehoiakim seized another prophet who spoke against Jerusalem and had him executed.

Jeremiah further angered Jehoiakim and the temple officials by symbolically acting out the destruction of Jerusalem. He took a pottery flask and went to the Potsherd Gate of the city, most likely the gate to the refuse dump. There he broke the flask and said: "Thus says Yahweh of hosts: So will I break this people and this city, as one breaks a potter's vessel, so that it can never be mended. In Topheth they shall bury until there is no more room to bury" (19:11).

Then he went to the temple court and spoke to the same effect in the presence of the people gathered there. For the first time the prophet was called on

Figure 12.3. Bulla with the name "Gemaryahu, son of Shaphan," a scribe in the court of Jehoiakim mentioned in Jeremiah 36:10–12, 25. A bulla is a lump of clay attached to a document and impressed with the owner's name. (Courtesy of Y. Shiloh, *Excavations of the City of David I, 1978–1982*, Qedem 19, Jerusalem, 1984, pl. 35:3)

to suffer bodily in Yahweh's service. Pashur, the priest, had him beaten and placed in stocks for a night. When he was released, he was forbidden admission to the temple area (36:5).

Rejected by his relatives and friends, exiled from the place of worship, and mocked because his words of doom went unfulfilled, Jeremiah gave bitter and unrestrained expression to his distress. In "confessions" or "prayers"[16] addressed to Yahweh, he angrily cried for vengeance on his enemies. He lamented his prophetic calling and even cursed the day of his birth (15:10; 20:14f). Certain that Yahweh had deceived him, he called Yahweh a "deceitful brook like waters that fail" (15:18). To these complaints the divine reply was encouraging and challenging:

> If you turn back, I will take you back,
>   and you shall stand before me.
> If you utter what is precious, and not what
>   is worthless,
>   you shall serve as my mouth. . . .
> And I will make you to this people
>   a fortified wall of bronze;
> they will fight against you,
>   but they shall not prevail over you. . . .
> I will deliver you out of the hand of the wicked,
>   and redeem you from the grasp of the ruthless.
>   [15:19b–21]

But Yahweh's response was also straightforward and realistic:

> If you have raced with men on foot,
>   and they have wearied you,
>   how will you compete with horses?
> And if in a safe land you fall down,
>   how will you fare in the thickets of the Jordan?
>   [12:5]

Later in Jehoiakim's reign, after the Babylonian victory at Carchemish in 605, Jeremiah was convinced that Judah's destiny was sealed. Babylon was

---

[16]Jeremiah 11:18–12:6; 15:10–21; 17:14–18; 18:18–23; 20:7–18. See studies of these in von Rad, "Konfessionen," pp. 265–76; and J. Philip Hyatt, "Introduction and Exegesis to Jeremiah," *Interpreter's Bible*, VI:777–93.

clearly the foe from the north and Nebuchadnezzar was Yahweh's appointed sovereign of the Near East (25:1–14). Jerusalem was doomed to complete destruction (16:1–17:8). The time was again right for the prophetic influence to be felt in the court. But Jeremiah was now under a ban and forbidden access to the temple. In order to fulfill his prophetic mission, his message had to assume a new form. Whereas it had been oral, now it was written on a scroll to be read to the people by Baruch. It was not a new message, but a summary of what Jeremiah had been preaching for more than twenty years. This was the scroll frivolously destroyed by Jehoiakim and later reproduced with additions by Jeremiah and Baruch.

Jeremiah and Judah's Last Days.   Chapters 26–35 of the book of Jeremiah are primarily narrative materials concerning the prophet's ministry during the period following the 597 exile. The materials were apparently gathered and organized by Baruch and clarify Jeremiah's relationship to the successors of Jehoiakim. The prophetic message during these days is a mixture of doom and hope. Jeremiah wanted to warn inhabitants remaining in Judah of the continued peril because of their sin and to encourage exiles in Babylon to prepare for an extended stay, taking seriously Yahweh's judgment on their apostasy. But the prophet also was confident that God's message went beyond punishment and exile. Yahweh had a new day and a new covenant for the people. Both emphases were important for the full word of Yahweh to be known.

Zedekiah, Jehoiakim's successor, genuinely respected Jeremiah, but lacked the necessary self-confidence to master the difficult situation that faced him. Unwisely goaded by those who hoped the Babylonian yoke could be cast aside, he again and again was tempted to rebel, in spite of continued counsel from the prophet to submit to Babylonian authority (chaps. 27–29).

An intended rebellion in 594 was forestalled by Jeremiah's drastic symbolic action. Wearing a wooden yoke on his shoulders, he called for submission to Babylon's yoke. When the temple prophet Hananiah countered by breaking the yoke and predicting Babylon's doom, Jeremiah announced for him an imminent death and replaced the broken yoke with one of iron as if to say, "Break this if you can." Hananiah's death after a few weeks explains Judah's unwillingness to participate in the revolt.

For a few years Judah and Jeremiah enjoyed peace, but then came the fatal revolt of 589 and the final siege of Jerusalem. Throughout the siege Jeremiah counseled submission to Nebuchadnezzer, Yahweh's instrument for Judah's punishment. The city's destruction was inevitable, but strangely Jeremiah affirmed a hope for the future. He bought a field near Anathoth, signed the deed before witnesses, and placed it in a jar for safekeeping.[17] By this act Jeremiah

---

[17]The transaction described in 32:1–16 illustrates the application of the law stated in Leviticus 25:25 and the usual procedure for exercising the right of property redemption.

revealed his faith in a restoration of Judah at some future date when fields in the war-torn countryside would again be valuable.

All the while, Judah's fortresses were being overrun and the city remained under siege. When only two of the fortresses, Lachish and Azekah,[18] were still offering resistance, Jeremiah determined to inform Zedekiah of the futility of continued opposition and to affirm surrender as the one option to save his life (34:1f.). Whatever hope Jeremiah may have had that his advice would be followed was crushed when an Egyptian army attacked Nebuchadnezzar and temporarily freed Jerusalem from siege (34:21; 37:5). The war party's hopes were high, and it predicted an end to Jerusalem's woes. Jeremiah, however, stood firm in his previous conviction and informed Zedekiah that the enemy would soon return.

During the absence of the Babylonians, Jeremiah left Jerusalem to visit Anathoth to claim the field he had purchased earlier. His enemies thought he was deserting to the Babylonians, whose cause he had appeared to champion throughout the siege. Without inquiring of the king, they had him beaten and imprisoned (37:11f.). Again Jerusalem was besieged and Zedekiah secretly sent for the prophet to ask, "Is there any word from Yahweh?" Jeremiah's reply was unchanged, "You shall be delivered into the hand of the king of Babylon" (37:17). Days of imprisonment, however, had taken their toll and the prophet pleaded not to be sent back to prison (37:20). Zedekiah, out of concern for the prophet's safety, transferred him to the "court of the guard" in the palace area and commanded that he be given food as long as any was available in the city.

From this more public place of confinement Jeremiah continued to speak to all who came near, encouraging their submission:

> Thus says Yahweh, Those who stay in this city shall die by the sword, by famine, and by pestilence; but those who go out to the Chaldeans shall live, they shall have their lives as a price of war, and live. Thus says Yahweh, This city shall surely be handed over to the army of the king of Babylon and be taken. [38:2–3]

The enraged princes called for Jeremiah's death, and with Zedekiah's toleration, he was thrown into a muddy cistern from which he was soon rescued by the speedy action of a palace official (38:7–13). He then remained in the "court of the guard" and until the capture of the city continued to advise the king to surrender. After the destruction of Jerusalem, Jeremiah was permitted to remain in Judah. He went to Mizpah and offered his services to Gedaliah, the Babylonian-appointed governor of the captured state.

---

[18]In the ruins of Lachish were found a number of military letters that vividly portray the rapid disintegration of the Judean opposition. Azekah fell, then Lachish, leaving the grim evidence of the thoroughness of the destruction in its ruins.

The New Covenant. Jeremiah had long plucked up and broken down, destroyed and overthrown; now it was time for him to build and to plant. The few months he spent with Gedaliah at Mizpah were perhaps the happiest of his life. He and the governor were in complete accord in their attempt to create order and purpose out of the chaos of 587. The destruction the prophet had predicted was past. Now he could devote himself to the constructive task of "strengthening the hands of a true patriot and servant of God in building up a new Israel on the ruins of the old."[19]

From this period came the promises of hope found in chapters 30–33, a section of the book commonly referred to as "The Book of Consolation." Although some of these materials may come from disciples of Jeremiah, the chapters depict the genuine optimism of a prophet who was able to see beyond Judah's immediate situation. Jeremiah believed that his nation had been punished to purge it of evil and call it to its senses. When the punishment had accomplished its purpose, however, Yahweh would restore the people:

> Thus says Yahweh:
> I am going to restore the fortunes of the
>   tents of Jacob,
>   and have compassion on his dwellings;
> the city shall be rebuilt upon its mound,
>   and the citadel set on its rightful site. . . .
> Their children shall be as of old,
>   and their congregation shall be established before me;
>   and I will punish all who oppress them. . . .
> And you shall be my people,
>   and I will be your God.
>
> [30:18, 20, 22]

At their head would be a prince submissive to Yahweh's will, the leader of a redeemed Judah:

> Their prince shall be one of their own,
>   their ruler shall come from their midst;
> I will bring him near, and he shall approach me,
>   for who would otherwise dare to approach me?
>   says Yahweh.
>   [30:21]

Both Judah and Israel would share in this bright future as Yahweh in redemptive love would make with them a new covenant, transcending in every way the old covenant of Sinai so often broken by the sinful people:

[19]John Skinner, *Prophecy and Religion* (Cambridge University, 1922), p. 279.

But this is the covenant that I will make with the house of Israel after those days, says Yahweh: I will put my law within them, and I will write it on their hearts; and I will be their God, and they shall be my people. No longer shall they teach one another saying, "Know Yahweh," for they shall all know me, from the least of them to the greatest, says Yahweh; for I will forgive their iniquity, and remember their sin no more. [31:33–34]

Note the tenacity of Judah's religious heritage. Even the prophet who had seen covenant broken, covenant reform fail, and the nation go to ruin now foresaw a future reestablishment of the relationship between deity and people that covenant implies.

This new covenant would be made effective by the free grace of Yahweh, which creates in the hearts of the people a knowledge of God and of God's ways, leading to obedience to God's law. Yahweh will be their God and they will be God's people in a fellowship unbroken by the sinful rebellions of the past. This hope of Jeremiah is the hope of Israelite faith.

One wishes that Jeremiah's story could have ended in peace-producing hope, but it did not. The tragedy that stalked his life struck again. Gedaliah was murdered and the leaders who remained fearful of Babylonian reprisal fled to Egypt, taking with them Baruch and Jeremiah. There they died.

Illustrate that Jeremiah is a tragic figure.

One closing word should be said about Jeremiah, because it is often wondered how he could endure a life of unending misery. How could he condemn the people he loved and predict the destruction of his land and city? Baruch wondered, too, and in prayer found an answer in a word from Yahweh: "I am going to break down what I have built, and pluck up what I have planted— that is the whole land" (45:4b). The land was Yahweh's land, the people Yahweh's people. Thus, the burden of Jeremiah's heart was the burden of the heart of God.

SUGGESTIONS FOR FURTHER STUDY

On Zephaniah, Habakkuk, and Nahum, see the basic commentaries and shorter articles in the Bible dictionaries. Donald E. Gowan, *The Triumph of Faith in Habakkuk* (John Knox, 1976), and J. Gerald Janzen, "Eschatological Symbol and Existence in Habakkuk," *Catholic Biblical Quarterly*, 44 (1982) 394–414, will help with Habakkuk. On Nahum, consult Walter A. Maier, *The Book of Nahum* (Concordia, 1987); Kevin J. Cathcart, *Nahum in the Light of Northwest Semitic* (Biblical Institute Press, 1973); and Alfred Halder, *Studies in Nahum* (Lundequist, 1947).

An article by James Crenshaw, "A Living Tradition," *Interpretation*, 37 (1983) 117–29, will introduce the serious student to significant research on

Jeremiah. Gerhard von Rad, "Die Konfessionen Jeremias," *Evangelische Theologie*, 3 (1936) 265–76, is old but still important for understanding that portion of the book. See also H. H. Rowley, "The Early Prophecies of Jeremiah in Their Setting," *Bulletin of the John Rylands Library*, 45 (1962) 198–234. Additional sources are listed in the General Bibliography.

Use the Bible dictionaries as listed in the General Bibliography to clarify the biblical books discussed in this chapter and to elaborate the meaning of the following terms: acrostic, eschatology, Book of Consolation, cultic reform, Day of Yahweh.

13

The Exile: Covenant Community Rediscovered (Isaiah 40; 42; 45; 49–55; Ezekiel 1–4; 11; 18; 23; 37; 47; Psalm 137)

The events surrounding 587 created for the covenant community a crisis of unbelievable proportions. Not only was social and political life in Palestine left in shambles, but also the very forms of covenant faithfulness were brought into question. Those who had seen Yahweh's faithfulness demonstrated in "covenant with David" now were left with only relics of the superstructures of their faith. Enemy soldiers had crossed borders of a holy land thought to be inviolate because Yahweh guarded them; the temple, God's symbolic dwelling place, was in rubble; David's son, Yahweh's vice-regent, had been taken away in disgrace. Faith was in genuine crisis. Could one continue to believe in Yahweh, whose concern for the people had been defined in Davidic terms? Had Judah's God perished with Jerusalem and Palestine? Some remembered the trauma and, overwhelmed with despair and not a little angry, asked with pathos, "How can we sing Yahweh's song in a foreign land?" (Psalm 137:4).

Some responded to the crisis by giving up their national identity. We know this because Hebrew names appear in later Babylonian documents. These persons had decided to settle in Babylon. But for the more devout, exile was a time for rethinking and rediscovering covenant faith. Just as when Abraham had no son and the Egyptian pharaoh "knew not Joseph," Yahweh's people were able to discover in exile new meaning of covenant and to build new structures of religion. The threatening place of chaos and death for the faithful became a place of new birth. During the traumatic exile, the nation maintained its identity and prepared for the time when, in the restoration, covenant could begin to take new and enduring form. To be sure, the emerging faith would not be simply a continuation of the traditional national cult. Yahweh's action in behalf of the people would be reinterpreted in light of the particular historical situation and would take on a form that would persist through the centuries of the future. This was the time of Judah's testing by fire, resulting in the emergence of refined Judaism—that is, the religion of the Jews as it took shape after the Babylonian exile.

The word "Jew" is derived from "Judah." It is technically applicable to the covenant people only following the Babylonian exile when the majority of the returnees to Palestine were from this prominent tribe.

Information about this period is at best sketchy. Data come piecemeal from diverse sources. A portion of the Chronicler's history, the only canonical history work relating to this period, tells us about the work of Ezra and Nehemiah. Considerable information is drawn by inference from the prophetic works of the exile and return. Ezekiel and Deutero-Isaiah are especially helpful. Babylonian and Persian royal archives, archeological finds, and the apocryphal 1 Esdras provide some data about the period. But all in all a great deal of cloudiness exists. We are largely dependent on inferences drawn from the more clearly delineated structure of Jewish life and faith during postexilic days. Nonetheless it is clear that these were days of rebuilding for the Jews, who came through the experience with (1) modified perspectives on covenant, (2) a diverse community, and (3) a new sense of responsibility toward the non-Jewish world.

LIFE IN JUDAH

Although disorganized, life continued in Judah after 587, but religious, social, and political life was at such a low ebb that the biblical story shifts to the exiles in Babylon. Hope for the future lay with them. But remember, the story is told by those who went into exile. There were still others in Judah who maintained covenant faithfulness.

Politically, the destruction of Jerusalem spelled the end of the Jewish state, at least temporarily. Although deportations to Babylon did not completely depopulate Palestine, Jewish political life ceased in the land of David. The territory became a Babylonian province. Clearly Nebuchadnezzar did not intend to leave strong political leaders in Judah and even Gedaliah may have been more a fiscal officer than a provincial governor.[1] Yet those Hebrews remaining in Palestine after 587 rallied around Gedaliah and attempted to go on with their lives. Jeremiah reflects on their effort: ". . . all the Judeans returned from all the places to which they had been scattered and came to the land of Judah, to Gedaliah at Mizpah; and they gathered wine and summer fruits in great abundance" (40:12). However, except for a brief period under the Maccabees,[2] an independent and autonomous Jewish nation would not again appear until the twentieth century C.E., with the birth of the modern state of Israel.

---

[1]Gray, *Archaeology*, p. 181.
[2]See below, pp. 470–474.

Although the national cult must have disintegrated with the destruction of the temple, some worship undoubtedly continued around an improvised or temporary sanctuary; "so sacred a site as that of the Jerusalem Temple could not have been thought to have lost its sanctity entirely."[3] The site was probably cleared and reused as a center of simplified worship. With Babylon firmly in control, worship of its gods may have been combined with the religious practice of the old Jerusalem sanctuary. Overall social, political, and religious life in Jerusalem after 587 was at a low ebb, but some of the traditional religion must have been continued. Some recent studies have claimed that the Judean community produced substantial and profound assessments of its experience and thereby contributed to the reconstruction of covenant theology. These suggest that the deuteronomic history work, that grand schematic interpretation of Israel's destiny found in Joshua–2 Kings,[4] may have arisen in this environment. More certainly Obadiah, several psalms (44, 74, 79, 102) and Lamentations[5] came from this segment of the covenant community.

The Book of Lamentations

The despair that prevailed in Palestine following the destruction of Jerusalem is reflected in the book of Lamentations. The book represents the presence of a creative stream in Judah during times not expected to produce literary excellence. The work is a collection of five lamentation poems and, because the poems correspond to the chapters, is quite easily outlined:

A. The agony of Jerusalem: chapter 1
B. Yahweh's judgment on the city: chapter 2
C. A lament of personal distress and prayer: chapter 3
D. Yahweh's wrath upon Jerusalem: chapter 4
E. A petition for Yahweh's mercy: chapter 5

Each has the rhythm of a dirge in a time of mourning and conveys a mood of grief. Chapters 1, 2, 3, and 4 are acrostic; they follow the letters of the Hebrew alphabet. Traditionally the poems were ascribed to Jeremiah, probably because of their common association with the fall of Jerusalem. Actually the poems are anonymous and were composed by Judeans left in Jerusalem after the exile began. They were brought together to provide liturgical materials for the annual remembrance of Jerusalem's fall.

Lamentations provides insight into the community's response to Nebuchadnezzar's siege, the fall of the city, and exile of the elite. The beginning of the

---

[3]Ackroyd, *Exile*, p. 29.

[4]Noth, *Überlieferungsgeschichtliche Studien: I* (Schriften der Könrgsberger Gelehrten-Gesellschaft, 3d ed., 1967), pp. 96f., 107ff.

[5]E. Jansen, *Juda in der Exilszeit* (Forschungen zur Religion und Literatur des Alten und Neuen Testaments, 69, 1956).

first poem reflects the intense feelings associated with these events. Grief became the mood of the day:

> She weeps bitterly in the night,
> tears on her cheeks;
> among all her lovers
> she has no one to comfort her.
>
> [1:2]

Explanation for travail was found in the traditional deuteronomic doctrine: Yahweh has caused it as punishment for a sinful people:

> Yahweh gave full vent to his wrath,
> he poured out his hot anger;
> and kindled a fire in Zion,
> that consumed its foundations.
>
> [4:11]

Obadiah

The book of Obadiah also comes from Judah after 587. It vents the frustrations of the poor after the fall of Jerusalem by expressing intense animosity toward the Edomites, with whom Jews had a longstanding compctition. Edomites had apparently taken advantage of Jerusalem's fall to move across the border and take territory from Judah. Their behavior, and Judah's reaction to it, reflected a tradition traced back to Jacob's (Israel's) superiority over Esau (Edom). The current circumstances agitated their enmity. Obadiah, a prophet about which we know nothing, gave vent to the vindictive hatred, anticipating Yahweh's judgment on the traditional enemy of his people:

> Your warriors shall be shattered, O Teman,
> so that everyone from Mount Esau
> will be cut off,
> For the slaughter and violence done to your brother Jacob,
> shame shall cover you,
> and you shall be cut off for ever.
>
> [9–10]

The brief book concludes with an emphasis on God's universal moral judgment "upon all the nations" through history. Judgment will come upon Edom and God's purpose will ultimately prevail, as stated by the closing words, "the kingdom shall be Yahweh's." The writing illustrates the frustrations of the oppressed Jewish community fighting for survival in a leaderless and desolate land and hints at some hope for the distant future.

Selected Psalms

Others who remained in Judah began to reinterpret their tradition to account for the disaster that had befallen them. Psalms from the period called to Yahweh:

> Rouse yourself! Why do you sleep, O Lord?
>   Awake! Do not cast us off forever!
> Why do you hide your face?
>   Why do you forget our affliction and oppression?
> For we sink down to the dust;
>   our bodies cling to the ground.
> Rise up, come to our help!
>   Redeem us for the sake of your
>   steadfast love!
>
> [Psalm 44:23–26]

> Do not remember against us
>   the iniquities of our ancestors;
>   let your compassion come speedily to meet us,
>   for we are very low.
> Help us, O God of our salvation,
>   for the glory of your name;
> deliver us, and forgive our sins,
>   for your name's sake!
> Why should the nations say,
>   "Where is their God?"
> Let the avenging of the outpoured blood
>   of your servants
>   be known among the nations
>   before our eyes!
>
> [Psalm 79:8–10]

If this represents the cult of the Judeans, it is apparent that they asked for vengeance, but also experienced a deeply moving sense of need and expression of hope. They were driven to plead with Yahweh for help; there was nowhere else they could turn for restoration of covenant.

The desperate situation also contributed to the development of the deuteronomic tradition, which condemned Israel for not realizing the possibilities of covenant and saw exile as judgment on a people who had been unfaithful to Yahweh. At the same time it promised salvation and hinted that, even in the sinister days of exile, redemption was possible because Yahweh would forgive.

Yet in spite of these attempts to hold on to covenant, those who remained in Judah were largely consumed by despair with little time for, or interest in, rethinking their religious commitments. Fortunately, Hebrew faith could also depend on those who had learned to sing Yahweh's song in a foreign land. In Babylon the culturally elite, political leaders, and religious enthusiasts were giving serious thought to the future of the Israelite people as the community of Yahweh.

LIFE IN BABYLON

Just how many Judeans were taken into exile is unknown. In 2 Kings 24:14–16 their number is given as eight to ten thousand, taken in the major deportations of 597 and 587. However, a reference in Jeremiah 52, probably an extract from an official Babylonian document, calculates the total number of deportees at less than five thousand. W. F. Albright conjectures that the discrepancy may be partly due to the heavy mortality of hungry and diseased captives in their long trek to Babylon.[6] Certainly the number of exiles must have been considerably smaller than the number who remained in Judah.

Identity Preserved.   To think of the Jewish exiles in Babylon as "captives" in the sense of a people in bondage is misleading. Certainly their life was not easy. They had to endure the hardships and humiliation of a displaced people, but they were not slaves to Babylonian taskmasters. One historian has described them as "recognized foreigners, affiliated to the plebean class of citizens and naturally without the privileges of the Babylonian aristocracy, but distinctly higher in status than the slave class."[7] The Babylonian experience was not a repetition of Egyptian bondage of earlier days. Further, the lot of Judah was quite favorable when compared with that of northern Israel. Whereas the dispersal of Israel by Assyria led to its loss of identity as a national group, the colonization of Judah in specific settlements around Babylon enabled it to preserve some unity.

At first many anticipated early deliverance from captivity. Later, following the advice of a letter written to them by Jeremiah, the exiles settled down in the strange land and tried to establish a routine that would make their ordeal bearable. They continued to marry and have families. They maintained their own communal organizations, probably reaching back to the days of Samuel for the pattern. "Elders" of the captivity occupied places of increased influence. The priest/prophet Ezekiel seems to have presided over the elders in much the same way Samuel had done in the days of tribal organization.[8] At several sites in Babylon "communities" of Jews existed with freedom of exchange between and among the groups. Jehoiachin, the king of Judah deported in 597, was soon brought out of prison by his Babylonian captors and given

[6]Albright, *Period*, p. 47.
[7]H. W. Robinson, *History*, p. 134.
[8]See Whitley, *Exilic*, pp. 78–79.

status among them. He dined at the king's table and was given an allowance for his personal needs (Jeremiah 52:31–34). Such an atmosphere of honorable treatment enabled the Jews to maintain their feelings of national and religious identity and undoubtedly contributed to their ability to revise covenant faith in their new circumstances.

Influence of Babylonian Culture.   Since Hebrews enjoyed considerable freedom in their captivity, Babylonian culture inevitably made inroads into the life of the Jews. They could not live in the most flourishing area of the east without being influenced by it. For one thing, the Aramaic language in official use in Babylon was akin to the native Hebrew of the captives. Inasmuch as the deported Jews were of higher classes, many of them would have had little difficulty in learning to use this tongue with facility. Hence, many displaced Jews began to use Aramaic in their dealings with the Babylonians[9] and this easy communication promoted cultural exchange.

The exile also offered dramatic vocational opportunities for a people whose way had been largely provincial. Opportunities unknown to them in Palestine were now accessible. Before exile, agricultural and pastoral callings were typical in Palestine, a "land of grain and wine, a land of bread and vineyards, a land of olive oil and honey" (2 Kings 18:32). Now these rural occupations were supplemented by more mercantile pursuits. Certainly many Jewish men were caught up in the "city of merchants." That they became involved in Babylonian trade and business is supported by the appearance of Jewish names in documents coming from later periods. Evidently some wealth developed.[10] Many must have become enamoured by the profitable life of the metropolis and lost their enthusiasm for return to the more strenuous agricultural life of Palestine. They were content to take their place in the new world, especially when it yielded abundant cultural and financial dividends. Hence, exile began to break down provincial barriers and expose covenant faith to non-Jewish influences, a process destined to continue dramatically over the next several centuries.

Religious Life.   A zealous core of Jews, however, were unwilling to accommodate to things Babylonian. They determined to maintain their identity with religion as the major bond. To them adaptation to life in the foreign land was a form of religious compromise, and they intended to preserve traditional faith, even if new forms were demanded. For them exile was only an interim in which they were sojourners in a strange land. They looked forward to the day when proud Babylon would come under the judgment of Yahweh and Israel would

---

[9]After the return from exile, Aramaic gradually replaced Hebrew as the language of Palestine. In New Testament times "Palestinian Aramaic" was the language of Jesus and the Apostles.

[10]Boadt, *Reading,* 394. Business tablets discovered at ancient Nippur, south of Babylon, list many Jewish names.

once again be established in Palestine. When their dreams of an immediate return went unrealized, believers interpreted their prolonged estrangement as the consequence of sins and transgressions (Ezekiel 33:10) and sought to revitalize Yahweh worship.

Of course, with the central Jerusalem sanctuary so far away, the cultus had to be transformed. Sacrifice could not be continued, but the devout could pray with faces toward Jerusalem. Other rituals not directly dependent on the temple, such as Sabbath observance and circumcision, could be observed and even given more emphasis. Probably to this period is to be traced the rise of the synagogue.[11] We cannot be sure just when, where, and how this new institution came into existence, but its presence in postexilic Judaism implies an origin during the exile as a temporary "tabernacle" in a foreign land. The intense study of scriptures later so characteristic of the synagogue must be rooted in the exilic concern for the past.

In reassessing the meaning of their religion, the faithful Jews turned with enthusiasm to the study and preservation of their religious literature. At various worship centers the literature of Israel's faith was collected and edited. The reality of the exile validated the work of various preexilic prophets and consequently authority was given to their work, assuring their preservation and hastening their inclusion in the canon. The Deuteronomist found the exile a fitting example of his theme that disobedience brings Yahweh's punishment, and so brought together traditional materials to make plain the nation's sins and Yahweh's purposes in judgment. Because the people were separated from the revered temple in Jerusalem, its cultic forms were cherished even more. Many of the psalms were collected. Torah took on its definitive shape with the Yahwistic and Elohistic epic materials combined with a priestly narrative. Thus, the disruption of ordinary patterns of religion pushed forward a concern for traditions expressed in the deuteronomic and priestly histories, a new appreciation of preexilic prophets, and the collection of certain psalms.

Perhaps the most dramatic alteration in Jewish religious life came in the area of the theology of national destiny. The fall of Jerusalem had obviously created a major theological problem. The existence of a Jerusalem sanctuary and the Davidic dynasty could no longer demonstrate Yahweh's faithfulness in keeping covenant with the nation. Now that temple was gone, what could be said about Yahweh's faithfulness? Was Israel's God, with David, gone forever?

The direction that the answers to these questions took is suggested by the prophetic stalwarts of the exile—Ezekiel and Deutero-Isaiah—who, along with the editors of Torah, undoubtedly had more to do with the religious reconstruction of the period than any other Jews. Their work clearly began to "dehistoricize" the temple and the David ideas, a process significant for the re-

---

[11]See Itzhak Magen, "Synagogues," in Stern et al., eds., *The New Encyclopedia*, IV, 1421–27, for a summary of archeological data regarding the synagogue.

building of Hebrew faith and important as well for early Christian formulations.

> Dehistoricizing refers to the process by which historical items come to be used symbolically.

Ezekiel

The prophet Ezekiel is a crucial figure in Israel's transition from preexilic to postexilic faith. His early oracles come prior to the destruction of Jerusalem and have led some interpreters to assume that he spent at least a part and possibly all of his ministry in Jerusalem. Certainly the holy city and its temple are the center of the prophet's early oracles, but the biblical tradition that Ezekiel spent his ministry in Babylon is as convincing as any reconstruction. The prophet's work is so thoroughly grounded in the exile that it is difficult to see how it may be disassociated from the actual historical situation.

Accordingly, Ezekiel, a priest in Jerusalem, was probably among those elite carried into Babylonian exile with Jehoiachin in 597. A few years after his deportation, his call to the prophetic office came through an ecstatic, awe-inspiring vision of Yahweh on a throne borne by a chariot. For the next two decades Ezekiel proclaimed Yahweh's message to the captives. Until the fall of Jerusalem the prophet's preaching was essentially an interpretation of the coming disaster. His message was delivered in Babylon, but directed to the situation in Jerusalem. After 587, the prophet addressed persons in exile. In this way Ezekiel was involved in the entire process of Judah's trauma and theological readjustment.

To say the least, Ezekiel was an unusual person. In any sophisticated society he would be considered an eccentric of first magnitude. His personal experience was extraordinary, bordering on the abnormal. His unusual temperament enabled him to visualize Yahweh enthroned in a storm or to feel himself bodily transported to Jerusalem to witness abominations practiced there. The same eccentricity enabled him to couch his message in dramatic symbolic acts. By digging through a wall, or carrying the baggage of a traveler, or dancing menacingly with a sword he simulated the fate of exiles leaving a beleaguered city. A valley of dry bones, a rusty caldron, or an eagle of multicolored plumage provided rich imagery for the graphic communication of his message. With brashness he talked of Jerusalem and Samaria as abhorred prostitutes. The individuality of the prophet gives his message a picturesqueness seldom seen in Hebrew scriptures. Further, the intensity with which Ezekiel proclaims the word of Yahweh epitomizes what is happening to the covenant community. The prophet, as the nation, experiences the reality of exile, not merely theory about it. His involvement in catastrophic disaster and in an awakening consciousness of God that followed it somewhat parallel what is happening to Israel. The harshness, almost violence, of his language suggests the intensity with which exile demanded a rethinking of destiny by the people of the covenant.

Ezekiel's message is a study in contrasts. With Jeremiah he shared the proclamation of unrelenting doom on Jerusalem prior to its fall. Before 587 he rebuked and condemned, declaring that the inevitable razing of the city would be no less than the accomplishment of the righteous judgment of Yahweh. Before holy Yahweh an apostate people could expect nothing other than the vindication of divine holiness. He envisioned Yahweh as having moved the divine presence (or glory) from the holy temple to areas outside the city.[12] However, after the fall of Jerusalem, Ezekiel's outlook became more optimistic. As if the fall of Jerusalem had been salve to his wrath, he changed from prophecies of woe to words of comfort and challenge. He sought to instill in his discouraged contemporaries a new faith for their trying times, a faith based on hope for an eventual glorious restoration of the Jewish nation. This restoration, like the destruction of Jerusalem, would be a miraculous act of Yahweh. Only when his despondent generation repentantly accepted responsibility for its sin would Yahweh intervene to reclaim the people. Then, like scattered sheep, the nation would be restored by the shepherd. Yahweh would be vindicated and a utopian Palestinian community would be created. Such optimism doubtless brought great courage to a downcast people.

The Book of Ezekiel

The major source of the book of Ezekiel is the prophet himself although, like other prophetic materials, the book in its present form was shaped by a circle of disciples. Clearly the book bears the mark of an editor's pen. Some poetic sections may predate the exile; other materials, notably chapters 38–39, seem to be later. The highly optimistic character of chapters 40–48 suggests a time closer to the return of the captives to Judah, but these probably originate with the sixth-century prophet. Within the circle of Ezekiel's disciples, original materials were compiled and additional oracles were added. Ezekiel himself may have begun the compilation, which was finished subsequent to his death. The result is a book arranged according to a clear outline:

A. Editorial introduction: 1:1–3
B. Account of Ezekiel's call: 1:4–3:27
C. Oracles of doom against Judah and Jerusalem: chapters 4–24; delivered between 597 and the destruction of Jerusalem in 587
D. Oracles against foreign nations: chapters 25–32. The lengthy poetic oracles

---

[12]Ezekiel 9:3; 10:15–19; 11:22f.

against Tyre and Egypt came from Ezekiel. The shorter prose ones against Ammon, Moab, Edom, Philistia, and Sidon were probably added by Ezekiel's disciples to complete the collection.

E. Oracles predicting the restoration of Judah and Jerusalem: chapters 33–39; delivered after 587

F. Ideal sketch of the restored community: chapters 40–48, delivered after 587

Many of these oracles are precisely dated and chronologically arranged. For the most part the chronological notices are in historical sequence (the major variation is the arrangement of the foreign oracles according to nations), but the materials in any one section do not necessarily belong to the date assigned to them. Evidently the editor wove together a group of oracles to which the prophet had affixed specific dates and a body of undated materials. The undated materials were placed here and there in the framework created by the dated oracles, producing some chronological confusion. The system of dating, however, faithfully represents the outline of a prophetic ministry divided between judgment and consolation, and suggests a prophetic career lasting from 597 to 571 B.C.E.

The Vision of the Call.   The character of Ezekiel is revealed by the visionary experience that culminated in his call to prophecy. Ezekiel had a vision of Yahweh's throne chariot, splendid beyond description and filled with Yahweh's glory. The majestic chariot moved in a storm from the north bringing a sense of Yahweh's presence to the priest in Babylon. Was there an actual storm as the "inspiration" of this vision? Perhaps, but we have no way of really knowing. Was there really a vision or is this account a "literary construct"? Again we have no way of knowing. Given the nature of prophetic understanding, any one or all of these could have been involved.

> Compare the "visions" in Amos with those in Ezekiel. Do you see differences and similarites in the experiences of the two?

Before the awesome holiness of "the appearance of the likeness of the glory of Yahweh," Ezekiel fell on his face, conscious of his human weakness and unworthiness in God's presence. The voice of Yahweh summoned him to receive his prophetic commission and Ezekiel, like the prophets before him, became captive to the divine word. This word, containing lamentation, mourning, and woe, was extended to him in the form of a scroll written on both sides. Ezekiel ate the scroll, symbolizing his willingness to incorporate Yahweh's word into his person and to give it expression by both bodily actions and proclamations. The prophet was told to proclaim the message, even though his preaching would not be heeded. Overwhelmed and appalled by the task given him, Ezekiel sat seven days silent in the midst of his fellow exiles before beginning to speak.

Symbolic Actions, Visions, and Allegories. Ezekiel spent the first portion of his ministry impressing his fellow exiles that not only would their exile continue, but they would be joined by their fellows from Jerusalem, a city whose doom was certain. The nation had forfeited its right to exist and stood under unalterable judgment from Yahweh. Little else mattered to the prophet in face of his compulsive concern for the bittersweet word of Yahweh that was his to declare. So impressed was he with his task and so unique was his personality that he went to extremes in the methods used to communicate the divine word. His humanity, in contrast to Yahweh's divine power, is accentuated throughout the book by Yahweh's addressing him ninety-three times as "son of man,"[13] an unusual form of address in the Hebrew scriptures except in the book of Ezekiel.

Earlier Israelite prophets had characteristically spoken their oracles, occasionally illustrating them by performing certain symbolic deeds,[14] but Ezekiel made bizarre symbolic action an integral part of his prophetic ministry.[15] Such behavior had a major role in his proclamations about the fate of Jerusalem and the character of exile. The prophet took a large, sun-dried brick incised with a picture of Jerusalem under siege and acted out a siege of the city (4:1–4). Then he lay on his left side and then his right side, symbolizing the length of exile for both Israel and Judah (4:4–8). With his face toward the brick portraying Jerusalem, he prophesied against the city. Daily for forty days he ate an odd mixture of three grains cooked over a dung fire (4:9–17), suggesting the scarcity of food in the besieged city and the dire circumstances of its rebellious inhabitants.

The fate of the people of Jerusalem was also graphically proclaimed. With a sword, the very symbol of war, the eccentric prophet shaved his head and beard (5:1–17). One third he burned on his model of Jerusalem, a third he cut to pieces with the sword, and a third he scattered to the wind. Thus Jerusalem's inhabitants would die in the besieged city, or be slain at its fall, or be scattered among the nations as exiles. However, a few of the hairs were bound in the skirt of the prophet's robe—not all of Yahweh's people would be lost. Finally, to represent Jerusalem's disastrous fall, Ezekiel dug through the wall of his house and carried his belongings through the hole (12:1–7). In this way he pictured for those already in exile the fate of their colleagues in Jerusalem.

These prophetic deeds were more than mere playacting to the prophet. They

---

[13]A "mortal" in NRSV.

[14]See Jeremiah 19:1–15; perhaps Isaiah acted out his "song of the vineyard," Isaiah 5:1–7.

[15]On the use and meaning of prophetic symbolism, see Lindblom, *Prophecy*, pp. 165–73. For Ezekiel's symbolic actions see Zimmerli, *Ezekiel*, pp. 28–29.

were "signs for the house of Israel," depicting Yahweh's sovereign purpose against Jerusalem. It was as if the deed were already done. For Ezekiel the symbolic action precipitated divine activity against Jerusalem. Prophetic behavior, like prophetic word, was alive to accomplish its end. A mind as suggestive as Ezekiel's had little difficulty envisioning Yahweh's deeds.

When Ezekiel was not symbolically acting out a sermon, he was having a surrealist vision or composing an allegory. No prophet before him had so used such peculiar media to convey his ideas. Nevertheless, his way certainly captured the attention and imagination of those who lived with him beside the river Chebar.

In vision he was transported to Jerusalem to see strange and terrible portents of evil and destruction. In a mysterious inner chamber of the temple he saw "portrayed on the wall all around . . . all kinds of creeping things and loathsome animals, and all the idols of the house of Israel" (8:10). Standing before them were the elders of the house of Israel with censers in hand, and the smoke of incense filled the room. Then, as if the priestly prophet had recoiled in horror and disbelief, Yahweh said to him, "You will see still greater abominations that they are committing" (8:13). In succession he was shown women weeping for Tammuz, a fertility deity, and men worshiping the sun, both within the sacred precincts of the temple. Forcefully Ezekiel proclaimed the judgment of Yahweh: "I will act in wrath; my eye will not spare, nor will I have pity; and though they cry in my hearing with a loud voice, I will not listen to them" (8:18).

Tammuz is known through the Gilgamesh Epic as a Sumerian god of spring vegetation. The fertility powers of the god were celebrated in an annual Babylonian cult that had numerous parallels in other areas of the East. The Tammuz practice included women entreating the deity for their own impregnation.

Visions of judgment followed as executioners descended upon the city to slaughter the inhabitants who remained after the righteous had been marked for deliverance. When the slaughter began, the prophet pleaded, "Ah Lord God! Will you destroy all who remain of Israel as you pour out your wrath upon Jerusalem?" (9:8) Yahweh's reply was decisive: "The guilt of the house of Israel and Judah is exceedingly great; the land is full of bloodshed, and the city full of perversity; . . . my eye will not spare, nor will I have pity, but I will bring down their deeds upon their heads" (9:9,10).

As if this were not sufficient to convince the exiles that the nation's doom was sealed, Ezekiel depicted its apostasy in vivid allegory.[16] Two of these (chap. 16 and 23) are reminiscent of Hosea's descriptions of Israel as a shameful harlot. The first allegory is the story of Jerusalem born in disgrace and aban-

[16]Ezekiel 15, the wild vine; 17:1–10, two eagles; 19:2–9, the lioness and her whelps; 19:10–14, the uprooted vine; 24:3–14, the caldron of judgment; and others.

doned: "Your origin and your birth were in the land of the Canaanites; your father was an Amorite, and your mother a Hittite. . . . You were thrown out in the open field, for you were abhorred on the day you were born" (16:3,5). Rescued and reared by Yahweh, the ungrateful child grew to maidenhood and became a harlot. This was Jerusalem; this was Judah.

The second allegory describes the prostitution of twin sisters, Oholah (Samaria) and Oholibah (Jerusalem).[17] Lewd Oholah was given to Assyria for punishment, but Oholibah did not heed this warning, actually becoming more corrupt than her sister. Therefore, she, too, would go to captivity. To her Yahweh said:

> You shall drink your sister's cup
>> deep and wide;
> you shall be scorned and derided,
>> it holds so much.
> You shall be filled with drunkenness and sorrow.
>> [23:32–33a]

The language of these allegories is bold, and was intended to shock. Ezekiel obviously had no time for niceties, and in the face of his message, who among the exiles would not believe that Judah and Jerusalem were doomed?

The Hope and Plan for Restoration.   Once Yahweh's judgment had fallen and Jerusalem was captured, Ezekiel ceased to be a prophet of disaster. His task then became constructive and visions of hope followed those of doom. The exiles were despondent because they felt caught by the inevitability of punishment. Their forefathers had sinned repeatedly and been punished, and so had they. If the hitherto inflexible principle of sin and retribution were correct, they were without hope. To counter their pessimism, Ezekiel challenged the older theology, proverbially expressed, "The parents have eaten sour grapes, and the children's teeth are set on edge" (18:2). He stressed that guilt is not fatalistically inherited, nor is it irremediable. The person who sins bears the guilt (18:10–13), but even so present righteousness may cancel past sin (18:21–23). Ezekiel stressed the individual's responsibility to Yahweh in the present situation. Any hope for the future rested on their relationship to Yahweh now. The exiles, therefore, had to act in righteous obedience to Yahweh for there to be a renewed Israel.

In a vision of restoration Ezekiel saw "dry bones which would live again" by the life-giving spirit of Yahweh (37:1–14). Exile was not the end for those of faith, for with them Yahweh would begin again: "I am going to open your graves, and bring you up from your graves, O my people; and I will bring you

[17]Ezekiel 23.

back to the land of Israel. And I will put my Spirit within you, and you shall live, and I will place you on your own soil" (37:12–14a).

First, however, Yahweh would replace their hearts of stone with hearts of flesh so that the covenant made with them might not be broken. Jeremiah had envisioned a new covenant from Yahweh in which the divine law would be put within the Israelites, upon their hearts, and Yahweh would be their God and they would be Yahweh's people. Ezekiel has Yahweh say, "A new heart I will give you, and a new spirit I will put within you" (36:26).[18] The internal, personal relationship with Yahweh is to prevail in the new beginning, the restoration, that lies ahead.

Chapters 40–48 of Ezekiel contain a vision that represents a major adaptation in Hebrew religious thinking. These chapters may have circulated as a unit before the book was put into its present form. In their present arrangement they bring the book to a fitting climax. The prophet takes the old ideas of David and Jerusalem, and builds on them an extended metaphor of future hope. Jerusalem becomes for him a symbol of an idealized rule of God over a theocratic state with the temple at its center. Around Jerusalem the restored tribes would live in orderly array occupying a territory extending from the "entrance of Hamath" to the "River of Egypt" (the boundaries of the Davidic empire). The priests would rule in the new state assisted by a prince in maintaining peace and order. No apostate kings would destroy the peace of restored Israel.

Ezekiel stressed the importance of ritual and cult in the new state, almost making purity of ritual as important as purity of heart. Nevertheless, he advocated obedience to covenant obligations and dreamed of a state in covenant with the holy Yahweh, who would be its king and its source of life. The apocalyptic anticipation of this picture of the restored nation is not surpassed in the Hebrew scriptures. From beneath the temple altar welled an artesian river of life that flowed from Jerusalem toward the Arabah, where it brought life to the Dead Sea (chap. 47). Along its bank grew fruitful trees in a delightful garden. All who lived in this Edenlike paradise would be blessed. Hence, for Ezekiel, Jerusalem's restoration was a symbol of what Yahweh had in store for the people's future.[19]

Hope proclaimed by Ezekiel made a significant contribution to the rebuilding of Israel's faith. In both destruction and reclamation he could see Yahweh's hand. Before 587 he encouraged those in Babylon and Palestine to move beyond resignation and despair to trust in Yahweh. The loss of all that Israel cherished—land, temple, king—spoke the name of Yahweh, who even in judgment could be known. Moreover, beyond judgment lay restoration. The holy

[18]See Jeremiah 31:33.
[19]The writer of Revelation draws on this imagery to convey hope to a distressed Christian community. See Revelation 21:1–4.

city would be rebuilt and named "Yahweh is there" (48:35). What better hope than that Yahweh's presence could be found in judgment!

Second Isaiah: The Exile's Great Unknown

The optimism injected into exilic theology by Ezekiel reached its crescendo in a prophet whose name is unknown. Because his work appears in later chapters[20] of the Isaiah scroll, he is designated Second or Deutero-Isaiah. This prophet lived several decades after the time of Ezekiel and consequently nearer the actual time of the restoration. He witnessed major changes in eastern politics—namely, the rise of Medo-Persian power—and interpreted what these changes meant to Israel. As a prophet with international vision, Second Isaiah was a crucial voice in formulating Israel's sense of responsibility for the nations.

From Isaiah to Second Isaiah: Prophetic Tradition and Reinterpretation. Although he remains anonymous, there can be no doubt about the tradition in which the unknown prophet of the exile stood. He belonged to the disciples of Isaiah of Jerusalem among whom that great prophet's ideas were preserved and passed on. In fact, he is the climax of the Isaian heritage, for in many ways the disciple surpassed the teacher. Taking the insightful themes of the prophet of Jerusalem, he interpreted the work of his predecessor, blending with it the insight of Amos, Hosea, Jeremiah, and Ezekiel, of whom he was also heir. With unequaled range of vision and passion of faith, he cast the best of their thought into a form expressive of both poet and prophet at their best, using a variety of literary structures. Poetry is commonplace and hymns resembling the psalms appear frequently. There are exhortations (51:1–8), legal argumentation as before a court of law (41:2–9), and a taunt song (chap. 47). The word "sing" appears often. Mastery of style and depth of theological perception give his oracles an exciting lilt and profound meaning. His work is a symphony in words, with theme and countertheme blending into one vibrant and pleasing whole so theologically exhilarating that to read it is to rejoice at the wonder of God.

The work of Second Isaiah is found in chapters 40–55 of the book of Isaiah. To these oracles, which come from the end of the period of the exile (c. 540), were added the oracles in chapters 56–66, which presuppose the return from exile and the restoration of Jerusalem. The latter chapters perhaps include materials from Second Isaiah himself, but they are composed largely of oracles from disciples of the unknown prophet who desired to continue the Isaiah tradition into the postexilic era. Some scholars set chapters 56–66 apart as a distinctive collection coming from Third or Trito-Isaiah because they presup-

[20]See above, p. 366.

pose return to the homeland. Rigid demarcation of units within the book, however, is somewhat arbitrary and may fail to recognize the complicated editorial work on each of these divisions over many years. Certainly Isaiah 1–66 is not simply the fusion of three independent prophetic works. Scholarly opinion on the literary unity of either 40–55 or 56–66 varies widely.[21] But the inclusion of the oracles of Isaiah of Jerusalem and these later materials in a single scroll testifies "that later followers continued to wrestle with the judgments and promises of Isaiah," giving "their minds and energies to the task of seeing that Israel did not lose sight of Yahweh's revelation through Isaiah."[22] From Isaiah of Jerusalem, through Deutero-Isaiah and associates in exile, to disciples of both in postexilic times, the great emphases appear again and again. The unity of the book, therefore, is not that of single authorship, but of prophetic concern to portray Yahweh's continued working through the covenant people.

The collection of prophetic oracles in chapters 40–66, the finest poems in the Hebrew scriptures, do not easily yield themselves to outline. The interplay of several themes ties them together, but no logical progression of thought or development of ideas is evident. Nor can we reconstruct their sequence from the historical situation of the prophet's life: he remains in every respect (except in perceptive theological thought) the great unknown. In a series of "ecstatic shouts" he speaks of the imminence of Yahweh's redemptive activity, the holiness of the incomparable Yahweh, God of the nations, creator and redeemer; and of Israel, sinful, repentant, redeemed, and redeeming. "His thoughts are poured out glowing and fluid, like molten metal before it has hardened into definite shape."[23]

Yahweh, Lord of History.   A pivotal assertion of the prophet-poet was that Yahweh is the one and only God—the sovereign Lord of all nations and events. The incomparable divine power has brought the world into existence and has absolute control over all history. All nations are under Yahweh's domain. The exile was Yahweh's judgment on the people, but Yahweh thereby sacrificed none of the divine dominion. Yahweh would continue acting by redeeming the repentant nation through the instrumentality of the foreign unbeliever, Cyrus of Persia (44:28–45:7).

Second Isaiah as the originator of a theology of world history considered Yahweh a God beyond compare:

> Thus says Yahweh, the King of Israel and
> his Redeemer, Yahweh of hosts;

---

[21]The Isaiah scroll of the Dead Sea Scrolls testifies to the early circulation of these materials as a unit.

[22]Harrelson, *Interpreting*, p. 228.

[23]R. H. Pfeiffer, *Introduction to the Old Testament* (Harper & Row, 1961), p. 465.

I am the first and I am the last;
　　besides me there is no god.
Who is like me? Let them proclaim it,
　　let them declare and set it forth before me.
Who has announced from of old the things to come?
　　Let them tell us what is yet to be.
Do not fear, or be afraid;
　　have I not told you from of old and declare it?
　　And you are my witnesses!
Is there any god besides me?
　　There is no other Rock; I know not one.
[44:6–8]

The exiles' hope for redemption rested on the sure foundation of Yahweh's sovereignty over creation and history (43:1–21). The creative activity of the holy God set the stage for a history of redemption. Surely the God of might, who by a creative word brought the world from the darkness of primordial chaos to radiant order and purpose, is more than able through an instrument of divine choice to rescue the people from exilic chaos to the light of freedom:

Thus says Yahweh,
　　the Holy One of Israel, and its Maker:
Will you question me about my children,
　　or command me concerning the work of my hands?
I made the earth,
　　and created humankind upon it;
it was my hands that stretched out the heavens,
　　and I commanded all their host.
I have aroused Cyrus in righteousness,
　　and I will make all his paths straight;
he shall build my city
　　and set my exiles free,
not for price or reward,
says Yahweh of hosts.
[45:11–13]

The people of God, therefore, would be tragically mistaken to forsake Yahweh for Babylonian deities, profitless and man-made idols that they were (44:9f.). Tragic and pathetic, indeed, was the experience of the one who trusted in Bel or Nebo, gods unable to redeem in time of crisis, becoming burdens to their devotees, so that deity and worshipers entered captivity together. With scornful irony the prophet ridicules the worshiper of idols as one who from the same tree makes bench, fire, and god:

Part of it he takes and warms himself, he kindles a fire and bakes bread. Then he makes a god and worships it, he makes it a carved image and bows down before it. Half of it he burns in the fire; over this half he roasts meat and eats it and is satisfied. He also warms himself and says, "Ah, I am warm, I can feel the fire!"

The rest of it he makes into a god, his idol, bows down to it and worships it; he prays to it and says, "Save me, for you are my god!" [44:15–17]

Second Isaiah, thus, called his people away from the enticements of Babylonian religion to Yahweh, whose activity of redemption was imminent.

> I bring near my deliverance, it is not far off,
>   and my salvation will not tarry;
> I will put salvation in Zion,
>   for Israel my glory.
>
> [46:13]

Proof of this was found in history. For the God who created the world ruled its affairs; nations and human beings were but instruments of the divine purpose. Yahweh ruled the nations, but Yahweh had chosen Judah to be a servant for the world's redemption. Hence if Israel had faith, it had nothing to fear; Israel would be strengthened, helped, and upheld by Yahweh's victorious right hand (41:10). In fact, Yahweh was at that moment shaping events in preparation for Israel's deliverance, choosing as the instrument of divine purpose Cyrus of Persia, who was destined to conquer Babylon and issue a decree permitting the exiles to return to Judah. Those who waited in faith would, therefore, with strength renewed, "mount up with wings like eagles," "run and not be weary," "walk and not faint," led by Yahweh in a new exodus.

A New and Greater Exodus.   Both Ezekiel and Second Isaiah draw on items that have a cherished history in Israel, but pour additional symbolic meaning into them. Exodus and Jerusalem are important images for the prophet, but they speak more of the future than of the past. Ezekiel has done this with Jerusalem, and now Deutero-Isaiah reinterprets the exodus. Yahweh had once led the people from Egyptian bondage across the sea, through the wilderness, to the land of promise, which it then seized in a holy war of conquest. What Yahweh did then, Yahweh was about to do again as redeemer of the chosen people:

> Thus says Yahweh,
>   who makes a way in the sea,
>   a path in the mighty waters, . . .
> "Do not remember the former things,
>   or consider the things of old.
> I am about to do a new thing.
>   now it springs forth, do you not perceive it?
> I will make a way in the wilderness
>   and rivers in the desert. . . .
> to give drink to my chosen people,
>   the people whom I formed for myself
> that they might declare my praise."
>
> [43:16, 18–21]

Yahweh would ransom Israel (43:3), act in judgment on its enemies (41:11–13; 49:25–26), and lead it home to Palestine (40:9–10, 55:12–13), where it would rebuild Jerusalem (49:16–17) and restore the land (44:26; 49:8). Sovereigns would be so subject to *the sovereign* Yahweh that there would be no hardening of rulers' hearts as in the time of Moses. Instead, Cyrus would act in accord with Yahweh's will as an instrument in the hand of the redeeming God:

> who says of Cyrus, "He, is my shepherd,
>> and he shall carry out my purpose";
> and who says of Jerusalem, "It shall be rebuilt,"
>> and of the temple, "Your foundation
>>> shall be laid."
>>>>> [44:28]

The opening oracle of Second Isaiah's work heralds this event in words of consolation unequaled in the Hebrew Bible:

> Comfort, O comfort my people,
>> says your God,
> Speak tenderly to Jerusalem,
>> and cry to her
> that she has served her term,
>> that her penalty is paid,
> that she has received from Yahweh's hand
>> double for all her sins.
>
> A voice cries out:
> "In the wilderness prepare the way of Yahweh,
>> make straight in the desert
>>> a highway for our God.
> Every valley shall be lifted up,
>> and every mountain and hill be made low;
> the uneven ground shall become level,
>> and the rough places a plain.
> Then the glory of Yahweh shall be revealed,
>> and all people shall see it together,
>> for the mouth of Yahweh has spoken."
>>>>> [40:1–5]

Across desert made to flower, on a highway prepared by Yahweh, the holy God would lead Israel home, to be welcomed by those to whom its return has been exultantly announced:

> Get you up to a high mountain,
>> O Zion, herald of good tidings;
> lift up your voice with strength,
>> O Jerusalem, herald of good tidings,
>> lift it up, do not fear;

> say to the cities of Judah,
>> "Here is your God!" . . .
> He will feed his flock like a shepherd,
>> he will gather the lambs in his arms,
> and carry them in his bosom,
>> and gently lead the mother sheep.
>>>> [40:9,11]

Listen to Handel's oratorio, "Messiah" and identify the oracles on which the composer draws. How does the music express the spirit of Second Isaiah?

Redemption Through Suffering: The Servant of Yahweh.   Scattered through the oracles of Second Isaiah are four poems about the "Servant of Yahweh."[24] These "Servant Songs" may have been the core around which the prophet organized other oracles. In them prophetic faith achieved a theological climax in its interpretation of the redemptive role of Yahweh's chosen people:

> Here is my servant, whom I uphold,
>> my chosen, in whom my soul delights;
> I have put my spirit upon him,
>> he will bring forth justice to the nations.
> He will not cry or lift up his voice,
>> or make it heard in the street;
> a bruised reed he will not break,
>> and a dimly burning wick he will not quench;
>> he will faithfully bring forth justice.
> He will not grow faint or be crushed
>> until he has established justice in the earth;
>> and the coastlands wait for his teaching.
>>>> [42:1–4]

In this quiet, unobtrusive way the servant would establish justice and Torah in the power of Yahweh's own spirit. He would be a "light to the nations" (49:6), spreading salvation to the ends of the earth. The world's redemption, however, would be bought with a price and the role of the servant would be hard:

> I gave my back to those who struck me
>> and my cheeks to those who pulled out the beard;

---

[24]Isaiah 42:1–4; 49:1–6; 50:4–9; 52:13–53:12. This delineation represents the majority opinion. However, because the break between the "songs" and their context is not always clear, some scholars are reluctant to define the "servant" sections of chapters 42 and 49 so precisely. Some scholars do not believe that these "servant songs" were written by the same poet who composed the rest of 40–55. There are certain differences of form, style, and content; nevertheless, the intimate relationship of the poems to their context and the great similarity of ideas and formal characteristics between the "songs" and the oracles among which they are placed speak for identity of authorship.

> I did not hide my face
> > from insult and spitting.
>
> > > > > [50:6]

Nevertheless, strengthened by Yahweh, he would see it through to an end of bitter rejection, suffering, and death:

> He was despised and rejected by others;
> > a man of suffering and acquainted with infirmity,
> and as one from whom others hide their faces
> > he was despised, and we held him of no account.
> Surely he has borne our infirmities
> > and carried our diseases;
> yet we accounted him stricken,
> > struck down by God, and afflicted.
> But he was wounded for our transgressions,
> > crushed for our iniquities;
> upon him was the punishment that made us whole,
> > and with his bruises we are healed.
> All we like sheep have gone astray;
> > we have all turned to our own way,
> and Yahweh has laid on him
> > the iniquity of us all.
>
> > > > > [53:3–6]

But the suffering of the servant is victorious, and the work of Yahweh triumphs in one who in humility and lowliness was utterly faithful to the divine purpose.

Despite their clear portrayal of the servant's mission, the songs do not make the identity of their subject clear, raising a question that has been a matter of extensive debate in biblical scholarship.[25] Who is the Servant of Yahweh? At first glance the answer seems to be "Israel personified," and the second song in fact makes that identification (49:3). A closer reading of all the poems, however, indicates that this answer is inadequate. The servant has a mission to Israel (49:6) and does a work that the nation Israel had proven unfit to accomplish. Perhaps, then, the prophet had in mind the redeemed and redeeming remnant of Israel or an individual king or prophet[26] who would represent Yahweh in a redemptive role.

Did the prophet, however, have a precise identification in mind? Probably not. He spoke more of a principle of redemption than of its precise means. He perceptively portrayed the salvation from Yahweh as coming through a servant—nation of Israel, redeemed remnant, individual—who would be like the

---

[25]The substance of this debate is well recorded in two works: Rowley, "The Servant of the Lord in the Light of Three Decades of Criticism," in *The Servant of the Lord*, and C. R. North, *The Suffering Servant in Deutero-Isaiah* (Oxford University, 2d ed., 1956).

[26]Cyrus, Uzziah, Hezekiah, Josiah, and Zerubbabel have been suggested among royal figures; Moses, Isaiah of Jerusalem, Jeremiah, and Second Isaiah himself are among prophetic figures.

one here described. The thought of the prophet appears to be fluid, moving from Israel, Yahweh's chosen covenant people who failed to be faithful, to the remnant purged and made holy by Yahweh. In this personification the prophet expresses a radically new vision of what it means to be the people of covenant— dedication, to the point of suffering, to fulfilling the redemptive purpose for which Yahweh had chosen the nation. This suffering servant could fulfill the destiny of Israel.

> Early Christians used the idea of the suffering servant to interpret Jesus. Can you demonstrate how the concept influenced the gospel materials?

Whoever the prophet had in mind in portraying the suffering servant, the idea itself was significant for Israel's understanding of exile. The trauma meant neither the end of covenant, nor forfeiture of Israel's mission. In the past, David had brought glory to a nation and fulfillment of Yahweh's promise. The same God who had been faithful in the past would continue to be involved in Israel's history, working through those who suffer to achieve the divine purpose. Centuries later, Christianity as an early sectarian group in Judaism, appropriated the idea to interpret "one like unto the son of David" destined to bring God's kingdom near.

In the two prophets Ezekiel and Deutero-Isaiah, then, we see the major expansion of Israel's faith that occurred during and after the exile. The old narrow provincialism that had been expressed in reverence for the Jerusalem sanctuary gave way to a broader and more sublime interpretation of Yahweh's concern for all people. The restricted horizons of Israel's earlier theology were pushed back to include Yahweh's dominion over other nations and a renewed sense of Israel's responsibility beyond its borders. During the centuries that lay ahead, Jewish religion would sometimes violate these ideals. Leaders, political and religious, would often encourage a narrow nationalism that went contrary to the prophetic dream for the nation. But with the exilic prophets the appreciation of Israel's universal destiny was given clear expression. Henceforth, it began to become in fact "a light to the nations."

SUGGESTIONS FOR FURTHER STUDY

For background information on the period, see Georges Contenau, *Everyday Life in Babylon and Assyria* (Edward Arnold, 1954), and Peter Ackroyd, *Exile and Restoration: A Study in Hebrew Thought of the Sixth Century B.C.* (S. C. M., 1968). Relevant sections from listed Histories in the General Bibliography will also be informative. Also in the General Bibliography are additional sources listed under Exile.

Consult the basic commentaries for help with the books of Lamentations,

Obadiah, Ezekiel, and Second Isaiah. Second Isaiah will be treated in volumes on Isaiah. See also the bibliography on Isaiah on page 379 and Claus Westermann, *Isaiah 40–66: A Commentary* (Trans. David Stalker, S. C. M., 1985). On Lamentations, Westermann also has a volume, *Lamentations: Issues and Interpretation* (Fortress, 1993). Give special attention to Walter Brueggemann, "Unity and Dynamic in the Isaiah Tradition," *Journal for the Study of the Old Testament*, 29 (1984) 89–107. For additional help with the book of Ezekiel, see Ralph W. Klein, *Ezekiel: The Prophet and His Message* (South Carolina, 1988), and Walther Zimmerli, *Ezekiel: A Commentary on the Book of the Prophet Ezekiel* (Hermeneia series, 2 vols., Fortress, 1979, 1983). Walter Brueggemann, *Hopeful Imagination: Prophetic Voices in Exile* (Fortress, 1986), treats Jeremiah, Ezekiel, and Second Isaiah.

See the General Bibliography for selected sources on Messiah and Messianism. The volume edited by James Charlesworth, *The Messiah: Developments in Earliest Judaism and Christianity* (Augsburg, 1992), and the one by George A. Riggan, *Messianic Theology and Christian Faith* (Westminster, 1967), tie together Hebrew and Christian ideas.

Consult the Bible dictionaries for further information on Palestinean Aramaic, suffering servant, allegory, and son of man.

14

Covenant Community Restored

RETURN AND RESTORATION
(HAGGAI; ZECHARIAH 1–6; EZRA 1–10; NEHEMIAH 1–13; MALACHI)

The Edict of Cyrus

Judah's years in exile coincided with the last days of the Babylonian empire. During the period, mastery over the east shifted to Persian hands. The supremacy of Babylon was primarily the work of Nebuchadnezzar, and during his reign the empire was able to dominate Near Eastern politics. The major threat to Babylonian dominance came from Media, who had been an ally in overpowering Assyria. During the long reign of Nebuchadnezzar, Media became a major power in the north, extending its control into the regions of Asia Minor. Nebuchadnezzar sought to maintain the balance of power by securing his hold on the Fertile Crescent. Probably the third deportation of the Jews, in 582 B.C.E., was a part of this effort.

Decline of Babylon. As long as Nebuchadnezzar lived, the Babylonian empire was held intact. With his death in 562 B.C.E., however, internal instability and intrigue rocked Babylon. Several weak kings followed and imperial power waned rapidly. While Babylon was declining, the forces of the east were being unified under Cyrus, the Persian. Revolting against Media, Cyrus seized its capital, blitzkrieged the empire, and was soon the ruler of the north.

Nabonidus (556–539), now Babylonian king, originally had supported Cyrus, hoping thereby to hold in check the Median threat. Following the successful revolution, however, Cyrus was feared more than Media had been. As a safeguard Nabonidus entered a defensive alliance with Egypt and Lydia. Cyrus, in turn, marched against the alliance and, after overrunning Lydia, stood on the borders of Babylonia. In these circumstances, Deutero-Isaiah

Figure 14.1. The Cylinder of Cyrus recording his capture of Babylon in 539. The inscription states his lenient policy, permitting captives to return to their native land where they would have freedom of worship. (Copyright, British Museum)

could see the hand of Yahweh moving to redeem Israel, now used to refer to the restored community.

Edict of Cyrus. Preoccupation with eastern opponents delayed Cyrus's invasion of Babylon for several years, but, when he did march against it, he captured the city with remarkable ease. Babylonian records state that the capital fell without battle, and the Cylinder of Cyrus reports that the "entire population . . . bowed to him [Cyrus] and kissed his feet. They were glad that he was king. Their faces lighted up. The master by whose aid the mortally sick had been made alive, all had been preserved from ruin. . . . [For this] they praised him and honored his name."[1] Obviously the Persian records overstate the popularity of Cyrus's reception, but they probably are not without some basis in fact. Nabonidus had fallen into disfavor with his subjects because he displaced Marduk, the chief Babylonian deity, in favor of other gods. Consequently, the city had little heart for defending his cause. A decisive battle turned in Cyrus's favor, and in October of 539 Babylon fell with little resistance.

The fall of "proud Babylon" set in motion Israel's deliverance. The Cyrus Cylinder announces an act of the Persian king's generosity toward captive peoples, allowing them not only to return to their homeland, but also to restore their religious sanctuaries. This edict of 538 does not mention the liberation of the Jews specifically, but Ezra 1:2–4 applies the policy directly to the covenant community:[2]

[1]From Cyrus Cylinder, as translated in Thomas, *Documents*, pp. 92–93.

[2]The attitude of Cyrus accounts for Deutero-Isaiah's high estimate of him as Yahweh's anointed deliverer. See Isaiah 44:24–45:13. The Chronicler also notes the edict in 2 Chronicles 36:22–23 and Ezra 6:3.

Thus says Cyrus king of Persia: Yahweh, the God of Heaven, has given me all the kingdoms of the earth, and he has charged me to build him a house at Jerusalem, in Judah. Any of those among you who are his people—their God be with them—are now permitted to go up to Jerusalem in Judah, and rebuild the house of Yahweh, the God of Israel—he is the God who is in Jerusalem; and let all survivors, in whatever place they reside, be assisted by the people of their place with silver and gold, with goods and with animals, besides freewill offerings for the house of God which is in Jerusalem.

This order of Cyrus marked the conclusion of exile and the beginning of the slow and sometimes tedious process of restoration.

The Chronicler of the Return and Restoration

For information about this important period of Israel's history, we are dependent on *The Chronicler*, a fourth century B.C.E. theologian who used historical materials to advance important theological themes. His work is found in the books of 1 and 2 Chronicles and Ezra and Nehemiah. His identity is otherwise unknown.[3] His work covers the whole of Israel's history down to his own time. In 1 and 2 Chronicles, he chose and arranged materials from Samuel–Kings, court records, temple records, genealogical lists, and other official documents to emphasize that Yahweh had directed Israel's past successes, the greatest of which was the establishment of the temple in Jerusalem. The worship of Yahweh and the study of Torah in this sacred center had shaped Israel into the community that Yahweh intended them to be. Throughout Chronicles the story of the northern kingdom is omitted and emphasis is given to those who contributed directly to the development of the worship system in Jerusalem. His chief hero is David, not as a slayer of giants or warrior king, but as a patron of Israel's cult. This concentration on Israel's worship distinguishes the Chronicler's work from all other traditions in Hebrew scripture. David's age is seen as the ideal for the restored nation in the future. Yahweh's covenant with David is referred to again and again. Here the Chronicler doubtless reflects the longing of his age for the restoration of the Davidic monarchy. But the Chronicler also has other concerns. Throughout he interprets history according to the doctrine of retribution. Events are presented to explain misfortunes as punishment for sins, particularly abuse of priests or prophets. In addition, the Chronicler notably emphasizes Yahweh's control of history through miraculous intervention.

In Ezra and Nehemiah, the Chronicler emphasized that the past community lived on in the exiles who returned from Babylon to Judah. He chose and arranged materials from sources like those used in Chronicles with special

---

[3]The ancient Jewish and Christian view that Ezra was the Chronicler is accepted only by the most conservative contemporary scholars.

emphasis on two narrative collections, the Ezra Memoirs (Ezra 7–10 and Nehemiah 8–10) and the Nehemiah Memoirs (Nehemiah 1–7; 12:27–43; 13:4–31), to demonstrate continuity between Israel's past successes and the achievements of the leaders of the restoration, namely, the return from Babylon as a new exodus; the rebuilding of the altar and the temple; the restoration of the worship of Yahweh there; the rebuilding of the walls of Jerusalem; and most important, the acceptance of Torah as a basis for a restored covenant relationship with Yahweh.

The Chronicler and the heroes of his narrative, the leaders and the common people who made the restoration possible, shared three important concepts:

1. Moral and ritual purity separated the covenant people from the rest of humanity. Any active impurity was understood as a threat to Israel's existence and even the existence of the world.
2. Jerusalem was the sacred center in which God's purposes of creation and redemption could be realized. It was the center of the earth, the highest mountain from which flowed rivers of life-giving water, the heavenly city come to earth, and the abode of God (Ezekiel 38:12; Zechariah 14:8–10; Ezekiel 47; Psalm 48:1–3; Ezekiel 40:1–4; Psalm 132:13–14). Its walls separated this holy place from the profane threatening world (Ezekiel 42:20). Even in the exilic chaos of foreign culture and power, Israel's roots still reached deep into the sacred ground of Jerusalem's sanctuary. Jerusalem was the source of salvation, justice, and law, the historical realities by which Yahweh's sacred presence made the world holy and secure.
3. Not only Jerusalem, but all of Palestine was a holy place filled with history that had profound meaning, which shaped the character of its people and their place in history. It was the place to which the Messiah would come (Haggai 2:23; Zechariah 6:9–14) to shape it into an Eden-like paradise.

For postexilic Israelite leaders, the return to Palestine and the restoration of worship in Jerusalem were essential if Israel was to have any future. Therefore, all measures necessary to assure purity of life in the restored Jerusalem were justifiable.

An outline of the Chronicler's work illustrates its theological and historical scope.

A. Judah's prehistory from Adam to Saul: 1 Chronicles 1–9
B. David: 1 Chronicles 10–29
C. Solomon: 2 Chronicles 1–9
D. From the revolt of 922 to the edict of Cyrus: 2 Chronicles 10–36
E. Restoration of the community of faith and worship in Jerusalem: Ezra 1–2
F. Rebuilding the Temple: Ezra 3–6
G. Preparing Jerusalem and the covenant community for the future: Ezra 7–10 and Nehemiah 1–13

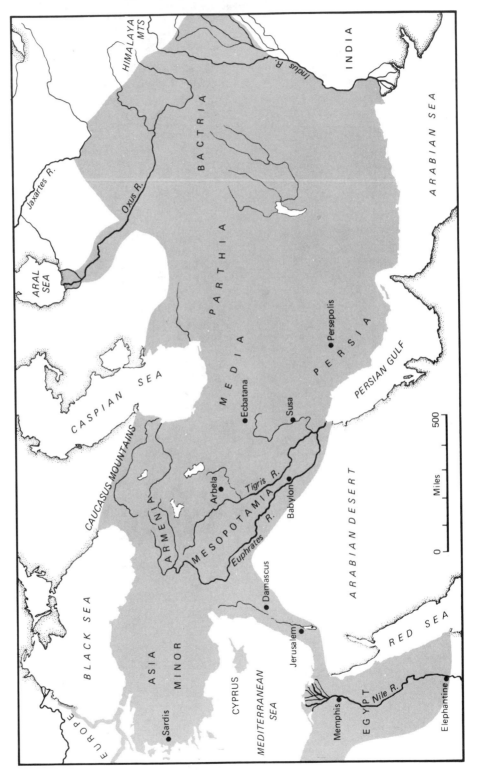

Figure 14.2. The Persian empire, c. 500 B.C.E.

Phase One: Restoration of the Community of Faith and Worship

The list of families who first returned to Jerusalem (Ezra 2:1–70) represents the restoration of the community of faith. It includes priests, Levites, other temple personnel, extended family groups, servants, horses, mules, camels, and donkeys. This is to say that the restoration could only be realized through cooperation of persons from all stations of life. Early Jewish readers would have taken pride that their family names were included in this list as among those willing to participate in such an enterprise. Since many Israelite names have theological meaning, often brief descriptions of God's activity, the early readers would have been sensitive to meanings of names like: Jeshua (Yahweh delivers), Shephatiah (Yahweh judges), Adonikam (the Lord has risen up), and so forth.

The first task was the restoration of the altar essential for the beginning of worship. Priests and lay people cooperated in laying natural unworked stones as required in the law of Moses (Exodus 20:25) on the site of the preexilic altar chosen by David, thus establishing continuity with the early worship of the preexilic community. When the altar was complete, the whole of preexilic worship was renewed: ongoing daily worship and prescribed worship on feast days for the entire community and for individuals the opportunity to make freewill offerings. Their first observance of the Feast of Booths, which was a time of rejoicing over God's gifts of the fruits of the land, must have been especially moving. They had returned from exile to eat again the produce of the holy land.

The altar was restored and worship begun in 538 B.C.E., but no work was done on the temple beyond the foundation until 520 B.C.E. The land to which the first returnees came offered little promise. A half-century earlier the army of Nebuchadnezzar had left Judah in ashes. In both the Shephelah and central hill country, practically every important town had been destroyed.[4] Also border regions in the Negeb, which had escaped the sword of Nebuchadnezzar, had become the possession of tribal groups who had moved in from the desert. With the nation's leadership in exile, little progress had been made during the interval in rebuilding the economy of Judah.

Further, the Jews who had remained in Palestine through the exilic period did not welcome returning captives as long-lost brothers. Through the years they had arduously eked out a living, and this immigrant group would have been a further threat to their economy. The fact that these returnees considered themselves the "true Israel" and looked with scorn on the "unclean" occupants of the land (Haggai 2:14) could only have intensified antagonism and distrust between the two groups.

Against the harsh reality of circumstances as they found them in Palestine, the sharp religious enthusiasm of the returnees was soon blunted. On the jour-

---

[4]See Wright, *Archaeology*, pp. 175–76.

Powers of Influence on Judah	Judah
Babylonia	
Nebuchadnezzar 605–562	587–538 Judah in exile in Babylonia
Amel-marduk 562–560	
Neriglissar 560–556	
Nabonidus 556–539	
(539—Fall of Babylon to Persia)	
Persia	
Cyrus 539–530	538—Edict of Cyrus permitting the
Cambyses 530–522	return of captives to Jerusalem
Darius I 522–486	520–516 Rebuilding of Jerusalem temple
Xerxes I 486–465	
Artaxerxes I 465–424	458—Mission of Ezra
	445– Nehemiah became
	governor of Judah
Xerxes II 423	
Darius II 423–404	
Artaxerxes II 404–358	
Artaxerxes III 358–338	
Arses 338–336	
Darius III 336–331	
(333—Battle of Issus; Persia fell to Greece	

The exilic and postexilic periods, 587–333 B.C.E.

Figure 14.3. The exilic and postexilic periods, 587–333 B.C.E.

ney back they may have cherished the dream of Deutero-Isaiah about a new exodus, but when faced with a desolate and harsh Palestine, the flowering hope of the desert began rapidly to wither and fade. Although almost no detailed information about the first two decades of the restoration is available, the words of Haggai looking back at the period must describe the situation accurately: "You have sown much, and harvested little; you eat, but you never have enough; you drink, but you never have your fill; you clothe yourselves, but no one is warm; and you that earn wages earn wages to put them into a bag with holes" [1:6].

Before the harsh economic reality of resettlement, the religious ideal of rebuilding the temple faced great obstacles. Those finding it almost impossible to build their own houses could generate little zeal for building the house of Yahweh. Opposition from the Samaritans served only to dishearten them the more. Also, when they began to compare what they were attempting to do with the magnificence of Solomon's temple, discouragement produced the conclusion that their ambition was futile. Small wonder that construction, hardly begun, was abandoned! In 520, eighteen years after reconstruction had been launched, the temple still had not been raised above the foundations. It appeared that the grand vision of a restored and triumphant Israel, with Yahweh reigning in Zion, would never be realized. The first stage of return thus turned out to be an ineffective attempt at restoration, frustrated by economic pressure and a lack of cooperation between returning exiles and the Judeans who had remained in Palestine.[5]

Phase Two: Rebuilding the Temple

A second phase in Israel's restoration focuses on Zerubbabel, Haggai, and Zechariah. Details are missing, but the general pattern of events is clear. At some time between 538 and 520 B.C.E. (probably nearer 538), Zerubbabel, a nephew of Sheshbazzar, arrived in Palestine as a Persian appointee to succeed Sheshbazzar as governor. The appointment undoubtedly had political overtones for the Persians. A stronger government in Palestine might serve as a defense against Egypt. However, the biblical materials are more interested in Zerubbabel as a religious leader. With him came another and perhaps larger contingent of Jews than the group that had come with Sheshbazzar.

During the early days of Zerubbabel's governorship, the power of Persia was unabated. Cyrus and his successor Cambyses (530–522) held the empire intact, and Judah remained a tiny and insignificant province with a population of barely twenty thousand[6] in a gargantuan and well-ordered empire. Compared with Persia, Israel seemed powerless and inconsequential. The "light to the nations" flickered as a candle on the verge of being extinguished. With hope for a messianic era teetering on the edge of despair, Israel needed more than the foundation of a temple around which to rally covenant faith.

At a time when Jews were too dispirited to return to temple building, encouraging events began to occur. Revolt rocked the Persian empire in 522. Media, Egypt, Armenia, Babylon, and Asia Minor were all in turmoil. For fully two years, the future of the Persian empire hung in the balance. During these troubled days for Persia, two prophets stirred Jewish hope and fanned the desire to complete the rebuilding of the temple. These prophets, Haggai and Zechariah, may have led an additional group of returnees.[7] Their preaching began around 520; both saw the rebellion against Darius as an opportunity for Judah. Their immediate purpose was to spur the lethargic religious spirit of the people to rebuild the temple and fully restore worship in Jerusalem.

The hopes of the exilic prophets had been grand and their poetic description of these hopes exceptional, but by 520 their hopes were still unrealized. No one in early postexilic Jerusalem imagined that the day of Yahweh's glory had dawned, that national life could be easily restored, or that a new covenant could face the future assured of Yahweh's presence. But Haggai and Zechariah did look to the future, speaking concretely and directly of the need to rebuild a

---

[5]James Smart, *History and Theology in Second Isaiah* (Westminster, 1965) pp. 281ff., interprets Isaiah 66 against this background.

[6]See Albright, *Period*, pp. 62–63.

[7]See Ackroyd, *Exile*, pp. 148–49.

sanctuary if the hopes of their more impressive predecessors were to be realized.

No one should say that Haggai and Zechariah were poorer prophets than the others, even though their themes were not as grand as those of the great prophets. They received a call like the others and were spokesmen for Yahweh to their contemporaries. The only proper criteria by which prophets should be judged are whether they were true ministers to their day and whether they succeeded or failed in their task. Both Haggai and Zechariah score well on these points.

Haggai.   Haggai is another of those prophets about whom personal details are lacking. He is mentioned only in the books of Haggai and Ezra and efforts to identify or characterize him move almost entirely on conjecture. The book that carries his name contains four oracles, all dated to the second year of Darius I (520). These oracles were given on four worship occasions at the time of the feast of tabernacles. Each oracle is introduced with a chronological reference and the prophetic formula, "the word of Yahweh came by Haggai the prophet":

A. Judgmental call to rebuild the temple and response from Zerubbabel and the people: 1:1–15a
B. Promise of the second temple's greatness: 1:15b–2:9
C. Torah on what is clean and unclean: 2:10–19
D. Eschatological hope and promise to Zerubbabel: 2:20–23

These oracles were compiled and edited by one of the prophet's friends or disciples who added the contextual elements that place the oracles in their historical setting. The short collection can hardly represent all that Haggai said on any of the four occasions he is reported to have spoken. They rather represent the disciple-collector's choice of oracles that most profoundly influenced the reconstruction of the temple. The book of Haggai, therefore, is a short history of the success of the prophet's preaching.

The central concern of Haggai is the cultic problem posed by worship in a ruined sanctuary. For the prophet this indicated lack of any proper sense of orientation and meaning. Absence of an adequate cultic center was evidence that the Jerusalemites were unaware of commitment to any reality large enough to hold them together. And, being uncommitted, they were unable to perceive what life was all about. Therefore, they were lost in the present and were threatened with no future.

Haggai approached the problem by encouraging the reconstruction of the ruined sanctuary. Persons cannot live without a center in which they find life full of meaning and reality—where the powers that create and sustain them can be encountered in their beneficial fullness. Therefore, the prophet promised the Jerusalemites and their leaders, Zerubbabel and the high priest Joshua, the blessings of Yahweh's presence in the new temple. This would be the temple's glory and the community's hope. National, religious, and cultic identity depended on the reestablishment of the cultic center. Jews could not know who they were apart from meaningful relationships with both God and covenant, to be accepted and proclaimed in the Jerusalem sanctuary. Haggai's concern went far beyond a building campaign. His interest was in an orientation that found meaning in the past and the present, and hope for the future, in the presence of God.

Haggai further anticipated that Yahweh's presence in the new sanctuary would have astonishing eschatological consequences. Cosmic upheavals would precede the elevation of Zion, treasures of the nations would come to Jerusalem, and Zerubbabel would be Yahweh's messiah. Although the prophet was overenthusiastic in his expectations for the temple, his preaching encouraged the Jews to get on with the rebuilding task. Further, his appreciation of divine presence and the need to symbolize that presence with sacred place were appropriate for any religious community.

Zechariah. The preaching of Zechariah overlapped and continued beyond the work of Haggai. More than likely this prophet was of priestly descent, but we have no information about the man himself. The book of Zechariah contains fourteen chapters, but it is almost universally accepted that only chapters 1–8 come from the sixth-century prophet. These chapters share Haggai's zeal for rebuilding the temple and the coming of the messianic age. Chapters 9–14 come from a later historical setting and are radically different in style. Chapters 1–8 show the following outline:

A. A plea for the people's repentance: 1:1–6
B. A series of eight dream visions: 1:7–6:8
C. The symbolic crowning of Joshua to depict the days of Zerubbabel ahead: 6:9–15[8]
D. Prophecies on restoration: 7:1–8:23

The major part of Zechariah's oracles utilize the dream vision with dialogue between God, prophet, and interpreting angel. Here, then, the form and imagery of Jewish apocalyptic are given major development. Apocalyptic uses symbols, fantastic descriptions, and cryptic language in distinctive ways.[9] Zechariah used apocalyptic visions to develop two major themes. Like Haggai he was concerned about the rebuilding of the temple, which for him meant the reestablishment of Yahweh's rule: "Thus says Yahweh, I have returned to Jerusalem with compassion; my house shall be built in it, says Yahweh of

---

[8]Most scholars agree that Zechariah 6:9–15 originally concerned Zerubbabel, not Joshua.
[9]For a fuller discussion, see the materials on Daniel in Chap. 15 below.

hosts. . . . My cities shall again overflow with prosperity; Yahweh will again comfort Zion and again choose Jerusalem" (1:16–17).

The prophet saw Yahweh moving to establish a triumphant rule in Zion. Because the temple was the focus of Yahweh's reign, the Jerusalemites were to get on with its construction.

Yahweh's presence in the restored sanctuary would also inaugurate a new age over which Zerubbabel would rule as Yahweh's anointed. As a descendant of David, he would be the "messiah" or "branch" through whom nationalistic hopes would be fulfilled. Alongside Zerubbabel, Joshua would serve as high priest, also as Yahweh's "messiah." The climax of Zechariah is reached in the assertion that the new age of salvation is meant for the whole world:

> Thus says Yahweh of hosts: Peoples shall come, the inhabitants of many cities; the inhabitants of one city shall go to another, saying, "Come, let us go to entreat the favor of Yahweh, and to seek Yahweh of hosts; I myself am going." Many peoples and strong nations shall come to seek Yahweh of hosts in Jerusalem, and to entreat the favor of Yahweh. Thus says Yahweh of hosts: In those days ten men from the nations of every language shall take hold of a Jew, saying, "Let us go with you, for we have heard that God is with you" [8:20–23].

Notice the contrast in how Haggai and Zechariah treat the "covenant with David" in comparison to Ezekiel and Deutero-Isaiah. The exilic prophets saw the temple and Davidic traditions more as symbols of Yahweh's future action, metaphors for an ideal age of divine rule. Haggai and Zechariah, however, focused on the immediate historical reconstruction of the temple that would bring in the messianic age. Stirred by their preaching Israelites returned to work on the temple. With messianic hope resurrected and centered in Zerubbabel, they began to prepare for the new day. Late in 520 they returned to the temple foundations, and by 516 the second temple had been completed.

Joel. Sometime after the restoration of the temple and before the Hellenic mark of Alexander had been stamped on the east, Joel made one of the infrequent breaks in postexilic prophetic silence. The book cannot be precisely dated, but it resembles both prophetic and apocalyptic writings. It is in three parts:

A. Locust plague and drought as signs of the imminent Day of Yahweh: 1:1–2:27
B. The outpouring of Yahweh's spirit upon Israel: 2:28–32
C. The eschatological Day of Yahweh: chapter 3

The first part of the work preserves themes akin to his predecessors. An ominous devastation of the area about his hometown Jerusalem by hordes of locusts is reminiscent of one of the visions of Amos's call to prophesy. Joel visualized the destroyers as Yahweh's agents punishing priests and people for their sins. He summoned the residents of the land to penitence in anticipation of God's merciful forgiveness:

> Yet even now, says Yahweh,
>> return to me with all your heart,
> with fasting, with weeping, and with mourning;
>> rend your hearts and not your clothing.
> Return to Yahweh, your God,
>> for he is gracious and merciful,
> slow to anger, and abounding in steadfast love,
>> and relents from punishing.
>
> [2:12–13]

This present disaster, though, presages a future Day of Yahweh, which will inaugurate better things. Beyond an awful judgment would come an age of divine bliss and bounty. This apocalyptic portion of Joel opens with a rapturous announcement from Yahweh:

> . . . I will pour out my spirit on all flesh;
> your sons and your daughters shall prophesy,
> your old men shall dream dreams,
> and your young men shall see visions.
>
> [2:28b]

But the Day of Yahweh will be a "great and terrible day, a time of judgment on all nations and the ultimate restoration of Jerusalem to glory." This dual emphasis portrays Yahweh's vindication of "Zion, my holy mountain," against its enemies and Yahweh's protection of the people:

> And Yahweh roars from Zion,
>> and utters his voice from Jerusalem,
>> and the heavens and the earth shake.
> But Yahweh is a refuge for his people,
>> a stronghold for the people of Israel.
>
> [3:16]

Phase Three: Preparing Jerusalem and the Covenant Community for the Future

The third, and perhaps most crucial phase of Israel's restoration came almost a century after the edict of Cyrus. The two most significant leaders in this restoration were Ezra and Nehemiah, who lived and worked during the last half of the fifth century B.C.E. They attempted to restate and reaffirm Israel's faith to the restored community in such a way that traditional covenant concepts were conserved and made relevant in forms suitable for a new age.

The interval between the completion of the Zerubbabel temple, 516 B.C.E., and the work of Nehemiah and Ezra is obscure. Isolated and meager sources provide what little information is available. The prophet Malachi gives a glimpse of life during the times, and the Chronicler in the books of Ezra and Nehemiah provides insight into religious and political conditions in Palestine. Largely, however, we must move with caution in describing the history of Israel prior to the mid-fifth century.

During the last part of the sixth and the first half of the fifth centuries, Palestine remained firmly under Persian control. It was part of one of the twenty provinces (satrapies) ruled by a governor (satrap). For three decades around the turn of the century, the strong and able hand of Darius I Hystaspis (522–486) guided the fortunes of Persia, and under his leadership the empire reached its zenith. Building flourished. A network of roads was cut across the whole empire. A standardized system of coinage was instituted. All of this meant an energetic economy. At the death of Darius in 486 B.C.E., however, Persia began to fare poorly. It encountered problems with the rising power of Greece. It became more and more evident that Persian power and prestige were on the decline.

In Palestine during this period the impact of world affairs was felt very little. The revived messianic hope that encouraged the temple's reconstruction was short-lived. Following its dedication, hope soon faded into disillusion. Optimism generated by the preaching of Haggai and Zechariah had centered in Zerubbabel, who was supposed to restore the Davidic dynasty. Suddenly, and quite mysteriously, Zerubbabel disappeared. Suspicions concerning his disappearance logically centered on the Persian king. To be sure, Darius could support the temple's restoration, but could he tolerate a petty prince of Judah about whom royal claims were made? With the passing of Zerubbabel, natural or unnatural, the high hopes of a restored nation faded. Leadership fell to a high priest named Joshua (Haggai 1:1) and his successors.

Life in Palestine through the first half of the fifth century continued to be confused and unpredictable. Although they possessed a temple, Jews in Palestine were an impoverished people, confined to an area not much more than twenty miles square, still struggling for existence—let alone significance. They enjoyed religious liberty, but remained politically dependent on Persia. Compatible relationships between the returned exiles and the resident Jews must have developed, but animosities against non-Jewish groups became more intense.

Religiously, these decades were years of complaint and skepticism. Discouraged Jews made little progress in reviving the Davidic state. They were content with the confederal union of groups bound loosely by social and national ties. Around Jerusalem they grubbed out a living relatively unconcerned about international movements. This low level of organizational and political concern fostered a casual attitude on the part of many. Neighboring peoples were permitted to move in with freedom. Marriages between Jews and non-Jews became more common and more acceptable. Many lost their enthusiasm for the pure faith and thereby became susceptible to foreign worship. Laxity in the payment of tithes forced Levites to abandon their sacerdotal duties to earn a living. Many worked their fields and crafts on the Sabbath. Some became slaves because of their debts. Social immorality prevailed. In short, the community of faith became thoroughly demoralized. The rebuilt temple did not, as some had hoped, reestablish Yahweh to the central place in the life of the people.

Malachi.   The low ebb of the spiritual life of the nation is addressed in the book of Malachi. The identity of the author is unknown. The present title comes from the word translated "my messenger," which appears in 3:1: "Behold, I send my messenger to prepare the way before me."

Whoever Malachi may have been, he stood in the tradition of the great prophets of Israel, denouncing the sin of both priest and people. However, in style of prophecy, he shows himself to be a precursor of later Judaism. The prophet drives home his message through the use of the dialectical question and answer: "You say, 'How have we despised your name?' By offering polluted food on my altar. And you say, 'How have we polluted it?' By thinking that Yahweh's table may be despised" (1:6b–7).

This method is more that of the scribe or of the law courts than that of the prophet. Instruction by disputation replaces the fiery oracles of earlier prophets. Reading the book, one senses that prophetic proclamation is being replaced by the scholastic procedures of later Jewish rabbis.

An outline of Malachi reveals how Judah's perversion of covenant relationship with Yahweh dominates the book:

A. Superscription: 1:1
B. Yahweh favors Israel, not Edom: 1:2–5
C. Priests corrupt worship and mislead the people: 1:6–2:9
D. Jerusalemites are idolatrous and degrade marriage: 2:10–16
E. They question the justice of Yahweh: 2:17–3:5
F. They are robbing Yahweh by not giving their tithes: 3:6–12
G. Yahweh's judgment is sure: 3:13–4:3
H. Subscription. 4:4–6

The message of Malachi includes some exalted themes. He suggests that all true worship, even that of the heathen, is offered to Yahweh (1:11); he denounces inhumane divorce as something that Yahweh hates (2:16); and he alludes to the fellowship of all persons (2:10). But the preaching of the prophet is mostly concerned with a form of organized religion to which adherents give only half-hearted devotion. He says little about social injustice. Social morality had degenerated (3:5), but Malachi is more concerned that tithes were withheld and imperfect animals offered in sacrifice (1:7–14; 3:8–10). If proper offerings were brought to the temple, Yahweh would bless the Jews and they would be great among the nations (3:10–12): "They shall be mine, says Yahweh of hosts. . . . For you who revere my name, the sun of righteousness shall rise, with healing in its wings" (3:17; 4:2).

The religion of this period certainly reflects the disappointment of the Jews over the failure of their messianic dreams. The longed-for Davidic state seemed a remote possibility, and although the temple had been restored, the glory of Solomon had not returned. The returnees had resettled the land, but the splendor of an anointed age was not apparent. The time for a new—and different— step in Jewish religious development was at hand. Into the opportune situation stepped Ezra and Nehemiah, who began to give Judaism a direction for centuries to come.

Both Ezra and Nehemiah were granted special commissions from Persian rulers to lead returns to Jerusalem and to carry out certain reforms in the restored community. Ezra's group returned in the seventh year of Artaxerxes I (458 B.C.E.).Nehemiah returned in the twentieth year of Artaxerxes I (445–444 B.C.E.). This is assuming that the chronological order given by the Chronicler can be defended against repeated arguments that Nehemiah must have returned before Ezra—Nehemiah returning during the reign of Artaxerxes I, Ezra during the reign of Artaxerxes II. Many have claimed that this order makes better sense in light of the fact that Ezra's work seems to presuppose the prior work of Nehemiah. Related to this question of date are questions about the extent to which the two men worked together and the relationship between their reform efforts.

The Chronicler associates them with one another only in a covenant renewal ceremony (Nehemiah 8:9) and in the ceremony celebrating the completion of the city wall (Nehemiah 12:33 and 36).

Ezra's Reform

Ezra was a priest who grew up and performed his early work among the Babylonian exiles. He was of that group of exiles who never lost their sympathies with the homeland and followed closely developments in Jerusalem. He became intensely concerned about reports of moral laxity among those who were privileged to be in Palestine. Distressed, he sought and received the authority of Artaxerxes I to head an expedition to Palestine for the purpose of regenerating the religious life of the people. Artaxerxes himself sent offerings to the temple and authorized Ezra to appoint magistrates and judges to punish those who refused to comply with the teachings of "the law of the God of heaven" (Ezra 7:11–26). In 458 B.C.E. Ezra and his colleagues arrived in Palestine and set to the task of implementing cultic and moral reforms.

Ezra's commission was to reform Jewish religious and social life "according to the law of your God which is in your hand" (Ezra 7:14). What does the phrase "which is in your hand" mean? Did Ezra carry a copy of the entire

Pentateuch from Babylon to be made available for the first time to the Jews who earlier had returned to Jerusalem? Surely the Pentateuch was already known to the Jews in Jerusalem since much of their activity assumed knowledge of it. Probably the phrase means that part of the law on which Ezra was an authority—the cultic laws, proper observance of which maintained society.

Ezra's reform focused on two matters, the problem of mixed marriages and the necessity for covenant renewal.

The Problem of Mixed Marriages (Ezra 9:1–10:44). Ezra learned soon after his arrival in Jerusalem that a number of men, including some priests and Levites, had married foreign women. By doing so they had violated the Laws of Holiness, which forbade the mixing of unlike things (Leviticus 19:19). Since some of them were priests and Levites, who were primarily responsible for ritual purity, they endangered the purity of the cultus and the community. Ritual purity was essential for the preservation of their world as a world of order. As Ezra saw it, this was not just a matter of racial purity, but a threat to the very existence of the community as the holy people of God. In a public act of mourning designed to attract attention, Ezra confessed to God all of Israel's past sins and denounced the present evil (mixed marriages) as a denial of God's love and of the responsibilities God had assigned to the returned exiles. He implied that the returned exiles could expect severe judgment for violating their very reason for being in Jerusalem. The people, impressed with this behavior so similar to the symbolic actions of earlier prophets, feared that his pronouncement would surely bring judgment on them and they grieved. Shecaniah, using language that implied that the marriages were not legitimate, confessed that such marriages were acts of faithlessness and suggested that all wives and children of the mixed marriages be sent away. Ezra persuaded the people to agree to Shecaniah's suggestion. This was done without any regard for prescribed rules for divorce (Deuteronomy 24:1–2; Jeremiah 3:8). This seems to have been a drastic and harsh solution to the problem, insensitive to the needs of the women and children who were expelled apparently without any measures being taken to provide for them. This harsh action raises questions in the mind of the modern reader. Where would they go? How could they live? Considering the tentative nature of the restored community and the difficulties and threats they faced, the purity of the community of faith had to be protected, but was it necessary to do this in such an extreme manner?

Covenant Renewal (Nehemiah 7:73b–9:37). The climax of Ezra's work was a day of national mourning and confession, a solemn ceremony of covenant renewal. In this ceremony, Ezra gives new place and meaning to the Law. The Law was not just a matter of concern for the priests, but was *Torah* (instruction) for all the people. The restored community should live under the rule of Law, which in effect was under the authority of God. Faithfulness to God would be demonstrated by faithfulness to the Law, not as slavish legalism, but as willing response to divine direction.

The people requested that Ezra read to them from the Law and gathered at the square before the Water Gate to hear him. He pronounced God's blessings on the people, an act intended to make them aware of God's real presence. Then he read from the Law for six hours. As he read, the Law was translated from Hebrew into the vernacular Aramaic and was explained to all the people—men, women, and children. In contrast to the necessity for priestly assistance to approach God through temple ritual, even a child could meet God in obedience of the Law. As they heard the reading and interpretation of the Law, they mourned because they had not adequately met its demands. Ezra acknowledged that mourning was an appropriate response. Worship should include remorse and confession, but should move toward joy. The God who requires obedience is the same God who forgives and saves. Ezra saw the Law as an expression of divine expectations that an authentic community of faith would be eager to meet. As the study of the Law continued on the following day, the people realized that it was time for the celebration of the Feast of Booths, a joyful celebration of harvest and a reminder of the deliverance from Egyptian bondage—the greatest divine act in their salvation history. They celebrated for seven days with great rejoicing.

The eighth day was a day of national mourning and confession. Ezra prayed a long public sermonic prayer of confession, juxtaposing the unfaithfulness of Israel and the faithfulness of God. Thus he reminded the people that the community of faith should regularly examine God's requirements, take appropriate action to meet these requirements, and commit themselves to their covenant obligations.

This presentation of the Law to the restored community in a way that helped them see its relevance for their individual and corporate life was Ezra's great achievement. In response to this teaching of Torah the restored community obligated themselves to an annual temple tax, to the maintenance of the altar, and to the giving of first fruits and the tithe (Nehemiah 10:32–39). In short, the Jews pledged themselves explicitly to the demands of the Law. They were becoming "a people of the book (or scroll)." With this reorganization of the community of faith around the requirements of the Law, something of the ancient religio-political philosophy that had undergirded the confederacy was restored in postexilic Judaism.

Ezra's work was accomplished rapidly. Probably within a year or two the major portion of his labor in Palestine was over. What happened to him we do not know. Josephus reports that he died soon after his mission and was buried in Jerusalem.

The impact of Ezra on Hebrew religion was enduring and many today refer to him as "the father of Judaism." His efforts to popularize the law started a trend that produced "the tradition of the elders." Inspired by the lead of Ezra, later teachers sought to interpret the law for the understanding of the people. In much the same way that the canonical scripture came to be looked upon with authority, the interpretation of revered leaders was accepted, organized, and preserved as authoritative tradition. Later sectarian groups within Judaism were often divided as to how much authority should be given to this oral tradition.

The work of Ezra may have contributed to a growing popularity of the synagogue in early Judaism. No tangible evidence is available regarding the origin of the synagogue.[10] Its beginnings are usually dated to the exile, when the Jews needed a center of worship to serve the purposes of fellowship and instruction formerly provided by the temple. Here the exiles would meet for prayer and discussion of Torah as they knew it. Ezra's practice of reading the law before the people may have inspired the synagogue practice of his day. Whether this were the case or not, Ezra's emphasis on teaching the commandments of the law gave a vigorous impetus to the instructional goals of Judaism. Inasmuch as instruction focused in the synagogue in later Judaism, the work of Ezra certainly played a significant role in the growing status of the synagogue during the postexilic period. Even after the temple was restored, the synagogue continued to function, assuming a role of its own following the emphasis of Ezra. Whereas the temple was the special precinct of the priesthood and high sacrificial system, the synagogue served ordinary people by providing continued instruction in Torah and common participation in worship. By the first century C.E., synagogues dotted the eastern world wherever Jews lived, and through them the Ezra instructional tradition was continued.

Nehemiah's Governorship

Nehemiah was a person of great distinction, a prime example of the Jew who did well in exile. When he appears in the biblical story, he is already a person of high rank, a cupbearer to King Artaxerxes I. Although in a position of honor in Persia, Nehemiah remained truly devoted to Israel's cause. Consequently, when he received news of unpleasant circumstances in Jerusalem, he was deeply distressed and sought the king's authority to lead a deputation to Jerusalem for the primary purpose of rebuilding the walls of the city.

Artaxerxes, undoubtedly anxious to fortify himself against the ever-restless Egypt, not only gave Nehemiah permission to refortify Jerusalem, but also provided materials for the enterprise. Additionally, Judah was made a separate

---

[10]Synagogues are not mentioned in the Hebrew Bible, but are prominent in the New Testament. Archeological information about synagogues prior to the first century C.E. is meager. See Filson, "Temple;" May, "Synagogues," pp. 185–200, 229–50; and especially Magen, "Synagogues," in Stern et al., eds., *New Encyclopedia*, IV, 1421–27.

province, and Nehemiah was appointed its governor. By 445 the new governor had arrived in Palestine and was addressing the task of inspiring the Jerusalem leaders to join his mission.

The mammoth project of building the walls was quickly accomplished. After a secret inspection of the breaks in the ancient walls, Nehemiah revealed his plans to the leaders. With their assistance, labor was conscripted, organized, and set to work. Within fifty-two days the basic structure of the wall was completed. To this were added in the next two years the necessary reinforcements and fortifications to complete the master plan.[11]

Nehemiah's project was opposed by Sanballat, the governor of Samaria, from whose district the new province of Judah had been separated. Sanballat was supported by Arabs, Ammonites, and Philistines, who obviously would not care to see Jerusalem strengthened. Several raids were made on Jerusalem, and a plot to murder Nehemiah was initiated. This opposition came to naught, however. Nehemiah was alert enough to avoid being lured into ambush and strong enough not to cower before threats on his life. He armed his construction crews; work proceeded on schedule. When the walls were completed, they were dedicated in solemn convocation. The dedication focuses on rituals of purification. Everything associated with the ceremony of dedication had to be pure. The walls were more than just a defensive barrier; they were a symbol of sacred space—the separation of Jerusalem from the chaotic outside, a threatening and dangerous world. They marked Jerusalem as a place full of meaning and value where full human potential could be realized in the presence of God. Two groups in procession, beginning from the same point and proceeding to the right and left to meet again, ritually enclosed the city with divine security. A tenth of the Judean population was then encouraged to move inside the refortified city.

Symbolically the restoration of Jerusalem was complete—an altar had been built in a ruined temple, a temple had been rebuilt in a ruined city, Torah had been presented and accepted as the basis of the restored community's commitment to God, and ruined walls had been rebuilt to protect the city of the restored community. Zion was secure and "the joy of Jerusalem was heard afar off" (Nehemiah 12:43).

Nehemiah's first tenure as governor lasted twelve years, after which he returned to Babylon. Shortly, however, he was back in Jerusalem and turned his attention to cultic reforms. He was particularly disturbed because the high priest had allowed an Ammonite to take up residence in a room of the temple formerly used for cultic purposes. The Ammonite and his household furnishings were "forcibly removed" and the temple room restored to its proper function. A series of executive orders designed to restore moral order to the land followed. The gates of the city were closed to Sabbath trading. The portions

[11]See Josephus, *Antiquities*, XI, v, 8.

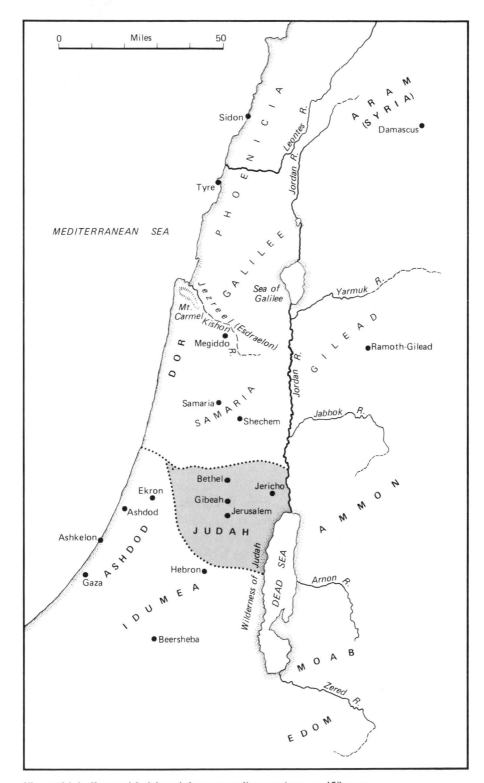

Figure 14.4. Restored Judah and the surrounding provinces, c. 458 B.C.E.

of the Levites were guaranteed. Usury was prohibited. Mixed marriages with women of Ashdod, Ammon, and Moab were strictly banned. A man who had married the daughter of Sanballet was run out of the city.[12] Nehemiah, like prophets before him, intended to protect the purity of Hebrew faith from outside influences.

THE PSALTER IN THE POSTEXILIC COMMUNITY
(SELECTED PSALMS)

Love of the temple and its worship, which dominates the Chronicler's history, is the context in which the Psalter came to be cherished in Israel. Although individual psalms come from across the whole range of Israel's history, their final collection and arrangement belongs to the postexilic period. These were Israel's prayers and praises[13] used for worship in the temple of Zerubbabel. Through these poems, known and loved by all in the Judeo-Christian tradition, Israel gave expression to many facets of its faith. In the study of the Psalter, therefore, one enters the worship life of Judaism at its best. The psalms express worshipers' griefs, sorrows, fears, and anxieties offered as prayer, but also their highest expressions of joy, confidence, and gratitude expressed as praise.

The Collection of the Psalter

The book of Psalms is an anthology of 150 poems divided into five sections, intended to correspond to the five divisions of Torah. Each section, with the exception of the last, ends with a benediction: 41:13; 72:19; 89:52; 106:48. These are not integral parts of the Psalms with which they are placed, but serve as benedictions for their section. The sections are: I, 1–41; II, 42–72; III, 73–89; IV, 90–106; and V, 107–150. Psalm 1 introduces the Psalter as a whole and Psalm 150 concludes the collection with a note of triumphant praise. Each of these sections contains psalms of many literary types with different subject matter, and from many different authors. This fivefold division of the Psalms was made in the postexilic period when Israel's religious poetry was again being used in Jerusalem worship.

Evidently the Psalter is a collection of collections, which have been rearranged into the present fivefold division. Several collections can be distinguished. (1) An Elohistic collection is characterized by the use of the divine name Elohim instead of Yahweh. Even in such widely used phrases as "O God,

---

[12]Josephus writes (Antiquities, XI, vii, 2 and viii, 2) that Sanballat compensated his son-in-law by building for him a temple on Mt. Gerizim to rival the one in Jerusalem as the divinely appointed place for worship. Josephus wrongly relates this to the time of Alexander the Great. By the time of Nehemiah the breach between Jew and Samaritan had become definite.

[13]Called the Tehillim, "Praises," by Jews.

my God" and "O God, God of my salvation," where the personal name Yahweh would be expected, Elohim is used. Probably this was an independent
collection in which, for some unknown reason, the name Yahweh was changed
to Elohim.[14]

Two collections based on subject matter are discernible: (2) The hallelujah
psalms (111–118, 135–136, 146–150)[15] are hymns of great praise and thanksgiving, often used as special songs for the festivals of Passover, tabernacles,
weeks, and dedication. (3) The "songs of ascent" (120–135) may have derived
their name from their use by pilgrims who "ascended" Mt. Zion at the time
of the great festivals.[16]

Four collections are designated according to personal names: (4) One of two
groups prefaced by the title "Psalm of David" is almost identical with book I
in the postexilic division.[17] (5) The second Davidic collection (51–65, 68–70)
is perhaps an anthology of prayers. (6) Eleven psalms (42–49, 84, 85, 87, 88)
are ascribed to "the sons of Korah," apparently a guild of temple singers mentioned in 1 Chronicles 9:19; 31; and 12:6. (7) A final collection (50, 73–83)
is ascribed to Asaph, either the individual mentioned in 1 Chronicles 16:5 or
a guild of singers alluded to in 2 Chronicles 29:13.

These collections overlap at many points, and it is obvious that many collections were available to the final compilers of the biblical book. Further, each
of these collections must have included more psalms than those preserved in
the Psalter. The appearance of many psalms in the Hebrew Bible outside the
Psalter indicates that psalmody was widespread in Israel and that the Psalter
collection is only a selective anthology.[18]

Origin of the Psalms

The complicated process by which various collections of psalms were made
and then used in the Psalter cannot be recovered. Walter Harrelson has sug-

---

[14]This is borne out in two particular instances. Psalm 14 and 53 are identical save that the
Yahwehs of Psalm 14 are changed to Elohim. The same is true of Psalm 40:14–17, which is
repeated in Psalm 70 with the same kind of alteration.

[15]Psalms 113–118 are called the Hallel and were used in the observance of Passover. Psalm 150
is a great Hallelujah to end the entire Psalter.

[16]Some suggest that the "ascents" refer to the steps leading from the court of the women to the
court of the Israelites on which the temple singers stood while singing. Others say that it refers to
the literary device of repeating in one verse certain key words contained in the preceding verse.
Kimchi, a Jewish rabbinical interpreter, said the "Ascent refers perhaps to the ascending of the
captives from Babylon" (quoted in Oesterley, *Psalms*, p. 500).

[17]The exceptions are Psalms 1, 2, 10, and 33 (10 was originally part of 9).

[18]Psalms appear in the prophetic books: Jonah 2:2–9; Nahum 1:8; Habakkuk 3; Isaiah 1:2–31;
Jeremiah 11:18–20. Poems contained in the Psalter are quoted at length in Hebrew prose works:
2 Samuel 22 is the same text as Psalm 18; 1 Chronicles 16:8–36 is composed of Psalm 105:1–15,
Psalm 96, and Psalm 106:1 and 47f. Two psalms in prose books do not appear elsewhere: "the
song of Moses" in Deuteronomy 32:1–43 and "the last words of David" in 1 Samuel 23:1–7.

gested a logical sequence:[19] (1) An initial body of cultic materials was produced for use in confederacy worship centers during and after the time of Joshua. (2) The establishment of Jerusalem as a worship center created a need for additional liturgical materials. David himself, by gift and inspiration, produced many hymns, laments, and confessions. (3) The division of the kingdom produced a rival temple in the north around which other psalms were written and collected. (4) Many of these found their way back to Jerusalem when the northern kingdom fell in 722. (5) During the Babylonian exile, the collection was put into writing and greatly expanded. (6) Finally, the postexilic community elaborated and rearranged the collection, perhaps added superscriptions and largely put the materials in their present order.

Obviously, the assumption that David was the author of the vast majority of the poems is unfounded. The Psalter itself ascribes many of them to poets other than David and probably only a minority of the so-called Davidic psalms originated with Israel's greatest king. The preposition in the Psalter title "Psalm of David" may be translated either "of," "by," "to," or "for." Thus, psalms so titled may be considered to be "in David's style" or "dedicated to David," or "of the Davidic collection."[20] By postexilic days David had become the patron of temple music. He reigned in memory as *the poet* and *the musician*. Further, the temple itself was traced to him and his son. Thus, as the tradition grew, a body of psalms gathered around his name and were attributed to the Davidic tradition.[21] David's major role, therefore, in the actual production of the Psalter was that of patron spirit and inspirational artmaster. Because the titles were not part of the original texts of the psalms, many added centuries after the origin of the psalms to which they are attached, they cannot be taken too seriously as descriptive of authorship or historical situation. The author or the actual historical occasion can be determined only for a dozen or so of the psalms.[22]

Studies that seek to place the psalms in their proper cultic role and bring them to life in the worship of ancient Israel are more productive. The psalms, like all great religious poetry, belong to both the individual and the group. Some were written by men who sought to express the experience of their inmost being with no desire that their thought become public. Later readers found these works to be sublime statements of their own feelings. In time private psalms became treasured possessions for public worship. They were

---

[19]*Interpreting*, pp. 407–8.

[20]Psalm 30 is inscribed "A Psalm of David." Under no circumstances could he be its author, for the title also describes it, "A Song at the Dedication of the Temple."

[21]The LXX shows a tendency to ascribe still more psalms to David.

[22]Whether a psalm came from the preexilic community or the community gathered around the second temple is often controversial. Opinion differs so widely that one scholar finds only one postexilic psalm, whereas another finds only two that belong to the preexilic period. The truth doubtless lies somewhere between these two extremes, with psalms coming from every period of Israel's history, more perhaps from the preexilic age.

recognized as expressing the feeling of all Israel. Other psalms were originally written for the cult by temple singers or by cultic prophets. When they were used in worship, they took on special and personal meaning for individuals and thus became "favorites." No one psalm, therefore, is strictly personal or totally public. Authorship, then, is of secondary importance. The vital question is, What place did a psalm play in the cult and what was its meaning in the experience of worship?

The Psalms as Poetry

The Psalter is the finest collection of Hebrew poetry from the ancient world.[23] Like much great poetry, psalms deal with matters of serious import: love and death, alienation and estrangement, despair and hope, life and eternity. They, however, are poems, not doctrinal treatises; they are poems to be sung or prayed. They must, therefore, be read as lyrics with all the characteristics of lyric poetry: formal structure (in this case, parallelisms), hyperboles, literary license, and emotional connections. The reader should look for metaphors, symbols, and images rather than logically structured argument. To read them literally loses their sensitivity in the letter of their words. The following brief examples illustrate these qualities:

> Yahweh is my shepherd,
>   I shall not want,
> he makes me lie down in green pastures.
> He leads me beside still waters;
>   he restores my soul.
> He leads me in right paths
>   for his name's sake.
>   [Psalm 23:1–4]

> O God, you are my God, I seek you,
>   my soul thirsts for you;
> my flesh faints for you,
>   as in a dry and weary land
>   where there is no water.
>   [Psalm 63:1]

> Blessed be Yahweh
>   who has not given us
>   as prey to their teeth!
> We have escaped as a bird
>   from the snare of the fowlers;
> the snare is broken,
>   and we have escaped.
>   [Psalm 124:6–7]

---

[23]See above, pp. 35–37, for a discussion of Hebrew poetry.

Praise Yahweh from the earth,
>   you sea monsters and all deeps,
fire and hail, snow and frost,
>   stormy wind fulfilling his command!
Mountains and all hills,
>   fruit trees and all cedars!
Wild animals and all cattle,
>   creeping things and flying birds!
[Psalm 148:7–10]

The Use of Psalms in Worship

More recent studies of the psalms have attempted to find their meaning in cult rather than in specific historical events.[24] Hermann Gunkel,[25] whose studies have influenced all major works on the Psalter since his day, distinguished the following five major classes of psalms, all associated with cult: (1) hymns, (2) communal laments, (3) royal psalms, (4) individual laments (5) individual songs of thanksgiving. He felt that two-thirds of all the psalms fell under those headings, and he had five subclasses for the others.[26] Careful examination of the Psalter in light of these classifications by literary types has led to a new understanding of Israel's worship. We modify Gunkel's classification slightly to include communal psalms of thanksgiving with individual songs of thanksgiving and add two categories, wisdom and covenant renewal psalms.

1. Hymns (Psalms 8, 30, 46, 47, 125 are examples). These psalms are either individual or communal expressions of praise to Yahweh because of who Yahweh is and what Yahweh has done. Some are related to thanksgiving, others to pilgrimage, trust, and to Yahweh's kingship.
2. Communal laments (12, 44, 60, 85, 126 are examples) and individual laments (5, 22, 51, 69, 141 are examples). Community laments arose from some shared experience of grief and sorrow, strife and difficulty. Individual laments grew out of personal distress, anxiety, and grief. They share a common sense of dependence on Yahweh to whom they call for a hearing, often make an offering, and plea for deliverance.
3. Royal psalms (2, 18, 45, 72, 110 are examples). These psalms relate directly to the life of King David. Some are coronation hymns (2, 110). Others express the king's gratitude to and faith in Yahweh or ask divine favor and blessing on the king (72). Others are royal pleas for help (144). One psalm is a song for a royal wedding (45).
4. Communal (15, 24, 66, 107 are examples) and individual (16, 23, 73, 116 are examples) psalms of thanksgiving. Some community thanksgiving psalms belong to

---

[24]The older tendency, found already in the titles of the psalms themselves, to relate certain hymns to incidents in Israel's history is particularly characteristic of the commentaries of C. A. Briggs and A. F. Kirkpatrick.

[25]Gunkel, *Psalmen*; Gunkel and Begrich, *Einleitung*.

[26]Songs of pilgrimage, e.g., Psalms 84, 122; community songs of thanksgiving, e.g., 67, 124; wisdom poetry, e.g., 1, 8, 37, 73, 127; two types of liturgies—Torah, e.g., 15, 24, 121, 134—and prophetic, e.g., 12, 53, 75, 91, 95; and mixes, e.g., 9–10, 36, 94.

the great religious festivals (15, 24). Others celebrate Yahweh as creator and lord of history (66), often reciting in detail Yahweh's redemptive work in Israel's past (107). Individual psalms of thanksgiving are thankful responses to Yahweh for deliverance from distress and trouble (16, 23). They are closely related to individual laments. Thanksgiving psalms often include serious pleas for further aid and blessing, whereas laments often praise Yahweh for the divine goodness and mercy even as they call out for more mercy and aid.

5. Wisdom psalms (1, 34, 49, 112 are examples). The theme of these psalms is faithfulness to divine guidance. That is wisdom! Love for divine guidance (Torah) leads to righteousness and blessing. Neglect of divine guidance leads to destruction. Torah is loved as the joy of life.

6. Covenant renewal psalms (50, 76, 78, 82, 111 are examples). These are psalms appropriate for the ceremony of covenant renewal at the fall festival of tabernacles.[27] They recite Yahweh's saving deeds, admonish obedience, and call the nations to judgment.

Psalms, therefore, were used in connection with almost every aspect of the temple ritual, and any adequate understanding of Israelite worship must imaginatively attempt to relate the Psalter to the book of Leviticus. Much of Leviticus is devoted to detailed descriptions of forms of worship. It served as a guide or handbook for those who presided at worship. The form of the ritual is presented without its liturgy and, therefore, stands stripped of its meaning: "Leviticus tells us what is to be done at this ceremony or that, and how it is to be done, but it does not tell us what was said, what ideas and emotions gathered around the rite, what it meant to those who participated in it.[28]

Because "it is the weakness of every cult-act that it is not self-explanatory, but may convey half a dozen meanings according to the mind of the worshiper who fulfills it,"[29] the religious leaders of Israel supplied rubrics that were repeated in connection with the rites, either by the worshiper or by the officiating priests. In general these rubrics contained an address to Yahweh, a statement as to Yahweh's nature, and a description of Yahweh's relationship to the worshiper or worshipers. They also stated the purpose of the offerings brought to the altar.

For the most part, the rubrics have been either lost or separated from the description of the ritual with which they originally were associated. Fortunately, however, two valuable and instructive illustrations of combined liturgy and cultic practice have been preserved. The confession worshipers were to recite when they brought first fruits to the sanctuary is recorded in Deuteronomy 26, along with the prescription for performing the act. The Israelite is

---

[27]Sigmund Mowinckel (*The Psalms in Israel's Worship*, I–II, Abingdon, 1962) goes a step further and interprets a number of psalms in relation to a New Year's festival, which he believes was celebrated in preexilic Israel.

[28]Nathaniel Michlem, "Leviticus" in *Interpreter's Bible*, II:5. See also Welch, *Psalter*, p. 70.

[29]Welch, *Prophet*, p. 110.

commanded to bring firstfruits in a basket and to present them before the priest. The priest places the basket before the altar and the worshiper repeats the following liturgical formula:

> A wandering Aramean was my ancestor; he went down into Egypt and lived there, few in number; and there he became a nation, mighty and populous. When the Egyptians treated us harshly and afflicted us, by imposing hard labor on us, we cried to Yahweh, the God of our ancestors, and Yahweh heard our voice and saw our affliction, our toil, and our oppression. Yahweh brought us out of Egypt with a mighty hand and an outstretched arm, with terrifying display of power and with signs and wonders; and he brought us into this place and gave us this land, a land flowing with milk and honey. So now I bring the first fruits of the ground that you, O Yahweh, have given me. [Deuteronomy 26:5b–10a]

Notice that what could be interpreted as a purely agricultural rite has been transformed by the liturgy into a ceremony inseparably bound with the acts of God in history. The liturgical formula is more than a personal prayer of thanks; "it is a confession or *credo*, which recapitulates the great saving acts which brought the community into being."[30]

Deuteronomy 21:1–9 contains a similar combination of formal instruction and liturgical utterance. A sacrifice was commanded upon the discovery of a dead person in the open field. An unworked heifer was to be taken to a valley with running water and there slain to make atonement for the blood of the victim. In the presence of the priests the elders of the city were to wash their hands over the body of the heifer while saying: "Our hands did not shed this blood, neither were we witness to it. Absolve, Yahweh, your people Israel, whom you redeemed; do not let the guilt of innocent blood remain in the midst of your people Israel. Then they will be absolved of bloodguilt" (21:7–8). Here there is both the sacrifice and the accompanying rubric, which explains the ritual's intention and desired efficacy.

Leviticus presents us with "the bare bones of such ceremonies, and such an external description of these rites may be unintelligible or even misleading without an imaginative grasp of the words and thoughts that properly accompanied them."[31] For these words and thoughts it is necessary to turn to the Psalter, for the two books belong side by side and were probably so used in the worship of Israel.

If it were known to what ceremonies the singing or petition of certain psalms was attached, the rites presented in Leviticus could be better understood. For example, the ritual form for a thank offering is given in Leviticus as follows:

> This is the ritual of the sacrifice of the offering of well-being that one may offer to Yahweh. If you offer it for thanksgiving, you shall offer with the thank offering unleavened cakes mixed with oil, unleavened wafers spread with oil, and cakes

---

[30]G. Ernest Wright, *The God Who Acts* (Regency, 1952), p. 71.
[31]Micklem, "Leviticus," in *Interpreter's Bible*, II:5.

of choice flour well soaked in oil. With your thanksgiving sacrifice of well-being you shall bring your offering with cakes of unleavened bread. From this you shall offer one cake with each offering, as a gift to Yahweh; it shall belong to the priest who dashes the blood of the offering of well-being. And the flesh of your thanksgiving sacrifice of well-being shall be eaten on the day it is offered; you shall not leave any of it until morning. [Leviticus 7:11–15]

An imaginative combination of this matter-of-fact statement with Psalm 116 as the spoken part of the liturgical act produces a realistic picture of persons at worship. Those wishing to give thanks to Yahweh presented themselves at the temple to pay a vow. In the presence of others they stood near the altar and recited the psalm, beginning with a general ascription of praise to Yahweh:

> I love Yahweh, because he has heard
>   my voice and my supplications.
> Because he inclined his ear to me,
>   therefore I will call on him as long as I live.
>   [Psalm 116:1–2]

Then they passed directly to the special reason for their gratitude:

> The snares of death encompassed me;
>   the pangs of Sheol laid hold on me;
>   I suffered distress and anguish.
> Then I called on the name of Yahweh:
>   "O Yahweh, I pray, save my life!"
>
> Gracious is Yahweh, and righteous;
>   our God is merciful.
> Yahweh protects the simple;
>   when I was brought low, he saved me.
>   [vv. 3–6]

Having expressed the reason for happiness and the occasion for sacrifice, they meticulously performed the ritual requirements for the payment of the vow. First, there was the libation of the drink offering, often an accompaniment of animal sacrifice. Lifting a cup, they poured out wine or water before the altar, at the same time reciting the proper liturgical formula:

> What shall I return to Yahweh
>   for all his bounty to me?
> I will lift up the cup of salvation
>   and call on the name of Yahweh,
> I pay my vows to Yahweh
>   in the presence of all his people.
> Precious in the sight of Yahweh
>   is the death of his faithful ones.
> O Yahweh, I am your servant,
>   child of your serving girl.
> You have loosed my bonds.
>   [vv. 12–19]

Then they presented to the priest their kid or lamb or whatever they had brought in payment of their vow, that it might be sacrificed on the altar. As they handed the animal to the priest they said:

> I will offer to you a thanksgiving sacrifice
> and call on the name of Yahweh.
> I will pay my vows to Yahweh
> in the presence of all his people,
> in the courts of the house of Yahweh,
> in your midst, O Jerusalem.
>   [vv. 17–19]

All now having been completed, the individual at the altar was joined by all who worshiped there in a cry of praise, "Hallelujah!!"

Using the relationship between Leviticus 7:11–15 and Psalm 116 as a guide, propose a relationship between I Kings 8 and Psalm 24.

Verses 1–2 and 12–19, exclusive of verse 15, may have formed the introduction and conclusion to a liturgical formula that accompanied the payment of vows other than that of deliverance from sickness. Between these passages worshipers, perhaps with the help of a priest, would articulate their own cause for thanksgiving. This practice would have been at first informal and spontaneous, but later would have become more stylized as the cultic officials became possessors of well-phrased formulas appropriate for all occasions.

Theology of the Psalter

The nature of the Psalter makes it difficult to speak of its theology. As has been seen, we are dealing with a collection of cultic materials brought together for use in worship. Thus the Psalter is not a "book" in the sense of developing an idea or ideas. The parts are not even unified by historical circumstances. Each psalm had its place in worship, each its emotion, and each its theology. Consequently we cannot speak of the theology of the Psalter in the same way that we refer to the theology of Isaiah or the Chronicler. Nevertheless, taken together these poems present a cross section of Israel's theological understanding. Sundry ideas from across Israel's history are incorporated into the book because the ideas were expressed in the community's worship. The Psalter, therefore, gathers the essence of Israel's thought and religion. The diversity of theological concepts preserved here is a chief factor in the popularity of the Psalter in both Jewish and Christian traditions.

Understandably, the theology of the Psalter centers on the character and activity of Yahweh because for Israel Yahweh was known by what Yahweh did. Throughout the Psalter Yahweh is seen as sovereign lord over nature, both its creator and sustainer. All creatures are objects of Yahweh's concern and care, and with love Yahweh pours out on them all good things. The storm obeys Yahweh's will; at Yahweh's command the sun courses the sky. For Israel, however, Yahweh is always much more than a nature deity: history is also within Yahweh's realm. The affairs of nations are under Yahweh's control, and the exodus of Israel, Yahweh's elect nation, was Yahweh's mighty act.

A large portion of the psalms, however, is not so sweeping in scope. In fact, many are almost or fully personal. In them Yahweh is God to be found in the sanctuary, a presence abiding on Mt. Zion as a resource and comfort to the weary pilgrims who wended their way to the holy sanctuary. Yahweh was in the holy temple, and all the earth had to be silent before Yahweh. In many psalms worshipers stand in Yahweh's presence in penitence, confession, petition, or praise. By doing so, they acknowledged the Lord of nature (Psalm 8) and history (78, 105, 106, 135, 136) as their God and the God of their people. Worshipers approached Yahweh in the sanctuary as one from whom they had received covenant blessings and to whom they owed covenant responsibilities. Thus, they were bold in prayer and praise. They were eager to obtain from God the grace and power to live life aright. They held nothing back; all their feelings were expressed openly. Doubt, fear, anger, hatred, belief, hopes, and loves were all clearly expressed. In effect, they trusted everything to God because they had confidence in God as holy, righteous, and steadfastly loving.

The personal quality of the Psalter gives this book a straightforward honesty in approaching life as it is. The gloomy and bitter side of experience comes in for its share of attention. The psalms praise, give thanks, reminisce, and reflect; they also lament and complain. They speak of the good that Yahweh has done (73:1) and question why Yahweh has not done more (73:3–14). From the depths of despair they lift to God a daring cry that sometimes borders on the blasphemous (58:10). They curse their fate, their enemies,[32] and almost, but not quite, even God. Such a realistic approach to life means that in the Psalter the integrity of Israel's faithful finds highest expression. They acknowledge life to be what it is, express their yearnings that it be different, and do both in the presence of the holy God whom they adore and who alone is their hope.

SUGGESTIONS FOR FURTHER STUDY

The Anchor Bible Dictionary and the *Mercer Dictionary of the Bible* are dependable sources for expanding the meaning of the following items: Jew, Judaism, elders, synagogue, tradition of the elders, apocalyptic vision.

On Judaism as it developed in the postexilic period, see two older works that are still helpful: Norman Snaith, *The Jews From Cyrus to Herod* (Religious Ed-

---

[32]Psalms 35, 59, 69, 70, 109, 137, 140 are commonly called "imprecatory psalms." They call for God's vengeance against enemies.

ucation, 1949), and A. C. Welch, *Post Exilic Judaism* (Blackwood, 1935). See also G.W.E. Nickelsburg, *Jewish Literature Between the Bible and the Mishnah* (Fortress, 1981). Other sources for postexilic Judaism are listed in the General Bibliography.

The basic commentaries should be consulted on Haggai, Zechariah, Chronicles, Ezra, and Nehemiah. Works on the Chronicler include: Peter R. Ackroyd, *The Chronicler in His Age* (*Journal for the Study of the Old Testament,* supplement 101, Sheffield, 1991); H. G. McConville, I & II *Chronicles* (Daily Bible Study, Westminster, 1984); J. D. Newsome, "Toward a New Understanding of the Chronicler and His Purpose," *Journal of Biblical Literature,* 94 (1975) 201–17; W. F. Stinespring, "Eschatology in Chronicles," *Journal of Biblical Literature,* 80 (1961) 209–19; Peter R. Ackroyd, "History and Theology in the Writings of the Chronicler," *Concordia Theological Monthly,* 38 (1967) 501–15; and R. L. Braun, "Solomonic Apologetic in Chronicles," *Journal of Biblical Literature,* 92 (1973) 503–16.

The bibliography on the Psalms and Psalter is extensive. A selection of sources is listed under Psalms, Psalter in the General Bibliography. Also consult the listing on Poetry, Hebrew.

15

The Emergence of Judaism

The battle for religious purity and sincere loyalty to Yahweh was not completely won by Nehemiah and Ezra. The struggle continued through the centuries between Ezra and the first century C.E.[1] During this time, Judaism as a structured religion was emerging and attaining a historical identity. Although Judaism has deep roots in the life and thought of earlier Israel, its character and structure are traced to significant developments in thought and practice coming after the Babylonian exile.

The postexilic period was marked by the appearance of a monumental cultural crisis. Under the leadership initially of Alexander the Great, Hellenism, the culture incorporating the ideals of classical Greece, spread rapidly through the Near Eastern world. Jewish motifs, like all other thought patterns of the area, were brought into the clash of cultures. Mosaic traditions were challenged, and syncretism with Greek culture became a possibility for Israel's religion. The encounter occurred during the crucial period when Judaism was struggling to find itself and was therefore susceptible to the powerful attraction of Greek culture. The threat was heightened by migration of Jews to all parts of the Mediterranean world and, in time, by the enforced imposition of Hellenism on Palestine by Greek overlords. Within this context and in face of this threat, Judaism as a religious system, developing out of that for which Ezra stood, began to take form.

Sources for Israel's religious and political developments during this period are scanty. The fortunes of Persia, Greece, and Rome are well documented, but the relevance of their affairs to the minor Palestinian province often remains obscure. Primary biblical histories are absent. Both the Deuteronomist and the Chronicler conclude their work prior to this period, and no additional

---

[1]This period has sometimes been called the "interbiblical" or "intertestamental" period on the erroneous assumption that no biblical writings came from these centuries.

Figure 15.1. Agate cylinder seal of Darius and its rolled-out impression of the king hunting lions from a chariot. (Copyright, British Museum)

canonical history covers the post-Ezra era. The apocryphal 1 and 2 Maccabees illumine the days of the Maccabean revolt, but this is only a small part of the period. Flavius Josephus, a Jewish historian writing toward the close of the first century C.E., covers this period in his expansive *Antiquities of the Jews* and *History of the Jewish Wars*, but he wants to make the Jews appear favorable to his Greco-Roman readers and so his reports must be read with reservation.

The most helpful source for understanding the rise of Judaism in the post-Ezra period is the nonhistorical biblical literature of the time. From them can be inferred some of the evolving patterns of the era. They are supplemented by various noncanonical writings dating to the same general period (early apocryphal and pseudepigraphical works, for example). All in all, however, we must proceed with caution because of the meager documentation of the period.

THE CHANGING POLITICAL SCENE

The Close of the Persian Period

The most dramatic feature of the fourth century was the gradual rise of Greece to dominate the Near East. Persia remained nominally in control of Palestine for most of the century following Ezra, but stinging defeats at Marathon Bay and Thermopylae made realization of its cherished purpose to conquer Greece more and more remote. During the last quarter of the fifth century, Darius II (423–404) was able to maintain Persian control of the eastern Mediterranean world primarily because the Peloponnesian wars kept Greece in turmoil. Persian influence on Palestine during this period is undocumented apart from some passing references in the Elephantine texts. We know that during the reign of Darius II, the Jews in Babylon continued to live as prosperous tradesmen, agriculturalists, and government officials, but the circumstances of the restored community in Palestine remain clouded in mystery.

The Elephantine Jews.   In contrast to the scarcity of information about Jews in Palestine, some data clarifying the state of the Jews in Egypt are available. A number of Aramaic papyri discovered at Elephantine in Egypt describe the life of a colony of Jews who lived there during the sixth and fifth centuries. Elephantine, located near the first cataract in southern Egypt, was the station for a frontier garrison composed of Jewish soldiers who enjoyed Persian patronage for serving as an outpost in its defenses in Egypt.

These papyri are mostly business and property documents, but two are especially helpful in understanding the religion of the colony. One contains a petition to Bagoas of Judah and Delaiah of Samaria, begging their intervention to secure Persian permission to restore the destroyed Elephantine temple. The other is the so-called "Passover papyrus," concerning the observance of a religious festival.[2]

The Jews of Elephantine felt a religious tie with Palestinian Jews, but they did not stand in the mainstream of Israel's historic faith. Deities other than Yahweh were included in their allegiance and worship. Alterations in the traditional modes of animal sacrifice were made to avoid offending Egyptians. Festivals of earlier days were sometimes altered or even avoided.[3] Evidently the Elephantine cult accommodated to the local situation and became highly syncretistic.

At Elephantine a rather elaborate temple served as the center of this modified Yahwism. Both the temple and the colony survived most of the fifth century. However, in 410 B.C.E. Egyptian rebels attacked the colony to protest Persian domination in Egypt, and the Jewish temple was destroyed. This was the occasion for the above-mentioned appeal to Persia for permission to rebuild. Persian permission was granted, and the temple was rebuilt probably soon after 408. However, the history of the colony suddenly comes to a close in 399 when the Persian garrison fell victim to a resurgence of Egyptian nationalism.

The Samaritans.   Another group that stood near but outside the circle of emerging Judaism was the Samaritans, a people that had arisen in central Palestine following the fall of Samaria in 722. As early as the divided monarchy, antagonism between Judah and the north had been pronounced; over subsequent centuries the communities drifted apart. The fall of Samaria and the

---

[2]A useful summary of the Elephantine finds may be read in Emil G. Kraeling's article, "New Light on the Elephantine Colony," in Wright and Freedman, ed., *Biblical Archaeologist Reader*, I:128–44.

[3]The "Passover papyrus" orders that a religious festival, probably the feast of Passover-unleavened bread, be observed according to the Jewish law.

consequent mixing of peoples widened the gap. Throughout the fifth century relationships between the Jews and Samaritans continued to worsen. The strict measures of Nehemiah and Ezra made little room for the Samaritans, whose ranks were probably swelled by many expelled from Jerusalem because of their noncomformity to the religious and political particularism of the reformers.[4] The appeals of the Elephantine colony to both Judah and Samaria reflect the division that existed between the two groups. Further, we know that Samaritans recognized only the Pentateuch as their scriptures, rejecting the prophetic writings, which were virtually canonical in Jerusalem by the third century B.C.E. Evidently by that time the breach with the Samaritans was complete.

Sometime prior to the early second century, the Samaritans built a temple on Mt. Gerizim to rival the Jerusalem sanctuary. The Hebrew scriptures give no account of this event, and we are left almost entirely to conjecture as to when the construction took place.[5] The Mt. Gerizim temple illustrated the depth of division between the two groups and made the question of whether to worship Yahweh in Jerusalem or Gerizim a real issue.[6] In New Testament days a story about a "good" Samaritan (Luke 10:25–37) would be pure fancy to the Jew, and a Jew whose "face was set toward Jerusalem" (Luke 9:53) would be unworthy of entertainment by a Samaritan.

The Fourth Century. Jews both inside and outside Palestine spent much of the fourth century under the influence of Persia, although this was a time of distress for the empire. Artaxerxes II (404–358), the successor of Darius II, spent most of his long tenure trying to maintain order. At the turn of the century Egypt successfully rebelled and remained independent throughout the remainder of his reign. On the heels of the Egyptian revolt came a rebellion by Cyrus the Younger, a brother of the king and satrap of Asia Minor. Artaxerxes maintained the upper hand only with great effort. The difficulty with Cyrus was followed by an unsuccessful revolt of western satraps, which failed more because of another uprising in Egypt than because of the power of Artaxerxes.

During the reign of Artaxerxes III (358–338), Persia appeared to mend, but its success was only temporary. The king was poisoned, and two years later his son and successor, Ares (338–336), was also assassinated. By the time of Darius III (336–331), Greece had been united under Philip of Macedon and was ready to move eastward under his illustrious son, Alexander.

Judah seems to have been little involved in these affairs. During the first three-quarters of the fourth century, it certainly was subject to Persia but en-

[4]See Nehemiah 13:28. A priest's grandson was expelled because he was married to Sanballat's daughter.

[5]An excellent, although technical, discussion of this problem may be found in Rowley's article, "Sanballat and the Samaritan Temple," *Bulletin of the John Rylands Library*, 38 (1955) 166–98.

[6]See 2 Chronicles 25:7; John 4:20–24.

joyed considerable internal freedom. It was relatively untouched by conflicts between Persia and Greece. It struck its own coinage and gradually began to use Aramaic, the official language of the Persian empire. The religious cult grew around the Jerusalem center, and the high priest rose to a place of unequaled prominence. Development and consolidation accomplished during this period prepared Judaism for the battles it was to face during the Greek period.

Greek Dominance

Alexander the Great.   During the time that Artaxerxes III was struggling to recover Persian power, Philip of Macedon (359–336) was unifying the Greek states around his leadership. By 338 all Hellas was under his control. Upon his assassination, the youthful Alexander succeeded in holding the Greek states together and assumed his father's role as leader. This event in 336 both spelled the end for the Persian empire and signaled an explosion of Greek culture into the Near East. In 334 Alexander crossed the Hellespont and routed a small Persian garrison at Granicus. Scarcely a year later, after marching across Asia Minor, he defeated the main Persian army at the pass of Issus. Darius III fled eastward for his life and gained a brief respite, but the days of the Persian empire were rapidly drawing to a close.

From Issus, Alexander turned southward to make the Mediterranean a Grecian sea before moving eastward in pursuit of Darius. Only the Phoenician city of Tyre resisted Alexander. After its fall in 332, the conqueror continued southward through Samaria and Judah, apparently receiving a warm welcome at every stop. The Egyptians welcomed Alexander as their liberator. When the victorious march through Palestine and Egypt had been completed, Alexander turned to finish with the Persians. Darius III made his final stand at Gaugamela near Arbela on the upper Tigris River, but his resistance was brief. In 331 Persia became the property of Alexander the Great. The conqueror continued his eastern march to the Indus River where, as legend has it, he wept because there were no more worlds to conquer. A few years later his brief career came to a sudden end when the young master of the world fell sick and died at the age of thirty-three.

The impact of Alexander the Great on the Near East was immeasurable. His conquests changed the face of the ancient orient and marked the beginning of a new era in its history. After Alexander, old cultural and political boundaries became less and less significant. Rapidly the east became dotted with Hellenistic colonies. Alexandria in Egypt, Sebaste (Samaria) in Palestine, and Antioch in Syria exemplify centers devoted to Alexander's aim to unify the world around Greek culture. Hellenistic gymnasiums, stadiums, and theaters sprang up in the major cities. Greek rapidly became the official language, and Greek thought provided a motif for thinkers grappling with old ideas in new formats.

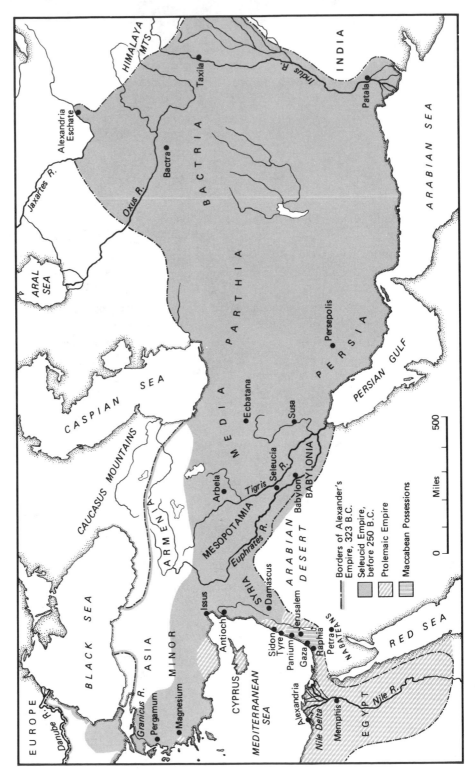

Figure 15.2. The Hellenistic world, c. 323 B.C.E.

Judah was not untouched by the arrival of Hellenism. Alexander's career brought to the foreground the issue of the relationship of covenant faith to non-Hebrew culture. How far could Jewish religion go in adapting to the developing Greek environment? This problem became acute in Palestine during the days of two groups of Hellenistic rulers who fell heir to portions of Alexander's empire—the Ptolemies of Egypt, and the Seleucids of Syria.

The Ptolemies. Following Alexander's death the empire was divided among his generals. Ptolemy gained control of Egypt and established himself in Alexandria; Seleucus won Babylonia, extending his rule to include Syria with control centered in Antioch. Phoenicia and Palestine lay between these two and predictably became objects of an extended struggle for their possession. During more than a century (323–198), the prize belonged to Ptolemy and his successors. Control of these Ptolemaic overlords influenced Jews very little. Old administrative patterns were maintained.[7] The high priest continued to

Figure 15.3. Judah, 323–63 B.C.E.

333–323 Control of Near East by Macedonian Empire under Alexander. Following his death, Ptolemies ruled Egypt and Seleucids ruled Syria		
Egypt	**Judah**	**Syria**
Ptolemy I 323–285	323–198 Judah under control of Ptolemies	Seleucus I 312–280
Ptolemy II 285–246 (Philadelphus)		Antiochus I 280–261
Ptolemy III 246–221		Antiochus II 261–246
		Seleucus II 246–226
		Seleucus III 226–223
	198 Battle of Panium in which Seleucids gained control of Palestine	Antiochus III 223–187 (the Great)
Ptolemy IV 221–203		
Ptolemy V 203–181		Seleucus IV 187–175
Ptolemy VI 181–146	167 Maccabean revolt	Antiochus IV 175–163 (Epiphanes)
		Antiochus V 163–162
(Egypt controlled by Rome after 180 and became Roman province in 30 B.C.E.)	165 Religious emancipation of Jews	
	142–63 Jewish political independence until Pompey established Roman rule over Jerusalem	

[7]The Zeno papyri, dating to the time of Ptolemy II Philadelphus, indicate that persons having authority from Persia were allowed to retain their positions.

occupy a place of privilege and leadership. Tribute was paid to Ptolemies, but the Jews enjoyed relative independence.

Under these congenial circumstances large numbers of Jews moved into Egypt, many seeking economic advantage. A large colony resided at Alexandria where they adopted Greek as their language, leading eventually to the production of the Septuagint. Over a period of years in the third century and perhaps under the patronage of the Ptolemies, who desired a copy of all literature translated into Greek for their great library, the scriptures of the Jews (primarily Torah) were translated into Greek. This significant development furthered communication between Jew and Greek and enhanced their mutual influence. Thus, the Septuagint represents a type of accommodation with Hellenism during the Ptolemaic period among Jewish communities living outside Palestine.

The Seleucids.   Hellenism created divisions within Judaism. Many were enamored with the new ways of doing things and became avidly Greek. These willingly adapted traditional Jewish laws and customs to the new situation. But for others such modifications threatened the pure faith. To them no compromise was tolerable. Although the majority of Jews thought little about the problem and simply drifted with events, the breach between the extremes had become quite apparent by the time Palestine came under the domination of the Seleucid rulers of Syria.

The story of Seleucid influences in Palestine is largely the tale of two kings— Antiochus III the Great (223–187) and Antiochus IV Epiphanes (175–163). Ptolemaic control of Palestine had been sustained by a series of provincial revolts that kept the Seleucid empire at bay. When Antiochus the Great came to the throne, he was determined to reverse the trend and gave his energies to the reexpansion of Seleucid borders. One successful campaign followed another until areas of Asia Minor, Mesopotamia, and Persia were restored to Seleucid control. Egypt, however, proved more difficult. For over two decades the issue remained in doubt, but finally in 198 B.C.E. at the battle of Panium (or Paneas) Egypt was defeated. Palestine was thus lost to the Ptolemies and joined most of the eastern Mediterranean world under Seleucid control.

If Josephus can be believed,[8] the Jews received the Seleucids as a welcome change from the Ptolemies, even taking up arms against the Egyptian garrison in Jerusalem. Their hopes were not in vain. Antiochus the Great treated the Jews with generosity, allowing them to "live according to the laws from their own country."[9] Priests and others connected with the cult were exempted from taxation, and the taxation of the general public was greatly reduced and for a time even discontinued. Antiochus supported the Jewish cult, even assisting in needed repairs to the temple. These actions undoubtedly won the loyalty of

[8] *Antiquities*, XII, iii, 3, 4.
[9] *Antiquities*, XII, iii, 3.

Figure 15.4. A tetradrachm of Antiochus IV Epiphanes from the mint of Antioch. Obverse shows the head of Antiochus; reverse shows Zeus on a throne. The inscription reads, *Basileos Antiochou Theou Epiphanou* ("King Antiochus, a god made manifest"). (Courtesy of the American Numismatic Society)

many Jews and lessened the hostility of many religious leaders. Consequently, as in the early days of Ptolemaic control, the patronizing support of Antiochus the Great made Hellenism attractive to the Jews.

The last decade of the rule of Antiochus again brought decline to the Seleucid empire. Rome had come to the foreground after Alexander's death, and Antiochus marched into the face of a formidable Roman force. He was defeated at Magnesia (190). Soon thereafter he was assassinated while trying to raise funds to pay Roman indemnities. Antiochus was followed by Seleucus IV (187–175), during whose twelve-year reign Jewish affairs worsened. The tolerant Hellenism of Antiochus the Great rapidly became bitter gall when Hellenism began to become obligatory. A plot to confiscate Jewish temple funds undoubtedly alienated many Jews who were already beginning to become suspicious of Hellenistic innovations.

The widening gap between ardent Jewry and its equally enthusiastic Hellenistic overlords came to an open crisis during the days of Antiochus IV (175–163), called Epiphanes because of his claims to divinity (*theos epiphanes*, "god manifest"). The policies of Antiochus Epiphanes were not new. From his predecessors he inherited an enthusiasm for unity under Hellenic culture and a claim to personal divinity. But Epiphanes was unique in the manner and intensity with which he enforced adoption of the Greek way of life. His extreme measures interfered with Jewish religious affairs and precipitated an open crisis.

Epiphanes was moved to drastic action by the growing threat of Rome. He inherited a disjointed empire in financial shackles to the power that was emerging as the dominant force of the Near East. To withstand Rome, the Seleucid provinces had to be united and all financial resources had to be tapped. The pressure caused Epiphanes to promote Hellenism with vigor and to bleed the empire of every possible source of revenue. Various temples, including the one at Jerusalem, came in for his plundering.

The strenuous policies of Antiochus naturally were opposed by those in Jerusalem who were already anti-Hellenic. His interference in selecting the high priest provided an additional point around which opponents could rally. Aspirants sought to buy the office from Epiphanes at a time when the ruler was concerned with garnering all available support in Jerusalem. On one occasion the legitimate high priest was outbid for the office by his brother Joshua, who used the Greek name Jason. The latter, in turn, was replaced by Menelaus, a person of questionable priestly heritage. Both Jason and Menelaus were ardent Hellenizers and operated with the full sanction of Epiphanes. Such intervention by a Greek in the religious affairs of the Jews increased both the zeal and the strength of their opposition.

Resistance in Palestine merely drove Epiphanes to more strenuous measures. By high hand and raw power, he began to force his way on the Jewish populace, property, and customs. To replenish his treasury, Antiochus rifled the Jerusalem temple of its vessels and stripped the gold leaf from its facade. He sent one of his generals to Palestine to enforce loyalty, and Jerusalem was treated as an enemy city. Its fortifications were destroyed, the city looted, copies of Torah burned, and many inhabitants slaughtered without cause. The temple was again ransacked and the regular cult suspended. An altar to Zeus was erected in the temple and offerings of swine were made on it, called the "abomination that makes desolate" in the book of Daniel (11:29–35). Sacrifices to Olympian deities and the eating of pork were made compulsory for the Jews. Completely reversing the policy of Antiochus the Great, Epiphanes outlawed the practice of Judaism under penalty of death. The offense of the infamous Seleucid had reached its maximum.

JEWISH INDEPENDENCE
(1 AND 2 MACCABEES)

The enforced Hellenism of Antiochus Epiphanes was met squarely by a zealous priestly family remembered as the Hasmoneans or Maccabees. Although some Jews accepted Syrian demands and others acquiesced by simply relying on Yahweh for deliverance, the makers of the new age were led by this family of active rebels who openly challenged the policies of Epiphanes.

> The name "Hasmonean" comes from the great-grandfather of Mattathias. "Maccabee" was apparently a nickname for Judas, the most prominent member of the family; it means "hammerer."

The Revolt (167–142 B.C.E.)

The spark that set off rebellion was struck in Modin, a remote mountain village that was the home of the priest Mattathias and his five sons. When an official of Epiphanes came to Modin to enforce compulsory sacrifice, Mattathias killed both the visiting officer and Jew who participated in the sacrifice. The event triggered revolt. Mattathias and his sons fled into the Judean hills and were soon joined by others willing to defend the worship of Yahweh with their weapons and their lives.

"Hasidim" comes from the Hebrew word, *chesed*, the same word used so frequently in Hosea. It is translated "steadfast love" in the RSV. The Hasidim were thus characterized by their steadfast faithfulness to the covenant.

Initially the revolt was more for religious than political purposes. Strong support came from devout religious groups. Chief among these were the Hasidim, or Pious Ones, a conservative segment of the Jewish nation opposed to most forms of Hellenization. For them modification of Jewish religious tradition was tantamount to apostasy, repudiation of divine covenant, and league with the heathen. Some of the Hasidim resisted independently and passively; others identified overtly with the organized Maccabean struggle. Both groups served the Maccabean objective of religious freedom.

The rugged mountain life proved too much for the aged Mattathias. Less than a year after the Modin incident, as he lay dying, he appointed his third son Judas as his successor and gave him the title "Maccabeus." Judas was the maker of the revolution. His accomplishment bordered on the miraculous. With few weapons and limited manpower, he forged untrained soldiers into a fighting guerilla unit seldom matched in military history. Because Epiphanes had his major forces engaged in a campaign against the Parthians, he dispatched one of his generals, Lysias, to handle the Palestinian uprising. The Seleucid strength was considerable and demanded of Judas ingenious military maneuvering. The rebels both outthought and outfought their Seleucid opponents. Capitalizing on their knowledge of the Judean hills, they used surprise attack and hurried withdrawal to win victory upon victory. Finally, in 165 B.C.E., Lysias was forced to negotiate the proscription of Epiphanes against Yahweh worship. Judas proceeded to Jerusalem, and with elaborate ceremony on the same day of its dedication to Zeus three years before, purged the temple and rededicated it to Yahweh. This winning of religious freedom is celebrated annually by Judaism in the feast of Hanukkah.

Religious freedom stirred Jewish hopes for political independence and furthered the spirit of resurging nationalism. When Epiphanes died, what had been resistance against Hellenism flared into a full-scale war for political liberty. Many Hasidim considered their objective gained and severed their ties with the military, but Judas launched a new offensive. He attacked the Idumeans, Ammonites, and Philistines; he rescued mistreated Jews in Gilead, while his brother Simon relieved others in Galilee. The liberators tasted nothing but victory until Judas launched an attack on the Acra, a fortified Syrian citadel at Jerusalem. Here he was forced to withdraw before the overpowering

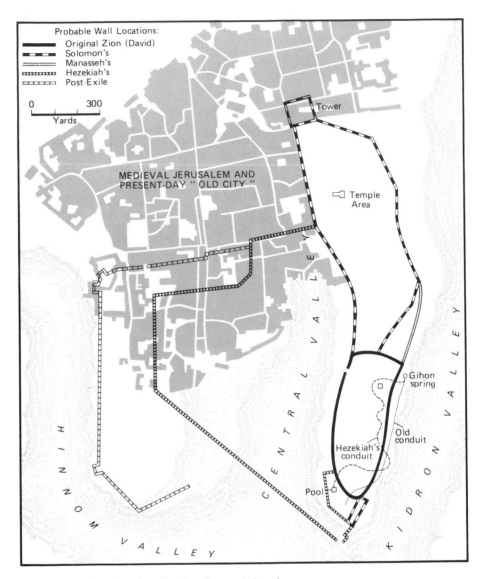

Figure 15.5. Jerusalem from David to Pompey's invasion.

Figure 15.6. A silver shekel dated to the second year of the Jewish revolt, about 67 C.E. The coin is inscribed "Jerusalem the holy." (Courtesy of the American Numismatic Society)

forces of Lysias and Antiochus V, temporary successor of Epiphanes. Shortly thereafter Judas was killed in battle.

Jonathan (161–143), fifth son of Mattathias, succeeded Judas, but initially his leadership was unpromising. The Hasidim gave him only limited support, and Jewish Hellenizers were in control of Jerusalem. Jonathan, however, was gifted with political as well as military ability. To his good fortune, disputes developed in the upper echelons of Syrian leadership, and Jonathan played the confused situation to the advantage of the Jews. His gains did not go unappreciated; among his several rewards was his appointment as high priest. Matters were going well until Jonathan's diplomatic flair, with its consequential successes, led to overconfidence. Lured into a trap by a Seleucid general, Jonathan's devotion to Syria was questioned, and he was imprisoned.

During Jonathan's tenure, Maccabean military forces were under the command of his brother Simon, whose successes along the coastal plain from Tyre to Egypt won for him the title "military governor" of the district. Simon attempted to ransom Jonathan, but his efforts were abortive, and Jonathan was executed. Simon (143–135) assumed full command and continued to make impressive gains. The most significant of several strategic military victories came in 142, when he forced the capitulation of the Acra in Jerusalem. Thereby Seleucid control in Palestine was finally broken, amounting to political freedom for the Jews.

As with Jonathan before, Simon was rewarded with the high priesthood. In addition, priestly authority was permanently conferred on his house. This action is especially noteworthy, for the Maccabees were not a traditional priestly family. Simon was also declared the civil ruler and commander-in-chief of the military. Consequently, as in earlier days, the political leader was also the religious leader, reminiscent of confederacy and kingship. The achievement of both religious and political independence under the Maccabees made heroes of the family long after the passing of Mattathias and his sons.

Maccabean Decline and the Coming of Rome

The Maccabees established an independent rule in Palestine that lasted for the better part of a century. Pride in the accomplishments of Mattathias and his sons continued through the second and into the first century, but the religious zeal with which the revolt had begun rapidly subsided. Concerns of state overshadowed religious matters. The period following the achievement of freedom was not a time of flourishing religion.

Maccabean leadership beyond the first generation is hardly worth recounting. The decline of Seleucid power gave the Hasmoneans respite and created an impression of peace. However, weak leadership in Palestine and the growing strength of Rome spelled a bleak future for Jewish independence.

The relative Jewish independence associated with Maccabean rule came to

an end in a series of events centering around two second-generation Maccabees, Aristobulus II and Hyrcanus II. Both desired the throne and neither
would yield to the other. Each appealed to Rome for support, but when Aristobulus resorted to arms, the Roman Pompey supported Hyrcanus. Pompey
not only defeated Aristobulus, but also marched on Jerusalem. His taking of
Jerusalem in 63 B.C.E. ended Hasmonean rule and is a convenient date for the
conclusion of Hebrew biblical history.

RELIGIOUS TRENDS IN EMERGING JUDAISM

The postexile years were crucial in the development of Israel's religion. The
period was characterized by radical cultural changes and continuous frustration
of Jewish national hopes. The coming of Hellenism and Israel's intense reaction
to it provided the setting within which Judaism as a religious system began to
take shape. Throughout the periods of Persian and Greek control of Palestine,
the Jewish community attempted to find its place in a troublesome world. The
Maccabean period began with great promise, but degenerated to force further
reevaluation of the basic tenets of Hebrew faith. Although no canonical works
review the history of these developments, late canonical and apocryphal books
suggest the general directions in which Jews attempted to preserve covenant
faith.

Particularism

Because exile and postexile forced Jews to look beyond their borders, their
relationship to the nations became a significant issue. As we have seen, Second
Isaiah interpreted Israel's role to be a unique people elected by Yahweh to be
a nation through whom divine blessings would be mediated to all nations.
Monotheistic faith carried as a corollary a redemptive mission to other peoples.
Yahweh alone was God, and Israel as Yahweh's people was to work toward
Yahweh's universal rule. The nation as a kingdom of priests could meet its
obligation by being Yahweh's chosen servant.

This ideal of national purpose, however, was pushed into the background
by the struggle for national identity during the postexilic era. Shut up in a small
area around Jerusalem and faced with threat to its very survival, the Jewish
community turned in on itself and created a sophisticated separatism. Although not all Jews adopted a particularistic narrowness, important elements,
which included many religious and political leaders, took this stance. Accordingly, the people of the covenant became in some measure a narrow and in-

> Compare this type of particularism with attitudes in fundamentalist Christianity
> and/or Shiite Islam.

tolerant community, overly concerned with the preservation of its own religious purity. Association with gentiles was frowned on, and intermarriage with them was strictly forbidden.[10] The returning exiles even refused to associate with kin they found living in Palestine. They held that those who had not been in Babylon were not really the people of God.

This disdain, even hatred, for the "non-Jew" created a bitterness so extreme that some passionately desired that God's wrath consume all Israel's enemies. Reacting to its insignificant role among powerful nations, Israel denounced neighbors and tried to underscore its own importance. The Jews were Yahweh's people, governed by Yahweh's Torah, chosen to be an elect nation. "We are God's people" easily became "We are the only people of God." Forgetting that God had chosen them when they were a no-people and made them a people for divine service, they came to look upon themselves as a people elected for privilege. This pride may have enabled Israel to survive in a threatening world, but it was hardly conducive to responsibility for the welfare of other peoples of the world.

Three canonical books address the exclusivistic, particularistic attitude that threatened covenant responsibility toward neighbors. Esther illustrates the narrowness that too often characterized Israel's religious thinking during this period; Ruth and Jonah, on the other hand, challenge exclusivism and remind Israel that the true people of covenant is obligated to be Yahweh's servant.

Esther. The book of Esther, against which Martin Luther directed scathing criticism, is a historical romance written to explain the origin of the Jewish festival of Purim. Purim was an extremely popular festival, although it had no specific authorization in Torah. In postexilic Judaism, Purim seems to have been the Jewish adaptation of a spring agricultural feast joyfully celebrating the overthrow of evil forces. But, whatever its origin, the festival came to be associated more with Yahweh's historical guidance of the people than with nature's cycles. In this, as in other cultic celebrations, Israel made sense of its existence, not through a mythological understanding of nature, but in the belief that Yahweh was active in history and that Israel could share Yahweh's purposes. At best, then, Purim was a celebration of Yahweh's sovereignty over historical events and nations. At the same time, it was capable of a narrow interpretation of Yahweh as the champion of Israel against the nations. As always, the grandeur of Israel's noblest theological explanation of reality could be misinterpreted.

Peripeteia (peripety) as applied to a literary work uses a sudden or unexpected reversal of circumstances. Esther demonstrates this literary technique.

---

[10]Jubilees 30:7–10. See also the policies of Nehemiah and Ezra.

The plot line of Esther rests on two earlier stories in Hebrew tradition: one is the tale of Esther becoming queen and the other is a story of palace intrigue in which the contestants are Haman and Mordecai. The early materials are woven together to demonstrate that good triumphs over evil. Heroic characters shrewdly maneuver to outwit the archetypical villain. The story is set in Susa during the reign of a Persian king, Ahasuerus (Xerxes, 486–465). It praises a young woman, Esther, whose Jewish identity is kept secret. She is chosen from among the most beautiful maidens in the kingdom to replace the deposed queen of Ahasuerus. With twists and turns in the plot, the story is told in three parts:

A. Esther becomes queen: chapters 1–2
B. Conflict between Mordecai and Haman: chapters 3–8
C. Observance of Purim: chapters 9–10

Artistically, the author demonstrates the futility of opposing Jews. Esther's position as queen enabled her to forestall a plot to liquidate the Jewish people and to turn it against the enemy. Haman, grand vizier of Persia, was offended by Mordecai,[11] the Jewish cousin and guardian of Esther, and persuaded the king to issue a decree calling for the massacre of all Jews because they refused to observe Persian customs. Esther intervened and the tables were turned. Haman was given the death sentence and hanged on the gallows intended for Mordecai. The Jews, allowed to defend themselves against their enemies, slaughtered seventy-five thousand in the provinces on one day and eight hundred ten in Susa, the capital, on the next day. Jews rejoiced over this slaughter and afterward observed with feasting and gladness the festival of Purim (so called because Haman fixed the day of the disaster by lot, *pur*).

Although the book may have been written toward the end of the Persian period,[12] more probably it comes from the Maccabean period when there was a strong spirit of Jewish nationalism and when proscriptions against Jews were common. Haman represents this anti-Jewish sentiment, and Purim celebrates a rather smug attitude toward Israel's enemies. The book, thus, does not represent the best in Hebrew faith, but must be understood in a context that encouraged a vindictive spirit. Postexilic Judaism is fighting for survival, a circumstance that does not typically promote altruism. Thus, vindictive Jewish particularism is understandable if unacceptable. The book itself does not claim to be history. Although it reflects an accurate knowledge of many Persian customs, the book is a polemical short story, clearly intending to say, "Be careful how you oppose the Jews or you will be hanged on your own gallows."

[11]Josephus (*Antiquities*, xi, 6) and a rabbinic tradition have Haman a descendant of King Agag, the Amalekite, and Mordecai a Benjaminite of the line of Saul, who slew Agag and Amalekites.
[12]See B. W. Anderson, "Esther," *Interpreter's Bible*, III:825–28.

Esther became one of five scrolls read on important Jewish festivals.[13] Although the writing does not even mention the name of God, it came to be regarded as the scroll par excellence and was given a place second only to Torah, illustrating again the intense spirit of nationalistic particularism that characterized postexilic Judaism.

The absence of the name of God gives the book a quite secular tone. Some have suggested that this silence may be intentional to show that Yahweh works for his people, even when his presence is not evident. The Additions to Esther, apocryphal materials in the Septuagint edition of Esther, may have been intended to add the religious dimension to an otherwise secular writing.

The tendency to downgrade Esther for its negative attitude toward outsiders should be tempered by the recognition that two canonical books coming from the same period challenge narrow exclusivism. Some Jews preserved their sense of covenant responsibility to the nations, hoping that all peoples would one day turn to the worship of Yahweh. The authors of Ruth and Jonah make this point with telling wit and irony: Yahweh is concerned for all humankind and, therefore, Israel as Yahweh's servant is obligated to be missionary.

Ruth.   The book of Ruth is one of the most beautiful short stories in ancient literature. Its scene is pastoral and the straightforward narrative focuses on family relationships. An anonymous author probably produced the story in the time of the confederacy, but a late postexilic theologian edited the earlier tale to produce the story as we now have it. It is a major argument against particularlism.

The central characters are Ruth, a Moabitess widow of a Judean from Bethlehem, and Naomi, her mother-in-law. Boaz, one of the great men of Bethlehem and kinsman of Ruth's first husband, plays a significant role, but clearly his part is secondary to the central figures. Although the main point of the story is elsewhere, the drama certainly portrays the two women as those chiefly responsible for preserving the family, an essential item in preserving the nation.

Through fidelity to Naomi, Ruth becomes a believer in Yahweh and chooses to leave her own people and return to Judah to share the destiny of God's people (chapter 1). Subsequently she wins the love of Boaz, and they have a child. This simple plot constitutes the story, but the crucial point, as edited, becomes clear in the last several verses (4:13–22). The child of the marriage of the Jew Boaz and the Moabitess Ruth is shown to be as ancestor of David, Israel's most illustrious king. The point is tellingly made: the lineage of the great king David includes a Moabitess!

With real skill, the editor holds before readers an outsider worthy of receiving

[13]Others were the book of Ruth (associated with Pentecost), Song of Solomon (Passover), Ecclesiastes (Tabernacles), and Lamentations (in remembering the 587 B.C.E. destruction of Jerusalem).

a reward from Yahweh (2:12). Morever, as an ancestress of David she was instrumental in mediating great blessing to Israel. In this light, Jewish particularism is shown to be unworthy. The covenant community is enlarged to include gentiles who desired to share faith in Yahweh, even including Israel's proverbial enemies. Here is a reminder that the true followers of God are always those who choose to serve Yahweh and, consequently, are not determined by purity of blood or correctness of genealogy.

Several important themes are woven into the plot of the unedited story. Events fall along lines intended by Yahweh in divine, beneficent providence. Also the book encourages fulfillment of traditional responsibilities when faced with difficult circumstances: Naomi seeks the good of her daughter-in-law rather than her own; Ruth respects Naomi above her own personal happiness; Boaz as a relative of the deceased husband nobly meets his traditional responsibilities. These dimensions of the book's purpose are illustrated in the comment of Boaz to Ruth: "May Yahweh reward you for your deeds, and may you have a full reward from Yahweh, the God of Israel, under whose wings you have come for refuge" (2:12). Nevertheless, the main theme, as edited in its canonical form, remains its challenge to particularism.

Jonah. Another critique of Israel's spirit of bitterness toward non-Jews is the book of Jonah. The book is placed in the canon with the prophetic books because it is a narrative about a prophet. Unlike other prophetic books, it contains no prophetic oracles and does not claim to have been written by a prophet. Its emphasis on universalism is more characteristic of the wisdom than the prophetic tradition.

In a story set in the eighth century (2 Kings 14:25), a prophetic voice after the exile reminded Israel of its covenant identity and missionary role. Parabolically Jonah is Israel; the book caricatures his attitude toward Nineveh, the capital of Assyria, whose brutality was proverbial. In stinging satire, the book shows the folly of Israel's rejection of foreigners, even those as detested as Ninevites:

A. Jonah is called to preach to a foreign people, but attempts to flee: 1:1–16
B. Jonah is swallowed by a great fish and released after his lament: 1:17–2:10
C. Obeying a second call, Jonah reluctantly preaches and Nineveh repents: 3:1–10
D. Jonah pouts and is rebuked by Yahweh: 4:1–11

All who heard or read the story of Jonah would have recognized the fugitive preacher as a personification of the narrow Jewish provincialism of the day. Commissioned to preach to Nineveh, Jonah fled in the opposite direction, lest he be instrumental in the redemption of Israel's hated enemies. The Jews understood his plight. They could not imagine that Yahweh would require them to be missionary to gentiles, especially Assyrians. Jonah, however, unable to escape Yahweh's call, was forced to preach in Nineveh. To his disgust the Assyrians repented and the doom he pronounced on the wicked city was averted. Disappointed and seeking shelter from the real world that included Nineveh, Jonah sat down in the shade of a vine. But the vine died, leaving the prophet exposed to the hot eastern sun—and to the inescapable call of God. In anger he rebuked God for allowing all this to happen. Yahweh, however, with a devastating last word reminded the rebellious prophet of the divine concern for all creatures and reprimanded Jonah for his greater care for his own comfort than for the lost multitude in Nineveh.

Small and recently restored Israel, suffering much from gentile hands, had judged all non-Jews unworthy of Yahweh's love and most certainly unworthy of Israelite time, patience, and concern. They needed to be reminded through the story of Jonah that Yahweh has pity even on the Ninevehs of the world and that Yahweh had chosen Israel as an instrument through whom the divine mercy might be extended. This was a hard lesson for Israel to learn. Through the postexilic centuries and on into the New Testament period, the nation often became shut up in its own pride. Continually the voice of the faithful had to be added to that of Ruth and Jonah to remind the people of the covenant that it was destined to be a kingdom of priests to the world, "a light to the nations."

The Wisdom Tradition

Another trend in postexilic Judaism is represented in Israelite wisdom. The disruptive experience of exile challenged easy answers to life's meaning and gave impetus to a search for wisdom quiescent in Israel's past. Some wise ones, or sages, approached life with practical intentions to provide counsel in proper standards of conduct. They understood their purpose in life to be to teach wisdom, and their vehicle was the wise and pithy saying "derived from a critical evaluation of human experience."[14] Although wisdom meant many things to them (practical sagacity, cunning, skill, craftsmanship), its goal was an "understanding of the highest ends of life and of the means of attaining them."[15] These wise ones were concerned with living decent, comfortable, and happy lives with high moral standards. They were in essence teachers of religious ethics. Although their writings do not appeal to the covenant idea and their advice is framed on grounds of human experience and sagacity, the mainspring and motive of their wisdom was "the fear of Yahweh"[16] and its normative principle was Torah. This "wisdom" was the condition of well-being and happiness brought about by conformity to the revealed will of Yahweh.

[14]Harrelson, *Interpreting*, p. 431.
[15]Rylaarsdam, *Revelation*, p. 11.
[16]Proverbs 1:7; 9:10; Psalm 111:10.

Other sages probed the question of the meaning of human existence with deep awareness of the anxieties and tensions of life. They had no ready advice or easy answers. In fact their wisdom often stands in judgment over the practically-oriented methods of other sages. They were frankly less optimistic about solutions to the human dilemma and often raised real questions to which they offered no answer. Nevertheless their realistic confrontation of crucial and critical issues is more satisfying than the less perceptive efforts of practical wisdom. They have left us some of the most existentially challenging literature in all of the Hebrew Bible.

The wise did not speak with the authority of the prophet nor the piety of the priest, but with prophet and priest, they molded the cultural and religious life of Israel. These earnest seekers of the good life aimed to teach their students what a good life was, or what fundamental, though difficult, questions must be asked. They directed their words to Israel's youth, teaching in public places and in private schools. In preexilic days, wisdom was taught at the city gate to all who would hear it. But in the restored community, schools of instruction were more structured, and youths of the upper classes, at least, were sent there to learn the maxims and principles that would guide them successfully through life.

Wisdom in the East.   Israel's wise ones stood in an international wisdom tradition. Wisdom writings are among the most prolific literary works found in the ancient Near East. Egyptian wisdom literature outnumbers all other documents from the third and the beginning of the second millennium B.C.E., centering on instructions for young men living in the court.[17] Egypt's wisdom also contained reflective essays on the meaning and significance of life.[18] From Babylon comes wisdom literature of these same two kinds, but in less abundance.[19] Edom, too, had a tradition of wisdom, as the Hebrew scriptures themselves attest.[20] Israel recognized Edom's excellence in this area and mentions some Edomites who were perhaps wise men (Heman, Calcol, and Darda) judged to be excelled by Solomon (1 Kings 4:30–31).

[17]Examples of these are "Instructions of Ptahhotep" (c. 2450 B.C.E.), the "Instruction of Prince Hordedof" (27th century B.C.E.), the "Satire on Trades" (c. 2150–1750 B.C.E.), the "Instruction of Amenemhet" (c. 2000 B.C.E.), and the "Instructions for King Merikare" (end of 22d century B.C.E.). Two later documents, Papyrus Lansing (c. 1100 B.C.E.) and the "Teaching of Amenemope" (1000–600 B.C.E.), are of the same general type.

[18]For example, "Dispute with His Soul of One Who is Tired of Life," and the "Admonitions of Ipuwer," both from the last half of the third millennium B.C.E.

[19]Only one sample of instructional material is known, "The Babylonian Book of Proverbs." It employs the term, "my son," characteristic of the book of Proverbs. Several reflective writings are extant: the "Bilingual Book of Proverbs," the "Babylonian Dialogue of Pessimism," the "Babylonian Job," and the "Wisdom of Ahikar." The last, Babylonian in origin, was circulated widely and became part of the wisdom collections of many peoples.

[20]Obadiah 8; Jeremiah 49:7.

Israel's Wisdom. Israel's wisdom literature is inseparably bound to this ancient Near Eastern heritage. Hebrew wise men did not hesitate to borrow materials they found suitable for their purpose. Solomon exchanged riddles and proverbs with the Queen of Sheba and with Hiram of Tyre (1 Kings 10:1). Agur and Lemuel, writers of some of the Proverbs,[21] were Arabs, and the characters in the book of Job were from localities famed for wisdom. Israel's literary forms and subject matter were often those of the wisdom literature of Egypt and Babylon; Proverbs 22:17–24:22 has thirty sections paralleling the wisdom of Amenemope. The concept of wisdom found in Proverbs 8–9 is of Canaanite origin, and many phrases and words throughout the book of Proverbs can be traced to Phoenician sources.[22] However, when Israel borrowed, it also "baptized." Whatever it adopted from other peoples was utilized to illustrate the theme that "the fear of Yahweh is the beginning of wisdom."[23] All wisdom has its source in Yahweh.

Although most of its wisdom literature (in its present form) comes from the postexilic period, wisdom in Israel "belonged to the ages." Its origin is lost in the period of oral preservation. Indications are that a widespread wisdom movement among the Canaanites was carried over into Israel during the period of the confederacy. The Joseph stories in Genesis reflect certain motifs from Egyptian wisdom, and Samson's riddles (Judges 14:12–19) and Jotham's fable (Judges 9:7–15) are classic types of eastern wisdom. By the time of the monarchy, a circle of wise women[24] and men was present in the Israelite community,[25] and by the time of Solomon, Israelite wisdom had begun to flourish.

Israelite wisdom gained its impetus from Solomon. Not only was he renowned as the wisest of kings and celebrated as a composer of proverbs by the thousands,[26] he also "realized the delights and supremacy of things of the mind"[27] and sponsored literary activity of all kinds. With this dawning of Israel's cultural life, wisdom became a staple part of the diet of Israel's intelligentsia. Inasmuch as Solomon became "patron saint of wisdom," later Israel ascribed to him the canonical books of Proverbs, Ecclesiastes, and Song of Songs, as well as the noncanonical writings of the Wisdom of Solomon, the Psalms of Solomon, and the Odes of Solomon. The tradition attributing them to Solomon is based on his proverbial fame as a wise man and springs from the custom of associating all literature of a given type with some great man of

---

[21]Proverbs 30:1ff.; 31:1ff.

[22]See Albright, *From the Stone Age to Christianity* (Doubleday, 1957), pp. 367–68, and "Some Canaanite-Phoenician Sources of Hebrew Wisdom," in Noth and Thomas, *Wisdom*, pp. 1–6.

[23]Proverbs 1:7; 2:5; 9:10; Job 28:28; Psalm 110:10; Ecclesiastes 12:13.

[24]E.g., "wisest ladies" of Judges 5:29; "wise woman" of Tekoa in 2 Samuel 14:2–20; the "wise woman" of Abel in 2 Samuel 20:16–22.

[25]See 2 Samuel 14:2; 20:16–22.

[26]1 Kings 4:29–34. Interestingly, Psalms 72 and 127 are ascribed to him.

[27]William A. Irwin, "The Wisdom Literature," in *Interpretor's Bible*, I:215. See 1 Kings 3:1 14, Solomon's prayer for wisdom instead of riches.

old known to have contributed literature of a similar nature. Later, during the period of the divided monarchy, there was a distinct class of wise ones set alongside the priest and the prophet.[28] Each of the three made its own contribution to the intellectual and spiritual life of the community, and each influenced the other.[29] Once firmly established on Israel's religious scene, the wise ones' approach to truth was not to be dislodged. Their growing influence in the postexilic community produced the final collecting and editing of much of the wisdom writing in Hebrew scriptures.

The wisdom tradition finds occasional expression throughout Hebrew literature,[30] but its major canonical expression is in three or four books representing the two streams of wisdom.[31] A practical, didactic, optimistic tradition is illustrated in the book of Proverbs and perhaps in the Song of Songs. Then a reflective and pessimistic trend in wisdom is represented by the books of Job and Ecclesiastes. The latter trend may illustrate a reaction against the counsel of sages who had become too facile or who had lost touch with practical experience.

The Practical Tradition: Proverbs and Song of Songs.

THE BOOK OF PROVERBS. The book of Proverbs contains about 375 sayings of Israel's sages intended to give prudential advice on how to live the good life. Wisdom is personified as woman (1:20–33; 3:15–20; 8:1–36). Sayings are heaped upon one another to distinguish the wise one from the fool, the good life from the bad. As in Israelite and other Semitic poetry, parallelism is characteristic of many proverbs, likely an aid to memorization. The book itself is a collection of collections, which may be divided as follows:

A. The proverbs of Solomon, son of David, king of Israel: 1:1–9:18
B. The proverbs of Solomon: 10:1–22:16
C. The word of the wise: 22:17–24:22
D. These also are sayings of the wise: 24:23–34
E. The proverbs of Solomon, which the men of Hezekiah, king of Judah, copy: 25:1–29:27
F. The words of Agur, son of Jakeh of Massa: 30:1–33
G. The words of Lemuel, king of Massa, which his mother taught him: 31:1–9
H. Praise of the good wife: 31:10–31

Each of these sections, except the last, contains material from various periods of Israel's history, as well as from the wider wisdom tradition of the ancient Near East. The book of Proverbs, therefore, is a distillation of the teachings of

[28]Jeremiah 9:23; 18:18; Isaiah 29:14.
[29]For a detailed study of one example, see McKane, *Prophets*.
[30]E.g., Psalms 1, 32, 34, 37, 49, 73, 112, 127, 133; Song of Solomon; Lamentations.
[31]Harrelson, *Interpreting*, pp. 431–33.

Israel's wise ones. It is exceedingly difficult to date the component parts from which the collections were made and there is considerable disagreement among scholars about the dates of the various collections themselves. The second collection (B) is regarded as the oldest, but all the first four collections (A–D) probably represent the best preexilic Israelite wisdom.[32] Much of the remainder of the book has the marks of foreign influence, and these sections are generally considered to be postexilic, although there is no definite evidence to preclude a much earlier date for much of the materials.[33]

In Proverbs the teaching of the wise is at its practical best. Whereas the law called for obedience and the prophets for response to the word of Yahweh, Israel's sages appeal to scrupulous observation of prudence. Approaching questions from the human side, with little reference to Israel's historical faith and with almost no emphasis on revelation,[34] they apply the principles learned by experience to the quest for a successful life. Their purpose was:

> For learning about wisdom and instruction,
>   for understanding words of insight,
> for gaining instruction in wise dealing,
>   righteousness, justice, and equity;
> to teach shrewdness to the simple,
>   knowledge and prudence to the young—
> Let the wise also hear and gain in learning,
>   and the discerning acquire a skill,
> to understand a proverb and a figure,
>   the words of the wise and their riddles.
>   [1:2–6]

The counsel of the wise took the form of practical and pithy sayings, the characteristic style of Proverbs:

> Keep your heart with all vigilance;
>   for from it flow the springs of life.
>   [4:23]
> When pride comes, then comes disgrace;
>   but wisdom is with the humble.
>   [11:2]
> A good name is to be chosen rather than great riches,
>   And favor is better than silver or gold.
>   [22:1]

---

[32]See Albright, *Stone Age*, pp. 367ff., and "Some Canaanite-Phoenician Sources of Hebrew Wisdom," pp. 1–15.

[33]Albright finds no postexilic materials anywhere in Proverbs. He holds that the materials are all sixth-century or older and that the book was edited in the fifth (possibly fourth) century ("Some Canaanite-Phoenician Sources of Hebrew Wisdom," p. 5, n. 1).

[34]The prophetic oracles are characterized by the opening, "Thus says Yahweh"; the teachings of the wise men appeal, "My son, hear my words."

Teachings like these maintained order in society as young persons embodied their principles in life and leadership.

THE SONG OF SONGS. The Song of Songs does not fit neatly into the category of Hebrew wisdom. Interpretations of the book have ranged widely: a drama with two or three characters, an anthology of secular love songs, a collection of wedding songs, an allegory of Yahweh's love for Israel, a simple love poem, or an allegory on the search for wisdom.[35] If wisdom is the context of the writing, the poems may be drawing on the imagery of wisdom as a woman. The ascription of the materials to Solomon, the patron of wisdom writings, supports this possibility.

Whatever the interpretive context, the Song is a celebration of the joyful nature of love between man and woman. There is no mention of God or appeal to covenant in the poems, and the language is often overtly erotic. Nevertheless, the Hebrews must have easily seen analogies between these reflections on human love and themes familiar in their traditions: the initial bliss of the Garden of Eden as a gift designed by Yahweh as a husband loving Israel as bride.

The Song of Songs was read at the feast of Passover and this connection undoubtedly contributed to its inclusion in the canon. Remember, too, that human love was not a mark of evil for ancient Israel. So the Hebrew could easily see a man's love for a woman as a reflection of "divine order which the community of faith continued to enjoy."[36]

Read the Wisdom of Solomon and/or the Wisdom of Jesus Son of Sirach from the Apocrypha and compare these to one of the Wisdom books from the Hebrew scriptures.

The Reflective Tradition: Ecclesiastes and Job.   Israel's wisdom tradition also includes an emphasis that reflects on the ambiguities of life and is skeptical of the easy answer. Some sages in Israel questioned the ease with which the Proverbialist assumed that the good life could be achieved. Experience for them included evil, as well as good, and the very presence of evil raised serious questions about the meaning of life. No merely human formula guaranteed success or happiness.

Life's harsh realities were brought home to Israel by the tragedy of the exile and compounded by the partial failure of all attempts to reconstruct the nation in the years that followed Cyrus's edict of emancipation. Israel had always been aware of evil as a fact as old as humankind (Genesis 3, 4), and the exile had encouraged explanation of evil as punishment for sin. How else could one understand the triumph of foreigners over God's covenant people? Exile and

---

[35]A full discussion of these options appears in Pope's, "Song of Songs," *Anchor Bible*, VII C: 89–229.

[36]Childs, *Introduction*, p. 579. Cf. also the basic imagery of Hosea.

postexile underscored for the nation that often innocent persons and nations suffer beyond what their sin justifies. The innocent often die young and evil often goes unpunished!

Some sought to resolve the problem by placing the blame for evil on Satan and demons rather than on Yahweh. Originally a semineutral prosecutor of sinful humans, the figure Satan became in the postexilic period the tempter and the originator of evil. The Jews were uncertain of Satan's origin, but they were increasingly sure that evil came from Satan. Satan ruled over a kingdom of darkness and was sovereign over a host of demons. Satan was evil personified, to be feared and yet respected for the cunning and power that Satan represented.

Other Jews were less interested in placing blame for evil than in explaining life in a world where evil was real. This attitude is typical of Ecclesiastes and Job. Both of these wisdom books contradict the accepted belief that evil is always the direct result of sin and that life's problems may be best resolved through the positive counsel of the sage.

ECCLESIASTES.[37] Authorship of Ecclesiastes (Qoheleth) is attributed to Solomon, which places it within the wisdom tradition. The language and thought of the book clearly suggest that Ecclesiastes belongs to the postexilic period,[38] probably the fourth or third century B.C.E. Judaism came to associate the book with the feast of tabernacles, "apparently in order to qualify the cheerfulness of that day with the thought that life and its joys are fleeting and that everything has its time."[39] Ecclesiastes contains many proverbs, rhetorical questions, allegories, and reflections, but it is without formal structure and therefore difficult to outline. Yet the perspective and sustained arguments of the book are clear:

A. The author's philosophy of life: chapters 1–4
   1. Life is vanity: 1:1–2:26
   2. God appoints a time for everything: 3:1–15
   3. The good and the evil share a common fate: 3:16–4:16
B. The author's advice in light of his philosophy: 5:1–12:8
C. Editorial description of Qoheleth and concluding admonition: 12:9–14

The book is permeated with melancholy skepticism. The writer did not believe it possible to find answers to questions raised by evil and suffering. He was cynical about all tradition and authority, even the authority of God. Although he believed in God, he could not find the ways of God in human

---

[37]The Hebrew root of the word "Qoheleth" means "assemblyman," much like "preacher" or "schoolmaster." The word is also used in the noncanonical Ecclesiasticus and and the Qumran scrolls.

[38]Gordis, in his *Koheleth, The Man and His World* (Jewish Theological Seminary of America, 1951), discusses this problem thoroughly.

[39]O. S. Rankin, "Ecclesiastes," *Interpreter's Bible*, V:4.

experience. He categorically denied those pious generalities of the past that directly associated sin and suffering, God and prosperity, but gave no alternative answer. He simply said, "Life has no meaning. It is like that, so live it as it comes":

> Vanity of vanities, says the Teacher,
>   vanity of vanities! All is vanity.
> What do people gain from all the toil at which
>   they toil under the sun?
> A generation goes, and a generation comes,
>   but the earth remains forever.
>
>   [1:2–4]

Such pessimism provides no answer, but neither does it oversimplify the problem of evil.

A skepticism like that of Ecclesiastes is not without its positive side. It may dislodge easy answers and thereby prepare the way for deeper faith. Ecclesiastes recognizes that simple formulas, whether theological or pietistic, cannot comprehend the ways of God. As far as Qoheleth is concerned, God remains the *unknown* and the *unknowable*. Although God may be disclosed in revelation, God's fullness remains to a large extent a mystery beyond human understanding. Luther later reminded the church that God was both *deus revelatus* and *deus absconditus.*[40] Glib equations make the uncritical assumption that a religious community knows propositionally all that there is to be known about God. Qoheleth apparently had had his fill of that kind of religious egotism. In reaction, he claimed that God is not really known in theology or in history. Doctrines derived from either source are at best partial and can never unravel the secrets of life or the character of God. Nevertheless, just because God cannot be known, it is not to be assumed that God does not exist. God is God; God's action in human affairs is indiscernible, and sometimes inscrutable.

This meant that persons are responsible for their own life. Hence, they must make the most of life in an alien and inhospitable environment. Above all, they must be realists. Pleasure and gain must not too quickly be taken as occasion for optimism, nor should sorrow and hard times lead to pessimistic despair. And although human purpose may end in the dust, God's unknown purpose is fulfilled. This questioning faith of Ecclesiastes is one basis of the book's existential relevance. God is after all God, whether or not humans are able to discern God's action in history. Almost as "agnostic believers," therefore, persons are called to live life and discover whatever meaning may be found in even ordinary things.

The sense of the value of activities in and of themselves is one of Qoheleth's most interesting concepts:

---

[40]The idea permeates Luther's thought. See his argument with Erasmus in *On the Bondage of the Will.*

For everything there is a season,
and a time for every matter under heaven:
    a time to be born, and a time to die;
    a time to plant, and a time to pluck
        up what is planted;
    a time to kill, and a time to heal;
    a time to break down, and a time to
        build up;
    a time to weep, and a time to laugh;
    a time to mourn, and a time to dance;
    a time to throw away stones, and a
        time to gather stones together;
    a time to embrace, and a time to
        refrain from embracing;
    a time to seek, and a time to lose;
    a time to keep, and a time to throw away;
    a time to tear, and a time to sew;
    a time to keep silence, and a time to
        speak;
    a time to love, and a time to hate;
    a time for war, and a time for peace.
What gain has the worker from his
    toil?

[3:1–9]

When life is lived under the sovereignty of God, nothing is trivial or merely routine. Each thing and action has its place and purpose. This is in fact one of God's good gifts (3:10–15), and every person should find enjoyment in toil (2:24; 3:12–13, 22; 5:18–20; 8:15; 9:7–10). At the same time, the transitory nature of things and of all human endeavor is a caution against the temptation to treat them as if they were eternal.

Therefore, by rejecting easy answers to complex historical and theological problems Qoheleth clears the air for honest and intelligent faith, offering a philosophy of life of significant value. The wisdom of this world is not on par with the wisdom of God. Humanity must await a wisdom "greater than that of Solomon" and carry on with faith that is both intelligent and strong until sufficient answers to life's great questions are revealed. The writing closes with these words: "Fear God, and keep his commandments; for this is the whole duty of everyone, for God will bring every deed into judgment, including every secret thing, whether good or evil" (12:13b–14).

JOB. The great drama of Job[41] also wrestles with the problem of evil and rejects the easy optimism of the Proverbialist. Here the issue is stated in terms of theodicy—that is, the reconciliation of evil and divine justice. Job, a man of

---

[41]The name "Job" is interpreted as "Where is (my) Father?" by W. F. Albright, "Northwest-Semitic Names in a list of Egyptian Slaves" (*Journal of the American Oriental Society*), 75 (1954) 222–33.

exemplary character and unwavering devotion, is stricken with disaster and disease. How can a benevolent God permit such suffering of a righteous man? Arguments and attitudes growing out of this question are themes in the book. The traditional deuteronomic doctrine that the righteous prosper and the evil suffer is summarily rejected, and new answers are sought.

The book of Job is not without its textual and literary problems.[42] It rivals Hosea in the number of vexing textual problems, and the issues of dating, authorship, and literary integrity are most difficult. Generally the book is best understood from a postexilic perspective in which both nation and individual Jew were confronted with the tragic predicament of suffering.

The book itself has been described as the "greatest poetic work produced by the Israelite community, in terms both of its poetic form and its intellectual honesty and perceptiveness."[43] Tennyson called it "the greatest poem of ancient and modern times." Actually, the prologue and epilogue are in prose and furnish the context for extensive poetic dialogues. The prose materials were probably part of Israel's cultural history prior to their use in Job. They apparently represent the Israelite version of an ancient Near Eastern story of the trials and sufferings of a righteous man. The poetic section,[44] however, is the heart of the book and exhibits a unity and "characteristic literary excellence which suggests the influence of a single personality."[45] The poet is steeped in the wisdom tradition, but with sensitive feeling and penetrating insight, he conveys raw realism as boldly portrayed in the experience of his hero. The outline of t' ꞌ book shows his procedure:

A. Prologue: chapters 1, 2
B. Job's complaint: chapter 3
C. Three cycles of debate with Eliphaz, Bildad, and Zophar: chapters 4–27
D. A wisdom discourse: chapter 28
E. Job presents his case of innocence: chapters 29–31
F. Elihu's arguments: chapters 32–37
G. God's speeches and Job's reply: 38:1–42:6
H. Epilogue: 42:7–17

The prologue sets the stage for the argument. Job is an extremely wealthy man and deeply pious. According to the traditional deuteronomic understanding of retribution, Job's wealth came because of his devotion. That catastrophe would strike such a man would be least expected. Yahweh had obviously approved Job by giving him "seven sons and three daughters . . . seven thousand

---

[42]A useful treatment of these appears in introductory discussion by Marvin H. Pope, "Job," *Anchor Bible*, XV:xiii–lxxxii.

[43]Harrelson, *Interpreting*, p. 443.

[44]Westermann, in his *Structure*, points out parallels between psalms of individual laments and the speeches of Job.

[45]Marvin Pope, "Job," *Anchor Bible*, XV:xxxvii.

sheep, three thousand camels, five hundred yoke of oxen, five hundred don-keys, and very many servants" (1:2–3). Yet before the heavenly court, Satan[46] accuses Job of serving God for profit. God's faith in Job prompts God to permit Satan to subject him to testing by affliction. Job loses his family, his posses-sions, and his health, but not his piety. In these circumstances he dares to ask, "Why?" Could a man dare believe that God watched over him (29:2) when loathesome sores covered his body? Had he not been eyes to the blind, feet to the lame, and father to the poor (29:15–16)? How, then, could a just God take away even friendship as his consolation? The depth of Job's plight and the futility of traditional answers to his situation is shown in the wife's advice: "Do you still persist in your integrity? Curse God, and die" (2:9).

Yet Job cannot resign himself to fate. His attempts to understand his own destitution and the God who does not fit the easy orthodoxy of reward and punishment form the heart of the book. In three cycles of debate, the poet sets the advice of friends (Eliphaz, Bildad, and Zophar) against the response of Job. Over and over, Job's comforters try to convince him that suffering is punish-ment for some sin against God:

> Think now, who that was innocent
> ever perished?
> Or where were the upright cut off?
> As I have seen, those who plow iniquity
> and sow trouble reap the same.
> By the breath of God they perish,
> and by the blast of his anger they are consumed.
> [4:7–9]

A young man, Elihu, adds to the argument of the friends that Job must be guilty of sin.[47] Job continually protests that he has done nothing deserving such severe punishment, but confesses his sense of estrangement from God. Out of distress he cries:

> I am blameless, I do not know myself;
> I loathe my life,
> It is all one; therefore I say,
> he destroys both the blameless and the wicked.
> [9:21–22]
> Oh, that I knew where I might find him,
> that I might come even to his dwelling!
> [23:3]

---

[46]The appearance of "the heavenly court" and "Satan" has regularly been cited in attempts to date the book by relating it to Persian and other Near Eastern influences.

[47]These speeches are disruptive to the ordered plan of the book and represent a later addition either by the poet himself or by an editor. The issues they raise had already been presented by the three friends and adequately refuted by Job's replies.

From the torment of physical and mental pain Job's thoughts "fly out like sparks struck from the iron as it lies between the hammer of God and the anvil of life."[48] Out of the void of the meaninglessness of his suffering and faced by death without assurance of life to come, he tries to find meaning.

The boldness with which Job questions God reveals the seriousness of the poet. He deals not simply with theological discussion, but with the possibility of faith. Is it possible to believe in God while facing life as it is? The book fails to explain why the innocent Job suffers, but it does speak to the reality of God in the midst of life. The discussion moves along several lines.

Clearly, the poet believes that Job is justified in defending his innocence; suffering is not a proof of sin. His appeal for an explanation is an act of faith, not defiance. Job's complaint is neither a rejection of God, who allowed his suffering, nor resignation to his fate. Rather, from an agonizing situation, he seeks to relate the moral God to his conviction of personal integrity. The poet, unlike the friends, refuses an easy explanation for the suffering and repudiates any who would condemn Job for raising the question Why? God vindicates Job in words addressed to Eliphaz: "My wrath is kindled against you and against your two friends; for you have not spoken of me what is right, as my servant Job has" (42:7).

The poet's "answer to Job"[49] is far more profound than mere reassurance amid travail. His confidence, presented in the Yahweh speeches (38:1–42:6), takes a different direction from that posed by Job's question. No explanation for Job's suffering is offered; in fact, Yahweh rejects presumptive questioning. "The complete evasion of the issue as Job has posed it must be the poet's oblique way of admitting that there is no satisfactory answer available to man, apart from faith."[50] Job himself has already acknowledged his finitude and helplessness (10:1–22), and now he must face the living God, whose character is fearsome and mysterious. The hard facts of life cannot be ignored, and Job is not denounced for daring to question. But neither can Yahweh be summoned as a witness to testify against Yahweh. Job's ultimate answer cannot be formulated in rational explanations, especially those of traditional deuteronomic outlook. Only a vision of God, who needs no more help in controlling the world than was needed in creating it, brings consolation to the inquirer. Such a vision comes only with struggle and agony, a pilgrimage essential to the discovery of trust. Job's closing confession shows the depths of his faith:

> Then Job answered Yahweh:
> "I know that you can do all things,
>   and that no purpose of yours can be thwarted.

---

[48]H. Wheeler Robinson, *The Cross in the Old Testament*, (S. C. M., 1955), p. 19. Chap. 1 of this book gives an excellent interpretation of Job.

[49]Carl G. Jung used this phrase as the title for a provocative book.

[50]Marvin Pope, "Job," *Anchor Bible*, XV:lxxv.

'Who is this that hides counsel
    without knowledge?'
Therefore I have uttered what I did not understand,
    things too wonderful for me, which I did not know.
'Hear and I will speak;
    I will question you, and you declare to me.'
I had heard of you by the hearing of the ear,
    but now my eye sees you;
Therefore I despise myself,
    and repent in dust and ashes.''

[42:1–6]

Job repents, not because his friends have been proven correct, but because this is what one must do when one confronts deity.

The prose epilogue seemingly reverts to the discredited doctrine of retribution. The vindicated hero is rewarded with the restoration of family and possessions to "twice as much as he had before" (42:10). Evidently this feature of the ancient material has been preserved by the author as a way of concluding the story without leaving the hero in utter despair. The deuteronomic conclusion, however, ought not detract from the main thrust of the book.

In the book of Job, the Hebrew Bible stamps its approval on individual sincerity and religious pilgrimage. From his dung heap, Job ultimately defies the sufferings that almost rob him of his faith in a mysterious God. Moreover, the book is a prophetic word to the Israelite community whose circumstances gave it birth. From the exile where city and temple and king had been taken away, the covenant people could trust in Yahweh, whose benevolence had been revealed in suffering and struggle, as also in the exodus and the gift of the land. Further, the book speaks a universal word: Job is everyman, reminding us that a deep and personal faith often comes by way of the long and sometimes shadowy corridor of sincere questions about the relevance of God for the agony in human existence.[51] The mystery of God's working shall never be fully comprehended. The book ultimately asserts that one who throws oneself on God, even though perplexed about life's evil, shall find God.

> Compare the book of Job, Ecclesiastes, and Archibald Maclish's play, *J. B.*, on their analysis and resolution of the problem of evil. Can you suggest other approaches that might be helpful with this problem?

Proverbs, Ecclesiastes, and Job are quoted or alluded to throughout the New Testament. Matthew 12:42 states of Jesus that "something greater than Solomon is here," and St. Paul calls him "the wisdom of God" (1 Corinthians 1:24). The Logos introduction to the Gospel of John, the Epistle of James, and

---

[51]James 5:11 makes Job a heroic example for Christians, to be steadfast in their faith amid great suffering.

other New Testament writings accentuate the role of the wisdom of God in the life, teaching, and accomplishment of Jesus. These references illustrate the staying power of the wisdom tradition in Judeo-Christian faith.[52]

The Community of Torah

No change in postexilic Jewish religious life was more significant than the increasing importance given to Torah. As we have noted, exile was a serious challenge to Davidic understandings of covenant and increasingly the utopian dream of an early restoration of the "day of David" was pushed into the future. The perspective of the period thus became eschatological—that is, the hope of the nation was known not so much in immediate politics as in the theology of what it by Yahweh's activity might become. Ultimately Yahweh's purposes for Israel would be realized. But what was to happen during the interval preceding Yahweh's intervention to fulfill Israel's history? How was the covenant community to live in light of continuing political disappointments? Judaism's answer to these questions was to reemphasize Sinai covenant concepts that centered on Torah. Quickened by the reforms of Nehemiah and Ezra, the Hebrews turned to observance of Torah as the most adequate way to prepare for the new day when Yahweh's Prince of Peace would rule over a new community established upon an everlasting covenant.

The popularity of Torah was both possible and necessary because of the loss of traditional centers of Jewish loyalty. Long destroyed was the cult of the north and its shrines at Dan and Bethel. The Jerusalem-centered national cult of the south, with its Davidic associations, lived on only in the continually frustrated hope for the reestablishment of national integrity. Jews were scattered throughout the known world (called diaspora), many never to return to the land of covenant promise. For them the old bond of national cult had little meaning. Even the successful reconstruction of the Jerusalem sanctuary was not enough to hold the community together. Moreover, those who returned to Judah had been unable to restore the old institutions. The promised future with the reestablishment of the Davidic state had not come, and all attempts to recapture the past proved tragically disappointing.

Even less possible was a return to the tribal league. Israel was far removed from the tribal way of life even though some of the confederal ideals had remained alive through monarchy and exile. Prophets such as Jeremiah (31:31–35) and Ezekiel (37:26) voiced hope for a new covenant, but fulfillment still lay in the distant future.

Therefore, a frustrated covenant people turned in a new direction to maintain continued existence. The key to survival was found in an estimation of Torah that established it as the basis of the community's life. This emphasis

---

[52]Illustrated in Israel's wisdom tradition by 4 Maccabees and the Wisdom of Solomon.

led to Israel's becoming a "people of the book." Confederal structure, nationalistic institutions, and temple cult gave way to a cult of Torah. Judaism was saturated with reverence for the Torah of Yahweh. James Sanders[53] suggests that Torah was canonized separately from the story of conquest for the simple reason that in exile Torah became Israel's master guide.

The Role of Torah.   Obedience to the law was not, of course, anything new in Israel. At the heart of the Sinai covenant had been the decalogue, the confederacy had centered on divine law, and the national life of Israel was always regulated by covenant law. Even Israel's great prophets, far from being "legalists" in their role as reformers, viewed the law as Yahweh's ordained guide for national and personal life. Thus, the role assigned Torah in the restored community was merely a rediscovery of one it had long held.

The Hebrew word *torah* means "instruction" or "direction," and its primary reference is to the directing that comes from Yahweh. The tribe of Levi was to teach "Jacob your ordinances and Israel your law (torah)" (Deuteronomy 33:10). Gradually, however, the word came to be used for a body of teaching, either prophetic or priestly. The code of Deuteronomy was called Torah and finally the word came to be applied to the "Law of Moses," the biblical books Genesis through Deuteronomy—that is, the Pentateuch. This extensive collection of written law from all periods of Israel's history was largely brought together during the exile. When Ezra returned to Jerusalem in 458 B.C.E., he brought with him a form of Torah and promulgated it as Yahweh's law by which the restored community was to structure its life. Thus, Torah, more than anything else, became determinative for Israel. Those who assumed the burden of this law were the true Israelites.

After the exile, Torah increasingly was considered the medium of revelation. The prophetic explanation of the exile as a judgment on disobedience made it natural for Judaism's leaders to deem obedience to the law the basis of any reestablishment and continuation of the people of Yahweh. No other course was open to them. Therefore, when prophecy declined during the postexilic period, the community turned to Torah to find Yahweh's word.

Gradually the law was accorded growing importance until finally it was absolutized. Separated from the historical context from which it sprang, the law came to be viewed as unchanging, unalterable, and eternal.[54] It was portrayed with absolute authority, preexistent to Sinai and Israel. The whole Torah was written on heavenly tablets, its prescriptions obeyed in heaven itself. By the Christian era, the law had reached its ultimate exaltation, being extolled as the

---

[53] *Torah and Canon*, p. 53.

[54] There is a hint of this in canonical literature (Psalm 119:89, 160), but it is made clear in apocryphal and pseudepigraphical writings: The Wisdom of ben Sirach, 16:26–17:24, and especially Jubilees 2:15–33; 3:8–14; 6:17f.; 16:20–31; 4:5; 5:13.

one possession left to Judaism apart from Yahweh. All the blessings of the world to come were promised to "those who had been saved by their works, and to whom the law hath now been a hope, and understanding an expectation, and wisdom a confidence."[55]

Cult and Torah.   Because the precepts of Torah included specific instructions for religious observances, the resurgence of Torah produced serious concern with correct cultic practice. Some changes from the cult of preexilic days are noticeable, but in large, the cultic traditions of the earlier temple were carried forward. Sacrifices continued as before, but with additional emphasis on sin offerings. The annual feasts and their historical significance were retained and two nationalistic festivals were introduced: Purim, celebrating the events described in Esther, and Hanukkah, recalling the dedication of the temple in 165 by the Maccabees. The Day of Atonement, the one fast day in Israel's liturgical calendar, gained importance because of the accentuated sense of sin brought on by the catastrophe of the exile.

Changes in keeping with emphasis on Torah are also discernible in the organization of cultic personnel. The high priestly office became hereditary, attaining an eminence unheard of in preexilic days. The high priest was the spiritual head of the community and often its secular ruler as well. The ordinary ranks of the priesthood were made up of those who were able to authenticate their Aaronic descent. The lower orders, all of whom had to claim descent from Levi, were for the most part descendants of the cultic leaders of the various Judean shrines outlawed during the Josianic reformation. These men were keepers of the temple, doorkeepers, and servants. A large group of them, however, made up the temple choirs, which played a vital role in community worship.

Cultic prophets associated with the temple played an increasingly important role in the liturgical services. Things that Yahweh had done and was doing for Israel were dramatically represented in the cult of proper worship. Yahweh's will had to be proclaimed, Yahweh's answers to prayers had to be communicated, and Yahweh's great deeds for the people in past days had to be recapitulated.

The Scribes.   The elevation of Torah also raised its study to a place of paramount importance and produced a class of men unrivaled in their devotion to the protection of the form and meaning of the law. If Torah was to retain its rightful place, it had to become the possession of all Israel, and the will of Yahweh found within Torah had to be known without question. Concern with these objectives produced a class of scribes devoted to the preservation, correct interpretation, and application of law. These men have preexilic counterparts,

---

[55]Apocalypse of Baruch 1:27.

but only in the days following Ezra did they really come into their own. The Sopherim, "men of the book/scroll," copied and safeguarded the scriptures from the exile to the first century B.C.E. The Masoretes, "men of the masora," continued the sacred discipline and by 900 C.E. had added vowels to the consonantal text. The scribes established elaborate procedures for protecting the form of the law. After the exile, they began to hedge Torah with Masora, a mass of detailed information about the text. They preserved the various text forms from which the Masoretic texts ultimately arose.

The scribes also were concerned with proper interpretation of Torah. Consequently, they established principles for its interpretation so that the law might be properly understood and applied. Scripture was explained in light of Torah and its commands given detailed definition. Care was observed to explain every implication of Torah lest the divine law inadvertently be broken. Under scribal influence, Judaism was becoming a religion of precept and rule in danger of losing the true spirit of its faith.

Sectarian Interpretation of Torah. The high place given to Torah made it inconceivable that any problem could arise that law did not address. Postexilic Israel was determined to bring all of life under control of law. Yet fluid cultural conditions often made the application of this instruction quite difficult. New circumstances, specific problems, or changing needs obviously would not be directly covered in old legislation. At the beginning the divine word might be clear, but the passing of time demanded new interpretations to keep Torah up-to-date. Out of such circumstances oral law developed as a means to keep Torah viable and applicable. This oral tradition developed over several centuries and gradually came to include a wide range of customs and decrees considered to be clarifications of original Torah.

The growing status of oral law in postexilic Judaism produced a variety of reactions within the religious community. All agreed that Torah was holy and ought to be made the basis for living. But could oral law rival written law in significance? Three options seemed to be open: (1) the covenant community could bend with historical circumstances and interpret law to meet changing conditions; (2) it could pretend that change had not occurred and focus on maintaining established cult and Torah under the supervision of a constituted priesthood; or (3) it could withdraw from the world and its flux, attempting to create a static environment. Groups within Judaism exercised each of these alternatives and toward the end of the postexilic period all these options were represented in Judaism: the Pharisees following the first alternative, the Sadducees the second, and the Essenes the third.

The most important faction arising in Judaism was that of the Pharisees.[56]

---

[56]The name "Pharisee" is derived from a Hebrew word meaning "separate."

as a distinct group sometime in the second century B.C.E. Pharisees were zealous in their obedience to Torah, which they explained to make it fit new situations. The result of their interpretation was a collection of oral law called
the "tradition of the elders." Pharisees traced the oral law to Moses and considered obedience to it morally obligatory. Eventually the "tradition of the
elders" was codified into the Mishnah (second law). The Mishnah in turn was
explained, amplified, and kept up-to-date. By the fifth and sixth centuries C.E.,
the Mishnah and its interpretations (*gemara*) had been combined into Talmud,
including both a Palestinian and a Babylonian version. Hence, following Torah
meant for the Pharisees also living by Talmud. Further, they also accepted the
prophetic books and certain of the Writings as religious authorities. They also
accepted doctrines not found in Torah. They believed in the resurrection of
the body, in angels and demons, and looked for the coming of the apocalyptic
kingdom. The Pharisees were never numerous, but they controlled the synagogues and their influence on Judaism was extensive. Pharisaism survived the
fall of Jerusalem in 70 C.E. and thus had a lasting influence on Judaism.

The Pharisees had no ambition for political power itself and disapproved of
revolutionary activity.[57] They exerted political influence only in times of im-
periled religious freedom. They felt that the kingdom of God would come when
the people of God kept the law, written and oral.

A second sect of Judaism was the Sadducees, the most conservative segment
of the Jewish population, both politically and religiously. They belonged to the
priestly aristocracy and the secular nobility of Jerusalem. Torah was their only
source of divine authority; they rejected the validity of the prophetic books and
the oral law of the Pharisees. They likewise rejected theological innovations
such as belief in resurrection, rewards, angels and demons, and most apocalyptic speculations. They were orthodox believers of the old school, "holding
fast to the spirit and the principles of genuine Yahwism as expressed in the
Torah,"[58] especially where it *centralized* religion on the temple and priesthood.

The Sadducees would go to any extreme to maintain the status quo and
generally followed a policy of collaboration and compromise with the powers
in control of the Jewish state during the later pre-Christian and early Christian
eras. Hasmonean priest-kings, like Roman procurators of a later period, found
support in Sadducee ranks. The political direction of the nation was a secondary concern to the proper administration of the temple cult and its law.

> A primary issue after 333 B.C.E. was the relationship between Judaism and its cultural
> environment. Discuss manifestations of this issue in contemporary culture and in-
> dicate how various religious groups manage the relationship.

[57]A radical left wing of Pharisaism produced a group of brave men who, unwilling to wait for
the rule of Torah to come, acted forcibly to establish God's dominion.

[58]C. Guignebert, *The Jewish World in the Time of Jesus* (Routledge and Kegan Paul, 1939), pp.
162–63.

Figure 15.7. Cave II adjacent to the Qumran settlement. In this and other nearby caves, numerous Hebrew scripture scrolls were hidden when Rome invaded Palestine, c. 70 C.E. They remained unclaimed until their accidental discovery in 1947. (*Illustrator* Photo/Ken Touchton)

In the face of continual pressure from outside Palestine, another sect of Jews withdrew from the world in an attempt to create an unchanging environment. These were the Essenes, who lived ascetic lives in community centers, some in towns, some in the countryside. They thought of themselves as the true Israel, that saving remnant through whom Yahweh's age-old promises might finally be realized. This self-styled community of the "new covenant" anxiously awaited the decisive inbreak of Yahweh. They felt that all prophecy was being fulfilled in their day and wrote commentaries on various biblical books to show that this was so. Semi-isolated from the world, they held goods in common, frowned on marriage, and enforced on themselves a strict discipline of scholarship, work, and worship. New members came from a constant stream of seekers who were admitted to the full fellowship of the communities only after they had proved worthy. Many scholars identify the Essenes with the famous "monastery" at Qumran in the Judean wilderness near the northwestern corner of the Dead Sea. Its members produced the Dead Sea Scrolls, an extremely valuable collection of biblical and nonbiblical manuscripts discovered first in 1947 and through the years since.

Figure 15.8. Clay jay for housing a scroll, used by the Essenes of Qumran to preserve their sacred texts when the community was threatened by Roman armies 66–70 C.E. (Copyright, British Museum)

Apocalyptic Interpretation of History

The Qumran experience suggests another theological trend in postexilic Judaism. Israel's undivided devotion to Torah enabled it to show faithfulness to Yahweh in the present, but Israel also had to be able to meet the future as God's people. Some, as those at Qumran, attempted a disciplined withdrawal as an act of preparation for Yahweh's ultimate victory on the last day; others chose to draw sword against the enemy, as those who fought with the Maccabees. Both groups were motivated by their conviction that Yahweh joins forces with the faithful people to oppose all powers of deception and evil.

Israel's hope in the ultimate triumph of God's cause was expressed in a novel type of Jewish literature that became popular in connection with the Maccabean revolt. This form is generally called "apocalypse," a Greek term meaning "revelation" or "unveiling," suggesting that the authors intended to reveal truths surrounded by mystery. Fragmentary samples of apocalyptic writing appear in prophetic oracles,[59] but the book of Daniel was the first full-fledged Jewish apocalypse. Response to the book's circulation won for the literary form a widespread prominence that lasted for almost three centuries. This literature, dating between about 200 B.C.E. and 100 C.E., is difficult to interpret: it is intentionally esoteric.

Character of Apocalyptic Literature. Apocalyptic writing had great appeal to its readers and its hearers. It captured the imagination with settings, creatures, events, and cryptic language whose immediate referent existed only in the minds of the author and his empathetic reader. Visions, exalted symbolism, ingenious manipulations of numbers, and fantastic descriptions (sometimes quite bizarre) served as vehicles to transport the responsive mind to the understanding intended by the writer. All apocalyptic symbolism should be interpreted according to its meaning for the author and his listeners.

Although the writing of apocalypse required creative genius and the occasional introduction of new concepts, the apocalyptist was not an originator of ideas. He built on foundations laid by prophetic predecessors and utilized literary imagery familiar to those for whom he wrote. The result was a powerful literary mode used with effectiveness in Judaism for several centuries.

Apocalyptic literature was written primarily during times of great distress and persecution. At historical moments that offered little or no hope, the apocalyptist lifted his sights to more distant horizons, willingly accepting defeat in the present, but remaining confident and optimistic about ultimate victory. He advocated a view of history consistent with his belief in a transcendent deity who was in control of the terminus of human affairs. His eschatological expectation was that Yahweh's sovereignty would be manifested at some end

---

[59]E.g., Isaiah 13–14; 24–27; Ezekiel 1, 28–39; Joel 2; 3; Zechariah 12–14.

time, that Yahweh's indestructible will would finally prevail over forces here and beyond, and that on a day of judgment, divine control would be fully asserted over all powers of evil. The eternal would be brought to bear on the temporal; divine good would defeat wickedness and bring great rejoicing to the people of God. Even the dead would be resurrected to share in the glory. To the apocalyptist, a great new age was in the making. The future was Yahweh's, who would bring it into being. Such an outlook was usually revealed to the apocalyptist by an otherworldly figure speaking the divine word.

For the apocalyptist the message was more important than the writer. He wrote pseudonymously, not reluctant to put his pronouncements under the name of some illustrious person of a era long past. Ascribing the writing to a celebrated ancient (such as Moses, Enoch, Isaiah, Baruch, or Ezra) enhanced the value of his message by making it read like a prediction of the present.

Inasmuch as the age of prophecy was thought to be gone, never to return, the apocalyptist could not claim prophetic authority for himself. Nonetheless, apocalyptic literature was heir of the prophetic movement in Israel and shared the burden of relating Yahweh's will to events in history. The apocalyptist, however, veered from the prophetic course in several ways. Whereas the prophet was primarily a spokesman, the apocalyptist was a writer. The prophet was concerned with the problems of a particular generation and addressed Yahweh's word to the people in ways relevant to the time. The apocalpytist looked with a general vision and telescoped vast expanses of time into a single gaze, often encompassing a succession of empires in his concern. The prophet directed his message to persons he deemed disloyal to God; the apocalyptist spoke to the faithful under persecution that tried their faith. The prophet thought of a kingdom of God established in this world through the ongoing processes of history; his apocalyptic counterpart emphasized a divine break in history to usher in the ideal age.

The apocalyptic writer contributed significantly to the advancement of Israel's religious ideas. He supported the reality of life after death and kept alive messianic hope. For him Yahweh was in control of history, not an indifferent spectator impotent to take a hand in affairs. He believed that Yahweh "had some purpose for the world He had made, and that His power was equal to its achievement."[60] The pious remnant of Israel, inseparably linked to Yahweh in its suffering, was engaged with Yahweh in a struggle for the accomplishment of the eternal purpose and will of God. Final victory would be accomplished in a coming Day of Yahweh. The best was yet to be and would surpass even the heightened imagination of Israel. Such a victory would originate and consummate in Yahweh and might involve all of eternity. The apocalyptic writer was not so concerned with specifying the calendar time when this might happen as with affirming the certainty of its coming.

[60]Rowley, *The Relevance of the Apocalyptic* (Lutterworth, 2d ed., 1947), pp. 151ff.

The Book of Daniel. Daniel is the chief example of apocalyptic writing in the Hebrew scriptures. The work had its precursors in chapters in Isaiah (13, 14, 24–27), Ezekiel (1, 28–39), Zechariah (12–14), and Joel (2,3). Several noncanonical writings later than Daniel follow the apocalyptic style. Enoch, the Testament of the Twelve Patriarchs, the Assumption of Moses, Baruch, the Sibylline Oracles, and the book of Jubilees form a wake trailing from the popular acceptance of the book of Daniel. Such literature also appears in the Qumran community. The final book of the New Testament, the Revelation of John, is an apocalypse.

Daniel is found among the Writings *(Kethu'bim),* the last section of the Hebrew Bible to be given canonical status. Because the book is written in late Hebrew, contains several Persian and a few Greek words, and has a large section in western Aramaic,[61] a postexilic date is clearly in evidence. The Wisdom of ben Sirach (c. 180) does not list Daniel in its catalogue of Israel's "famous men,"[62] but the book is referred to soon after the middle of the second century B.C.E. in the Sibylline Oracles (3:381–400). These factors suggest that the book was written during the strenuous early days of the Maccabean revolt, or about 168–165 B.C.E., after the desecration of the temple but before the victories of Judas and the temple's rededication.

Daniel presents many literary-critical problems. The combination of simple human-interest stories with complicated apocalyptic visions, shifts from the first to the third person, and the combination of Aramaic and Hebrew suggest multiple authorship. The chronology does not always coincide with what is known of the history of the period, such as the misdating of the beginning of the Babylonian exile in the third year of Jehoiakim (1:1). In fact, the number of historical inaccuracies has led Walter Harrelson to suspect the author to have deliberately misrepresented the historical events as a subtle indication to his readers that he was actually writing in a much later period with a quite different historical enemy of God's people in mind.[63] Whether or not the errors are intentional, they illustrate that the author writes later than the events and recasts materials in light of his own purpose to inspire persons of faith to endure temptation and hardship.

The book of Daniel reflects important turns in the development of Israel's religious ideas. The notion of angels, belief in resurrection of individuals from death, and the vicarious efficacy of martyrdom are all included in the book as ideas accepted in the Israelite community. But more significantly, apocalyptic judgment has clearly become a part of Judaism's view of history. Daniel affirms real confidence in an approaching rule of God on earth and exhorts Israel to be prepared to meet that day with unwavering commitment. God's interven-

---

[61]Daniel 2:4b–28. The postexilic Ezra has an Aramaic section, 7:12–26.
[62]Ecclesiasticus 44:1–50:24.
[63]*Interpreting,* p. 458.

tion alone would be sufficient to save faithful Jews. The covenant community is solemnly responsible to share the rule of the sovereign Lord of all nations. Thus, although the book was directed to a specific age with the distinctive purpose of reassuring Yahweh's people in a time of distress, Daniel further intends to proclaim Yahweh's sovereignty over all history, a theological reality to inspire both confidence and commitment.

The theme of Daniel is that hope is best placed in Yahweh, who controls the final engagement with evil and who, at the divinely appointed time, will usher in the final kingdom. The author seems to have been one of the Hasidim who suffered under the oppressive policies of Antiochus IV Epiphanes and, convinced that Yahweh would redeem, intended to encourage support for the Maccabean revolt. Using well-known stories of the heroism of a certain Daniel who struggled faithfully and successfully against Babylonian tyranny, he sought to encourage his contemporaries in their distress. If Jews persecuted by Antiochus would follow Daniel's example, persevere in faith, display real courage, and endure martyrdom, they would preserve the rich tradition of those who had kept alive faith in Yahweh's ultimate victory. Faithful commitment in the present difficulty was necessary to share in the glory of Yahweh's final triumph. Although the book did not promise immediate success for Maccabean resistance, opposition to Syrian tyranny must have been strengthened by its confidence in the future. The book systematically develops its themes:

A. Stories about Daniel and his friends: chapters 1–6
    1. Introduction—Daniel and his four friends: 1:1–21
    2. First story—interpreting Nebuchadnezzar's dream: 2:1–49
    3. Second story—enduring the fiery furnace: 3:1–30
    4. Third story—Nebuchadnezzar's madness: 4:1–37
    5. Fourth story—Belshazzar's banquet: 5:1–31
    6. Fifth story—Daniel in the lions' den: 6:1–28
B. Daniel's apocalyptic visions: chapters 7–12
    1. First vision—the four beasts: 7:1–28
    2. Second vision—the ram and he-goat: 8:1–27
    3. Third vision—the seventy weeks: 9:1–27
    4. Fourth vision—the last days: 10:1–12:13

Chapters 1–6 dramatically relate the adventures of four young Jewish men employed by the Babylonian government during the exile. Like Joseph in Egypt, these Israelite aliens in a foreign land impressively interpreted dreams for their captors: "The king said to Daniel, 'Truly, your God is God of gods and Lord of kings, and a revealer of mysteries, for you have been able to reveal this mystery' " (2:47)!

They remained true to the ritual requirements of their faith, keeping the letter of the law. Their faithfulness to Yahweh initially brought promotion in position, but later they incurred the disfavor of the Babylonian sovereign by refusing to worship an idol set up by the king. These Jewish devotees could not be separated from their steadfastness, even if it meant death:

> If our God whom we serve is able to deliver us from the furnace of blazing fire and out of your hand, O king, let him deliver us. But if not, be it known to you, O king, that we will not serve your gods and we will not worship the golden statue that you have set up (3:17,18).

Devotion of this character caused even the foreign rulers to acclaim Israel's God:

> for he is the living God,
> enduring for ever:
> his kingdom shall never be destroyed,
> and his dominion has no end.
> He delivers and rescues,
> he works signs and wonders
> in heaven and on earth, . . .
>   [6:26b–27a]

Throughout the first part of the book, the lonely four stand as a minority against the crowds, which capitulate to the will of tyrants. They had faith that with "a stone cut out, not by human hands" (2:34), God demolishes the temporal powers of this world.

The apocalyptic visions contained in chapters 7–12 parade four empires across the screen of Yahweh's vision. Babylonians, Medes, Persians, and Greeks are symbolized in varied and clear imagery. In due course the wisdom and power of Yahweh had prevailed over Babylonian and Persian emperors. Masters of earthly empires are shown to come and go, but Yahweh and Yahweh's kingdom last forever. The kingdom moving on divine power prevails over those built on military strength. Then attention is focused on the Greek age of the writer. These chapters make it clear that the contemporary agonies of devout Jews under the tyrannical pressures of Antiochus Epiphanes are analogous to the trials of Daniel and his friends. The heroic behavior of the captives in exile is exalted as a pattern for Jewish conduct to be followed with greater fidelity in the presence of Epiphanes' "abomination of desolation."

In the first vision, four awesome beasts emerge from the sea. The beasts represent the Babylonian, Median, Persian, and Greek imperial powers. The fourth beast had ten horns symbolizing the succession of Seleucid rulers. It was the most terrible beast of all and its little horn was Antiochus Epiphanes, the reigning monster in Jewish eyes. Yahweh, "the Ancient One," sentenced this beast to death and gave the eternal kingdom to "one like a son of man,"[64] who was identified as belonging to the "holy ones of the Most High"—that is, the faithful under oppression (7:18). The writer is telling the struggling Jews

---

[64]Daniel 7:13,14. "Son of man" appears in the Aramaic translation of the passage. New Testament gospel narratives use the phrase to refer to Jesus.

that hope rests in the action of God, who is forever in control of the destiny of those who trust in God.

For the apocalyptist one powerful visionary statement of a theme would not suffice. Therefore the idea of divine judgment on Antiochus is repeated in additional fantasies. The second vision represents the victory of Greece (a he-goat) over Medo-Persia (a two-horned ram). The "great horn" of the he-goat was Alexander the Great, who was broken while strong and succeeded by four other horns, representing the divisions of his empire. From one of these horns emerged a "little horn," Antiochus Epiphanes, an arrogant, proud tyrant who would ravage and plunder for three years (168–165 B.C.E.).

In the third vision Jeremiah's prediction of a seventy-year exile (25:11, 12) is restated as "seventy weeks" (9:24). Gabriel, the angel interpreter of the vision, discloses that Babylonian, Persian, and Greek power had been broken by the strength of Yahweh, who therefore would ultimately destroy Antiochus and his oppressive rule. Yahweh would remain sovereign over history. The fourth vision continues the theme of Yahweh's ultimate victory. It covers the period from the third year of Cyrus of Persia to an end "at the time appointed" (11:27, 29) beyond Antiochus Epiphanes. In apocalyptic imagery, history is traced through Alexander, the Ptolemies, and the Seleucids to Antiochus Epiphanes. In due time the Seleucid oppressor "shall come to his end, with none to help him" (11:45).

The impact of the vision leaves Daniel impatiently asking a question quite typical of apocalyptic literature, How long shall it be till the end of these wonders? He received assurance and the admonition: "Happy are those who persevere . . . . But you, go your way, and rest; and you shall rise for your reward at the end of the days" (12:13).

The book of Daniel was written to a specific age with the distinctive purpose of reassuring Yahweh's people in a time of distress. Its religious values, however, are abiding and apply to men and women of all the ages. H. H. Rowley has summarized these values:

1. Obedience to the will of God is the purpose of life, more important than life itself.
2. God is active in history. Only men of folly fail to take him into account.
3. Religion is not just "peace and poise of spirit," but life lived in fellowship with God and service of men.
4. Peace is God's gift to a world that does his will, not man's achievement.
5. To spread the spirit of loyalty to God is one's highest contribution to the well-being of the world.
6. Loyalty to God is loyalty to a person, not to an idea.
7. Life extends beyond death. In the Hebrew Bible only the book of Daniel teaches a bodily resurrection.
8. An urgency of decision is known in the choice between loyalty or disloyalty to God.[65]

[65]H. H. Rowley, "The Meaning of Daniel for Today," *Interpretation*, 15 (1961) 387–97.

Moreover, the latest book of the Hebrew canon serves a fitting connection between the Hebrew scriptures and the New Testament. The author of Daniel understands perfectly well that Yahweh's authority is conferred on the transformed and purified people of God, "saints of the Most High," through whose dedication all nations of the earth will be blessed. Covenant is known when Yahweh rules over a devout people living with the confidence of Yahweh's sovereignty over history. Therein is the true kingdom of God. Such an idea is the basis of Jesus' teaching and the New Testament affirmation of a kingdom in which God reigns until the final day.

CONCLUSION

Maccabean rule, which proved a signal disappointment, was short-lived. Less than a century after winning independence in 142, Israel became subject to Rome, never again (in ancient times) to be free. As a nation, Israel was dead. Its faith, however, was in Yahweh, and its hope lived on. The God who had chosen Abraham to father a great nation would still act to bless all peoples through Israel. Knowing that faith is hope, Israel looked for the coming of Yahweh's kingdom and the doing of Yahweh's will. Nothing could stand in the way of its realization; its coming would be Yahweh's doing.

Thus, Israel's hope was the expectation of the work of sovereign Yahweh, whose ways are mysteriously beyond finding out. The shape of that hope had not crystallized by the close of the Hebrew biblical period. The hope was one, but its expressions were many. The prophets looked for the historical establishment of a kingdom ruled over by Yahweh's anointed ("messiah") who would rule in righteousness, embodying the ideal of the Davidic monarchy. The apocalyptists yearned for the divine arrival of an extramundane kingdom of glory that would be ushered in by the coming of "a son of man," bringing an end to the present evil age. Some saw the realization of Yahweh's purpose through the unselfish redemptive suffering of the Servant of Yahweh, whether Israel, the remnant, or some individual. In some sense all who had religious perception longed for the establishment of a new and ideal covenant between Yahweh and Yahweh's people, a covenant that would never be broken and would ultimately include both Israel and the nations.

For Judaism these hopes are being fulfilled in the life of the Jewish community. Christians, drawing on their Jewish heritage, understand God's continuing action in history to be demonstrated in Jesus of Nazareth. For these believers, both Jewish and Christian, expectations developed across the centuries of Hebrew history anticipate the future reality of the kingdom of God established with persons of faith in a new covenant.

SUGGESTIONS FOR FURTHER STUDY

A number of items in this chapter may require further reading in the Bible dictionaries: Samaritans, Hellenism, Hasmoneans, Maccabees, Hasidim, Purim, wisdom, scribes, Pharisees, Essenes, Sadducees, Talmud, Mishnah, Gemara, tradition of the elders, theodicy, diaspora. The dictionaries will be helpful to those who are interested in second- and third-generation Maccabees or more details regarding the Ptolemies or Seleucids.

For the impact of Hellenism on the East, consult a biography of Alexander, such as Peter Green, *Alexander the Great* (Praeger, 1970), or N. G. L. Hammond, *Alexander the Great: King, Commander, and Statesman* (Noyes, 1980). Erich S. Gruen, *The Hellenistic World and the Coming of Rome* (Cornell, 1993), and Frank W. Walbank, *The Hellenistic World* (rev. ed. Harvard, 1993), are competent treatments of the subject. Samuel K. Eddy, *The King Is Dead: Studies in the Near Eastern Resistance to Hellenism (334–31* B.C.*)* (University of Nebraska, 1961), will clarify the response to Alexander and Hellenism.

Consult the basic commentaries, especially *The Anchor Bible* and *The Interpreter's Bible*, to expand your understanding of biblical books discussed in this chapter. Additional bibliographies on the book of Job, apocalyptic literature, wisdom and wisdom literature, the Dead Sea Scrolls, postexilic Judaism, and Messianism will be found under these headings in the General Bibliography.

Several journal articles will help with Job: T. W. Tilley, "God and the Silencing of Job," *Modern Theology* 5 (1989) 257–70; Matitiahu Tsevat, "The Meaning of the Book of Job," *Hebrew Union College Annual* 37 (1966) 73–106; and James L. Crenshaw, "Popular Questioning of the Justice of God in Ancient Israel," *Zeitschrift fur die altestamentlich Wissenschaft* 82 (1970) 380–95.

On theodicy, see Walter Brueggemann, "Theodicy in a Social Dimension," *Journal for the Study of the Old Testament* 33 (1985) 3–25, and James L. Crenshaw, *Theodicy in the Old Testament* (Fortress, 1983).

Other items which may be helpful with the period: Werner Foerster, *From the Exile to Christ* (Fortress, 1964), gives a picture of Palestinian Judaism during this period; William McKane, *Proverbs: A New Approach* (Westminster, 1970), and *Prophets and Wise Men* (S. C. M., 1965); E. W. Heaton, *The Book of Daniel* (S. C. M., 1956); Roland E. Murphy, *The Song of Songs* (Hermeneia series, Fortress, 1990); and Othmar Keel, *The Song of Songs* (Continental Commentary series, Fortress, 1994).

Chronology of the Hebrew Biblical Period[1]

I. The ancient world before the patriarchs
   A. The Stone Age, beginning at least 100,000 years ago. This era is usually divided into the Old, Middle, and Late Stone Ages, which cannot be dated with precision. Culture appeared and began to take on refinements as early as 8000 B.C.E. Agriculture is in evidence in the Near East in the Middle Stone Age; villages and pottery appear in the 6th–5th millennia.
   B. The Copper Stone Age, 4th millennium. Writing developed in Babylonia by 3500 B.C.E.
   C. The Early Bronze Age, 3rd millennium. Great states of Egypt and Mesopotamia emerge: Sumer, Akkad, Ebla, Egypt's Old Kingdom and Intermediate Empire.
II. Premonarchical Hebrew history, c. 2000–1020 B.C.E.
   A. The Patriarchal Age, c. 2000–1500. Canaan was under Egyptian influence during this period. Abraham, probably 19th century.[2] Migrations into Canaan continued through the 14th century.
   B. Backgrounds of National Formation, c. 1700–1020.

---

[1]Chronology for all periods is based on the revised edition of *The Westminster Historical Atlas to the Bible*, G. Ernest Wright and Floyd V. Filson, editors. This scheme largely follows a chronology developed by W. F. Albright (see *Bulletin of the American Schools of Oriental Research*, 100 [December 1945] 16–22).

[2]See Albright, "Abraham the Hebrew: A New Archaeological Interpretation," *Bulletin of the American Schools of Oriental Research*, 163 (October 1961) 36–54.

Israel	*Egypt*	
SOJOURN IN EGYPT, C. 1700–1300 Israel's movement into Egypt began c. 1700	Hyksos domination of Egypt	1710
	18th Dynasty, Egyptian re-surgence	1570
Additional migrations throughout the period	Independence won by Ah-mose I	1570–1546
	Egyptian strength reached peak	
	Thutmose III	1490–1435
	Religious revolution, discon-tent, weakness in Amarna period	1370–1353
Oppression of the Hebrews	19th Dynasty, building and strength	1310
	Establishment of delta capital Seti I	1308–1290
EXODUS FROM EGYPT, C. 1280, MOSES	Ramses II	1290–1224
CONQUEST OF CANAAN, C. 1250–1200, JOSHUA	20th Dynasty	1200
CONFEDERACY, C. 1200–1020		
Struggle with Canaanites, c. 1100	Ramses III	1175–1174
Philistines dominated southern Canaan by time of Saul	Defeat of sea peoples result-ing in settlement of Philis-tines in Canaan	
	End of Egyptian empire	1065

III. Period of Hebrew kings, c. 1020–587 B.C.E.

Near Eastern Power of Influence in Palestine	*Palestine*			
	1. United Monarchy, 1020–922 B.C.E.			
	Saul, 1020–1000			
	David, 1000–961			
	Solomon, 961–922			
	2. Divided Monarchy, 922–587 B.C.E.			
EGYPT	JUDAH		ISRAEL	
Shishak invaded 918 Judah	Rehoboam	922–915	Jeroboam I	922–901
	Abijah	915–913		
	Asa	913–873	Nadab	901–900
SYRIA			Baasha	900–877
Benhadad I c. 880–842	Jehoshaphat	873–849	Elah	877–876
			Zimri	876
			Tibni*	876–?
			Omri*	876–869

*a period of coregency

Near Eastern Power of Influence in Palestine		Palestine			
(853—Battle of Karkar)				Ahab	869–850
				Ahaziah	850–849
Hazael	c. 842–806	Jehoram or Joram	849–842	Jehoram	849–842
		Ahaziah	842		
		Athaliah	842–837	Jehu	842–815
		Joash or Jehoash	837–800	Jehoahaz	815–801
		Amaziah	800–783	Joash	801–786
		Uzziah*	783–742	Jeroboam II	786–746
REZON	c. 740–732	Jotham*	750–735	Zechariah	746–745
(Fall of Damascus to Assyria—732)				Shallum	745
				Menahem	745–736
				Pekahiah	736–735
ASSYRIA		Ahaz	735–715	Pekah	735–732
Tiglath-pileser	745–727			Hoshea	732–722
Shalmaneser V	727–722				
(724–722—Siege of Samaria)					
Sargon II	722–705				
(722—Fall of Samaria)					
Sennacherib	705–681	Hezekiah	715–687		
(701—Siege of Jerusalem)					
Esarhaddon	681–669	Manasseh	687–642		
Asshurbanapal	669–633?	Amon	642–640		
Assuretililani	633–629?	Josiah	640–609		
Sinsharishkum	?629–612				
(Fall of Nineveh to Babylonia—612)					
EGYPT					
Necho	609–593	(Battle at Megiddo; Josiah killed by Necho of Egypt—609)			
BABYLON					
Nabopolassar	626–605				
		Jehoahaz	609		
Nebuchadnez-zar	605–562	Jehoiakim	609–598		
(Battle of Carchemish; defeat of Necho—605)					
(First expedition of exile—597)		Jehoiachin	598–597		
(Fall of Jerusalem to Babylon—587)		Zedekiah	597–587		

*a period of coregency

IV. Exilic and postexilic periods, 587–333 B.C.E.

Powers of Influence on Judah		Judah	
BABYLON		Judah in exile in Babylon	587–538
Nebuchadnezzar	605–562		
Amel-marduk	562–560		
Neriglissar	560–556		
Nabonidus	556–539		
(539—Fall of Babylon to Persia)			
PERSIA			
Cyrus	539–530	Edict of Cyrus permitting the return of captives to Jerusalem	538
Cambyses	530–522		
Darius I	522–486	Rebuilding of Jerusalem temple	520–516
Xerxes I	486–465		
Artaxerxes I	465–424	Mission of Ezra	458
Xerxes II	423	Nehemiah became governor of Judah	445
Darius II	423–404		
Artaxerxes II	404–358		
Artaxerxes III	358–338		
Arses	338–336		
Darius III	336–331		
(Battle of Issus; Persia fell to Greece—331)			

V. The Hellenistic period, 333–63 B.C.E.

Control of East by Macedonian empire under Alexander. Following his death, Ptolemies controlled Egypt and Seleucids controlled Syria, 331–323

Egypt		Judah		Syria	
Ptolemy I	323–285	Judah under control of Ptolemies	323–198	Seleucus I	312–280
Ptolemy II (Philadelphius)	285–246			Antiochus I	280–261
				Antiochus II	261–246
Ptolemy III	246–221			Seleucus II	246–226
				Seleucus III	226–223
Ptolemy IV	221–203	Battle of Panium in which Seleucids gained control of Palestine	198	Antiochus III (the Great)	223–187
				Seleucus IV	187–175

Egypt		Judah		Syria	
Ptolemy V	203–181	Maccabean revolt	167	Antiochus IV (Epiphanes)	175–163
Ptolemy VI	181–146	Religious emancipation of Jews	165	Antiochus V	163–162
Egypt controlled by Rome after 180 and became Roman province in 30 B.C.E.		142–63		Jewish political independence until the establishment of Roman rule over Jerusalem	

Glossary

ACROSTIC. A literary device in which successive lines or verses begin with letters in alphabetical order.

AETILOGY. *See* Etiology.

AMALEKITES. Desert tribe living south of Canaan in Negeb and Sinai peninsula. Biblical tradition traces them from Amalek, son of Esau. They were enemies of Israel up to the time of the monarchy.

AMMONITES. Amorite people of Transjordan. Lived along the Jabbok watershed. Although from the same racial stock, they were enemies of Israel. Biblical tradition traces them from Lot.

AMORITES. Semitic people from northwest Mesopotamia. Flooded the Fertile Crescent after 2000 B.C.E. The migration of Israel's ancestors to Canaan was part of this movement. Name means "westerners" (Babylonian) or "highlanders" (Hebrew).

AMPHICTYONY. A religious confederation centered in a sanctuary. Term derived from Greek word meaning "to gather around." Appropriate for Israel's religio-political organization between the conquest and monarchy, only if used to designate their bond on grounds of common religious commitment. Israel's amphictyonic center was first located at Shechem, later at Shiloh.

ANATOLIA. Ancient geographic name for Asia Minor.

ANTHROPOMORPHISM. The ascription of human form, personality, or attributes to that which is not human, especially deity.

'APIRU. *See* Habiru.

APOCALYPTIC. From a Greek term meaning "to reveal" or "to unveil." Type of literature common in Judaism in the late centuries B.C.E. and early centuries C.E. Characterized by symbolic language and elaborate imagery. Best example in the Hebrew Bible is the book of Daniel. A book written in apocalyptic style is called an Apocalypse.

APOCRYPHA, HEBREW. 1. Generally, noncanonical literature. 2. Specifically for Protestants, books included in the Septuagint and Vulgate, but not in the Hebrew Bible.

APODICTIC LAW. Unconditional law, such as the decalogue.

ARABAH. Arid desert plain between the Dead Sea and the Gulf of Aqabah. Rich in mineral deposits, especially copper and iron.

ARAMAIC. The language of the Arameans; spread by merchants throughout western Asia, it became the lingua franca of the ancient Near East. Became the common language of the Persian empire after 500 B.C.E. and, in time, the language of postexilic Jews. Portions of the Hebrew Bible were written in Aramaic.

ARAMEANS. Semitic peoples who entered the Fertile Crescent 1500–1000 B.C.E. Established small kingdoms in Syria. Some of them were among Israel's ancestors.

ARCHEOLOGY. The scientific study by excavation, examination, and publication of the remains of ancient civilizations.

ARK. 1. The boxlike boat of the biblical story of the flood. 2. The portable throne of Yahweh symbolizing the divine presence among the people. First kept in the tabernacle; then in the inmost chamber of the temple.

ASHDOD REBELLION. A revolt against Assyria by Ashdod of Philistia, possibly with participation by Hezekiah of Judah, 714–711 B.C.E.

ASHERAH. Female goddess of Canaan, Baal's consort. Fertility goddess of sex and war. In the Hebrew Bible, Asherah is used loosely of the goddess, her wooden image, or the tree or pole used as her symbol.

ASSYRIA. Empire on upper Tigris River. Its culture dates to the third millennium B.C.E. Assyrians dominated the Fertile Crescent between 1100 and 612 B.C.E. Nineveh was the capital of the empire during its period of dominance.

ATON. Egyptian sun god. Championed by Akhnaton as *the one* deity.

ATONEMENT, DAY OF. *See* Fast Day.

BAAL. Name applied to various local Canaanite deities, but also used as a substitute for Hadad, the chief Canaanite god of fertility in whom the other deities were merged. Baal was the personification of natural forces that produce rain and vegetation.

BABEL. Mythological location of a tower in an etiological story (Genesis 11) accounting for language differences; a polemic against Babylon.

BABYLON. City on middle Euphrates, capital of Old Babylonian and Neo-Babylonian empires. The city gave its name to the surrounding territory and the empire that was centered there.

BABYLONIAN CHRONICLE. A clay tablet recording and dating the battle of Carchemish and the capture of Jerusalem in 597 B.C.E.

B.C.E. Years "before the common era," sometimes designated B.C., "before Christ."

BEHISTUN ROCK. A trilingual inscription from Darius I of Persia which was a key to deciphering cuneiform.

BIBLICAL CRITICISM. The scholarly effort to understand biblical materials through rational analysis. More specific labels, often overlapping, have been applied to this approach: (1) Textual criticism: The attempt to establish a dependable text by careful comparison of extant manuscripts. (2) Historical criticism: Reconstructing the place and time from which biblical materials come in order to understand their meaning in their original environment. (3) Literary criticism: Study that focuses upon the literary type (genre), usually including sources used by the author and the development and characteristics of the genre. Concerned with plot structure, characterization, climax, and symbolism. (4) Form criticism: Attempt to break larger bodies of material into small units (forms) assumed to have developed in the oral and written preservation of materials. (5) Source criticism: Analysis of sources used in the construction of larger literary units. (6) Redaction criticism: Attempt to determine the final editor's purposes as disclosed by his arrangement, editing, and modification of the materials. (7) Tradition criticism: Study of the development of themes in larger canonical collections—e.g., the ideas of kingdom, covenant. (8) Structuralism: A system of interpretation that focuses on the function and structure of language rather than the structure of a text, on the assumption that relationships of language precede elements in the text. *See also* Feminine Hermeneutics.

BOOK OF CONSOLATION.   Jeremiah 30–33.

CANAAN.   Name for the land between the Jordan and the Mediterranean from Egypt to Syria. The name may mean "land of purple," so called because of purple dye made from the murex shellfish found along the coast. Later called Palestine.

CANON.   A collection of authoritative sacred books.

CANONIZATION.   The process by which a collection of works becomes authorized— i.e., forms a canon.

C.E.   Years of the "common era," sometimes designated A.D., *anno Domini.*

CHALDEANS.   1. Mountain people who founded the Neo-Babylonian empire. 2. As- trologers of the postexilic period so called because of the proficiency of Baby- lonian priests in astronomy.

CHARISMATIC.   A leader by virtue of extraordinary gifts or ability.

CHEREM.   The "ban" of the holy war. The word means "to set apart" or "to dedicate," but in the Hebrew Bible was sometimes interpreted to mean the total destruction of enemies.

CHERUBIM.   Symbolic creatures of composite type, half-animal, half-human. Cheru- bim were the guardians of Yahweh's earthly throne.

CHESED.   Term meaning "covenant love," a key concept in Hosea.

CHRONICLER.   The historian who compiled and edited the books of Chronicles, Ezra, and Nehemiah, a continuous telling of Israel's story.

CIRCUMCISION.   The removal of the male foreskin; used in Jewish tradition as a ritual of induction into the covenant community.

CODEX.   Handwritten manuscripts in book form.

CONFEDERACY.   A loosely structured grouping of Israelite tribes to perform functions of common interest. Typical of Hebrew organization from about 1200 to 1020 B.C.E. Their bond was a common commitment to covenant with Yahweh. *See also* Amphictyony.

COSMOLOGY.   Conception of the structure of the universe.

COURT HISTORY OF DAVID.   2 Samuel 9–24 and 1 Kings 1–2, the deuteronomic story of David's rule. Frank and realistic. Also called the succession narrative.

COVENANT.   1) Agreement between individuals or groups. 2) Specifically in the He- brew Bible, an agreement between the sovereign Yahweh and Israel. Yahweh agrees to be Israel's God; Israel in turn is to be Yahweh's people and respond in faithfulness.

COVENANT CODE.   A succinct ethical elaboration of the decalogue found in Exodus 20:22–23:33.

CULTUS (CULT).   A system of worship.

CUNEIFORM.   Wedge-shaped Semitic writing characteristic of Mesopotamia.

DAVIDIC COVENANT.   The covenant emphasis developed after the reign of David, stressing the importance of preserving the Davidic tradition, particularly keeping a descendant of David on the throne and honoring the Jerusalem sanctuary.

DEAD SEA SCROLLS.   Numerous biblical and nonbiblical manuscripts and fragments found since 1947 in caves on the northwest side of the Dead Sea; they came from the library of the Essene community of Qumran. *See also* Essenes.

DECALOGUE.   The "ten words." The Ten Commandments found in Exodus 20 and Deuteronomy 5.

DEUTERO-ISAIAH, or SECOND ISAIAH.   The part of the book of Isaiah written during the exile by a prophet or prophets in the tradition of Isaiah of the 8th century. Includes chaps. 40–55 and perhaps 56–66, although many scholars believe the latter to be the work of still another prophet (or prophets) whom they designate Trito-Isaiah.

DEUTERONOMIC HISTORY. An extensive "history" of Israel that took final form during or just after the exile. It includes Deuteronomy, Joshua, Judges, Samuel, and Kings. Sometimes called "D." The author (or authors) of the history is known as the Deuteronomist.

DIASPORA. Jews living outside Palestine after the time of the exile.

DIVINATION. "Divining" the message of deity by interpreting omens, such as oil and water in a cup, celestial phenomena, and dreams. Oracles so produced were known as "omen texts."

DOCUMENTARY HYPOTHESIS. Theory of the authorship of the Pentateuch assuming four separate authors or groups of authors. *See* Yahwistic history, Elohistic history, Deuteronomic history, and Priestly history.

EBLA. A locale in Syria where a cache of texts has been found, possibly clarifying the background of the Hebrew patriarchal period.

ECSTASY. Literally "to stand outside." The ecstatic trance was used in ancient Near Eastern prophecy to produce a message from deity.

EDOMITES. A Semitic people who lived in the Arabah and Negeb, south of the Dead Sea. According to the Hebrew Bible, the descendents of Esau.

EISEGESIS. The interpretive approach that "reads meaning into" the biblical text. *See* Exegesis.

EL. The Semitic root is expressive of divinity. El was the name of the great "high" god of the Canaanite pantheon. In the Hebrew Bible, the name is applied indiscriminately to all gods but also used as a proper name of a particular deity. When referring to Israel's god, El is most often followed by a modifying word (El Bethel, El Roi, El 'Olam, El Shaddai, etc.) The Hebrew Bible prefers the plural word Elohim, perhaps to show that Yahweh was God in the highest sense of the word.

ELOHISTIC HISTORY. A "history" of Israel's beginnings covering the period from creation to the conquest. Written sometime around 900 B.C.E. in the kingdom of Israel from the perspective of the northern tribes. Sometimes called "E." Its author (or authors) is known as the Elohist.

ENUMA ELISH. "When on high," the opening words of the Mesopotamian story of creation, commonly used as title of the work.

EPHRAIM. 1. Son of Joseph. 2. Most important of the northern tribes. 3. Poetic name for the kingdom of Israel.

EPONYM. The person from whom a family, race, city, or nation is supposed to have taken its name.

ESCHATOLOGY. The study of last or final things, as death, the end of the age, etc.

ESDRAELON. *See* Jezreel.

ESSENES. Ascetic Jewish sect of late Hebrew Bible times. Lived in monastic-type establishments, the most famous of which was at Qumran.

ETIOLOGY. The explanation of cause or reason.

EXEGESIS. The interpretive approach that derives meaning "out of" the biblical text. *See* Eisegesis.

FAST DAY. The one regular fast day in the Israelite liturgical calendar was the Day of Atonement, a most sacred day when atonement was made for the sins of all the people.

FEAST. Three major festivals in the Israelite liturgical year: (1) Passover-unleavened bread *(Pesach-Mazzoth)*; great celebration of the exodus deliverance. The first feast of the liturgical year. (2) Weeks *(Shabhuoth)*, also called Pentecost in later

Judaism. Agricultural festival at the end of the barley harvest. Fifty days after the feast of unleavened bread. (3) Ingathering *(Sukkoth)*, also called tabernacles or booths. Harvest festival of thanksgiving. Also commemorative of the deliverance from Egypt. Eventually this festival was celebrated in connection with New Years and became the time of covenant renewal at the beginning of the year.

Two minor or later festivals: (1) Purim, a nationalistic celebration of events recorded in the book of Esther. (2) Dedication (Hanukkah), also called feast of lights. Celebration of the rededication of the temple during the Maccabean revolt.

FEMININE HERMENEUTICS. An approach to biblical interpretation that aims to overcome patriarchal orientations in biblical literature.

FERTILE CRESCENT. A semicircular region of fertility between mountains and desert extending northwestward from the northern tip of the Persian Gulf through the Tigris-Euphrates valley to Haran and bending southwestward through Syria, Phoenicia, and Palestine into the Nile River valley. The term was first used by James H. Breasted, a noted Egyptologist.

FERTILITY CULTS. Systems of worship centered around the rhythmic cycle of nature, and rituals appropriate to deities primarily associated with the needs of primitive agricultural peoples. Orgiastic rites involving sex in some form largely characterized their religious practices.

GEMARA. Commentary on the Mishnah (oral law). The two together comprise the Talmud.

GILEAD. Region east of Jordan, between Yarmuk and Arnon rivers.

GILGAMESH EPIC. An ancient Mesopotamian tale dealing with the quest for immortality, includes a flood story with features both similar and dissimilar to the Genesis account.

HABIRU. A nondescript group of persons of varied ethnic backgrounds who ranged across the ancient Near East in the third and second millennia B.C.E. Although the term is cognate with Hebrew, it seems to have a wider application both temporally and geographically.

HAGIOGRAPHA. *See* Writings.

HANUKKAH. *See* Feasts.

HASIDIM. The Pious Ones who resisted by both active and passive means the oppressive policies of Antiochus Epiphanes. Probably the precursors of the Pharisees.

HASMONEANS. *See* Maccabees.

HEBREW. 1. A Semitic tongue learned by the Israelites from Canaanites. The language of the Hebrew Bible—except for certain late section in Aramaic, the tongue that replaced Hebrew in Jewish usage. 2. An Aramean branch of Semites who traced themselves to Eber of Genesis 10:24. A term often used as a synonym for the preexilic Israelite.

HEILSGESCHICHTE. An interpretation that sees history as the arena of God's activity, thus, "salvation history."

HELLENISM. The culture incorporating the ideals of Classical Greece.

HENOTHEISM. Belief in a single deity without denying the existence of others.

HERMENEUTICS. The science of interpretation, especially of biblical materials. Usually defined more narrowly in terms of the goals and methods of the interpreter. *See* Biblical criticism.

HEXATEUCH. Term used for the first six books of the Hebrew Bible as a unit. Preferred to the traditional term "Pentateuch" by some scholars in that (1) Joshua provides fulfillment to the promise of the Pentateuch and (2) the priestly source runs from Genesis through Joshua.

HITTITES. Non-Semites and probably Aryans, who formed a cultural tie between Europe and the Near East. Their formidable kingdom was centered in Asia Minor and Syria in the second millennium B.C.E.

HIEROGLYPHICS. The picture writing of ancient Egypt. These "sacred carvings" probably originated with the priests.

HOLINESS CODE. A collection of laws in Leviticus 17–26 dealing with life and worship acceptable to God.

HOREB. *See* Jebel Musa.

HYKSOS. A Semitic people who overran Egypt and ruled there 1710–1570 B.C.E.; capital, Memphis.

INTERPOLATION. The interruption of the biblical text by additions or comments.

ISRAEL. 1. The name given Jacob, twin son of Isaac, after his religious experiences at the Jabbok ford. 2. The people and its descendents bound together by religious and political ties formally established at Sinai. 3. The northern kingdom, as opposed to Judah, following the division of the Israelite monarchy in 922 B.C.E. 4. God's chosen people. The religious nation, rather than a political state.

JAMNIA. The Palestinian town where Jewish scholars assembled in 90–100 C.E. to consider the canon of the Hebrew Bible. Their work led to a Hebrew Bible containing those books found in modern Protestant editions of the Hebrew scriptures.

JEBEL MUSA. Mountain in southern part of Sinai peninsula. The traditional Mt. Sinai. The name means "mountain of Moses."

JEBUSITES. Early Canaanite residents of Jebus, the city that became Jerusalem.

JEHOVAH. *See* Yahweh.

JEWS. Common name for Israelites after the exile. A derivative of Judah, the tribe of which most of returnees to Palestine were members.

JEZREEL. 1. A town on the edge of Mt. Gilboa overlooking the plain. 2. A valley, also known as the plain of Esdraelon, which extends from the north of Mt. Carmel on the west to a pass to the Jordan on the east. An important battlefield of Palestine.

JORDAN CLEFT. The geological fissures through which the Jordan River runs. Extends through the valley between Lebanon and Anti-Lebanon mountains in the north and Gulf of Aqabah and Red Sea in the south.

JOSIANIC REFORMATION. The most epochal of Judah's several religious revivals. Begun about 626 B.C.E. under the leadership of King Josiah, it was catapulted to great heights in 622 B.C.E. by the discovery of "a scroll of the law" (probably the core of our book of Deuteronomy). Centralization of worship in Jerusalem was a primary objective of the reforms.

JUDAH. 1. The fourth son of Jacob and Leah. 2. The tribe named eponymously for (1). 3. The southern kingdom after the division of the Israelite monarchy in 922 B.C.E. 4. In postexilic days, the region around Jerusalem.

JUDAISM. The religion of the Jews as it developed after the exile.

JUDEA. A Greco-Roman term for the Judah of postexilic times. The extent of the area varied greatly until 70 C.E.

JUDGE OF ISRAEL. The central leader of Israel during the period of tribal confederacy, who presided at the confederal sanctuary. Illustrated in Eli and Samuel.

JUDGES. 1. Tribal heroes of Israel in the era of the confederacy, *shophet*s. They became both civil and military leaders on the basis of their charismatic sanction. 2. A book in the Hebrew Bible in the group known as the Former Prophets.

KENITES. Early Midianite metalsmiths living in the Arabah. Worshipers of God by the name of Yahweh.

KENITE HYPOTHESIS. The belief held by many that the name Yahweh and certain religious practices came to Israel through Midian, possibly via Jethro, Moses' father-in-law.

KETHU'BIM. *See* Writings.

LAW. *See* Torah.

LEGEND. A story, usually about a hero or heroine of the distant past, often popularly thought to be historical, but traditionally preserved to entertain or to convey values.

LEVITES. Those of the Israelite tribe named eponymously for Levi, the third son of Jacob and Leah. Priests whose entire function was cultic were supposed to come from this tribe. Its members who were not officiating priests performed menial cultic tasks.

LITTLE APOCALYPSE. Isaiah 24–27.

LXX. *See* Septuagint.

MACCABEES. The family that heroically commanded the successful Jewish war of independence against Seleucid oppression. Gained religious freedom in 165 B.C.E. and political freedom in 142 B.C.E. Remained in control until 63 B.C.E. Also called Hasmoneans, from Hasmon, the great-grandfather of Mattathias, who launched the revolt.

MASORA. Instructional and informational annotations placed in the margins of Hebrew manuscripts. Begun by the Sopherim and extended by the Masoretes ("men of the Masora").

MASORETES. "Men of the Masora." Jewish scribes who copied manuscripts. They added vowel points to the consonantal text in the 7th to 9th centuries C.E.

MASORETIC TEXT. The text of the Hebrew Bible that became standardized between the 7th and 10th centuries C.E. Owes its existence to the work of the Masoretes.

MEGILLOTH. The canonical Hebrew scrolls—Ruth, Esther, Ecclesiastes, Song of Songs, and Lamentations—read on festival occasions.

MESOPOTAMIA. The area on either side and "between the rivers" Tigris and Euphrates. In general terms, the valley region between ancient Haran and the Persian Gulf.

MESSIAH. The anticipated "anointed" ruler of Davidic descent or deliverer of the Jewish people. In Greek, "the Christ."

MIRACLE. In the Hebrew Bible, a mighty act, natural or supernatural, in which Yahweh is seen to work in behalf of the covenant community.

MISHNAH. The mass of Jewish oral, legal traditions accumulated across several centuries and reduced to written form by Rabbi Judah ha-Nasi (c. 135–220 C.E.). The basic section of the Talmud.

MOABITES. In biblical tradition, the eponymous descendents of Moab, a son of Lot, and one of Lot's daughters. Residents of the land east of the Dead Sea and inveterate enemies of Israel.

MONOTHEISM. The belief that there is only one God.

MYTH. 1. A story about God or godlike beings. 2. A story that symbolically accounts for the origin of a belief, practice, or phenomenon. 3. The hypostatization or personification of an abstract idea.

NAB'I. The term most used to refer to the Hebrew prophet. Means "spokesman."

NEVI'IM. *See* Prophets.

NEGEB. The largely arid region south of Judea.

OMEN TEXTS. *See* Divination.

OMRIDS. Those of the dynasty of Omri, king of Israel.

OPHEL. The southernmost portion of the hill in Jerusalem on which the temple rested.

ORACLE. 1. A divine declaration. 2. The medium of a divine disclosure. Used of a person, place, or thing. 3. Short, stylized unit of prophetic speech.

ORAL TRADITION. The preservation of sacred materials by word of mouth.

OSTRACA. Ancient fragments of pottery or clay tablets used for records and correspondence.

PALESTINE. Name applied to the land between the Jordan valley and the Mediterranean Sea after the time of the Philistines, from whom the name is derived. *See* Canaan.

PAPYRUS. An aquatic plant commonly used as writing material by superimposing a horizontal layer of thin wet strips on a vertical layer and pressed to dry.

PARALLELISM. The most characteristic feature of Hebrew poetry: the couplet with intimate correspondence between the two lines.

PARAPHRASE. A restatement of the meaning of a biblical passage without undue concern for precise transfer of linguistic forms.

PARCHMENT. Animal skin prepared as writing material.

PASSOVER. *See* Feasts.

PENTATEUCH. The first five books of the Hebrew Bible, Genesis–Deuteronomy. Also known as Torah.

PENTECOST. *See* Feasts.

PESHITTA, or PESHITO. The standard Syriac version of the Hebrew Bible.

PHARISEES. The post-Maccabean Jewish religious group that continued the tradition of the Hasidim. Devoted to the law, written and oral.

PHILISTINES. A group of non-Semitic peoples who settled along the southern end of the maritime plain of Palestine during the twelfth century B.C.E. They were a continual menace to the Israelites until the time of David.

PHOENICIA. An ancient country lying between the Lebanon mountain range and the Mediterranean Sea. Its chief cities were Tyre and Sidon, seaports of repute. In times of friendliness, Phoenicia gave Israel access to the ports of the Mediterranean world.

POLEMIC. A disputation unit that intends to degrade or attack an idea or subject, as illustrated in the Tower of Babel (Genesis 11:1–9) story, which pokes fun at Babylon and its worship.

POLYTHEISM. Belief in gods.

POSTEXILE. The period of biblical history after the Babylonian exile, specifically designates the period from 539 B.C.E. until the beginning of the Roman period about 63 B.C.E.

PREEXILE. The period of biblical history before the Babylonian exile.

PRIESTLY HISTORY. The exilic–postexilic "history" of Israel used in the writing of the Hebrew Bible, so called because of its orientation toward Israelite cultic legislation. Sometimes designated "P."

PROPHETS. The second division of the Hebrew scriptures including the former prophets (Joshua, Judges, Samuel, and Kings) and the latter prophets (Isaiah, Jeremiah, Ezekiel, and the Book of the Twelve).

PROVERB. A short, direct statement that intends to draw a conclusion from life's experience. Some come from popular culture; others are framed by sages to make a judgment and instruct in values. Many proverbs use simile to make their point.

PSEUDEPIGRAPHA. A group of noncanonical writings from the postexilic period, so called because some were "falsely inscribed" with the name of some outstanding and revered person.

PTOLEMIES. Name given to the dynasty of Macedonian rulers of Egypt following the death of Alexander the Great. The dynasty took its name from Ptolemy I, surnamed Soter.

PURIM. *See* Feasts.

QARQAR. Scene of a battle in 853 B.C.E. between Shalmaneser III of Assyria and a coalition of kings of Syria-Palestine under Benhadad of Syria. Precise Assyrian dating of this battle makes it a pivotal event for biblical chronology.

QUMRAN.   The monastic community of the Essenes in the foothills of the Judean wilderness near the Dead Sea. Members of this Essene community produced the Dead Sea Scrolls.

RAS SHAMRA.   Locale in northern Syria where in 1929 were discovered numerous Canaanite religious texts revealing the fertility emphasis of Baal religion. *See* Baal.

ROSETTA STONE.   A stone with a trilingual inscription found by a member of a Napoleonic military expedition to Egypt that provided clues for deciphering hieroglyphics.

SADDUCEES.   A Jewish religious group arising during the late pre-Christian era. Conservative and aristocratic. Rejected the authority of oral tradition and theological beliefs in afterlife. Held fast to Torah.

SAMARIA.   1. The village enlarged and made capital of the northern kingdom by Omri. 2. Geographically, the middle of three north–south divisions of Palestine. Extended between the Jordan and Mediterranean from the plain of Esdraelon in the north to the territory of Benjamin in the south.

SAMARITANS.   A racially mixed people arising in the region of Samaria after the Assyrian conquest of 722 B.C.E. Assyrians were moved to the north and intermarried with native Israelites.

SCRIBE.   A copyist charged with both the preservation and interpretation of the Jewish scriptures.

SECOND ISAIAH.   *See* Deutero-Isaiah.

SELEUCIDS.   Name given to the dynasty of Macedonian rulers of Syria following the death of Alexander the Great. The dynasty took its name from Seleucus I.

SEMITES.   "Shemites," supposed descendents of Shem. A group of nations from the Near East forming a linguistic, but not a racial, unit. Babylonians, Assyrians, Phoenicians, Syrians, Israelites, Moabites, Ammonites, and others were Semitic.

SEPTUAGINT.   The Greek translation of the Jewish scriptures dating to the 3d century B.C.E. Its name (from Latin, "seventy") is derived from the legend that 72 scholars did the work of translation in 72 days. Abbreviated LXX.

SHEMA.   The key confession of faith in Jewish liturgy. Opens with Deuteronomy 6:4–9 and focuses on the phrase, "Hear, O Israel, the Lord our God is one Lord."

SHEOL.   The Hebrew equivalent of the Greek Hades. The place of the dead; a vague, shadowy, gloomy region beneath the earth to which all persons go at death. No idea of reward or punishment.

SHEPHELAH.   The "lowlands" of Judah's western frontier. The region of low rolling hills between the Judean hill country and the Philistine plain.

SHOPHETS.   *See* Judges.

SINAI.   *See* Jebel Musa.

SINAI COVENANT.   The covenant idea as given form around the Sinai tradition, emphasizing observance of the law as the proper response to Yahweh's deliverance of Israel from Egyptian bondage.

SON OF MAN.   A phrase in the Hebrew Bible typically meaning simply a human being. Ezekiel used the phrase as God's address to him, and Daniel used the title to symbolize those who rule over the kingdom of God.

SONS OF THE PROPHETS.   Guilds gathered around a prophetic hero.

SOPHERIM.   The "men of the book," a group of scholars charged with publishing and safeguarding the manuscripts of the Jewish scriptures. Began their work in 4th century B.C.E. and continued into the early Christian era. Responsible for dividing manuscripts into sentences and sections.

STELE.   A stone pillar bearing an inscription, carving, or design, usually set up to memorialize a person, deity, or event.

SUCCESSION NARRATIVE.   *See* Court history of David.

SUCCOTH, also SUKKOTH.   The Jewish feast of tabernacles. *See* Feasts.

SUFFERING SERVANT.   A figure of speech used by Second Isaiah to describe the obedient, self-sacrificing servant of God.

SYNAGOGUE.   The local institution for Jewish religious instruction and worship. Not mentioned in the Hebrew Bible but prolific in the New Testament. Probably arose during or just after the exile.

SYRIA.   The northern part of the land bridge between Asia and Egypt. Area included Phoenicia on the coast and the inland kingdom of Aram, whose capital was Damascus.

TABERNACLE.   The portable tent-sanctuary of the Israelites used during the exodus wanderings period.

TABERNACLES, FEAST OF, also SUKKOTH.   *See* Feasts.

TALMUD.   The combination of Mishnah (the codified "tradition of the elders") and Gemara (the explanation of Mishnah). A Palestinian Talmud was completed about 275 C.E.; a Babylonian Talmud was completed about 500 C.E..

TARGUM.   An Aramaic paraphrase of the Jewish scriptures, coming from early in the Christian era when Aramaic replaced Hebrew as the common language of the Jews.

TEMPLE.   The sanctuary in Jerusalem, the center of Jewish religion after the time of Solomon. It served as the central Yahweh shrine throughout its history. The first temple in Jerusalem was built by Solomon; the second by Zerubbabel upon return from the Babylonian exile. Herod the Great began a renovation, which was not completed until c. 65 C.E. The history of the temple concludes with its destruction by the Romans in 70 C.E.

TESTAMENT.   A "will" or "covenant." The word itself is a Latin rendition of the Greek word for "covenant." It was first used in connection with the Bible by Tertullian and Origen in the early century 3rd C.E. *See also* Covenant.

TEXTUAL CRITICISM.   The scholarly attempt to determine the original wording of a biblical text. Also called "lower criticism."

THEOPHANY.   A manifestation of God to humans through an appearance, such as an angel or some natural phenomenon.

THEO-POLITICS.   Term coined by Martin Buber to designate Isaiah's idea that a covenant people should avoid political alliances, depending only on Yahweh.

TORAH.   Hebrew, "instruction" or "law." Sometimes used to refer generally to scriptures of Judaism, but specifically means the Pentateuch, the "law" of Moses.

TRANSCOLONIZATION.   Practice of cross-colonizing as exercised by Assyrians after their capture of Jerusalem in 722 B.C.E. *See* Samaritans.

TRANSJORDAN.   The plateau region lying between the Jordan cleft and the arid areas of the Arabian Desert. Extends from Bashan in the north to Edom in the south.

TWELVE, THE BOOK OF THE.   The "minor" prophets, including Hosea, Joel, Amos, Obadiah, Jonah, Micah, Nahum, Habakkuk, Zephaniah, Haggai, Zechariah, and Malachi.

VULGATE.   The Latin translation of the scriptures prepared by Jerome near the end of the 4th century C.E. under the auspices of the Roman Church.

WEEKS, FEAST OF, Also, PENTECOST.   *See* Feasts.

WRITINGS.   The third division of the Hebrew Bible, including Psalms, Proverbs, Job, Song of Solomon, Ruth, Lamentations, Ecclesiastes, Esther, Ezra, Nehemiah, and Chronicles. Also called Hagiographa or *Kethu'bim*.

YAHWEH.   The Israelite personal name for God. Because the name was regarded as too sacred to be pronounced, the Masoretes attached to the consonantal *YHWH* the vowels from *Adonai*, which means "my Lord." The KJV and RSV indicate the use of the word by LORD (or sometimes GOD).

YAHWISTIC HISTORY.   The earliest of several "histories" of Israel used in the writing of the Hebrew Bible. It covers the period from creation to conquest. Its name is derived from its preference for the divine name *Yahweh*. Sometimes designated "J." Its author or authors is usually referred to as the Yahwist.

ZIGGURAT.   An ancient Babylonian or Assyrian temple in the form of a step-pyramidal tower.

ZION.   Literally, the ridge of Ophel on which early Jerusalem was located. Used poetically to refer to the city itself.

ZION THEOLOGY.   Idea that the Jerusalem temple should remain central in Jewish cultic practice.

General Bibliography

Entries are grouped according to subject or type, listed alphabetically, and cross-referenced with listings elsewhere in the book. References within commentary series, dictionaries, or collections are usually not listed separately. References noted at conclusion of each chapter are usually not entered here.

Alexander the Great. *See* Hellenism.

Amos. *See* p. 354.

Apocalyptic Literature, Eschatology

Collins, John J. *Daniel: With an Introduction to Apocalyptic Literature.* The Forms of Old Testament Literature series, Rolf Knierim et al., eds. Eerdmans, 1984.

———. "The Jewish Apocalypse." *Semeia,* 14 (1979) 21–59.

———. ed. "Apocalypse: The Morphology of a Genre." *Semeia,* 14 (1979) 1–217.

Gowan, Donald E. *Eschatology in the Old Testament.* Fortress, 1986.

Hanson, Paul D. *The Dawn of Apocalyptic: The Historical and Sociological Roots of Jewish Apocalyptic Eschatology.* Fortress, 1975.

Russell, D. S. *The Method and Message of Jewish Apocalyptic.* Old Testament Library. Westminster/John Knox, 1980.

Schmitals, Walter. *The Apocalyptic Movement: Introduction and Interpretation.* Abingdon, 1975.

Wilson, R. D. "From Prophecy to Apocalyptic: Reflections on the Shape of Israelite Religion." *Semeia,* 21 (1981) 79–95.

Apocrypha and Pseudepigrapha

Charlesworth, James H., ed. *The Old Testament Pseudepigrapha.* 2 vols. Doubleday, 1986.

Nickelsburg, G. W. E. *Jewish Literature Between the Bible and the Mishnah.* Fortress, 1981.

Sparks, H. F. D., ed. *The Apocryphal Old Testament.* Oxford, 1984.

Stone, Michael E., ed. *Jewish Writings of the Second Temple Period.* Augsburg/Fortress, 1984.

Archeology

Included here are general works on archeology and the Hebrew scriptures. Works on specific sites are found at the end of the appropriate chapter or in the footnotes.

Aharoni, Yohanan. *The Archaeology of the Land of Israel.* Westminster, 1982.

Albright, W. F. *Archaeology and the Religion of Israel.* 5th ed. Johns Hopkins, 1965.

Ben-tor, Amnon, ed. Trans. R. Greenberg. *The Archaeology of Ancient Israel.* Yale, 1992.

Blaiklock, E. M., and R. K. Harrison, eds. *The New International Dictionary of Biblical Archaeology.* Zondervan, 1983.

Dever, William G. *Recent Archaeological Discoveries and Biblical Research.* Washington, 1990.

———. "The Middle Bronze Age: The Zenith of the Urban Canaanite Era." *Biblical Archaeology,* 50 (1987) 148–77.

Drinkard, Joel F., Jr. et al., eds. *Benchmarks in Time and Culture: An Introduction to the History and Methodology of Syro-Palestinean Archaeology.* Scholars, 1988.

Freedman, David N., and E. F. Campbell, Jr., eds. *The Biblical Archaeology Reader, II–IV.* Doubleday, 1964, 1970, 1983.

Gray, John. *Archaeology and the Old Testament World.* Nelson, 1962.

Lapp, Paul W. *Biblical Archaeology and History.* World, 1988.

Leonard, A., Jr. "The Late Bronze Age." *Biblical Archaeology,* 52 (1989) 4–39.

Mazzar, Amihai. *Archaeology of the Land of the Bible, 10000–586.* Anchor Bible Reference Library. Doubleday, 1990.

Moorey, Peter R. S. *A Century of Biblical Archaeology.* Westminster/John Knox, 1992.

Negev, Auraham, ed. *The Archaeological Encyclopedia of the Holy Land.* Rev ed. Nelson, 1986.

Perdue, Leo G., Lawrence Toombs, and Gary Johnson, eds. *Archaeology and Biblical Interpretation.* John Knox, 1987.

Pritchard, James B. *Archaeology and the Old Testament.* Princeton, 1958.

Sanders, James A., ed. *Near Eastern Archaeology in the Twentieth Century: Essays in Honor of Nelson Gleuck.* Doubleday, 1970.

Smick, Elmer B. *Archaeology of the Jordan Valley.* Baker, 1973.

Stern, Ephraim et al., eds. *The New Encyclopedia of Archaeological Excavations in the Holy Land, I–IV.* Israel Exploration Society, 1993.

Williams, Walter G. *Archaeology in Biblical Research.* Abingdon, 1965.

Wright, G. Ernest. *Biblical Archaeology.* Rev. ed. Westminster, 1966.

Wright, G. Ernest, and David N. Freedman, *The Biblical Archaeologist Reader, I.* Doubleday, 1961.

Ark Narrative. *See* p. 292.

Atlases. *See* Geography.

Authority. *See* Inspiration.

Canon, Text, and Versions

Barr, James. *Holy Scripture: Canon, Authority, Criticism.* Westminster, 1983.

Bruce, F. F. *History of the Bible in English.* 3d ed. Oxford, 1978.

Brueggemann, Walter. *The Creative Work: Canon as A Model for Christian Education.* Fortress, 1962.

Coates, G. W., and B. O. Long, eds. *Canon and Authority.* Fortress, 1977.

Ewert, David. *From Ancient Tablets to Modern Translations.* Zondervan, 1983.

Fredricks, E. S., ed. *The Bible and Bibles in America.* John Knox, 1988.

Leiman, Sid Z. *The Canon and Masorah of the Hebrew Bible: An Introductory Reader.* KTAV, 1974.

Ostborn, Gunner. *Cult and Canon: A Study in the Canonization of the Old Testament.* B. Lundequistska, 1951.

Robinson, H. Wheeler, ed. *The Bible and Its Ancient and English Versions.* Oxford, 1940.

Sanders, James A. *From Sacred Story to Sacred Text: Canon in Paradigm*. Fortress, 1986.
———. *Torah and Canon*. Fortress, 1972.
Tucker, Gene M., David L. Petersen, and Robert R. Wilson, eds. *Canon, Theology, and Old Testament Interpretation*. Fortress, 1988.
Walsh, J. P. M. "Contemporary English Translations of Scripture." *Theological Studies*, 50 (1989) 1336–58.
Wurthwein, Ernst. Trans. E. F. Rhodes. *The Text of the Old Testament*. Eerdmans, 1979.

Chronicles, Book of.   *See* p. 320, 460.

Chronology
Bickerman, Elias J. *Chronology of the Ancient World*. Cornell, 1968.
Bimson, John J. *Redating the Exodus and Conquest*. Almond, 1981.
Finegan, Jack. *Handbook of Biblical Chronology*. Princeton, 1964.
Hayes, John H., and Paul K. Hooker. *A New Chronology for the Kings of Israel and Judah and Its Implications for Biblical History and Literature*. Westminster/John Knox, 1988.
Thiele, Edwin R. *A Chronology of the Hebrew Kings*. Zondervan, 1977.
———. *The Mysterious Numbers of the Hebrew Kings*. 3d ed. Eerdmans, 1983.
Wiseman, D. J. *Chronicles of Chaldean Kings (626–566 B.C.) in the British Museum*. Trustees of the British Museum, 1956.

Commentaries
The Anchor Bible. William F. Albright and David N. Freedman, eds. 44 vols. Doubleday, 1964 onward.
The Broadman Bible Commentary. Clifton J. Allen et al., eds. 12 vols. Broadman, 1969–1972.
Hermeneia: A Critical and Historical Commentary. Frank M. Cross, Jr. et al., eds. Fortress, 1979 onward.
Interpretation: A Bible Commentary for Teaching and Preaching. James L. Mays, Patrick D. Miller, and Paul J. Achtemeier, eds. Westminster/John Knox, 1983 onward.
The Interpreter's Bible. George A. Buttrick et al., eds. 12 vols. Abingdon, 1952.
Jerome Biblical Commentary. Raymond E. Brown, Joseph A. Fitzmyer, and Roland E. Murphy, eds. Vol. 1 *(Old Testament)*. Prentice-Hall, 1968.
The Old Testament Library. John Bright, James Barr, and Peter Ackroyd, eds. 25 vols. Westminster, 1961 onward.

Conquest and Settlement.   *See also*, pp. 255–56.
Aharoni, Yohanan. "The Israelite Occupation of Canaan." *Biblical Archaeologist Reader*, (May/June 1982) 14–23.
Albright, William F. *Yahweh and the Gods of Canaan: A Historical Analysis of Two Contrasting Faiths*. Doubleday, 1968.
Boling, R. G. *Judges; Introduction, Translation, and Commentary*. The Anchor Bible, vol. 6A. Doubleday, 1975.
Borowski, Obed. *Agriculture in Iron Age Palestine: The Evidence From Archaeology and the Bible*. Eisenbrauns, 1987.
Bottero, Jean. *Le probléme des Habiru à la 4e Rencontre Assyriologique Internationale*. Imprimerie Nationale, 1954.
Blenkinsopp, Joseph. "Structure and Style in Judges 13–16." *Journal of Biblical Literature*, 82 (1963) 65–76.
Brueggemann, Walter. *The Land: Place as Gift, Promise, and Challenge in Biblical Faith*. Overtures to Biblical Theology series. Fortress, 1977.

Crenshaw, James L. *Samson: A Secret Betrayed, A Vow Ignored.* John Knox, 1978.

Cross, Frank M., Jr. "The Priestly Tabernacle." *Biblical Archaeologist Reader,* vol. I, (1961), 201ff.

Greenburg, Moshe. *The Hab/piru.* American Oriental Society, 1955.

Mayes, Andrew D. *Israel in the Period of the Judges.* Alec R. Allenson, 1974.

Mendenhall, George E. "The Hebrew Conquest of Palestine." *Biblical Archaeology,* 25 (1962) 66–87.

von Rad, Gerhard. "Verheissenes Land und Jahwes Land in Hexateuch." *Zeitschrift des deutschen Palastin-Vereins,* 66 (1943) 191–204.

Court History of David.   See p. 292.

Covenant

Baltzer, Klaus. Trans. David E. Green. *The Covenant Formulary.* Fortress, 1971.

Gerstenberger, E. "Covenant and Commandment." *Journal of Biblical Literature,* 84 (1965) 38–51.

Hillars, Delbert R. *Covenant: The History of a Biblical Idea.* Johns Hopkins, 1969.

McCarthy, Dennis J. *Old Testament Covenant: A Survey of Current Opinions.* Blackwood, 1972.

———. *Treaty and Covenant.* 2d ed. Analecta Biblica series, vol. 21, Biblical Institute, 1978.

Mendenhall, George E. *Law and Covenant in Israel and the Ancient Near East. Biblical Archaeologist,* 2 (1954) 26–46; 17, 3 (1954) 49–76.

Nicholson, E. W. *God and His People: Covenant and Theology in the Old Testament.* Oxford, 1986.

Creation.   *See also* pp. 131–32.

Anderson, Bernhard W. *Creation Versus Chaos: The Reinterpretation of Mythical Symbolism in the Bible.* Fortress, 1987.

———. *From Creation to New Creation.* Fortress, 1994.

———, ed. *Creation in the Old Testament.* Fortress, 1984.

Coote, Robert B., and David R. Ord. *In the Beginning: Creation and Priestly History.* Fortress, 1991.

Hamilton, Virginia. *In the Beginning: Creation Stories From Around the World.* Harcourt, Brace, Jovanovich, 1988.

Hyers, M. Conrad. *The Meaning of Creation: Genesis and Modern Science.* John Knox, 1984.

Lambert, W. G., and Simon B. Parker. *Enuma Elis: The Babylonian Epic of Creation.* Clarendon, 1966.

Lenowitz, Harris, and Charles Doria, eds. *Origins: Creation Texts from the Ancient Mediterranean.* Anchor, 1976.

O'Brien, Joan V. *In the Beginning: Creation Myths from Ancient Mesopotamia, Israel and Greece.* Scholars, 1982.

van Till, Howard J. et al. *Portraits of Creation: Biblical and Scientific Perspectives on the World's Formation.* Eerdmans, 1990.

Westermann, Claus. Trans. John J. Scullion. *Creation.* Fortress, 1974.

Criticism.   *See also* Textual Criticism; Form Criticism; Literary Criticism; Tradition Criticism; Interpretation; Social Sciences; Feminist Hermeneutics.

Barton, John. *Reading the Old Testament: Method in Biblical Study.* Westminster, 1984.

Brueggemann, Walter, and Hans Wolff. *The Vitality of Old Testament Traditions* 2d ed. John Knox, 1982.

Dobbs-Allsopp, F. W. *Weep, O Daughter of Zion: A Study of the City-Lament Genre in the Hebrew Bible*. Editrice Pontificio Institutio Biblico, 1993.

Gunn, D. "New Directions in the Study of Hebrew Narrative." *Journal for the Study of the Old Testament*, 39 (1987) 65–75.

Keegan, Terrance J. *Interpreting the Bible: A Popular Introduction to Biblical Hermeneutics*. Paulist, 1985.

Levenson, Jon D. *The Hebrew Bible, The Old Testament, and Historical Criticism*. Westminster/John Knox, 1993.

McKenzie, S. L., and S. R. Haynes. *To Each His Own Meaning: An Introduction to Biblical Criticism and Their Application*. John Knox, 1993.

McKnight, Edgar V. *Meaning in Texts: The Historical Shaping of a Narrative Hermeneutics*. Fortress, 1978.

Mendenhall, George E. *The Tenth Generation: The Origins of Biblical Tradition*. Johns Hopkins, 1973.

Rogerson, John W. *W. M. L. de Welte: Founder of Modern Biblical Criticism*. Journal for the Study of the Old Testament series, no. 126. Cornell, 1991.

Sanders, James A. *Canon and Community: A Guide to Canonical Criticism*. Fortress, 1972.

Smith, T. C. *How We Got Our Bible*. Smith & Helwys, 1994.

Van Seters, John. *In Search of History: Historiography in the Ancient World and the Origins of Biblical History*. Yale, 1983.

Wuellner, W. "Where Is Rhetorical Criticism Taking Us?" *Catholic Biblical Quarterly*, 49 (1987) 448–63.

Criticism, Form

Culley, Robert C. *Studies in the Structure of Hebrew Narrative*. Fortress, 1976.

Hayes, John H., ed. *Old Testament Form Criticism*. Fortress, 1974.

Koch, Klaus. *The Growth of the Biblical Tradition: The Form Critical Method*. Scribner's, 1969.

Lohfink, Gerhard. *The Bible: Now I Get It: A Form-Criticism Handbook*. Doubleday, 1979.

McKnight, Edgar V. *What Is Form Criticism?* Fortress/Augsburg, 1969.

Muilenburg, James. "Form Criticism and Beyond." *Journal of Biblical Literature*, 88 (1969) 1–18.

Tucker, Gene M. *Form Criticism of the Old Testament*. Fortress, 1971.

Criticism, Literary

Alter, Robert. *The Art of Biblical Narrative*. Basic Books, 1981.

Gros Louis, R. R., ed. *Literary Interpretation of Biblical Narratives*. Abingdon, 1974.

Habel, Norman C. *Literary Criticism of the Old Testament*. Fortress, 1971.

McKnight, Edgar V. *The Bible and the Reader: An Introduction to Literary Criticism*. Westminster, 1985.

Schwartz, Regina M., ed. *The Book and the Text: The Bible and Literary Theory*. Blackwell, 1990.

Sternberg, Meir. *The Poetics of Biblical Narrative*. Indiana, 1987.

Criticism, Textual

Ap-Thomas, D. R. *A Primer of Old Testament Textual Criticism*. Rev. ed. Fortress, 1971.

Brotzman, Ellis R. *Old Testament Textual Criticism: A Practical Introduction*. Baker, 1993.

Goshen-Gottstein, M. H. "Textual Criticism of the Old Testament: Rise, Decline, Rebirth." *Journal of Biblical Literature*, 102/3 (1983), 365–99.

Klein, Ralph W. *Textual Criticism of the Old Testament: The Septuagint after Qumran.* Fortress, 1974.

McCarter, P. Kyle, Jr. *Textual Criticism: Recovering the Text of the Hebrew Bible.* Fortress, 1986.

Tov, Emanuel. *Textual Criticism of the Hebrew Bible.* Fortress, 1992.

Weingreen, Jacob. *Introduction to the Critical Study of the Text of the Hebrew Bible.* Oxford, 1982.

Wurthwein, Ernst. *The Text of the Old Testament: An Introduction to Biblia Hebraica.* Blackwell, 1957.

Criticism, Tradition History

Knight, Douglas A., ed. *Tradition and Theology in the Old Testament.* Fortress, 1977.

Rast, Walter E. *Tradition History and the Old Testament.* Fortress, 1972.

Daniel.   *See* Apocalyptic Literature; Son of Man; *also* p. 506.

Dead Sea Scrolls

Burrows, Millar. *The Dead Sea Scrolls.* Viking, 1955.

———. *More Light on the Dead Sea Scrolls.* Viking, 1958.

Cross, Frank M., Jr. *The Ancient Library of Qumran and Modern Biblical Studies.* Fortress, 1995.

Cross, Frank M., Jr., and Shemaryahu Talman, eds., *Qumran and the History of the Biblical Text.* Harvard, 1973.

Davies, Philip R. *Behind the Essenes: History and Ideology in the Dead Sea Scrolls.* Scholars, 1987.

Dupont-Sommer, A. Trans. G. Vermes. *The Essene Writings from Qumran.* Peter Smith, 1973.

Fitzmyer, Joseph A. *Response to One Hundred One Questions on the Dead Sea Scrolls.* Paulist, 1992.

Milik, Joseph T. *Ten Years of Discovery in the Wilderness of Judea.* Alec R. Allenson, 1959.

Ringgren, Helmer, *Faith of Qumran: Theology of the Dead Sea Scrolls.* Crossroad, 1993.

Shanks, Hershel, ed. *Understanding the Dead Sea Scrolls: A Reader from the Biblical Archaeology Review.* Random House, 1992.

Vermes, Géza. *The Dead Sea Scrolls in English.* Viking/Penguin, 1988.

———. *The Dead Sea Scrolls: Qumran in Perspective.* Rev. ed. Fortress, 1981.

Wilson, Edmund. *The Dead Sea Scrolls: 1947–1968.* Oxford, 1969.

Yadin, Yiguel. *The Message of the Scrolls.* Simon and Schuster, 1957.

———. *The Temple Scroll: The Hidden Law of the Dead Sea Sect.* Random House, 1985.

Decalogue.   *See* Law in the Hebrew Bible.

Deutero-Isaiah.   *See* p. 429.

Deuteronomy

Clements, R. E. *God's Chosen People: A Theological Interpretation of the Book of Deuteronomy.* Judson, 1969.

Clifford, Richard. *Deuteronomy: With an Excursus on Covenant and Law.* Liturgical, 1982.

Craigie, Peter C. *Commentary on the Book of Deuteronomy.* New International Commentary of the Old Testament. Eerdmans, 1976.

Cunliff-Jones, H. *Deuteronomy: Introduction and Commentary.* S. C. M., 1951.

Lindblom, Johannes. "The Lawbook of the Josianic Reform." *Catholic Biblical Quarterly,* 38 (1976) 293–302.

Mayes, A. D. *Deuteronomy.* New Century Bible. Attic, 1979.

McBride, S. Dean, Jr. "Polity of the Covenant People: The Book of Deuteronomy." *Interpretation*, 41 (1987) 229–44.

Miller, Patrick D. *Deuteronomy. Interpretation: A Biblical Commentary for Teaching and Preaching.* John Knox, 1990.

von Rad, Gerhard. *Studies in Deuteronomy.* Studies in Biblical Theology, no. 9, S. C. M., 1953.

Weinfeld, Moshe. *Deuteronomy and the Deuteronomic School.* Clarendon, 1972.

Dictionaries

The Anchor Bible Dictionary, I–VI. David N. Freedman, ed. Doubleday, 1992.

Catholic Bible Encyclopedia. John E. Steinmueller and Kathryn Sullivan, eds. J. F. Wagner, 1959.

New Catholic Encyclopedia. Catholic University of America. McGraw-Hill, 1967–1989.

Encyclopaedia Judaica. Yearbook produced annually. Macmillan, 1971 onward.

Harper's Bible Dictionary. Paul J. Achtemeier, gen. ed. Harper, 1985.

The Interpreter's Dictionary of the Bible, I–IV. Keith Crim, gen. ed. Abingdon, 1962. Supplement, 1976.

Leick, Gwendolyn. *A Dictionary of Ancient Near Eastern Architecture.* Routledge, 1988.

———. *A Dictionary of Ancient Near Eastern Mythology.* Routledge, 1991.

Mercer Dictionary of the Bible. Watson E. Mills, ed. Mercer University, 1990.

Theological Dictionary of the Old Testament. G. Johannes Botterweck and Helmer Ringgren, eds. 6 vols. Eerdmans, 1978–1986.

The New Westminster Dictionary of the Bible. Henry S. Gehman, ed. Westminster, 1970.

Documents

The New Oxford Annotated Bible with the Apocryphal/Deuterocanonical Books. Bruce M. Metzger and Roland E. Murphy, eds. Oxford, 1991.

Pritchard, James B., ed. *The Ancient Near East: An Anthology of Texts and Pictures.* Princeton, 1965.

———. *Ancient Near Eastern Texts Relating to the Old Testament.* 3d ed. Princeton, 1969.

———. *The Ancient Near East in Pictures Relating to the Old Testament.* 2d ed. Princeton, 1969.

Thomas, D. Winston, ed. *Documents from Old Testament Times.* Harper Torchbooks. Harper, 1961.

Ebla. *See* p. 84.

Ecclesiastes. *See* Wisdom and Wisdom Literature.

Eschatology. *See* Apocalyptic Literature.

Exile

Ackroyd, Peter R. *Exile and Restoration: A Study of Hebrew Thought of the Sixth Century B.C.* S. C. M., 1968.

———. *Israel under Babylon and Persia.* New Clarendon Bible. Oxford, 1975.

Contenau, Georges. *Everyday Life in Babylon and Assyria.* Edward Arnold, 1954.

Klein, Ralph W. *Israel in Exile: A Theological Interpretation.* Fortress, 1979.

Newsome, James D. *By the Rivers of Babylon: An Introduction to the History and Theology of the Exile.* John Knox, 1979.

Smith, D. L. *The Religion of the Landless: The Social Context of the Babylonian Exile.* Indiana, 1989.

Whitley, Charles F. *The Exilic Age.* Longmans, 1957.

Ezekiel. *See* p. 429.

Feminine Hermeneutics. *See also* Women's Studies.

Achtemeier, Paul J., ed. "The Bible, Theology and Feminists Approaches." *Interpretation*, 42/1 (1988) 3–72.

Bal, M. *Lethal Love: Feminist Literary Reading of Biblical Love Stories*. Indiana, 1987.

Brenner, Athalya, ed. *A Feminist Companion to Genesis*. Journal for the Study of the Old Testament, 1993.

Collins, Adele Y., ed. *Feminist Perspectives on Biblical Scholarship*. Scholars, 1985.

Day, Peggy L., ed. *Gender and Difference in Ancient Israel*. Fortress, 1989.

Fewell, Dana N. "Feminist Reading of the Hebrew Bible: Affirmation, Resistance and Transformation." *Journal for the Study of the Old Testament*, 39 (1987) 77–87.

Fiorenza, Elizabeth S. *Bread Not Stone: The Challenge of Biblical Interpretation*. Beacon, 1985.

———. *But She Said: Feminist Practices of Biblical Interpretation*. Beacon, 1987.

Laffey, Alice L. *An Introduction to the Old Testament: A Feminist Perspective*. Fortress, 1988.

Newsome, Carol A., and Sharon H. Ringe, eds. *The Women's Bible Commentary*. Westminster/John Knox, 1992.

Russell, Letty M., ed. *Feminist Interpretation of the Bible*. Westminster, 1985.

Tolbert, Mary A., ed. *The Bible and Feminist Hermeneutics*. Semeia, 28 (1983) 3–126.

Trible, Phyllis. *God and the Rhetoric of Sexuality*. Fortress, 1978.

———. *Rhetorical Criticism: Context, Method, and the Book of Jonah*. Fortress, 1994.

———. *Texts of Terror: Literary-Feminist Readings of Biblical Narratives*. Fortress, 1984.

———. "Depatriarchalizing in Biblical Interpretation." *Journal of the American Academy of Religion*, 41 (1973) 30–48.

———. "The Effects of Women's Studies on Biblical Studies." *Journal for the Study of the Old Testament*, 22 (1982) 3–72.

———. "Five Loaves and Two Fishes: Feminist Hermaneutics and Biblical Theology." *Theological Studies*, 50 (1989) 279–95.

Genesis, Book of

Barr, James. *The Garden of Eden and the Hope of Immortality*. Fortress, 1993.

Brueggemann, Walter. *Genesis: A Bible Commentary for Teaching and Preaching*. John Knox, 1982.

Coates, George W. *Genesis*. Eerdmans, 1983.

Gunkel, Hermann. *The Legends of Genesis: The Biblical Saga and History*. Schocken, 1987.

Sarna, Nahum M. *Understanding Genesis: The Heritage of Biblical Israel*. Schocken, 1970.

Speiser, E. A., ed. *Genesis*. The Anchor Bible. Vol. 1. Doubleday, 1964.

Vawter, Bruce. *On Genesis: A New Reading*. Doubleday, 1977.

von Rad, Gerhard. *Genesis: A Commentary*. Old Testament Library, Rev. ed. Westminster, 1973.

Westermann, Claus. Trans. John J. Scullion. *Genesis 1–11*. Continental Commentary. Augsburg/Fortress, 1984.

———. Trans. John J. Scullion. *Genesis 12–36*. Continental Commentary. Augsburg/Fortress, 1985.

———. Trans. John J. Scullion. *Genesis 37–50*. Continental Commentary. Augsburg/Fortress, 1986.

Geography

Aharoni, Yohanan. Trans. A. F. Rainey. *The Land of the Bible: A Historical Geography*. Rev. ed. Westminster, 1979.

Aharoni, Yohanan, and Michael Avi-Yonah. *The Macmillan Bible Atlas*. Rev. Macmillan, 1977.

Baly, Denis. *Basic Biblical Geography*. Fortress, 1987.

Grollenberg, L. H. *Atlas of the Bible.* Nelson, 1957.

Kark, Ruth. Trans. Michael Gordon. *The Land That Became Israel: Studies in Historical Geography.* Yale, 1990.

Kraeling, Emil. *Rand McNally Bible Atlas.* McNally, 1956.

May, Herbert G., ed. *Oxford Bible Atlas.* 3d ed. Oxford, 1984.

Negenman, Jan H. Ed. H. H. Rowley. *New Atlas of the Bible.* Doubleday, 1969.

Noth, Martin. Trans. Victor I. Gruhn. *The Old Testament World.* Fortress, 1966.

Orni, Ephraim, and Elisha Efrat. *Geography of Israel.* 3d ed. Jewish Publication Society, 1973.

Pritchard, James B., ed. *The Harper Atlas of the Bible.* Harper, 1987.

Wright, G. Ernest, and Floyd V. Filson, eds. *The Westminster Historical Atlas of the Bible.* Rev. ed. Westminster, 1956.

Habakkuk. *See* p. 404.

Haggai. *See* p. 460.

Hellenism. *See* p. 506.

Histories (Works that treat the entire Hebrew scriptures, unified by either history or book-by-book.)

Ahlström, Gösta. Ed. Diana Edelman. *The History of Ancient Palestine: The Palaeolithic Period to Alexander's Conquest.* Fortress, 1993.

Anderson, Bernhard W. *Understanding the Old Testament.* 4th ed. Prentice-Hall, 1986.

Beebe, H. Keith. *The Old Testament: An Introduction to Its Literary, Historical, and Religious Traditions.* Dickenson, 1970.

Boadt, Lawrence. *Reading the Old Testament: An Introduction.* Paulist, 1984.

Bright, John. *A History of Israel.* 3d ed. Westminster, 1981.

Buck, Harry M. *People of the Lord.* Macmillan, 1965.

Cate, Robert L. *An Introduction to the Old Testament and Its Study.* Broadman, 1991.

Childs, Brevard. *Introduction to the Old Testament as Scripture.* Fortress/Augsburg, 1979.

Crenshaw, James L. *Story and Faith: A Guide to the Old Testament.* Macmillan, 1986.

Harrelson, Walter. *Interpreting the Old Testament.* Holt, Rinehart and Winston, 1964.

Jagersma, Henk. *A History of Israel in the Old Testament Period.* Fortress, 1983.

Kuntz, Kenneth. *The People of Ancient Israel: An Introduction to Old Testament Literature, History and Thought.* Harper, 1974.

Lemche, N. P. *Ancient Israel: A New History of Israelite Society.* Sheffield, 1988.

Miller, J. Maxwell, and John H. Hayes. *A History of Ancient Israel and Judah.* Westminster, 1986.

Noth, Martin. *The History of Israel.* 2d ed. A. & C. Black, 1960.

Pixley, Jorge. *Biblical Israel: A People's History.* Fortress, 1992.

Scoggin, J. Alberto. *A History of Ancient Israel: From the Beginnings to the Bar Kochba Revolt, A.D. 135.* Westminster, 1985.

Shanks, Hershel, ed. *Ancient Israel: A Short History from Abraham to the Roman Destruction of the Temple.* Prentice-Hall, 1988.

Hosea. *See* p. 354.

Inspiration, Authority

Achtemeier, Paul J. *The Inspiration of Scripture: Problems and Proposals.* Westminster, 1980.

Albertz, Rainer. Trans. John Bowden. *A History of Israel's Religion in the Old Testament Period.* Vol. 1 (From the Beginnings to the End of the Monarchy). Westminster/John Knox, 1994.

Barr, James. *The Scope and Authority of the Bible.* Westminster, 1980.

Craigie, Peter C. *The Old Testament: Its Background, Growth, and Content.* Abingdon, 1987.

Kelsey, David H. *The Uses of Scripture in Recent Theology.* Fortress, 1975.

Orr, James. *Revelation and Inspiration.* Eerdmans, 1952.

Trembath, K. Robert. *Evangelical Theories of Biblical Inspiration: A Review and Proposal.* Oxford, 1987.

Vawter, Bruce. *Biblical Inspiration.* Westminster, 1972.

Warfield, Benjamin B. *The Inspiration and Authority of the Bible.* 2d ed. Presbyterian and Reformed, 1948.

Interpretation

Anderson, Bernhard W. *Creation Versus Chaos: The Reinterpretation of Mythical Symbolism in the Bible.* Association, 1967.

———, ed. *The Old Testament and the Christian Faith.* Harper, 1963.

Barr, James. *Old and New in Interpretation.* S. C. M., 1965.

Boadt, Lawrence et al., eds. *Biblical Studies: Meeting Ground of Jews and Christians.* Paulist, 1980.

Brueggemann, Walter. *Texts under Negotiation: The Bible and Postmodern Imagination.* Fortress, 1993.

Clements, Ronald E. *One Hundred Years of Old Testament Interpretation.* Westminster, 1976.

Gordis, Robert. *Poets, Prophets, and Sages: Essays in Biblical Interpretation.* Indiana, 1971.

Grant, Robert M., and David Tracy. *A Short History of the Interpretation of the Bible.* 2d ed. Fortress, 1984.

Hayes, John H., and Carl R. Holladay. *Biblical Exegesis: A Beginner's Handbook.* John Knox, 1982.

Knight, Douglas A., and Gene M. Tucker, *The Hebrew Bible and Its Modern Interpreters.* Fortress, 1985.

Morgan, Robert. *Biblical Interpretation.* Oxford, 1988.

Sandmel, Samuel. *The Enjoyment of Scripture: The Law, the Prophets, and the Writings.* Oxford, 1972.

Isaiah of Jerusalem. *See* p. 379.

Jeremiah. *See also* pp. 404–5.

Blank, Sheldon. *Jeremiah: Man and Prophet.* Hebrew Union College, 1961.

Carroll, Robert P. *From Chaos to Covenant: Prophecy in the Book of Jeremiah.* Crossroads, 1981.

Clements, Ronald E. *Jeremiah.* Interpretation commentary. John Knox, 1988.

Holladay, William L. *The Architecture of Jeremiah 1–20.* Bucknell, 1976.

———. *Jeremiah: Spokesman of Our Time.* United Church Press, 1974.

Huey, F. B., Jr. *Jeremiah, Lamentations.* The New American Commentary, vol. 16. Broadman, 1993.

Hyatt, J. Phillip. *Jeremiah: Prophet of Courage and Hope.* Abingdon, 1958.

Leslie, Elmer A. *Jeremiah.* Abingdon, 1964.

Nicholson, E. W. *Preaching to the Exiles: A Study of the Prose Tradition in the Book of Jeremiah.* Blackwell, 1970.

Overholt, Thomas W. *The Threat of Falsehood: A Study in the Theology of the Book of Jeremiah.* Studies in Biblical Theology, 2d ser, no. 16. S. C. M., 1970.

Jerusalem

Kenyon, Kathleen. *Digging Up Jerusalem.* Praeger, 1974.

Mare, W. Harold. *Archaeology of the Jerusalem Area.* Baker, 1987.

Mazzar, Benjamin. *The Mountain of the Lord.* Doubleday, 1975.

Peters, Francis E. *Jerusalem: The Holy City in the Eyes of Chroniclers, Visitors, Pilgrims, and Prophets.* Princeton, 1985.

Purvis, James D. *Jerusalem: The Holy City: A Bibliography.* ATLA Bibliography Series, 20. 2 vols. Scarecrow, 1988, 1991.

Shanks, Hershel. *The City of David: A Guide to Biblical Jerusalem.* The Biblical Archaeology Society, 1975.

———. "The City of David After Five Years of Digging." *Biblical Archaeology Review,* 11 (November/December 1985) 22–38.

Shiloh, Yigal. "City of David Excavations, 1978." *Biblical Archaeologist,* 42 (2979) 165–71.

Yadin, Yigael, and R. Grafman, eds. Trans. R. Grafman. *Jerusalem Revealed: Archaeology in the Holy City, 1968–1974.* Yale, 1976.

Job. *See also* Wisdom and Wisdom Literature; *and* p. 506.

Crook, Margaret B. *The Cruel God: Job's Search for the Meaning of Suffering.* Beacon, 1959.

Duquoc, Christian, and Casiano Floristan, eds. *Job and the Silence of God.* T & T Clark, 1983.

Gordis, Robert. *The Book of God and Man: A Study of Job.* University of Chicago, 1965.

———. *The Book of Job: Commentary, New Translation and Special Studies.* Jewish Theological Seminary, 1978.

Gutierrez, Gustavo. Trans. Martha J. O'Conner. *On Job: God-Talk and the Suffering of the Innocent.* Orbis, 1987.

Habel, Norman C. *The Book of Job: A Commentary.* Old Testament Library. Westminster, 1985.

Perdue, Leo G., and W. Clark Gilpin, eds. *The Voice from the Whirlwind: Interpreting the Book of Job.* Abingdon, 1991.

Pope, Marvin H., *Job.* 3d ed. The Anchor Bible, vol. 15. Doubleday, 1973.

Robinson, T. H. *Job and His Friends.* S. C. M., 1954.

Snaith, Norman H. *The Book of Job: Its Origin and Purpose.* Alec R. Allenson, 1968.

Tsevat, Matitiahu. *The Meaning of Job and Other Biblical Studies.* KTAV, 1981.

Vawter, Bruce. *Job and Jonah.* Paulist, 1983.

Westermann, Claus. *The Structure of the Book of Job.* Fortress, 1981.

Zerafa, P. P. *The Wisdom of God and the Book of Job.* Rome, 1978.

Jordan River, Valley. *See* p. 84.

Journals. *See* Periodicals.

Judaism, Postexilic. *See also* pp. 459–60.

Bickerman, Elias J. *From Ezra to the Last of the Maccabees: Foundations of Post-Biblical Judaism.* Schocken, 1962.

Cohen, Shaye J. D. *From the Maccabees to the Mishnah.* Westminster, 1987.

Davies, W. D., and I. Finkelstein, eds. *The Cambridge History of Judaism.* Vol. 1 (The Persian Period). Cambridge, 1984.

Epstein, I., ed. *The Babylonian Talmud.* Socino, 1948.

The Jewish People: Past and Present. Jewish Encyclopedic Handbooks. Central Yiddish Culture Organization, 1946.

Neusner, Jacob. *From Testament to Torah: An Introduction to Judaism in Its Formative Age*. Prentice-Hall, 1988.

Russell, David S. *The Jews from Alexander to Herod*. The New Clarendon Bible, vol. 5. Oxford, 1967.

Sandmel, Samuel. *Judaism and Christian Beginnings*. Oxford, 1978.

Schiffman, Lawrence H. *From Text to Tradition: A History of Second Temple and Rabbinic Judaism*. KTAV, 1991.

Steinberg, Milton. *Basic Judaism*. Harcourt, Brace and World, 1947.

Stone, Michael E. *Scripture, Sects, and Visions: A Profile of Judaism from Ezra to the Jewish Revolt*. Fortress, 1980.

Ulrich, Eugene, et al., eds. *Priests, Prophets, and Scribes: Essays on the Formation and History of Second Temple Judaism in Honor of Joseph Blenkinsopp*. Journal for the Study of the Old Testament, 1992.

Widoger, Geoffrey, ed. *The Encyclopedia of Judaism*. Macmillan, 1989.

Kings, Book of. *See* p. 292.

Law in the Hebrew Bible. *See also* p. 221.

Alt, Albrecht. "The Origins of Israelite Law," *Essays in Old Testament History and Religion*. Trans. R. A. Wilson. Doubleday, 1968.

Daube, David. *Studies in Biblical Law*. Cambridge, 1947.

Davidson, Joy. *Smoke on the Mountain: An Interpretation of the Ten Commandments*. Westminster, 1985.

Harrelson, Walter. *The Ten Commandments and Human Rights*. Fortress, 1981.

———. "Law in the Old Testament." *Interpreter's Dictionary of the Bible*, vol. 3, 77–89.

Nasuti, H. P. "Identity, Identification, and Imitation: The Narrative Hermeneutics of Biblical Law." *Journal of Law and Religion*, 4/1 (1986) 9–23.

Nielson, Eduard. *Law, History, and Tradition*. G. E. C. Gads, 1983.

Noth, Martin. Trans. D. R. Ap-Thomas. *The Laws in the Pentateuch*. Fortress, 1967.

Patrick, Dale. *Old Testament Law*. John Knox, 1985.

Phillips, Anthony. *Ancient Israel's Criminal Law: A New Approach to the Decalogue*. Schocken, 1970.

Malachi. *See* pp. 443–44.

Messiah, Messianism

Becker, Joachin. Trans. David E. Green. *Messianic Expectation in the Old Testament*. Fortress, 1980.

Charlesworth, James H., ed. *The Messiah: Developments in Earliest Judaism and Christianity*. Augsburg, 1992.

Durham, John. "The King as 'Messiah' in the Psalms." *Review and Expositor*, 81 (Summer 1984) 425–35.

Greenstone, Julius M. *The Messiah Idea in Jewish History*. Greenwood, 1972.

Klausner, Joseph. *The Messianic Idea in Israel*. Macmillan, 1954.

Mowinkel, Sigmund. *He That Cometh*. Abingdon, 1954.

Riggan, George A. *Messianic Theology and Christian Faith*. Westminster, 1967.

Ringgren, Helmer. *The Messiah in the Old Testament*. S. C. M., 1956.

Ruether, Rosemary. *The Radical Kingdom: The Western Experience of Messianic Hope*. Harper, 1970.

Scholem, Gershom. *The Messiah Idea in Judaism and Other Essays in Jewish Spirituality*. Schoken, 1971.

Micah. *See* p. 379.

Moses. *See* p. 221.

Myth, Folklore

Cross, Frank M., Jr. *Canaanite Myth and Hebrew Epic*. Harvard, 1973.

Eliade, Mircea. *Myth and Reality*. Harper, 1963.

Gunkel, Hermann. Trans. Michael D. Rutter. *The Folktale in the Old Testament*. Almond, 1987.

Hooke, S. H. *Myth, Ritual, and Kingship*. Clarendon, 1958.

Kitagawa, Joseph H., and Charles H. Long, eds. *Myths and Symbols: Studies in Honor of Mircea Eliade*. University of Chicago, 1969.

Kramer, Samuel N., ed. *Mythologies of the Ancient World*. Doubleday, 1961.

Leick, Gwendolyn. *A Dictionary of Ancient Near Eastern Mythology*. Routledge, 1991.

Loew, Cornelius. *Myth, Sacred History, and Philosophy*. Harcourt, Brace, and World, 1967.

Long, Charles. *Alpha: The Myths of Creation*. George Braziller, 1963.

McCurley, Foster R. *Ancient Myths and Biblical Faith: Scriptural Transformations*. Fortress, 1983.

O'Brien, Joan, and Wilfred Major. *In The Beginning: Creation Myths from Ancient Mesopotamia, Israel and Greece*. Scholars, 1982.

Roberts, J. J. M. "Myth Versus History: Relaying the Comparative Foundations." *Catholic Biblical Quarterly*, 38 (1976) 1–13.

Rogerson, J. W. *Myth in Old Testament Interpretation*. De Gruyter, 1974.

Nahum. *See* p. 404.

Patriarchs

Albright, W. F. "Abraham the Hebrew: A New Archaeological Interpretation." *Bulletin of the American School of Oriental Research*, 163 (October 1961) 36–54.

Millard, A. R., and D. J. Wiseman, eds. *Essays on the Patriarchal Narratives*. Eisenbrauns, 1983.

Thompson, Thomas L. *The Historicity of the Patriarchal Narratives: The Quest for the Historical Abraham*. De Gruyter, 1974.

Van Seters, John. *Abraham in History and Tradition*. Yale, 1975.

Pentateuchal Studies. *See also* Genesis, Book of; Patriarchs; Deuteronomy.

Brueggemann, Walter, and Hans W. Wolff. *The Vitality of Old Testament Traditions*. Westminster/John Knox, 1985.

Fretheim, Terrence. *Deuteronomic History*. Abingdon, 1983.

Howard, D. M., Jr., "The Case for Kingship in Deuteronomy and the Former Prophets." *Westminster Theological Journal*, 52 (1990) 87–101.

Lohfink, Norbert. Trans. Linda M. Maloney. *Theology of the Pentateuch: Themes of the Priestly Narrative and Deuteronomy*. Fortress, 1994.

Moberly, R. W. L. *The Old Testament of the Old Testament: Patriarchal Narratives and Mosaic Yahwism*. Fortress, 1994.

Noth, Martin. *The Deuteronomic History*. Journal for the Study of the Old Testament, 1981.

———. Trans. Bernhard W. Anderson. *A History of Pentateuchal Traditions*. Scholars, 1981.

O'Brien, Mark A., and Anthony A. Campbell. *Sources of the Pentateuch*. Fortress, 1992.

Plaut, W. Gunter. *The Torah: A Modern Commentary*. Union of Hebrew Congregations, 1981.

Sanders, James A. *Torah and Canon*. Fortress, 1972.

Van Seters, John. *Der Jahwist als Historiker*. Theologischer Verlag, 1987.

———. *The Life of Moses: The Yahwist as Historian in Exodus-Numbers*. Westminster/ John Knox, 1994.

———. *In Search of History: Historiography in the Ancient World and the Origins of Biblical History*. Yale, 1983.

Whybray, Robert N. "The Making of the Pentateuch." *Journal for the Study of the Old Testament*, Supp. 53. Journal for the Study of the Old Testament, 1987.

Periodicals

Biblical Archaeologist. American Schools of Oriental Research.

Biblical Archaeology Review. Biblical Archaeology Society.

Catholic Biblical Quarterly. Catholic Biblical Association of America, Catholic University of America.

The Expository Times. T. & T. Clark.

Interpretation. Union Theological Seminary in Virginia.

Journal of Biblical Literature. Society of Biblical Literature.

Journal for the Study of the Old Testament. Sheffield. Academic Press.

Vetus Testamentum. International Organization for Study of the Old Testament.

Poetry, Hebrew. *See also* Psalms, Psalter.

Alter, Robert. *The Art of Biblical Poetry*. Basic Books, 1985.

Cross, Frank M., Jr., and David N. Freedman. *Studies in Ancient Yahwistic Poetry*. Scholars, 1975.

Culley, Robert C. *Oral Formulaic Language in the Biblical Psalms*. University of Toronto, 1967.

Geller, Stephen A. *Parallelism in Early Biblical Poetry*. Scholars, 1979.

Kugel, James L. *The Idea of Biblical Poetry: Parallelism and Its History*. Yale, 1981.

O'Connor, Michael. *Hebrew Verse Structure*. Eisenbrauns, 1980.

Petersen, David L., and Kent H. Richards. *Interpreting Hebrew Poetry*. Fortress, 1992.

Priest, Priesthood

Anderson, Gary A., and Saul Olyan, eds. *Priesthood and Cult in Ancient Israel*. Journal for the Study of the Old Testament series, no. 125. Cornell, 1991.

Cody, Aelred. *Ezekiel: With an Excursus on Old Testament Priesthood*. M. Glazier, 1984.

———. *A History of Old Testament Priesthood*. Pontifical Biblical Institute, 1969.

Cross, Frank M., Jr. "The Priestly Tabernacle." *Biblical Archaeology Reader*, I (Doubleday, 1961) 201–28.

Gayford, Sydney C. *Sacrifice and Priesthood*. 2d ed. Methuen, 1953.

James, E. O. *The Nature and Function of Priesthood: A Comparative and Anthropological Study*. Vanguard, 1961.

Sabourin, Leopold. *Priesthood: A Comparative Study*. Brill, 1973.

Welch, A. C. *Prophet and Priest in Old Israel*. S. C. M., 1936.

Prophecy (Works on individual prophets are usually noted at the end of the appropriate chapters.) *See also* p. 338.

Anderson, Bernhard W., and Walter Harrelson, eds. *Israel's Prophetic Heritage*. Harper, 1962.

Blenkinsopp, Joseph A. *A History of Prophecy in Israel from the Settlement in the Land to the Hellenistic Period*. Westminster, 1983.

Bright, John. *Covenant and Promise: The Prophetic Understanding of the Future in Pre-exilic Israel*. Westminster, 1978.

Brueggemann, Walter. *The Prophetic Imagination.* Fortress, 1978.

Buber, Martin. *The Prophetic Faith.* Macmillan, 1949.

Clements, Ronald E. *Prophecy and Tradition.* John Knox, 1975.

Coggins, Richard, Anthony Phillips, and Michael Knebb, eds. *Israel's Prophetic Tradition.* Cambridge, 1982.

Crenshaw, James L. *Prophetic Conflict and Its Effects upon Israelite Religion.* Walter de Gruyter, 1971.

Halder, Alfred. *Association of Cult Prophets Among the Ancient Semites.* Almquist and Wiksells Boktryeheri, 1945.

Heschel, Abraham. *The Prophets.* Harper, 1963.

Koch, Klaus. *The Prophets: The Assyrian Period.* Fortress, 1982.

————. *The Prophets: The Babylonian and Persian Periods.* Fortress, 1984.

Lindblom, Johannes. *Prophecy in Ancient Israel.* Fortress, 1982.

Mays, James L., and Paul J. Achtemeier, eds. *Interpreting the Prophets.* Fortress, 1987.

McKane, William. *Prophets and Wise Men.* S. C. M., 1965.

Orlinsky, H. M., ed. *Interpreting the Prophetic Tradition.* Hebrew Union College, 1969.

Overholt, Thomas W. *Channels of Prophecy: The Social Dynamics of Prophetic Activity.* Fortress, 1989.

————. *Prophecy in Cross-Cultural Perspectives: A Sourcebook for Biblical Researchers.* Scholars, 1986.

Peterson, David L. *The Role of Israel's Prophets.* Journal for the Study of the Old Testament, supp. 7. Journal for the Study of the Old Testament, 1981.

————, ed. *Prophecy in Israel.* Fortress, 1987.

Rowley, H. H., ed. *Studies in Old Testament Prophecy.* T. & T. Clark, 1950.

Sawyer, John F. A. *Prophecy and the Prophets of the Old Testament.* Oxford, 1987.

Scott, R. B. Y. *The Relevance of the Prophets.* Macmillan, 1968.

von Rad, Gerhard. *The Prophetic Message.* S. C. M., 1968.

Ward, James M. *Thus Says the Lord: The Message of the Prophets.* Abingdon, 1991.

Westermann, Claus. *Basic Forms of Prophetic Speech.* Westminster, 1967.

Wilson, Robert R. *Prophecy and Society in Ancient Israel.* Fortress, 1980.

Winward, Stephen. *A Guide to the Prophets.* John Knox, 1977.

Wood, Leon J. *The Prophets of Israel.* Baker, 1979.

Zuker, David J. *Israel's Prophets: An Introduction for Christians and Jews.* Paulist, 1994.

Psalms, Psalter. *See also* Hebrew Poetry.

Anderson, Bernhard W. *Out of the Depths: The Psalms Speak for Us Today.* Rev. ed. Westminster, 1983.

Berry, Donald K. *The Psalms and Their Readers.* Journal for the Study of the Old Testament, 1993.

Brueggemann, Walter. *Israel's Praise: Doxology against Idolatry and Ideology.* Fortress, 1988.

Durham, John. "The King as 'Messiah' in the Psalms." *Review and Expositor,* 81 (Summer 1984) 425–35.

Gunkel, Hermann. *Die Psalmen.* Vandenhoeck and Ruprecht, 1926. Eng. trans., *The Psalms.* Fortress, 1967.

Gunkel, Hermann, and Joachin Begrich. *Einleitung in die Psalmen.* Vandenhoeck and Ruprecht, 1933.

Holladay, William L. *The Psalms Through Three Thousand Years.* Fortress, 1993.

Keel, Othmar. Trans. Timothy J. Hallett. *The Symbolism of the Biblical World: Ancient Near Eastern Iconography and the Book of Psalms.* Seabury, 1978.

Kraus, Hans J. *Psalms 1–59.* Continental Commentary series. Augsburg/Fortress, 1987.

————. *Psalms 60–150*. Continental Commentary series. Augsburg/Fortress, 1989.

————. *Theology of the Psalms*. Continental Commentary series. Fortress, 1992.

Leslie, Elmer A. *The Psalms*. Abingdon, 1949.

Mays, James L. *Psalms*. Interpretation: A Commentary for Teaching and Preaching. Westminster/John Knox, 1994.

Miller, Patrick D. *Interpreting the Psalms*. Fortress, 1986.

Mowinckel, Sigmund. *The Psalms in Israel's Worship, I–II*. Abingdon, 1962.

Oesterley, W. O. E. *The Psalms*. S. P. C. K., 1955.

Ringgren, Helmer. *The Faith of the Psalmists*. S. C. M., 1963.

Rogerson, J. W., and J. W. McKay. *Psalms*. Cambridge Bible Commentary. Cambridge, 1977.

Weiser, Artur. *The Psalms*. Old Testament Library. Westminster, 1962.

Westermann, Claus. *Praise and Lament in the Psalms*. Westminster, 1984.

Ruth. *See* Women's Studies.

Samuel, Book of. *See* p. 292.

Second Isaiah. *See* Deutero-Isaiah.

Social Science Studies (Sociology, Anthropology, Folklore)

Brueggemann, Walter, and Patrick Miller, eds. *A Social Reading of the Old Testament*. Fortress, 1994.

Clements, Ronald E., ed. *The World of Ancient Israel: Sociological, Anthropological, and Political Perspectives*. Cambridge, 1989.

Culley, Robert C., and Thomas W. Overholt, eds. *Anthropological Perspectives on Old Testament Prophecy*. Semeia 21. Scholars, 1981.

Eilberg-Schwartz, Howard. *The Savage in Judaism: An Anthropology of Israelite Religion and Judaism*. Indiana, 1990.

Gottwald, Norman K. *The Hebrew Bible: A Socio-Literary Introduction*. Fortress, 1985.

————. *The Hebrew Bible in Its Social World and in Ours*. Scholars, 1993.

————. *Social Scientific Criticism of the Hebrew Bible and Its Social World: The Israelite Monarchy*. Semeia 37. Scholars, 1986.

————. "Religious Conversion and the Societal Origins of Ancient Israel." *Perspectives in Religious Studies*, 15 (1989) 49–65.

Hahn, Herbert F. *The Old Testament in Modern Research*. Fortress, 1966.

Kirkpatrick, P. G. *The Old Testament and Folklore Study*. Journal for the Study of the Old Testament, Monograph Series 62. Sheffield, 1988.

Long, Burke O. "The Social World of Ancient Israel." *Interpretation*, 37 (1982) 243–55.

Niditch, Susan. *Folklore and the Hebrew Bible*. Fortress, 1993.

Rogerson, John W. *Anthropology and the Old Testament*. Blackwell, 1978.

————. "The Use of Sociology in Old Testament Studies." *Vetus Testamentum Supplement*, 36 (1985) 245–56.

Smith, D. L. *The Religion of the Landless: The Social Context of the Babylonian Exile*. Indiana, 1989.

Wilson, Robert R. *Sociological Approaches to the Old Testament*. Fortress, 1984.

Wolff, Hans W. Trans. Margaret Kohl. *Anthropology of the Old Testament*. Fortress, 1974.

Son of Man. *See* p. 417.

Song of Songs. *See* p. 506.

Ten Commandments. *See* Law in the Hebrew Bible.

Themes in the Hebrew Bible. *See also* Theology and the Hebrew Bible; Covenant.

Ballentine, Samuel. *The Hidden God: The Hiding of the Face of God in the Old Testament.* Oxford, 1983.

———. *Prayer in the Hebrew Bible.* Fortress, 1993.

Boecker, Hans J. Trans. Jeremy Moiser. *Law and Administration of Justice in the Old Testament and the Ancient Near East.* Augsburg, 1980.

Brueggemann, Walter. *The Land: Place as Gift, Promise, and Challenge in Biblical Faith.* Fortress, 1977.

Crenshaw, James L., and J. T. Willis, eds. *Essays in Old Testament Ethics.* KTAV, 1974.

Culley, Robert C. *Themes and Variations: A Study of Action in Biblical Narrative.* Scholars, 1992.

Daniella, G. A. *Studies in the Name Israel in the Old Testament.* Appelbergs Boktrycheri, 1946.

Davidson, Robert F. *The Courage to Doubt: Exploring an Old Testament Theme.* S. C. M., 1983.

Gammie, John G. *Holiness in Israel.* Fortress, 1989.

Greenberg, Moshe. *Biblical Prose Prayer: As A Window to the Popular Religion of Ancient Israel.* University of California, 1983.

Hasel, Gerhard F. *The Remnant: The History and Theology of the Remnant Idea from Genesis to Isaiah.* 3d ed. Andrews, 1980.

Hutton, Rodney R. *Charisma and Authority in Israelite Society.* Fortress, 1994.

Kaiser, W. C., Jr. *Toward Old Testament Ethics.* Zondervan, 1992.

Levenson, Jon D. *Sinai and Zion: An Entry into the Jewish Bible.* Winston, 1985.

Mason, Rex. *Old Testament Pictures of God.* Regent's Study Guide 2. Smith and Helwys, 1993.

Mendenhall, George E. *Law and Covenant in Israel and the Ancient Near East.* Biblical Colloquium, 1955.

Mettinger, Tryggve. *In Search of God: The Meaning and Message of the Everlasting Names.* Fortress, 1988.

Muilenberg, James. *The Way of Israel: Biblical Faith and Ethics.* Torchbooks. Harper, 1965.

Ringgren, Helmer. *Sacrifice in the Bible.* Association, 1963.

Roberts, J. J. M. "The Davidic Origins of the Zion Tradition." *Journal of Biblical Literature,* 92 (1973) 329–44.

Sandmel, Samuel. *The Several Israel's.* KTAV, 1971.

Westermann, Claus. *Prophetic Oracles of Salvation in the Old Testament.* Westminster/John Knox, 1991.

———. *What Does The Old Testament Say About God?* John Knox, 1979.

Theology and the Hebrew Bible

Brueggemann, Walter. *Old Testament Theology: Essays on Structure, Theme, and Text,* ed. Patrick D. Miller. Fortress, 1991.

Childs, Brevard S. *Biblical Theology in Crisis.* Westminster, 1970.

———. *Biblical Theology of the Old and New Testaments.* Fortress, 1993.

———. *Old Testament Theology in a Canonical Context.* Augsburg/Fortress, 1985.

Clements, Ronald E. *Old Testament Theology: A Fresh Approach.* John Knox, 1979.

Dentan, R. C. *Preface to Old Testament Theology.* Rev. ed. Seabury, 1963.

Eichrodt, Walther. *Theology of the Old Testament.* 2 vols. Westminster, 1961, 1967.

Goldingay, John. *Theological Diversity and the Authority of the Old Testament*. Eerdmans, 1987.

Hasel, Gerhard F. *Old Testament Theology: Basic Issues in the Current Debate*. 3d ed. Eerdmans, 1982.

Hayes, John H., and Frederick C. Prussner, *Old Testament Theology: Its History and Development*. John Knox, 1985.

Jacob, Edmund. *Theology of the Old Testament*. Harper, 1958.

Kohler, Ludwig. *Old Testament Theology*. Lutterworth, 1957.

Levenson, Jon D. *Sinai and Zion: An Entry into the Jewish Bible*. Winston, 1985.

McKenzie, John. *A Theology of the Old Testament*. Doubleday, 1974.

Nicholson, E. W. *God and His People: Covenant and Theology in the Old Testament*. Oxford, 1986.

Perdue, Leo G. *The Collapse of History: Reconstructing Old Testament Theology*. Fortress, 1994.

Tsevat, Matitiahu. "Theology of the Old Testament: A Jewish View." *Horizons in Biblical Theology*, 8 (1986) 33–50.

von Rad, Gerhard. Trans. D. G. Stalker. *Old Testament Theology*. 2 vols. Harper, 1962, 1965.

Vriezen, T. C. *An Outline of Old Testament Theology*. Blackwell, 1958.

Westermann, Claus. Trans. D. Stott. *Elements of Old Testament Theology*. John Knox, 1982.

Zimmerli, Walther. Trans D. Green. *Old Testament Theology in Outline*. T. & T. Clark, 1978.

Warrior-God. *See* p. 292.

Wisdom and Wisdom Literature

Blenkinsopp, Joseph. *Wisdom and Law in the Old Testament*. Oxford, 1983.

Crenshaw, James L. *Old Testament Wisdom: An Introduction*. John Knox, 1981.

Crenshaw, James L., ed. *Studies in Ancient Israelite Wisdom*. KTAV, 1976.

Johnson, L. D. *Israel's Wisdom: Learn and Live*. Broadman, 1975.

Murphy, Roland E. *Tree of Life: An Exploration of Biblical Wisdom Literature*. Doubleday, 1992.

———. *Wisdom Literature: Ruth, Esther, Job, Proverbs, Ecclesiastes, Canticles*. Eerdmans, 1981.

Noth, Martin, and D. Winton Thomas, eds. *Wisdom in Israel and in the Ancient Near East*. Brill, 1955.

Perdue, Leo G. *Wisdom and Creation: The Theology of Wisdom Literature*. Abingdon, 1946.

Perdue, Leo G., Bernard B. Scott, and William J. Wiseman, eds. *In Search of Wisdom*. Westminster/John Knox, 1993.

Rylaarsdam, J. C. *Revelation in Jewish Wisdom Literature*. University of Chicago, 1946.

Scott, R. B. Y. *The Way of Wisdom in the Old Testament*. Macmillan, 1971.

von Rad, Gerhard. Trans. James O. Marton. *Wisdom in Israel*. S. C. M., 1972.

Women's Studies. *See also* **Feminine Hermeneutics.**

Darr, Katheryn P. *Far More Precious Than Jewels: Perspectives on Biblical Women*. Fortress, 1991.

Day, Peggy L., ed. *Gender and Difference in Ancient Israel*. Fortress, 1989.

Dresner, Samuel H. *Rachel*. Fortress, 1994.

Jeansonne, Sharon P. *The Women of Genesis: From Sarah to Potiphar's Wife*. Fortress, 1990.

LaCocque, Andre. *The Feminine Unconventional: Four Subversive Figures in Israel's Tradition*. Fortress, 1990.

Meyers, Carol L. *Discovering Eve: Ancient Israelite Women in Context*. Oxford University, 1988.

Mollenkott, Virginia R. *The Divine Feminine: The Biblical Image of God as Female*. Crossroads, 1983.

———. *Women, Men and the Bible*. Abingdon, 1977.

Newsome, Carol A., and Sharon H. Ringe, eds. *The Women's Bible Commentary*. Westminster/John Knox, 1992.

Otwell, John H. *And Sarah Laughed: The Status of Women in the Old Testament*. Westminster, 1977.

Ruether, Rosemary R., ed. *Religion and Sexism: Images of Women in the Jewish and Christian Traditions*. Simon and Schuster, 1974.

Terrien, Samuel L. *Till the Heart Sings: A Biblical Theology of Manhood and Womanhood*. Fortress, 1985.

Worship.   *See also* Psalms, Psalter, Priest, Priesthood.

Harrelson, Walter. *From Fertility Cult to Worship*. Scholars, 1980.

Heschel, Abraham J. *The Sabbath: Its Meaning for Modern Man*. Farrar, Strauss and Young, 1951.

Kraus, Hans-Joachim. Trans. Geoffrey Buswell. *Worship in Israel: A Cultic History of the Old Testament*. John Knox, 1966.

Rowley, H. H. *Worship in Ancient Israel: Its Forms and Meaning*. S. P. C. K., 1967.

Zephaniah.   *See* p. 404.

Author Index

542

Subject Index